Law for Professionals

Chiara Tincani

Contract for the International Carriage of Goods by Road

Springer

Chiara Tincani
Department of Law
University of Verona
Verona, Italy

ISSN 2662-141X ISSN 2662-1428 (electronic)
Law for Professionals
ISBN 978-3-031-08486-7 ISBN 978-3-031-08487-4 (eBook)
https://doi.org/10.1007/978-3-031-08487-4

This Springer imprint is published by the registered company Springer Nature Switzerland AG
The registered company address is: Gewerbestrasse 11, 6330 Cham, Switzerland

A mio marito e a mio figlio

Preface

The Geneva Convention on the International Carriage of Goods by Road is a fundamental text of uniform law. It has played a substantive role in fostering economic exchange and consequently social development in Europe and a part of Asia, such as Turkey, which sits beyond the furthest edges of the European Union. The Convention has facilitated trade and created a standardized system that everyone in the industry understands. For more than six decades, operators have been able to rely on a single set of rules, favoring awareness of the issues involved when carrying goods, even in times of political change, such as post-1991 or the recent decisions taken by the United Kingdom.

In the last few decades at least, the main works published in English, and hence those that have enjoyed the most widespread reach, have relied on the ideas of authoritative common law academics. These definitely provide a reference framework for all. There are also some extremely complex and systemically important works penned in German, French, Spanish, and Italian, providing more of a view of people versed in continental law. This project is inspired by the wish to make a contribution in this field, retaining the same continental cultural framework but using the language most widely adopted in Europe (and beyond), in the hope of facilitating comparison between experiences in continental systems and those of common law. Despite the enormous theoretical efforts of the authors, the interpretations between the two sides do differ frequently and it might well be necessary to engage in further discussion and debate to refine the final analysis and improve the comparison of ideas. The Convention itself is based largely, if not entirely, on the traditional theories of civil law systems, with a very significant contribution being made by case law and precedent in these countries.

As I hope to show convincingly, I firmly believe the numerous gaps left and questions raised by the CMR can be more robustly resolved through the limited use of national law and, if anything, by exploring all the resources of the text, which is as stimulating as it is complex. Such a point of view is debatable and not that common. Objections might well be raised, but I am ready for these as I have dedicated the opening chapters to justifying this approach as far as is possible. The very structure of the Convention and its overall logic support such an approach, precisely because the CMR is concerned with the regulation of freight transport as a whole, so that legitimate business activity, and consequently trade, can benefit.

Since the audience is readers across the globe, no effort has been made to consider how the CMR has been integrated by national legislations, including in Italy. The sole focus of the work is uniform law and not its interaction with the various systems, as it would have been impossible to consider even all the main ones (let all alone of them). The considerations are aimed at people who are interested in the implementation of the CMR, regardless of where such people might reside or the sectoral indications of the law in their home countries. The sole exceptions are the regulations of the European Union, in terms of applicable law and jurisdiction, and the Lugano Convention, in terms of relations with Switzerland. This departure from the general rule is justified, given the importance of the points in question.

Following a study that lasted nearly three years, made especially taxing and problematic by the pandemic (as happened to other authors around the world in just about every field), the CMR has proved to be a surprisingly modern text, although some critical revision is needed—something that has been announced on more than one occasion, but never actually happened. The goals envisaged in 1956 have been achieved with great clarity and success that, at times, might even be surprising. The CMR is perhaps a little out of date as it does not take into account (and could not have) modern means of communication, namely those means familiar to everyone by now, such as e-mail and mobile phones, but also the tools used currently by businesses, typically programs enabling the constant traceability of goods and the progressive integration, into their logistics, of functions associated with the carriage of goods but different in nature, albeit provided by the same enterprise. Specifically for these aspects, an effort has been made to underscore where problems in interpretation arise and where, at times, current strategies do not match the provisions. This problem is set to become more acute in the short term and will need to be monitored closely, otherwise there is the risk of losing a fundamental asset provided by the CMR, namely a common regulatory framework for the carriage of goods that can favor growth in all the signatory nations and, ultimately, improve the lives of their inhabitants for generations to come.

Verona, Italy Chiara Tincani

Contents

Chapter 1
Contract for the International Carriage of Goods by Road

Contents

1.1 Purpose of the Geneva Convention

1.1.1 The Standardization of Transport Law

As expressed in the preamble, the CMR aims to regulate the contract for carriage in a uniform way so that the parties can refer to a single legislative text, without having to know and apply domestic laws. Thus, simplification speeds up operations, with a significant boost to this economic sector. The more complete and exhaustive the uniform law regulation, the less interference there is with national law; thus, the former does not lose consistency and does not break up into different and, at times,

C. Tincani, *Contract for the International Carriage of Goods by Road*, Law for Professionals, https://doi.org/10.1007/978-3-031-08487-4_1

conflicting domestic sources. Accordingly, an autonomous body of norms related to individual systems is created among the ratifying States;[1] in fact, "the general aim of the movement towards uniform law is grounded in a firm conviction that uniform international complex of norms is essential to give full effect to international legal relations".[2] Overall, the initiative is part of a broader process, which began with the Berne Convention of 14 October 1890, about the transport of goods by rail,[3] and continued with that of Brussels of 25 August 1924, related to the unification of certain rules on the bill of lading,[4] and with that of Warsaw[5] of 12 October 1929, about air transport.[6]

The CMR was opened for signature on 19 May 1956 and, on that same date, was signed by the representatives of Austria, the Federal Republic of Germany, France, Luxembourg, the Netherlands, Poland, Sweden, Switzerland, and the then Yugoslavia. The Convention entered into force on 2 June 1961, with the filing of the ratifications of the first five States (Austria, France, Italy, the Netherlands, and the then Yugoslavia). In 1968, the United Kingdom and Northern Ireland ratified the Convention and it applied to the territories of Gibraltar and the Isle of Man. The CMR does not operate in trade between the United Kingdom and the Republic of Ireland. Fifty-eight countries have signed up to date.[7]

Since 1956, the Convention has undergone only two modifications. The first was introduced by the Protocol of 5 July 1978, which entered into force on 15 March 1982.[8] This Protocol introduced the new unit of account proposed by the

---

[1]Cf. Haak (1986), p. 11 ff.

[2]Cf. Haak (1986), p. 11 ff. See also Pesce (1995), p. 9 ff.; Rodière (1970), p. 621 ff.

[3]Today, the Convention relating to the International Carriage of Goods by Rail is that of Bern approved on 9 May 1980, which entered into force on 1 May 1985, as amended by the 1999 Vilnius Protocol.

[4]The 1924 Brussels Convention was amended by subsequent Protocols of 23 February 1968 and 21 December 1979. Consider the Convention of 31 March 1978, signed in Hamburg and entered into force on 1 November 1992, but ratified by a limited number of States, while the conditions for its entry into force have not been fulfilled for the so-called Rotterdam Rules.

[5]Today, the 1929 Warsaw Convention, as amended by the 1955 Hague Protocol, applies if the Montreal Convention of 28 May 1999, does not apply.

[6]Cf. Putzeys (1981), p. 9 ff.; Loewe (1976), p. 312 ff.; Ramberg (1974), p. 10 ff.; Van Ryn (1966), p. 639 ff.; Capel Ferrer (2006), p. 517 ff.

[7]These countries have joined the CMR: Afghanistan, Albania, Armenia, Austria, Azerbaijan, Belarus, Belgium, Bosnia - Herzegovina, Bulgaria, Croatia, Cyprus, Czech Republic, Denmark, Estonia, Finland, France, Georgia, Germany, Greece, Hungary, Iran (Islamic Republic), Ireland, Italy, Jordan, Kazakhstan, Kyrgyzstan, Latvia, Lebanon, Lithuania, Luxembourg, Malta, Mongolia, Montenegro, Morocco, Netherlands, North Macedonia, Norway, Oman, Pakistan, Poland, Portugal, Moldova, Romania, Federation Russia, Serbia, Slovakia, Slovenia, Spain, Sweden, Switzerland, Syria, Tajikistan, Tunisia, Turkey, Turkmenistan, Ukraine, United Kingdom and Northern Ireland and Uzbekistan.

[8]The following States have ratified the Protocol of 5 July 1978: Albania, Armenia, Austria, Belarus, Belgium, Bosnia - Herzegovina, Croatia, Cyprus, Czech Republic, Denmark, Estonia, Finland, France, Georgia, Germany, Greece, Hungary, Iran (Islamic Republic), Ireland, Italy, Jordan, Kyrgyzstan, Latvia, Lebanon, Lithuania, Luxembourg, Malta, Netherlands, North Macedonia,

"International Monetary Fund", for the determination of the compensation limit, replacing the germinal gold franc. The second modification was due to the Protocol on the electronic consignment note of 20 February 2008, which entered into force on 5 June 2011.[9] Overall, the CMR has worked; although affected by its time, for some aspects, this text is an important tool for a homogeneous regulation. In fact, "the guarantee that the Convention offered operators to be able to rely on (...) solid foundations (...) constituted an essential prerequisite for the development of traffic".[10] However, as progress has facilitated faster transport, it has highlighted some weaknesses of the Convention. For instance, the 2008 Protocol combined the traditional consignment note with the electronic one, with a partial modernization. The Protocol governs an electronic act containing all the significant elements, but does not consider that, by now, many other means are used, such as e-mail messages and mobile phones or palmtop computers communications. Moreover, larger companies envisage a "traceability" of the load guaranteed in a continuous way.[11] Due to these factors, the regulatory homogeneity imagined in 1956 has been partly lost.

Meanwhile, the complexity of the operations means that the contract for carriage is enriched with services other than a simple journey, albeit related from a teleological point of view. In this regard, the question arises to what extent a deep interpretation of the provisions is possible, so as to include new agreements such as, for example, that of logistics.[12] In this study, the point is often considered with regard to various institutions, looking for an overview. Finally, as a result of technical progress, the notion of vehicle has entered into crisis, because it is not able to envisage self-driving trucks, a reality currently not far from complete realization.[13] In front of telematics and IT innovations, it is possible to evaluate the opportunity to prepare a new convention or foresee further amendments to the current one.[14]

This last solution was preferred with the 2008 Protocol and did not have the hoped-for success, given that few States have ratified it. A new overall text would presuppose the accession of the major industrialized countries and, in particular, of those that have ratified the original CMR, but it is not easy. Moreover, in the context of maritime transport, the partial success of the 1978 Hamburg Convention

---

Norway, Pakistan, Poland, Portugal, Moldova, Romania, Russian Federation, Serbia, Slovakia, Slovenia, Spain, Sweden, Switzerland, Tunisia, Turkey, Turkmenistan, Ukraine, United Kingdom and Northern Ireland, and Uzbekistan.

[9]The following States have ratified the Protocol of 20 February 2008: Belarus, Belgium, Bulgaria, Czech Republic, Denmark, Estonia, Finland, France, Iran (Islamic Republic), Latvia, Lithuania, Luxembourg, Netherlands, Norway, Oman, Poland, Portugal, Moldova, Romania, Russian Federation, Slovakia, Slovenia, Spain, Sweden, Switzerland, Tajikistan, Turkey, Ukraine, United Kingdom and Northern Ireland, and Uzbekistan.

[10]Cf. Silingardi et al. (1994), p. 4 ff.

[11]Cf. Putzeys (2006), p. 523 ff.; Sánchez-Gamborino (2006), p. 677 ff.; Bon-Garcin (2006), p. 706 ff.

[12]Cf. Verheyen (2016), p. 453 ff.

[13]Cf. Verheyen (2016), p. 453 ff.

[14]Cf. Antapasis (2017), p. 240 ff.

demonstrates how the efforts made in its drafting have not been fully reflected, due to the small number of ratifications.[15] An alternative scenario is a recourse to the international conference, foreseen for the revision of the CMR, pursuant to Article 49. With the reshaping of some of its projections, the most urgent problems could be solved, for example, with regard to multimodal transport.[16] To date, Article 49 has never been implemented.

However, although the innovations stratified over the decades have brought new problems and undermined some aspects of the original plant, the CMR remains crucial, as evidenced by the intense jurisprudential debate. Above all on a systematic level, the Convention is not always an easy meeting ground between continental and common law, with notable differences in the interpretation of some rules and, sometimes, in the conception of the structure of the Treaty. A critical evaluation of the intense analysis of doctrine and case law can contribute to a better understanding of the issues under discussion.

1.1.2 The Draft Revision of Some Provisions of the CMR

In the seventies, a working group created within the *Comité des transports intérieurs de la Commission économique pour l'Europe des Nations Unies* proposed the opportunity to modify some provisions of the CMR, pursuant to Article 49. In this regard, having received the issue, Unidroit prepared a summary of the various proposals,[17] including those presented by the United Kingdom, the International Chamber of Commerce (ICC) and the International Union of Road Transport (IRU), already examined by the Unidroit in a previous study.[18] In particular, many ratifying States and various organizations had proposed to provide for the carrier to be exempted from liability in the event of nuclear disasters, so that the Convention would align with those on rail transport, which had opted for this solution. Then, with regard to the provisions of the CMR, a variation of Article 1, fourth paragraph, letter a), was discarded, so that postal transport should have been included in the operational scope of CMR. At the same time, a more precise formulation of Article

[15] Cf. Antapasis (2017), p. 240 ff.

[16] Cf. Antapasis (2017), p. 240 ff.; Haak (2006), p. 325 ff.

[17] In a study presented by Unidroit: "*le groupe du travail a accepté l'offre de l'Unidroit d'élaborer un document préliminaire destiné à faciliter l'examen de la documentation existante*". It is a study presented by Unidroit in 1971, requested by the "*groupe ad hoc du groupe de travail des transports routiers de la Commission économique pour l'Europe des Nations Unies, sur les observations concernant une révision éventuelle de la CMR*".

[18] This is the 1969 study prepared by Unidroit at the request of the "*Sous - Comité des transports routiers de la Commission économique pour l'Europe des Nations Unies, sur les propositions concernant une révision de la CMR*".

2 on the stacked transport was requested.[19] Above all, this suggestion had applicative importance, while the others concerned marginal aspects.

Then, the emphasis was placed on the advisability of adopting a single model of the consignment note. In this regard, the IRU revealed a model conforming to that adopted by the UN, which was gradually introduced in road transport starting from 1 January 1971. Furthermore, the need to re-examine the formulation of the so-called "paramount" clause was highlighted, as well as the inclusion of a further letter in Article 6, first paragraph, precisely letter l). Therein should have been indicated whether the loading or unloading had to be the responsibility of the transporter or the stowage could not be carried out by the same operator. This suggestion, which had a considerable applicative importance, should have been accepted, but it was not.

In general, the modifications concerned interpretative difficulties attributable to differences between the two official versions of the text. In particular, with regard to the verification obligation incumbent on the carrier at the time of receipt of the goods, pursuant to Article 8, first paragraph, for the French text, "*le transporteur est tenu de vérifier*", while, according to the English version, "the carrier shall check". To clarify the provisions, it was suggested to delete the reference to the freight forwarder in Article 11, third paragraph, to resolve the difficulties relating to the identification of the applicable law on the basis of the private international law. In the same sense, a new formulation of the rules on the power of counter-order has been foreshadowed, so that it could be extinguished not with the delivery of the consignment note to the addressee, but with the withdrawal of the goods.

Without claiming to be exhaustive, we have to mention the suggested modification of Article 22 on the transport of dangerous goods, which would have been necessary to provide for the stipulation of a special agreement between the shipper and the carrier, with detailed information on the load and with the obligation to recall this agreement in the consignment note. The same declaration of value regulated by Article 24 and that of special interest to redelivery governed by Article 26 should have been anticipated by an agreement with the carrier. Furthermore, with regard to Article 26, another paragraph was proposed that excluded moral damage from additional one. Finally, with a partial modification of Article 41, which establishes the mandatory nature of the Convention, it was suggested to make the carrier's liability regime derogable in favor of the entitled person, with his unilateral act, outside the cases provided for by the Convention itself.

In 1972, the working group created within the *Comité des transports intérieurs de la Commission économique pour l'Europe des Nations Unies* decided that no changes were necessary, because unanimous consensus on the presented ideas had not been obtained. A revision based on simple or qualified majority would have meant that the effects of significant amendments would be produced only in relation to the States that had approved them. This would have created a division of the countries part of the CMR in two groups and would have discouraged other countries

[19] Cf. Loewe (1976), p. 403 ff.

from ratifying it.[20] However, the story deserves to be remembered, albeit after some time, because some indications were important and responded to objective problems.

1.1.3 *The Two Official Texts and the Reservations of Some Countries*

The CMR has two official texts, one in English and one in French, and they have equivalent authority.[21] Their coexistence has created interpretative problems for the use of terms with a different semantic value. Attached to each text is a signature protocol according to which "*les soussignés, dûment autorisés, sont convenus des déclarations et précisions suivantes: la présente Convention ne s'applique pas aux transports entre le Royaume - Uni de Grande Bretagne et d'Irlande du Nord et la République d'Irlande*". Since both States are now signatory to the Convention, this limitation of the scope appears superfluous. However, it is debated[22] whether its abrogation can be ordered by a unilateral act by the United Kingdom, the only one to have signed the Protocol.

This solution would run counter to the final provisions of the Convention itself. In fact, for Article 47, any divergence between two or more signatory countries on the interpretation or application of CMR, not resolved by negotiations or otherwise, can be brought before the International Court of Justice, upon the request of one of the States. According to Article 48, when signing or ratifying the CMR, each country can make a reservation with regard to Article 47, but, pursuant to Article 48, third paragraph, no other is allowed. Therefore, the two States mentioned in the Protocol can neither unilaterally nor consensually revoke this reservation. Rather, for the latter to be eliminated, an international agreement accepted by all countries[23] would be needed.

Then, at the time of its accession, Spain stated that it would not apply the CMR in Gibraltar, which falls within the scope of the Convention, following a declaration by the United Kingdom. Spain's decision does not constitute a reservation, which would be void pursuant to Article 48, but refers to Article X of the Treaty of Utrecht of 13 July 1973, which does not authorize Gibraltar to carry out land transport with Spain.[24]

Until now, no country has applied Article 49, according to which, by means of a notification addressed to the Secretary-General of the UN, it is possible to convene a

[20] Cf. Loewe (1976), p. 405 ff.

[21] Cf. Clarke (2014), p. 16 ff., according to whom "the English and the French texts are of equal authority".

[22] Cf. Czapski (2006), p. 558 ff.

[23] Cf. Czapski (2006), p. 558 ff.

[24] Cf. Czapski (2006), p. 559 ff.

conference to review the Convention.[25] In particular, the Secretary must notify all States of this request and may convene the conference if he obtains the consent of at least a quarter of these within four months of notification. Finally, according to Article 44, each country can denounce the Convention with a communication to the UN Secretary-General and the denunciation takes effect twelve months after the date on which the Secretary receives the notice.

1.1.4 A Possible Interpretation of Article 1, Fifth Paragraph, on the Amendments to CMR

According to Article 1, fifth paragraph, the signatory States undertake not to introduce changes to the CMR with agreements between two or more of them. The provision aims to preserve the uniformity of the Convention, avoiding its disarticulation in several bilateral pacts. Therefore, any ratifying State can rely on the full application of the CMR.[26] This principle was called into question with the adoption of the Protocol of 5 July 1978, which entered into force on 28 December 1980, and emended Article 23, third paragraph, inserting the seventh, eighth and ninth paragraphs. Since only a part of the States that had originally ratified the CMR accepted the Protocol, it kickstarted the fragmentation process of the Convention, resulting in the adoption of the Protocol of 27 May 2008, on the electronic consignment note, eventually entered into force on 5 June 2015.[27]

There have been several attempts to heal this fracture of the system of the CMR[28] and, initially, an orientation[29] considered the modification of Article 23 coherent with Article 49 of the same Convention, but a conference has never been convened, with a request addressed to the Secretary-General of the United Nations for the revision of the CMR, as required by the same Article 49. Then, the solution,[30] according to which the limit of liability would be calculated on the basis of special drawing rights also for the States that have not ratified the relative Protocol, has given way to the more recent one,[31] for which the relative text applies only to countries who have stipulated the Protocol; for the others, Article 23 in its original version still applies. This latter approach is more convincing, as it assumes that an agreement can produce its effects only if it is accepted. Basically, the question is whether the adaptation of the CMR to the new requirements causes an implicit repeal

[25] Cf. Loewe (1976), p. 403 ff.

[26] Cf. Loewe (1976), p. 522 ff.; Rogov (2005), p. 464 ff.

[27] Cf. Czapski (2006), p. 551 ff.

[28] Cf. Rogov (2005), p. 465 ff.

[29] Cf. Rogov (2005), p. 465 ff.

[30] Cf. Rogov (2005), p. 465 ff.

[31] Cf. Rogov (2005), p. 465 ff.

of Article 1, fifth paragraph, or if the adoption of amending protocols leads to a violation of the Treaty.

For political and economic reasons, the protocols consistent with the structure of the CMR have been considered in light of the principles established by the 1969 Vienna Convention on treaties. In spite of its Article 4, which sanctions the nonretroactivity of the same Vienna Convention, this did not prevent the application of its criteria to the treaties prior to its entry into force, due to the general relevance of the same canons.[32] Therefore, according to Article 40, fourth paragraph, of the 1969 Convention, the agreement containing amendments does not bind States that are already parties to the treaty, but do not accept the latter agreement. Article 30, fourth paragraph, letter b), of the same Convention operates, according to which, if there are two treaties, one of which is a later one, in relations between a country that has ratified both and a State that has signed only one of the two, the one which has been signed by both shall apply. Based on this persuasive reconstruction, the additional protocols to the CMR are binding only for the countries that apply them. The fragmentation of the Geneva Convention into single bilateral relations threatens the system as a whole and, in particular, this process has repercussions on Article 31, third paragraph, with the weakening of the principle established to supervise the enforceability of judicial decisions against all signatory States.

1.2 Transport Covered by the Geneva Convention

1.2.1 The Definition of Road Transport

According to Article 1, the CMR applies to international road freight transport.[33] Without giving a precise definition,[34] this provision outlines the distinctive features of this contract,[35] in addition to indicating some cases that do not fall within the scope of validity of the Convention.[36] Therefore, it refers to a consensual contract

---

[32] Cf. Rogov (2005), p. 468 ff.

[33] Cf. BGH 17 July 2008, in *Europ. transp. law.*, 2009, no. 44, 196, according to which "unless provided otherwise the direct application of the CMR provisions is restricted in principle to cross - border unimodal transport contracts"; LG Aachen 21 March 2017, in *TranspR*, 2018, 22, according to which a transport framework contract involves the application of the CMR, in the presence of the related requisites referring to the single trip. See also Gruber (2017), p. 11 ff.; Antapasis (2017), p. 13 ff.; Sánchez-Gamborino (2001), p. 843 ff.; De La Motte and Temme (2013), p. 58 ff.

[34] Cf. Haak (1986), p. 55 ff., according to whom "the CMR does not contain a definition of transport contract, from which elements could be distilled by which to delimit other contracts in the transport sphere"; Ferrari (2018), p. 1244 ff.

[35] Cf. Silingardi et al. (1994), p. 12 ff.; Ferrari (2018), p. 1243 ff. See also App. Grenoble 10 September 2020, in *Le Lamy transp.*, 2021, vol. I, 473.

[36] Cf. App. Aix-en-Provence 30 October 2014, in *Bull. transp. logist.*, 2014, 694; Rodière (1970), p. 622 ff.

and, for its stipulation, the written form is not required.[37] Agreements concluded orally, by telephone or fax,[38] are valid, and the delivery of the goods to the carrier is necessary for the custody service to begin,[39] but not for the completion of the agreement. The CMR regulates contracts concerning the transfer of "*marchandises*"[40] and, in particular, since it does not give a definition of goods, for some[41] the problem could be referred to domestic law. This argument is not convincing, as, to safeguard its uniform character, the Convention must be interpreted in its legal system.[42] Moreover, excluding some transports, Article 1, fourth paragraph, letters a), b), and c), implicitly define the notion of goods as any object other than those mentioned. Therefore, pursuant to Article 1, a significant load may include goods that move on wheels or have no commercial value, but Article 1 does not refer, for example, to postal transport.

The notion of "*marchandises*" must not be understood in a restrictive sense, with reference only to the transfer of loads relating to a sale, as the expression does not consider the underlying relationships between the sender and the consignee and, therefore, the reasons that may push the shipper to conclude his agreement. Rather, the term "*marchandises*" refers to "tangible movable goods in general".[43] So, as an accessory to the transfer of persons, baggage is not a "*marchandises*" and its movement is not subject to the CMR. Then, the container would not be good for Article 1, second paragraph, as it would be the envelope of the load, so that the CMR would not regulate its possible damage.[44] Without entering into the merits of an evaluation of its nature, the argument is not convincing, as the Convention itself considers the goods with their packaging, as, for example, can be inferred from Article 24, which refers to the gross weight.[45] Furthermore, the trailer made

[37] Cf. Putzeys (1981), p. 20 ff.; Loewe (1976), p. 317 ff.; De La Motte and Temme (2013), p. 58 ff. See also Hof Antwerp 31 October 2011, in *Europ. transp law,* 2013, no. 48, 82, according to which "carriage by couriers can fall under the CMR Convention provided that the cumulative conditions of the Convention are fulfilled".

[38] Cf. Loewe (1976), p. 318 ff.

[39] Cf. Putzeys (1981), p. 20 ff.

[40] The French version of Article 1 reads, "*la présente Convention s'applique à tout contrat de marchandises par route à titre onereux*". The English version of Article 1 reads, "the present Convention shall apply to every contract for the carriage of goods by road (. . .) for reward". Cf. De La Motte and Temme (2013), p. 85 ff.

[41] Cf. Clarke (2014), p. 30 ff.

[42] Cf. Haak (1986), p. 55 ff., according to whom "application of criteria drawn from a particular national system in order to ascertain the content of the transport contract would put in danger the principal aim of the Convention, namely, to lay down a uniform regulation of the carrier's liability".

[43] Cf. Loewe (1976), p. 319 ff.

[44] Cf. RB Antwerp 7 January 1977, in *Europ. transp. law,* 1977, no. 12, 420; RB Antwerp 27 October 1972, *ibid.,* 1972, no. 7, 1054.

[45] Cf. Clarke (2014), p. 31ff.; Rodière (1970), p. 622 ff., according to whom "it is of no great significance whether the goods are carried as separate packages or in 'containers'".

available free of charge to the carrier by the sender is considered as "*marchandises*", together with the goods loaded at a later time.[46]

Finally, the transfer must be carried out "*par route*", with the only exception of overlapping transport, regulated by Article 2.[47] The carrier must not be a professional, as the Convention is silent on this role; therefore, any transport performed outside the entrepreneurial activity could fall within the scope of the CMR,[48] although this scenario is rare, even more so in an era like ours, in which the complexity of operations requires the intervention of organized companies.

The transfer must be for consideration.[49] However, this does not necessarily imply a "cash payment",[50] but, only that it is commensurate with the complexity of the trip. Therefore, free transport, that made by friends or those carried out for symbolic amounts are excluded. Then, according to Article 1, third paragraph, the Convention operates for transfers made by States, government institutions or bodies. The purpose of the provision was to favor the accession of the then socialist countries and avoid conflicts in implementation in the States in which transport was subject to nationalization measures.[51]

In defining the transport itself, Article 1 is affected by its time and, therefore, gives a meager notion of it. This has favored raids by national laws, raids aimed at filling any relative gaps, to the detriment of a uniform application of the Convention. According to Article 1, the CMR operates if the contract is valid, but domestic law does not apply, as the question must be resolved only according to the Convention orders.[52] In the event that the shipper entrusts a load that the carrier should not have accepted, because of a higher value than that permitted in his general conditions, any receipt of the goods by him is sufficient for the application of the CMR[53] and there is no case of a null and void contract. Although the contrary has been stated,[54] such a clause of the general conditions is not invalid, as it delimits the commitment of the carrier, who is under no obligation to accept any assignment, nor is this required by Article 41. In any case, there is no reference to national law,[55] not having any area of its own. As part of the ongoing relationship, the carrier may limit his availability to perform the transport. This pertains to the subject of the contract and does not

[46] Cf. RB Rotterdam 6 July 2011, in *Europ. transp. law,* 2011, no. 46, 655.

[47] Cf. Loewe (1976), p. 319 ff.; De La Motte and Temme (2013), p. 87 ff.; Ferrari (2018), p. 1247 ff.

[48] Cf. Loewe (1976), p. 320 ff.

[49] Cf. De La Motte and Temme (2013), p. 61 ff.

[50] Cf. Silingardi et al. (1994), p. 13 ff.; Loewe (1976), p. 320 ff.

[51] Cf. Silingardi et al. (1994), p. 14 ff.; Rodière (1970), p. 623 ff., according to whom "the detail is particularly useful in making effective the membership of socialist countries".

[52] Cf. Verheyen (2016), p. 444 ff.

[53] Cf. *Datect Electronic Holdings Limited and Others* c. *United Parcels Service Limited and Another,* in *Unif. law rev.,* 2005, 624.

[54] Cf. OLG Keulen 25 March 2004, in *TranspR,* 2004, 358; BGH 17 July 2008, *ibid.,* 2008, 365; Hof Amsterdam 28 August 2008, in *S&S,* 2011, 79.

[55] Cf. Verheyen (2016), p. 444 ff.

conflict with any provision of the CMR, regardless of whether it is done with general conditions or in another way. In fact, each operator can define his activity and, at the same time, derogate from what was originally imagined.

Over time, new organizational methods have developed, with dystonic features compared with the traditional transport of goods. In the field of logistics, "freight integration contracts" are increasing, in which the mode of transport is indeterminate at the time of stipulation. If these agreements provide for a journey, if international, the CMR always applies, although opposing arguments have been formulated,[56] wrongly influenced by domestic law, which has no relevance. For instance, for the Belgian one,[57] the road transport contract for goods is such if there is an agreement on the vehicle at the time of stipulation. Conversely, for Germany[58] and the Netherlands,[59] it is possible to define at a later stage how the transfer takes place. This is relevant for national agreements, but these previsions do not affect the interpretation of the CMR, which considers the international transports exclusively and comprehensively. In no way is its application precluded if the contract is included in a broader consensual scheme and, for example, in a mixed agreement, according to an expression of both Italian and German law. Failing that, illegitimately it would be easy for the parties to evade the operation of the CMR, using more articulated consensual schemes in which transport is included, in contrast with the spirit and letter of the CMR.

Obviously, the Convention can only be invoked if the carriage is on road and international, regardless of the fact that these characteristics appear in one part of the journey and are not predetermined at the conclusion of the contract. For instance, with regard to a "freight integration contract", it does not matter that some transfers are international or by road and others do not have these characteristics, because, for example, the goods are forwarded to the station and proceed by rail. Only in the first scenario does the Convention operate, and it is mandatory, so that an opposite consensual indication would not be valid.

Similar conclusions must be drawn with regard to a recent case, the so-called "green last mile logistic",[60] in which the last part of the journey is carried out with bicycles or "pedestrian couriers". The CMR regulates transport on trucks, as stated by Article 1.[61] Therefore, it applies to the journey up to the point at which the cycling section begins. If the parties are free to opt for this ecological solution, it is an ancillary service, but subsequent to road transport and the achievement of its

---

[56] Cf. Verheyen (2016), p. 449 ff.

[57] Cf. Cass. Belgium 8 November 2004, in *Europ. transp. law,* 2006, no. 41, 228, according to which, "if the contract between parties does not mention the mode of transport and if it is not clear from the circumstances of the case that parties has a road transport in mind, then the CMR is inapplicable". See also Verheyen (2016), p. 449 ff.

[58] Cf. BGH 4 March 2004, in *TranspR,* 2004, 460.

[59] Cf. Hof Gravenage 28 November 2007, in *S&S,* 2009, 28 ff.

[60] Cf. Verheyen (2016), p. 455 ff.

[61] Cf. Jung (1997), p. 150 ff.

destination, in the sense of the Convention. The opposite evolutionary interpretation[62] is against the literal tenor of the CMR.

1.2.2 The Presumed Relevance of the Consignment Note in Determining the Scope of the Geneva Convention

Pursuant to Article 1, to apply the CMR, the place of receipt and the one envisaged for delivery must be located in two different countries, of which at least one has signed the Convention.[63] It is an objective requirement and, if it is met, the uniform law text applies, regardless of whether the sender or carrier is aware of it. With an isolated solution, according to the Italian case law, the operation would be conditioned by an explicit clause of the contractors, affixed in the consignment note. In accordance with an orientation dating back over time,[64] for a decision,[65] "the applicability of the Geneva Convention (. . .) requires that the parties have expressed their will in this sense, both by inserting the indication in the consignment note for which the transport is subject to the regime provided for by the aforementioned Convention, pursuant to Article 6, first paragraph, letter k), or, failing that, with agreements, even oral, demonstrable by any means".

For this approach, the purpose of Article 6, first paragraph, letter k), would be to leave the freedom to decide whether to apply the CMR. Article 4 should be coordinated with Article 6, first paragraph, letter k), and Article 7, third paragraph. In particular, this last provision would not make sense in case of the indication of Article 6, first paragraph, letter k), as no expense and no prejudice could arise to the entitled person if the agreement was subject to the Convention. Then, in the absence of an express declaration, the desire to refer to the uniform law text could be demonstrated in another way. Therefore, the Convention would be mandatory, pursuant to Article 41, only if recalled.

Italian case law made the error not to grasp the sense of the mandatory nature of the reference to the CMR in the consignment note. In fact, Article 6, first paragraph, letter k), refers to the "paramount clause", that is to an agreement under which the applicability of the Convention is extended to nonadhering countries. Although the Italian legal theory[66] has always criticized this approach and underlined its dystonic character with respect to the clear literal tenor of Article 1, with the exception of

[62] Cf. Verheyen (2016), p. 455 ff.

[63] Cf. Van Hee (2017), p. 17 ff.; Kolacs (2017), p. 23 ff.; Katauskas (2017), p. 29 ff.

[64] Cf. Cass. Italy 28 November 1975, no. 3983, in *Giur. it. mass.,* 1975.

[65] Cf. Cass. Italy 7 February 2006, no. 2529, in *Giur. it mass.,* 2006. See also Cass. Italy 5 March 2019, no. 6316, *ibid.,* 2019.

[66] Cf. Pesce (1995), p. 55 ff.; Silingardi (1987), p. 613 ff.; Tullio (1992), p. 192 ff.

isolated contrary decisions,[67] the case law has remained firm on its positions, in open contrast with the interpretation given by other legal systems, in which the CMR has unconditional binding force, according to known points of view.[68]

The consequences of this erroneous statement are evident; in particular, in Italian law, the CMR has been transformed from "uniform legislation of necessary application into pact discipline".[69] The function of regulating the compensation of damages if the contract is not governed by the Convention, due to the lack of reference in the consignment note, is attributed to Article 7, third paragraph. On the contrary, for Article 7, third paragraph, the restoration of the prejudice is connected to the more limited scenarios in which the uniform law text does not have a binding force, because it is invoked by countries that are not part of the Convention. Finally, expressed will was identified as an essential prerequisite for the operation of the Convention, in contrast with the wording of Article 6, first paragraph, letter k), instead aimed at extending the same CMR to States that have not ratified it.

Basically, for the Italian case law, the Convention would be optional, but it would become mandatory if recalled. In this way, Article 4 is refuted,[70] so that, in the event of an express declaration not being made, the entire Convention would be inapplicable. Furthermore, the compilation of the consignment note has nothing to do with the operation of uniform law. Finally, as noted,[71] "a now acquired principle is being called into question (. . .), by virtue of which the legal certainty to which the adoption of internationally uniform measures is addressed cannot be compromised by the use of negotiation autonomy as a criterion of connection for the purpose of identifying the material law applicable to the specific relationship".

1.2.3 Types of Carriage Excluded from the Scope of the Geneva Convention

According to Article 1, fourth paragraph, letter a), b) and c), the "*transports effectués sous l'empire de conventions postales internationals*", the "*transports funéraires*"

---

[67] Cf. App. Brescia 1 June 2001, in *Dir. transp.*, 2002, 573 ff., according to which the CMR has a binding nature, without the need for a reference expressed in the contract, when the transport ends in a country other than the one in which it started, pursuant to Article 1; Trib. Lucca 24 April 2013, in *Giur. it. mass.*, 2013.

[68] Cf. Clarke (2014), p. 63 ff.; Messent and Glass (2018), p. 95 ff.; Loewe (1976), p. 338 ff.; Libouton (1973), p. 27 ff.

[69] Cf. Silingardi et al. (1994), p. 20 ff.

[70] Cf. Cass. Italy 7 February 2006, no. 2529, in *Giur. it. rep.*, 2006; Cass. Italy 28 November 1975, no. 3983, *ibid.*, 1975; Cass. Italy 1 March 1978, no. 1034, *ibid.*, 1978; Cass. Italy 26 November 1980, no. 6272, *ibid.*, 1980; Cass. Italy 2 October 2003, no. 14680, *ibid.*, 2003.

[71] Cf. Silingardi et al. (1994), p. 20 ff.

and, finally, the "*déménagement*" ones are not governed by the CMR.[72] Funeral transport is excluded because it presupposes a "particular specialization of carriers in correlation with health regulations"[73] and is disciplined by a specific convention.[74] Human and animal bodies fall into this category, provided that, in the latter case, the journey is intended for their burial. Flowers and crowns accompanying the coffin are considered ancillary goods[75] and, therefore, they are not subject to the CMR, as opposed to funeral articles, such as caskets, as they are also "*marchandises*".[76]

International postal transport is also regulated by a specific convention and, therefore, does not fall within the scope of the CMR.[77] Due to the way it is organized, even the move has been excluded from the scope of the Convention; in fact, "the application of the CMR to removals would be time-consuming and inappropriate",[78] and although an independent regulation would have been desirable for this case as well, a convention has never been concluded. Furthermore, as containers are used more and more frequently for removals, the question arises whether a specific regulation is necessary.[79]

As, in practice, the two cases overlap, to make sense of Article 1, fourth paragraph, letter c), and define the scope of the CMR, identifying the dividing line between transport in the strict sense and moving operations is necessary.[80] Thus, activities aimed not only at transferring the goods, but also at preparing and packing them pertain to the latter.[81] Therefore, a transport in which the furniture is placed in two containers is not a moving operation, because the preparatory phases of picking up the objects and their packaging are lacking and, therefore, the transport itself falls back into the area of the CMR.[82] However, characteristics of the vehicle used are

[72] The French version of Article 1, fourth paragraph, let. a), letter b), and letter c). The English text reads, "carriage performed under the terms of any postal conventions", "funeral consignments" and "furniture removal".

[73] Cf. Pesce (1995), p. 84 ff.

[74] This is the Convention on the carriage of human remains stipulated in Strasbourg on 26 October 1973.

[75] Cf. Loewe (1976), p. 324 ff.; Messent and Glass (2018), p. 51 ff.

[76] Cf. Clarke (2014), p. 32 ff.

[77] Cf. LG Düsseldorf 23 November 2001, in *TranspR,* 2002, 28, according to which postal transports are not regulated by the CMR; LG Bonn 20 December 2001, *ibid.,* 2002, 443, according to which postal administration are not regulated by the CMR. See also De La Motte and Temme (2013), p. 102 ff.

[78] Cf. Clarke (2014), p. 32 ff.

[79] Cf. Clarke (2014), p. 32ff.; Haak (1986), p. 51 ff.; Rodière (1970), p. 622 ff., according to whom, "if one takes into consideration today the number of things conveyed by containers, such a special exception for those containers involved in the removal trade is hard to justify"; Fillers (2020), p. 178 ff.

[80] Cf. Loewe (1976), p. 325 ff.; De La Motte and Temme (2013), p. 104 ff.

[81] Cf. Rodière (1970), p. 620 ff.

[82] Cf. RB Antwerp 1 April 1980, in *Europ. transp. law,* 1980, no. 15, 461 ff.; Hof Antwerp 16 October 1985, *ibid.,* 1986, no. 21, 377; OLG Düsseldorf 3 May 1984, in *TranspR,* 1984, 198; *Parr* c. *Clark & Rose Ltd.* in *S. C. R. L.*, 2002, 222.

irrelevant.[83] Then, emphasis was placed on the fact that the move presupposes a transfer from one building to another. Therefore, it does not fall under Article 1, fourth paragraph, letter c), the movement of furniture from the shop in which it is purchased to the office to be furnished,[84] as opposed to what happens if the operation is aimed at moving it from the main office of an English company to a secondary one in Paris.[85] However, for a more restrictive argument,[86] the transfer of some personal furniture does not fall within the exception of Article 1, fourth paragraph, letter c), because there would be no need for a change of residence, so that the transport falls back into the scope of the CMR. This idea is not convincing because, in any case, it is a journey destined to satisfy the interests of the family and requires the packaging of the goods.

1.2.4 The Definition of Vehicle in the Geneva Convention

With regard to the means, pursuant to Article 1, second paragraph, "vehicles" include motor ones, articulated vehicles and semi-trailers, as defined by Article 4 of the Convention for road traffic, signed in Geneva on 19 September 1949.[87] In turn, it was replaced with that on road traffic, signed in Vienna on 8 November 1968, which entered into force on 21 May 1977. In particular, according to Article 4 of the Vienna Convention, a "motor vehicle" is that intended for the transport of people or goods by road and the "trailer" is any vehicle that must be towed by a motor one. This term includes the concept of "semi-trailer". This expression defines any trailer intended to be joined to a motor vehicle, so that a part rests on the latter and a considerable component of its mass is supported by the motor vehicle itself. Finally, an "articulated vehicle" is the set of vehicles consisting of a motor one and a semi-trailer connected to the first. Thus, travel carried out by means other than those expressly indicated by the Vienna Convention,[88] starting with bicycles, is not international transport, according to the CMR.

In recalling the 1949 Geneva Convention, the CMR has made it binding on every State that has ratified the same CMR, albeit within the narrow limits of Article 1, second paragraph, with regard to those systems that have not adhered to the 1949

[83]Cf. OLG Hamburg 3 July 1980, in *VersR*, 1980, 1075.

[84]Cf. Putzeys (1981), p. 41 ff.

[85]Cf. OLG Hamburg 28 February 1985, in *TranspR*, 1985, 436.

[86]Cf. OLG Hamburg 28 February 1985, in *TranspR*, 1985, 436.

[87]Cf. De La Motte and Temme (2013), p. 95 ff.; Ferrari (2018), p. 1249 ff.

[88]Cf. Rodière (1970), p. 622 ff., according to whom that "effected by vehicle excluded (though in those circumstances would be possible to speak properly of a contract of carriage?)" is not transport.

Convention. On the contrary, according to some,[89] the Vienna Convention, which modified that of 1949, precisely because it was not referred to in Article 1, would not be applicable in the States that have ratified it. It would not be enough for a country to have stipulated the CMR, but the argument is not acceptable. Although there is no express reference, the 1968 Convention follows the fate of the 1949 Geneva one and, furthermore, the former affects Article 1, second paragraph, of the CMR, although the reference has changed. Therefore, the States that have signed the CMR must ensure the implementation of the Vienna Convention[90] for the limited purposes of international transport.

The 1968 Vienna Convention[91] does not only define the vehicle but, after having indicated the different types, the same Article 1, letter v), considers the figure of the driver and identifies him in every person who takes the helm of a vehicle, motor vehicle or other (including cycles). There is a correlation between circulation and the driver, and this is confirmed by Article 8, first paragraph, according to which every vehicle or every set of moving means must have a driver; for Article 8, fifth paragraph, of the Vienna Convention, he must have constant control of the vehicle.

In particular, according to Article 13, in each juncture, the driver must remain a master of driving, so that he can comply with criteria of prudence and is able to carry out all the relevant maneuvers, for instance, by adjusting the speed in relation to the state of the road, the atmospheric conditions and traffic intensity. Basically, the driver must be in a position to slow down and, if necessary, to stop, if situations require it.

With technological progress, the idea of circulation changes, no longer anchored to the necessary human presence. In perspective, traditional driving can be an alternative to a self-driving mode and, albeit in a future projection, usual traffic could be significantly reduced. To adapt the Vienna Convention to technological innovation, in 2014, the *Working Party on the Road Traffic Safety* of *United Nations Economic Commission for Europe* (UNECE) approved an amendment to the same Vienna Convention, and it entered into force on 23 March 2016.[92] According to Article 8, fifth paragraph *bis,* the driver can remove his hands from the steering wheel, as long as he is able to deactivate the automatic driving system and regain control at any time.

---

[89] V: Messent and Glass (2018), p. 51 ff., according to whom, with regard to the applicability of the 1968 Convention, "it is doubtful whether this can be done in this country in the absence of specific legislative enactment".

[90] Cf. Loewe (1976), p. 322 ff., according to whom, "in cases where States parties to CMR are not parties to that Convention, the relevant definitions contained in it become part of their law on the basis of the reference appearing in CMR".

[91] Cf. Pastore (1997), p. 45 ff. Consider also the United Nations Convention on Road Traffic signed in Geneva on 19 September 1949.

[92] Although in the different sphere of the Convention relating to the contract for the international carriage of goods by road, signed in Geneva on 19 May 1956, cf. Kolacs and Hopster (2017), p. 150 ff., according to whom "the interpretative framework of the CMR allows for the evolutionary interpretation of terms included in the convention".

1.2.5 Regulatory Prospects for International Freight Transport by Driverless Vehicles

The CMR dates back to 1956 and transport was carried out only with traditional vehicles; autonomous driving still was a distant idea. Regardless of the reference to the Vienna Convention, the CMR presupposes the role of the pilot. Rather than reiterating the correlation between transport and driver, taken for granted during those times, the reference to the 1968 Convention responded and still today satisfies the need to define the notion of vehicle. In the CMR, the role of the pilot is crucial, identified with the carrier or one of his auxiliaries.

For instance, pursuant to Article 12, first paragraph, the sender can change the initial program along the journey. The shipper holds a unilateral power[93] and its exercise is not conditional on any assumption, but is the expression of a free choice.[94] Finally, the counter-order is exercised against the carrier, who must comply with the instructions, without being able to investigate their motivations, which are irrelevant. Any variations may concern all the profiles of the original journey, from the itinerary, if agreed, to the identification of the consignee, to that of the place of destination. Furthermore, the CMR provides for a system of reserves, which can be formulated by the carrier when he takes delivery of the goods or by the recipient upon arrival. According to Article 8, the transporter must verify the accuracy of the information given in the consignment note and related to the number of packages and the markings. Moreover, he must ascertain the apparent state of the goods and their packaging.

Then, for the entire journey, he must behave in a collaborative spirit. In fact, according to Article 14, first paragraph, the occurrence of events hindering[95] the execution of the journey according to the original indications requires the carrier to ask for instructions and warn of the impediment, to allow the sender to identify an alternative strategy, suitable to guarantee the conclusion of the operation. Thus, the driver is a central stakeholder in the system of the CMR. Its regulation presupposes that a person transfers the goods from one place to another and, during the journey, the main obligation is enriched by other instrumental ones, the most important of which is that of safekeeping. Although not essential, the consignment note is intended for traditional transport, performed with a driver, and it would not make sense if the delivery of the goods was not made by a human being.

On the contrary, in the case of a journey with automated trucks on predefined lines, the CMR does not allow any partial revision, as such intervention would overwhelm its entire framework. Not only the notion of vehicle should be changed,

---

[93] Cf. Silingardi et al. (1994), p. 87 ff.; Clarke (2014), p. 83 ff., according to whom "this right unilaterally to alter the terms of the contract is referred to as the right of disposal". See also Temme (2013), p. 300 ff.

[94] Cf. Wesolowsky (2013), p. 354 ff.

[95] Cf. Rodière (1971), p. 3 ff., according to whom "obstacle (. . .) indicates any event which prevents the execution of the contract in accordance with the terms laid down in the consignment note".

but, for instance, the reserve system should be eliminated. Therefore, such a transformation is unrealistic, because it would have to affect the whole regulation in a substantial way and it would be difficult to apply a text that would have become fragmented.

The idea of putting discipline back on individual national law is not reasonable, because, since 1956, Europe has experienced an important discipline of uniform law, with undoubted benefits for trade and for the serenity of the operators involved, accustomed to dealing with a text only. Looking ahead, the renunciation of this model for services performed with self-driving trucks could create problems for enterprises, which are not used at all to identify the applicable domestic law. A more promising option is a supranational discipline, such as a regulation or a directive of the European Union, even if, in this latter case, many States that have joined the CMR would be excluded. A more inclusive instrument could be offered by a second and distinct international convention.

In perspective, if the option of a supranational discipline or of an international treaty law is adopted, it becomes necessary to deal with the new concept of truck, with the progressive disappearance of the driver and of ancillary obligations, first of all, to comply with the counter-order and provide information. The loading and accommodation of the goods in the vehicle would become a focal point for the carrier's liability, because the reserve system would have to change entirely. In fact, before the journey, if there were no driver, it would no longer be possible to check the condition of the cargo in a discussion between the sender and the transporter. First and foremost, the pilot has now to focus on the location of the load on the vehicle. Given the fact that automated ones cannot be controlled remotely, the fact of giving further intermediate indications by the shipper would be no longer possible. As the system is already set up from the start, the counter-order power would be compressed and, at the same time, the focus on the sender's needs would be reduced.

The impediments that arise during the execution of the contract should be subject to a new uniform regulation. Furthermore, the rules on liability for loss or damage should consider the role of the producer of the information systems alongside that of the carrier. In fact, the load may suffer damage due to a construction defect of the vehicle or poor maintenance. Therefore, it is possible to imagine a different division of liability between the manufacturer of the self-driving vehicle and the transporter, obviously only if they are different subjects.

In sum, with the use of a truck without a driver, on the one hand, the relationships among the sender, the carrier and the consignee would change radically, as, for example, the space reserved for possible second thoughts on the journey would be reduced. On the other hand, the inclusion of a new subject, such as the manufacturer of the vehicle, could make the rules on liability more complex. We should not ask ourselves what the features of a possible regulation should be; however, if this reflection is not current, it is about to become. It would be serious if the supranational structures and those aimed at favoring the adoption of treaties did not understand the importance of the choice made in 1956, namely the creation of a uniform system of law that has been in place for over sixty years. The road to take is not the one of domestic regulations; indeed, the shorter and more linear path would be an initiative of the European Union, because it could trigger a more complex international convention.

1.2.6 The So-called Platooning

Technological advances in self-driving vehicle construction are combined with a new form of traffic, the so-called platooning. Its use is already frequent with current techniques and, at the moment, it consists in the arrangement of a convoy composed of trucks, each with its own driver; each of them follows the indications of the first. In this way, the vehicles can proceed at a constant speed with greater safety, guaranteed by a regular and synchronous movement.[96] The direction of the column is entrusted to the pilot of the first truck; therefore, any mistake he makes may result in damage to one of the following vehicles.

Platooning has no affinity with cumulative transport, governed by Articles 34 ff. of the Convention. In fact, platooning envisages the intervention of several carriers in the execution phase. Undoubtedly, this applies only if the trucks are from different companies, but operate simultaneously and are not under the same contract. According to Article 1 of the CMR, for there to be a transport, both the "navigation of the cargo"[97] and the "propulsion"[98] are necessary, that is, the management of the vehicle. Therefore, as the initial driver is entrusted with the task of directing the convoy, each operator independently responds for damage caused to the goods transported.[99]

Basically, if, following an imprudent behavior of the first pilot, the vehicle in the column were to suffer prejudice, the other carriers would still respond on the basis of the CMR.[100] The fact to align with the indications of others has no relevance for any exemption from liability. According to a recent argument,[101] the first driver would be an auxiliary of subsequent transporters, pursuant to Article 3 of the CMR and, therefore, the latter would answer for his acts and omissions. The statement is correct; the fact that the CMR regulates only the liability of the carrier toward the sender and the consignee does not exclude the use of a particular driving strategy. However, this does not affect the liability of the transporter, even for the impact of these methods and, consequently, for the trust placed in the first driver. The problem of internal relations between different operators is quite different, especially with respect to the one in which the pilot of the first vehicle in the column works. As there

[96] Cf. Verheyen (2016), p. 452 ff.
[97] Cf. Verheyen (2016), p. 452 ff.
[98] Cf. Verheyen (2016), p. 452 ff.
[99] Cf. Verheyen (2016), p. 453 ff.
[100] Cf. Verheyen (2018), p. 22 ff.
[101] Cf. Verheyen (2018), p. 19 ff.

is no cumulative transport, the topic is entirely outside the scope of the CMR and is governed by domestic law, according to which any liability must be assessed.

1.2.7 The International Nature of Transport

The CMR pertains to international transport and, according to Article 1, the place of delivery of the goods to the carrier and their destination must be located in two different States, of which at least one must have signed the Convention.[102] The provision is independent of the reference to the residence or nationality of the contracting parties and defines the international character in relation to the transfer of the load[103] and the extreme points of the relative journey; these factors can be inferred from the contract. Thus, despite the stipulation of two agreements, of which the first is functional to transport from Marseille to the Italian border and the second to the subsequent redelivery in Milan, the entire operation falls within the scope of the CMR, as the journey begins in a State other than the one of destination and its breakdown into two parts, subject to different contracts, does not prevent the application of the same Article 1. Failing that, it would be easy to elude the uniform law.[104] Then, according to an Austrian decision,[105] the CMR would not apply to an entire transport performed abroad. The solution is not convincing, because although the transport does not take place in Austria, it can still be subjected to the CMR if the itinerary involves two States. The fact that not even a part of it takes place in Austria is irrelevant, without prejudice to the identification criteria of the judge of the State having jurisdiction, pursuant to Article 31.

Furthermore, the Convention applies if, having become impossible to reach the destination, the goods are returned to the sender; then, the fact that most of the journey is made in the same State or that the cargo does not arrive is irrelevant.[106] Actually, it is enough to plan the trip in compliance with the criteria of Article 1, and the failure to perform the journey pertains to the pathological events of transport, which are in any case regulated by the Convention. Then, a national path that precedes or follows the international one falls within the scope of CMR if it is part

[102] Cf. Haak (1986), p. 44 ff.; Rodière (1970), p. 624 ff.; Krings (1999), p. 142 ff.; De La Motte and Temme (2013), p. 56 ff.; Ferrari (2018), p. 1252 ff. See also Cass. France 25 May 1993, in *Europ. transp. law,* 1994, no. 29, 366, according to which "*en matière de transport international, la CMR l'emporte sur les lois nationales*". See also the 1962 study by Unidroit on the interpretation of Article 1, first paragraph, carried out at the request of the IRU, according to which with Article 1, first paragraph, the scope of application of the Convention has to be extended as far as possible.

[103] Cf. Loewe (1976), p. 327 ff.

[104] Cf. Putzeys (1981), p. 87 ff.

[105] Cf. OGH 19 January 2011, in *TranspR,* 2011, 255.

[106] Cf. *Quantum Ltd.* c. *Plane Trucking Ltd.,* in *Lloyd's rep.,* 2001, 131; Clarke (2014), p. 53 ff.; Rodière (1970), p. 624 ff.

of the overall operation.[107] On the contrary, the transfer is governed by domestic law if it is covered by a separate contract with exclusive internal significance.[108] In particular, the consignment note may not cover the transport to its final destination,[109] or the last part of the route may be "*entre deux points du territoire français*" and entrusted to a subsequent carrier.[110] In both situations, as already stated, the second contract would be governed by domestic law.[111] For the last case, the conclusion is correct and, for the first, the consignment note alone is not relevant, pursuant to Article 4; the overall will must be considered, regardless of the means by which it is proved.

According to some,[112] it would be possible to enter into subsequent national agreements, provided that there is a so-called breaking of the load at the border, with the entrusting of the goods to a different carrier. On the contrary, one contract performed by multiple transporters would fall within the scope of the CMR. This argument is correct with regard to the second case;[113] moreover, this one is regulated by the same Convention as cumulative transport. The first statement is not persuasive, because the intention is to plan an international transport in any case and the breaking down of the route into internal journeys within a single country does not affect this aspect.[114]

---

[107] Cf. App. Lyon 18 October 1985, in *Bull. transp.*, 1986, 744, according to which it falls within the scope of the CMR the entire route Sarezzo (Italy), Lyon, Sochaux; in this case, the last leg is relevant because it is the final destination; Cass. com. France 30 June 2009, *ibid.*, 2009, 447; App. Versailles 5 November 2009, *ibid.*, 2010, 61; App. Versailles 24 June 2004, *ibid.*, 2004, 595; App. Versailles 14 September 2004, *ibid.*, 2004, 102; App. Chambéry 16 November 2010, *ibid.*, 2012, 632; Cass. com. France 21 November 1995, in *Le Lamy transp.*, 2021, vol. I, 476; Cass. com. France 18 March 1986, in *Bull. transp.*, 1986, 607; App. Paris 23 October 1996, *ibid.*, 1997, 106.

[108] Cf. Cass. France 21 June 1982, in *Bull. transp.*, 1982, 427; App. Paris 21 January 1986, *ibid.*, 1986, 742; App. Dijon 22 November 1988, ibid., 1989, 566; App. Lyon 3 March 1983, *ibid.*, 1983, 359; App. Paris 15 October 1986, *ibid.*, 1987, 72; App. Versailles 15 January 1986, *ibid.*, 1986, 741; App. Poitiers 18 January 1989, *ibid.*, 1990, 101; App. Paris 14 December 1977, *ibid.*, 1978, 289, according to which, if the national journey is a matter of a few meters, it is ancillary to international transport and, therefore, is subject to the CMR.

[109] Cf. App. Paris 28 March 2002, in *Le Lamy transp.*, 2021, vol. I, 475.

[110] Cf. Cass. com. France 25 March 1997, in *Le Lamy transp.*, 2021, vol. I, 475; App. Versailles 17 January 2002, in *Bull. transp. logist.*, 2002, 1999; App. Versailles 15 January 1986, *ibid.*, 1986, 741; App. Versailles 24 October 1996, *ibid.*, 1997, 491; App. Nîmes 26 May 1982, *ibid.*, 1982, 407; App. Paris 17 December 1970, *ibid.*, 1971, 49; Cass. com. France 21 June 1982, *ibid.*, 1982, 427.

[111] Cf. Cass. com. France 12 May 1987, in *Bull. transp.* 399; Trib. com. Beauvais 4 July 2002, *ibid.*, 2002, 603.

[112] Cf. Putzeys (1981), p. 87 ff.

[113] Cf. Cass. com. France 6 July 1993, in *Le Lamy transp.*, 2021, vol. I, 475; Cass. com. France 1 March 2016, *ibid.*, 2021, vol. I, 475; App. Paris 4 June 2008, in *Bull. transp. logist.*, 2008, 433; App. Bordeaux 12 December 2016, *ibid.*, 2017, 14; Trib. com. Aix-en-Provence 23 June 2003, *ibid.*, 2003, 494.

[114] Cf. AG Canton of the City of Basel 12 May 2000, in *TranspR*, 2000, 372, according to which the international character of the transport is relevant for the purposes of Article 1, first paragraph, and

If the consignee rejects the goods and, upon the shipper's instructions, the carrier delivers them to another recipient in the same State, the second transfer concerns the conclusion of the original contract.[115] The solution is consistent with Article 15, which, in fact, invites the transporter to ask for instructions in the event of impediments to delivery. Usually, the place of departure and that of destination are indicated in the consignment note;[116] if it is not so, proof can be given by other means.[117] In case of discrepancy between what results from the consignment note and what has been agreed, the actual intention prevails.[118]

1.3 The So-called "*superposé*" Transport

1.3.1 The Conditions for the Applicability of Article 2

Article 2 of the CMR identifies the risk-sharing criteria for transport performed by various means. The provision does not have "the role of a sufficient regulatory basis to support the development of multimodal transport".[119] In fact, Article 2 considers only a case characterized by the nonbreaking of the load,[120] that is, by the absence of transshipment from one vehicle to another;[121] basically, the Article considers a situation where the cargo is transferred by sea or by other means.[122] The purpose of the provision is to extend the CMR to cases which, due to the travel arrangements, would not fall within its scope of operation.[123] However, in the same road route, it is possible to transfer goods from one vehicle to another[124] or to unload them for inspections to be performed or the cargo to be rearranged or redirected.[125] However, its possible rupture does not prevent the application of the CMR to road sections if

must not be assessed with regard to the transfer. For example, the two distinct outward and return relationships from one country to another are international, with separate agreements.

[115]Cf. OLG Munich 12 April 1991, in *TranspR,* 1991, 298; Putzeys (1981), p. 86 ff.

[116]Cf. Haak (1986), p. 44 ff.

[117]Cf. App. Rouen 16 June 1972, in *Europ. transp. law,* 1972, no. 7, 1040.

[118]Cf. Clarke (2014), p. 54 ff.; Loewe (1976), p. 327 ff.; BGH 17 April 1997, in *Unif. law rev.,* 1998, 206; App. Aix-en-Provence 12 May 1992, in *Le Lamy transp.*, 2021, vol. I, 476; App. Paris 28 March 2002, *ibid.,* 2021, vol. I, 476.

[119]Cf. Silingardi et al. (1994), p. 29 ff.; Haak (1986), p. 92 ff.; Putzeys (1981), p. 94 ff.; Sánchez-Gamborino (2001), p. 849 ff.; Loewe (1976), p. 331 ff.

[120]Cf. App. Angers 15 May 2012, in *Le Lamy transp.*, 2021, vol. I, 478; Rodière (1970), p. 623 ff.; Clarke (2014), p. 28 ff., who underlines how lo - lo transport is excluded from Article 2; Laurijssen (2001a), p. 799 ff.; Putzeys (1990), p. 107 ff.; Fremuth (2013), p. 113 ff.

[121]Cf. App. Nîmes 26 May 2011, in *Le Lamy transp.*, 2021, vol. I, 478.

[122]Cf. App. Douai 6 April 2017, in *Bull. transp. logist.,* 2017, 259.

[123]Cf. Haak (1986), p. 96 ff.

[124]Cf. Silingardi et al. (1994), p. 32 ff.; Messent and Glass (2018), p. 57 ff.

[125]Cf. Clarke (2014), p. 39 ff.

they are part of an international journey, pursuant to Article 1.[126] Nearly always, the CMR applies regardless of the importance of the route traveled with a vehicle other than the motor one.[127] In fact, Article 2, second paragraph, provides for an exception if the entitled person proves that the damage or delay occurred in a part of the nonroad route is not caused by any act or omission of the relative carrier, but is the result of a fact that only nonroad transport could have caused.[128] Therefore, the CMR fully applies in case of nondefined prejudice.[129] Then, if, after having agreed to perform the journey by various means, after the transshipment, the transfer ends without breaking the load, the original prevails over the actual method of execution, with the consequent exclusion of the application of the CMR.[130]

Since the notion of vehicle in Article 1, second paragraph, refers to the list of the 1949 Geneva Convention on road traffic, neither the so-called swap body nor the container can be included, as they were unknown at that time. The opposite extensive interpretation is not persuasive,[131] as, in addition to being against the literal interpretation of Article 1, second paragraph, of the CMR, it violates its intent to anchor the concept of vehicle to the relevant definition of the 1949 Convention. Moreover, as they are removable superstructures and not parts of the vehicle, the swap body and the container cannot lead to a combined transport regulated by the CMR. In fact, only the latter is loaded onto the ship,[132] not the truck as a whole. The same conclusions can be reached if the tank is moved.[133] Finally, only the road carrier is the interlocutor of the shipper and the consignee, who have no relationship with the sea or rail transporter.[134]

If the parties use the overlapping carriage, they can insert the ban on transshipment in the consignment note, pursuant to Article 6, second paragraph, letter a). In fact, the unjustified breaking of the load does not entail the inapplicability of the CMR, as the nonfulfillment cannot be resolved in a benefit for the same carrier. On the contrary, the Convention does not apply if the consignment note itself does not preclude the transshipment and the journey is international, pursuant to Article 1, but performed by different means, after breaking the load, admitted at least implicitly.

[126] Cf. Silingardi et al. (1994), p. 32 ff.; RB Antwerp 9 December 1977, in *Europ. transp. law,* 1990, no. 25, 2014.

[127] Cf. App. Orléans 20 January 1982, in *Bull. transp.,* 1982, 233; App. Versailles 4 November 1987, in *Le Lamy transp.*, 2021, vol. I, 478.

[128] Cf. Cass. com. France 23 September 2014, in *Bull. transp. logist.,* 2014, 517.

[129] Cf. App. Versailles 15 October 1992, in *Bull. transp. logist.*, 1993, 239.

[130] Cf. Haak (1986), p. 98 ff.; Clarke (2014), p. 38 ff.

[131] Cf. Silingardi et al. (1994), p. 32 ff.

[132] Cf. Cass. Netherlands 27 April 1989, in *Europ. transp. law,* 1989, no. 24, 345; Haak (1986), p. 98 ff.; Loewe (1976), p. 331 ff.; Rodière (1970), p. 625 ff.

[133] Cf. App. Rouen 29 June 2017, in *Bull. transp. logist.,* 2017, 451.

[134] Cf. Cass. com. France 5 July 1988, in *Bull. transp.,* 1989, 449, according to which the road carrier cannot oppose his customer with a clause relating to the bill of lading; Putzeys (1981), p. 99 ff.

Moreover, the person entitled to redelivery must be informed of changes in the mode of transport, if they can exclude the applicability of the CMR. Thus, the nonfulfillment of the obligation to inform exposes the carrier to compensation for damages, if the claims of the entitled person are affected by the operation of a discipline less favorable to him than that of the 1956 Geneva Convention.[135] On the contrary, Article 2 is without prejudice to the provision of Article 14. Therefore, in the event of supervening impediments, the breaking of the load is irrelevant if it is authorized by the party who has the right to dispose of the cargo, as a suitable solution to safeguard the successful outcome of the journey.[136]

1.3.2 The Case in Which CMR Is Not Applicable According to Article 2, Second Paragraph

Article 2 provides for an articulated discipline for the international transfer of goods by various means. In line with the objective of uniformly regulating transport, pursuant to Article 2, the CMR applies although parts of the route are not a road.[137] In particular, Article 2 refers to the relationships between the entitled person and the road transporter with whom one enters into the contract;[138] the internal relations between the road carrier and the others are regulated on the basis of the specific legislation of the transport involved,[139] intended to discipline the exercise of any recovery action. Furthermore, combined transport differs from cumulative one because, for Articles 34 ff. of the CMR,[140] the journey is broken down with the intervention of the road carriers only, subject to their adherence to the overall agreement, and each one of them responds jointly. On the contrary, in overlapping transport, only the road transporter concludes the contract, while the others, chosen by the first, are liable for the prejudices that occurred along their journey.[141]

---

[135] Cf. Silingardi et al. (1994), p. 34 ff.

[136] Cf. Silingardi et al. (1994), p. 35 ff.; Haak (1986), p. 97 ff.; Loewe (1976), p. 331 ff.; Clarke (2014), p. 39 ff.; Messent and Glass (2018), p. 60 ff.; Rodière (1970), p. 624 ff.

[137] Cf. Messent and Glass (2018), p. 62 ff.; Bombeeck et al. (1990), p. 118 ff.; Czapski (1990), p. 173 ff.; Rodière (1970), p. 623 ff.; Sánchez-Gamborino (2001), p. 849 ff.; Hill (1976), p. 183 ff.; Fremuth (2013), p. 117 ff. See also Trib. com. Paris 11 March 1983, in *Europ. transp. law,* 1990, no. 25, 2017, according to which the road carrier can invoke sea risk as a cause for exemption from liability, pursuant to Article 17, second paragraph, of the CMR if it causes damage to the goods; Trib. com. Paris 14 September 1983, *ibid.,* 1990, no. 25, 212; RB Antwerp 28 January 1985, *ibid.,* 1990, no. 25, 211.

[138] Cf. Putzeys (1981), p. 95 ff.

[139] Cf. Hof Antwerp 1 October 2018, in *Europ. transp. law,* 2018, no. 53, 386, according to which the sea carrier can be released from liability for the theft of the vehicle after disembarkation, according to the Hague Rules; Czapski (1990), p. 173 ff.

[140] Cf. Loewe (1976), p. 331 ff.; Delebeque (2006), p. 569 ff.

[141] Cf. Putzeys (1981), p. 99 ff.

According to Article 2, the CMR does not apply if three conditions are met,[142] namely the fact that the loss, damage or delay in delivery takes place on the nonroad journey;[143] is not caused by any act or omission of the relative carrier; and derives from a circumstance that occurred during the course of the transfer due to the same nonroad section.[144] On the contrary, the Geneva Convention applies to prejudices caused by an unknown cause and if the causal link between the damage and the situation relating to the aforementioned nonroad section is not demonstrated. The burden of proof falls on whoever invokes the different discipline.[145]

In particular, according to Article 2, to not apply the CMR, the prejudice must not be absolutely attributable to the road carrier; therefore, the Convention can be invoked if the latter contributes to the realization of the damage itself. Then, application difficulties arise if this provision is interpreted in the light of Article 3, for which the transporter is liable for the acts and omissions of his employees and of those whose activities he uses. The argument suggesting that the behavior of the auxiliaries for the purposes of Article 2, first paragraph, is relevant because they collaborate in the execution of the service and their negligent conduct cannot exclude the operation of the CMR. More questionable is the extensive exegesis of Article 3,[146] according to which the road carrier would also be liable for the work of the one using a different means of transport. This approach would exclude from the matter covered by the Article 2, first paragraph, most of the cases in which the prejudice occurs along the route executed in another way. In fact, the CMR would not be applicable only if the damage is caused by an unrelated third party, as in the case of a collision at sea attributable to the other ship.[147] The intermediate solution,[148] more consistent with Article 2, can be preferred, for which Article 3 refers to the collaborations that the carrier uses only for the road routes.

Furthermore, according to Article 2, the prejudice must take place during[149] and due to off-road transport. With regard to this last scenario, the question[150] arise whether the concept of cause of damage should be interpreted in a restrictive or extensive way; in the first case,[151] only events specific to that mode of transport would be significant, such as, for instance, the collision between ships. In the second

[142] Cf. Haak (1986), p. 101 ff.; Loewe (1976), p. 332 ff.; Bombeeck et al. (1990), p. 119 ff.; Czapski (1990), p. 173 ff.

[143] Cf. Ruitinga and De Haan (2001), p. 833 ff.

[144] Cf. Ruitinga and De Haan (2001), p. 835 ff.

[145] Cf. Silingardi et al. (1994), p. 37 ff.

[146] Cf. *Thermo Engineers Ltd.* c. *Ferrymasters Ltd.*, in *Lloyd's rep.*, 1981, 200.

[147] Cf. Messent and Glass (2018), p. 65 ff.

[148] Cf. Messent and Glass (2018), p. 65 ff.

[149] Cf. App. Paris 23 March 1988, in *Bull. transp.*, 1988, 265, according to which the road carrier is responsible for lack of stowage; App. Versailles 15 October 1992, *ibid.*, 1993, 239, according to which the road carrier responds for having loaded the goods on a trailer in poor condition.

[150] Cf. Silingardi et al. (1994), p. 38 ff.; Messent and Glass (2018), p. 66 ff.

[151] Cf. Hof Gent 30 April 1997, in *Europ. transp. law*, 1997, no. 32, 606; BGH 15 December 2011, in *TranspR*, 2012, 330, according to which fire on board is a typical damage of maritime transport.

case, all the facts that create damage in the course of nonroad transport should be considered, regardless of their traceability among the facts typical of that mode of transport. In this way, relevance is attributed to common events, such as fire[152] or strike, if they occur in a nonroad part of the route.[153] *A fortiori*, this latter interpretation is preferable.[154]

Having met the requirements of Article 2, first paragraph, the liability of the road carrier is regulated in the manner in which that of the nonroad transporter would have been governed if a contract had been concluded between the latter and the sender, in accordance with the mandatory provisions on nonroad carriage. The different rules apply with regard only to the liability, as the CMR operates for all other aspects, such as, for instance, the statute of time limitations.[155] Doubts have arisen about the concept of mandatory rule, partly fueled by a different wording of the provision in the two official texts of the Convention.[156] In fact, the French version refers "*aux dispositions imperatives*", while the English one refers to the "conditions prescribed by law". This last expression seems to include not only imperative, but also dispositive provisions. The restrictive solution has to be preferred, because it is anchored to the univocal concept of mandatory precepts. Then, it is necessary to identify the mandatory provisions referring to the different modes of transport. In general, the regulation of the carrier's liability at both national and international levels has a frequent mandatory nature to the detriment of the rights of the person entitled to redelivery. Therefore, many sections of mixed transport should be subject to their own rules, as they are mandatory.

Despite conflicting arguments,[157] the CMR can be replaced by a different, partly mandatory, regulation,[158] if it is nonbinding in favor of the entitled person. Otherwise, it would be impossible to apply most of the provisions on nonroad transport, due to their limited and partial mandatory nature. The scenario of nonroad carriage

---

[152] Cf. OLG Munich 23 December 2010, in *TranspR,* 2011, 158, according to which fire is a risk considered by Article 2, first paragraph, of the CMR; OLG Hamburg 14 April 2011, *ibid.*, 2011, 181; OLG Düsseldorf 12 January 2011, in *Europ. transp. law,* 2012, no. 47, 87; Cass. Netherlands 14 June 1996, in *Europ. transp. law,* 1996, no. 31, 558.

[153] Cf. App. Paris 13 October 1986, in *Bull. transp.,* 1986, 689; App. Reims 22 January 2007, *ibid.,* 2007, 95; Cass. com. France 23 September 2014, *ibid.,* 2014, 571; App. Paris 25 September 2003, *ibid.,* 2003, 793; App. Aix-en-Provence 27 June 1986, in *Le Lamy transp.*, 2021, vol. I, 479.

[154] Cf. Silingardi et al. (1994), p. 38 ff.; Messent and Glass (2018), p. 66 ff.; Czapski (1990), p. 173 ff.; *Thermo Engineers Ltd.* c. *Ferrymasters Ltd.,* in *Lloyd's rep.,* 1981, 200.

[155] Cf. *Le Lamy transp.*, 2021, vol. I, 480.

[156] Cf. Bombeeck et al. (1990), p. 125 ff.; Czapski (1990), p. 181 ff., who proposes to solve the interpretative difficulties by specifying in the consignment note that, in the case of combined transport, it is meant Article 2, first paragraph, in the English text.

[157] Cf. *Thermo Engineers Ltd.* c. *Ferrymasters Ltd.,* in *Lloyd's rep.,* 1981, 200.

[158] Cf. OLG Düsseldorf 12 January 2011, in *Europ. transp. law,* 2012, no. 47, 87, according to which "the Hague Rules are imperative regulations in the sense of Article 2"; RB Antwerp 17 January 1997, in *Europ. transp. law,* 1998, no. 33, 53, according to which, if the parties do not invoke Article 2, first paragraph, it is not necessary for the judge to assess the carrier's liability on the basis of the mandatory provisions relating to the nonroad section.

regulated by entirely nonmandatory rules is different; for instance, consider the so-called roll-on/roll-off,[159] in which the vehicles are loaded on the deck and not in the hold and for which negotiable bills of lading are not issued,[160] because the transport is governed by binding rules also in favor of the carrier, i.e., by Article 1, letter b), and by Article 6 of the 1924 Brussels Convention.[161] In this case, the CMR applies, and the road transporter can invoke its Article 17, second paragraph, in the event of nautical fault or fire, while the storm is not an inevitable circumstance, as the fact that loading on the deck was not essential can be opposed to the carrier.[162] Furthermore, if he places part of the vehicle on the deck and another in the hold, an intersection of sources can be generated to the detriment of the uniformity the CMR tends to establish.[163]

To overcome the difficulties generated in identifying the applicable and mandatory discipline, the rules on nonroad transport would operate, although the parties regulate the relationship on the basis of nonbinding principles,[164] as, for example, happens with the loading of the vehicle on the bridge and without the issuance of any bill of lading.[165] Therefore, the imperative nature would have to be verified not with regard to the modalities with which nonroad[166] transport is performed, but with reference to the relationship that, hypothetically, would have occurred between the sender and the nonroad carrier; in essence, the nonbinding rules would be the expression of a uniform imperative discipline with respect to which they would be

[159] Cf. Laurijssen (2001b), p. 791 ff.; Fremuth (2013), p. 147 ff. See also Cass. France 5 July 1988, in *Europ. transp. law,* 1990, no. 25, 221, according to which Article 2 of the CMR applies in the absence of mandatory provisions relating to maritime transport; Arrond. Antwerp 18 November 1987, *ibid.,* 1990, no. 25, 251.

[160] On the contrary, see Cass. Netherlands 29 June 1990, in *Le Lamy transp.*, 2021, vol. I, 480, according to which, if the failure to issue the bill of lading precludes the application of the maritime regulations, it would be regulated by the CMR most of the road transport. This argument is not acceptable because the wording of Article 2 clearly refers only to the mandatory rules.

[161] Cf. Clarke (2014), p. 47 ff.; Cass. com. France 5 July 1988, in *Bull. transp.,* 1989, 119, according to whom for the bridge transport the CMR applies.

[162] Cf. App. Aix-en-Provence 12 September 1989, in *Le Lamy transp.*, 2021, vol. I, 480; App. Aix-en-Provence 16 January 1990, *ibid.,* 2021, vol. I, 480; App. Paris 23 March 1988, in *Bull. transp.,* 1988, 265; App. Versailles 15 October 1992, in *Bull transp. logist.,* 1993, 239; RB Gent 19 June 1990, in *Europ. transp. law,* 1991, no. 26, 377, according to which the carrier is not liable if he places on the deck of a ship the closed vessel capable of withstanding normal atmospheric conditions.

[163] Cf. Silingardi et al. (1994), p. 43 ff.; *Le Lamy transp.*, 2021, vol. I, 480.

[164] Cf. Cass. Netherlands 29 June 1990, in *Europ. Transp. law,* 1990, no. 25, 589; App. Paris 25 September 2003, in *Bull. transp. logist.,* 2003, 793; RB Antwerp 25 February 2000, in *Europ. transp. law,* 2000, no. 35, 527; BGH 15 December 2011, in *TranspR,* 2012, 330.

[165] Cf. Messent and Glass (2018), p. 72 ff., according to whom, "starting from an objective basis, the background facts of the transport in issue are used to resolve the difficulties involved in applying an abstract solution, which in effect applies the uniform rules without regarding to the specific rules governing their application, in particular, the requirement that a bill of landing be issued"; Clarke (2014), p. 50 ff.

[166] Cf. Czapski (1990), p. 173 ff.

mere exceptions. In this manner, the relations between the person entitled to redelivery and the road transporter and between these and the other operators would be made homogeneous. This is because the same uniform discipline would apply, for instance, with the possibility for the road carrier to oppose to whoever requests compensation the same compensation limit from which, for example, the maritime carrier benefits. This would occur without the recovery action being nullified due to the occurrence of the so-called excepted danger, such as nautical fault. Although suggestive, this argument is not acceptable,[167] since, rightly or wrongly, the CMR guarantees uniformity, extending its application to the greatest number of cases,[168] with the sole exception of the one in which the parties refer to the mandatory provisions of the international convention which regulates the nonroad transport.

Then, in some cases, the transporter can choose whether to continue the journey on a road or on a sea route, such as the overcoming of the English Channel, after the creation of the tunnel. Therefore, if he opts for maritime transfer, he must inform the sender of the risks associated with such navigation and may be called upon to compensate for the damages resulting from the violation of this obligation,[169] for example, because the lack of warning does not allow the shipper to stipulate an adequate insurance coverage.[170] However, the shipowner must work diligently and, therefore, in winter or in bad weather, he cannot leave the vehicle in the most exposed part of the deck, especially if delicate or perishable goods are placed in a trailer covered by a tarpaulin.[171] Furthermore, the carrier bears the detrimental consequences of his choice;[172] just think of the prejudice attributable to the delay due to the truck being stopped in the port of destination because of the nonpresentation of documents which would be unnecessary in the case of road transport.[173]

---

[167] Cf. Silingardi et al. (1994), p. 46 ff.

[168] Cf. Clarke (2014), p. 50 ff.

[169] Cf. App. Toulouse 6 January 1987, in *Bull. transp.*, 1988, 78.

[170] Cf. *Le Lamy transp.*, 2021, vol. I, 480.

[171] Cf. Cass. com. France 7 January 1997, in *Le Lamy transp.*, 2021, vol. I, 482; App. Aix-en-Provence 16 January 1990, *ibid.*, 2021, vol. I, 482; App. Aix-en-Provence 19 June 1991, *ibid.*, 2021, vol. I, 482. See also App. Aix-en-Provence 12 September 1989, *ibid.*, 2021, vol. I, 482, according to which the road carrier responds because he has not requested the accommodation of the vehicle in the hold, given the delicate nature of the load.

[172] Cf. Trib. com. Marseille 4 February 1986, in *Europ. transp. law,* 1990, no. 25, 223, according to which the road carrier responds if he does not ask for the accommodation of the vehicle in the hold, even knowing that the goods would have required an allocation in conditions of perfect impermeability.

[173] Cf. App. Paris 15 February 1982, in *Bull. transp.* 1982, 141; App. Paris 23 March 1978, *ibid.*, 1978, 265; App. Pau 16 January 1980, *ibid.*, 1980, 91, according to which the carrier responds if he performs part of the transport for the Middle East by sea, despite the traveler asking for a land trip *de bout en bout*.

In the internal relations between the road carrier and the other ones, there are no particular issues, unless the former causes damage with his conduct;[174] in this case, he responds exclusively. The compensation limit applies for each damaged package; for the shipping carrier, it operates by reason of the vehicle and the load, considered as a single entity, unless the relative document indicates the number of packaging and identifies them with appropriate marks or symbols.[175] Finally, the road transporter can act against port intermediaries chosen by himself; thus, if a shipping agency makes a mistake in filling out the bill of lading and declares a number of packages lower than the actual one, he must compensate the road carrier for the damage created by the vehicle being stopped at the customs offices of the country of destination.[176]

Then, if a semi-trailer without a driver on board arrives, it is considered delivered to the road carrier only if it is coupled to the tractor.[177] Therefore, we have to consider null and void the clause included in the bill of lading aimed at excluding the liability of the shipping carrier for damage or theft committed during disembarkation and before the truck is entrusted to the road transporter.[178] Furthermore, if the shipping carrier proves that the prejudice is caused by a so-called peril of the sea, he does not have to demonstrate that the semi-trailer was correctly coupled; if anything, this burden falls on the terrestrial transporter.[179] Then, the shipowner must give evidence that the vessel equipped with a refrigeration system is connected to the electrical circuit on board. In fact, the lack of connection falls within the commercial fault and not within the nautical one.[180] Furthermore, the shipper is not liable to the road carrier for the loss of the vehicle following a shipwreck, although the former has organized the transport by sea.[181] Finally, in determining the prejudice suffered by the land transporter for the destruction of the vehicle, the value of the equipment recently acquired, such as the tarpaulin or new tires; the cost of repairs, if significant; and any rental costs of a replacement truck must be considered.[182]

---

[174] Cf. App. Paris 23 March 1988, in *Bull. transp.*, 1988, 265, according to which the road carrier is responsible because he has not adequately placed the goods inside the vehicle; App. Douai 6 April 2017, *ibid.*, 2017, 259; App. Aix-en-Provence 10 September 1992, *ibid.*, 1993, 349, according to which the road carrier is liable for damage resulting from the torn sheet of the semi-trailer.

[175] Cf. App. Toulouse 8 December 1983, in *Bull. transp.*, 1984, 457; App. Aix-en-Provence 13 June 1984, in *Le Lamy transp.*, 2021, vol. I, 481.

[176] Cf. App. Aix-en-Provence 12 January 1982, in *Le Lamy transp.*, 2021, vol. I, 481. See also App. Aix-en-Provence 12 July 1983, *ibid.*, 2021, vol. I, 481; App. Aix-en-Provence 17 November 1987, in *Bull. transp.*, 1987, 624.

[177] Cf. Cass. com. France 5 July 1994, in *Bull. transp. logist.*, 1994, 690; App. Aix-en-Provence 6 January 1994, in *Le Lamy transp.*, 2021, vol. I, 481.

[178] Cf. App. Aix-en-Provence 6 January 1994, *Le Lamy transp.*, 2021, vol. I, 482.

[179] Cf. App. Aix-en-Provence 13 September 1989, in *Le Lamy transp.*, 2021, vol. I, 482.

[180] Cf. App. Aix-en-Provence 19 March 1985, in *Le Lamy transp.*, 2021, vol. I, 482.

[181] Cf. App. Paris 10 June 1986, in *Le Lamy transp.*, 2021, vol. I, 482.

[182] Cf. App. Aix-en-Provence 5 December 1996, in *Le Lamy transp.*, 2021, vol. I, 482.

As Article 2, first paragraph, makes the fulfillment of the three requirements "to the extent that it is proved" conditional, there may be a concurrence of the liability of the road carrier with that of the other one.[183] For example, if the former causes damage to the load and the shipping carrier loses part of it, the CMR applies for the initial prejudice and for the sea route only if the relative rules are nonbinding. Finally, according to Article 2, second paragraph, if the road transporter deals with the nonterrestrial section, his liability is always regulated by Article 2, first paragraph, as if the dual function were exercised by two different people.[184] This scenario is rarely applied, because it is unlikely that a road transporter is to perform the activity in a different way. However, if the injury occurs in the road part, the CMR applies, as in the case of the unknown cause.[185] Furthermore, if the prejudice takes place during the maritime section and if the three requisites are met, the relative provisions apply, provided they are mandatory. If the road transporter contributes to the prejudice or if the regulation on maritime transfer is nonbinding, the CMR applies.[186]

1.3.3 Intermodal Transport and the Geneva Convention

Article 2 considers combined transport without breaking the load and does not regulate the other cases in which each section performed in a different way is preceded by transshipment.[187] Therefore, the Convention cannot be applied to multimodal carriage as a whole.[188] According to some decisions,[189] the convention applicable to multimodal transport should be identified on the basis of national law; in this regard, the former would be governed by the law regulating the prevailing route.[190] Therefore, the CMR could concern the entire multimodal transport if the overland journey is the longest. The solution is not convincing, because it is against the spirit and the literal tenor of the CMR, as scenarios such as these are not contemplated and are inconsistent with Article 2.

---

[183] Cf. Messent and Glass (2018), p. 73 ff.

[184] Cf. Messent and Glass (2018), p. 73 ff.

[185] Cf. Messent and Glass (2018), p. 73 ff.

[186] Cf. Messent and Glass (2018), p. 74 ff.

[187] Cf. Clarke (2014), p. 34 ff.; Ha Ngoc (2016), p. 470 ff.

[188] Cf. Puetz (2018), p. 122 ff. See also BGH 17 July 2008, in *TranspR,* 2008, 365, according to whom the CMR applies only to contracts for the transport of goods by road carried out with this exclusive means; OLG Karlsruhe 17 October *ibid.,* 2008, 471, according to which the CMR does not apply to multimodal transport.

[189] Cf. *Quantum Ltd.* c. *Plane Trucking Ltd.,* in *Lloyd's law rep.,* 2001, 133, according to which the Convention on International Air Transport applies on the basis that the air route is prevailing.

[190] Cf. Verheyen (2016), p. 451 ff.

Then, for the entire multimodal carriage, Article 31 of the CMR cannot be applied.[191] As it is not desirable to identify the jurisdiction with regard to each part of the route, due to the risk of "facing legal claims in an infinite number of *fora*",[192] the Regulation (EU) 1215/2012 applies, while waiting for the adoption of a new convention on multimodal transport concerning the States of the European Union. Therefore, in the absence of an arbitration clause, the multimodal operator could be called in front of the judge of the State where he has his head office or where the services have been or should have been performed. In addition, if the same operator acts for recovery against the road carrier, Article 31 of the CMR applies, because the internal relations are entrusted to the specific regulation of each section of the journey.

There have been attempts to govern multimodal transport with the Rotterdam Rules, the text of which was approved on 28 January 2008, with the title "Draft Convention on contract for the International carriage of goods wholly or partly by sea".[193] In reality, the reference to this Convention is not convincing. Thus, without prejudice to the fact that it has not entered into force, pursuant to its Article 82, letter b), it would not preclude the operation of any international agreement regulating the carriage of goods by road if, according to its provisions, it applies to the transport of goods when the motor vehicle is loaded onto a ship.[194] The Rotterdam Rules create problems with the CMR[195] because they seem to limit the scope of this Convention to the maritime phase. According to a more coherent reading,[196] this reference concerns the overall provisions of the CMR, which extend their effects beyond their normal scope.

Then, according to Article 26 of the same Rotterdam Rules, if the damage or delay in delivery occurs in the part of the transport before or after the sea section, the Rotterdam Rules themselves would yield to the mandatory provisions governing the different route and to those on liability, compensation limit and prescription.[197] Other aspects such as jurisdiction or travel documents would fall within the scope of the Rotterdam Rules,[198] but it is redundant to elaborate the concept here, given that they have not entered into force.

---

[191] Cf. BGH 17 July 2008, in *TranspR*, 2008, 365; Cass. Netherlands 8 November 2011, in *Unif. law rev.*, 2005, 628; Cass. Netherlands 1 June 2012, in *TranspR,* 278.

[192] Cf. Puetz (2018), p. 122 ff.

[193] These rules have not entered into force.

[194] Cf. Ha Ngoc (2016), p. 482 ff.

[195] Cf. Clarke (2014), p. 36 ff.

[196] Cf. Messent and Glass (2018), p. 79 ff.

[197] Cf. Ha Ngoc (2016), p. 473 ff.

[198] Cf. Messent and Glass (2018), p. 79 ff., but see Clarke (2014), p. 37 ff, according to whom "one wonders about the consequences of (unspecified but important) rules, for example, concerning jurisdiction".

References

Antapasis MH (2017) Is CMR a uniform law? The Greek perspective on Article 1. In: Aa. Vv., Verheyen W (ed) CMR 60 years. Time for retirement or future proof? Paris, p 13 ff

Bombeeck M, Hamer P, Verhaegen B (1990) La responsabilité du transporteur routier dans le transport par car – ferries. Eur Transp Law 25:113 ff

Bon-Garcin I (2006) Les 50 ans de la Convention CMR – Avenir et perspectives du transport international par route. Unif Law Rev:699 ff

Capel Ferrer J (2006) La Convention CMR – Pilier du trasport international par route. Unif Law Rev:517 ff

Clarke MA (2014) International carriage of goods by road: CMR. New York, ed. VI

Czapski W (1990) La responsabilité du transporteur routier lors du transroulage et du ferroutage. Eur Transp Law 25:173 ff

Czapski W (2006) Application et interprétation de la Convention CMR à la lumière du droit international. Unif Law Rev:545 ff

De La Motte H, Temme J (2013) Art. 1. In: Aa. Vv., Thume KH (ed) CMR: über den Beförderungsvertrag im internationalen Strassengüterverkehr. Frankfurt am Main, ed. III, p 49 ff

Delebeque P (2006) La Convention CMR, les transports superposés et multimodaux. Unif Law Rev:569 ff

Ferrari F (2018) Art. 1 der CMR. In: Aa. Vv., Internationales Vertragsrecht. Munich, p 1241 ff

Fillers A (2020) The CMR in the practice of Letvian courts. Unif Law Rev:169 ff

Fremuth F (2013) Art. 2. In: Aa. Vv., Thume KH (ed) CMR: über den Beförderungsvertrag im internationalen Strassengüterverkehr. Frankfurt am Main, ed. III, p 110 ff

Gruber A (2017) How Article 1 of the CMR Convention is interpreted by the French courts. In: Aa. Vv., Verheyen W (ed) CMR 60 years. Time for retirement or future proof? Paris, p 11 ff

Ha Ngoc J (2016) La Convention CMR et les Règles de Rotterdam. Unif Law Rev:469 ff

Haak KF (1986) The liability of the carrier under CMR. The Hague

Haak KF (2006) "Revision der CMR"? TransR:325 ff

Hill DJ (1976) Carriage of goods by road to the Continent. Eur Transp Law 11:182 ff

Jung C (1997) The Convention on the contract for the International carriage of goods by road (CMR): survey, analysis and trends of recent German case law. Unif Law Rev:148 ff

Katauskas T (2017) Interpretation of Article 1 of the CMR Convention in Lithuania. In: Aa. Vv., Verheyen W (ed) CMR 60 years. Time for retirement or future proof? Paris, p 29 ff

Kolacs MC (2017) Country report on Article 1. In: Aa. Vv., Verheyen W (ed) CMR 60 years. Time for retirement or future proof? Paris, p 150 ff

Kolacs MC, Hopster G (2017) When technology takes the wheel. In: Aa. Vv., Verheyen W (ed) CMR 60 years. Time for retirement or future proof? Paris, p 150 ff

Krings E (1999) CMR: examen de la jurisprudence des Cours de Cassation de France et de Pays – Bas (première partie). Unif Law Rev:140 ff

Laurijssen P (2001a) "Water en weg – Botsing wan wetten" Stapelvervoer onder artikel 2 CMR. Eur Transp Law 36:799 ff

Laurijssen P (2001b) Kombinierter Transport Roll – on – Roll – off. Eur Transp Law 36:791 ff

Libouton J (1973) International road transport. Convention on the contract for the international carriage of goods by road. Review of Court decisions 1965 – 1971. Eur Transp Law 8:6 ff

Loewe R (1976) Commentary on the Convention of 19 May 1956 on the contract for the international carriage of goods by road. Eur Transp Law 11:311 ff

Messent A, Glass DA (2018) CMR: contracts for the international carriage of goods by road. New York, ed. IV

Pastore F (1997) Circolazione stradale internazionale: Convenzione di Vienna 7 ottobre – 8 novembre 1968 e accordi europei di Ginevra 1 maggio 1971 e 13 marzo 1973 sulla circolazione e segnaletica stradale commentati e comparati tra di loro e con il nuovo Codice della strada. Rimini

Pesce A (1995) Il trasporto internazionale di merci. Torino
Puetz A (2018) Rules on jurisdiction and recognition or enforcement of judgments in specialized Conventions on transport in the aftermath of TNT: dynamite or light in the dark? Eur Legal Forum:117 ff
Putzeys J (1981) Le contrat de transport routier de marchandises. Brussels
Putzeys J (1990) Le droit superposé ou les paradoxes de l'Article 2 CMR. Eur Transp Law 25:107 ff
Putzeys J (2006) L'adaptation de la Convention CMR à l'ère informatique. Unif. Law Rev:523
Ramberg J (1974) The law of carriage of goods. Attempts at harmonization. Eur Transp Law 9:2 ff
Rodière R (1970) The Convention on road transport. Eur Transp Law 5:622 ff
Rodière R (1971) The Convention on road transport. Eur Transp Law 6:3 ff
Rogov S (2005) New interpretation of art. 1, para. 5, of the CMR Convention? Eur Transp Law 40: 463 ff
Ruitinga P, De Haan RJ (2001) Gabriële Wehr revisited. Eur Transp Law 36:831 ff
Sánchez-Gamborino FJ (2001) La Convención CMR según la Jurisprudencia del "Tribunal Supremo" de España. Eur Transp Law 36:843 ff
Sánchez-Gamborino FJ (2006) La lettre de voiture CMR 'IRU 1976' et le nouveau modèle en projet. Unif Law Rev:677 ff
Silingardi G (1987) La CMR: da normativa uniforme di applicazione necessaria a disciplina pattizia. Dir Comm Int:613 ff
Silingardi G, Corrado A, Meotti A, Morandi F (1994) La disciplina uniforme del contratto di trasporto di cose su strada Turin
Temme C (2013) Art. 12. In: Aa. Vv., Tume KH (ed) CMR: über den Beförderungsvertrag im internationalen Strassengüterverkehr. Frankfurt am Main, ed. III, p 300 ff
Tullio L (1992) La CMR convenzione di diritto uniforme. Dir Trasp:192 ff
van Hee L (2017) The applicability of the CMR Convention from a Dutch perspective. In: Aa. Vv., Verheyen W (ed) CMR 60 years. Time for retirement or future proof? Paris, p 17 ff
Van Ryn J (1966) Une nouvelle étape dans l'élaboration du droit des transport: la Convention de 1956 relative au transport international de marchandises par route (CMR). Eur Transp Law 1: 639 ff
Verheyen W (2016) National judges as gatekeepers to CMR Convention. Unif Law Rev:441 ff
Verheyen W (2018) Platooning cooperation as a model towards sustainable road Transport. https://ssrn.com/abstract=3119656
Wesolowsky K (2013) A review of judicial decisions of the Polish Supreme Court within the scope of CMR. Eur Transp Law 48:354 ff

Chapter 2
The Mandatory Nature of the Geneva Convention

Contents

2.1 The Concept of Binding

2.1.1 The Importance of the Binding Nature of the Geneva Convention System

For Article 41, the Convention is binding; accordingly, the parties may not stipulate clauses modifying the regulations of uniform law.[1] Failing that, such clauses are null

[1]Cf. Messent and Glass (2018), p. 393 ff.

C. Tincani, *Contract for the International Carriage of Goods by Road*, Law for Professionals, https://doi.org/10.1007/978-3-031-08487-4_2

and void;[2] in fact, "any stipulation that directly or indirectly derogates from the provisions of this Convention shall be null and void".[3] The regulation is thus unchangeable.[4] Overall, Article 41 is not designed so much for the protection of an allegedly weak contracting party as to establish a homogenous set of regulations of necessary application,[5] mostly aimed at the need "to avoid undue competition between individual transport enterprises that might wish to attract clients by offering terms that were actually or allegedly better".[6] Within the CMR structure, in fact, parties are placed on the same level, consistent with the logic of organized enterprises that operate on the market.

The invalidity of clauses derogating from the Convention does not sweep away other contractual prescriptions. For instance, the principle of safeguarding the agreement, which operates even where the clause is essential to its conclusion, enjoins to automatically replace the Convention following any indications that are in conflict with it.[7] For this purpose, relevance is attached to any derogation clauses from the carrier's liability regime, such as those pursuant to which the carrier is liable for prejudices arising from packaging or loading defects notwithstanding that such activities are entrusted to the sender.[8] In one interesting case,[9] an agreement that excluded both parties' monitoring of the load at the time of its delivery was held to be null and void. Conversely, agreements that delimit assumed obligations and their scope are valid.[10]

Moreover, clauses limiting liability to the amount set by way of indemnity in an insurance contract are null and void.[11] The same conclusions are reached when the carrier undertakes providing the necessary documents to complete customs operations; the transporter is not liable in case they are not complete because that would

[2] Cf. OLG Düsseldorf 21 November 2007, in *TranspR,* 2008, 36, according to which a contractual provision that excludes monitoring by both parties of the delivered goods is null and void.

[3] This is how the English text is expressed; in the French version, we read "*est nulle et de nul effet toute stipulation qui, directement ou indirectement, dérogerait aux dispositions de la présente Convention*".

[4] Cf. Clarke (2014), p. 286 ff. Cf. OGH 18 February 2013, in *TranspR,* 2013, 344, according to which, as Article 41 lays down the mandatory nature of the CMR, the national rules of private international law are irrelevant and do not apply.

[5] Cf. Silingardi et al. (1994), p. 17 ff.

[6] Cf. Loewe (1976), p. 401 ff.; Messent and Glass (2018), p. 393 ff.

[7] Cf. Silingardi et al. (1994), p. 17 ff.

[8] Cf. Messent and Glass (2018), p. 394 ff., nt. 7.

[9] Cf. OLG Düsseldorf 21 November 2007, in *TranspR,* 2008, 38.

[10] Cf. BGH 26 March 2009, in *TranspR,* 2010, 76, according to which a clause that regulates the nature of goods covered by a contract and, consequently, delimits what the carrier's obligation involves is valid. There is, therefore, no conflict with Article 41; OGH 6 July 2016, *ibid.*, 2016, 461, according to which Article 41 does not prevent the conclusion of an agreement aimed at determining whether the loading must be attended to by the sender or by the carrier.

[11] Cf. Cass. France 17 May 1983, in *Bull. transp.,* 1983, 445; RB Brussels 12 February 1977, in *Europ. transp. law,* 1978, no. 13, 285; RB Antwerp 4 May 1977, *ibid.*, 1978, no. 13, 478.

conflict with Article 11, second paragraph.[12] Likewise, the agreements whereby the transporter accepts an interest rate of more than five percent are null and void. In this scenario, although he does not object, the party entitled to the goods may only obtain interest to the extent laid down by Article 27, first paragraph.[13]

More generally, clauses that aggravate the carrier's liability are invalid,[14] such as those that impose on him a penalty in case of a delay.[15] Only, the declaration of value or of special interest at the redelivery, in accordance with Articles 24 and 26, is excluded from the scope of invalidity. For some,[16] the reason for this choice operated by uniform law[17] lies in the difficulty of identifying the economically strong party in practice, given the need to not upset the market balance. From a critical viewpoint,[18] it should be highlighted that the components of the market could be influenced differently. Therefore, if this is the objective of Article 41, it remains partly unfulfilled. However, Article 41 itself ensures the carriers that they will not lose their rights toward the sender and the recipient.[19]

The mandatory nature of uniform law is strict, does not make room for exceptions and operates even where the derogation works against the carrier. However, not all Convention provisions have this characteristic; in fact, on the issue of cumulative transport, Article 40 allows the amendment of Articles 37 and 38. Moreover, Articles 31 and 33[20] grant a limited freedom in the conclusion or enforcement of a single contract. In fact, Article 31 selects the jurisdiction identification criteria from which the parties must choose at the time of exercising the action, whereas Article 33 provides for arbitration as an alternative to the judicial resolution of a dispute. Viewed as a whole, however, these provisions are binding too. In reality, a consensual clause on jurisdiction based upon parameters differing from those of Article 31 is null and void, precisely in terms of Article 41. The same conclusions can be reached for

---

[12]Cf. App. Paris 27 January 1971, in *Bull. transp.*, 1971, 115.

[13]Cf. Arrond. Rotterdam 12 April 1972, in *S & S*, 1972, 103; Hof Brussels 13 January 1972, in *Europ. transp. law,* no. 7, 151.

[14]Cf. App. Paris 27 January 1971, in *Bull. transp.,* 1971, 115; Clarke (2014), p. 286 ff.

[15]Cf. OLG Monaco 26 July 1985, in *TranspR,* 1985, 395.

[16]Cf. Loewe (1976), p. 401, according to whom "the reasons for this are, first, that there was no way of knowing which party to a contract for the carriage of goods would be the strongest economically and therefore in a position to exercise pressure on the person with whom he has contracted and, second, that it seemed advisable to avoid competition between individual transport enterprises, which might wish to attract clients by offering them terms which were actually or allegedly better".

[17]Cf. Clarke (2014), p. 286 ff., who highlights how the solution of the Convention runs contrary to The Hague – Visby rules for international maritime carriage of things, under which clauses that aggravate the carrier's liability may be stipulated.

[18]Cf. Clarke (2014), p. 286.

[19]Cf. OGH 5 July 1977, in Clarke (2014), p. 286 ff., nt. 344.

[20]Cf. Messent and Glass (2018), p. 393 ff.

arbitration,[21] with special emphasis on some contractual provisions typical of the Dutch legal system and deemed by German case law[22] to be in conflict with Article 33. Despite the existence of past judgments taking the opposite view,[23] under Article 41 these provisions are null and void. The level of autonomy recognized by a rule is one thing, but another is a consensual regulation that differs from it.

As regards Article 41, issues of application have arisen in relation to the role of the freight forwarder; in particular, the question has been posed[24] on whether he can refer to the conditions that limit his liability, introduced on the basis of national law. In this regard, we need to assess the freight forwarder's role in the transport; if he takes the carrier's position, any attempts to refer to such clauses restricting his liability, according to the domestic law, will be useless, as the Convention and its Article 41 will apply.[25]

Moreover, by virtue of the last-mentioned rule, the transporter cannot creatively regulate the operations ancillary to the transfer of goods, if they fall within the scope of application of the CMR. For example, he may not limit his own liability. Rightfully, however, German case law[26] considers the assignment of a task to the sub-carrier to be unfettered, because this agreement cannot find any conflicting prescription. Furthermore, the parties can have at their disposal contractual profiles not regulated by the CMR; so it is possible to conclude an agreement on the safety of the trip[27] or on the performance of the service, such as a clause that excludes the set-off between the mutually conflicting credits of the sender and carrier.[28]

Sometimes, attempts are made to circumvent Article 41 by fragmenting the trip into several national transfers, with the idea that each would be regulated by the law of the individual State. In case of simulation and fraudulent intents, the solution violates Article 41, besides Article 1. Rather, the carrier may reduce the scope of his liability in conformity with the prescriptions of uniform law. For instance, loading and unloading obligations can be incurred by the sender, whereupon the transporter would not be responsible for the relative prejudices,[29] even though German case law[30] enjoins an obligation on the transporter to check the safety of the motor vehicle

[21] Cf. *A. B. Bofors – UVA* v. *A. B. Skandia Transport,* in *Lloyd's rep.*, 1982, 410, according to which the arbitration clause drawn up in conflict with the requirements laid down by Article 33 is invalid under Article 41.

[22] Cf. OLG Stuttgart 22 February 2007, in *TranspR,* 2007, 249.

[23] OLG Cologne 28 May 2005, in *TranspR,* 2005, 472.

[24] Cf. Messent and Glass (2018), p. 394 ff.

[25] Cf. Hof Brussels 23 December 1971, in *Europ. transp. law,* 1972, no. 7, 865, according to which a freight forwarder may not rely on the national rules that limit his liability, because, in international transport, the forwarder can be deemed a carrier and, as such, is covered by the CMR.

[26] Cf. OLG Munich 21 July 2017, in *TranspR,* 2017, 62; LG Cottbus 8 July 2008, *ibid.,* 2008, 370.

[27] Cf. OGH 18 May 1982, in *TranspR,* 1983, 48.

[28] Cf. Clarke (2014), p. 287 ff.

[29] Cf. Clarke (2014), p. 287 ff.

[30] Cf. OLG Brema 8 February 2007, in *TranspR,* 2008, 252.

before the beginning of the journey.[31] A special case was examined in Germany on the application of the CMR, as a result of an agreement about a national transport, but with the specific contractual reference to the CMR regulation. Therefore, there was not a peremptory delimitation of its operational scope, but a consensual solution.[32] In such a scenario, it was persuasively argued that it would be possible to derogate from the CMR, precisely because the prerequisite for its operation was the contractual will itself and the limit was not established by the rules of the Convention, but by possible mandatory provisions of national laws, according to the nature of the journey.

2.1.2 The Invalidity of Agreements That Conflict with Mandatory Provisions

In case carriage is covered by the CMR, Article 41 makes its rules and regulations mandatory, with a possible conflict between the Convention and individual contracts. For some legal systems, such as the Italian or German ones, a decisive role is played by the principle of good faith, understood as the "'pervasive rule of the entire contractual doctrine",[33] aimed at "introducing itself in the different aspects or moments that mark the life of the contract".[34]

Accordingly, good faith identifies the duties which parties must respect, despite the fact that not all of them are expressly contemplated by the agreement or by the law. Questions have arisen[35] as to whether such a criterion might operate with regard to the Convention. Perhaps, the question is slightly overestimated. Given that, in fact, the CMR regulates the carrier's liability in detail, there is not much room for any integration with good faith, even in the application of the UNIDROIT Principles of International Commercial Contracts 2016. Overall, uniform law is in itself exhaustive. An exception is presented by the German decisions that emphasize the importance of the shipper's warning on the characteristics of the goods at the time of contract stipulation,[36] so that the transporter is duly informed and able to pre-establish suitable organizational solutions. In reality, this is not as much relevant for the purposes of Article 17, as for the fact that, pursuant to Article 29, the compensatory limit does not operate. In any event, for those legal systems in which good faith takes on a role of integration of obligations, it is inevitable to pay regard to it to determine the commitment required by the carrier, often with the

[31] Cfr. Otte (2018), p. 1596 ff.

[32] Cf. BGH 19 January 2006, in *TranspR,* 2006, 121; BGH 28 February 2018, *ibid.,* 2013, 290.

[33] Cf. Di Majo (1997), p. 153 ff.

[34] Cf. Di Majo (1997), p. 153 ff.

[35] Cf. Clarke (2014), p. 286 ff.

[36] Cf. BGH 20 January 2005, in *TranspR,* 2005, 311.

reiteration of usual models inferred from the principles of domestic regulation, referred to the international transport.

In general, the problem of Article 41 concerns the compatibility of uniform law with the so-called "standard trading conditions".[37] Thus, the carrier may not rely on an arbitration clause included in the "Nordic conditions",[38] because it does not comply with Article 33,[39] which imposes the respect of some specific formal requirements. The solution is consistent with the principle of the mandatory nature of Article 41. The same was held for some indications specific to the Dutch legal system.[40] In contrast, there are some German judicial decisions concerning arbitration clauses stipulated in agreements that are not compatible with Article 33 (specifically for the Dutch legal system). In fact, they are legally effective for some judgments and, thus, not null and void under Article 41,[41] while the opposite solution was adopted for others.[42]

Conversely, if, in the role of the transporter, the freight forwarder is liable for having performed the redelivery in breach of the instructions received, it is uncertain whether the latter can invoke the clause limiting his liability.[43] For a decision,[44] he may not rely on the national law on clauses reducing his responsibility, because it would be in conflict with Article 41. This thesis is not convincing with regard to aspects ungoverned by uniform law; the parties are allowed to stipulate an autonomous consensual regulation and, *a fortiori*, that is true of other contracts, such as the shipping one. However, if the freight forwarder is also a carrier, Article 41 operates, as the entire Convention applies to regulate the transporter's obligations.

Because the CMR contemplates cash on delivery only, the indications on redelivery that do not relate to such scenario may be included in specific agreements; their breach would not preclude the freight forwarder from invoking the most favorable consensual regulation. Furthermore, "it was held" for good reason "that although the Road Haulage Association (RHA) terms could not apply to the international carriage by virtue of Article 41, they are applicable to the period of storage following the termination of the international carriage".[45]

The same conclusions should be reached in the insurance field, in case the transporter requests disbursement of indemnity when found liable for the personal injuries suffered by an employee during the unloading process, following the

[37] Cf. Messent and Glass (2018), p. 395 ff.

[38] Cf. Messent and Glass (2018), p. 395 ff.

[39] Cf. *A. B. Bofors – UVA* v. *A. B. Skandia Transport,* in *Lloyd's rep.,* 1982, 410.

[40] Cf. OLG Cologne 28 May 2005, in *TranspR,* 2005, 472.

[41] Cf. OLG Stuttgart 22 February 2007, in *TranspR,* 2007, 249.

[42] Cf. OLG Cologne 28 May 2005, in *TranspR,* 2005, 472; LG Giessen 31 July 2008, *ibid.,* 2008, 370.

[43] Cf. *Eastern Kayam Carpets Ltd.* v. *Eastern United Freight Ltd.,* in *Lexis citation,* 1983, 1311.

[44] Cf. *Eastern Kayam Carpets Ltd.* v. *Eastern United Freight Ltd.,* in *Lexis citation,* 1983, 1311.

[45] Cf. *T Comedy (U. K.) Ltd.* v. *Easy Managed Transp Ltd.,* in *Lloyd's rep.,* 2007, 397.

inadequate arrangement of the load, an operation entrusted to his care.[46] The solution is correct; the clause does not derogate from the discipline on liability under Articles 3 and 17, because it complies with an aspect not covered by the Convention. It would be different if the request for insurance indemnity were related to detriments to the goods.[47] In this case, for the relevant civil liability insurance contract to operate, the carrier's responsibility must be ascertained on the basis of the CMR.

A mooted point[48] concerns the compatibility with Article 41 of a clause whereby the transporter is entitled to check the packaging and refuses to load other goods. If unbeknown to the carrier such goods are on the vehicle and arrive in a damaged condition, the question arises[49] as to whether he might exclude his liability by invoking the mentioned clause. This has been denied for being in breach of Article 41, because the same clause would derogate from Article 17.[50] The solution is not persuasive, because the CMR does not structure the carriage on a single organizational model, but leaves to the parties the power to decide how to perform it and for which cargo. Therefore, we have to consider valid a clause allowing the carrier to accept goods before loading and executing the latter operation, as it often occurs.

German case law is possibly in conflict with Article 41.[51] This case law rules that, in the event of unlimited liability, in accordance with Article 29, the aggrieved party could choose whether to refer to Article 23, first and second paragraphs, or to national law. Even before impairing the binding nature of the Convention, the solution is unfounded. In fact, although there is full liability, it is still covered by the CMR and, therefore, by Article 23. *A fortiori*, Article 41 is refuted by the well-known Italian case law[52] in terms of which, if no consignment note is drawn up, the whole Convention would not be applicable. Once again, the orientation is fallacious, because drafting the consignment note has nothing to do with the application of uniform law.[53]

46 Cf. *Noble* v. *The R. H. Group*, in Messent and Glass (2018), p. 395 ff.

47 Cf. Messent and Glass (2018), p. 395 ff.

48 Cf. *Datec Electronic Holdings Ltd.* v. *United Parcels Service Ltd.*, in *Lloyd's rep*, 2007, 114.

49 Cf. *Datec Electronic Holdings Ltd.* v. *United Parcels Service Ltd.*, in *Lloyd's rep*, 2007, 114.

50 Cf. *Datec Electronic Holdings Ltd.* v. *United Parcels Service Ltd.*, in *Lloyd's rep*, 2007, 114.

51 Cf. BGH 30 September 2010, in *TranspR*, 2010, 437.

52 Cf. Cass. Italy 7 February 2006, no. 2529, in *Giur. it. rep.*, 2006; Cass. Italy 28 November 1975, no. 3983, *ibid.*, 1975; Cass. Italy 1 March 1978, no. 1034, *ibid.*, 1978; Cass. Italy 26 November 1980, no. 6272, *ibid.*, 1980; Cass. Italy 2 October 2003, no. 14680, *ibid.*, 2003.

53 Cfr. Otte (2018), p. 1593 ff.

2.1.3 The Specific Cases Considered by Article 41, Second Paragraph

According to Article 41, second paragraph, clauses whereby the carrier "*se ferait céder le bénéfice de l'assurence de la marchandise ou toute autre clause analogue, ainsi que toute clause déplaçant le fardeau de la preuve*" are null and void.[54] Even without such provision, invalidity would still attach to an agreement by which, once an insurance against damages has been stipulated, the party entitled to the goods has to transfer the indemnity credit to the carrier. In fact, in that case, the latter would be relieved of any liability, with a derogation running counter to Article 41, first paragraph.[55] This prohibition does not extend to responsibility insurance, unless proof is adduced that the relevant premium is paid by the shipper.[56] With economic burdens resting on him, in fact, the transporter is free to insure his civil liability and, actually, such reasonable practice must be encouraged, because it complies with the criterion of professional diligence.

Overall, Article 41, second paragraph, interferes with the insurance matter, which is not covered by the Convention, because this is restricted to carriage only. The aim is to avoid including clauses in the contract that involve the party entitled to the goods and his insurers, whereby the latter waive the subrogation action.[57] Thus, an attempt is made to safeguard the risk allocation system defined by the CMR. The concept of subrogation is deemed by uniform law to be easily intelligible and refers to the compensatory claim formulated against the responsible person by the insurer against damages after payment of indemnity.

Accordingly, we have to consider null and void an agreement[58] whereby the transporter accepts to compensate for any detriment only where the party entitled to the cargo stipulates an insurance contract in which the company undertakes not to exercise the subrogation action against the transporter himself. The same conclusions ought to be reached if such a waiver is not included in the contract of carriage, but only relates to the regulation of the relationship between the insurer and his beneficiary. The last-mentioned thesis cannot be supported. If there is no evident connection between the contract of transport and the insurance one, the CMR, which pays regard only to the former, cannot be applied. Therefore, the carrier is entitled to rely on a clause waiving the subrogation action not referred to in the contract of

[54] This is how Article 41, second paragraph, is expressed in the French version; in the English text, we read "a benefit of insurance in favour of the carrier or any other similar clause or any clause shifting the burden of the proof shall be null and void".

[55] Cf. OGH 15 December 1977, in *VersR*, 1978, 980.

[56] Cf. Clarke (2014), p. 289 ff.

[57] Cf. Messent and Glass (2018), p. 396 ff.

[58] Cf. Trib. com. Brussels 10 November 1971, in *J. P. A.*, 1971, 227; OGH 24 June 1999, in *TranspR*, 2000, 370.

transport, because it does not infringe Article 41.[59] It is harder to deny an interference with the latter contract if the insurance premium is taken into account in the consideration agreed to with the transporter.

Moreover, in France,[60] a clause included in the contract of carriage by which the shipper binds himself to take out a transporter liability insurance is held to be valid even within the scope regulated by the Convention. Considering that the carrier is sometimes responsible for the entire prejudice, in accordance with Article 29, these clauses would guarantee an adequate indemnity. The thesis favoring their validity cannot be endorsed, because they entail a breach of Article 41, second paragraph; we are, in fact, dealing precisely with the scenario prohibited by it.

Lastly, according to Article 41, second paragraph, agreements affecting the burden of proof are null and void. Even in this case, in order for Article 41, second paragraph, to operate, the clause must concern aspects regulated by the Convention. The solution is reasonable;[61] the *onus* of proof is governed by the CMR and the principle of Article 41, second paragraph, is redundant, because the consequences can be inferred from the first paragraph. The application-linked centrality of the problem justifies the specification, which draws attention to an essential aspect.

2.2 The Binding Nature of the Geneva Convention and the Laws of the Various States

2.2.1 The Direct References in the CMR to National Law

The aim of the CMR is to uniformly regulate the most significant profiles of the contract of carriage, so that the parties can refer to a single text, without having to know and apply all the national laws involved. Simplification speeds up operations, leading a significant impulse to this economic sector. The more complete and exhaustive the rules of uniform law are, the less interference there is with domestic one, with the result that the former does not lose consistency and does not break up into different and, at times, conflicting national sources. Article 41 aims at accomplishing this objective by enshrining the mandatory nature of the CMR, save for some sporadic exceptions, which do not alter the overall framework. If the Convention has been a success story,[62] especially if we consider that the text dates back to 1956, some of its parts refer to domestic law.

Indeed, the CMR uses different criteria to identify the applicable national law. For instance, Articles 29 and 32 refer to that of the presiding judge related to negligence

[59] Cf. App. Paris 26 June 1981, in *Bull. transp.*, 1981, 395; Cass. Belgium 9 April 1981, in *E. L. D.*, 1983, no. 11, 31.

[60] Cf. Trib. Poitiers 7 December 1983, in *Bull. transp.* 1985, 425; Clarke (2014), p. 289 ff.

[61] For the opposite view, cf. Loewe (1976), p. 401 ff., who offers no justification.

[62] Cf. Herber (2004), p. 93 ff.

equated to willful default, as well as the scenarios of suspension and interruption of prescription differing from those contemplated in Article 32. Actually, both provisions are a cause of perplexity, not so much because it is unreasonable to mention the law of the presiding judge, but, because, in such instances, the CMR could have regulated the problems in a direct and all-inclusive fashion, thereby avoiding integration with national systems.

A different case is that of Article 16, fifth paragraph, regarding the method for selling the goods after the end of the journey. Here, reference is made to the law of the place in which the cargo is found, and this solution is reasonable. The Convention could not have tackled the problem because it would have been too time-consuming and it would have required integration with the national trial system. Moreover, the place in which the selling must take place influences the choice of the law. Further, with regard to the alleged loss, if the party entitled to the goods fails to comply with the prescriptions of Article 20, fourth paragraph, the carrier can dispose of the load recovered, in conformity with the national law of the place where it is found. The rule is questionable, because there is no possible control over the position in which the goods are found. Therefore, it is not possible to provide a realistic proof conflicting with the allegations of the carrier and he could influence the choice of national law, abstractly at least, because the issue is almost non-existent in practice.

In all these rules, the Convention places its own criterion for the identification of national law and such a choice is buttressed by the mandatory nature of Article 41, so that it prevails over any other consensual solution. Therefore, the usual criteria for the connection and resolution of private international law conflicts do not operate, but there is a direct binding prescription, which prevails over any other indication.

2.2.2 *The Provisions of the Convention That Presuppose the Application of National Law, Without Its Identification*

The Convention does not always identify national law; various rules imply it without providing any indication about its choice. Thus, in accordance with Article 11, third paragraph, for the purposes of customs operations, the carrier acts as the shipper's agent. It follows that any relevant regulation is remitted to national law, because the Convention does not tackle such aspects. Besides, there is a necessary integration in Article 5, first paragraph, in the part wherein it allows the signature of the consignment note to be replaced by the affixing of stamps on the part of the shipper or the carrier, if that is regulated precisely by the national law. Again, as regards the internal relationships between successive transporters in the cumulative carriage, Article 38 governs the scenario where one of them becomes insolvent and, because the Convention does not specify when that would occur, domestic law must be applied.[63]

Furthermore, in the CMR, the definition of prejudice caused by delay is very concise and, inevitably, given the complexity of the problem, what is laid down by Article 23, fifth paragraph, is insufficient. This is especially true as far as the most delicate cases are concerned and also for the related determination of the compensable prejudice; the law of each State is of assistance. What is more, as Article 27, first paragraph, only concerns the interest paid by the carrier on compensations owed, national law is applied where the transporter institutes action to request relief for any damages or consideration.

In other scenarios, the silence of the CMR does not justify the reference to national law. Thus, for example, despite the fact that Articles 17 and 18 only consider liability for loss, damage and delay, the Convention regulates the entire issue and, therefore, breach of the obligation to perform the journey. Moreover, the shipper may not benefit from the compensatory limit laid down by the national legal system in the event of liability for omitted information on the dangerous nature of the goods, under Article 22, as the Convention fully regulates the problem, despite contrasting opinions.[64] Then, with regard to the instances of prejudices caused by delay, loss and damage, the burden of proof rests on the party invoking relief, based on the criteria set by Article 23, first, second and fifth paragraphs. This topic falls within the scope of uniform law and that of the trial is irrelevant, as the regulation is of substantive nature.

Furthermore, despite the fact that Article 31 does not prescribe any formal requirement for the agreement on jurisdiction, there is no reference to national law, although the contrary thesis has been endorsed.[65] This is because in the absence of a contrary provision in Article 31, formal freedom must be accepted.[66] Then, notwithstanding contrary views,[67] Article 32 applies to the action against the carrier for incomplete execution, because the scenario is regulated by the CMR, if we admit that it is independent from loss or delay. In addition, Article 32, first paragraph, letter a), rather than national law, operates where goods are refused and brought back to the sender, having arrived damaged.[68] After all, according to some,[69] Article 32, first paragraph, letter c), would not apply to loss, damage or delay that were not traceable back to the specific provisions of Article 32, first paragraph, letter a) and letter b),

[63] Cf. Messent and Glass (2018), p. 380 ff.

[64] Cf. Putzeys (1981), p. 356 ff.

[65] Cf. Loewe (1976), p. 388 ff.; Messent and Glass (2018), p. 295 ff.

[66] Cf. Puetz (2018), p. 122 ff. See also Cass. Belgium 29 April 2004, in *Europ. transp. law,* 2004, no. 39, 688.

[67] Cf. BGH 18 February 1972, in *Europ. transp. law,* 1972, no. 7, 860; Polish Supreme Court 7 March 2017, II CSK 242/2016.

[68] For a contrary view, see *Moto Vespa S. A.* v. *Mat (Britannia express) Ltd.,* in *Lloyd's rep.,* 1979, 175, according to which national law applies in that event.

[69] See: *Moto Vespa S. A.* v. *Mat (Britannia express) Ltd.,* in *Lloyd's rep.,* 1979, 175.

with the result that we should refer to national law. However, the problem does not arise, because either the goods arrive and letter a) operates accordingly, or reference has to be made to letter b).

In addition, in case there is no indication of the instructions concerning the conclusion of the insurance contract on the consignment note, in accordance with Article 6, second paragraph, letter e), there is no room for domestic law, as the specific case is entirely governed by the Convention, despite the existence of contrasting opinions.[70] Thus, compensation for damages caused during loading or stowage operations is not governed by national law, considering that the CMR does not mention it, because they are activities instrumental to the carriage and, as such, falling within the scope of uniform law. Article 27, regarding the interest charged on the sum to be paid as compensation, indicates a predetermined annual rate and the effective date from which it accrues. It does not, therefore, leave room for national law, although there have been plenty of judgments taking the opposite view.[71] Moreover, interest can neither run from a time preceding the adoption of one of the two acts envisaged by Article 27, first paragraph, nor can domestic law be invoked for that purpose, because Article 27 itself tackles the issue exhaustively.

Lastly, despite the lack in uniform law of an express notion of redelivery, not even in this case is reference made to national law,[72] and the Convention regulates the entire issue. For the same reasons, any provisions of each country on unloading do not apply. Otherwise, the idea of homogeneous regulation would fail. Therefore, because the CMR intervenes, it must be applied to the custody that follows the unloading process, in accordance with Article 16, second paragraph, without the need to invoke national law, which is not mentioned, unlike what occurs in Article 16, last paragraph. Further, Article 16 repeatedly underlines the carrier's right to seek redressal against the goods or the price obtained, in order to satisfy his claims, and uniform law regulates the entire matter. Finally, in terms of Article 30, the parties' mutual verification of the state of the goods at the time of redelivery does not allow recourse to procedures specific to each country, notwithstanding the existence of opposite viewpoints.[73]

In conclusion, although the CMR does not regulate all aspects of the contract meticulously, an extensive interpretation enables its implementation to be defined in such a manner as to guarantee a uniform regulation. For those profiles that eschew its application based on literal criteria and for which the Convention does not identify national law to be taken into account, we must refer to the system adopted by each country for the resolution of the conflict of laws. Thus, for instance, the national one

[70] Cf. Messent and Glass (2018), p. 97 ff.

[71] Cf. Cass. com. France 6 June 1995, in *Le Lamy transp.*, 2020, vol. I, 517; Cass. com. France 3 March 1998, in *Bull. transp. logist.*, 1998, 231; Cass. com. France 18 January 2000, in *Le Lamy transp.*, 2020, vol. I, 517; Cass. com. France 28 January 2003, *ibid.*, 2020, vol. I, 517; App. Rouen 1 March 2012, *ibid.*, 2020, vol. I, 517. See also Clarke (2014), p. 307 ff.; Krings (1999), p. 779 ff.

[72] Cf. App. Paris 22 October 1997, in *Bull. transp.*, 1997, 779; App. Versailles 3 September 2013, *ibid.*, 2013, 518; Cass. com. France 10 March 2015, in *Le Lamy transp.*, 2020, vol. I, 479.

[73] Cf. Silingardi et al. (1994), p. 253 ff.; Pesce (1995), p. 315 ff.

chosen by the parties will operate according to the Turkish legal system,[74] failing which must apply the law that shows the closest connection to the contract. Therefore, if the carrier's head office is situated in the same State in which the loading or unloading is performed or in which the sender's head office is located, reference will be made to the law of that country, as long as it is compatible with the principles of Turkish public order; otherwise, Turkish law will operate.[75] For non-Member States, the rules on the resolution of the conflict vary according to each State's indications and its international Conventions. However, the solution is more linear for Member States of the European Union, for which Regulation (EC) 593/2008 on the law applicable to contractual obligations (Rome I) operates.[76]

2.2.3 The Regulatory Gaps in the CMR and in the Conventions of Uniform Law

There is a known orientation in legal theory[77] aimed at imagining a close correlation between the CMR and the applicable national law. According to this thesis, faced with the difficulty of implementing provisions of uniform law, we should postulate the frequent recourse to domestic one after its identification, just on the basis of the criteria of private international law. This thesis is not convincing,[78] because it weakens the complete regulation of the contract of carriage, as per the objective we can infer from Article 1 of the CMR.

As we have sought to do in this research when examining problems individually, the solution to the questions surrounding application should be found within the CMR system and not outside it. This is consistent with what has been stressed for other texts of uniform law, especially for the Vienna Convention on the sale of goods.[79] As it can be observed in this regard,[80] assuming this is the desired option in the text, it is difficult to identify any general principle that can help solve gaps. Such an attempt must be made as a matter of priority,[81] before referring to the UNIDROIT

[74] Cf. Dicleli (2012), p. 71 ff., according to whom, "in cases where the parties did not include a choice-of-law agreement in their contract, their contractual relationship is governed by the law that is most closely connected with the contract".

[75] Cf. Dicleli (2012), p. 71 ff.

[76] Cf. Fillers (2020), p. 174 ff.

[77] Cf. Clarke (2014), p. 307 ff.; Krings (1999), p. 779 ff.

[78] Cf. Messent and Glass (2018), p. 310 ff.; Clarke (2014), p. 307 ff.; Silingardi et al. (1994), p. 253 ff.; Pesce (1995), p. 315 ff.

[79] Cf. Witz (2020), p. 508 ff.

[80] Cf. Witz (2020), p. 510 ff., according to whom, in regards to the Vienna Convention on the international sale of goods, "*la principale difficultée est la détermination des principes generaux dont la Convention s'inspire*".

[81] Cf. Pesce (1997), p. 506 ff.

Principles on international trade contracts[82] or to the ones of the European Contract Law.[83]

Precisely, the critical examination of the CMR system can suggest its reconstruction, which would allow us to solve the gaps without having to refer continuously to national law. In reality, if we compare the 1980 Vienna Convention with the Geneva one, we can discern dystonic elements. On the one hand, the CMR lacks detailed general conditions in the practice,[84] whereas the consignment note indications are concise and operational, as we can infer from Article 6 of the CMR. On the other hand, the strong organizational factors characterizing the carriage and a more limited scope of the regulation can help us unravel the interpretative doubts. This can happen if we recognize that the necessary promotion of its own self-sufficiency is something intrinsic to uniform law, unless we were to modify the underlying reason for its very existence. Notwithstanding the fact that the Court of Justice of the European Union has denied that it is called upon to interpret the CMR,[85] what is lacking is a homogeneous application entrusted to transversal jurisdictional bodies, and we could also discuss the relevance of foreign decisions in each legal system.[86]

One of the objectives of this research is to ascertain whether there are any comparable orientations. Albeit with contradictions and substantial differences in the decisions of the various countries, these emerge if we share a universalist objective when interpreting uniform law.[87] The first target is to limit the relevance of domestic one. We must, therefore, infer from the CMR the aim of providing a complete regulation, given that only in that case could we aspire for a realistic uniformity. Having established this criterion, which is certainly questionable and yet widespread in contemporary law,[88] the justification of a reduction in interference with the national legal system cannot be founded beforehand and in a general way. From time to time, we need to verify possible gaps and establish whether, within the Convention, there are resources to overcome them. This is the idea the present study has drawn inspiration from, and only a critical reading thereof can tell us not so much whether the goal has been achieved as whether, at least, it has been pursued consistently. However, it postulates acceptance of the close relevance of the CMR to the categories of continental law to be resorted to in order to circumscribe and fill the gaps, without prejudice to the reference to the Treaty of Vienna on international agreements.[89]

---

[82] Cf. Hondius (2001), p. 419 ff.

[83] Cf. Hondius (2001), p. 419 ff.

[84] Cf. Schlechtriem and Witz (2008), no. 27.

[85] Cf. Court of Justice, Grand Chamber, 4 May 2012, C – no. 533 of 2008, *TNT Express Nederland BV* c. *AXA Versicherung AG.*

[86] Cf. Witz (2020), p. 512 ff.

[87] Cf. Witz (2003), p. 54 ff.

[88] Cf. Witz (2020), p. 512 ff.

[89] Cf. Witz (2020), p. 512 ff.

2.3 The Geneva Convention and the European Union's Rules on Determining the Applicable Law

2.3.1 The Geneva Convention Model and Regulation (EC) 593/2008 on the Law Applicable to Contractual Obligations (Rome I)

For those EU States that have joined the CMR, the identification of applicable domestic laws presupposes an examination of the relationship of such Convention with Regulation (EC) 593/2008. Viewed as a whole, the latter is part and parcel of the "known process of communitarization of private international law"[90] and has a clear structure. According to Article 24, second paragraph, it replaces the previous Rome Convention of 1980. In fact, any reference to the latter "is understood to be made to the (...) Regulation".[91] Conversely, for Article 25, the Regulation does not prevent the application of international conventions signed by one or more Member States if they govern conflicts of laws regarding contractual obligations. For such a provision to operate, however, the Regulation has imposed that, by 17 June 2009, the conventions adopted by the Member States should have been notified to the Commission.

With a recurring pattern (think of Article 71 of Regulation (EU) 1215/2012 relating to the jurisdiction, recognition and execution of decisions in civil and commercial matters),[92] we get confirmation of "the pliable nature of the Regulation"[93] in favor of uniform law texts stipulated by EU countries. Then, according to Article 25, second paragraph, "the (...) Regulation prevails, among Member States, on the conventions concluded exclusively between two or more of them, to the extent that they" concern issues disciplined by the Regulation itself. This provision, however, does not question the relationship with the uniform law Conventions related to carriage. In fact, "the latter prevails as they lay down rules equipped with a title of exclusive applicability".[94] Accordingly, for those situations regulated by uniform law, the conflict-of-law provisions set out in the Regulation become "permissive conflict-of-law rules"[95] and, as such, are bound not to be implemented. Thus, the CMR prevails over Regulation (EC) 593/2008 in all those instances in which it lays down its own criterion of identification of national law, as in the aforementioned scenarios of Article 16, fifth paragraph, in relation to the sale of the

[90] Cf. Tonolo (2009), p. 309 ff.; Kohler (1999), p. 1 ff.; Basedow (2000), p. 687 ff.; Pocar (2000), p. 873 ff.

[91] Cf. Article 24, last paragraph, of Regulation (EC) 593/2008.

[92] Before such a regulation, along the same lines, see Article 71 of Regulation (EC) 44/2001.

[93] Cf. Tonolo (2009), p. 312 ff.

[94] Cf. Tonolo (2009), p. 313 ff.

[95] Cf. Sadikov (1985), p. 191 ff.

goods, Article 29 with regard to the forfeiture of the compensatory limit and Article 32 on prescription.[96]

An opposite solution is reached for profiles not directly regulated by the Convention but entrusted to national law, without there being any rule for its identification; to these, we must add those aspects on which the CMR is silent. This last-mentioned area shrinks if we opt for an extensive interpretation of the provisions of uniform law, in such a manner as to ensure a homogeneous regulation. Be it as it may, more generally, for that part of the contract that eludes the CMR, we need to refer to the discipline adopted by each country for the resolution of the conflict. Accordingly, for Member States of the European Union, reference should be made to Regulation (EC) 593/2008. In particular, Article 5 concerns contracts for the carriage of goods. In the first place, it refers to Article 3 on the choice of law, on the strength of which the parties identify the applicable domestic law. This choice must be explicit or clearly specified in the agreement or susceptible of being inferred from the circumstances.

In the latter event, we can reconstruct the common intention from the convergence toward a single legal system of the most significant aspects relating to the execution of the contract.[97] It could be, for instance, the place of its conclusion coinciding with that of loading or unloading. In this regard, the choice for a carrier based in a specific country might be relevant. We could indeed infer from such connection that the sender's intention is to submit the service performance to the related legal system. Altogether, by its reference to Article 3, Article 5, first paragraph, underlines the centrality of the parties' autonomy.[98]

In the absence of any agreement, Article 5 makes reference to the law of the country of the carrier's habitual residence, as long as it corresponds to the place of receipt of the goods or of delivery, or to the law of the State of the shipper's habitual residence. Failing that, the law of the agreed upon place of delivery will operate and, in the latter instance, a clear alternative emerges, capable of resolving any uncertainties. Of further assistance is the reference to the law of the transporter's habitual residence, as European regulations on the conflict of laws are often inspired by this criterion. Moreover, such principle is tempered by the necessary connection with one of the parameters indicated by Article 5 itself, in its first paragraph, so that any imbalances can be corrected. The reference to the shipper's place of habitual residence is in his favor, because he can thereby know in advance which law will be applied.

Lastly, according to Article 5, last paragraph, in the absence of the choice of law, we resort to the so-called escape clause,[99] by virtue of which the law of the State showing the closest connections with the contract is implemented.[100] The country

[96] Cfr. Otte (2018), p. 1594 ff.

[97] Cf. Cass. Italy 9 October 1984, no. 5028, in *Riv. dir. int. priv. proc.*, 1985, 625.

[98] Cf. Carella (1999), p. 105 ff.

[99] Cf. Vismara (2017), p. 63 ff.

[100] Cf. Baratta (1991), p. 177 ff.; Lopes Pegna (2006), p. 756 ff.

thus identified can be different from what would have been selected pursuant to Article 5, first paragraph.[101] The escape clause (*clause échappatoire*) has a subsidiary nature in the field of carriage, because it only intervenes if none of the conditions of Article 5, first paragraph, are met, for instance, where there is no coincidence between the carrier's habitual residence and either the place of receipt of the goods or of delivery or the country of the shipper's habitual residence, and the redelivery is performed in a place other than the one agreed upon.[102]

2.3.2 The Geneva Convention Model and Regulation (EC) 864/2007 on the Law Applicable to Extra-Contractual Obligations (Rome II)

Regulation (EC) 864/2007, in Article 1, concerns the conflict of laws as regards extra-contractual obligations in the civil and commercial fields.[103] Since Article 28 of the CMR disciplines the scenario of the carrier's extra-contractual liability in relation to cases of loss, damage or delay in redelivering the cargo, we need to coordinate such text with the Regulation. By delimiting the respective contexts, the criteria for identifying the national law can be defined, if the countries involved have adhered to the CMR and are members of the European Union.[104]

Given the notions of "extra-contractual obligation", "event" and "damage" according to Article 2 of the Regulation, for Article 3, national law applies even where it is not that of an EU country. Moreover, in terms of Article 4, first paragraph, the law is identified on the basis of the place in which the prejudice occurs, regardless of the State in which the causative fact arises or the one in which the indirect consequences manifest.[105] Therefore, the principle of the *lex loci commissi delicti* (the law of the place where the fact was committed), relied upon by most EU States,[106] was replaced by that of the *lex loci damni* (the law of the place where the prejudice took place), a criterion which, unlike the former, "determines the right balance between the interests of the alleged culprit and those of the aggrieved

[101] Cf. Tonolo (2009), p. 342 ff., according to whom the interpreter is tasked with "establishing the extent of the connection with the contract and the legal system it is linked to, within the framework of a hermeneutical activity aimed at bringing to focus, case by case, the closest law to the contractual relationship".

[102] Cf. Vismara (2017), p. 65 ff. More generally, on the escape clause, see Knoepfler (1982), p. 113 ff.; Von Overbeck (1999), p. 128 ff.; Castel (2007), p. 565 ff.

[103] Cf. Kadner Graziano (2008), p. 457 ff.

[104] Denmark does not participate in the adoption of the Regulation (EC) 864/2007. Cf. Kadner Graziano (2008), p. 448 ff.

[105] Cf. Zournatzi (2018), p. 269 ff.

[106] Cf. Busnelli (1991), p. 539 ff.

party".[107] An exception is provided by Article 4, second paragraph, which considers the case where the parties habitually reside in the same country and, in this situation, the relative law applies. Lastly, Article 4, third paragraph, introduces an exception that operates if the unlawful fact displays close connections with a State other than the one that would have been selected pursuant to Article 4, first and second paragraphs.

As in Regulation (EC) 593/2008, a space is reserved for contractual autonomy.[108] In fact, for Article 14, the parties can reach an agreement to establish which law to apply. However, unlike what is laid down by the 2008 Regulation, such a clause must be subsequent to the fact that occasioned the prejudice, unless the parties exercise a commercial activity. In general, this choice must be explicitly formulated or has to be inferred from the circumstances, but cannot undermine the rights of third parties.

In addition, specific criteria for the resolution of the conflict are introduced with regard to unjust enrichment,[109] *negotiorum gestio*[110] and *culpa in contrahendo* (fault in the conclusion of the contract).[111] Thus, for Article 10, first paragraph, if an obligation arising from unjust enrichment is linked to a relationship, such as the one that stems from a contract or from an unlawful fact, the law that governs them applies. Failing that, the law is that of the country in which the parties habitually reside, in accordance with Article 10, second paragraph. Lastly, if the first and second paragraphs of Article 10 do not provide a solution, the law of the State in which the enrichment was generated is referred to.

On the model of Article 10, Article 11 regulates the extra-contractual obligations arising from a *negotiorum gestio*, whereas, according to Article 12,[112] the instances of so-called *culpa in contrahendo* (fault in the conclusion of the contract) are regulated by the law applicable to the contract. Failing that, the law of the State in which the prejudice originates or in which the parties habitually reside will operate.

In terms of Article 28, the Regulation does not prevent the execution of international conventions stipulated by one or more Member States at the time of its adoption and aimed at disciplining the conflict regarding extra-contractual liability. To this end, only the uniform law texts communicated to the Commission by 11 July 2008 are relevant. Thus, the CMR operates if the loss, damage or delay give rise to extra-contractual actions against the carrier or his assistants. Based on that, only the extra-contractual liability claims promoted by the party entitled to the goods within the scope of the transport are regulated by the Convention. Furthermore, Article 28 of the CMR does not concern third parties; therefore, if these are citizens of the Union, they must resolve the conflict pursuant to Regulation (EC) 864/2007. It is not

---

[107] This is how the sixteenth recital reads.

[108] Cf. Zournatzi (2018), p. 271 ff.

[109] Cf. Zournatzi (2018), p. 273 ff.; Tubeuf (2008), p. 535 ff.

[110] Cf. Tubeuf (2008), p. 535 ff.

[111] Cf. Kozyris Phaedon (2008), p. 496 ff.

[112] Cf. Volders (2007), p. 127 ff.; Lagarde (2009), p. 598 ff.

always easy to identify the borderline between the two sources because there are doubtful scenarios, such as the unjust enrichment action. If, as contended in this research, it is not disciplined by the Convention, we must refer to Article 10 of the Regulation; otherwise, if the opposite thesis is endorsed,[113] reference should be made to Article 28 of the CMR.

2.4 The Interpretation of the Geneva Convention

2.4.1 The Criteria for Interpreting Provisions of the Geneva Convention

The 1969 Vienna Convention on international treaties devotes its third section to the method of interpretation. Despite being more recent than the CMR, for a correct understanding of the latter we should consider the criteria of the 1969 Convention. After all, they embody consolidated principles.[114] Article 31 calls for a literal exegesis based on the common meaning of the provisions, whereas Article 32 refers to complementary means of interpretation, if it is necessary to draw confirmation of the exegesis determined by the application of Article 31, or if the overall sense of the rules is still ambiguous or obscure or a textual reading would lead to an absurd or illogical solution.[115] In reality, the reference to the 1969 Vienna Convention should not be overestimated, with its attention to the centrality of the text, because such an indication must be traced back to the systematic construction objectives characteristic of a uniform law treaty, which imposes a panoramic reflection, especially with a view to remove gaps and reduce references to national law. If the aim of the CMR analysis is to enhance an integrated reconstruction thereof, in favor of an overall regulation of the conduct of operators, a textual exegesis might not always be enough. Therefore, Article 31 of the Vienna Convention represents a reference point, but its mention of literal interpretation ought not to be overestimated.

Common law countries have always shown perplexity on the need to resort to alternative tools, with a preference for a system revolving around a textual reading that makes little room for judges' creative intervention, so much so that, "in Britain, the judiciary finds it difficult to deviate from a clear text even if that text would lead to unintended results".[116] Instead, the teleological method proposes an interpretation that takes into account the scope and purpose of the CMR. Its aim is "to standardize conditions under which international carriage of goods is undertaken".[117] Therefore,

[113] Cf. LG Graz 5 April 2000, in *Europ. transp. law,* 2002, no. 37, 360.

[114] Cf. Clarke (2014), p. 6 ff., according to whom "the provisions of Vienna Convention codify already existing public international law"; Verheyen (2016), p. 442 ff.

[115] Cf. Verheyen (2016), p. 443 ff.; Czapski (1998), p. 461 ff.

[116] Cf. Clarke (2014), p. 7 ff. See also Messent and Glass (2018), p. 5 ff.

[117] Cf. *Quantum Ltd.* v. *Plane trucking Ltd.* in *Lloyd's rep.*, 2001, 133.

the relevant provisions should be interpreted pursuant to such parameters. For some,[118] this would not have a subsidiary character but rather prevail over the literal one. For common law countries there is no risk that "the judges become legislators, but that they may become legislators with widely differing, and perhaps unduly legalistic, views of the policy which is, or ought to be, behind the legislation",[119] whence the proposal is to mitigate such principle, supplementing it with further elements.[120]

Defining the purpose of the Convention is facilitated by the examination of preparatory works, which might, for example, lend meaning to the silence on certain aspects; with all that, in general, the emphasis[121] falls on the difficulty of dominating the relevant documents. It is not always the case, in fact, that we can understand the scope of a decision on an amendment, because the motivations might have differed. This difficulty has been discerned by common law countries,[122] which have seldom resorted to preparatory works. In addition, we can refer to the examination of foreign decisions, which can serve as a guide for the solutions adopted or for their motivational ground. As is well known, in common law countries, where decisions are of a binding nature,[123] there is reluctance to depart from the precedent,[124] even where such departure could avail a more complete interpretation.

2.4.2 Interpretation of the CMR as a Text of Uniform Law Based on the Logic of Continental Law

The need to safeguard uniformity is not felt only for the CMR, as there have been similar requests with regard to the 1980 Vienna Convention on international sales. In the case of this Treaty, it was highlighted[125] that the risk of divergent interpretations might jeopardize the search for uniformity. Unlike the CMR, the 1980 Convention offers a criterion that has provided inspiration to subsequent texts,[126] in particular,

[118]Cf. OLG Düsseldorf 27 March 1980, in *Europ. transp. law*, 1983, no. 18, 89.

[119]Cf. Haak (1986), p. 17 ff.; Messent and Glass (2018), p. 5 ff.

[120]Cf. Clarke (2014), p. 9 ff.

[121]Cf. Clarke (2014), p. 9 ff.

[122]Cf. *Fothergill* c. *Monarch Airlines Ltd.*, in *AC*, 1981, 278.

[123]Cf. Clarke (2014), p. 11 ff.; Messent and Glass (2018), p. 9 ff. Cf. *Ulster – Swift Ltd.* v. *Taunton Meat Haulage Ltd.*, in *Lloyd's rep.*, 1977, 346.

[124]Cf. Messent and Glass (2018), p. 9 ff. But see *J. J. Silber Ltd.* v. *Islander Truckin Ltd.*, in *Lloyd's rep.*, 1985, 243, where two foreign decisions were considered.

[125]Cf. Witz (2020), p. 508 ff.

[126]Cf. Article 7 of the 2001 United Nations Convention on the assignment of credits in international trade and Article 5 of the 2005 Convention on the use of electronic communications in international contracts.

UNIDROIT Principles.[127] According to Article 7 of the 1980 Convention, we must consider its international nature, the need to promote its uniform application[128] and due compliance with good faith; furthermore, gaps must be resolved in light of its canons. This approach has a more general character, that is, it can be followed for other texts. After all, Article 7 of the 1980 Vienna Convention explicitly formulates some objectives that are already partly present in the recital of the CMR, according to which the purpose is to regulate carriage uniformly.

On the one hand, the 1980 Vienna Convention identifies the purposes the exegesis must aim for,[129] but, on the other hand, it does not consider any traditional hermeneutical criterion. The need to enhance the international profile partly hinders the application of the parameters followed by the national legal system. Given that, according to some,[130] the principles conceived for treaties other than those of uniform law may not be implemented because they are built on a codification of material law.[131] We could, therefore, elaborate specific methods, drawing them from continental tradition.[132] Based on this, we can first proceed with a literal interpretation, though the text must be read by disengaging ourselves from any conditioning created by the individual legal system,[133] so that "*l'interprétation soit dénationalisée et se coule dans un moule intérnational*".[134]

Therefore, a self-sufficient system can be formed[135] and, if a textual reading is not exhaustive, the teleological one, aimed at clarifying the purpose of the rule, will provide assistance.[136] In that case, we can opt for an evolutionary research, allowing us to bring the provisions in line with new economic–social processes. Overall, the method brings to mind that of continental law,[137] but it lodges it in a uniform logic, so that a solution can be sought that is consistent with the international nature of the

---

[127] Cf. Witz (2020), p. 508 ff.

[128] Cf. Deumier (2018), p. 265 ff.

[129] Cf. Ferrari (2017), p. 244 ff.

[130] Cf. Witz (2020), p. 509 ff.

[131] Cf. Schlechtriem and Schwenzer (2016), p. 23 ff., nt. 1.

[132] Cf. Witz (2020), p. 509 ff.

[133] Cf. Witz (2020), p. 509 ff., according to whom "*il importe de lire attentivement, en s'abstenant de chauffer ses 'lunettes de juriste national'*"; Honnold (1988), p. 208 ff.

[134] Cf. Racine (2018), p. 18 ff.

[135] Cf. OLG Munich 21 July 2016, in *VersR*, 2017, 583, in terms of which the CMR represents a complete and self-contained regulatory system, without any need to refer to civil law institutions. Cf. Jesser-Huß (2017), p. 358 ff.; Verheyen (2016), p. 447 ff.; Pesce (1997), p. 505 ff., according to whom "the introduction to the uniform rules (. . .) is intended to underline that unification of the law (. . .) means that that same identity is open to (identity of) interpretation through the renunciation of the principles of domestic law and the acceptance that, under a system of uniform rules, the relative jurisdictional institutions are autonomous".

[136] Cf. Cerqueira and Nord (2020), p. 517 ff.

[137] Cf. Putzeys (2016), p. 424 ff.

problems and is as detached as possible from purely local assessments.[138] Often, in fact, some terms might reflect different concepts in the two contexts.

With this view, decisions play a relevant role;[139] if a constant orientation has been formed on a controversial issue, it can be followed for the sake of safeguarding uniformity, and the national judge should know foreign case law.[140] Thus, judicial decisions that refer solely to the precedents of domestic law, without ascertaining their relevance, with the risk of perpetuating questionable solutions, have to be discouraged.[141] To unify objectives, the most significant of which is the promotion of uniformity, this system can be applied to the CMR (based on the 1980 Vienna Convention), albeit in the absence of a specific provision. The risks of exegetical divergences is one of the most serious threats to the effectiveness of the CMR. This is because, by favoring solutions inspired by the individual legal systems, they lead to disintegration and open the way to the so-called forum shopping. Accordingly, even for the Geneva Convention we could autonomously review the logic peculiar to continental law, on which it is based.

Although the contract of carriage has but a distant connection with those relating to international trade, due to its specific, prevalently technical character, there is, however, a point in referring to the UNIDROIT Principles, particularly to good faith. The latter, in fact, are rules common to many legal systems and consistent with the needs of international contracts. As they are also a criterion of interpretation, they have no binding force and their application depends on their persuasive value.[142] In particular, for Article 1. 7 of the UNIDROIT Principles, the contracting parties must act in good faith and may not exclude or limit such duty.[143]

As the principles follow an approach typical of civil law systems in a sufficiently clear manner, good faith is understood as a supplementary source of the identification of obligations to integrate those directly mentioned by the agreement. After all, due to the influence of continental culture, considerable relevance has to be attributed to the phase preceding the conclusion of the contract. In case negotiations are not conducted in good faith, the aggrieved party may request compensation for damages. In contrast, traditionally common law countries reject such a criterion, given their usual distrust of general clauses. Even when they admit good faith, they confine it to the executive phase.

Therefore, compared to the UNIDROIT Principles, which entail an articulate reading, good faith can be understood either as a supplementary source or as a duty pertaining to the moment of implementation. Even for a correct understanding of the CMR, good faith plays a decisive role; in particular, by resorting to it, German case

[138] Cf. Verheyen (2016), p. 449 ff.

[139] Cf. Legros (2016), p. 427 ff.; Schelin (2016), p. 434 ff.

[140] Cf. Lookofsky and Flechtner (2005), p. 512 ff.

[141] Cf. Lookofsky and Flechtner (2005), p. 512 ff.

[142] Cf. Bonell (2004), p. 137 ff.; Di Majo (1997), p. 153 ff.; Gutierrez Falla (2005), p. 503 ff.; Ferrari (2017), p. 244 ff.

[143] Cf. McKendrick (2008), p. 518 ff.; Hartkamp (1994), p. 65 ff.

law has integrated some obligations of parties. For example, it has recognized that the sender has saddled with a duty to provide information on the nature of the goods. Thus, if at the time of delivery the transporter is not informed about their specific value, his liability is limited, particularly in the event of theft,[144] and the shipper has to face with the risks deriving from his behavior. These judgments echo the German conception of good faith as a mechanism for integrating obligations and, partly at least, simultaneously enhancing mutual reliance, bestowing a significant weight on preventive information.

References

Baratta R (1991) Il collegamento più stretto nel diritto internazionale privato dei contratti. Milan

Basedow J (2000) The communitarization of the conflicts of laws under the Treaty of Amsterdam. Common Mark Law Rev:687 ff

Bonell MJ (2004) Un 'codice' internazionale del diritto dei contratti. I principi Unidroit nei contratti commerciali internazionali. Milan

Busnelli F (1991) Itinerari europei nella 'terra di nessuno fra contratto e fatto illecito': la responsabilità da informazioni inesatte. Contr Impr:554 ff

Carella G (1999) Autonomia della volontà e scelta di legge nel diritto internazionale privato. Bari

Castel JG (2007) The uncertainty factor in Canadian private international law. McJill Law J:565 ff

Cerqueira VG, Nord N (2020) Retour sur le silence des parties à propos de l'application de la Convention de Vienne sur le vente internationale de marchandises. AJ Contrat:517 ff

Clarke MA (2014) International carriage of goods by road: CMR. New York, ed. VI

Czapski W (1998) Interprétation de la Convention CMR à la lumière du droit international public. Eur Transp Law 33:461 ff

Deumier P (2018) La Convention de Vienne, source vivifiante pour les questions d'interprétation. Mélanges Claude Witz:265 ff

Di Majo A (1997) L'osservanza della buona fede nei principi Unidroit sui contratti commerciali internazionali. In: Aa. Vv., Bonell MJ, Bonelli F (eds) Contratti commerciali internazionali e principi Unidroit. Milan, p 153 ff

Dicleli SU (2012) Liability of the carrier under the CMR Convention. sudicleli@gsimeridian.com articletter, 71 ff

Ferrari F (2017) Autonomous interpretation versus homeward trend versus outward trend in CISG case law. Unif Law Rev:244 ff

Fillers A (2020) The CMR in the practice of Latvian courts. Unif Law Rev:168 ff

Gutierrez Falla LF (2005) Good faith in commercial law and the Unidroit principles of international commercial contracts. Penn State Int Law Rev:507 ff

Haak KF (1986) The liability of the carrier under CMR. The Hague

Hartkamp AS (1994) The concept of good faith in the Unidroit principles for international commercial contracts. J Int Comp Law:65 ff

Herber R (2004) Überblick über die gesetzlichen Regelungen in Deutschland und in internationalen Übereinkommen. TranspR:93 ff

Hondius E (2001) La convention de Vienna après l'arrêt Cofratel. In: Etudes offertes à Jacques Ghistin, Le contrat au début du XXI siècle, LGDJ, p 419 ff

Honnold J (1988) The sales Convention in action – uniform international words: uniform words: uniform application? Jill Com:207 ff

[144] Cf. BGH 1 December 2005, in *TranspR,* 2006, 115; OGH 26 March 2004, *ibid.,* 2004, 364.

Jesser-Huß H (2017) Article 41 CMR und verbleibende Möglichkeiten der Vertragsgestaltung. TranspR:358 ff
Kadner Graziano T (2008) Le nouveau droit international privé communautaire en matière de responsabilité extracontractuelle (règlement Rome II). Rev droit int privé:448 ff
Knoepfler F (1982) Utilité et dangers d'une clause d'exception en droit international privé. In: Hommage à Raymond Jeanprêtre, Neuchâtel, p 113 ff
Kohler C (1999) Interrogations sur les sources du droit international privé après le Traité d'Amsterdam. Revue critique:1 ff
Kozyris Phaedon J (2008) Rome II: tort conflicts on the right track! A postscript to Symeon Symeonidis 'Missed opportunity'. Am J Comp Law:406 ff
Krings E (1999) CMR: examen de la jurisprudence des Cours de Cassation de France et de Pays – Bas (deuxième partie). Unif Law Rev:779 ff
Lagarde P (2009) La culpa in contrahendo à la croisée des règlements communautaires. In: Aa. Vv., Venturini G, Bariatti S (eds) Nuovi strumenti del diritto internazionale privato. New instruments of private international law. Nouveaux intruments du droit international privé. Liber Fausto Pocar, Milan, p 598 ff
Legros C (2016) Modalités de l'interprétation uniforme de la CMR. Quelles difficultées? Quelles remèdes? Unif Law Rev:426 ff
Loewe R (1976) Commentary on the Convention of 19 May 1956 on the contract for the international carriage of goods by road. Eur Transp Law 11:311 ff
Lookofsky J, Flechtner H (2005) Nominating Manfred Forberich: the worst decisions in twenty-five years? J Int Comm Law Arbitr:199 ff
Lopes Pegna O (2006) Il rilievo del collegamento più stretto della Convention di Roma alla proposta di regolamento 'Roma I'. Riv Dir Int:756 ff
McKendrick E (2008) Contract law. Text, cases and materials. Oxford
Messent A, Glass DA (2018) CMR: contracts for the international carriage of goods by road. New York, ed. IV
Otte K (2018) Art. 41 der CMR. In: Aa. Vv., Internationales Vertragsrecht. Munich, p 1592 ff
Pesce A (1995) Il trasporto internazionale di merci. Turin
Pesce A (1997) Uniform law on international carriage of goods: a system of special rules. Eur Transp Law 32:503 ff
Pocar F (2000) La comunitarizzazione del diritto internazionale privato: una 'European conflict of laws revolution'? Riv Dir Int Priv Proc:873 ff
Puetz A (2018) Rules on jurisdiction and recognition or enforcement of judgments in specialized Conventions on transport in the aftermath of TNT: dynamite or light in the dark? Eur Legal Forum:117 ff
Putzeys J (1981) Le contrat de transport routier de marchandises. Brussels
Putzeys J (2016) La CMR soixante ans et plus. Unif Law Rev:420 ff
Racine J-B (2018) L'application par les jurisdictions françaises du droit uniforme et des Conventions internationales. In: Lauvaux P, Massot J (eds) L'application du droit étranger, in SLC, p 19 ff
Sadikov N (1985) Conflict of laws in international transport law. Recueil des cours:191 ff
Schelin J (2016) CMR Convention in a law and economic perspectives. Unif Law Rev:434 ff
Schlechtriem P, Schwenzer I (2016) Commentary on the UN Convention on the international sale of goods. Oxford
Schlechtriem P, Witz C (2008) Convention de Vienne sur les contrats de vente internationale de marchandises. Paris
Silingardi G, Corrado A, Meotti A, Morandi F (1994) La disciplina uniforme del contratto di trasporto di cose su strada. Turin
Tonolo S (2009) La legge applicabile ai contratti di trasporto nel regolamento Roma I. Riv Dir Int Priv Proc:309 ff
Tubeuf C (2008) Enrichissement sans cause, gestion d'affaires et 'culpa in contrahendo'. Rev Droit Comm Belge:535 ff

Verheyen W (2016) National judges as gatekeepers to the CMR Convention. Unif Law Rev:441 ff

Vismara F (2017) Le clausole di eccezione nel diritto internazionale privato. Milan

Volders B (2007) Culpa in contrahendo in the conflicts of laws. A comment on Article 12 of the Rome II regulation. Yearb Priv Int Law:127 ff

Von Overbeck A (1999) The fate of two remarkable provisions of the Swiss statute on private international law. Yearb Priv Int Law:128 ff

Witz C (2003) La quête de l'universalisme dans l'interprétation. In: La Commission des Nations Unies pour le droit commercial international: à propos de trente - cinq ans d'activité, LPA, p 54 ff

Witz C (2020) Le défi de l'interprétation uniforme. AJ Contrat:508 ff

Zournatzi C (2018) La disciplina dei regolamenti Ce 593 / 2008 (Roma I) e Ce 864 / 2007 (Roma II) sulla legge applicabile alle obbligazioni contrattuali e extracontrattuali nel contract of carriage e nel diritto della navigazione. Dir Mar:269 ff

Chapter 3
Stipulation of the Contract and the Consignment Note

Contents

3.1 Stipulation of the Contract

3.1.1 The Concept

Article 1, first paragraph, indicates the prerequisites for the applicability of the Convention; it requires that a contract of carriage is concluded for consideration and that the places of receipt and redelivery are situated in two different countries, at least one of which has signed the text of the uniform law. Accordingly, no written form is prescribed for the agreement, which can be reached in any manner, orally as well; essentially, a principle of freedom applies, on the strength of which the parties'

C. Tincani, *Contract for the International Carriage of Goods by Road*, Law for Professionals, https://doi.org/10.1007/978-3-031-08487-4_3

intention may be expressed in any way, even implicitly, for instance, through conclusive conduct.[1]

With equal incisiveness, the Convention defines the function of the consignment note and, according to Article 4, "*le contrat de transport est constaté par une lettre de voiture*".[2] This document reproduces the agreement in its essential features, although, again in terms of Article 4, its "*absence, irrégularité ou perte n'affectent ni l'existence ni la validité du contrat de transport*".[3] It follows that the recourse to the consignment note is neither a requirement for the validity of the contract nor a necessary prerequisite for the application of the Convention. However, drawing it up is remitted to a discretional evaluation,[4] although its draft, which is considered the most reasonable and frequent solution, is encouraged in every way by Article 5.[5] The document is a means of proof,[6] failing which other avenues may be resorted to,[7] in order to prove the agreements that have been reached.[8]

Even if it is not a necessary act, there is clear benefit in the note, as it identifies obligations and duties with sufficient precision,[9] and both shipper and carrier can

---

[1] Cf. Clarke (2014), p. 59 ff., according to whom "no particular form is required of the contract of carriage".

[2] This is how Article 4 is formulated in the French version. As for the English version, we read "the contract of carriage shall be confirmed by the making out of the consignment note".

[3] This is how Article 4 is formulated in the French version. As for the English version, we read "the absence, irregularity or loss (...) shall not affect the existence or the validity of the contract of carriage".

[4] Cf. BGH 22 May 2014, in *TranspR,* 2015, 33, according to which receipt of the goods by the carrier can be evinced by any document, even one signed by the driver alone, so long as he had a chance to check the load and ascertain its consistency.

[5] Cf. Cass. com. France 17 February 1970, in *Bull. transp.,* 1970, 158; Cass. com. France 15 May 2001, in *Le Lamy transp.*, 2020, vol. I, 471; App. Versailles 5 October 2006, in *Bull. transp.,* 2006, 711; App. Lyon 11 May 2006, *ibid.,* 2007, 78; App. Warsaw 17 December 2014, I ACa 971/2014; App. Krakow 12 October 2017, I ACa 510/2017; App. Bialystok 25 March 2015, I ACa 952/2014.

[6] Cf. Messent and Glass (2018), p. 86 ff., according to whom "the consignment note is not intended to be a document of title, but merely a method of evidencing the contract". See also Hill (1976), p. 183 ff., in terms of whom "it is not intended to be a document of title, but merely a method of laying down standard conditions of contract for the international carriage of goods by road". See Putzeys (1981), p. 126 ff., according to whom "*la lettre de voiture est un instrument de preuve d'une rencontre de volontés qui existe et subsiste indépendamment de cet instrument*". Likewise Loewe (1976), p. 334 ff.; Libouton (1973), p. 23 ff.; Sánchez-Gamborino (2001b), p. 644 ff.; Fillers (2020), p. 183 ff.

[7] Cf. App. Segovia 10 November 1999, no. 288, in *Ac,* 1999, 8028.

[8] Cf. Cass. France 18 July 1966, in *Bull. transp.,* 1966, 286. Cf. Putzeys (1981), p. 126 ff., for whom, "*puisque la lettre de voiture fait foi des conditions du contrat, son absence ou sa perte (...) obligera le juge à dégager ces conditions des autres éléments qui seront soumis à son appréciation*". See also Sánchez-Gamborino (2001a), p. 644 ff.; Teutsch (2013a), p. 208 ff.

[9] Cf. Silingardi et al. (1994), p. 56 ff., according to whom "a regular consignment note" ensures "a sufficient framework of legal certainty as regards the relationships between parties of the contract of carriage"; Fillers (2020), p. 183 ff.

easily know and prove their agreements.[10] Thus, in accordance with Article 7, first paragraph, the sender is liable for all costs and must give compensation for the damage suffered by the transporter as a result of the inaccuracy or insufficiency of the indications prescribed by Article 6. Think of the damage caused to the consignee by a delay stemming from a wrong indication of the address or from a surcharge ascribable to an inaccurate declaration of the weight of the goods.[11] Article 7 still operates, by virtue of Article 4, despite the fact that the information is not incorporated into the consignment note, with all that this is the most convenient solution. Not only Article 7, first paragraph, but also various other provisions pay heed to the essential document for a correct structuring of the collaboration.

Conversely, failure to draw it up raises inevitable practical questions as regards proof of the agreement and of its provisions.[12] Thus, the circumstance that a carrier possesses the so-called TIR card of another transporter does not mean that he is an assistant of the latter[13] and the receipt issued by the carrier without examining the content along with the statement "a pallet with three hundred pieces" provides no proof of the actual content of the load.[14] Moreover, in the event of an agreement concluded by telex, the person organizing the transport can be seen as a shipper rather than a forwarder,[15] regardless of the non-existence of the consignment note. In fact, that does not prevent adducing evidence of the agreement through different means.

Then, as regards payment of the consideration, the carrier can prove that he has concluded a contract regulated by the Convention by providing evidence that the sender accepts the invoices.[16] Lastly, in the event that the document is lost following theft of the vehicle in which it was kept, the conclusion of the contract may be demonstrated by exhibiting the customs documents, from which we can infer the

---

[10]The consignment note is not a means of proof sufficient to exclude tax evasion. Cf. Court of Justice, second section, 6 September 2012, Case c - no. 273 of 2011, *Mecsek – Gabona Kft* v. *Nemzeti Adó – és Vámhivatal Dél – dunántùli Regionális Adó Foigazgatósága;* Court of Justice, fourth section, 20 October 2016, Case C – no. 24 of 2015, *Josef Plöckl* v. *Finanzamt Schrobenhausen*; Court of Justice, fourth section, 10 June 2021, Case c - no. 279 of 2019, *The Commissioners for Her Majesty's Revenue and Customs.*

[11]Cf. App. Colmar 16 June 1972, in *Bull. transp.*, 1972, 320. See, for a contrary view, Cass. com. France 16 May 2006, in *Le Lamy transp.*, 2020, vol. I, 471.

[12]Cf. Messent and Glass (2018), p. 87 ff. See also (2014), p. 59 ff., according to whom, "although a consignment note is not essential, its absence can cause difficulties". See, in addition, Paris 27 June 1972, in *Europ. transp. law,* 1972, no. 7, 1040; App. Versailles 5 November 2009, in *Bull. transp.,* 2010, 61.

[13]Cf. App. Paris 4 December 1970, in *Bull. transp.,* 1970, 407. Cf. Libouton (1973), p. 24 ff.

[14]Cf. OLG Düsseldorf 14 November 2001, in *TranspR,* 2002, 73.

[15]Cf. Hof Brussels 19 October 1972, in *Europ. transp. law,* 1973, no. 8, 503; Supremo Tribunal Da Justiça, Portugal, 17 November 1994, in *Unif. law rev.,* 1997, 200, according to which the lack of a consignment note and the production of a receipt by the forwarding agent do not prevent the Convention from applying to the actual carrier.

[16]Cf. RB Mechelen 14 February 1973, in *Europ. transp. law,* 1973, no. 8, 630; Trib. com. Paris 12 October 1971, in *Unif. law rev.,* 1973, 268.

names of the shipper, the addressee and the carrier, in addition to the weight and nature of the goods.[17] Similarly, any error in drawing up the note does not exclude the applicability of the Convention; however, by virtue of Article 4, we must investigate the relationship that has been established. With good reason, therefore, a forwarder who issues instructions to the transporter but whose name does not appear on the document must be deemed part of the agreement, as the sender.[18] Thus, if the consignment note sets out a place of destination differing from the one planned, the carrier is bound to execute the redelivery in the place agreed upon where the same can be inferred in another way.[19]

Further, the manner the relevant facts can be proved is a question entrusted to national procedural law, as such falling outside the scope of the Convention. The latter, aware of the unavoidable problems of application, not surprisingly underlines the importance of the document, which guarantees everyone, regardless of domestic indications on preliminary procedural investigation, with a logic of programming the texts written and known in every country, based on commonly used forms. This is in line with the practice of the 1956 economic society, founded on the importance of documents, when the idea of their stability was felt more acutely than it does now.

Although there is unanimous consensus in considering the consignment note irrelevant for the existence and validity of the contract, some[20] take the view that its draft is necessary for the Convention to operate in certain cases. According to Article 12, fifth paragraph, letter a), to exercise the power of counter - order, the sender should produce the first copy containing the new instructions. The statement fails to convince, especially if we consider that, by now, modern technology dominates and, owing to it, changes to the initial program can be notified through other means, such as a simple email message or one sent by a mobile phone. If the legal theory relating to countermand necessarily requires the document to be drawn up, this would conflict with the spirit of the Convention, being in breach of Article 4.

Similarly, we cannot endorse the thesis[21] whereby the lack of the document allegedly precludes the formulation of reservations under Article 9, second paragraph. The consignment note, in fact, simplifies the conduct and, as it is conceived as a probative tool, it allows the shipper and the carrier to clarify their respective position from time to time. However, any reservations could also be relied upon in another way, verbally, in particular. Precisely, in accordance with Article 4, albeit with greater difficulty, the transporter can always show that he did actually put them

[17] Cf. App. Nancy 29 November 1994, in *Bull. transp.,* 1995, 17. A contrary position was adopted in App. Paris 28 September 1981, cited in *Le Lamy transp.*, 2020, vol. I, 472, in terms of which "*un T2 ou un carnet TIR n'équivaut nullement à une lettre de voiture, pas plus qu'un 'manifeste d'entrée' document douanier étranger, ne saurait constituer une preuve de la livaison*".

[18] Cf. Trib. com. Antwerp 20 April 1972, in *J. B. C.,* 1972, 466.

[19] Cf. RB Antwerp 3 April 1977, in *Europ. transp. law,* 1977, no. 12, 411; Hof Brussels 17 November 1977, *ibid.,* 1980, no. 15, 319.

[20] Cf. Messent and Glass (2018), p. 86 ff.; Clarke (2014), p. 60 ff.; Loewe (1976), p. 334 ff.

[21] Cf. BGH 9 February 1979, in *Europ. transp. law,* 1980, no. 15, 215. See also Messent and Glass (2018), p. 86 ff.

forward.[22] Furthermore, the declaration of special interest at the redelivery is valid and effective even if it is not set out in the note, although divergent opinions have been expressed on this point.[23]

Moreover, Article 6 does not limit itself to mentioning, among possible profiles to be comprised in the document, informational elements concerning which errors or omissions could and should be rectified. Reference is also made to specific clauses of an enacting nature, such as the one on cash on delivery or the paramount clause. In such instances, and in all others in which consensual commitments are envisaged, it is not possible to modify a written clause in a signed text that documents the expression of intention and the fact that the agreement was reached, without possibly invoking Article 4. Although this rule makes reference to the lack of documentary support, this does not affect the conclusiveness of the documents related to any clauses reduced to writing and, on that ground alone, not susceptible to any tacit amendment. Despite the lack of any explicit confirmation in Article 4, the tone is unequivocal, given that the existence and validity of the contract in the absence of the document are emphasized, whereas in no way is the prevalence of a different will postulated when it is expressed in the note, as is the case with the declaration of special interest at the redelivery.

The Convention does not require written forms, leaving it to the parties' autonomy to decide how to set out the indications of Article 6. For a better and more streamlined regulation of traffic, in 1976, the International Road Union[24] developed a model with a typical format, reproduced in four copies. Each one has a different color, red for the shipper, green for the carrier, blue for the consignee, and a further one in black, unsigned, reserved for the fulfillment of administrative formalities.[25] Thus, the draft of the document has been made uniform and its transmission has been facilitated; it is the refinement of a paper model.

3.1.2 Functions and Purpose

Apart from expressing the contractual will, the consignment note is a means of proof that finds a cogent set of regulations in the Convention, which allow all parties to

[22]Cf. Messent and Glass (2018), p. 89 ff., according to whom "it is clearly desirable that a consignment note (. . .) be drawn up so that the disputes can be kept to a minimum".

[23]Cf. Messent and Glass (2018), p. 86 ff.; Putzeys (1981), p. 127 ff., according to whom "*les déclarations d'intérêt spécial et de valeur spéciale doivent, pour être opposables au transporteur, être portées sur la lettre de voiture*". See also Loewe (1976), p. 334 ff. You can also check App. Paris 9 July 1980, in *Bull. transp*., 1980, 449; App. Reims 13 July 1977, *ibid.*, 1977, 406.

[24]The so-called IRU. Cf. Teutsch (2013a), p. 206 ff.

[25]Cf. Sánchez-Gamborino (2006), p. 677 ff.

easily demonstrate their agreements.[26] The uniform law encourages recourse to this document,[27] while simultaneously excluding that it is a necessary prerequisite for the application of the CMR. Article 5 does not require any specific formal elements,[28] and the document may thus be drafted in any manner, without the domestic law being capable of intervening. In terms of Article 5, the note must be set in three original copies, all of them signed by the sender and by the carrier.[29] The signature may be replaced by a stamp[30] wherever that is permitted by the law of the country in which the document is drawn up;[31] this is the only supplementary national intervention allowed. However, in case the note is signed by a representative, as the issue is not regulated by the CMR, we must refer to the domestic law as identified pursuant to the general principles.[32] In addition, according to Article 5, the first copy is delivered to the shipper, the second follows the goods and the third is retained by the carrier.[33]

The Convention does not identify the party that must draw up the consignment note, whether the carrier or the shipper,[34] although, given the way the provision is phrased, it should refer to the former.[35] Indeed, for Article 5, "*le troisième exemplaire est retenu par le transporteur*".[36] The problem is examined in particular in Article 7, second paragraph, which takes for granted its legitimate and frequent draft by the transporter, even in those parts in which the information originates with the sender. It is therein specified that the former operates as an agent of the latter, unless otherwise disciplined, which may be proven in any way. While the carrier frequently fills in the three copies, the initiative can be taken by the sender and the issue is hardly relevant from a practical viewpoint. In fact, for Article 7, what matters is not so much the identity of the drafter of the text as the joint signature thereof.

---

[26] Cf. LG Hamburg 5 December 2007, in *TranspR,* 2008, 264, according to which the main function of the consignment note is to document the agreements and specify the goods delivered to the carrier, allowing him to append reservations.

[27] Cf. Messent and Glass (2018), p. 89 ff.

[28] Cf. Messent and Glass (2018), p. 89 ff., according to whom "the Convention makes no provisions as to the form the consignment note should take".

[29] Cf. Teutsch (2013a), p. 211 ff.

[30] Cf. Teutsch (2013a), p. 212 ff.

[31] Cf. Rodière (1971), p. 625 ff.

[32] Cf. BGH 25 October 2012, in *TranspR,* 2013, 239.

[33] Cf. Polish Supreme Court 13 October 2016, V CSK 712/2015.

[34] Cf. Clarke (2014), p. 60 ff., according to whom "the identity of the person responsible for preparing the consignment note is not stated by the CMR". See, in addition, Loewe (1976), p. 335 ff. Cf. OGH 29 January 2014, in *TranspR,* 2014, 375, according to which the CMR does not prescribe who is to fill in the consignment note and any party to the contract can do so.

[35] Cf. Loewe (1976), p. 335 ff., according to whom "this is clear from the wording of the third sentence of paragraph 1, which states that the first copy shall be handed to the sender, while the third copy shall be retained by the carrier".

[36] This is how the text is expressed in the French version. As for the English version, it reads "the third shall be retained by the carrier".

In the absence of one of the signatures,[37] the document fails to produce the effects contemplated by Article 9, because the note does not comply with Article 5.[38] Therefore, according to Article 4, the contract is valid; however, we must rely on other means of proof to establish whether the party that does not sign is nevertheless involved in the contractual relationship.[39] However, without prejudice to the rules on the issue of evidence in the national law of the presiding judge, in some legal systems a text departing from the directions of Article 5 might still retain relevance, as it can influence or determine the judge's conviction about the agreements that have been reached, although the topic is not covered by the Convention and is entrusted to the procedural principles of each country.

Moreover, according to some,[40] the driver is allowed to sign on the carrier's behalf by virtue of an implicit power of representation arising from his position of employment or at least that of an assistant. The thesis can be endorsed,[41] because a general criterion of the Convention consists of the fact that an enterprise is held responsible for its collaborators' actions and, after all, the note frequently serves as acknowledgment of valid agreements, albeit expressed verbally. If anything, the principle should not be invoked only for the transporter. For the traceability of the document, a relevant aspect is whether it can be connected to the organization without the need to confer a power of representation, let alone expressly or in writing. In most cases, in fact, drivers and assistants are the ones who sign the note, without any objection being raised.

Furthermore, regardless of the 2008 Protocol on the electronic consignment note, the question arises as to whether it can be sent by telefax or by telex. The Convention does not clarify the problem, and that is inevitable, as it dates back to 1956. However, at least for the telefax, which reproduces the image of the document, the extensive thesis is persuasive,[42] although the Protocol is strict on formal constraints. Due to this, we can exclude the legitimate use of a normal email communication, because, at least for the countries that have ratified it, compliance with said Protocol is required.

No measure is contemplated for the refusal to sign, as legal theory presupposes the consent of the interested parties and a joint filling in of the note. The thesis[43] according to which such refusal would always enable the counterparty to terminate the contract due to breach is not convincing. The rule says nothing in that regard and

[37] Cf. Teutsch (2013a), p. 213 ff.

[38] Cf. *City Vintages Ltd* v. *SCAC Transport International,* in *Lloyd's rep.,* 1987, 1053. See also App. Paris 6 January 1971, in *Bull transp.,* 1971, 40; App. Douai 11 March 1982, *ibid.,* 1982, 199; App. Paris 11 June 1974, *ibid.,* 1974, 49; App. Paris 8 November 1995, *ibid.,* 1996, 132.

[39] Cf. Clarke (2014), p. 61 ff.

[40] Cf. Jung (1997), p. 151 ff.

[41] For an opposite view, see Schmid (2013), p. 190 ff.

[42] Cf. Putzeys (2006), p. 528 ff.

[43] Cf. Clarke (2014), p. 61 ff., according to whom the "refusal by one party to the contract of carriage by road to co-operate in the creation of a consignment note would justify the other party in electing to terminate the contract of carriage". See also Loewe (1976), p. 335 ff.

the failure to sign does not preclude the execution of the program agreed upon. If anything, we must consider the reasons for the hindering conduct to establish whether non-compliance stems from an instrumental attitude, aimed at making the proof hard, without a plausible motivation, pursuant to an initiative in bad faith. A refusal, however, might be the result of occasional circumstances or of divergent views on contractual aspects and, if they are essential, there could be no complete and binding agreement. As confirmation that the Convention does not assign an unambiguous effect to the refusal to sign, Article 5 does not specify when the document should be filled in and, once again, leaves the decision to the parties.[44] If, however, the note is drawn up after taking charge of the goods, the carrier must prove actual delivery in another way,[45] while the contract is in any event valid, effective and subject to the uniform law.

According to Article 5, second paragraph, if the cargo must be loaded on different vehicles or there are goods of various kinds or distinct batches, the transporter and the shipper must draw up as many notes as the trucks used or as the number of items involved. In this case, too, the parties will establish the method of documentation and, therefore, whether to resort to the provision of Article 5, second paragraph. Problems of application might emerge as regards exercise of the power of countermand, inasmuch as, for Article 12, fifth paragraph, letter c), it is impermissible to split the load, and the carrier must not factually take on the economic function of "distributor".[46]

3.1.3 The Mandatory Content

Article 6 regulates the content of the note. In the first paragraph, it identifies the mandatory elements for filling it up completely; the second paragraph outlines the indications to be added only with the prior express consent of sender and shipper, and the last paragraph considers those identified from time to time.[47] Article 6, first paragraph, letter a), lays down the duty to specify the place at and date on which the document is drawn up, as these useful details allow the determination of the time and place of conclusion of the contract.[48] Indeed, although the agreement might be concluded at a different time than that in which the note is drafted, and no

[44] Cf. Messent and Glass (2018), p. 92 ff., according to whom "when it is done will therefore depend upon the parties' convenience and local practice". For a restrictive viewpoint, see Polish Supreme Court 13 October 2916, V CSK 712/2015, which demands that the consignment note be issued from as early as the start of the trip.

[45] Cf. Messent and Glass (2018), p. 92 ff. See also App. Rouen 16 June 1972, in *Europ. transp. law,* 1972, no. 7, 1040.

[46] Cf. Messent and Glass (2018), p. 111 ff.; Rodière (1971), p. 625 ff.; Teutsch (2013a), p. 215 ff.

[47] Cf. Clarke (2014), p. 62 ff.; Loewe (1976), p. 336 ff.; Libouton (1973), p. 25 ff.; Rodière (1971), p. 626 ff.

[48] Cf. Teutsch (2013b), p. 220 ff.

coincidence between those two acts is required, we could infer such a coincidence, subject to possible dispute, pursuant to social normality criteria. It is thus possible to identify the applicable national law in accordance with Article 5, regarding the replacement of the signature with a stamp.[49]

According to Article 6, first paragraph, letters b), c), and e), it is necessary to set out the names and addresses of both the sender and the transporter and those of the consignee as well;[50] thus, the parties are duly identified.[51] In the opinion of some,[52] the unsigned note might be raised against the shipper, so long as he draws it up. The thesis cannot be subscribed to, as Article 5 requires the signature or at least the affixing of a stamp, although that does not subtract relevance from the incomplete document for the purposes of demonstrating the agreement, if we can draw such a conclusion from domestic procedural law, on how to discharge the burden of proof. The note, however, would show discordance with Article 5, which means that Article 9 would be inapplicable.[53] It is then always possible to show that the contract has not been concluded, despite the draft of the document, and, specifically, its possible compliance with Article 5, for instance as regards signatures.[54]

Additionally, there is a duty to describe the place and date of receipt of the goods[55] and the place stipulated for redelivery, under Article 6, first paragraph, letter d). This provision facilitates the verification of the prerequisites of applicability of the Convention by virtue of Article 1, which makes reference to the scheduled redelivery in a country other than that of departure.[56] Furthermore, it is necessary to specify the destination, so that the transporter can be fully acquainted with his obligations and how to discharge them.[57] Moreover, as regards the identification of jurisdiction, in accordance with Article 31, first paragraph, letter b), the same jurisdiction belongs to the judges of the State appointed for redelivery. To this end, importance is attached to the indication of the locality in the note, an indication that prevails, although counter - order is exercised.

It is necessary to describe the nature of the goods[58] and the method of their packaging, to specify the recognized name of the dangerous load[59] and declare the

[49]Cf. Silingardi et al. (1994), p. 61 ff.

[50]Cf. App. Poznań 8 September 2017, I Aca 281/2017.

[51]Cf. Teutsch (2013b), p. 221 ff. Cf. OLG Hamburg 6 November 1980, in *VersR,* 1982, 556.

[52]Cf. Cass. com. Paris 5 October 1983, in *Le Lamy transp.*, 2020, vol. I, 472.

[53]Cf. OLG Monaco 23 April 2013, in *TranspR,* 2015, 449.

[54]Cf. *Tetroc Ltd* v. *Cross – con (Intrenational) Ltd,* in *Lloyd's rep.,* 1981, 192; App. Paris 6 January 1971, in *Unif. law rev.,* 1971, 149.

[55]Cf. Teutsch (2013b), p. 222 ff.

[56]Cf. Cass. Paris 21 November 1995, in *Unif. law rev.,* 1996, 594.

[57]Cf. Copenhagen Maritime and Commerciale Court 16 September 1996, in *Europ. transp. law,* 1998, no. 33, 71, according to which the carrier who delivers in conformity with the instructions issued by an appointee of the consignee indicated in the consignment note is not liable for failure to deliver even where a different address is set out in the consignment note.

[58]Cf. Teutsch (2013b), p. 223 ff.

[59]Cf. Loewe (1976), p. 336 ff.; Libouton (1973), p. 25 ff.

packages and their gross weight.[60] This relates to the precise understanding of the object of the transport, not only in anticipation of recorded reservations, but also so that the carrier, even regardless of such essential activities, might know what he has to transfer and, accordingly, adopt the necessary measures. It follows that, irrespective of the expressions found in Article 6, first paragraph, letters f), g), and h), in any event precisely, the load must be identified in every detail, as confirmed by Article 7, first paragraph, letter a), from which we draw the indispensable completeness of the description.

After all, when the goods leave the sender's sphere of control and enter the carrier's one, the latter must be equipped with all possible useful knowledge, on the basis of prognostic, albeit precautionary, criteria. This is even more true if there is any possible danger, thus for the obvious sake of protecting safety. It is no coincidence that we infer from Article 7, first paragraph, letter a), the insufficiency of a textual application of Article 6, first paragraph, because the sender is saddled with a more articulate duty to collaborate, in good faith. He is indeed the one with the best knowledge of the goods, so he can be neither reticent nor absent-minded or negligent, without prejudice to the fact that, in accordance with Article 4, the information can be provided in another way, without including it in the document, despite the difficulty of demonstrating it.

Pursuant to Article 6, first paragraph, letter i), within the limits of what is known at the time of departure, the consideration[61] must be described in detail and the customs charges duly spelled out, along with the specific liability for omission or for defective declarations, in relation to any damages, in accordance with Article 8. The shipper, therefore, must clarify the estimated costs, especially customs ones, and provide any useful indication. Conversely, the consideration must be highlighted by the transporter and, in any case, it is included within the agreements to be documented. In addition, Article 6, first paragraph, letter k), refers to the so-called paramount clause[62] and, notwithstanding the conflicting and unjustified Italian case law,[63] the omission is irrelevant for the purposes of giving effect to the Convention. Indeed, as legal theory (unsuccessfully but in a manner we can subscribe to) has sought to explain, its applicability is objective and unrelated to any manifestation of will.[64]

---

[60] Cf. Teutsch (2013b), p. 224 ff.; Otte (2018a), p. 1290 ff.

[61] Cf. Teutsch (2013b), p. 225 ff.

[62] Cf. Clarke (2014), p. 62 ff.; Loewe (1976), p. 337 ff.; Libouton (1973), p. 26 ff.; Teutsch (2013b), p. 226 ff.

[63] Cf. Cass. Italy 7 February 2006, no. 2529, in *Giur. it. rep.,* 2006; Cass. Italy 28 November 1975, no. 3983, *ibid.,* 1975; Cass. Italy 1 March 1978, no. 1034, *ibid.*, 1978; Cass. Italy 26 November 1980, no. 6272, *ibid.,* 1980; Cass. Italy 2 October 2003, no. 14680, *ibid.,* 2003. For a contrary standpoint, see App. Florence 2 February 1981, in *Giur. it. rep.,* 1981; App. Brescia 1 June 2001, *ibid.,* 2001; Trib. Tortona 8 May 2005, *ibid.,* 2005; Trib. Lucca 24 April 2013, *ibid.,* 2013. Rightfully, the approach is criticized by Teutsch (2013b), p. 226 ff.

[64] Cf. Fadda (1984), p. 554 ff.; Maresca (1981), p. 366 ff.; Valaperta (1976), p. 100 ff.; Lana (1972), p. 751 ff.; Pesce (1995), p. 55 ff.

3.1.4 The Optional Content

Apart from the indications contemplated by Article 6, first paragraph, the consignment note might set out additional ones, if agreed upon.[65] Thus, pursuant to Article 6, second paragraph, letter a), transhipment can be prohibited, although the Convention does not clarify the meaning of the term.[66] We could have transhipment in two instances: when a plurality of vehicles of different types is used to execute the same transfer or when you replace the initial truck with another one of the same nature, for example, in the event that the first breaks down in such a manner as to make it unusable. In the first scenario, Article 2 applies, whereupon infringement of the prohibition could entail the termination of the contract for breach, if damage to the goods is discovered. Nevertheless, such a scenario is rare, as it is unlikely for the sender to be aware of this fact while the trip is in progress and, after it has ended, termination of the contract would no longer make sense. If anything, the problem arises where several transfers are stipulated through a single agreement. Thus, any violation of the prohibition can be relied upon to prevent further collaboration. Lastly, the thesis[67] whereby unauthorized use of a different type of vehicle would always entail termination of the contractual relationship is unfounded, given that, in any event, there has to be a judicial action by the shipper, pursuant to the national law. The topic, indeed, is not regulated by the Convention. Nonetheless, the compensatory limit laid down by Article 23 does not apply because, in breach of an express clause, the transporter acts at least with default equated to willful misconduct and is liable as such for the entire damage caused by his breach.

Furthermore, the carrier could undertake not to replace the truck, for example, because the goods require special refrigeration or the transport involves considerably unwieldy machinery, and its transfer could generate prejudice that may be hidden, as well as hard to detect at the time of redelivery, in accordance with Article 30, first paragraph. The breach in any event entails responsibility for the damage, without prejudice to the need to replace the vehicle. This could be, for instance, the breakdown of the refrigeration system that cannot be repaired on the spot or a major failure of the truck preventing its further use.

Based on Article 6, second paragraph, letter b), it is possible to indicate "*les frais que l'expéditeur prend à sa charge*".[68] More generally, the provisions contemplated in the second paragraph "must be based on conditions stipulated by parties at the latest at the time of signature of the consignment note".[69] This preclusion, however, does not exclude the possibility of proving by other means an agreement subsequent

[65] Cf. Clarke (2014), p. 62 ff.; Messent and Glass (2018), p. 96 ff.

[66] The French version reads "*transbordement*". Cf. Teutsch (2013b), p. 229 ff.

[67] Cf. Messent and Glass (2018), p. 96 ff.

[68] In the English text, we read, "the charges which the sender undertakes to pay". Cf. App. Montpellier 27 May 2003, in *Bull. transp. Logist.*, 2003, 437, according to which the charges are borne by the consignee if the shipper fails to state that he will bear them in whole or in part.

[69] Cf. Loewe (1976), p. 339 ff.

to the draft of the note,[70] as per Article 4. This is possible if it does not contradict the express signed clauses, which, on the contrary, take precedence on the contractual program.

According to Article 6, second paragraph, letter c), cash on delivery clause could be stipulated. Thus, once the mandate to collect the price the goods are saddled with has been accepted, the transporter must demand it before executing the redelivery; otherwise, "*est tenu d'indemniser l'expéditeur à concurrence du montant du remboursement, sauf son recours contre le destinataire*",[71] in terms of Article 21. In addition, aiming for a higher consideration, the sender may declare a value exceeding the limit set out in Article 23, third paragraph, so that, in the event of loss or damage, full compensation can be secured. A similar function is discharged by the declaration of special interest at the redelivery,[72] a declaration which, in turn, presupposes a higher fee. The compensation can, in fact, include the further damage, if proved, up to the value of the declared interest.[73] In any case, the incomplete draft of the note or its disappearance do not deprive the relevant declarations of legal effect, except that they render the probative effort by the party intending to rely on them more difficult.

In terms of Article 6, second paragraph, letter e), the sender may issue instructions on concluding the insurance contract for the goods and the carrier must abide by them.[74] If this indication is omitted, he is not liable for the damage in the event that the insurance company stipulates an indemnity falling short of the one imagined by the shipper or payment of what is due has more stringent requirements than the desired ones. There is no room for recourse to the national law, as the scenario is regulated by the Convention. This is so regardless of the existence of contrary theses.[75]

The consignment note can set out the deadline within which the load must be redelivered, whereupon the maximum binding duration of the trip is defined.[76] Lastly, a list of documents delivered to the transporter might be present. Thus, according to Article 11, the shipper must transmit whatever might enable customs operations to be performed and is liable for the prejudices arising from the lack or incompleteness of the material.[77]

---

[70] Cf. Loewe (1976), p. 339 ff.

[71] This is how the English text reads "the carrier shall be liable to the sender for compensation not exceeding the amount of such charge, without prejudice to his right of action against the consignee". Cf. Fremuth (2013), p. 577 ff.

[72] Cf. Teutsch (2013b), p. 231 ff.

[73] Cf. Messent and Glass (2018), p. 96 ff.

[74] Cf. Teutsch (2013b), p. 231 ff.

[75] Cf. Messent and Glass (2018), p. 97 ff., according to whom "no specific mention is made in the Convention of the question of the failure of the carrier to effect insurance when instructed to do so, so this will depend upon the provisions of the national law in question".

[76] Cf. Messent and Glass (2018), p. 97 ff.

[77] Cf. Messent and Glass (2018), p. 97 ff.

3.1.5 Determining the Route and Establishing the Methods of Performance

For Article 6, last paragraph, additional indications may be included, even if not simultaneously with the original draft of the note. This provision emphasizes contractual autonomy in the definition of the consensual content, although Article 41 prevents any derogation from the uniform law, which is of imperative nature. After all, the list of Article 6, first and second paragraphs, is complete, and it is not easy to imagine any further clauses, given that the most frequent elements of transport are all mentioned.

The new instructions recorded on the first copy of the note pursuant to the counter - order cannot be traced back to the provision of Article 6, last paragraph, although different opinions have been expressed.[78] This is because, according to Article 12, any variations stem from a unilateral power regulated by the Convention in the interest purely of the shipper. Accordingly, they are not shared changes, as required by Article 6, third paragraph, which underlines that both parties should deem them useful. Thus, Article 6, third paragraph, does not apply if, as soon as the carriage has begun, the load is moved and, after repositioning it correctly, the transporter informs the shipper, who decides to insert a warning in the note.[79] In this case, too, consent is lacking, and we are dealing with a unilateral decision of the sender, aimed at ensuring safety.

Article 6, third paragraph, refers to the information and clauses additional to those mentioned by Article 6, first and second paragraphs, which, however detailed, do not exhaust all conceivable variants.[80] Think of the methods of storing perishable goods,[81] which require a motor vehicle with specific characteristics, for example, one equipped with a sophisticated refrigeration system. In this regard, Article 6, first paragraph, letter f), which merely requires "the description in common use of the nature of the goods and the method of packing, and, in the case of dangerous goods, their generally recognized description",[82] might not be enough. Sometimes, the truck must be indicated with the sectoral characteristics and, to that end, consent is necessary. The carrier must be aware and accept that the transfer presupposes the use of a specific vehicle, as this profile pertains to the consensual program.

[78] Cf. Messent and Glass (2018), p. 97 ff.

[79] See, for the contrary approach, *Harrison & Sons Ltd.* v. *R. T. Steward Transport Ltd.*, in *Europ. transp. law,* 1993, no. 28, 747, according to which the annotation of the warning can be traced back to the rules of Article 6, third paragraph.

[80] Cf. Teutsch (2013b), p. 233 ff.

[81] Cf. OLG Karlsruhe 24 March 2011, in *VersR*, 2011, 1546; OLG Monaco 5 May 2010, *ibid.*, 2010, 1521; OLG Düsseldorf 30 May 1988, in *TranspR*, 1988, 423.

[82] This is how the English text reads. As for the French version, we have "*la dénomination courante de la nature de la marchandise et le mode d'emballage, et, pour les marchandises dangereuses, leur dénomination généralement reconnue*".

Similarly, instructions may be stipulated on loading and unloading methods, if, for instance, safety demands that some specific kind of accommodation be provided. The sender is familiar with the goods and their specificity and, therefore, he is able to illustrate their correct arrangement adequately, whereas the carrier might ignore the most suitable procedure. These indications need not be always included in the document, as they can be contained in technical specifications or, to ensure speed, stamped on the packages. Nevertheless, they have binding effects on the transporter, if agreed upon. Therefore, it is possible to supplement the note with additional information, precisely in accordance with Article 6, last paragraph.

Generally, the carrier chooses the most appropriate itinerary, because, within his operational structure, he can identify executive strategies better than others. In Article 6, first and second paragraphs, there are no elements relating to the route. There is, however, no prohibition against its specification if, for some reason, the shipper has an interest in it and the carrier agrees. In that event, he must execute instructions, unless, during the trip, that becomes impossible or counterproductive. In those scenarios, he must request instructions by virtue of Article 14. In case he does not obtain new directions, he can choose an alternative route allowing him to conclude the trip, in accordance with Article 14, last paragraph. Thus, if the vehicle is unable to proceed due to a local strike of the customs offices, in the absence of instructions, the carrier is entitled to evaluate an alternative at his discretion.

In summary, the clauses stipulated by Article 6, last paragraph, align the note to the needs that, either simultaneously with its draft or in a subsequent phase, emerge for the sender, due to the characteristics of the transfer or those of the load. Cases are not frequent and, in particular, we do not have any judicial decisions, but Article 6 stresses contractual autonomy and a possible structuring of the consensual program that is best suited to the needs that emerge. Article 6, third paragraph, can apply where the carriage is linked to other agreements pertaining to prior or subsequent phases, for example, those revolving around storage or logistics.

3.1.6 Electronic Documents

Notwithstanding the linguistic differences, electronic progress has simplified the relationships between carriers and their customers. Meanwhile, the complexity of operations has made it necessary to constantly ensure the so-called "traceability" of goods, and there is dissociation between the contract and the overall activity. The shipper, indeed, may not deliver the goods, being already stored in the carrier's warehouse, and the latter may resort to subtransporters quite frequently. Thus, we have to consider partially modified the *modus operandi* ("*mode opérative*") conceived by the CMR as "*mode binaire: un expediteur réel de la marchandise, un destinatiare réel qui, à un moment donné, prend sa place et un tranporteur tout aussi réel qui les relie*".[83] If several parties intervene, a stringent real-time control is required and the electronic note should allow everyone to check the progress of the load at any time, with the possibility of exercising the powers and rights envisaged by the uniform law.

On 27 May 2008, a supplementary Protocol to the CMR was concluded on the electronic consignment note.[84] Prepared by the Inland Transport Committee of the Economic Commission for Europe, it came into force on 5 June 2011.[85] According to Article 2, first paragraph, any question, request, reservation, or other declaration pertaining to the execution of the contract may be formulated by electronic communication. In compliance with Article 2, second paragraph, a note drawn up in conformity with the Protocol has the same value as a written one and is therefore a means of proof.

For Article 4, the electronic note must meet all the requirements laid down by the original Convention.[86] Therefore, it must be signed by both the shipper and the carrier, whereas an inaccurate or defective draft thereof does not affect the validity of the contract. Rather, the note must bear an electronic signature capable of linking it to the document. Based on Article 3, the method selected for the signature is presumed to be reliable where it unequivocally identifies the person appending it, is created with means enabling the author to exercise an effective control, and is connected to the information recorded therein, so that any variation thereof can be detected. Pursuant to Article 6, first paragraph, at the shipper's request, the carrier must provide all the information that allows the former to access the electronic note. Similarly, the documents to be delivered to the transporter under Article 6, second paragraph, letter g), including for the purposes of performing customs operations, must be transmitted by electronic communication, as long as there is an IT connection with the note itself.

The 2008 Protocol confirms the original idea of the Convention. While the content and criteria for drawing up the note are reproduced in electronic form, no intervention is attempted on the structure of the document, the most significant features of which are simply reiterated. A sizable part of the Protocol focuses on IT aspects and is aimed at identifying a simple and clear procedure;[87] not surprisingly, Article 5 regards a technical regulation. Thus, the crisis of the note is attributed to the written form, while being oblivious to the fact that the problems are more complex; that is so as the 1956 model is in any event out of line with the speed of

[83] Cf. Putzeys (2006), p. 527 ff. See also Martius (2007), p. 301 ff.

[84] Its ratifying signatories are France, Great Britain, Northern Ireland, Belarus, Bulgaria, Czechoslovakia, Denmark, Estonia, Iran, Luxembourg, Poland, Portugal, Moldova, Romania, Russia, Slovakia, Slovenia, Spain, Tajikistan, Turkey, and Ukraine.

[85] According to Article 8 of the 2008 Protocol, "this Protocol shall enter into force on the ninetieth day after five of the States referred to in article 7, paragraph 3, of this Protocol, have deposited their instruments of ratification or accession".

[86] Cf. Martius (2007), p. 302 ff.

[87] Cf. Putzeys (2006), p. 528 ff., who hopes for a streamlined system capable of solving practical questions. For instance, "*le téléx et le télécopieur sont - ils des 'communications électoniques?'*".

traffic. It is not so much a question of replacing the written document with the electronic one, because new means of proof, simpler and more streamlined, should be conceived, as the problem is the dynamism of relationships. Indeed, the so-called "traceability" presupposes a quick procedure, in conflict with the idea of a detailed note signed by shipper and carrier in triplicate form.

Despite being often perceived as an important sign of innovation,[88] the Protocol has a conservative structure and, not incidentally, its success has been partial, with some important countries, first of all Germany, declining to subscribe to it. The reason lies in the strategic approach, innovative only in part, as the aim is to transpose the 1956 regulatory structure into electronic form, by, for instance, overcoming doubts surrounding the possible use of *telefax* or *telex*[89] for transmitting the document. In the season of "traceability" and structural connection between logistics and transports, with large-sized enterprises integrating with many sub-carriers, the main operators on the international market nevertheless prefer to refer to their own systems, in the entrenched belief that they will accordingly enjoy tighter controls and more efficient informational lines. Conversely, in the constant contact between all the persons involved in a trip, communications by telephone, voice, or message take place continuously.

Essentially, the Protocol conceives that email communications or similar tools accompanied by electronic signature be sent *in lieu* of the traditional note. This can certainly happen, with a correction of the inconveniences inherent in the written form. However, if the Protocol reasonably accomplishes its set objectives, it brings about a partial modernization and validates the need for a text containing all the significant elements at a time when other means are used in any event and major enterprises allow "traceability" ensured in a different way. Given the limited ratifications of the Protocol, a substantial review does not seem feasible in the short term, whereas the solution to the problem cannot be entrusted to a new treaty, which would be exposed to the same risks. If anything, it is up to case law to guide the innovation, because judicial proof involves the appreciation of techniques the Convention could not have imagined. At the time the Protocol had been drawn up, technological resources were already quite different from current ones, which are continuously evolving.

For today's means of communication to be considered, novel developments very often revolve around the evidence, regulated by the national law. Although this emerges in relation to the electronic note, it is a more general subject. Precisely, the limited success of the Protocol conveys that, in assessing the execution of contracts, judges are often faced with something else, that is, email messages, immediate phone calls, communications sent by mobile phones, or the use of Personal Digital Assistants (PDAs). In this sense, we partly lose the homogeneity sought after in 1956; in fact, currently, the problem is mainly the proof and the law of the seized judge

[88] Cf. Lespagnon (2006), p. 673 ff.; Sánchez-Gamborino (2006), p. 677 ff.

[89] Cf. Putzeys (2006), p. 528 ff.

becomes relevant. There are various solutions, and operators bound to participate in a trial held in a foreign State will experience difficulties.

The question, therefore, would not have been how to regulate the dispatch of the transport document by email, but, if anything, whether to extend the scope of the Convention to some profiles of the judicial evidence. After all, major companies operating on the international market adapt to the conduct of their interlocutors by producing consensual models and systems of homogeneous execution of services; the programs on "traceability" are a glaring example. Thus, the dialogue with senders is extensively influenced by the information system of carriers, and this tendency is destined to be strengthened further. Conversely, there is no point in thinking that everything is written by certified email or similar methods, when, in fact, drivers, warehouse workers and employees find it more convenient to phone each other or send messages by mobile phone.

3.2 Liability for Withholding Information, Drawing Up the Consignment Note Incorrectly and with Regard to Packaging

3.2.1 The Incomplete Drafting of the Consignment Note

The consignment note identifies the obligations of both the sender and carrier. According to Article 7, the former is liable for the inaccuracy or incompleteness of the information entrusted to his care, based on Article 6, if, due to such breaches, the latter incurs costs or suffers prejudices.[90] The transporter is not saddled with additional costs or damages arising from a negligent conduct or omission by the shipper. Think of an inaccurate declaration of weight;[91] if the declared weight differs from the actual one, the prejudice might consist of a tire bursting with resultant capsizing of the vehicle[92] or even in the truck being set on fire.[93] These are examples drawn from well-known cases on the actions of the transporter. Rather, less dramatically, he might find it hard to locate the consignee where the address is incorrect, or he might neglect the necessary precautions for the transfer of dangerous goods or fail to understand which measures he should adhere to, because of inadequate information on the characteristics of the load.

Article 7 refers to the elements laid down by Article 6, first and second paragraphs, falling within the sender's sphere of control, such as the recipient's name and address or the scheduled place of redelivery; this is information the carrier is unable

[90]Cf. Teutsch (2013c), p. 235 ff.; Otte (2018b), p. 1294 ff.

[91]Cf. App. Colmar 16 June 1972, in *Bull. transp.*, 1972, 320.

[92]Cf. Cass. France 6 November 1967, in Putzeys (1981), p. 349 ff., nt. 852. See also Loewe (1976), p. 342 ff.

[93]Cf. Cass. France 27 November 1962, in Putzeys (1981), p. 349 ff., nt. 853.

to verify.[94] Article 7, first paragraph, uses the terms "inaccuracy"[95] and "inadequacy",[96] but its scope includes omission and, where the informational defect causes "loss, damage, or delay, the sender may be liable under Article 7".[97] Regardless of the expressions used, Article 7 must be given an extensive interpretation and applied to any negligent or reckless behavior, capable as such of provoking an error or preventing adoption of the necessary precautions.

Although, in road trips, the issue is felt far less in social sensitivity than with sea or air travel, transport is viewed by Article 7 as a dangerous activity, which means that the carrier is obliged to adopt every measure aimed at preventing the risk, while the sender has to provide the information necessary for the adoption of the best precautionary rules. By setting forth the liability associated with the breach of the Article 6 obligations, Article 7 foists on it a teleological vision, so that, regardless of the lists, all news that facilitates a better arrangement of the trip must be transmitted. A breach also arises with regard to the profiles not expressly mentioned, provided that the shipper can foresee and understand the usefulness of his declarations. The sender can fill in the note in an imprecise or defective way; however, because of its probative value, it is always possible to demonstrate the information actually conveyed through different means. For example, based on Article 6, first paragraph, letter f), the nature of the goods must be set out, but the lack of written specification of their dangerousness does not preclude the possibility of highlighting the carrier's awareness, at least for the information that is received verbally.

The breach of Article 6 triggers the Article 7 liability only in the presence of an etiological nexus with a prejudice suffered by the transporter, and there is no room for the national law, because the entire scenario is regulated by the Convention. The CMR distinguishes between costs and damages, whereas, based on the most widespread theses, at least in continental law, the former are included in the latter. If the carrier wastes time at the destination to search for the consignee and is forced to stay there overnight, the fee paid to the hotel is a damage, irrespective of its unambiguous determination, at least according to the opinions of various legal systems, such as the Italian one. Even at the cost of some conceptual imprecisions, some relevance attaches to the separate reference to "*frais*"[98] and "*dommages*",[99] as the intention is to give an all-inclusive slant to the precept to avoid discrepancies induced by possible, divergent orientations on the part of the individual countries. This is confirmation that the issue is fully traced back to the Convention. If anything, if the sender's infringement occasions an extension of the trip, the transporter may ask not only relief for the prejudice but also an additional fee for the unforeseen effort needed to overcome the impediment. The foregoing does not affect the obligation to

[94] Cf. Teutsch (2013c), p. 236 ff.

[95] This is what we find in the English text. In the French version, we read "*inexactitude*".

[96] This is how the English text reads. As for the French version, we have "*insuffisance*".

[97] Cf. Clarke (2014), p. 63 ff.

[98] This is how the French text is expressed, whereas in the English version it reads "expenses".

[99] As per its formulation in the French text. In the English version we find "loss and damage".

notify or solicit instructions pursuant to Article 14, as that must occur despite the difficulty being created by the shipper.

Important as it was in 1956, Article 7 has lost much prominence, not so much because senders have become more precise, although they are aided by computer resources, but because, during transfers, omissions or inadequacies can be corrected rather easily, and, if these attempts are successful and no damage is produced, the compensatory obligation no longer stands; after all, the consignment note is not the only source of information.

Moreover, in terms of Article 7, second paragraph, the shipper is entitled to ask the carrier to fill in the document as far as the elements that relate to his person are concerned. For such a provision to operate, a request by the sender, implicit as well, is needed. It might, for example, be a request we can infer from a conclusive behavior, without prejudice to the fact that the carrier is not obliged and may refuse, given that the issue is entrusted to contractual autonomy. Unless proved otherwise, it is presumed that the transporter acts as agent for the shipper; so, he must precisely reproduce the indications as they have been reported to him. On the one hand, therefore, this liability may be excluded by an opposite indication in the contract. On the other hand, according to Article 7, second paragraph, the carrier takes charge of the task he is liable for as an agent and must act diligently, asking for the necessary news (without being obliged to check whether the answers are exact) and completing the note scrupulously. If, for instance, the sender requests that a clause on cash on demand be included and his request is not acceded to, the transporter is held responsible in the event that the consignee fails to pay the consideration precisely because the necessary, preventive payment has not been specified.[100]

3.2.2 The So-called Paramount Clause and Liability for Failure to Stipulate It

Article 1 identifies the prerequisites for application of the Convention and, in particular, requires that the place of receipt and the one stipulated for redelivery be situated in two different countries, at least one of which has signed the Convention. This is sufficient for the uniform law text to apply, based on an objective requirement, regardless of the fact that the sender or the carrier is aware of it. Accordingly, one of the elements necessary for correctly drawing up the note is the paramount clause, in accordance with Article 6, first paragraph, letter k), and it is compulsory.[101] Notwithstanding the opposite orientation of Italian case law,[102] this clause

[100] Cf. BGH 17 April 1997, in *Unif. law rev.*, 1999, 206. See also Clarke (2014), p. 63 ff.

[101] Cf. Teutsch (2013c), p. 241 ff.; Mankowski (2019), p. 475 ff.; Otte (2018a), p. 1291 ff.

[102] Cf. Cass. Italy 7 February 2006, no. 2529, in *Giur. it. rep.*, 2006; Cass. Italy 28 November 1975, no. 3983, *ibid.*, 1975; Cass. Italy 1 March 1978, no. 1034, *ibid.*, 1978; Cass. Italy 26 November 1980, no. 6272, *ibid.*, 1980; Cass. Italy 2 October 2003, no. 14680, *ibid.*, 2003.

consensually extends the application of the Convention to those legal systems that have not ratified it, while having no impact on its application in signatory countries, particularly in Italy.

Linked to Article 6, first paragraph, letter k), Article 7, in its third paragraph, considers the carrier liable for the damages and costs resulting from the omitted indication of the paramount clause: "*l'ayant droit à la marchandise*"[103] is entitled to act, hence, depending on the scenarios, the shipper or the consignee. Despite the fact that Article 6, first paragraph, does not specify the party who must fill in the note, Article 7, third paragraph, becomes clear, as it is mostly the carrier who draws up such document. Rarely have judicial decisions tackled the breach of Article 6, first paragraph, letter k), because many countries have ratified the Convention and only in a few instances are the transporter and shipper prejudiced by the failure to include the paramount clause. As rightfully confirmed by some,[104] it seeks to apply the Convention to the contractual relationship even if the State under whose jurisdiction the dispute arises has not ratified it, and the judge seized with the matter cannot refer to it on the basis of the principles of his domestic law. In particular, by accepting the redelivery, the consignee is bound by all contractual clauses, including the paramount one.

Drawn up according to Article 6, first paragraph, letter k), the consignment note documents the agreement and prevails over any contrary intention that is not confirmed in writing.[105] On this point, it is not possible to rely on any different factual relationship established between the sender and carrier. Article 4 is irrelevant, as it relates to the failure to fill in or to the incorrect filling in of the note. However, if the same is complete and signed, it operates precisely because it is impossible to provide a proof running counter to its content, in conflict with the spirit of the Convention. If, therefore, the paramount clause is included in a signed note, it demonstrates the signing parties' consensual and binding will and it applies to the recipient as well when he asks for redelivery.

In terms of Article 7, third paragraph, the person entitled to dispose of the goods may request compensation for the prejudice and reimbursement of the expenses. The sender, for example, can sign a declaration of special interest at the time of redelivery to avoid the situation where the compensatory limit is raised against him in the event of loss or damage. The failure to stipulate the paramount clause might produce a prejudice if it is shown that the relief obtained pursuant to the law of the State that is not a party to the Convention falls short of what would have been secured had the CMR been implemented,[106] and evidence is seemingly easy. By introducing Article 6, first paragraph, letter k), the Convention aims to treat international carriage

---

[103] Thus, it is spelled out in the French text, whereas the English version reads "the person entitled to dispose of the goods".

[104] Cf. Clarke (2014), p. 63 ff.; Messent and Glass (2018), p. 95 ff.; Loewe (1976), p. 338 ff.; Libouton (1973), p. 27 ff.

[105] Cf. Loewe (1976), p. 338 ff.

[106] Cf. App. Aix-en-Provence 22 March 1990, in *Bull. transp.*, 1990, 796.

uniformly, involving on a consensual basis legal systems that, not having ratified it, would not be entitled to invoke it. The selected mechanism refers to contractual autonomy, despite the mandatory nature of the clause, under Article 41 as well. Perhaps the modest success of the rule is because nearly all European countries have ratified the Convention and, possibly, to the inclusion of such clauses in the most frequently used printed models.

3.2.3 Liability for Customs Operations

Based on Article 11, first paragraph, besides providing all information to the carrier, the shipper must deliver the documents necessary for customs operations[107] or for the discharge of other administrative formalities, such as, for instance, those relating to a health check or to import or export restrictions.[108] The note must set out both the list of documents in accordance with Article 6, second paragraph, letter g), and the indications on customs in accordance with Article 6, first paragraph, letter j), and the shipper is liable for inaccuracies where the same cause the transporter to suffer a prejudice.[109]

The carrier is not saddled with an obligation to provide advice and does not have to ascertain the sufficiency and adequacy of the material.[110] Article 11 only imposes on him a duty to perform the transit operation legitimately, for example, by exhibiting the so-called TIR card[111] if the goods are waiting.[112] Although it is an infrequent occurrence, the transporter can bind himself to execute the customs operations comprehensively.[113] This possibility, however, does not fall within the scope of operation of the Convention, which only regulates the different scenario of Article 11, and this means that in all the other instances the national law applies. According to some continental law systems, if he incurs this additional obligation, the carrier can act as an authorized customs representative or pursuant to a power

[107] Cf. Messent and Glass (2018), p. 106 ff.; Clarke (2014), p. 63 ff.

[108] Cf. Loewe (1976), p. 351 ff.

[109] Cf. Cass. Belgium 3 January 1997, in *Europ. transp. law,* 1998, no. 33, 825; Rogov (1998), p. 649 ff.

[110] Cf. Messent and Glass (2018), p. 105 ff. See OLG Düsseldorf 23 December 1997, in *TranspR,* 1997, 422, according to which the carrier should make sure that he has all the documents necessary for the fulfillment of customs formalities; failing that, he will be liable for any delay.

[111] V. BGH 9 September 2010, in *TranspR*, 2011, 178, according to which, as the TIR card relates to an administrative duty more than to customs formalities, it would fall outside the scope of article 11. Cf. Messent and Glass (2018), p. 105 ff.; Putzeys (1981), p. 155 ff.

[112] Cf. App. Nîmes 16 May 2012, in *Le Lamy transp.*, 2020, vol. I, 475, according to which "*le transporteur est responsable du transit, mais non de l'accomplissement des formalitées douanières*".

[113] Cf. App. Versailles 20 November 1985, in *Bull. transp.,* 1986, 264.

conferred on him by the owner.[114] For example, in this role, the transporter must pay the amount due for the import. Large-size enterprises can perform the dual role of the carrier and authorized customs representative, inasmuch as their structure enables them to tackle this kind of commitment. The opposite situation can occur of the customs representative replacing the carrier in material operations, in which event the latter must deliver the documents received to the former, pursuant to Article 11.

For Article 11, third paragraph, the transporter acts as an agent of the shipper,[115] which entails behaving with professional diligence in discharging formalities.[116] If he fails to attend to them or fulfills them incompletely, he must refund the penalty applied against his customer, without prejudice to the provision of redress for any additional damages.[117] The rule refers to the role of the agent and the relevant regulation is entrusted to the domestic law, varying as such depending on which legal system is involved.[118] The reference to the "*commissionaire*"[119] makes it unavoidable to accommodate for the regulations of each country, as the Convention does not cover such a matter and does not clarify the implications of the expression used. If we accept this approach, even the fault mentioned in Article 11, second paragraph, should be assessed in a similar fashion. Indeed, the liability is uniform in Article 11, second and third paragraphs, and must be examined pursuant to the same criteria. Nevertheless, this reference to sources lying outside the Convention strikes a strident note, and the question arises as to whether there was no way to avoid it. Nonetheless, Article 11 applies in any event and prevails over any contrary national indications, which only concern the expected diligence and the level of collaboration and initiative owed by the carrier. It is difficult to get an easy integration between the sources, yet it is inevitable, as it is induced by the explicit textual reference to the agent.

The transporter is liable for the loss or incorrect use of the document[120] and thus for events that can be foreseen through a prudent conduct. We might think here of the loss of a document serving to identify the goods or to determine the importer's profit margin.[121] It follows that the liability imposed by Article 11, second paragraph, is unrelated to defects that are intrinsic to the documents and deals, rather, with

[114] Cf. *Le Lamy transp.*, 2020, vol. I, 475.

[115] Cf. Putzeys (1981), p. 156 ff.; Loewe (1976), p. 351 ff. Cf. Hof Antwerp 22 February 2021, in *Europ. transp. law,* 2020, no. 61 56.

[116] Cf. Rodière (1971), p. 635 ff.

[117] Cf. App. Paris 23 September 1981, in *Bull. transp.,* 1981, 538.

[118] Cf. Rodière (1971), p. 635 ff.; Putzeys (1981), p. 156 ff.

[119] Thus it reads in the French version, whereas the English text has "agent".

[120] Cf. App. Paris 15 February 1982, in *Bull. transp.,* 1982, 141; Cass. com. France 10 June 1976, *ibid.,* 1986, 402; Cass. com. France 28 September 2004, in *Europ. transp. law,* 2005, no. 40, 552; Hof Antwerp 15 May 2006, in *Europ. transp. law,* 2006, no. 41, 658, according to which in this case, too, the rules on prescription laid down by Article 31 of the CMR apply. Cf. Messent and Glass (2018), p. 106 ff.

[121] Cf. App. Lyon 7 October 1994, in *Bull. transp. logist.,* 1994, 757.

infringements in their use.[122] The shipper must ascertain that they are complete and precise, since the carrier, his agent, is only obliged to transmit them to the competent offices, not to check them as well.[123]

A compensatory limit operates in favor of the transporter and, according to Article 11, third paragraph, the relief cannot exceed what is due in the event of loss of the load.[124] The provision only applies to damages caused by the carrier as an agent, that is, in terms of Article 11, second and third paragraphs, while it is unrelated to the scenario where more complex duties in the field of customs are taken up. If, in fact, the transporter undertakes to perform all the activities, his responsibility is no longer regulated by the Convention but by the domestic law, which can impose full compensation. If he, when attending to formalities and material operations, and thus under Article 11, second and third paragraphs, acts with a default equated to willful misconduct, Article 29 applies, and, as he is barred from invoking the limit, he must provide full compensation. Moreover, the limit of Article 11, third paragraph, is always the one introduced for the loss of goods, although the problem arisen at customs causes a delay, that is, not the application of penalties but non-compliance with the deadline for restitution for prolonged operations. The provision of a compensatory limit of the uniform law for a liability largely regulated at the national level is quite odd.

Article 11, second paragraph, rules that the shipper is responsible for any prejudice suffered by the carrier by virtue of the defectiveness or incompleteness of the material. Due to inaccurate documents, the stop at the border could be extended,[125] in which case the transporter would be entitled to request compensation for damage attendant on lack of circulation of the vehicle or on repayment of the penalty inflicted on him.[126] In any event, he is not liable for any delay.[127] Similarly, the shipper is responsible for the load getting frozen in a truck forced to be parked at the Mont Blanc tunnel at the end of November, stemming from the failure to transmit a document, where such a situation can provoke prejudice to the vehicle.[128] Furthermore, if the transporter suffers theft of the goods while waiting for documents to be completed, he is not liable for the loss of the load, because, according to Article 11, second paragraph, the event is causally linked to the breach by the shipper

[122] Cf. App. Paris 27 January 1971, in *Bull. transp.,* 1971, 115.

[123] Cf. Putzeys (1981), p. 156 ff.; Loewe (1976), p. 351 ff.; Libouton (1973), p. 29 ff.

[124] Cf. Cass. France 28 May 2002, in *Europ. transp. law,* 2002, no. 37, 509, according to which Article 32 does not apply to the actions arising from the mandate of Article 11. The thesis cannot be validated, given that Article 11 makes reference to provisions specific to the Convention, such as that of the compensatory limit.

[125] Cf. App. Rennes 19 March 1987, *Le Lamy transp.*, 2020, vol. I, 475.

[126] Cf. App. Montpellier 24 April 2001, in *Bull. transp. logist.,* 2001, 525; Cass. com. France 28 September 2004, *ibid.,* 2004, 668.

[127] See App. Paris 7 December 1981, in *Bull. transp.,* 1982, 73; App. Lyon 7 May 1981, *ibid.,* 1981, 410.

[128] Cf. App. Lyon 7 May 1981, in *Bull. transp.,* 1981, 410; App. Paris 2 December 1981, *ibid.,* 1982, 73; Cass. com. France 28 September 2004, *ibid.,* 2004, 668.

himself, which lays the foundation for a dangerous situation.[129] The solution is convincing, as the theft occurs during the enforced stop, imposed for incompleteness of the material, only if it depends on the original conduct of the sender and it is not possible to guard the truck better.

The shipper must provide the information necessary to allow compliance with formalities, in accordance with Article 11, first paragraph.[130] The provision does not specify the nature of the news, but it pertains to the shipment and thus to the goods and to the identification of the consignee. The scope of Article 11, instead, does not extend to the administrative regulations on the carrier's performance, as he must know it or must commit himself to obtaining any necessary information, taking on the obligation to transfer the load along with the associated tasks.

3.2.4 The Packaging

Among the mandatory elements mentioned in the consignment note, Article 6, first paragraph, letter f), identifies "*le mode d'emballage*",[131] without indicating, however, who should tackle it. The shipper is usually the party responsible for the packaging. Based on this, at the time of receipt, the carrier must check the apparent state of the packaging itself; this presupposes, in fact, that the delivered item is already in its wrapping. Article 8, first paragraph, letter b), does not spell out a peremptory principle because such an aim is not in line with the spirit of the Convention, which adapts to the widespread practice free from any prescriptive objectives. By prior agreement, in fact, the transporter can see to the packaging. Despite the rarity of such scenario, this can be an obligation accessory to the carriage. In this case, the content of the contract is expanded, whereupon the issue is regulated by the Convention, given that it concerns any activity due pursuant to the agreement and, even under Article 6, third paragraph, there is full autonomy in extending the transporter's services.

More frequently, he attends to the packaging within the scope of a different agreement. For instance, the packaging can be regulated by a clause included in a deposit contract executed before the trip. Pursuant thereto, the carrier undertakes to safeguard the goods for a certain period and, sometimes, operates on them, collecting them in anticipation of the forwarding and preparing their wrapping. Sometimes, these activities are described as falling under logistics and, as such, are not regulated by the Convention, but are instead fully disciplined by the national law and the services are performed through complex organizational models. If the deposit contract regulates the packaging obligation, the CMR does not apply, given that it only governs the carriage; to this end, the subordination of the overall agreements to

---

[129] See Krings (1999), p. 160 ff.

[130] Cf. Messent and Glass (2018), p. 105 ff.

[131] Thus in the French text. As for the English version, it reads "the method of packing".

a single integrated goal is of no relevance. Faced with an operation broken down into different activities, such as deposit, preparation of the goods, and their adaptation in anticipation of distribution, we must rebuild consensual will and establish whether the packing obligation is conceived as a performance accessory to the transport or part of a different, albeit connected, contract. The CMR can be invoked only where the carrier undertakes to package the load within the scope of the transport. Statistically, the scenario is irrelevant, at least as far as we can understand, as contractual texts are confidential, and each logistics company avoids their disclosure.

However, although we can only infer what emerges from the organization of specialized companies, the packaging precedes the start of the transfer and, for the most part, it is a component of other operations. If these take place pursuant to a single agreement, the carriage is in any event regulated by the uniform law and such obligations must be kept separate, although the overall agreement considers a variety of them from a perspective of instrumental connection. Separating the profile of the transport is not as hard as one would imagine, as the creditor of the complex performance must order the enterprise to transfer the cargo; from that moment, the journey and application of the CMR begin. In these cases, given the electronic nature of the most of the connections, drafting the written consignment note is hardly plausible and, often, no recourse is made to the electronic one either. However, even if the packaging is done after notification of the shipment, it mostly concerns the component of the agreements not regulated by the Convention.

Article 10 identifies the sender's liability for defective packaging, whereas its repercussions on that of the transporter are dealt with by Article 17, fourth paragraph, letter b).[132] Where the packing is done by the carrier, neither of the two rules applies. If the performance is an accessory to the transport, it comes within the purview of the Convention; yet, it is regulated neither by Article 10 nor by Article 17, fourth paragraph, letter b), whereas, when it is executed within the scope of a logistics contract, it is governed by the domestic law. Both Article 10 and Article 17, fourth paragraph, letter b), pay regard only to the packaging performed by the shipper. In compliance with the former provision, he is liable to the carrier for damages "*aux personnes, au matériel ou à d'autres marchandises*"[133] and for costs as well.[134]

According to Article 10, the prejudice could pertain to "equipment", "*materiel*" in the French version. Therefore, the transporter would not be entitled to claim damages for the replacement of the mudguards, as they do not fall within such a concept, despite the fact that the event is provoked by defective packaging.[135] However, this thesis is unfounded, as the notion of Article 10 is all-inclusive. In addition, imperfect packaging might cause prejudice to a person; yet, he cannot act against the shipper, not even if he is the driver, as the Convention only regulates the carriage. Article

[132] Cf. Loewe (1976), p. 349 ff.; OGH 20 January 2020, in *Europ. transp. law,* 2021, no. 61, 67.

[133] Thus in the French text. The English version reads "to persons, equipment or other goods".

[134] Cf. Silingardi et al. (1994), p. 77 ff.; Loewe (1976), p. 349 ff.

[135] See OGH 2 April 1982, in *TranspR,* 1984, 151.

10 defines the scope of liability, not the persons entitled to bring the related action for compensation. Thus, if, due to insufficient packaging, a third party unrelated to the trip suffers damage, Article 10 does not entitle him to institute any action. However, if the transporter is responsible according to the national law, the CMR regulates recourse against the sender. A third party could bring a direct action against him only if the domestic law acknowledges it.[136] A similar reasoning applies in the event of damage to other parts of the groupage cargo, with the resultant action against the carrier, this time governed by the Convention. If responsible for the loss or damage of other goods, the transporter may invoke Article 10 against the shipper who packaged his load wrongly.

Furthermore, the sender is liable for the expenses caused by an imperfect package. This expression is inaccurate, though, because we are dealing in any event with damages, at least in accordance with traditional principles of continental law. Although at the cost of an inaccuracy, Article 10 aims to extend its reach in an all-inclusive direction, highlighting that it relates to all possible scenarios. If the carrier recreates the package or suspends the transfer, he can obtain an increased consideration; indeed, the concept of "*frais*"[137] comprises "*prix*",[138] as we can infer from Article 6, first paragraph, letter i).

According to Article 10, the sender is not responsible if the imperfection is apparent or known at the time of receiving the goods; yet, the transporter does not insert any reservations.[139] In particular, if the packaging defect is not patent but known to the carrier, the latter may not invoke compensation for damages unless he formulates reservations.[140] According to some,[141] if the transporter receives the load from an appointee of the shipper, the latter's assistant cannot be held liable, as he is not a party to the contractual relationship. The Convention does not concern the direct action against the third party, given that its sphere of interest is the contract (of carriage). Conversely, the sender is liable for the conduct of his collaborators.

---

136 Cf. Loewe (1976), p. 349 ff.; Messent and Glass (2018), p. 104 ff.

137 Thus in the French text, whereas the English version reads "charges relating to carriage".

138 Thus in the French text. In the English version we read "carriage charges".

139 Cf. Loewe (1976), p. 350 ff.

140 Cf. Loewe (1976), p. 350 ff.

141 Cf. Libouton (1973), p. 29 ff., according to whom "the party who in actual fact hands over to the carrier at the instruction of the sender is neither the sender nor a party to the contract of carriage; he is not liable under article 10 of the CMR". See also Messent and Glass (2018), p. 104 ff. Cf. App. Liegi 18 December 1967, in *Europ. transp. law,* 1969, no. 4, 965.

3.3 Reservations

3.3.1 The Carrier's Reservations at the Time of Delivering the Goods to Him

By receiving the goods, the transporter takes on the obligation to safeguard them, instrumental to the carriage one, and it is presumed that the load is transmitted in conformity with what is stated in the consignment note.[142] Because of this, Article 8, first paragraph, letter a), rules that the carrier must verify the accuracy of the document with regard to the "*nombre de colis, ainsi qu'à leur marques et numéros*"[143], and check the appearance of goods and their packaging, in accordance with Article 8, first paragraph, letter b).[144] Thus, he will ascertain the size of the load, the conditions of the goods and their packaging. If, for example, upon indication by the shipper, the carrier pulls a trailer ostensibly devoid of defects, which, as a result of capsizing, causes damage to the cargo, he is not liable if he can prove that he could not have possibly known that the truck was unsuitable.[145] As regards Article 8, first paragraph, letter b), if the carriage takes place at a controlled temperature, checking integrity implies verification of the temperature too,[146] but the transporter can limit himself to examining merely the apparent state of conservation,[147] along with the consequences moreover of Article 9, second paragraph, that is, with the presumption in favor of the sender.[148] In the absence of motivated reservations, in fact, it is

[142] Cf. Clarke (2014), p. 67 ff.; Teutsch (2013d), p. 246 ff.; Otte (2018c), p. 1299 ff.

[143] This is how the French text is formulated. As for the English version, it reads "number of packages and their marks and numbers". Cf. Trib. com. Marseille 30 April 1966, in *Le Lamy transp.*, 2020, vol. I, 466, according to which "*le transporteur se doit de contrôler que les conteneurs comportent leur plomb d'origine*".

[144] Cf. OLG Hamburg 18 August 1999, in *TranspR*, 2000, 220, according to which the carrier is saddled with a specific obligation to check the apparent condition of the goods at the time of their receipt.

[145] Cf. Messent and Glass (2018), p. 104 ff., nt. 125 and nt. 124.

[146] Cf. App. Paris 20 November 1979, in *Bull. transp.*, 1980, 190; App. Montpellier 18 September 1986, in *Le Lamy transp.*, 2020, vol. I, 466; OLG Munich 8 March 2011, in *TranspR*, 2013, 31, in terms of which the temperature of the goods is one of the profiles of their external conditions taken into account by Article 8, first paragraph, letter b), with the resultant application of the presumption of conformity, in accordance with Article 9, second paragraph. See Libouton (1973), p. 28 ff.; Teutsch (2013d), p. 251 ff.

[147] Cf. App. Paris 14 February 1991, in *Bull. transp. logist.*, 1991, 289; App. Montpellier 21 March 2000, *ibid.*, 2000, 350, according to which the decision to limit the examination purely to the apparent state is entrusted to the carrier, because "*il incombe au transporteur de s'assurer que la marchandise au départ ne présentait pas une température trop élevée qui ne pouvait pas être abaissait par le système frigorifique*".

[148] Cf. Teutsch (2013d), p. 254 ff.

presumed that the carrier receives the load at the predetermined temperature.[149] In the scenario tackled by Article 8, first paragraph, letter a), if the transporter does not detect any discrepancies, he will confirm the number of recorded packages, and such a declaration will prevail over any other one.[150]

For Article 8, second paragraph, the carrier can formulate two different orders of reservations.[151] In one case, he declares himself unable to conduct the inspection but must justify the reasons.[152] Think of the delivery of a sealed container.[153] Declarations must be specific and their justification objective and, thus, with a precise validation. In the other scenario, during verification of the apparent state of the load and its packaging, the transporter can detect possible discrepancies between what is mentioned in the document and what emerges from actual inspection.[154] In this event, too, reservations must be motivated, with an analysis of the integrity of the load and of its packaging.

The nature of reservations varies depending on the shipper's acceptance or objection, and silence is tantamount to the latter. The reservations must therefore be formulated in joint consultation with the sender, who, in case he endorses them, binds himself, without the possibility of any further refutation, not even in judicial proceedings. According to Article 8, second paragraph, acceptance must be explicit[155] and be evinced by the consignment note.[156] As it has a purely probative relevance, consent may be manifested in another form, although that renders its proof far more difficult. However, reservations that are accepted without being transcribed into the note are effective between shipper and carrier and impact the sphere of the consignee only if brought to his knowledge. In this sense, the document of Article 8, second paragraph, does not only satisfy proof-related requirements but also has the effect of allowing what has been stated to be raised against the recipient. This is a fairly good advantage considering that, so long as they remain unknown to the consignee, accepted reservations are given no effect and do not circumscribe the carrier's liability *vis-à-vis* his person.

---

[149] Cf. App. Montpellier 14 September 2010, in *Le Lamy transp.*, 2020, vol. I, 466; App. Montpellier 10 September 2019, *ibid.*, 2020, vol. I, 466; App. Paris 4 April 2007, in *Bull. transp. logist.*, 2007, 388; Cass. com. France 10 July 1990, *ibid.*, 1990, 697.

[150] Cf. App. Paris 7 October 1993, in *Bull. transp. logist.*, 1993, 741. Cf. Teutsch (2013d), p. 249 ff.

[151] Cf. Teutsch (2013d), p. 251 ff.

[152] Cf. App. Bordeaux 7 February 1983, in *Le Lamy transp.*, 2020, vol. I, 466.

[153] Cf. App. Rouen 11 February 1993, in *Bull. transp. logist.*, 1993, 583; App. Paris 5 April 1990, *ibid.*, 1991, 223. Cf. Putzeys (1981), p. 139, according to which "*la notion de moyens raisonnables est laissée à l'appréciation du juge en fonction des circostances de fait*". See also Clarke (2014), p. 69 ff.; Haak (1986), p. 187 ff.

[154] Cf. Teutsch (2013d), p. 252 ff.

[155] Cf. Putzeys (1981), p. 150 ff., in terms of whom express acceptance should be construed as referring to the one formulated in such a way as to leave no room for doubt. See also Haak (1986), p. 187 ff.

[156] Cf. Messent and Glass (2018), p. 102 ff.; Loewe (1976), p. 347 ff.

Conversely, if the shipper does not uphold the transporter's remarks, the reservations are not binding on him,[157] and the assessment of their cogency is deferred to a subsequent moment, especially to the stage of possible judicial proceedings.[158] Lastly, based on Article 8, third paragraph, the sender may request that the carrier verify the gross weight or the quantity of the goods otherwise expressed, in addition to the content of the packages.[159] The outcome of this ascertainment must be evinced by the note and the transporter is entitled to claim reimbursement of the expenses[160] and an increase in his fee if such operation is not agreed upon at the start and results in an extension of the trip. The provision aims to create certainty on significant elements by joint consultation, in those instances where their verification is complex and the carrier can object that he is unable to comply with Article 8, first paragraph. The provision relates in fact purely to patent problems, on which, by their nature, feedback can be readily provided at once. If the occurrence of this scenario is doubtful, Article 8, third paragraph, lays down a concise procedure for solving the problem.

In short, reservations presuppose a verification of the elements identified by Article 8. Accordingly, remarks set out in the note and untraceable back to any of those profiles are not reservations and cannot overcome the presumption of conformity laid down by Article 8, second paragraph.[161] In logistics and subsequent transfer contracts, the transport could relate to goods deposited with the carrier, and the delivery takes place a long time prior to the start of the trip. Therefore, it occurs within the confines of a different relationship, albeit one instrumental to the further forwarding of the load. Any disputes on the integrity of it, on its packaging, or on other profiles are not susceptible of reservations as per Article 8, because the CMR does not apply for a deposit that is preparatory to a subsequent transfer.

---

[157] Cf. Messent and Glass (2018), p. 102 ff. See App. Aix-en-Provence 9 December 1980, in *Bull. transp.,* 1981, 143; OLG Düsseldorf 24 September 1992, in *TranspR,* 1993, 54 ff.

[158] Cf. Loewe (1976), p. 347 ff., according to whom "the sender, when he is willing not only to agree to the reservation but also to waive the presumption referred to in article 9, paragraph 2, has no other possibility than to break the contract". The thesis must be jettisoned because the failure to accept the reservations has the sole effect of not binding the shipper, free therefore to dispute them in judicial proceedings. The contract is not terminated and the national law does not apply to ascertain any possible liability on the carrier's part.

[159] Cf. App. Rouen 4 June 1992, *Le Lamy transp.*, 2020, vol. I, 467, according to which the carrier is not bound to conduct such verification, although the same must be performed if the sender requests it. See also App. Rennes 25 May 1988, *ibid.,* 2020, vol. I, 467; App. Paris 17 March 1977, in *Bull. transp.*, 1977, 196. Cf. Clarke (2014), p. 69 ff., in whose view the ascertainment referred to in Article 8, third paragraph, may only be requested by the shipper because he "is the one who stands to lose most as a result of any delay that checks might cause and who (...) must pay the cost of checks". See furthermore Putzeys (1981), p. 142 ff.; Teutsch (2013d), p. 259 ff.

[160] Cf. Messent and Glass (2018), p. 102 ff.; Otte (2018c), p. 1307 ff.

[161] Cf. Rodière (1971), p. 628; Clarke (2014), p. 70 ff.

3.3.2 *The Presumption on the Delivery of the Goods and the Presumption on Their Apparent Good Condition*

According to Article 9, first paragraph, unless proven otherwise, the consignment note attests to the contractual terms agreed upon and to receipt of the goods. The rule envisages a relative presumption, which can be rebutted by evidence of different facts.[162] Thus, if the document is drawn up before delivery of the load, never performed, the transporter may prove that it had never been entrusted to him. For Article 9, first paragraph, to operate, the note must be drafted in conformity with Article 5, signed therefore by both the shipper and the carrier. A defective draft, in fact, does not exclude the possibility of adducing other evidence of what is set out in the document, but no presumption arises as regards receipt of the load and terms of the contract.

In particular, Article 6 indicates the elements to be included. Some relate to factual data, such as the name and address of the sender, whereas others concern operative clauses, such as the paramount one or the stipulation of cash on delivery. The presumption outlined in Article 9, first paragraph, cannot refer to such agreements because they become binding once they are stipulated in writing. Conversely, if there are discrepancies about factual elements, they may be proven even when they conflict with what has been declared.[163] Simultaneously, however, the contrary demonstration cannot concern the obligations incurred. In general, the relevant *onus* rests on the party disputing what is established by the presumption, but the CMR does not regulate any means of proof.

Furthermore, in terms of Article 9, second paragraph, in the absence of reservations, the goods and their packaging are presumed to be in a good apparent condition at the time of their receipt.[164] The same applies to the number of packages, their markings, and their numbers, in conformity with the consignment note.[165] In the absence of motivated reservations with regard to the packaging scenario, the presumption is extended to its content because the transporter always has a chance to inspect the packages. Accordingly, if no objection is raised, it is presumed that the delivered load is intact even where the transporter does not verify it due to

[162] Cf. Messent and Glass (2018), p. 99 ff.; Rodière (1971), p. 629 ff.; Sánchez-Gamborino (2001a), p. 644 ff.; Jung (1997), p. 152 ff.; Teutsch (2013e), p. 264 ff.; Fillers (2020), p. 185 ff.

[163] Cf. Putzeys (1981), p. 151 ff.

[164] Cf. App. Lyon 22 March 1985, in *Le Lamy transp.*, 2020, vol. I, 468, according to which the lack of motivated reservations is inferred from the fact that the wetness observed by the consignee was not there at the time of departure. See also App. Nancy 16 February 2011, in *Bull. transp. logist.*, 2011, 205. Cf. Teutsch (2013e), p. 266 ff.; Koller (2019), p. 1 ff.

[165] Cf. OLG Cologne 16 April 2015, in *TranspR*, 2015, 449, in terms of which Article 9, second paragraph, gives rise to a legal presumption on the number of pieces delivered to the carrier.

operational difficulties.[166] According to some judicial decisions,[167] the reservations marked "*conteneur plombé*" and "*impossibile de contrôler la quantité et la qualité du chargement*" are insufficient. The solution is not convincing, as it imposes on the carrier a greater diligence effort than what is required of a cautious operator and does not find confirmation in Article 9.

In addition, it is not possible to adduce proof in conflict with the presumption,[168] and the failure to dispute the integrity of the goods or their packaging renders what is set out on the note unchangeable. In fact, according to the categories of continental law, the presumption is absolute. It follows that the patent defects of the packaging undetected at the time of delivery may no longer be highlighted at the end of the trip,[169] and the transporter is liable for any deviation of the load from what is reflected in the document.[170] To prevent the presumption from being triggered, some motivated reservations must be formulated and these must therefore find objective confirmation and exclusively pertain to apparent damages. If the reservations are accepted by the shipper, what has been agreed is the last word on the issue, cancelling out the possibility of adducing proof to the contrary. If an objection during joint examination ends with the sender's acceptance, there is no presumption. As confirmation of its absolute nature, case law takes the view that it is not even allowed to allege a material error.[171]

Lastly, if, pursuant to Article 8, third paragraph, and upon the sender's request, the transporter verifies the gross weight of the load or the content of the packages, the issue thus arisen is settled through a joint ascertainment, which the parties bind themselves to. The problem of the presumption does not come into play, because, at that point, the difficulty that had emerged has been dealt with. Indeed, according to

[166] Cf. App. Paris 17 March 1977, in *Bull. transp.*, 1977, 196. Cf. Teutsch (2013e), p. 269 ff.

[167] Cf. App. Douai 17 June 2004, in *Bull. transp. logist.*, 2004, 508.

[168] Cf. Costanzo (1984), p. 14 ff. But see Messent and Glass (2018), p. 101, for whom, "if the carrier fails to comply with article 8, the sanction is that laid down by article 9, paragraph 2, then it will be presumed, unless the contrary is proved, that the goods and their packaging appeared to be in good condition". The thesis should be rejected because Article 9, second paragraph, unlike its first paragraph, does not allow contrary proof to be adduced. For the approach herein criticized, see Loewe (1976), p. 348 ff.; Silingardi et al. (1994), p. 71 ff. The majority view does not however pay heed to the clear textual difference.

[169] Cf. Messent and Glass (2018), p. 100 ff., according to whom "there is a presumption of fact that that damage is *in transit*". See also Loewe (1976), p. 349 ff. V. Trib com. Brussels 26 October 1972, in *Europ. transp. law,* 1973, no. 8, 516; App. Paris 10 December 1971, in *Unif. law rev.*, 1972, 274; App. Paris 19 December 1971, in *Bull. transp.,* 1972, 35; Trib. comm. Charleroi 26 June 1977, in *Europ. transp. law,* 1977, no. 12, 776; Cass. com. France 13 June 2006, in *Bull. transp.* 2006, 452.

[170] Cf. App. Montpellier 10 September 2019, in *Le Lamy transp.*, 2020, vol. I, 468; Cass. com. France 2 February 1982, in *Bull. transp.,* 1982, 152; App. Paris 30 May 1973, *ibid.,* 1973, 304; App. Versailles 29 February 1984, *ibid.,* 1984, 249.

[171] Cf. Jung (1997), p. 152 ff., nt. 27, according to whom, in the event of sealed goods being delivered, if a discrepancy exists between the quantity recorded on the consignment note and the lesser one actually delivered, it is irrelevant for the purposes of alleging a material error in the way in which the note was drawn up, that at the end of the trip the seals are intact, given that those seals could well have been restored in case of theft by the very criminals who committed the offence.

continental law, a presumption established by law draws from a demonstrated fact proof of an uncertain one, but this cannot happen in case a joint verification is conducted on an empirical situation that is explicitly clarified. Because of this, Article 8, third paragraph, cannot inevitably entail any presumption.[172]

3.3.3 *Loading and Stowage*

The CMR does not regulate loading and stowage. In fact, the methods of executing the carriage can differ depending on the goods; this is the case, for instance, of particularly cumbersome machinery. If the loading obligation usually rests on the carrier, the rule is not absolute,[173] and the parties may stipulate otherwise.[174] We must examine the contract, that is, the parties' will, which, if not expressed, can be inferred from conclusive facts, as well as from criteria for determining the consideration. If the loading is paid with regard to its determination, the transporter must attend to it. In any event, we must consider the characteristics of the goods and "*un colis est généralement chargé par le transporteur, mais pas une bobine de tôle de treize tonnes*".[175] The same holds true for particularly unwieldy machinery, whose specificities are known to the sender alone if he happens to be its manufacturer.[176]

The clause "*l'éxpediteur assume seul la responsabilité de la manutention et du chargement*" may be affixed to the consignment note, and it applies despite the carrier taking part in such operations or performing a verification to ensure the safety of the vehicle and traffic.[177] Breach of the monitoring obligation triggers the transporter's liability if he fails to put forward reservations in the presence of a patent defect, in case it results in damage to the goods.[178] In general, the repercussions on the carrier's responsibility are regulated by Article 17.

---

[172] But see Van Ryn (1966), p. 648 ff., in whose opinion Article 9, second paragraph, applies to the scenario under examination. The reasons given in the text are confirmed.

[173] Cf. OGH 19 December 2018, in *TranspR,* 2019, 324, according to which the CMR does not establish whether the carrier must see to the loading or to the stowage, and if no contrary indication is found in the contract, such activities must be undertaken by the sender.

[174] Cf. Putzeys (1981), p. 159 ff., according to whom "*le chargement consitute une modalité d'éxecution du contrat du transport et c'est au contrat qu'il faut se référer pour répondre concrétement*".

[175] Cf. Putzeys (1981), p. 161 ff.

[176] Cf. Trib. Charleroi 1 October 1968, in *Unif. law rev.,* 1969, 327.

[177] Cf. Putzeys (1981), p. 160 ff.

[178] Cf. Cass. com. France 3 May 1976, in *Bull. transp.,* 1976, 317; Cass. com. France 1 December 1992, in *Le Lamy transp.*, 2020, vol. I, 467; Cass. com. France 1 February 2011, in *Bull. transp. logist.,* 2011, 107; App. Lyon 16 March 2012, *ibid.,* 2012, 250; App. Lyon 22 June 2012, in *Le Lamy transp.*, 2020, vol. I, 467; App. Douai 17 June 2004, in *Bull. transp. logist.,* 2004, 504; App. Versailles 27 October 2005, *ibid.,* 2005, 731.

Although Article 10 concerns packaging defects, the provision can be applied by analogy to the loading performed by the sender, while simultaneously inferring the transporter's obligation to monitor it. If, therefore, he proves the causal nexus between the sender's poor loading and the damage to his truck, he can obtain compensation.[179] In the event of death of a person hit by the goods leaking out of a poorly sealed container, the carrier may seek compensation from the sender, even if he does not dispute immediately the defective way in which the item was closed because such a defect is not patent.[180] Similarly, if, due to inadequate placement, the load falls and causes damage to the trailer, the transporter may claim compensation by virtue of Article 10.[181]

Separate from the loading is the stowage, which follows the former and consists of arranging the cargo in such a manner as to avoid displacements during the trip. The Convention does not mention anything about this; therefore, the contract can indicate the obliged party,[182] who is usually the carrier. In fact, he, more than anyone else, knows the vehicle and the stresses the load is subjected to. Thus, the transporter is in the best condition to place the goods so as to distribute their weight, thereby preventing the risk of overturning or reducing the one arising from circulation; however, this does not preclude a different agreement. Once again, Article 10 applies by analogy. Thus, if the sender places the load in a hardly appropriate manner due to imperfect packaging, without acknowledging the last-mentioned defect, the carrier cannot exercise an effective control when goods are being arranged and does not have to raise immediate reservations.[183]

Lastly, compensation for prejudice caused during loading or stowage is not regulated by the national law, even though the Convention does not discipline it.[184] The two operations nonetheless fall within the scope of the uniform law, as they are activities instrumental to the transport and an intrinsic part of its execution. In particular, they complete delivery, and no reason exists to regulate in a different way phases pertaining to the same activity. They are segments of a single operation; therefore, they must be traced back to the same regulation. The Convention will operate accordingly.

---

[179] Cf. App. Paris 8 February 1974, in *Bull. transp.*, 1974, 104; App. Paris 7 July 1994, in *Le Lamy transp.*, 2020, vol. I, 468; App. Metz 5 December 2013, in *Bull. transp. logist.*, 2014, 15.

[180] Cf. App. Lyon 21 February 1991, in *Bull. transp.*, 1992, 166.

[181] Cf. App. Lyon18 December 2008, in *Bull. transp. logist.*, 2009, 483.

[182] Cf. Putzeys (1981), p. 164 ff.

[183] Cf. App. Liège 27 October 1992, in *J. T.*, 1993, 538.

[184] For an opposite view, see App. Metz 5 December 2013, in *Bull. transp. logist.*, 2014, 15; App. Pau 5 May 2008, *ibid.*, 2008, 559; App. Paris 10 April 2014, *ibid.*, 2014, 698; App. Douai 28 June 2018, *ibid.*, 2018, 413. In support of the thesis we are disputing here, see Clarke (2014), p. 75 ff.; Silingardi et al. (1994), p. 81 ff.

References

Clarke MA (2014) International carriage of goods by road: CMR. New York, ed. VI

Costanzo E (1984) Il contratto di trasporto internazionale nella CMR. Milan

Fadda E (1984) Ancora sui presupposti per l'applicabilità della CMR. Dir Mar:554 ff

Fillers A (2020) The CMR in the practice of Latvian courts. Unif Law Rev:169 ff

Fremuth F (2013) Article 21. In: Aa. Vv., Tume KH (ed) CMR: über den Beförderungsvertrag im internationalen Strassengüterverkehr. Frankfurt am Main, ed. III, p 577 ff

Haak KF (1986) The liability of the carrier under CMR. The Hague, 1986

Hill DJ (1976) Carriage of goods by road to the continent. Eur Transp Law 11:182 ff

Jung C (1997) The Convention on the contract for the international carriage of goods by road (CMR): survey, analysis and trends of recent German case law. Unif Law Rev:148 ff

Koller I (2019) Die Beweislast für den ordnungsgemäßen Zustand des Gutes bei dessen Übernahme, insbesondere für die Vorkühlung. TranspR:1 ff

Krings E (1999) CMR: examen de la jurisprudence des Cours de Cassation de France et de Pays–Bas (première partie). Unif Law Rev:160 ff

Lana AG (1972) Presupposti di applicazione della CMR. Dir Trasp:751 ff

Lespagnon F (2006) Une expérimentation réussie: le modèle de la lettre de voiture électronique de l'OCIR (France). Unif Law Rev:673 ff

Libouton J (1973) International road transport. Convention on the contract for the international carriage of goods by road. Review of Court decisions 1965–1971. Eur Transp Law 8:6 ff

Loewe R (1976) Commentary on the Convention of 19 May 1956 on the contract for the international carriage of goods by road. Eur Transp Law 11:311 ff

Mankowski P (2019) Rechtszersplitterung durch Rechtsvereinheitlichung. TranspR:475 ff

Maresca M (1981) Ambito di applicazione della CMR e ruolo della volontà delle parti. Dir Mar:366 ff

Martius HPAJ (2007) The use of electronic means of communication under the Convention on the contract for the international carriage of goods by road. Eur Transp Law 41:297 ff

Messent A, Glass DA (2018) CMR: contracts for the international carriage of goods by road. New York, ed. IV

Otte K (2018a) Art. 6 der CMR. In: Aa. Vv., Internationales Vertragsrecht. Munich, p 1285 ff

Otte K (2018b) Art. 7 der CMR. In: Aa. Vv., Internationales Vertragsrecht. Munich, p 1295 ff

Otte K (2018c) Art. 8 der CMR. In: Aa. Vv., Internationales Vertragsrecht. Munich, p 1300 ff

Pesce A (1995) Il trasporto internazionale di merci. Turin

Putzeys J (1981) Le contrat de transport routier de marchandises. Brussels

Putzeys J (2006) L'adaptation de la Convention CMR à l'ére informatique. Unif Law Rev:523 ff

Rodière R (1971) The Convention on road transport. Eur Transp Law 6:574 ff

Rogov S (1998) Zollhaftung und Verhalten des Frachtführers bei CMR–Transporten nach Rußland. Eur Transp Law 33:649 ff

Sánchez-Gamborino FJ (2001a) La jurisprudence du Tribunal Supremo espagnol en matière de CMR. Unif Law Rev:644 ff

Sánchez-Gamborino FJ (2001b) La Conventión CMR según la Jurisprudencia del "Tribunal Supremo" de España. Eur Transp Law 36:842 ff

Sánchez-Gamborino FJ (2006) La lettre de voiture CMR 'IRU 1976' et le nouveau modèle en projet. Unif Law Rev:677 ff

Schmid RT (2013) Article 3. In: Aa. Vv., Thume KH (ed) CMR: über den Beförderungsvertrag im internationalen Strassengüterverkehr. Frankfurt am Main, ed. III, p 190 ff

Silingardi G, Corrado A, Meotti A, Morandi F (1994) La disciplina uniforme del contratto di trasporto di cose su strada. Turin

Teutsch C (2013a) Article 5. In: Aa. Vv., Thume KH (ed) CMR: über den Beförderungsvertrag im internationalen Strassengüterverkehr. Frankfurt am Main, ed. III, p 207 ff

Teutsch C (2013b) Article 6. In: Aa. Vv., Thume KH (ed) CMR: über den Beförderungsvertrag im internationalen Strassengüterverkehr. Frankfurt am Main, ed. III, p 217 ff

Teutsch C (2013c) Article 7. In: Aa. Vv., Thume KH (ed) CMR: über den Beförderungsvertrag im internationalen Strassengüterverkehr. Frankfurt am Main, ed. III, p 235 ff

Teutsch C (2013d) Article 8. In: Aa. Vv., Thume KH (ed) CMR: über den Beförderungsvertrag im internationalen Strassengüterverkehr. Frankfurt am Main, ed. III, p 246 ff

Teutsch C (2013e) Article 9. In: Aa. Vv., Thume KH (ed) CMR: über den Beförderungsvertrag im internationalen Strassengüterverkehr. Frankfurt am Main, ed. III, p 264 ff

Valaperta G (1976) La CMR è facoltativa? Trasp 10:100 ff

Van Ryn J (1966) Une nouvelle étape dans l'élaboration du droit de transports: la Convention de 1956 relative au transport international de marchandises par route (CMR). Eur Transp Law 1: 639 ff

Chapter 4
The Different Negotiation Models and the Participation of Several Subjects in the Stipulation and Execution of Multiple Modes of Transport

Contents

4.1 The Freight Forwarder

4.1.1 The Relationship Between the Freight Forwarder and the Carrier

Article 1 limits the scope of the Convention to the transport contract. It does not give a definition just as it does not describe the sender or carrier. Other operators intervene with different roles, as in the case of freight forwarders.[1] Because their activity is organizational and preparatory to the transfer, they do not assume any obligation in this regard; however, they identify the carrier willing to fulfill the

[1] Cf. Hof Antwerp 20 December 1999, in *Europ. transp. law,* 2000, no. 35, 687, according to which the person "who, in addition to the delivery costs, also advances the import duties (...) and customs clearance charges, deposits, administrative charges, demurrage charges and detention charges, must be regarded as a forwarding agent".

C. Tincani, *Contract for the International Carriage of Goods by Road*, Law for Professionals, https://doi.org/10.1007/978-3-031-08487-4_4

transport.[2] If, to qualify the respective contracts, the freight forwarder and the carrier have distinct roles, from an application point of view it is not always easy to distinguish one from the other. In fact, the intensification of international traffic and the inclusion of more operators in the execution of the same service have created doubts concerning the notion of transporter. In particular, we cannot accept the thesis[3] according to which he would always be a freight forwarder who assumes the obligation but entrusts the entire execution to other parties with separate agreements. The party that makes the trip but concludes the contract and undertakes to perform the service is a carrier. In fact, the methods of execution are irrelevant for applying the CMR and a subcarrier can be employed. Nevertheless, the role of the transporter must be broken down into contractual and *de facto*.

The Convention does not regulate the position of the freight forwarder but refers to domestic law,[4] identified on the basis of the general criteria of private international law. In fact, the qualification of the contract between transport and shipping is based on the analysis of the different conducts and of assumed obligations.[5] Thus, according to a known approach,[6] it would always be a carrier that agrees to operate at fixed costs. The solution is not convincing, as determining the consideration can never be decisive to classify the contract. Instead, a more articulated reconstruction of the parties' will is needed.[7] Furthermore, it is not the freight forwarder but the carrier that agrees with the shipper on a different, and usually higher, consideration than what is required by the material executor of the journey.[8] On the contrary, the freight forwarder often asks for consideration equal to that paid to the transporter, plus an additional sum as the remuneration of his activity.[9]

In many civil law systems, shipping is subject to specific regulations and is usually equivalent to a mandate. For instance, in French law, "*le commissionaire de transport*" entrusts a journey in whole or in part to others[10] and the use of

[2]Cf. Schmid (2013a), p. 953 ff.

[3]Cf. *Tetroc Ltd.* v. *Cross–Con (International) Ltd.*, in *Lloyd's rep.*, 1981, 192, in which "the defendants performed no part of the carriage, having sub-contracted its performance to other carriers. They argued that they were forwarders only".

[4]Cf. Loewe (1976), p. 318 ff.; Wesolowski (2013), p. 340 ff., nt. 14.

[5]Cf. Supreme Court of Poland 27 August 2019, V CSK 191/2018.

[6]Cf. OLG Köln 27 September 2005, in *TranspR,* 2007, 316.

[7]Cf. Loewe (1976), p. 318 ff.

[8]Cf. Clarke (2014), p. 27 ff. See *Tetroc Ltd.* v. *Cross–Con (International) Ltd.*, in *Loyd's rep.*, 1981, 198; OLG Hamburg 18 May 1989, in *TranspR,* 1990, 188; OLG Munich 5 July 1989, *ibid.*, 1990, 16; OGH 14 July 1993, *ibid.*, 1994, 189: OLG Munich 4 December 1996, *ibid.*, 1997, 195; OLG Munich 31 March 1998, *ibid.*, 1998, 353; OLG Hamm 14 June 1999, *ibid.*, 2000, 29; BGH 14 February 2008, in *Europ. transp. law,* 2008, no. 43, 1227; Cass. Belgium 17 September 1987, *ibid.*, 1998, n. 23, 201.

[9]Cf. *Marston Excelsior* v. *Arbuckle, Smith & Co,* in *Lloyd's rep.*, 1971, 306.

[10]Cf. Putzeys (1981), p. 31 ff., according to whom "*le commissionnaire de transport accepte d'effectuer un transport (...). Mais il fait effectuer le transport en son nom et pour son propre compte*". See Libouton (1973), p. 14 ff.

sub-transport indicates the intervention of the "*commissionnaire de transport*". However, the relations between the latter and the shipper[11] are regulated by national law.[12] Although they are not subject to the CMR, the Convention is applied indirectly by way of the doctrine of "*en ce qui concerne l'étendue de la résponsabilité*",[13] on the basis of the principle according to which "*le commissionnaire ne est plus responsable vis à vis de son client que ses substitués ne le sont légalement envers lui – même*".[14]

The "*entre commissionnaires successifs*"[15] relationships are similarly regulated, that is, by the national law, while "*les rapports du commissionnaire de transport et du transporteur*" are covered by the Convention.[16] To establish whether the operator acts as a carrier or as a "*commissionnaire de transport*", it is often necessary to evaluate "*la commune intention des parties*".[17] This is entirely logical if one considers the necessary identification of the obligations undertaken. Then, according to French law, the "*commissionnaire – expéditeur*"[18] is also a freight forwarder, who undertakes to conclude transport contracts in his name and on behalf of the customer. Therefore, he does not assume any transfer obligations and is a simple agent. Thus, the assignment of "*expédier*" is addressed to the freight forwarder,[19] while the issue of the transport invoice made by those that do not execute the journey can involve the assumption of the more articulated position of the "*commissionaire de transport*".[20] However, for our limited purposes, the importance of this distinction can be reduced, because, in any case, the Convention does not apply.

---

[11] Cf. Cass. com. France 18 September 2007, in *Bull. transp. logist.*, 2007, 587; Cass. com. France 11 December 2007, *ibid.*, 2007, 771; Cass. com. France 16 February 1970, *ibid.*, 1970, 144; Cass. com. France 27 October 1975, *ibid.*, 1975, 526; Cass. com. France 12 May 1981, *ibid.*, 1981, 355; Cass. com. France 12 November 1991, in *Le Lamy transp.*, 2020, vol. I, 454; App. Paris 9 April 2008, *ibid.*, 2020, vol. I, 454, according to which "*tout contrat de commission est régi par le droit national*". See App. Lyon 28 October 2004, in *Bull transp. logist.*, 2005, 525, according to which the "*CMR n'est pas applicable à l'action du destinataire contre le commissionnaire de transport ou à celle d'un assureur subrogé*"; App. Versailles 29 November 2001, *ibid.*, 2002, 127.

[12] Cf. Bon-Garcin (2016), p. 510 ff.

[13] Cf. Cass. com. 18 September 2007, in *Le Lamy transp.*, 2020, vol. I, 454.

[14] Cf. Cass. com. France 16 June 1981, in *Bull. transp.*, 1981, 419; App. Versailles 30 March 1995, in *Le Lamy transp.*, 2020, vol. I, 454.

[15] Cf. Cass. com. France 21 June 1982, in *Bull. transp.*, 1982, 513; Cass. com. France 5 February 2002, *ibid.*, 2002, 52; App. Paris 18 December 1996, *ibid.*, 1997, 570; App. Paris 28 September 2006, in *Le Lamy transp.*, 2020, vol. I, 454; App. Nîmes 13 December 2007, *ibid.*, 2020, vol. I, 454.

[16] Cf. Cass. com. France 18 March 1986, in *Bull. transp.*, 1986, 607; App. Paris 17 March 1993, *ibid.*, 1993, 488.

[17] Cf. App. Montpellier 18 September 2012, in *Le Lamy transp.*, 2020, vol. I, 454.

[18] Cf. Putzeys (1981), p. 36 ff.

[19] Cf. Hof Brussels 26 June 1974, in *Europ. transp. law,* 1975, no. 10, 235.

[20] Cf. Hof Brussels 21 January 1969, in *Europ. transp. law,* 1969, no. 4, 943.

Who takes an action based on the CMR must prove the stipulation of a transport contract, according to Article 1. Despite some different rulings,[21] there is no possible way to subvert this distribution of the burden of proof. Indeed, in case of the sender or recipient requesting for compensation resulting from loss, damage or delay due to the carrier's responsibility, "*l'ayant droit*" must demonstrate the existence of the related contract of transport. If he fails to do so, the problem of the possible assumption of the position and responsibility of the freight forwarder remains unsolved. This refers to the structure of the agreement in each legal system and to the corresponding contractual provision of the obligation. So, the reasoning can no longer be led by the interpretation of CMR, which, if anything, sets the distinctive criteria of the carrier's position and of the related agreement, proposing them in relation to any different operator considered by the law of each country.

4.1.2 Other Parties That Interfere with the Execution of the Transport Without Assuming the Role and Responsibility of the Carrier

With the intensification of transport, the carrier tends to expand his activity and take on additional functions, which are different from transport and are often preparatory, such as storage, packaging, and assembly of goods. The organizational integration of these functions with transport has led to the creation of a contractual model that has gained wide response in practice, the so-called logistics contract.[22] This covers cases wherein the transporter undertakes to perform operations other than simple travel, albeit related from a teleological point of view. However, in terms of the qualification of the agreement, a service does not lose its individuality and, therefore, the contract does not *per se* fall within the scope of the Convention. The opposite solution must be adopted if we are to discuss mere ancillary services, included in the transport, which, at that point, falls entirely within the scope of the CMR. The difference can be highly nuanced and its detection implies a careful examination of the consensual texts.

Similarly, the charter with the driver is not regulated by the CMR under which the same charter makes his work available in driving a vehicle, but does not assume any obligation of custody, as this falls within the renter's sphere of risk.[23] The line between transport and hire contracts is blurred in some national laws, such as in the Italian one,[24] as, albeit in different ways, both operators contribute to the realization of the journey. A distinctive criterion, which, although adopted in some States, is not

[21] Cf. RB Antwerp 27 February 1967, in *Europ. transp. law,* 1968, no. 3, 1244; Cass. com. France 5 May 1985, in *Bull. transp.*, 1986, 350.

[22] Cf. Messent and Glass (2018), p. 30 ff.; Kneefel (2000), p. 371 ff.

[23] Cf. Putzeys (1981), p. 21 ff.

[24] Cf. Gragnoli (1989), p. 698 ff. For the German legal system, cf. Schmidt (2019), p. 249 ff.

very convincing, refers to the methods of determining remuneration. Thus, the consideration fixed on the basis of the length of the route would impose the qualification of the contract as charter.[25] On the contrary, if the same consideration is fixed, the contract has to be regarded as transport.[26] If a charterer distinguishes his vehicle with the colors and markings of the company with which he collaborates permanently, his activity could be included in the charter agreement and, therefore, would not fall within the scope of the Convention.[27] More generally, in the charter agreement, a hirer has more power of control over a driver from different points of view, that is, from itinerary identification to load arrangement.[28]

With the "haulage"[29] or "traction"[30] contract, the owner of the tractor makes himself available to the transporter, who has only the trailer, so that the latter can make the delivery. The person who drives the tractor does not replace the carrier, as he does not assume the obligation to deliver, and their relationship is governed by the different "*contrat de traction*".[31] However, a separate agreement may exist between the two parties, for instance, if they enter into a subcontract and, even in this case, it would not be possible to apply the CMR because of the extraneousness of this situation to its scope. If the trailer were made available to the carrier, with his tractor under the "haulage" contract, things would be different. The first is considered a commodity and, therefore, if it suffers damage because of improper handling of the goods loaded therein, the transporter is liable for breach of contract but not for the violation of traffic safety requirements.[32]

Finally, the so-called "*transitaire*"[33] undertakes to transfer goods from the first transporter to the next, fulfilling the related administrative obligations and complying with orders limited to the receipt and return of the load. He plays a role similar to that of the freight forwarder; however, the latter performs a more limited intervention, with agreements outside the operational scope of Convention.

---

[25] Cf. Cass. com. France 23 October 1980, in *Bull. transp.,* 1980, 598; OGH 8 September 1983, in *Europ. transp. law,* 1985, no. 20, 282.

[26] Cf. Cass. com. France 13 November 2001, in *Bull. transp. logist.,* 2001, 804.

[27] On the contrary, see App. Paris 22 February 1980, in *Bull. transp.*, 1980, 239, according to which it would be a transport contract.

[28] Cf. OGH 8 September 1983, in *Europ. transp. law,* 1985, no. 20, 287.

[29] Cf. Clarke (2014), p. 30 ff.

[30] Cf. Putzeys (1981), p. 24 ff.

[31] Cf. Putzeys (1981), p. 26 ff., according to whom "*il n'y aura contrat de traction à proprement parler que si l'entrepreneur qui confie la semi–remorque au tractionnaire est lui–même un professionnel du transport*".

[32] Cf. RB Antwerp 1 February 1996, in *Europ. transp. law,* 1996, no. 31, 579.

[33] Cf. Libouton (1973), p. 17 ff.; Clarke (2014), p. 28 ff.

4.2 Subcontracted Transport Services

4.2.1 *The Importance of Subcontracted Transport Services in the Geneva Convention System*

The subcontract is not regulated by the Convention. However, this has not prevented the widespread diffusion of the institute, which is frequent, particularly because the carrier needs the collaboration of other operators to execute the transfer fruitfully and economically. Indeed, this agreement has always met with a favorable response from operators as it allows their cooperation. For this remarkable application, this organizational solution has been very successful, so that the carrier assumes the obligation to perform the entire transfer in relation to the sender and makes use of another transporter designated by himself, only with an internal division of tasks.

The strategic choices on the methods of execution of the service are left to the original transporter, who may decide to entrust, in whole or in part, to different operators the implementation of his consensual obligations.[34] To this end, he stipulates a separate agreement with the carrier, the collaboration with whom he intends to use. This contract is linked to the former by a functional link, as it pertains to the same operation.[35] In fact, the subcarrier has no relationship with the original shipper,[36] but cooperates in the execution of the same program[37] and, in turn, may use another subcarrier.[38]

This contractual model has been born from practice, particularly for the rapid movement of goods between often highly distant locations and for the implementation of integrated services, given the inadequacy of an individual operator to execute complex transfers within acceptable times. Unsurprisingly, this solution has been considered even in relation to information technology as a sign of modern organizational system.[39] This observation is correct, because the increase in traffic leads to operators' specialization, as they are often likely to treat limited segments of the overall economic function more efficiently. This integration is inevitable and does

[34] Cf. OGH 16 May 2002, in *TranspR,* 2002, 403, according to which, if the place of destination cannot be reached and the carrier turns to another, for the completion of the journey, Article 16, second paragraph, does not apply. The carrier is not only liable for *culpa in eligendo*, but also for the actual fulfillment of his obligation.

[35] Cf. OLG Karlsruhe 15 December 2016, in *TranspR,* 2017, 217, according to which the carrier can ask the defendant sub-carrier in recourse to reimburse the costs of the so-called *Vorprozess*.

[36] Cf. OLG Düsseldorf 5 September 2018, in *TranspR,* 2019, 73, according to which the conviction of the carrier to pay damages is not in itself sufficient to obtain that of the sub-carrier.

[37] Cf. Bon-Garcin (2016), p. 510 ff.

[38] Cf. RB Mechelen 18 November 1999, in *Europ. transp. law,* 2000, no. 35, 432. But see Hof Antwerp 9 March 1998, in *Europ. transp. law,* 1998, no. 33, 707, according to which there is a link between the shipper and the sub-carrier; thus, the latter and the principal carrier would be jointly and severally liable toward the sender. For the very structure of sub-transport, this thesis is unacceptable.

[39] Cf. Putzeys (2006), p. 528 ff.

not deserve any negative judgment, because it corresponds to the reasonable desire of each operator to devote himself to tasks of which he has full knowledge and for which he is equipped.

We cannot accept the idea according to which "the relationship between the first carrier and the subsequent ones in international transport (. . .) must always be framed in the rules" of uniform law, "when there is no specific contrary aspect, that is, a transport with reshipment is imagined from its origin".[40] Meanwhile, sub-transport has a structure that implies a distinct agreement, and it is not mentioned in the Convention because it is different from cumulative transport.[41] As the CMR rules only the latter, sub-carriage does not fall within its scope;[42] however, the two models cannot be forcefully equated.

The opposite approach[43] sees a permissive component in the provisions of uniform law on cumulative transport; namely, the CMR would allow the presence of several carriers only in regulated cases, as though other, general, contractual solutions of the opposite sign were forbidden. That is not persuasive. Regardless of its questionable nature in this aspect and the failure of this strategy, the Convention has decided to regulate cumulative transport but not sub-carriage, and this approach must be accepted; however, the alleged prohibition of the second model cannot be derived from the CMR. The interpretation suggested herein has a precise textual basis, because the Convention does not preclude sub-transport, as it does not deal with it. We cannot accept the idea that the roles examined by the CMR would be the only possible ones, because this solution has no textual basis and excessively limits private autonomy. For example, the use of a subcontractor, resulting from the unilateral choice of the original carrier, cannot entail the unlimited liability of Article 29.[44]

Simultaneously, it is not possible to agree with the approach of those who perceive the subcarrier, identified as party of a separate contract, as a mere assistant to the original transporter. Hence, the activity of the former would be traced back to Article 34.[45] Meanwhile, in sub-transport, there is an agreement distinct from the

---

[40] Cf. Pesce (1995), p. 73 ff. In the sense sustained in the text, cf. Silingardi et al. (1994), p. 300 ff.; Musi (2017), p. 185 ff.

[41] Cf. OLG Munich 21 July 2016, in *TranspR,* 2017, 25, according to which the last subcontractor is not a contractual counterparty of the sender, who cannot act against the subcontractor due to the inapplicability of Article 34.

[42] Cf. Hof Antwerp 8 November 1989, in *Europ. transp. law,* 1990, no. 25, 83, according to which the relationship between the main carrier and the sub carrier is not regulated by CMR, but is governed by national law. But see App. Alicante 25 October 2019, n. 1181, in *Jur,* 2020, 88714, according to which the first carrier and the sub-transporter would be jointly and severally liable according to CMR. This supposition is not acceptable because it is in contrast with the very structure of sub-transport. In the sense that is criticized here, see App. Barcelona 13 February 2003, in *Jur,* 2004, 14188.

[43] Cf. Pesce (1995), p. 73 ff.

[44] Cf. Lg Cottbus 8 July 2008, in *TranspR,* 2008, 368.

[45] Cf. Clarke (2014), p. 171 ff., according to whom the sub-transporter "accepts the goods and the note also on behalf (. . .) of the subcontractor higher up the chain of delegation"; HR 11 September

original one,[46] which is intervened with the shipper, and only the carriers are part of it. This makes it impossible to recall the cumulative transport, which, according to Article 34, occurs when subsequent carriers adhere to the agreement originally stipulated and undertake toward the shipper to perform a part of the journey. Nor does the Convention leave room for ambiguous contractual solutions, such as the "artificial statutory contract between the actual carrier and the owner of the goods",[47] as this agreement would allow the application of uniform law in the absence of an explicit regulation.[48]

On the contrary, the setting of the CMR is easier. In fact, sub-carriage is a transport contract and is subject to uniform law if the conditions of Article 1 of the Convention are met, that is, first and foremost, the international nature of transport itself.[49] However, this happens quite rarely because subtransporters often traverse routes within a single country, with the consequent application of the relevant national law. As a result, because only domestic law applies to sub-carriage, in such frequent occurrences, operators are not very familiar with the national legal framework, with the consequent failure to achieve the objectives of the Convention.

4.2.2 Subcontracting and Legal Frameworks of Individual Countries

Sub-transport is an internal agreement between the carrier and the operator that executes all or part of the journey, so that the original shipper may not be aware of the agreed upon sub-transport. In fact, in respect of the sender, the obligation falls only on the carrier and the methods of implementation do not matter from a more general viewpoint. Because this agreement produces effects only between the carrier and the sub-transporter, the latter has no relationship with the consignee. For example, although executed out by the subcarrier, the redelivery is understood to have been made in the name of the original transporter and under his responsibility, because it is performed on his behalf. It is necessary to distinguish between material execution, entrusted to the subcarrier, and the redelivery executed by the main carrier, from the legal viewpoint, albeit with the intervention of the subtransporter. Inevitably, the effects of the subtransport are reflected in the compensation plan, because any related action can be exercised by the shipper only against the main

2015, in *Europ. transp. law,* 2016, no. 51, 109, according to which "Article 34 of the CMR is to be interpreted extensively so that there is also a case of successive carriage when the principal carrier (...) subcontracts the whole of the carriage to another haulier".

[46] Cf. Cass. Belgium 30 June 1995, in *Europ. transp. law,* 1996, no. 31, 544.

[47] Cf. Clarke (2014), p. 171 ff.

[48] Cf. Silingardi et al. (1994), p. 300 ff.

[49] Cf. OLG Schleswig Holstein 18 December 2014, in *TranspR,* 2015, 157; OGH 29 March 2017, *ibid.,* 2017, 315.

transporter. From the point of the original carriage contract, the role of the sub-carrier is not relevant.

Although the Convention does not specifically regulate sub-transport, the latter does not escape the discipline of uniform law, given that it is a carriage contract, in case the conditions of Article 1 are met and, particularly, the one referring to the international character of the journey entrusted to the subcarrier. In fact, the main transporter assumes the position of shipper toward him and the same carrier exercises all the powers vested by the CMR in the sender, for example, the counter-order. Furthermore, in the event of sudden impediments occurring during the journey, the sub-transporter must ask the original carrier for instructions. Then, in the event of incomplete compilation of the consignment note or its absence, which is a rare situation, the agreement on an international sub-transport is valid according to Article 4 of the same Convention.

On the contrary, the CMR is not relevant if, as it often happens, the part of the journey performed by the sub-transporter takes place within a single country. In this case, national law applies, with all the implementation difficulties for the operators. It is impossible to examine here what happens in each State. In fact, there are various possible solutions, which can range from a specific framework related to sub-transport to its regulation based on, however domestic, general principles. To give just one example, consider that, in Italy, according to case law,[50] the recipient, but not the sender has direct action against the subcarrier. Regardless of the rationale for this conclusion, because the digression would be excessively ample, the solution is unusual and controversial,[51] but presently supported by many decisions.[52] If Italian law applies, any recipient could ask for compensation from a subcarrier, and the question arises concerning whether such a specific orientation can be applied in another country, despite there being an impact on the recipient, that is, on one of the parties to the original international contract. The problem is fundamental, because sub-transport is in every case linked to the initial agreement and pursues the same objective; however, the selective text editing of the Convention leaves

[50]Cf. Cass. Italy 28 September 2009, no. 20756, in *Giur. it. rep.*, 2009, according to which, "if the carrier has entrusted on his own initiative the total or partial execution of the transport of things to another carrier, the possibility of a contract in favor of third parties of Article 1411 cod. civ. and the quality of third party must be recognized, also for the sub-transport contract, to the recipient, the adherence of whom with the request for the return of the transported goods corresponds to the third party's declaration of wanting to benefit from the stipulation in his favor". See also Cass. Italy 14 May 1979, no. 2773, in *Giust. civ.*, 1979, I, 1899; Cass. Italy 17 April 1992, no. 4728, in *Arch. giur. circ.*, 1992, 825; Cass. Italy 26 April 1995, no. 4620, in *Nuova giur. civ. comm.*, 1996, I, 263.

[51]Cf. Tincani (2012), p. 11 ff.; Alvisi (2008), p. 135 ff.

[52]Cf. Cass. Italy 28 September 2009, no. 20756, in *Giur. it. rep.*, 2009, according to which "it is up to the recipient, as the beneficiary of the sub-transport contract, to exercise the rights toward the subcontractor who, once the return has been requested, is entitled to pursuant to Article 1689 cod. civ., including that of requesting compensation for damage for the loss or damage of the things transported". Cf. also Trib. Bari 29 November 2008, in *Giur. it. rep.*, 2008; Cass. Italy 2 March 2006, no. 4656, *ibid.*, 2006.

ample room for the different legal frameworks of each country and partly defeats the purpose of uniform law.

4.3 Cumulative Transport

4.3.1 The Concept

According to Article 34, cumulative transport requires a single contract and the participation of several carriers. Everyone adheres to the agreement, undertakes to execute a portion of the journey, and is liable to the person entitled to the goods.[53] Therefore, it is not attributable to this case a situation wherein, in the execution of a service, the sender involves several operators based on distinct agreements,[54] precisely due to the lack of uniqueness of the contractual constraint required by Article 34. Similarly, it is not cumulative transport but sub-carriage[55] when the transporter entrusts all or part of the transfer to another operator on the basis of a separate agreement.[56]

The scenario is different in case, despite having concluded a cumulative transport, the carrier decides to execute his section using a subcarrier. Article 34 underlines how, in cumulative transport, the service must be performed by several operators,[57] without affecting their further organizational choices. The fact that a transporter employs a subcarrier does not undermine his position in the cumulative contract, precisely because the sub-transport concerns internal relations and does not affect the original sender.[58] Therefore, it is not possible to accept the approach[59] according to which Article 34 would not apply to any carrier that has others make his journey,

---

[53] Cf. Anfray (2003), p. 733 ff.; Schmid (2013a), p. 947 ff.; Lemont-Black (2017), p. 161 ff.; Sánchez-Gamborino (2001), p. 875 ff.; Marchand (1996), p. 578 ff.; Van Dijk and Spijker (2016), p. 341 ss; Musi (2016), p. 435 ff.; Busti (1980), p. 138 ff.; Otte (2018a), p. 1567 ff.

[54] Cf. Messent and Glass (2018), p. 346 ff., according to whom Article 34 does not apply "to the situation where a sender of goods has themselves contracted more than one carrier for successive carriage".

[55] Cf. OGH 4 June 1987, in *Europ. transp. law,* 1988, no. 23, 714. Cf. Schmid (2013a), p. 950 ff.; Bon-Garcin (2016), p. 510 ff.; Marchand (1996), p. 578 ff.

[56] Cf. Spanjaart (2016), p. 522 ff., who wonders whether the organizational model of cumulative transport has not been exceeded in the face of the increasingly frequent use of sub-transport.

[57] Cf. Schmid (2013a), p. 949 ff.; Van Acker (2001), p. 717 ff.

[58] Cf. Messent and Glass (2018), p. 346 ff. See App. Paris 10 March 1992, in *Bull. transp.,* 1992, 647; App. Paris 10 October 2012, *ibid.,* 2012, 647; OGH 4 June 1987, in *Europ. transp. law,* 1988, no. 23, 714. But see LG Duisburg 10 May 1968, *ibid.,* 1969, no. 4, 979; OLG Düsseldorf 8 May 1969, *ibid.,* 1970, no. 5, 446, according to which the sub-transporter would be "subsequent carrier". The thesis is in contrast with the one held here, according to which the sub-transport has effects only between the parties. In this sense, see OGH 4 June 1987, *ibid.,* 1988, no. 23, 714; OGH 29 January 2002, *ibid.,* 2002, no. 37, 809.

[59] Cf. Loewe (1976), p. 396 ff. But see Haak (1986), p. 112 ff.

because the provision would refer to the transport "performed by successive carriers".[60] In fact, Article 34 identifies the parties obliged to execute the service, but does not place any prohibition on the use of others.

According to the very same Article 34, the carriers following the first become parties of the contract with the acceptance of the goods[61] and with the delivery of the consignment note.[62] For some,[63] the document would be necessary and its presence binding, so that, in its absence, the rules on cumulative transport could not be invoked. According to this approach, based on a literal exegesis,[64] it would not be possible to apply Article 4, pursuant to which omission or incomplete compilation of the consignment note would not affect the validity of the agreement. Otherwise, the specific reference to the same note provided for in Article 34 would be frustrated. Moreover, as Article 4 is part of a separate chapter of the CMR from that on cumulative transport, it could not be applied to the latter, except with an express reference, which is absent in the same Article 34.[65] The solution is not convincing; the fact that the Convention is divided into chapters does not help to identify the sphere of operation of the rules present in each one, but aims to give a merely formal and systematic order to a complex of provisions intended to regulate a problem in a homogeneous way. Therefore, Article 4 also operates for a contract with multiple carriers, and failure to deliver the consignment note to the next one does not prevent the agreement from being classified as cumulative, but involves the use of more complex means of proof.[66] In fact, it is necessary to consider the relationships

---

[60] It says so in the English version. The French version reads as follows: "*exécuté par des transporteurs routiers successifs*".

[61] Cf. Schmid (2013a), p. 957 ff.; Otte (2018a), p. 1570 ff.

[62] Cf. Supreme Court of Poland 4 December 2015, I CSK, 1063/2014, according to which, pursuant to Article 34, the next carrier is the one who accepts the goods and the consignment note; Supreme Court of Poland 18 February 2016, II CSK 111/2015; OLG Hamm 27 January 2011, in *TranspR,* 2011, 181; *Dresser UK Ltd.* v. *Falcongate Freight Management Ltd.,* in *Europ. transp. law,* 1991, no. 26, 798, according to which the delivery of the consignment note would be necessary.

[63] Cf. Messent and Glass (2018), p. 348 ff.; Putzeys (1981), p. 105 ff., according to whom, with "*l'acceptation de la lettre de voiture et de la marchandise (...), le transporteur succesif s'intègre dans le contrat initial, dont il assume la corresponsabilité*"; Haak (1986), p. 107 ff.

[64] Cf. Messent and Glass (2018), p. 348 ff.; Hill (1976), p. 197 ff.

[65] Cf. Messent and Glass (2018), p. 348 ff., according to whom "Article 4 is included in Chapter III (...). Then, a totally separate Chapter VI deals with 'Provisions relating to carriage performed by successive carriers.' It is therefore arguable as a question of strict interpretation that Article 4 in a totally separate chapter cannot impliedly override Article 4".

[66] In the sense that it is criticized here, see *Harrison & Sons Ltd.* v. *R. T. Steward Transport Ltd.,* in *Europ. transp. law,* 1993, no. 28, 747; *Dresser U. K. Ltd.* v. *Falcongate freight management Ltd., ibid.,* 1991, no. 26, 798; Cass. Belgium 12 April 2013, in *Europ. transp. law,* 2014, no. 49, 109. Cf. also Loewe (1976), p. 396 ff., according to whom "the requirement of acceptance of the consignment note was introduced as a partial answer to the danger that a successive carriage might find themselves bound by an international contract of carriage of which they are ignorant". But see HR The Netherlands 11 September 2015, in *Europ. transp. law,* 2016, no. 51, 109, according to which the delivery of the consignment note is not necessary; Laurijssen (2016), p. 121 ff.

between carriers as they unfold, not to evaluate them on the simple basis of a formal requirement, such as the successful delivery of the consignment note.

For some,[67] if a transporter only has a semi-trailer and assigns another to perform the service, equipped with the road tractor, the latter would be a subsequent carrier only if he accepted the consignment note pursuant to Article 34. Failing that, he should be considered a subcontractor. However, the delivery of the document is not relevant and, in the aforementioned case of sub-transport, the intervention of the second carrier concerns the same route as that of the main one, while, according to Article 34, in the context of cumulative transport, the next carrier should undertake to perform a different segment of the journey. Therefore, Article 34 does not operate, but, rather, in the mentioned scenario, there is a sub-transporter, even though this conclusion is reached on the basis of a different reasoning from that proposed by some authors.[68]

Pursuant to Article 34, a joint and several passive obligations arise from cumulative transport; therefore, each carrier is responsible for not only his route but also the entire journey. Thus, if, as often happens, the last segment takes place in a single country, the relative national law does not apply, but the activity is regulated by Article 34 as a service provided in fulfillment of a joint and several liability obligation.[69] Inevitably, the regulation of cumulative transport affects responsibility. For example, the effects of Article 29, which provides for the forfeiture of the compensation limit benefit for behaviors committed with willful misconduct or with equivalent fault, extend to all carriers and not merely to the perpetrator of the act.[70]

4.3.2 *Carriers' Joint Liability in Cumulative Transport*

According to the Convention, in cumulative transport, each carrier is liable for not only his own route but also for what happens during the entire journey.[71] If Article 35 provides for a joint and several responsibility obligation, Article 36 limits its effects,[72] because the shipper or the recipient can claim compensation for loss, damage or delay only against the first carrier, the last one, or the person executing

[67] Cf. Messent and Glass (2018), p. 361 ff. Cf. also *Texas Instruments Ltd.* v. *Nason (Europe),* in *Lloyd's rep.*, 1991, 146; *Walek & Co.* v. *Chapman & Ball (International) Ltd., ibid.,* 1980, 279; *Rosewood Trucking Ltd.* v. *Brian Balaam,* in *Unif. law rev.*, 2005, 624.

[68] Cf. Messent and Glass (2018), p. 361 ff.

[69] Cf. Messent and Glass (2018), p. 341 ff. See also RB Antwerp 16 April 1975, in *Europ. transp. law,* 1975, no. 10, 548; Hof Hertogenbosch 21 December 1965, *ibid.,* 1966, n. 1, 698; Cass. France 16 October 2012, in *Bull. transp.,* 2012, 632.

[70] Cf. Messent and Glass (2018), p. 362 ff.

[71] Cf. Schmid (2013a), p. 949 ff.; Otte (2018b), p. 1575 ff.

[72] Cf. Rodière (1971), p. 583 ff.; Bon-Garcin (2016), p. 518 ff.; Van Acker (2001), p. 721 ff.

the part of the transfer wherein the fact occurred.[73] Furthermore, the same action can be brought against more than one of these transporters and this solution can be convenient if the entitled person fears that one of them may be insolvent.[74] In this regard, there is no certainty that the competing actions fall within the jurisdiction of the same State. Therefore, the criterion envisaged by Article 31, first paragraph, letter a), according to which the jurisdiction of the country in the territory of which the defendant has the branch or agency with which the contract operates, applies to the first carrier as the others adhere at a later time, with agreements concluded with the first transporter.[75]

He is the one that enters into the original agreement. Then, to identify the carrier under whom the prejudice occurs, it is necessary to prove that the injurious act occurred precisely in that segment. The last transporter[76] is considered the one who makes the final journey and completes the redelivery, concluding the transfer. In case the goods are lost in a physical sense during the journey, it is not possible to take action against the last carrier according to Article 36.[77] In fact, per Article 35, the transporter assumes responsibility for the cumulative relationship with the receipt of the load and, consequently, following the destruction or loss of the cargo in an intermediate phase, the role of the "last carrier" does not exist, precisely because the goods have not been delivered to him.[78] On the contrary, the omitted transmission of the consignment note is not relevant, because Article 4 applies, although there is no lack of discordant voices.[79]

The scenario wherein the goods arrive at their destination damaged or delayed is different, because, in any case, redelivery takes place and this implies that the last carrier receives the load from the previous one.[80] From an application-oriented perspective, it is easier for the sender or the recipient to act against the first or the last transporter, because the section wherein the fact takes place is not always easily identified. For example, the carrier following the one whereon the goods are

[73] Cf. RB Antwerp 28 March 1966, in *Europ. transp. law,* 1966, no. 1, 708; RB Brussels 28 February 1975, *ibid.,* 1975, no. 10, 231. Cf. Schmid (2013b), p. 965 ff.

[74] Cf. Rodière (1971), p. 583 ff.

[75] Cf. Messent and Glass (2018), p. 368 ff., according to whom, moreover, "an agreed jurisdiction clause within Article 31, paragraph 1, would not be binding on a successive carrier unless included in the consignment note or otherwise communicated to him before or at the time of his taking over the goods". Cf. *British American Tabacco Denmark A/S* v. *Kazemier* in *Lloyd's rep.,* 2016, 463.

[76] So it reads in the English version. In the French version, it reads as follows: "*le dernier transporteur*".

[77] Cf. Silingardi et al. (1994), p. 128 ff.

[78] Cf. Messent and Glass (2018), p. 366 ff.; Loewe (1976), p. 398 ff. But see Silingardi et al. (1994), p. 303 ff., according to whom "the carrier to whom the goods were contractually entrusted could be sued, even if the shipment was lost in a fraction of the transport preceding the one owed by them".

[79] V. Messent and Glass (2018), p. 366 ff., according to whom, "since the performing carrier has not taken over both the goods and the consignment note", he cannot be considered as the next carrier and, in this case, would operate the national law.

[80] Cf. Messent and Glass (2018), p. 366 ff.

damaged can forget to put reservations on the note.[81] Therefore, more generally, prejudice can be noticed only at the time of redelivery.

Article 36 provides for compensation for events due to loss, damage or delay.[82] Therefore, it is not possible to act on the basis of this provision to obtain reimbursement of the amount paid in excess.[83] The idea[84] according to which failure to collect the cash on delivery would fall within the concept of "loss"[85] is not acceptable, as the phrasing of Article 36 indicates that it refers to a loss in a physical or economic sense, because this notion appears alongside references to damage and delay. As these are terms alluding either to the intrinsic condition of the goods or to their condition at the time of their arrival, a compensation action for violation of the obligations of asking for cash on delivery has a different nature and cannot be equated with loss in an economic sense,[86] because the latter presupposes the end of any usefulness of the asset.

Moreover, Article 36 provides for an exemption because it does not matter whether the carrier is the first, the last, or the one who performs the segment of the journey during which the fact takes place, if claims of the sender or the recipient for compensation due to loss, damage or delay are asserted in a lawsuit brought by the same transporter. For example, he might do so to obtain payment of the consideration. In fact, in this case, the entitled person can present a counterclaim or formulate an "*exception*" regardless of the position the transporter has in the cumulative contract. The rule responds to a principle of procedural economy[87] and aims at preempting the situation wherein, if sued by a carrier other than the operators identified by Article 36, the sender or the recipient are forced to establish a separate trial to enforce their claims.

4.3.3 Internal Relationships Between Carriers

Pursuant to Article 35, the carrier that accepts the goods from the previous one must issue a dated and signed receipt, as well as indicate his name and address on the second copy of the consignment note. This provision does not require a particular format for the first document and, therefore, the receipt might result from a copy of

[81] Cf. Messent and Glass (2018), p. 366 ff.

[82] Cf. Otte (2018c), p. 1578 ff.

[83] Cf. Messent and Glass (2018), p. 366 ff.

[84] Cf. Messent and Glass (2018), p. 367 ff.

[85] Thus, Article 36 reads in the English version. In the French version, it reads as follows: "*perte*".

[86] Cf. BGH 10 December 2009, in *TranspR,* 2010, 78; BGH 13 February 1980, in *VersR,* 1980, 533; BGH 15 October 1992, in *TranspR,* 1993, 137.

[87] Cf. Putzeys (1981), p.107 ff.; Pesce (1984), p. 364 ff.; Musi (2017), p. 2013 ff.

the same consignment note.[88] Failure to deliver the receipt or lack of these indications does not preclude the assumption of the position by the next transporter, as Article 35 only facilitates identification and as failure to implement the rule does not alter the relationships between the various carriers. The same consignment note is not necessary to perfect the adhesion later, at least according to the preferred setting.[89]

According to Article 35, first paragraph, both on the second copy of the consignment note and on the receipt, the next carrier can make reservations similar to those provided for by Article 8, second paragraph. Therefore, they may concern the number of packages and markings on one hand and the apparent state of the goods and their packaging on the other. Moreover, they must be motivated and, if accepted by the previous transporter, they are binding on him, failing which the assessment of their validity is postponed to a subsequent juncture, particularly to a judicial decision.

Article 35 does not refer to Article 8, third paragraph, wherefor the shipper may ask the carrier to verify, in addition to the contents of the packages, the gross weight or the quantity of the goods otherwise expressed. The rule only concerns the initial phase of the transfer and aims at creating, in contradiction with the sender, certainty on elements significant for the execution of the agreement. The provision cannot be applied to cumulative transport and passages between the various transporters. In fact, in this case, the assignment of the load concerns the execution of the journey, as well as, due to the speed of traffic, it would be difficult to wait for the outcome of a procedure, albeit succinct, such as the one provided for by Article 8, third paragraph.

Article 35, second paragraph, refers to Article 9 in relations between carriers and, therefore, until proven otherwise, the consignment note gives evidence to the receipt of the goods by the next transporter. However, failure to refute the integrity of the load or its packaging renders what is indicated on the document unchangeable, because the presumption of Article 9 is absolute and cannot be overcome by demonstrating the simultaneous issue of a receipt with reservations. Article 9 assumes that the consignment note is drafted in compliance with the provisions of Article 5. Only clear and motivated reservations lead to overcoming the presumption of Article 9, which is not applicable in case of omission or of inexact compilation of the consignment note. However, such occurrences do not prevent the relationships between the previous and subsequent carriers from being proven in another way, although the demonstration is more difficult. In this case, the delivery of a receipt with reservations indicates the intention of the next transporter to challenge the integrity of the load taken over. In the particular case where the first carrier receives a sealed container, he must demonstrate that he has delivered the goods intact to the second transporter so that the loss is attributable to the latter. This

[88] Cf. Messent and Glass (2018), p. 367 ff., according to whom "the receipt is not required to be in any particular form and may be on a copy of the consignment note".

[89] Cf. Schmid (2013a), p. 958 ff.

applies, in particular, to situations where the container is sealed in the transition phase between the first and the second carriers.[90]

Article 37 contemplates the action of recourse in the context of internal relations between transporters.[91] According to Article 40, the parties may provide for a different regulation and only in failing to do so can Article 37 be applied, notwithstanding the general principle of Article 41. According to Article 37, the carrier that pays the indemnity on the basis of the CMR can act in recourse to recover the amount paid, in addition to interest and expenses, from other transporters.[92] Unlike Article 36, the scope of which is limited to actions for loss, damage and delay, Article 37 applies indistinctly to all those relating to "*une indemnitée payées en vertu de la Convention*",[93] regardless of the title on which the claims are based. Consequently, Article 37 can be invoked to recover the expenses incurred for "*formalités en douane*"[94] or for "*emboursement ou défaut d'avis de souffrance*".[95]

Pursuant to Article 37, letter a), the action of recourse must be exercised exclusively against the transporter who is liable for the prejudice.[96] This provision refers to the "carrier responsible for the loss and damage",[97] but does not expressly regulate the prejudice caused by delay. According to a well-known approach,[98] the Convention would opt for an extended notion of the concept of "loss and damage", including both the prejudice resulting from delay and that from a non-collected payment in case of cash on delivery that has been agreed upon. Instead, Article 37 must be read in conjunction with Article 36. Because the latter expressly disciplines liability for loss, the notion of damage in Article 37 must be interpreted in a similar manner; otherwise, if the person entitled obtains compensation for the prejudice due to delay, pursuant to Article 36, the carrier would be deprived of the right of recourse against the other transporters or, at least, that would not be regulated by the Convention, which is preferable. Furthermore, because of how it is formulated, Article 36 refers to material damage[99] and, from the same viewpoint, based on a consistent reading of the rules on cumulative transport, the reference to damage in Article 37 has to be

[90] Cf. OLG Munich 25 November 2004, in *TranspR,* 2005, 473.

[91] Cf. Federal Court of the Swiss Confederation 22 November 1983, in *Sistema informatico della Corte federale*, according to which Article 37 of the CMR also applies to the action of the main carrier against the sub-carrier. This view is not shareable.

[92] Cf. Schmid (2013c), p. 967 ff.; Otte (2018d), p. 1580 ff.; Van Acker (2001), p. 723 ff.

[93] So it reads in the French version. The English version reads as follows: "compensation in compliance with the provisions of this Convention".

[94] Cf. *Le Lamy transp*., 2020, vol. I, 542 ff.

[95] Cf. *Le Lamy transp*., 2020, vol. I, 542 ff.

[96] Cf. Schmid (2013c), p. 969 ff.

[97] So it reads in the English version. In the French version, it reads as follows: "*le transporteur par le fait duquel le dommage a été cause*".

[98] Cf. Messent and Glass (2018), p. 377 ff.

[99] See Messent and Glass (2018), p. 377 ff., according to whom "the word 'loss' would seem wide enough to cover loss caused through delay, and through failure collect C. O. D. charges".

seen in the same sense. Therefore, Article 37 operates on the issue of delay and not on that of non-fulfillment of obligations to receive cash on delivery.

In case of apparent defects, to identify the responsible carrier, it is necessary to refer to Article 35, second paragraph, for which internal relations are regulated by Article 9, in case the consignment note is completed. We have to accept the approach[100] that considers the last transporter responsible for damage to the goods against which the recipient draws up reservations upon delivery unless he proves that his predecessor had already formulated the same reservations. In this last regard, that is on the possibility of contrary proof in the absence of written reservations, Article 9, second paragraph, provides for an absolute presumption on the apparent perfect condition of the goods, their packaging, the conformity of the number of packages, and their markings with the indications of the consignment note. Consequently, failure to record reservations formulated by a previous carrier does not allow the last operator to demonstrate in another manner how the defects alleged by the recipient had already been identified.

According to Article 37, letter b), if two or more transporters are responsible for the events, each must pay a sum proportional to his component of liability.[101] When this cannot be determined, payment shall be made in relation to the amount of consideration contemplated for the respective journeys. It is often difficult to affix liability, as it is complex to divide the respective responsibilities. In the cases provided for by Article 37, letter a) and b), action is often taken against all carriers involved,[102] unless the perpetrator of the fact is identified. In fact, in this case, "*le transporteur qui a payé indemmité ne peut agire que contre lui et n'a pas d'action contre les autres transporteurs non fautifs*".[103]

Pursuant to Article 37, letter c), if it is not possible to identify the responsible carriers, the indemnity is divided among everyone on the basis of the criteria provided for by Article 37, letter b).[104] This situation often occurs in case non-apparent defects are ascertained by the recipient at the time of removal of the packaging, that is, after the redelivery. The rule also operates in other situations, for example, if the damage is provoked by the vehicle overturning due to the lack of loading executed by the previous transporter.[105]

To complete the regulation on internal relations, Article 38 states that the insolvency of one of the carriers involves the division of his possible share among the others in proportion to the consideration due to them.[106] The Convention does

[100] Cf. Cass. com. France 19 January 1976, in *Bull. transp.*, 1976, 149; Cass. com. France 5 July 1988, *ibid.*, 546; App. Paris 24 April 1984, in *Le Lamy transp.*, 2020, vol. I, 543.

[101] Cf. App. Paris June 4, 2008 in *Bull. transp. logist.*, 2008, 433.

[102] Cf. Silingardi et al. (1994), p. 305 ff.; Schmid (2013c), p. 969 ff.

[103] Cf. Cass. Belgium 30 May 1980, in *Europ. transp. law*, 1980, no. 15, 79.

[104] Cf. Schmid (2013c), p. 970 ff.

[105] Cf. App. Pau 10 September 2007, in *Bull. transp. logist.*, 2008, 83.

[106] Cf. Schmid (2013d), p. 971 ff. Cf. RB Rotterdam 19 June 2019, in *Europ. transp. law*, 2020, no. 55, 309.

not say when the debtor is insolvent; for this profile, it is necessary to refer to national law.[107] Article 38 applies even though the insolvent operator is solely responsible.[108] This solution responds to substantial justice, as it is intended to prevent the entire economic burden of the damage from falling on the carrier that fulfills the compensation obligation asked by the person entitled, on the basis of his mere convenience.

4.3.4 Actions Between Carriers

According to Article 39, a carrier against whom the action for recourse is exercised cannot challenge the fact that the payment is due, provided that he is notified of the introductory act, which entitles such a transporter to take part in the trail, if the compensation is determined in court. In any case, the possibility remains for the defendant operator to prove that he is responsible for the damage himself.[109] Furthermore, as Article 33 allows the insertion of an arbitration clause in the transport contract, the related decision may have a binding effect toward subsequent carriers, if this provision is included in the consignment note or, failing that, it is otherwise brought to the attention of the transporter later, upon receipt of the goods.[110]

The expression "judicial authority"[111] refers to the one of the State that has jurisdiction according to the principles established by the Convention. Pursuant to Article 39, second paragraph, the carrier acting in recourse[112] can opt for the country wherein one of the transporters concerned has his habitual residence, head office, branch, or any agency through which he reached the agreement, and the action can be exercised against all other operators. This way, the duplication of the causes is avoided.[113] When compared with Article 31, Article 39 does not consider the judge of the State where the place of receipt of the goods or that intended for redelivery are located. We cannot accept the German case law idea, according to which the recourse action can also be proposed in the latter countries, on the basis of Article 31. On the contrary, Article 39, second paragraph, would not express an exclusive

[107] Cf. Messent and Glass (2018.), p. 380 ff.

[108] Cf. *Le Lamy transp.*, 2020, vol. I, 543 ff.

[109] Cf. Schmid (2013e), p. 973 ff.; Van Acker (2001), p. 727 ff.

[110] Cf. Messent and Glass (2018), p. 385 ff.

[111] So it reads in the English version. The French version reads as follows: "*décision de justice*".

[112] Cf. BGH 19 April 2007, in *Europ. transp. law,* 2008, no. 43, 94, according to which Article 39, second paragraph, concerns the internal relations between successive carriers, in the sense of Article 24.

[113] Cf. Messent and Glass (2018), p. 387 ff. V. *Harrison & Sons* v. *R. T. Steward Transport Ltd.*, in *Europ. transp. law,* 1993, no. 28, 747. See also Schmid (2013e), p. 974 ff.

criterion for identifying the jurisdiction.[114] In fact, there are no literal indications to support the German interpretation.

Article 39, first and second paragraphs, seeks to concentrate judicial cognition at least on the existence of the right to compensation, so that the problem is solved with regard to all subsequent carriers, without prejudice to the possible dispute of the responsibility of each one. This brings with it some elements of complexity, because the two provisions must be set in many procedural systems and in the equally articulated perspective of arbitration. However, such difficulties are inevitable, and the Convention is careful to indicate the aim, rather than to enter into the merits of the procedural institutes, thus assuming a cautious stance. Then, implementation depends on individual legal systems and cannot be examined in a general way.

Article 39, third paragraph, refers to Article 31, third and fourth paragraphs. Therefore, once a decision has become enforceable, it is such for all the concerned countries, as soon as each one fulfills the formalities prescribed by its legal system.[115] According to Article 31, fourth paragraph, only decisions made in contradiction or *in absentia* and judicial settlements are relevant. Provisional executive rulings and those condemning the compensation for damages and expenses following total or partial rejection of the action are excluded from the scope of the rule. Article 39 only concerns the contracting States. Therefore, if a person opts for the jurisdiction of a different one, on the basis of Article 39, second paragraph, the decision that has become definitive in this legal system produces effects in relation to the other countries concerned, according to the ordinary principles of international procedural law.

Pursuant to Article 39, fourth paragraph, claims are subject to a different limitation period, of either one or three years, in case of willful misconduct or equivalent default. The duration of the limitation period has been provided for by the Convention for disputes relating to transport wherein the CMR applies, pursuant to Article 32, first paragraph.[116] According to Article 39, the term starts from the date of a definitive decision[117] that determines the compensation in accordance with the provisions of uniform law. Failing that, the term starts from the day of actual payment.[118] If neither of the two cases occurs, the limitation period does not run, at least on the basis of a fairly unavoidable literal interpretation. However, the solution leaves much to imagination, because it does not protect the certainty of the relationships, as, in general, the regulation of the limitation period should do.

---

[114] Cf. OLG Munich 16 March 2017, in *TranspR*, 2017, 369.

[115] Cf. Schmid (2013e), p. 975 ff.

[116] Cf. Schmid (2013e), p. 975 ff.

[117] Cf. App. Paris 27 June 1989, in *Le Lamy transp.*, 2020, vol. I, 543; App. Versailles 10 May 2012, in *Bull. transp. logist.*, 2012, 378; Cass. Belgium 30 June 1995, in *Europ. transp. law*, 1996, no. 31, 544.

[118] Cf. Cass. com. France 3 March 1988, in *Bull. transp. logist.*, 1998, 231; App. Paris 31 May 2000, in *Le Lamy transp.*, 2020, vol. I, 543; App. Paris 14 September 2011, in *Bull. transp. logist.*, 2011, 539; App. Versailles 3 September 2013, *ibid.*, 2013, 539; App. Paris 22 May 2014, in *Le Lamy transp.*, 2020, vol. I, 543; App. Gand 20 June 1986, in *Europ. transp. law*, 1986, no. 22, 371.

Article 39, fourth paragraph, applies only to actions between successive carriers;[119] therefore, those exercised by the freight forwarder against the transporter do not fall within its scope.[120] However, this provision allows the carrier that has paid the indemnity according to the CMR to act in recourse to recover the paid amount. Therefore, the different schemes prescribed by Article 32 apply if the carrier proposes to obtain the agreed consideration.[121] However, the transporter against whom the right of action is taken might no longer be in a position to ask for his fee.[122] This is because of the completed prescription period and, according to Article 32, fourth paragraph, the claim can no longer be the subject of a counterclaim nor invoked as an "*exception*".[123]

References

Alvisi C (2008) Il trasferimento dei diritti nel contratto di trasporto di cose. Bologna
Anfray AI (2003) Pluralité de transporteurs en régime CMR: étude comparative sur un problème de qualité à defendre. Unif Law Rev:733 ff
Bon-Garcin I (2016) Distinction entre transporteurs successifs, sous–traitant et commissionaire de transport en droit français. Unif Law Rev:510 ff
Busti S (1980) Il trasporto cumulativo nella CMR. Trasp:136 ff
Clarke MA (2014) International carriage of goods by road: CMR. New York, ed. 6
Gragnoli E (1989) Considerazioni sul noleggio di autoveicoli adibiti al trasporto di merci. Dir Mar:698 ff
Haak KF (1986) The liability of the carrier under CMR. The Hague
Hill DJ (1976) Carriage of goods by road to the Continent. Eur Transp Law 11:183 ff
Kneefel AOE (2000) From CMR to logistics. Eur Transp Law 55:371 ff
Laurijssen P (2016) Successive carriage within the meaning of articles 34 and following of the CMR. Eur Transp Law 51:121 ff
Lemont-Black S (2017) Evaluation of the rules on successive carriage. The concept of the successive CMR, carrier on trial. In: Aa. Vv., Verheyen W (ed) CMR 60 years. Time for retirement or future proof? Paris, p 161 ff
Libouton J (1973) International road transport. Convention on the contract for the international carriage of goods by road. Review of Court decisions, 1965–1971. Eur Transp Law 8:6 ff
Loewe R (1976) Commentary on the Convention of 19 May 1956 on the contract for the international carriage of goods by road. Eur Transp Law 11:311 ff
Marchand S (1996) La pluralité de transporteurs routiers selon la CMR. Eur Transp Law 31:577 ff
Messent A, Glass DA (2018) CMR: contracts for the international carriage of goods by road. New York, ed. 4
Musi M (2016) Il trasporto con vettori successivi tra jus positum e jus in fieri. Dir Mar:419 ff

[119] Cf. App. Lyon 30 November 2017, in *Bull. transp. logist.*, 2017, 739.

[120] Cf. App. Paris 14 September 2011, in *Bull. transp. logist.*, 2011, 539; App. Lyon 2 March 1978, *ibid.*, 1978, 382; Trib. comm. Tarbes 5 February 1979, *ibid.*, 1979, 196; App. Paris 17 November 1983, *ibid.*, 1984, 390; Cass. com. France 3 March 1988, *ibid.*, 1998, 231.

[121] Cf. *Muller Batavier Ltd.* v. *Laurent Transport Co. Ltd.*, *Lloyd's rep.*, 1977, 411.

[122] Cf. *Muller Batavier Ltd.* v. *Laurent Transport Co. Ltd.*, *Lloyd's rep.*, 1977, 411.

[123] Cf. Messent and Glass (2018), p. 390 ff.

Musi M (2017) Evaluation of the rules on successive carriers. Carriage performed by successive carriers. In: Aa. Vv., Verheyen W (ed) CMR 60 years. Time for retirement or future proof? Paris, p 187 ff

Otte K (2018a) Art. 34 der CMR. In: Aa. Vv., Internationales Vertragsrecht. Munich, p 1568 ff

Otte K (2018b) Art. 35 der CMR. In: Aa. Vv., Internationales Vertragsrecht. Munich, p 1574 ff

Otte K (2018c) Art. 36 der CMR. In: Aa. Vv., Internationales Vertragsrecht. Munich, p 1577 ff

Otte K (2018d) Art. 37 der CMR. In: Aa. Vv., Internationales Vertragsrecht. Munich, p 1581 ff

Pesce A (1984) Il contratto di trasporto internazionale di merci su strada, Padova

Pesce A (1995) Il trasporto internazionale di merci. Turin

Putzeys J (1981) Le contrat de transport routier de marchandises. Brussels

Putzeys J (2006b) L'adaptation de la Convention CMR à l'ère informatique, in Unif. law rev., 523 ff

Rodière R (1971) The Convention on road transport. Eur Transp Law 6:574 ff

Sánchez-Gamborino FJ (2001) La Conventión CMR según la Jurisprudencia del 'Tribunal Supremo' de España. Eur Transp Law 36:842 ff

Schmid RT (2013a) Aricle 34. In: Aa. Vv., Thume KH (ed) CMR: über den Beförderungsvertrag im internationalen Strassengüterverkehr. Frankfurt am Main, ed. 3, p 947ff

Schmid RT (2013b) Article 36. In: Aa. Vv., Thume KH (ed) CMR: über den Beförderungsvertrag im internationalen Strassengüterverkehr. Frankfurt am Main, ed. 3, p 964 ff

Schmid RT (2013c) Article 37. In: Aa. Vv., Thume KH (ed) CMR: über den Beförderungsvertrag im internationalen Strassengüterverkehr. Frankfurt am Main, ed. 3, p 967 ff

Schmid RT (2013d) Article 38. In: Aa. Vv., Thume KH (ed) CMR: über den Beförderungsvertrag im internationalen Strassengüterverkehr. Frankfurt am Main, ed. 3, p 971 ff

Schmid RT (2013e) Article 39. In: Aa. Vv., Thume KH (ed) CMR: über den Beförderungsvertrag im internationalen Strassengüterverkehr. Frankfurt am Main, ed. 3, p 972 ff

Schmidt P (2019) Der Lohnfuhrvertrag im Lichte jüngerer Rechtsprechung, Fata morgana order Realität? TranspR:249 ff

Silingardi G, Corrado A, Meotti A, Morandi F (1994) La disciplina uniforme del contratto di trasporto di cose su strada. Turin

Spanjaart M (2016) The successive carrier: a relic from the past. Unif Law Rev:522 ff

Tincani C (2012) La natura del trasporto stradale di merci. Milan

Van Acker M (2001) Beförderung durch aufeinanderfolgende Frachtführer gemaß art. 34 ff. C. m. r., in Europ. transp law, n. 36 717 ss

van Dijk R, Spijker A (2016) Beförderung durch auf ein anderfolgende Frachtführer (Art. 34–40 CMR). TranspR:2341 ff

Wesolowski K (2013) A review of judicial decisions of the Polish Supreme Court within the scope of CMR. Eur Transp Law 48:337 ff

Chapter 5
The Journey and Execution of the Contract

Contents

5.1 The Sender's Authority

5.1.1 General Problems Regarding the Execution of the Contract

The Convention contemplates as its characterizing element the compilation of the consignment note,[1] regardless of the validity of the contract, even in the event of deficiency or incompleteness. Article 6 provides for a detailed breakdown of the elements to be included and, this way, those identified at the time of stipulation must be reported. In executing the journey, the initial program might be subject to deviations, for example, due to the exercise of the counter-order, according to Article 12, or the occurrence of unforeseeable or inevitable circumstances pursuant to Article 14. Regardless of the adequacy of the document and its indications, in

[1] Cf. Silingardi et al. (1994), p. 99 ff.; Messent and Glass (2018), p. 89 ff.; Clarke (2014), p. 61 ff.

C. Tincani, *Contract for the International Carriage of Goods by Road*, Law for Professionals, https://doi.org/10.1007/978-3-031-08487-4_5

such cases, the carrier must take immediate action. In 1956, communication was slow and not suitable for the current rapid circulation of goods. Smartphones did not exist and issues such as the difficulty of finding a fixed location and the complexity of international conversations were challenging without today's tools, which, moreover, sometimes give evidence of what is said. It would have been difficult to leave a written record of the statements, for example, in the case of one made by phone, provided the driver was able to reach a telephone booth quickly. Therefore, the Convention has regulated the deviations from the initial program by providing for the compilation of the consignment note with regard to all the subjects involved.

The Convention wants decisions to be proven, underlining the relational dimension of the execution of the transport, characterized by the exercise of powers and the fulfillment of obligations by all the parties. They are called to cooperate, according to a scheme governed in detail, with the possible unforeseen events to be faced and the forms of reaction to be planned, as they have to be based upon collaboration of all parties of the contract. The measures taken during the journey should be documented, either because the sender decides to change the original program or because the carrier must be given new instructions, so that the impediments that have arisen are overcome. Moreover, it is necessary to confirm the acts that take place after arrival.

Uniform law focuses on regular compilation of the consignment note, but, according to Article 4,[2] its absence, irregularity, or loss does not affect the validity of the contract. Today, thanks to the technological progress, it is possible to resort without any difficulty to e-mails or more immediate solutions, such as the so-called *WhatsApp* messenger, and to certify receipt of the statement in real time, with new indications or information on a situation, including that which may hinder the continuation of the journey. Largely, the practical problems recognized in 1956 have been overcome. However, this new scenario does not change the overall principles of the Convention.

The consignment note is entrusted with the proof of declarations.[3] In the absence of relevant annotations, the demonstration by any other means is allowed and modern technological tools give substantial help to this end. Therefore, Articles 12 ff. often focus on the compilation of the consignment note and its three copies, but the relative provisions do not affect the validity of the same acts. However, Article 4 has to be observed and, in the case of omitted annotations, the declarations are valid, but there is the need to demonstrate their existence and content in another

[2]The English text reads, "the absence, irregularity or loss of the consignment note shall not affect the existence or the validity of the contract of the carriage which shall remain subject to the provisions of this Convention". The French text reads, "*l'absence, l'irrégularitée ou la perte de la lettre de voiture n'affectent ni l'existence ni la validité du contrat de transport qui reste soumis aux dispositions de la présente Convention*".

[3]Cf. Putzeys (1981), p. 117 ff.

way.[4] This interpretation was already important in 1956, and it has become even more relevant today, when, despite the distance, it is easier to give evidence. The Convention pays particular attention to the reciprocal relations between the parties involved, always regulating their powers and obligations, just in case there is an unforeseen event. Article 4 regulates the form of the contract, and no restrictive principles can be derived from it on the validity of the declarations or limitations to the proof, as they are neither stated nor recognizable from the exegesis of the CMR.

5.1.2 The Power of Disposal

According to Article 12, first paragraph, during the journey, the sender can change the initial program, "asking the carrier to stop the goods in transit, to change the place at which delivery is to take place or to deliver the goods to a consignee other than the consignee indicated in the consignment note".[5] The shipper holds unilateral power[6] and its exercise is not conditional on any prerequisite, but is the expression of free choice.[7] The transporter must comply with the instructions without having the power to investigate the shipper's motivations, as they are irrelevant, and the changes may affect all the profiles of the original journey, from the itinerary, if agreed, to the identification of the recipient, to that of the destination.

The power pertains to the transport contract,[8] the sender acquires the same power with the stipulation of the agreement[9] and, when exercising it, the impact that such a decision could have on the external relations with the recipient is irrelevant.[10]

---

[4]Cf. Putzeys (1981), p. 126 ff., according to whom, "*puisque la lettre de voiture fait fois des conditions du contrat, son absence ou sa perte obligera le juge à degager ces conditons des autres éléments qui seront soumis à son appréciation*".

[5]So reads Article 12, first paragraph, in the English version. The French text reads, "*en demandant au transporteur d'en arrêter le transport, de modifier le lieu prévu pour la livraison ou de livrer la marhandise à un destintaire différent de celui indiqué sur la lettre de voiture*". See Temme (2013a), p. 298 ff.

[6]Cf. Silingardi et al. (1994), p. 87 ff.; Clarke (2014), p. 83 ff., according to whom "this right unilaterally to alter the terms of the contract is referred to as the right of disposal". See also Temme (2013a), p. 300 ss.; BGH 21 September 2017, in *Europ. transp. law,* 2017, no. 52, 631.

[7]Cf. Wesolowski (2013), p. 354 ff.

[8]Cf. BGH 21 September 2017, in *TranspR,* 2018, 11, according to which the power of counter-order does not depend on the existence and regular compilation of the consignment note, or on the stipulation of the contract.

[9]Cf. OLG Munich 18 October 2001, in *TranspR,* 2002, 27, according to which, for the purposes of identifying a total loss, the condition of the goods at the place of destination must not be considered, but at the place of departure, if the recipient refuses to receive them and they are returned to the sender.

[10]Cf. Messent and Glass (2018), p. 110 ff., according to whom "it should be borne in mind (. . .) that the right of disposal (. . .) does not necessarily reflect the ownership of the goods". See also Putzeys (1981), p. 179 ff. Cf. App. Piraeus 173/2011, according to which, if a sale contract with an ex-store

Therefore, the counter-order would be legitimate and binding even if it were to result in a breach of contract in the underlying relationships.[11] Let us consider the scenario of a sale[12] wherein the transfer of ownership to the recipient–buyer takes place with the delivery to the carrier. If, during the journey, the sender–seller identifies another consignee, the change is legitimate and the fact that it is a violation of the obligations deriving from the same sale is irrelevant. In no case can the transporter investigate these aspects.

According to Article 12, second paragraph, the shipper can no longer exercise the counter-order when the second copy of the consignment note is delivered to the recipient or when the latter requests the transmission of the document after the arrival of the goods pursuant to Article 13, first paragraph;[13] with the acceptance of the consignee who has been identified in the contract, the sender is no longer the holder of the power of counter-order and the recipient takes over.[14] He and the shipper cannot hold power simultaneously and the carrier cannot be subjected to conflicting instructions. Then, as per Article 12, fourth paragraph, if the recipient orders redelivery to another person, that one is not granted a similar power.[15] With good reason, CMR wants to avoid postponing the extinction of the relationship and therefore the completion of the journey.[16]

In 1956, transport was slower and the sender could hardly communicate with the carrier. In fact, because of the inadequacy of the means, it was difficult to transmit instructions in time. To be enforceable, the order would often have had to arrive before transport had begun and it would have been contrary to fairness to expect the carrier to reorganize the journey, for example, when the itinerary was almost completed. Once near the agreed place, the transporter could be instructed to deliver in a different and distant destination from the one scheduled. However, in the past, these scenarios were rarer, because of the limited means of communication. Today, the context has changed dramatically and this happens not only because of fast movements, often with remote control on their execution, but also thanks to modern technologies, because of the quick notification of changes, with a simple e-mail or mobile phone message.

If warned early enough, the transporter can satisfy his customer by rescheduling the activity, and the framework has changed, above all, from the evidentiary point of view. While in the original setting, the drafting of the consignment note was

---

clause is stipulated by virtue of which the risk of transport is transferred to the recipient from the moment of delivery, it does not mean that the buyer–recipient becomes the holder of the power to counter-order.

[11] Cf. Krings (1999), p. 160 ff.

[12] Cf. Temme (2013a), p. 303 ff.

[13] Cf. RB Limburg 28 February 2018, in *Europ. transp. law,* 2018, no. 53, 481.

[14] Cf. Temme (2013a), p. 307 ff.

[15] Cf. Messent and Glass (2018), p. 113 ff., according to whom "a consignee nominated by the original consignee (. . .) does not have a similar right, but there is no similar express restriction on the sender or on the consignee who is exercising his right under Article 12, paragraph 3".

[16] Cf. Silingardi et al. (1994), p. 94 ff.

necessary to this end, now everything is solved much more easily in alternative ways. For example, we have to consider the anachronistic fact that Article 12, second paragraph, refers to the delivery of the second copy of the consignment note, when the important point is the arrival of the goods and the transmission to the recipient. The lack of transcription in the consignment note cannot be referred to in a limiting sense, as though it could prevent the exercise of the counter-order, pursuant to Article 12, second paragraph.

In fact, the transfer of power from the sender to the recipient takes place with the redelivery of the load and its acceptance, and the transmission of the document is of less importance.[17] The scenario wherein this happens without acceptance of the cargo is just theoretical and has no practical meaning.[18] In fact, this second moment sanctions the extinction of the shipper's power and the rise of that of the recipient, except in cases where, pursuant to Article 12, third paragraph, the recipient is given the exclusive power from the beginning, at any rate as an alternative to that of the sender. The latter can dispose of his counter-order with the annotation on the consignment note or, anyway, with the manifestation of the relative will in any form,[19] as the agreement can be proved without limits.[20] Therefore, it is not convincing the idea of those Authors[21] according to whom, in its exercise and its manifestation, the counter-order would be related to the correct compilation of the consignment note.[22]

These provisions refer to a historical situation wherein, usually, there was a substantial time between the conclusion of the agreement and the beginning of the journey such that making changes could be difficult, because only before the journey had begun was it possible to make annotations on the consignment note. Moreover,

[17] Cf. Cass. Italy 10 February 2003, no. 1935, in *Europ. transp. law,* 2003, no. 38, 776. On the contrary, which is criticized here, cf. Messent and Glass (2018), p. 110 ff., according to whom "there is the procedural requirement for production of the first copy of the consignment note endorsed with the amended instructions". Cf. also Clarke (2014), p. 83 ff., according to whom "the right of disposal is linked to possession of the consignment note. If the sender has no consignment note, the sender has no right of disposal". Cf. Temme (2013a), p. 307 ff.

[18] Cf. Clarke (2014), p. 85 ff., according to whom "the consignee is entitled to the second copy immediately after the 'arrival' of the goods, which may be earlier than delivery. Moreover, in practice, although not entitled to it, the consignee may persuade the carrier to hand over the second copy to arrival, thus ending the sender's right of disposal". It is no coincidence that the author does not cite any precedent.

[19] Cf. Temme (2013a), p. 301 ff.

[20] On the contrary, which is criticized here, see Loewe (1976), p. 352 ff., according to whom, "for the consignee to avail himself of the right of disposal (. . .), it is necessary that an entry to this effect should be made in the consignment note and that the consignee, at the time when he wishes to exercise his right of disposal, should already have in his possessions the copy of the consignment note originally handed to the sender".

[21] Cf. Loewe (1976), p. 352 ss.; Messent and Glass (2018), p. 110 ff.

[22] Cf. Clarke (2014), p. 85 ff., according to whom "the person exercising the right of disposal must produce 'the first copy of the consignment note,' i.e. the one originally handed to the sender. Production of the note proves a person's right of disposal". See also BGH 27 January 1982, in *Europ. transp. law,* 1985, no. 20, 249.

this idea of a prolonged wait can be felt in Article 32 and many other provisions, which envisage an executive phase lasting for weeks, wherein the material transfer was not immediate. On one hand, these rules have little to do with today's commercial practices; on the other hand, Article 12 wants to guarantee the exercise of the counter-order, and a literal interpretation that imposes impossible writings would be against its spirit, as it would prejudice the reasonable implementation of power. Although this is rarely invoked, lavishing too much attention to the format would not contribute to the realization of the parties' interests, would impose unrealistic constraints and would try to pass on a by now obsolete idea of the centrality of the document, especially the paper one.

Any discrepancy from the indications of the Convention does not affect the validity of the consignment notes pursuant to Article 4, and the same applies to Article 12, third paragraph. In a convincing way, it is noted[23] that there are no limits to the proof of the immediate conferral of power to the recipient, who can exercise it before delivery, as soon as he is aware of this possibility. To this end, the consignee must not have anything, neither the first nor the second copy of the consignment note, and the opposite ideas[24] give a formalistic interpretation, hostile to the speed of traffic. On the contrary, the consignment note is not a bill of loading, nor is it a credit title in general. It helps in showing evidence, but it is not the only means to do so.[25]

5.1.3 The Consequences of Exercising the Power of Disposal

Pursuant to Article 12, fifth paragraph, letter a), new instructions must be included in the first copy of the consignment note. The act retains its own probative significance, but the carrier must comply with orders transmitted in another manner.[26] In fact, the assertion is even more true today, as the transporter might have already completed the journey if, to execute the new indications, he had to wait for the consignment note. In 1956, its absence or imperfection would have exposed the transporter to a

[23] Cf. App. Douai 18 November 2008, in *Bull. transp.,* 2008, 735, according to which the annotation of the new instructions would only have evidential value and would not preclude the sender from giving the order in any other way. See also Cass. France 21 November 2011, *ibid.,* 2006, 728; BGH 27 January 1982, in *Europ. transp. law,* 1985, no. 20, 348; OLG Stuttgart 11 November 2009, in *TranspR,* 2010, 149, according to which the lack of the consignment note would not prevent the sender from requesting the goods; BGH 4 July 2002, in *Europ. transp. law,* 2002, no. 37, 817, according to which the carrier is required to comply with the new provisions, despite the fact that the first copy has not been delivered or the same had not been included in the consignment note.

[24] Cf. Clarke (2014), p. 85 ff.; Loewe (1976), p. 352 ff.; Messent and Glass (2018), p. 110 ff.

[25] Cf. App. Douai 18 November 2008, in *Bull. transp.,* 2008, 735, according to which the fact that the new instructions are indicated in the first copy of the consignment note is provided for by Article 12, first paragraph, for evidential purposes.

[26] On the contrary, cf. Clarke (2014), p. 85 ff.; Loewe (1976), p. 352 ff.; Messent and Glass (2018), p. 110 ff.

greater probative effort,[27] as he would have had to demonstrate that the indications differing from those planned had been provided and, in the event of lack of evidence, would have risked compensation for prejudices.

The transporter is obliged to comply with new orders only if they are "*réguliers*" and, if not, he is responsible for the damage caused.[28] Therefore, any party that agrees to change the place of destination following a telephone call does not act in a very prudent manner. This is even truer if, without any checks, the carrier executes the instructions given by an unidentified third party. In these situations, the former is liable for the entire prejudice and does not operate the limit, because he is in default equivalent to willful misconduct.

The counter-order must be executable, which means that, according to a criterion of social normality, it must intervene in a segment of the journey compatible with the transporter's possibility of reorganizing it,[29] without prejudice to the necessary professional diligence of the carrier, limited to his usual activity, often referring only to specific countries and itineraries. The transporter cannot be expected to comply with the instructions when they are sent when the journey is almost completed or if they involve unsustainable detours. The importance of Article 12, fifth paragraph, does not reside in the request for annotation, which is now outdated; rather, it must be established whether compliance is possible and whether the indication allows the transporter to execute them without compromising his functionality. Therefore, it is necessary to proceed to a fair balancing of the opposing interests, to avoid a situation wherein the exercise of power violates the area reserved for the strategic assessments of the carrier or, more generally, can cause prejudice to other senders or recipients. As the rule has pointed out well, the instructions must not hinder the normal action of the transporter.[30]

The order might not be feasible and, because of this, there are some limits.[31] Once impossibility has been reported, the shipper must evaluate the further solutions to be adopted and, for example, can opt for the unloading of the goods or ask for them to be returned to himself. In this case, a new delivery deadline can be agreed, with a modification of the consideration, including additional expenses, pursuant to Article 12, sixth paragraph. Then, as per Article 12, seventh paragraph, the carrier is liable

---

[27]Cf. Cass. France 21 November 2011, in *Bull. transp.,* 2006, 728; BGH 27 January 1982, in *Europ. transp. law,* 1985, no. 20, 348; OLG Stuttgart 11 November 2009, in *TranspR,* 2010, 149; BGH 4 July 2002, in *Europ. transp. law,* 2002, no. 37, 817.

[28]Cf. Cass. France 19 July 1976, in *Bull. transp.,* 1976, 3641, according to which "*le destinatarie initial, frustré de la livraison, est alors fondé à lui réclamer des dommages–interêts en réparation du préjudice subi par suite d'une violation des prescriptions de CMR*". Cf. also Cass. com. France 29 May 1984, in *Le Lamy transp,* 2020, vol. I, 476; Cass. com. France 24 April 1990, *ibid.,* 2020, vol. I, 476. Cf. Temme (2013a), p. 309 ff.

[29]Cf. Loewe (1976), p. 352 ff., according to whom "the right of refusal exists only if the carrying out of the instructions will seriously interfere with the normal activities of the carrier's enterprise".

[30]Cf. Temme (2013a), p. 303 ff.

[31]Cf. Silingardi et al. (1994), p. 88 ff.

for prejudices caused by failure to comply with the new instructions[32] and, in any case, even if he cannot fulfill what is ordered, he has two obligations from which he cannot escape. First, he can no longer execute what was established at the beginning and, then, he must provide immediate notice, pursuant to Article 12, sixth paragraph, except for damages, on the basis of Article 12, seventh paragraph. Therefore, the counter-order always has effects, at least negative ones, preventing the implementation of the original program and imposing that the sender and the transporter discuss the matter.

Then, subsequently, as per Article 12, fifth paragraph, letter c), it is not possible to split the load and the carrier must not actually assume the economic function of "distributor".[33] Finally, the counter-order cannot be exercised with fraudulent intent,[34] for example, when in a malicious manner an attempt is made to impose the conclusion of the trip in the country of departure. If the initial destination were real (and, therefore, there were no simulation), the variation of the place of arrival would not prejudice the application of the Convention. On the contrary, if the uniform law were invoked for internal transport, the requirement of internationality would be missing and the Convention would not apply. In this case, its principle would be circumvented with a subsequent modification that sends the load to a place in the country of departure. Anyway, these cases are rare, if not practically non-existent, not only because of the illegitimacy of the conduct, but because malicious efforts would be superabundant with respect to the objectives. However, the case must be kept in mind and, if this were to happen, the Convention would not be applicable for a fraudulent counter-order.

5.2 The Carrier's Obligations

5.2.1 The Duty to Provide Information

As per Article 14, first paragraph, events[35] hindering the execution of the journey according to the original indications require the carrier to ask for instructions[36] and the provision strengthens the necessary collaborative spirit. The transporter must warn of the impediment, so as to allow the person entitled to dispose of the goods to identify an alternative strategy, suitable for guaranteeing the conclusion of the

[32] Cf. Temme (2013a), p. 312 ff.

[33] Cf. Messent and Glass (2018), p. 111 ff.

[34] See: Silingardi et al. (1994), p. 95 ff.; Loewe (1976), p. 351 ff.

[35] Cf. Rodière (1971), p. 3 ff., according to whom "obstacle (. . .) indicates any event which prevents the execution of the contract in accordance with the terms laid down in the consignment note". Cf. also Temme (2013b), p. 333 ff.; Otte (2018a), p. 1345 ff.

[36] Cf. OLG Hamburg 9 March 2000, in *TransR,* 2000, 253.

operation. According to some,[37] the carrier must also give information in the event of definitive and irremediable impossibility, for example, following the removal of the load, despite any indication being useless for continuing the itinerary. This observation is exact, not only because the correctness imposes a timely notice, but also because various decisions could be taken, both in relation to the insurers and in those between the recipient and the shipper, who must receive immediate notice. Although the rule talks about impossibility,[38] Article 14 can be applied to any impediment.

It refers to any event preventing to go on respecting the plan of the consignment note or, in its absence, of the consensual declarations however formulated. The reason[39] is irrelevant and it could be a previous breach of the contract by the same carrier.[40] In this case, the latter should anyway be required to ask for information and, if he did not do so, he would be responsible for the damage caused by this illegitimate omission, without prejudice to the relief related to the original, imperfect execution of the service. Then, because of an incorrect assessment, the transporter could consider applicable Article 14, first paragraph, in the hypotheses where the itinerary could have been executed in accordance with the original program, that is, if his request could be tiring or overabundant, due to difficulties of little importance. This would be the least of the problems, because unnecessary questioning causes minimal disturbance without bringing about real responsibility. In practice, the decision is left to the carrier, and his conduct must be examined with reference to the degree of diligence that can be expected from a professional operator. The concept of impediment of Article 14, first paragraph, is a relative one[41] and is related to the situation, without prejudice to the fact that the same impediment can be original or supervening.[42]

Then, as per Article 14, first paragraph, the request for instructions must be addressed to the person entitled of the goods,[43] and that is not always the sender as, for example, in the case of Article 12, third paragraph. The transporter is asked to try to identify the person entitled to dispose of the load that should receive the news.

[37] See: Silingardi et al. (1994), p. 103 ff.

[38] Cf. Messent and Glass (2018), p. 123 ff., according to whom "the article applies only to impossibility; it will therefore not apply where it has merely become onerous, difficult or expensive to perform". Cf. also Loewe (1976), p. 355 ff.; Rodière (1971), p. 3 ff. See App. Paris 27 May 1980, in *Bull. transp.*, 1980, 435; App. Orléans 12 November 1996, *ibid.*, 1997, 159.

[39] Cf. Messent and Glass (2018), p. 123 ff., according to whom there are "no explicit limitations of causes of impossibility". See also Rodière (1971), p. 3 ff.

[40] Cf. Clarke (2014), p. 91 ff.

[41] Cf. Clarke (2014), p. 91 ff.

[42] The French text reads, "*l'éxecution du contrat dans les conditions prévues à la lettre de voiture est ou devient impossible avant l'arrivée de la marchandise au lieu prévu pour la livraison*". The English text reads, "it is or becomes impossible to carry out the contract in accordance with the terms laid down in the consignment note before the goods reach the place designated for delivery".

[43] Cf. Messent and Glass (2018), p. 123 ff.

Failing that, he is exposed to an action for prejudices,[44] although the risk can be easily avoided by writing to both the sender and the recipient, who could both answer in disagreement and, in that situation, the conflict should be resolved. As has rightly been pointed out,[45] Article 14, first paragraph, does not apply if the transporter proposes different methods of execution, because there is "a bilateral modification of the contract",[46] where everything depends on its acceptance. Similarly, it is not possible to apply Article 14, first paragraph, if an alternative solution has already been envisaged in the consignment note, without prejudice to the obligation to explain what has happened.

As Article 14, first paragraph, refers to Article 12, the instructions must comply with the regulations on the counter-order and, therefore, must be reported on the first copy of the consignment note. Failing that, the transporter is at any rate required to observe them, pursuant to Article 4. Although, in practice, the importance of Article 14, first paragraph, is underestimated and the rule is not always observed with the necessary scruples, this is one of the fundamental principles of the Convention, because it provokes a discussion in good faith on overcoming the impediment and at any rate requires rapid information. This criterion has become fundamental with modern means of communication, which, making it easier to fulfill the obligation of Article 14, first paragraph, accentuate the responsibility in case of non-compliance. Finally, the instructions have the same effects as the counter-order, pursuant to Article 12, resulting in a unilateral modification of the relationship and, according to Article 16, with regard to expenses and consideration.[47]

Then, as per Article 14, second paragraph, the journey can continue with a detour from the itinerary; however, not obtaining the indications in good time, the carrier may be forced to adopt the most reasonable measures. Where applicable, the transporter's responsibility must be assessed with reference to not only the adequacy of the solution but also the legitimacy of the decision not to wait for suggestions. The rule does not provide for specific criteria, but refers to individuals' own choice, referring to the best measures.[48] However, the interest to be safeguarded is that of the person entitled to the goods[49] and it is preferable to set up a discussion between the same person and the carrier, also for weighing up the final determination.

Several reasons could dissuade the transporter from waiting for orders, such as excessive prolongation of the stop, preexisting commitments incompatible with a long wait, or the perishable nature of the goods. Therefore, the reasons may concern

---

[44] Cf. Hof Antwerp 14 May 2007, in *Europ. transp. law,* 2008, no. 43, 99, according to which Article 14, first paragraph, applies to the carrier if the loader does not warn of the breakdown of the refrigeration system.

[45] See: Silingardi et al. (1994), p. 103 ff.

[46] See: Silingardi et al. (1994), p. 103 ff.

[47] The issue concerns the determination of remuneration and is dealt with in the relative chapter.

[48] The English text reads, "he shall take such steps as seem to him to be in the interest of the person entitled to dispose of the goods." The French text reads, "*il prend les mesures qui lui paraissent les meilleures dans l'intérêt de la personne ayant le droit de disposer de la marchandise*".

[49] Cf. Messent and Glass (2018), p. 123 ff.

his activity or the nature of the load, and the criterion of the best solution cannot be absolute, but must refer to the circumstances, considering the degree of diligence that might be required on the basis of a professional evaluation.[50] Therefore, valuable goods could be entrusted to another carrier for return or for continuation of the journey, and an appropriate transporter must be chosen at the lowest possible cost. For example, verification of the adequacy of this consideration must be consistent with the fact that the carrier may be in a country the language or business practice of which is unknown, mostly in the presence of imminent commitments to be honored. In any case, the transporter must ask what initiative to take and whether he should choose between returning the cargo to the sender or applying Article 16.[51] Article 14, second paragraph, responds to the concerns of its time as well, that is, when communications were difficult. Today, instructions can be requested by e-mail or mobile phone, and the carrier can acquire them in real time. There should not be a long interval between the request and the reception; therefore, the transporter should apply Article 14, second paragraph, decreasingly, avoiding the risk of being challenged on the appropriateness of the decision taken.

If, then, the indications do not arrive, it can be complex to establish the preferable determination, because for the carrier the haste and the need to dedicate himself to other trips must be considered on one hand. On the other hand, he must use all modern technologies and communication or research tools compatible with the fact of being at a distance from the base, but with the employment of the most sophisticated solutions available. Respect for professional diligence and fulfillment of the obligations of Article 14, first and second paragraphs, must be assessed on the basis of incisive criteria, because the commitment must be proportionate to the interests of others and correspond to the widespread competence on the market, according to the best practices of economic operators. This conclusion can create problems for those that occasionally venture into international transport. This is not surprising, because one of the objectives of the Convention is to select qualified carriers and, by prescribing a high level of competence, to progressively improve their efficiency. For what these considerations may be worth, this has been happening steadily over the past sixty years.

5.2.2 *The Impossibility to Transport*

The logic of Article 14, first paragraph, revolves around the concept of "impossibility" and, as a cause of termination of the relationship, it must be understood in an absolute sense,[52] although the request for instructions might concern a simple

[50] Cf. Clarke (2014), p. 91 ff., according to whom "the level of the carrier's duty is not absolute". See also Putzeys (1981), p. 162 ff.; Loewe (1976), p. 356 ff.

[51] Cf. Messent and Glass (2018), p. 124 ff.

[52] Cf. Temme (2013b), p. 334 ff.

impediment. This makes the execution of the trip more difficult and it might impose higher costs for its continuation, but it is not final.[53] Thus, it is not such a temporary factor as the strike of some customs officers, while a national abstention from work would be different, because the journey could not be continued, not even with a detour. In fact, impossibility must preclude any alternative solution and lead to a definitive interruption of the transport. The extreme and best-known scenarios are theft and robbery, because the subtraction of the load prevents the completion of the journey, marking the conclusion of the relationship, although it is not the physiological outcome as is the redelivery.

Although the request for instructions might take place in other situations, precisely of impediment,[54] impossibility extinguishes the relationship, as it happens for the breakdown of the refrigeration system, when the condition of the goods is compromised. In this regard, the instructions must be consistent with the mandatory regulations and, if the carrier were to depart from them, that would be illegitimate, with the prohibition to comply with. Therefore, if, in the face of damage due to the loss of the pre-established temperature, the entitled party still wished to deliver the load as though it were intact, the indication should be disregarded, because it would be unlawful to suggest a conduct in contrast with administrative or criminal provisions, which are widespread in many countries.

Another typical causative factor of impossibility is a road accident. If it provokes the destruction of the load, it is necessary to issue a warning even if the loss is total, although there are no possible instructions. Instead, Article 14, first paragraph, has to be completely applied if it is necessary to provide for the part of the goods that has remained intact. Furthermore, the accident can cause damage to the vehicle and, in this case, the carrier is not released from his obligation. Once the discussion has been established with the sender or the recipient, the transporter must resort to repairing or replacing the truck, but he does not need any further authorization, because this falls within the fulfillment of the original obligation, which must be brought to final execution at higher costs.[55] This is a concept opposite to that of impossibility. If anything, the instructions may concern the temporary arrangement of the load, pending the solution of the problem.

The concept of absolute impossibility refers to transport as it is conceived in the contract. A typical example is given by the recent blockade of borders by many countries for health reasons. Although it cannot last more than a certain period, this choice precludes the execution of the agreement, because the obligation of performing the service cannot last for months, in wait of an opposite administrative or legislative measure. On the contrary, if only one passage at the border is closed, there is no impossibility and the carrier must go for another one, subject to notice of the mere impediment, if relevant, pursuant to Article 14, first paragraph.

---

[53] Cf. Temme (2013b), p. 336 ff.; Otte (2018a), p. 1350 ff.

[54] Cf. Temme (2013b), p. 336 ff.

[55] Cf. Messent and Glass (2018), p. 124 ff.

The obligation to transport concerns any initiative that is necessary and compatible with social normality criteria, with respect to the achievement of the agreed objective, although this is to be seen in reference to the situations of time and place, as prerequisites of the contract. However, within these limits, the carrier's effort must be maximal and aimed at overcoming non-definitive impediments, because they must be borne in mind at the time of stipulation, in the calculation of the consideration and for the acceptance of the obligation. Article 12 is different, as it considers a change imposed unilaterally, not agreed upon, and the relevance of which has not been weighed.

5.2.3 The Impossibility or Impediment to Redelivery

Article 15 regulates the impediments to redelivery, and this is achieved with the passage of detention of the goods from the carrier to the recipient, assuming the arrival of the load at the agreed location and its acceptance.[56] It cannot be shared the approach according to which, in the absence of an express definition of redelivery in uniform law, one should refer to the national one.[57] The Convention regulates the entire matter, except in cases of express referral to domestic law, such as the prescription.[58] Moreover, in the very same Article 15, refusal[59] is considered and, implicitly, the redelivery is identified as an event wherein consent is required, in addition to the acquisition of material availability of the cargo.

For the same reasons, national rules on unloading do not apply.[60] Otherwise, the idea of regulating trafficking in a unitary manner would disappear and, on the contrary, there is a strong need for simplification. In this regard, the silence of Article 15 does not count as a reference to a State discipline, but as acceptance of private consensual solutions, with autonomy not limited by mandatory provisions, neither by a uniform law nor by the one of individual country. Therefore, the contract establishes the person that should perform the unloading and, if this is not done at the

[56]Cf. Temme (2013c), p. 340 ff.; Jung (1997), p. 153 ff.; Otte (2018b), p. 1351 ff.

[57]Cf. App. Paris 22 October 1997, in *Bull. transp.*, 1997, 779; App. Versailles 3 September 2013, *ibid.*, 2013, 518; Cass. com. France 10 March 2015, in *Le Lamy transp.*, 2020, vol. I, 479.

[58]Cf. Article 32.

[59]Cf. OLG Munich 2 December 2015, in *TranspR,* 2016, 69, according to which, if the sender orders the goods to be returned to the place of departure in response to the refusal to receive the goods, the carrier has no right of retention of the goods, according to German law, since the transport ends with the arrival at the point of departure and at that moment the transporter is entitled to payment.

[60]Cf. App. Amiens 23 November 1990, in *Bull. transp.*, 1990, 292; App. Paris 21 May 2003, *ibid.*, 2003, 438; App. Versailles 27 October 2005, in *Le Lamy transp.*, 2020, vol. I, 479. For all these decisions, the law of the place of destination would apply. Cf. App. Lyon 18 April 2006, in *Bull. transp.*, 2006, 667, according to which, in France, reference has often been made to the Rome Convention of 19 June 1990, now replaced by the European Union regulation of 17 June 2008, no. 593, to determine the applicable law on the basis of the criteria of private international law.

time of stipulation, the solution can be found during execution. So, if, in derogation of commercial practice, the carrier intervenes in place of the recipient, he assumes the relative responsibility.

Redelivery can be proven in any way and, if the consignment note has been drawn up, pursuant to Article 13, first paragraph, the consignee can request the release of the second copy.[61] However, the omission of, or the irregularity in the consignment note does not affect the validity of the contract, pursuant to Article 4. Thus, for some,[62] the proof is not given if the clause "*déniée par le destinataire*" appears on the consignment note, but without the stamp being affixed to it. In this case, the attempted redelivery must be inferred from other circumstances,[63] for example, from the fact that the carrier calls the recipient on the day indicated in the document and speaks about the end of the transport.[64]

Furthermore, the behavior of the carrier that delivers without verifying the identity of the recipient would be legitimate if the party to whom the goods are entrusted signs the "*bon de livraison*" and is "*à l'adresse de livraison*".[65] The solution is not convincing, as the transporter must act according to the necessary professional diligence and, therefore, his verification cannot be stopped at appearances (particularly if they are so generic); on the contrary, all suitable steps must be taken for exact identification.[66]

We cannot consider redelivery the fact that the goods are taken into the customs warehouse, waiting for the administrative office or its representatives to check on them,[67] because there is no passage in the detention and, above all, the public structure operates for regulatory or fiscal reasons, not in the interest of the recipient. The same applies if the warehouse is transformed into a temporary customs structure because of the lack of space in the institutional premises. In this context, it is not equivalent to the redelivery the deposit in the recipient's building,[68] which has become a customs warehouse. On the contrary, the opposite must be considered if the recipient orders to arrange the load at a trusted third party and not at his headquarters or, in any case, if the redelivery is executed by the will of the same consignee and is functional to his organizational needs and to the best location of the assets.

---

[61] See also OLG Koblenz 9 March 2016, in *TranspR*, 2017, 109, according to which, in case of lack of consignment note, Article 13 leaves the regulation of redelivery to national law. The thesis is not acceptable, due to the probative nature of the consignment note.

[62] Cf. Cass. com. France 15 May 1984, in *Bull. transp.*, 1984, 526; App. Paris 26 February 2003, *ibid.*, 2003, 289; App. Aix - en - Provence 2 March 2000, in *Le Lamy transp.*, 2020, vol. I, 480.

[63] Cf. Cass. com. France 5 July 1988, in B*ull. transp.*, 1988, 530.

[64] Cf. Cass. com. France 5 July 1988, in B*ull. transp.*, 1988, 530.

[65] Cf. App. Paris 11 March 2009, in *Bull. transp.*, 2009, 290.

[66] Cf. Clarke (2014), p. 92 ff., according to whom "the carrier must make inquiries even though this takes time and may be inconvenient".

[67] Cf. Cass. com. France 24 November 1987, in *Bull. transp.*, 1988, 42.

[68] Cf. Cass. com. France 6 February 1985, in *Le Lamy transp.*, 2020, vol. I, 480.

According to Article 15, first paragraph, redelivery can be precluded because of the occurrence of impediments, identified as "*empechêments*".[69] An extensive interpretation must be given to the rule to make it consistent with Article 14 and, therefore, it includes the scenarios of both impediment in the proper sense and absolute impossibility. According to Article 15, as well, the latter must be assessed in relation to the circumstances, for example, in cases of non-delivery because of unavailability of the recipient; on the contrary, the impediment translates into a difficulty that can be overcome with alternative solutions, although sometimes they cause an increase in costs. An example of this second occurrence is the delay in receipt,[70] an event often linked to the disorganization of the consignee, but which does not preclude the subsequent fulfillment of the obligation, although with a patrimonial burden for the carrier, who can obtain a corresponding increase in the consideration and, if anything, compensation for prejudices.

An impediment[71] is sufficient for the transporter to ask for instructions, pursuant to Article 15.[72] If the recipient adheres to the contract, according to Article 13, first paragraph, and later realizes the occurrence of impediments, he can give the necessary orders, at least according to Article 12.[73] Even if Article 15, first paragraph, seems to imply the opposite thesis,[74] "there are situations in which (. . .) the recipient has still counter-order power".[75] Finally, the Convention does not provide for a deadline within which information must be requested and, in general, the carrier's notice must be immediate.[76]

Then, per Article 15, second paragraph, despite having refused the goods, the consignee can change his position until the carrier receives instructions to the contrary from the sender.[77] Therefore, an absolute impossibility, such as refusal, is conceived as reversible, and the goods remain available until the transporter obtains indications to the contrary.[78] It is a rare scenario and, in fact, it implies that the carrier has a warehouse in the place of destination to store the load temporarily, failing

---

[69]The English text reads, "where circumstances prevent delivery".

[70]Cf. OLG Düsseldorf 18 November 2017, in *TranspR,* 2018, 197, according to which the carrier's custody obligation continues when there is a delay in redelivery due to an impediment of short duration or destined to resolve, pending acceptance by the recipient.

[71]Cf. Clarke (2014), p. 92 ff.

[72]Cf. Temme (2013c), p. 342 ff.

[73]Cf. Silingardi et al. (1994), p. 108 ff.

[74]According to Article 15, first paragraph, if there are impediments to redelivery, the carrier asks the sender for instructions.

[75]Cf. Silingardi et al. (1994), p. 108 ff.

[76]Cf. Rodière (1971), p. 5 ff., according to whom "the carrier must apply for instructions to the sender. It should be added to the text that he must inform (the sender) of the reason why delivery is impossible and that he must take action within a reasonable period of time".

[77]Cf. Messent and Glass (2018), p. 125 ff.; Loewe (1976), p. 357 ff.; Putzeys (1981), p. 183 ff.

[78]Cf. Putzeys (1981), p. 183 ff., according to whom "*le refus du destinataire de recevoir la marchandise empêche qu'il soit mis fin au contrat de transport. Le contrat se poursuivant, le transporteur reste responsable vis - à -vis de la marchandise à laquelle il doit ses soins*".

which the case could not take place. Once again, the rule is affected by its era, characterized by slow communications, as, in the past, a long time could have passed between the request and the response and, in reference to this situation, the choice made by the Convention is justified. Today, with technological innovation, the provision does not have great practical importance, as the new instructions should be immediate, with there being no time for an afterthought. Then, if the transporter does not notify the shipper about the refusal of the recipient, the same carrier should answer for the prejudices provoked to the sender, for example, because the latter cannot immediately give the necessary information to third parties,[79] because the goods become unsaleable[80] or he continues to ship to the consignee himself, unaware of his decision[81] and of the previous breach of the contractual assignment. Missing or late notice gives rise to compensation for prejudices.

Then, as per Article 15, third paragraph, if the impediment occurs after the recipient has indicated another person to whom to redeliver, pursuant to Article 12, third paragraph, the consignee replaces the sender and the new party replaces the recipient for the application of Article 15, first and second paragraphs.[82] The provision contemplates the hypothesis wherein the consignee exercises the counter-order pursuant to Article 12, third paragraph, but operates although the instructions are given on the basis of Article 12, second paragraph,[83] for the identity of the effects. Despite acquiring relative power on the basis of Article 12, second paragraph, the recipient can order the transfer of the goods to another person.

5.2.4 The Possible Instructions in Case of Impediments to the Redelivery

According to Article 15, first paragraph, the occurrence of impediments to redelivery requires the carrier to ask the sender for instructions and the former must always contact the shipper if the recipient refuses the goods.[84] In this case, by expressed provision, the shipper is not required to show the first copy of the consignment note, also because he may have already sent it to the consignee. For some,[85] the problem

[79] Cf. App. Paris 30 April 1985 in *Le Lamy transp.*, 2020, vol. I, 480.

[80] Cf. App. Lyon 24 March 1983, in *Bull. transp.*, 1984, 166.

[81] Cf. Cass. com. France 13 December 1982, in *Bull. transp.*, 1983, 64.

[82] Cf. Messent and Glass (2018), p. 125 ff.; Otte (2018b), p. 1355 ff.

[83] On the contrary, cf. Loewe (1976), p. 357 ff., according to whom the reversal of roles "cannot be extended to cover the case in which the consignee has acquired his right of disposal under Article 12, paragraph 2".

[84] Cf. Jung (1997), p. 153 ff.

[85] Cf. Clarke (2014), p. 93 ff., according to whom, "if the cause of prevention is some cause other than the refusal of the consignee, the interference has been drawn, *a contrario*, that the sender can give instructions only in accordance with Article 12". Cf. also Rodière (1971), p. 6 ff.

would arise as to how the sender should behave in the event of an impediment other than refusal, if he is unable to present the document. In fact, the transporter should ignore any indication and proceed with the unloading or, alternatively, with the sale, pursuant to Article 16, second and third paragraphs. It is a consequence of a strict and literal interpretation of Article 12, and the solution is not convincing, because the shipper's failure to show the consignment note does not exempt the carrier from otherwise verifying which party is able to give instructions, for example, "through consultations with the sender or recipient in order to prevent compensation claims".[86]

In the event of an impediment, the shipper's indications must identify alternative solutions suitable for concluding the journey. In Article 15, there is no provision similar to that of Article 14, second paragraph, for which the transporter would be authorized to take the most appropriate measures if he fails to receive orders in good time. However, this discipline also applies to events that prevent redelivery and the carrier has an interest in ensuring that the stop does not continue, for example, to not compromise the condition of the goods, if perishable, or to not jeopardize his further activities. Despite its different drafting, Article 15 does not see the initiatives of Article 16, second and third paragraphs, as an immediate alternative to the sending of instructions, because, before reaching that step, the transporter must evaluate other suitable solutions, with an extensive application of Article 14. Think of the importance of returning the load of extreme value to the sender if everything suggests bringing it back. If even the shipper remains silent, the transporter must opt for the most rational measure. To this end, he can refer to Article 14, second paragraph, because, while waiting to proceed as suggested by Article 16, second and third paragraphs, he must explore every option, less traumatic than those of Article 16, on the basis of a principle of graduality. This one, before the definitive unloading or sale and after the unsuccessful request for instructions, passes through the search for another strategy, although the point is not mentioned in Article 15.

The recipient's refusal leaves the counter-order to the sender alone, albeit within the limits set by Article 15, second paragraph.[87] Having lost interest in getting the goods back, the shipper can ask the carrier to get rid of them and, obliged to behave according to criteria of social normality and professional diligence, the latter must assess whether the conditions exist to perform the operation legitimately. For example, the transporter could identify a suitable place, even more so if it is a bulky load. He might be in a foreign country, either the language or any specific provisions of which on waste disposal are unknown and, therefore, he might not always be able to do what is necessary and again must consult the shipper. Only apparently, the destruction of a load of vile value is the most reasonable remedy,

[86]Cf. Silingardi et al. (1994), p. 109 ff.

[87]The English text reads, "even if he has refused the goods, the consignee may nevertheless require delivery so long as the carrier has not received instructions to the contrary from the sender". The French text reads, "*même s'il a refusé la marchandise, le destinataire peut toujours en demander la livriason tant que le transporteur n'a pas reçu d'instructions contraires de l'expediteur*".

because it can be a very complex strategy fraught with risks of violation of the specific discipline, which must be avoided.

As often happens, the sender can request for the load be returned to him. In this case, he must agree on a possible new delivery deadline and can redefine the consideration. Because Article 12, fifth paragraph, applies, the carrier may refuse to execute the return journey, should this result in prejudice to the normal performance of his business or in obstacles to the fulfillment of his commitments toward other customers. In fact, even if Article 15, first paragraph, does not refer to Article 12, fifth paragraph, the rule must be applied, because, in any case, there are instructions to be performed, with a significant modification of the original obligation of the transporter, who, in planning the journey, was not in a position to weigh this eventuality. Therefore, the frequent case of the return of the load due to impediments to delivery and for refusal of the recipient is governed by Article 12, fifth paragraph. Further, the request to bring the goods back to the shipper is counter-order, so that the sender becomes the recipient at the same time and his decision is binding within the limits of any other measure adopted, pursuant to Article 12.

5.3 The Redelivery and Its Alternatives

5.3.1 Cash on Delivery

According to Article 21, having accepted the assignment to collect the price for which the goods are charged, if sold, as is usually the case, the carrier must request it before executing the redelivery. Otherwise, "*est tenu d'indemniser l'expéditeur à concurrence du montant du remboursement, sauf son recours contre le destinataire*".[88] According to some Authors,[89] this further obligation would be the subject of an accessory contract, in some civil law systems attributable to a mandate with representation. Instead, for a more convincing reconstruction,[90] it is a clause of the only transport agreement, regarding a further performance than the typical one, and this enriches the obligations of the transporter.[91]

[88] The English text reads, "the carrier shall be liable to the sender for compensation not exceeding the amount of such charge, without prejudice to his right of action against the consignee". Cf. Fremuth (2013), p. 577 ff.

[89] Cf. Silingardi et al. (1994), p. 186 ff.

[90] Cf. Cass. Italy 13 July 1993, no. 7697, in *Arch. civ.,* 1994, 631; Cass. Italy 10 May 1989, no. 2137, in *Dir. trasp.,* 1990, 345; Cass. Italy 21 January 1994, no. 561, *ibid.,* 1995, 273.

[91] Cf. OLG Düsseldorf 13 December 2006, in *TranspR,* 2007, 25. Cf. Messent and Glass (2018), p. 218 ff. See also Fremuth (2013), p. 580 ff.; Riguzzi (2006), p. 190 ff.

Once again, the lack of indication in the consignment note does not invalidate the related provision,[92] as the document has only a probative value, pursuant to Article 4,[93] and the sender can demonstrate by any other means that he asked for the sum to be collected, although, in these situations, this can be difficult, because the documents are very useful. Precisely because cash on delivery must not necessarily result from the consignment note, the recipient cannot demand delivery if the obligation cannot be inferred from this specific act and, therefore, the carrier can prove the agreement on cash on delivery in any way against the consignee, even if the case is brought in front of a judge.

The institute is different from the collection of the costs and the consideration of the transport from the recipient.[94] In fact, in the latter case, the interest of the carrier and not the one of the shipper is relevant. The two matters are heterogeneous, because, as it is obvious, a problem of the transporter's liability arises only in terms of cash on delivery. Therefore, with good reason, the Convention strictly distinguishes the institutions, although both can be provided for the same transport. Regarding the cash on delivery, which usually has the price[95] as its object, the fact that the sender conditions the redelivery to the payment of additional amounts when compared with the consideration for the sale is irrelevant, if clear indications are given on what must be required.

Accuracy is necessary in the definition of the assignment,[96] regarding both the collection methods and the amount. For the carrier to execute the contractual provision, the service must be adequately defined. Thus, the clause "*le règlement s'effectue en contre documents vue sur la banque*", for the generic reference, has not been considered effective, as the transporter could not have refused the return "*en l'absence de remise de documents précis*".[97] Likewise, the expression "*contre*

[92]Cf. Cass. France 22 January 2002, in *Bull. transp.,* 2002, 110; App. Paris 21 October 1970, *ibid.*, 1970, 307; BGH 10 January 1982, in *Europ. transp. law,* 1983, no. 18, 32; Hof Hertogenbosch 13 January 1970, *ibid.*, 1971, no. 6, 817; OLG Düsseldorf 3 December 1990, in *TranspR,* 1991, 91; Cass. Greece 471/2006.

[93]Cf. Silingardi et al. (1994), p. 186 ff.; Putzeys (1981), p. 236 ff.; Pesce (1995), p. 255 ff.; Cabrera Cánovas (2012), p. 150 ff.

[94]Cf. Article 13, second paragraph.

[95]With good reason, see also Messent and Glass (2018), p. 219 ff., according to whom, "for example, the consignee may have agreed with the sender to pay the carriage charges, costs of packing, insurance and these can equally be made the subject matter of Article 21". Cf. *Eastern Kayam Carpets Ltd.* v. *Eastern United Freight Ltd.,* Lexis citation, 1983, 1311; App. Aix - en - Provence 6 November 1981, in *Bull. transp.,* 1982, 258. See also Fremuth (2013), p. 582 ff.

[96]Cf. Messent and Glass (2018), p. 220, according to whom "the sender must take care to ensure that he has communicated his instructions with sufficient clarity". Cf. OLG Düsseldorf 13 December 2006, in *TranspR,* 2007, 25. Cf. also Fremuth (2013), p. 593 ff.

[97]See App. Paris 23 May 2019, *Le Lamy transp.*, 2020, vol. I, 483. See also OLG Düsseldorf 21 April 1994, in *TranspR,* 1995, 67; Cass. France 14 May 2008, in *Europ. transp. law,* 2008, no. 43, 611; GH Hertogenbosch 13 January 1970, *ibid.,* 1971, no. 6, 817.

documents pour solde de notre facture"[98] has been considered obscure, because the desire to subordinate the redelivery to the "*justification du paiement par le destinire du solde du prix des marchandises*"[99] could not be inferred. This last decision is less persuasive, because, albeit badly expressed, the indication of the shipper was quite transparent. On the contrary, a description[100] referring to an "*attestation de blocage de fonds*", an "*attestation bancaire de paiement*" or a "*justificatif de l'ouverture d'un accréditif bancaire*" has been considered sufficient. This conclusion is reasonable, because the will was unambiguously expressed, albeit with imprecise jargon. In a convincing ruling, the carrier was held responsible because he had not realized that he had accepted the copy and not the original of the "*attestation bancaire*", as expected.[101] Then, if the redelivery must be made "*contre attestation de paiement de 65.000 F*",[102] the obligation is not fulfilled if it is not clearly demonstrated that the bank transferred the sum to the shipper's account.

More generally, the sender's order to execute the redelivery after the return of certain documents would not be binding on the transporter, who would not be required to verify their accuracy before accepting them. In fact, for some Authors, one should apply Article 11 of the Convention, according to which the carrier does not have to check the documents for customs operations and, therefore, the request of cash on delivery would only concern the collection of a sum of money.[103] This idea is not convincing, because Article 11 refers to a non-comparable case and, regarding the cash on delivery, the transporter must perform an ancillary service to the main one, aimed at satisfying a particular interest. Therefore, he must act according to professional diligence and execute all the necessary checks to guarantee correspondence between what he receives and what is requested.

So, neither Article 11, invoked in a non-persuasive way, nor Article 21, which, meanwhile, concerns cash on delivery refer exclusively to the collection of money.[104] This would not be conceivable in modern economic society, because of either the complexity of payment methods or the articulation of possible agreements between sender and recipient, normally regarding buying and selling. Therefore,

[98] Cf. Cass. France 21 October 1970, in *Bull. transp.,* 1970, 367. See also App. Paris 19 January 1978, *ibid.,* 1978, 161; Hof Gent 13 September 1995, in *Europ. transp. law,* 1997, no. 32, 602; App. Paris 21 October 1970, in *Bull. transp.,* 1970, 307; App. Paris 26 January 1973, *ibid.,* 1973, 73; Cass. com. France 22 July 1976, *ibid.,* 1976, 416.

[99] Cf. Cass. France 21 October 1970, in *Bull. transp.,* 1970, 367.

[100] Cf. App. Paris 16 January 1991, in *Bull. transp.,* 1991, 173. Cf. also Arrond. Breda 16 February 1969, in *Europ. transp. law,* 1970, no. 5, 67.

[101] Cf. Cass. com. France 20 May 1997, in *Le Lamy transp.*, 2020, vol. I, 483. See also App. Paris 21 April 1989, *ibid.,* 2020, vol. I, 483; App. Versailles 2 March 2000, *ibid.,* 2020, vol. I, 483; Cass. com. France 20 December 1987, *ibid.,* 2020, vol. I, 483.

[102] Cf. App. Paris 27 April 1978, in *Bull. transp.,* 1978, 408.

[103] Cf. App. Paris 23 May 2019, *Le Lamy transp.*, 2020, vol. I, 483; App. Lyon 27 January 1989, *ibid.,* 2020, vol. I, 483.

[104] Cf. Sánchez Gamborino (2001), p. 646 ff.

redelivery can be conditional on any solving behavior of the consignee[105] and, in particular, on the transmission of documents or checks.[106] In the past, the carrier would have been in trouble if he had been entrusted with documents in a foreign language[107] but, today, the problem does not arise. In fact, with a minimum of patience and with modern means of communication, he can ask the shipper for confirmation and, for his peace of mind, he must do so, avoiding putting himself in a condition where this is impossible. For instance, one has to avoid to arrive at the recipient's when, because of the time or a holiday, the sender is not available.

In general, if he is required to deliver after being paid in cash, the transporter can only accept money or a cashier's check, which, if not counterfeit, entails certain fulfillment.[108] When discussing other documents, if he is not sure about their nature or their content, he must withhold the goods and ask for confirmation, thus overcoming many issues. In particular, with regard to the redelivery contingent on the collection of checks, this topic would be left to national law,[109] but this idea cannot be accepted, because it is not clear as to what this should establish and, in any case, the transporter can demand precise instructions to reduce the risk of accepting incorrect payment methods.[110]

Then, as per Article 21, if the carrier fails to comply with his obligation, the sender can act against him and request compensation within the limit of the price, without prejudice to the transporter's action toward the recipient.[111] According to the French version, the carrier must "*indemniser l'expéditeur à concurrence du montant du remboursement*", while the English text says, "the carrier shall be liable to the sender for compensation not exceeding the amount of such charge", and this

---

[105] Cf. Fremuth (2013), p. 588 ff., for the cases of payment by credit card, by check with bank guarantee or by bank check.

[106] Cf. Fremuth (2013), p. 586 ff., for the hypothesis of payment by bank draft or by bank transfer. See Cass. Greece 471/2006.

[107] Cf. Cass. Belgium 18 February 1994, in *Europ. transp. law,* 1994, no. 29, 464, according to which the carrier, which should have collected certified checks, is responsible, before carrying out the delivery, if he accepts documents written in Greek with different completions. Cf. also App. Versailles 2 March 2000, in *Bull. transp.,* 2000, 408; Cass. France 28 September 2004, *ibid.,* 2004, 669, according to which the carrier is not responsible if the bank has refused a check drawn up with slight irregularities.

[108] Cf. BGH 25 October 1995, in *Europ. transp. law,* 1996, no. 31, 404, according to which "acceptance of a check in payment instead of cash does not, in principle, constitute proper performance of the obligation to obtain cash on delivery within the meaning of Article 21 of the CMR".

[109] Cf. Messent and Glass (2018), p. 219 ff., according to whom, "as to whether the carrier is entitled to accept a check in payment of the C. O. D. charges, this is a matter for the relevant national law".

[110] Cf. App. Paris 31 January 1983, in *Bull. transp.,* 1983, 83; Cass. France 28 September 2004. *ibid.,* 2004, 669, according to which the carrier must verify the apparent conformity of the check. Cf. Audienca Provinciale de Alicante 15 June 2005, quoted by Messent and Glass (2018), p. 221 ff., nt. 106, which recognizes the carrier's responsibility in the event of a false check, even more so, if there were elements in this sense.

[111] Cf. Fremuth (2013), p. 613 ff. Cf. BGH 10 October 1991, in *Europ. transp. law,* 1992, no. 27, 262.

has given rise to application uncertainties.[112] In fact, for the French description, the shipper can ask for the total amount in any case, while, based on the indications in English, to obtain the same result, he should demonstrate that he has suffered the corresponding damage. However, the French version captures the spirit of the rule, which requires the transporter to pay what he should have demanded and, thus, the sender can receive the due amount.[113] Truth be told, despite the actual difference between the two versions, significant problems can rarely emerge, because if the consignee's debt is not honored, the prejudice is equal to the full amount. Evidently, if bank checks or documents are to be sent, the carrier is only responsible for their exact receipt, not for the creditworthiness of the issuer. In general, if the latter does not execute what is requested, the transporter must not proceed with the redelivery, but ask for instructions.

Article 21 provides for a compensation limit in favor of the carrier, where it is not required to reimburse further damages with respect to the amount identified in the contract and not collected. Then, he can act against the consignee and, although it is reported concisely, this is subject to uniform law. For example, as regards prescription and jurisdiction, there is no need for referring to national law, although Article 21 is laconic. In fact, the rule is sufficient to circumscribe the object of the request and is in line with the general principles, for which the default of the transporter or malicious behavior that misleads him cannot be to the advantage of the consignee, if he receives the goods without paying.[114]

Article 21 also applies in the case of theft of valuables during the return journey and, furthermore, if the redelivery takes place without payment is requested. Therefore, Article 21 covers any breach by the carrier, with a very incisive liability, despite the compensation limit. Consequently, the consensual provision of the cash should lead to a reasonable increase in the consideration, if only because, in many countries, the transporter has difficulty in agreeing on insurance coverage.

5.3.2 Unloading and Termination of Transport

Article 16, second paragraph, regulates the unloading by the carrier on behalf of the entitled party.[115] By virtue of the reference to Article 14, first paragraph, and Article 15, in many countries, such as Italy, the transporter can resort to this remedy only if

[112] Cf. Messent and Glass (2018), p. 222 ff., according to whom Article 21 "contemplates an award of less than that sum"; Clarke (2014), p. 112 ff.

[113] Cf. App. Grenoble 17 January 2012, in *Bull. transp.*, 2012, 97, according to which the carrier must first pay the recipient and then act against the recipient, and the argument is well founded, because if it does not suffer damage, the carrier cannot act against the recipient. See BGH 10 October 1991, in *Europ. transp. law,* 1992, no. 27, 262, according to which the shipper can demand interest on the amount paid late by the carrier and this argument is also well founded.

[114] Cf. Fremuth (2013), p. 614 ff.

[115] Cf. Temme (2013d), p. 352 ff.; Jung (1997), p. 153 ff.; Otte (2018c), p. 1356 ff.

irreparable impossibility occurs during the journey or at the time of redelivery, and Article 16 does not clarify the relationship between the unloading and the measures of Articles 14 and 15. However, from a joint reading, it can be deduced that the former is an extreme solution, which can be used when it is not possible to comply with new orders, if any, and to those arrived with intolerable delay.

Article 16, second paragraph, presupposes an impossibility of completing the journey, and this one does not concern the fate of the load but another obstacle, which cannot be overcome by the carrier. In fact, the trip does not end because of his declaration, despite the text of the Convention, but due to the objective impossibility of the service, of which the unloading is the result, if there are no other instructions or if a better outcome cannot be seen. The end of the obligation to transport does not depend on the unloading itself, but on the fact that the journey cannot be completed and, excluding the others, this residual measure protects the interests of the sender and the recipient.

The carrier has no power to choose, except for the sale, because he cannot apply Article 16, second paragraph, if there are more useful measures and, at any rate, he can do so only if transport becomes impossible. His original obligation is extinguished for this last reason and if he asks for instructions and either they are not given or they do not offer a better solution. Thus, unloading does not put an end to the obligation to transport, but to the one to wait for directions or to engage in other less traumatic behaviors. Today, with modern means of communication, the carrier should often receive instructions in good time and, therefore, in practice, the application of Article 16, second paragraph, is not frequent, as testified by the few decisions on the matter.

However, if he opts for unloading, the transporter has the right to receive the consideration for the activity performed,[116] of course, if the impediment is beyond his sphere of control. Instead, he keeps on having to hold onto the goods, pursuant to Article 16, second paragraph, and can organize himself as he wishes by coming up with suitable solutions.[117] Thus, he can deposit in the place he is in, if there is a warehouse; however, if he decides to bring the load back if he does not receive compliant indications from the shipper, he is not entitled to compensation for the return, because this is not agreed upon.

According to Article 16, second paragraph, the unloading extinguishes the main obligation, but does not affect the ancillary ones, which continue to be regulated by the transport contract and, therefore, by the Convention. So, the carrier remains in charge of his custody obligation, while waiting for the definitive accommodation of the load, with the application of uniform law, although there are different opinions.[118] But, as the Convention applies, it must regulate further custody, without the

---

[116] Cf. Hof Antwerp January 6, 2014, in *Europ. transp. law,* 2014, no. 49, 341, according to which even in this case the right to compensation is subject to the prescription of Article 31.

[117] Cf. Temme (2013d), p. 354 ff.

[118] On the contrary, cf. Messent and Glass (2018), p. 127 ff.; Clarke (2014), p. 96 ff., for whom the custody activity executed by the carrier after unloading would fall within the national framework.

need to invoke national law, which is not mentioned, unlike what is ruled by Article 16, last paragraph.

Then, if the carrier does not have an establishment *in loco*, he can enter into a deposit agreement with third parties[119] and, in this situation, he is liable only for *culpa in eligendo*, pursuant to Article 16, second paragraph. Therefore, he must choose according to professional diligence, making use of all modern technological resources and research tools compatible with the fact that he is far from his base, such as when he is in a country that speaks an unknown language. So, he must look for an adequate party that is a recognizable operator with his own structure, and negotiate a reasonable price, with reference to both the context and the value of the load. Thus, he is responsible if the warehouse is not suitable for guaranteeing the conservation of the goods, because of a defect that is immediately recognizable.

Then, as per Article 16, second paragraph, the unloading is executed on behalf of "*l'ayant droit*"[120] and, because with this measure the obligation to transport is extinguished, one has to consider this moment to identify the person entitled to it. Therefore, if, at that time, the recipient has not yet acquired the rights, pursuant to Article 12, third paragraph, the shipper still has the power to dispose of the cargo.[121] According to Article 16, second paragraph, "*la marchandise reste grevée des créances résultant de la lettre de voiture et de tous autres frais*".[122] Consequently, if provided, the obligations concerning the cash on delivery and the so-called "assigned port" are not extinguished, but the transporter must inform the depositary of their existence. Upon failing to do so, at the time of delivery, the latter is not liable if he does not collect the consideration for the sale, pursuant to Article 21, or the fee for the transport, on the basis of Article 13, second paragraph, and the relative prejudice remains in the responsibility of the transporter because of his omission.

Finally, uniform law does not regulate the deposit; Article 16 says nothing and domestic law applies, which must be identified on the basis of the general criteria of private international law.[123] Therefore, if this is possible on the basis of the same domestic law, the carrier can stipulate both in his own name and in that of others, that is, presenting himself as the representative of the entitled party, as both solutions are compatible with the Convention, if the claims of the sender and the recipient are not affected. In fact, for those that work in a foreign country, who cannot know the regulation of which in depth, the conclusion of the deposit is not always easy and, to simplify it, the carrier can conclude the contract in his own name, provided that the entitled party is notified. There should be no overwhelming difficulty in transferring

[119] Cf. Temme (2013d), p. 354 ff.

[120] The English text reads, "for account of the person entitled to dispose of them".

[121] Cf. Silingardi et al. (1994), p. 113 ff.

[122] The English text reads, "the charges due under the consignment note and all other expenses shall remain chargeable against the goods".

[123] Cf. Loewe (1976), p. 358 ff., according to whom "there is no particular reason for arguing that the applicable national law should be that to which the contract of carriage would have been subject if CMR had not been applicable". See also Clarke (2014), p. 96 ff.

the load to the entitled party, of course, after the payment of the consideration to the warehouse is made.

5.3.3 Sale

According to Article 16, third paragraph, the carrier can sell the goods under certain circumstances.[124] The perishable nature of the load, its particular condition, or the excessive burden of the deposit, when compared with the value, may lead to resorting to this measure without waiting for instructions from the entitled party. The reference to "*l'état de la merchandise*"[125] is somewhat obscure and, perhaps, such an occurrence could be encountered when, although not perishable by its nature, the load may undergo an alteration in its composition or in its appearance, because of exposure to a risk induced more by contingencies than by the intrinsic characteristics of the wares. Basically, Article 16, third paragraph, draws an institution that is in some way extreme, as it is aimed at remedying situations of urgency, wherein the conservation of assets would be contrary to the interests of the entitled party.

The sale can also be arranged if, within a reasonable yet not precisely identified timeframe, the transporter does not receive different orders, the execution of which can be demanded and feasible.[126] Hence, alienation is an alternative solution to unloading and any other less drastic measure. If the instructions are received in time, the carrier may oppose to the entitled party the same limits as in Article 12, fifth paragraph, letter b), provided for the counter-order.[127] In any case, the transporter must take some suitable initiative to preserve the interests of the shipper and, thus, if the recipient refuses the redelivery, the former is held responsible if a long period of time passes by before any definitive step is taken, especially if the goods are then alienated at low price.[128] Not only urgency justifies the sale, but it is the same if a standstill is too long.

[124] Cf. Temme (2013d), p. 356 ff.; Jung (1997), p. 153 ff.

[125] The English text reads, "their condition warrants such a course".

[126] Cf. Loewe (1976), p. 359 ff., according to whom the carrier cannot execute those instructions "which are so unreasonable that they would involve the loss of or at any rate some serious deterioration in the value of the goods, since the carrier might in such a case suffer a loss from the fact that he would no longer be able to consider the goods as sufficient security for his expenses".

[127] Cf. Loewe (1976), p. 359 ff., according to whom "the instructions which the carrier may reasonably be required to carry out are instructions which comply with the requirements of Article 12, paragraph 5, letter b), provided that such instructions can be carried out". See also Messent and Glass (2018), p. 129 ff.

[128] Cf. Cass. com. France 23 May 1977, in *Bull. transp.*, 1977, 388; App. Paris 25 October 1995, *ibid.*, 1995, 362.

Article 16 does not explicitly address the connection between the institutions of the second and third paragraphs. However, if the custody after the unloading lasts too long, the sale must be made, except in case of an agreement on the return journey, which is always possible. Basically, the proceeds of the alienation must be kept at the disposal of the entitled party,[129] and the carrier can withhold the costs that affect the goods, but must return any remainder. In case costs are higher, he is entitled to the difference, which must be paid by the shipper.[130]

According to some,[131] the sale should always be preceded by the unloading, pursuant to Article 16, second paragraph. Therefore, the transporter would be the depositary and only in that capacity would he be required to ask the entitled party for instructions before the alienation of the goods. This idea is unfounded, because, as mentioned, the unloading pursuant to Article 16, second paragraph, extinguishes the obligation to transport, not the overall relationship, and the carrier always remains bound by a single contract, without ever assuming a different responsibility. Furthermore, national law does not apply. Meanwhile, if, after the sale, the buyer asks the transporter to deliver the load to himself, to execute this transfer the carrier can sign another contract,[132] although this scenario is unlikely to happen.

With regard to the methods of sale, Article 16, fifth paragraph, refers to the domestic law of the place where the goods[133] are located. The rule is complex to implement, as the transporter should know the regulations of the country of destination and have a person *in loco* to assist him in the related operations. Failing to do so, he is bound to face issues. Anyway, the Convention could not have opted for a different solution, because the place wherein the alienation must be executed influences the choice in an unavoidable way and recourse must be made to the relevant national law.

---

[129] Cf. Messent and Glass (2018), p. 129 ff.

[130] The French text reads, "*si la marchandise a été vendue (...), le produit de la vente doit être mis à la disposition de l'ayant droit, déduction faite des frais grevant la marchandise. Si ses frais sont supérieurs au produit de la vente, le transporteur a droit à la différence*". The English text reads, "if the goods have been sold (...), the proceeds of sale, after deduction of the expenses chargeable against the goods, shall be placed at the disposal of the person entitled to dispose the goods. If the charges exceed the proceeds of sale, the carrier shall be entitled to the difference".

[131] Cf. Messent and Glass (2018), p. 129 ff, according to whom, "at the time of sale, the goods must have been unloaded as provided for by Article 16, paragraph 2 and are being either by the carrier himself or by a third party". See also Loewe (1976), p. 359 ff., according to which "the second sentence must be understood to mean, though this is not stately expressly, that, if the conditions referred to in the first sentence are not satisfied, the carrier which has become a depositary must first seek instructions from the person entitled to dispose of the goods if he wants to sell them".

[132] Cf. Messent and Glass (2018), p. 129 ff., according to whom, "where the goods have not been unloaded and the sale involves further carriage, this will of course be subject to a fresh contract of carriage with the buyer".

[133] Cf. Temme (2013d), p. 358 ff.

References

Cabrera Cánovas A (2012) Jurisprudencia del Tribunal Supremo español en materias reguladas por el Convenio CMR. In: Sánchez-Gamborino F, Cabrera Cànovas A (eds) El convenio CMR: el contrado de transporte internacional de mercancías por carretera. Barcelona, p 129 ff

Clarke MA (2014) International carriage of goods by road: CMR. New York, ed. 6

Fremuth F (2013) Article 21. In: Aa. Vv., Thume KH (ed) CMR: über den Beförderungsvertrag im Internationalen Strassengüterverkehr. Frankfurt am Main, ed. 3, p 577 ff

Jung C (1997) The Convention on the contract for the international carriage of goods by road (CMR): survey, analysis and trends of recent German case law. Unif Law Rev:148 ff

Krings E (1999) C. M. R.: examen de la jurisprudence des Cours de Cassation de France et de Pays – Bas (première partie). Unif Law Rev:160 ff

Loewe R (1976) Commentary on the Convention of 19 May 1956 on the Contract for the International Carriage of Goods by Road. Eur Transp Law 10:311 ff

Messent A, Glass DA (2018) CMR: contracts for the international carriage of goods by road. New York, ed. 4

Otte K (2018a) Art. 14 der CMR. In: Aa. Vv., Internationales Vertragsrecht. Munich, p 1345 ff

Otte K (2018b) Art. 15 der CMR. In: Aa. Vv., Internationales Vertragsrecht. Munich, p 1351 ff

Otte K (2018c) Art. 16 der CMR. In: Aa. Vv., Internationales Vertragsrecht. Munich, p 1359 ff

Pesce A (1995) Il trasporto internazionale di merci. Turin

Putzeys J (1981) Le contrat de transport routier de marchandises. Brussels

Riguzzi M (2006) I contratti speciali. Il contratto di trasporto. In: Tratt. dir. priv., directed by Bessone, vol XIV. Turin

Rodière R (1971) The Convention on road transport. Eur Transp Law 6:1 ff

Sánchez Gamborino FJ (2001) La Conventión CMR según la Jurisprudencia del 'Tribunal Supremo' de España. Eur Transp Law 36:842 ff

Silingardi G, Corrado A, Meotti A, Morandi F (1994) La disciplina uniforme del contratto di trasporto di cose su strada. Turin

Temme J (2013a) Article 12. In: Aa. Vv., Thume KH (ed) CMR: über den Beförderungsvertrag im Internationalen Strassengüterverkehr. Frankfurt am Main, ed. 3, p 304 ff

Temme J (2013b) Article 14. In: Aa. Vv., Thume KH (ed) CMR: über den Beförderungsvertrag im Internationalen Strassengüterverkehr. Frankfurt am Main, ed. 3, p 333 ff

Temme J (2013c) Article 15. In: Aa. Vv., Thume KH (ed) CMR: über den Beförderungsvertrag im Internationalen Strassengüterverkehr. Frankfurt am Main, ed. 3, p 340 ff

Temme J (2013d) Article 16. In: Aa. Vv., Thume KH (ed) CMR: über den Beförderungsvertrag im Internationalen Strassengüterverkehr. Frankfurt am Main, ed. 3, p 352 ff

Wesolowski K (2013) A review of judicial decisions of the Polish Supreme Court within the scope of CMR. Eur Transp Law 48:341 ff

References

Chapter 6
Charges

Contents

6.1 Nature of Charges

6.1.1 Determining Charges

The contract of carriage regulated by the Convention is for consideration,[1] as confirmed by Article 1, which explicitly states that point, with the consequence that any free-of-charge contractual relationships are not subject to uniform law. This is in congruence with the intention of considering ordinary commercial traffic and with the idea of a regulation of professional activity, not of occasional trips undertaken for friendship or various reasons. These rare cases are excluded from the application of the Convention, within the scope of which the right to payment is fully included, despite its determination being left to the unconditional exercise of negotiating autonomy, without any specific provision.[2]

[1]Cf. Putzeys (1981), pp. 15 ff., according to whom "*le contrat de transport est un contrat onéreux, ce qui exclut du champ de notre examen le transport bénévole*". See also Messent and Glass (2018), pp. 19 ff.; Silingardi et al. (1994), pp. 13 ff.; De la Motte and Temme (2013), pp. 86 ff.

[2]Cf. Putzeys (1981), pp. 61 ff., according to whom "*la fixation du prix peut ne pas être concomitante à sa formation*".

C. Tincani, *Contract for the International Carriage of Goods by Road*, Law for Professionals, https://doi.org/10.1007/978-3-031-08487-4_6

No contradiction exists between the necessary correspondence between the remuneration of the carrier's performance and the lack of rules on the criteria for quantifying the former. In fact, Article 1 defines the scope left to the intervention of the Treaty, which refrains from establishing how the price is to be calculated, although the Convention covers the related credit in full, for instance, with regard to the provisions on the jurisdiction,[3] arbitration[4] or prescription.[5] Completed in 1956, the CMR reflects its time, in which a regulation of remuneration would have appeared, on one hand, detrimental to contractual freedom and, on the other hand, superfluous, due to the trust placed in market mechanisms. At least in some national contexts, different approaches have been considered over the years; in road traffic, it was deemed necessary to peremptorily regulate the amount of fee[6] on the recommendation of the European Union.[7] However, these transformations have not affected the Convention, which has remained faithful to its original structure, and, truth be told, discordant voices are few.

The nonexistence of a provision on the calculation of remuneration does not prevent the operation of national law if the matter is covered by a set of rules, and the silence of the Convention does not count as a prohibition of the same regulation; rather, it underlines the irrelevance of the problem *vis-à-vis* the objectives of uniform law. These conclusions are confirmed in Article 6 regarding the necessary information to be recorded in the consignment note, which is required to summarize all significant elements for the contract and the trip. In fact, Article 6, first paragraph, letter i), and Article 6, second paragraph, letter b),[8] require the specification of both the payment and the expenses, indicated with univocal expressions in the English[9] and French[10] texts.

Both contrast the consideration with "charges" or different "*frais*", proposing a synthetic list and using notions of common experience, without a definition or a specific regulation. In fact, these concepts belong to the common practice of any country and do not need any particular clarification, if ever specific clauses in the agreements stipulated, precisely with confirmation in the consignment note or, in any

[3]Cf. Article 31.

[4]See Article 33.

[5]Cf. Article 32.

[6]In Italy, the fork tariff system was introduced with law no. 298 of 6 June 1974.

[7]Cf. the EEC regulation of 30 July 1968, no. 1174, which was followed by the EEC regulation of 12 December 1977, no. 2831.

[8]Cf. Messent and Glass (2018), pp. 92 ff.; Clarke (2014), pp. 20 ff.

[9]The English text of Article 6, first paragraph, letter i), reads, "charges relating to the carriage (carriage charges, supplementary charges, customs duties, and other charges incurred from making of the contract to the time of delivery); in Article 6, second paragraph, letter b), it reads, "the charges which the sender undertakes to pay".

[10]The French text of Article 6, first paragraph, letter i), reads, "*les frais afférents au transport (prix de transport, frais accessoires, droits de douane et autres frais surveneant à partir de la conclusion du contra jusqu'à la livraison)*"; in Article 6, second paragraph, letter b), it reads, "*les frais que l'expéditeur prend à sa charge*".

case, in the contract, without prejudice to Article 4,[11] for which the nonexistence and, *a fortiori*, the incompleteness of the consignment note do not cause any invalidity. The parties normally agree on a lump sum price, which may be nonmodifiable[12] or reviewable if one of them changes the transaction terms or fails to fulfill completely its obligations.[13] Thus, if a transporter agrees on an overall fee inclusive of customs clearance costs, the amount also covers those related to the stop necessary for these operations.[14]

After so many years, the Convention's decision not to deal with the amount and criteria for determining the consideration should be considered wise, not because such a provision should be viewed as unreasonable in itself, considering that there have been indications from the European Union law.[15] However, due to the enormous geographical scope of the Convention, there cannot be such an extensive unitary market and there cannot be a credible lawgiver with regard to its economic aspect. Uniform law pertains to the fundamental provisions of the contract, while the possible regulation of the fee is aimed at market configuration and settlement of expectations of the relative operators. It would be unrealistic to pursue such an aim for dozens of countries that apply the Convention. In each State, the structure and the *modus operandi* of the companies are often different. From this perspective, uniform law has successfully overcome several decades of intense application precisely because of the original prudence of its approach; within the limits of its aims, it has understood well the difference between an impossible unitary regulation of the market and an indispensable regulation of the agreement. This does not prevent a synthetic reflection on the consideration within the scope of the Convention itself, as some rules refer to it, albeit in line with other provisions, starting with those relating to the consignment note.

---

[11] See: Messent and Glass (2018), pp. 87 ff.; Clarke (2014), pp. 59 ff.; Putzeys (1981), pp. 117 ff., according to whom "*the lettre de voiture routière est un document here contains the contracts of transport, ma ne le constitue pas*".

[12] Cf. App. Chambéry 22 June 1982, in *Le Lamy transp.*, 2020, vol. I, 484.

[13] Cf. App. Paris 15 February 1985, in *Le Lamy transp.*, 2020, vol. I, 484, for a scenario where the consideration is reduced, due to the sudden costs incurred by the client for organizational shortcomings attributable to the freight forwarder. See also App. Paris 16 September 1992, *ibid.*, 2020, vol. I, 484; App. Lyon 16 February 2010, *ibid.*, 2020, vol. I, 484. See also Cass. com. France 19 November 1996, in *Bull. transp. logist.*, 1996, 878, according to which significant modifications of the consideration subsequent to the stipulation of the contract can justify the carrier's refusal to perform according to the various conditions and lead to the termination of the contract.

[14] Cf. App. Paris 21 April 1983, in *Le Lamy transp.*, 2020, vol. I, 484. See also App. Orléans 20 January 1982, in *Bull. transp.*, 1982, 233, for which the lump price cannot be changed because a foreign country has established a "*taxe de transit*"; App. Paris March 13, 1986, in *Le Lamy transp.*, 2020, vol. I, 484; Cass. com. France 20 March 1990, *ibid.*, 2020, vol. I, 484, according to which the lump price cannot be changed following the increase in the rate of the currency used for payment.

[15] Cf. Regulation (EC) no. 1174 of 30 July 1968, which was followed by Regulation (EC) no. 2831 of 12 December 1977.

6.1.2 Charges and the Consignment Note

Article 6 describes in detail the content of the consignment note, indicating in the first paragraph the necessary elements, i. e., those that cannot be ignored when drafting it and those to be added only if contemplated in the specific agreements in the second paragraph. The payment is included in the first group; in particular, according to Article 6, first paragraph, letter i), expenses must be reported and divided into "*prix de transport, frais accessoires, droits de douane et autres frais survenant à partir de la conclusion du contrat jusqu'à la livraison*".[16] It is not always easy to identify in advance what costs may have supervened between the conclusion of the agreement and the redelivery of goods and, in this regard, doubts have arisen regarding the appropriateness of the described rule, with good reason.[17] The additional expenses can often be quantified only after the end of the journey, with an obvious forecasting difficulty at the time when the consignment note is filled in.

According to some,[18] the calculation of the precise amount should be postponed to a later stage without compromising the carrier's reasons, as an initial general reference would be sufficient. Although reasonable, the solution is not consistent with Article 6, first paragraph, letter i), which identifies in detail the items into which travel costs are divided. The failure to immediately specify the expenses that may arise involves a violation of the same Article 6, especially because the first paragraph groups the fundamental elements and the rule is mandatory, according to Article 41, regardless of the consequences of the omission, considering Article 4. There is no reason to depart from the conclusions reached on the whole system of the note. Thus, in the event of failure to report the expenses to be borne by the consignee, if the relative amount is not requested from him upon redelivery, he does not have to pay it pursuant to a subsequent request, at least according to a ruling dating to some time back,[19] but it would be different if the recipient's awareness of the consensual provision of such disbursements could be demonstrated in another way, as, in the event of deficiencies in the note, it is always possible to provide proof of agreements in a different manner.

According to Article 6, second paragraph, letter b), the parties may indicate "*les frais que l'expéditeur prend à sa charge*".[20] More generally, the regulation

---

[16]The English text reads, "carriage charges, supplementary charges, customs duties, and other charges incurred from making of the contract to the time of delivery".

[17]Cf. Messent and Glass (2018), pp. 94 ff., according to whom "this requirement can rarely be completely satisfied, as often it is not clear what supplementary charges have been incurred until after delivery".

[18]Cf. *T Comedy (U. K.) Ltd.* c. *Easy managed Transport Ltd.*, in *Lloyd's rep.*, 2007, 397.

[19]Cf. OLG Hamm 12 November 1973.

[20]In the English text, we read: "the charges which the sender undertakes to pay". Cf. App. Montpellier 27 May 2003, in *Bull. transp. logist.*, 2003, 437, according to which the costs are to be borne by the consignee if the shipper does not declare that he will bear them in whole or in part.

contemplated in the second paragraph "must be based on conditions stipulated by parties at the latest at the time of signature of the consignment note".[21] However, this does not preclude demonstrating by other means an agreement subsequent to the compilation of the note,[22] pursuant to Article 4. According to Article 7, first paragraph, the shipper is liable for the losses and damages suffered by the carrier for the "inaccuracy"[23] and "inadequacy"[24] of elements contemplated in Article 6, second paragraph. The incorrect indication of transport charges entails the liability to the carrier for consequent damages and the effects of this provision extend to the failure to mention what is laid down in Article 6, second paragraph, letter b), after the agreement with the carrier.[25]

6.1.3 Changes to the Charges While the Carriage Is Being Conducted

The Convention contemplates some hypotheses of modification of the "*frais afférents au transport*" during the journey. In the first place, exercise of the power of counter—order involves changes in the itinerary. In regulating the methods of implementation, Article 12, fifth paragraph, letter a), allows the carrier to request, in addition to any compensation for damages, reimbursement of the expenses incurred to comply with the new instructions.[26] The provision is consistent with the objective of encouraging collaboration between the sender and carrier. The former's power to create deviations from the original program must be coordinated with the latter's need to recover the high costs associated with such order; however, the rule does not specify how the quantification should take place. Just like the shipper, the transporter exercises a unilateral power over the consideration and, within the limits of reasonableness, the parties must cooperate for the benefit of faster circulation of goods.

Article 12, fifth paragraph, letter a), distinguishes various consequences of the countermand, lest the interest of the carrier be damaged, a problem unrelated to that of the consideration. These prejudices are distinguished from the increase in the fee of a contractual nature and related to the greater professional commitment required for the unexpected modification of the itinerary. Although the rule does not express itself on the quantification criteria and there is no regulation, at least implicitly the

[21] Cf. Loewe (1976), pp. 339 ff.

[22] Cf. Loewe (1976), pp. 339 ff.

[23] The French text reads, "*de l'inexactitude*".

[24] The French text reads, "*de l'insuffisance*".

[25] Cf. Loewe (1976), pp. 339 ff., according to whom "the terms 'inaccuracy' and 'inadequacy' cover also the absence of these particulars, since if inadequacy gives rise to responsibility, the same consequence must follow *a fortiori* in the absence of the particulars in question".

[26] Cf. Temme (2013a), pp. 304 ff.

contrast between compensation for prejudices and stipulation of a high consideration emphasizes how the latter must be calculated in a balanced way and reasonably correspond to the objective expectations, if taking into account the sudden nature of the request. Since that of counter—order is a power recognized by the uniform law, its exercise cannot be thwarted by exorbitant requests, in contrast with the spirit of Article 12, even if its text says nothing to that effect.

For Article 14, first paragraph, the carrier who is unable to continue under the conditions indicated in the consignment note or, in any case, as agreed at the beginning, must ask for instructions from the person who has the right to dispose of the goods,[27] pursuant to Article 12. In this case, any variation of the original itinerary does not depend on a subjective evaluation by the sender, but on an unexpected event, which requires finding alternative solutions, suitable for guaranteeing the conclusion of the trip. Thus, in the presence of a supervened impediment, the transporter must identify the person to contact to ask for instructions and, in turn, this person may issue them, showing the first copy of the note.

Despite the different premises, the instructions have the same effects as those provided for by Article 12, as they determine a unilateral modification of the relationship, making compliance therewith binding, except for what is laid down on expenses by Article 16, first paragraph: this rule reflects the approach of Article 12, fifth paragraph, letter a).[28] Therefore, the carrier can recover the additional costs caused by his request for instructions or consequential on their execution, with the exception of those attributable to his possible negligent behavior,[29] pursuant to Article 16, first paragraph.[30] For some,[31] this rule would enjoin an assessment of the transporter's conduct with reference not only to the request for instructions, but also to the supervened events, which made normal execution of the journey impossible. If they were attributable to the negligent conduct of the carrier, the latter could not recover the expenses necessary for the implementation of alternative solutions, aimed at allowing the end of the journey and planned by the subject entitled to dispose of the goods.[32] Furthermore, the fault of the transporter is equated to that of his "servants or agents",[33] as, even in this case, Article 3 of the Convention would apply. Therefore, payment of the additional costs incurred to resolve difficulties created by unwary assistants could not be requested.

---

[27] The English text reads, "from the person entitled to dispose of the goods in accordance with the provisions of the Article 12"; the French text reads, "*à la personne qui a le droit de disposer de la marchandise conformément à l'Article 12*".

[28] Cf. Temme (2013b), pp. 349 ff.

[29] The French text reads, "*à moins que ses frais ne soient la conséquence de sa faute*"; the English text reads, "unless such expenses were caused by the wrongful act or neglect of the carrier".

[30] Cf. Temme (2013b), pp. 347 ff.; Jung (1997), pp. 153 ff.; Fillers (2020), pp. 190 ff.

[31] Cf. Messent and Glass (2018), pp. 126 ff.; Loewe (1976), pp. 357 ff.; Rodière (1971), pp. 7 ff.

[32] Cf. Loewe (1976), pp. 357 ff.; Rodière (1971), pp. 7 ff.

[33] Cf. Messent and Glass (2018), pp. 126 ff.

Both these ideas are well-founded, as they allow for a balanced settlement of the interests involved. If the problem can still be traced back to a default by the carrier, the high costs have to be borne by him and he cannot assert them against whoever offers him instructions. If anything, the contrast inherent in Article 16, first paragraph, between the expenses caused by the request for instructions and those due for their execution, is even too detailed, as, in any case, the same complex situation is being discussed.

For Article 16, first paragraph, with some fussiness, it is necessary to distinguish between the costs caused by the interruption of the journey and the request for instructions and those, more likely, related to their implementation. The former one depends on the need to suspend or slow down the transfer narrowly understood, and the latter one is connected to the possible modification of the itinerary. In this regard, the similarity with the exercise of the counter—order is even clearer. Moreover, Article 12, fifth paragraph, letter a), and Article 16, first paragraph, belong to the same regulatory context and underline how the original consideration must be referred to the initial agreements. The correspondence of the contract causes a transformation of the price if there are significant changes in the obligations of the carrier, without prejudice to his duty to allow the completion of the journey in the two aforementioned cases. Therefore, these rules reinforce the principle of correspondence, providing for its application also in the case of a change in obligations.

6.1.4 Recovery of Expenses

The Convention introduces further hypotheses of modification of the consideration. In fact, Article 10 establishes, on one hand, a liability of the shipper for damage to persons or goods resulting from packaging defects and, on the other hand, the possibility for the carrier to recover the costs incurred due to defective packaging.[34] The first considers the damage in all its variants and, therefore, does not concern the consideration. Conversely, the second part of Article 10 regarding costs is relevant. The provision does not specify them, but refers, in general, to the "expenses resulting from defective package".[35] Therefore, according to some, Article 10 would refer both to the expenses related to the adoption of measures necessary to prevent the damage and to those aimed at remedying it, once it occurred.[36] The observation is acceptable, as the overall effort of the shipper for the implementation of the initial program, with his transcendence of obstacles that appeared at any time, must be considered. There is no responsibility of the sender if the imperfection of the wrapping is apparent or known at the time of receipt and the transporter formulates

---

[34]The English text reads, "for any expenses due to defective package of the goods"; the French text reads, "*les frais, qui auraient pour origine la défectuosité de la marchandise*".

[35]Cf. Messent and Glass (2018), pp. 104 ff.

[36]Cf. Messent and Glass (2018), pp. 104 ff.

no reservations. To recover the expenses, pursuant to Article 10, he must prove that the defect is not identifiable at the beginning of the journey; alternatively, if, at that juncture, the anomaly is evident or known, the relative reservations must be appended to the consignment note.

Then, according to Article 14, first paragraph, and Article 15, both of which are quoted in Article 16, in the presence of impediments occurring during the journey or at the time of redelivery, the carrier must ask for instructions from the person entitled to dispose of the goods. Only if such indications do not arrive on time can he opt for other measures taken on his own initiative, if in keeping with the interests of the person entitled to disposal of the goods; in fact, unloading is considered "the *extrema ratio* which can be used in the absence of other solutions"[37] and, once this operation is completed, the journey is considered finished and the carrier assumes the custody of the goods, unless he decides to entrust it to a third-party.[38] According to Article 16, second paragraph, the cargo "*reste grevée des créances résultant de la lettre de voiture et de tous autres frais*"[39] and, therefore, in addition to the consideration, the transporter can request other costs, connected with unloading and the subsequent phase. Since, with the deposit, the trip has ended, but the obligatory relationship is not extinguished, the expression "*autres frais*"[40] must not only include out-of-pocket expenses, represented by the necessary disbursements, but also the hoped-for profit for the attainment of which the carrier agrees to execute the transport. The parties must reach an agreement, as a meeting point between opposing interests; in entirety, Article 16, second paragraph, "anticipates the consequences envisaged by the subsequent third paragraph (. . .), concerning the sale".[41]

In fact, according to Article 16, third paragraph, without waiting for instructions, the carrier can order the alienation in three cases: when the goods are perishable or their state suggests it; when there is no proportion between the storage costs and the value; and, finally, when the person entitled to dispose of the load has not given contrary indications, within a reasonable time. In essence, alienation is a further hypothesis compared with continuation of the journey and redelivery and contrasts with unloading, which the transporter can trail after a certain period. For Article 16, fourth paragraph, the proceeds must be made available to the person entitled to dispose of the goods, "*déduction faite des frais grevant la merchandise*".[42] As in the

---

[37] Cf. Silingardi et al. (1994), pp. 112 ff.

[38] Cf. OGH May 15, 2002, in *Europ. transp. law,* 2003, n. 38, 512, according to which, "where, as a result of technical traffic problems, the place of delivery could not be reached by road carriage and consequently the carrier by road transferred the goods on a smaller vehicle to another carrier who performed the subsequent carriage, such action does not constitute the termination of the carriage within the meaning of Article 16, second paragraph".

[39] The English text reads, "the charges due under the consignment note and all other expenses shall remain chargeable against the goods". Cf. Temme (2013b), pp. 359 ff.

[40] The English text reads, "all other expenses".

[41] Cf. Silingardi et al. (1994), pp. 113 ff.

[42] The English text reads, "after deduction of the expenses chargeable against the goods". Cf. Temme (2013b), pp. 359 ff.

case of custody, in determining costs, not only those strictly incurred for the procedure must be calculated, but also the expected profit, quantified by agreement. In this way, the interest in a balanced consideration is safeguarded, under the principle of correspondence that leads to a modification of the fee for all significant changes in the obligations. Finally, for Article 16, fourth paragraph, if the expenses are higher than the proceeds, the carrier may sue for the difference.[43]

In all these cases, we refer to the concept of "expenses",[44] because the rules ramify from situations outside the sphere of control of the transporter, such as to cause him obstacles, with consequent disservices. Therefore, the initial project is altered, thereby impacting the linear development of the activity and original organizational strategy. However, as the carrier is asked to deal with issues caused by events outside his sphere of control, the mere reimbursement of the out-of-pocket costs incurred and the amounts paid to third-parties is not enough. On the contrary, it is necessary to rebalance the consideration, so that the transporter's economic interest is safeguarded, despite the fact that he faces unfavorable contingencies, which must not reduce his reasonable profit. As the Convention lacks a quantification of the consideration, even when its adjustment is postulated, it is still left to private autonomy, without expressly providing for a judicial intervention to settle any conflicts. If anything, the limited extent of the amounts helps in favor of reaching an agreement, and the lack of jurisprudential precedents demonstrates the reasonableness of the choice of the uniform law.

In Article 16, the right of the carrier to seek redress against the goods or the price obtained for the satisfaction of his claims is stressed several times and, if this solution has been generally successful in transport law, it is, in any case, a derogation from the its normal criteria. The approach is rational, especially if one thinks of 1956s Europe, when, at a great distance from the place of departure, it could have been convenient for the carrier to have a regulatory resource for fulfilling his claims. Presently, amid the frenzy of contemporary traffic, this vestige from past times could induce a smile from us, as the primary objective is not to keep vehicles parked. It would be strange if a transporter had opposite ideas and was interested in exercising his right against goods or the price obtained, when there are much simpler forms of credit protection, in court, albeit without certainty of the result. In summary, the practical importance of this part of Article 16 is negligible. In addition, the Convention does not provide for "rights of lien"[45] on load; for some,[46] the exercise of these rights would be governed by the national law. The thesis is not very convincing, as uniform law has regulated the matter by recognizing a right in favor of the carrier, mentioned in Article 16. Aspects not covered by the Convention cannot be supplemented by the domestic law.

[43] Cf. Temme (2013b), pp. 358 ff.

[44] The French text reads, "*frais*".

[45] Cf. Messent and Glass (2018), pp. 128 ff.

[46] Cf. Messent and Glass (2018), pp. 128 ff.

6.2 The Carrier's Right to Charges

6.2.1 Charges and Delivery

With the delivery, the carrier concludes the carriage operation and, having fulfilled his obligation, can ask for compensation, if the contract does not provide otherwise. In congruence with the principle of correspondence, the right arises with the implementation of the consensual program. Any agreements between the sender and transporter on payment methods are irrelevant, because one thing is to regulate the time and another is to establish its prerequisite. For example, if advance payment is stipulated, the amount must be returned if the carrier fails to complete the journey. According to Article 16, second paragraph, following the occurrence of impediments during the transfer or redelivery, the carrier can opt to unload the goods. By express provision, once this operation has been conducted, the journey is considered complete, but the obligatory relationship continues, so that the load remains burdened by credits linked to the consideration;[47] this is related to the performance by the carrier and its execution triggers the right, even if the transfer does not end in a physiological sense with the redelivery, as in the scenario dealt with in Article 16, second paragraph.

In the absence of redelivery or an equivalent fact, the carrier may not obtain the consideration, and this is the case of total loss or destruction of the entire load, also pursuant to Article 23, fourth paragraph. The two hypotheses are analogous, as they prevent the right to compensation from arising, considering that the common goal is not achieved, as a German decision highlights.[48] If the price has been paid, it must be returned. Total loss presupposes the nonarrival of goods, while, if destroyed, the load reaches its destination, but is compromised in its entirety and, therefore, is useless: in this case, we would talk of loss in an economic sense.[49] Complete destruction or loss is identical in consequences and do not entitle one to consideration, but oblige a party to pay compensation, if there is liability.

Delays and damages are different as, unlike other scenarios, they involve redelivery. In both cases, the cargo arrives at its destination with some anomaly, either because the deadline within which it should have arrived is not complied with, or due to an alteration of its condition, capable of partially compromising its integrity. Despite the imperfections, the consignee may have an interest in the redelivery and, if requested, the carrier is entitled to the consideration, as the transport ends, but the carrier himself is required to pay compensation for damages. Simultaneously, the transporter is a creditor and debtor; thus, by considering both profiles, the reciprocal reasons are defined through an ordinary algebraic operation. The violation of the redelivery deadline, in particular, and the consequent delay do

[47] Cf. Messent and Glass (2018), pp. 126 ff.

[48] Cf. OLG Munich 18 October 2001, in *TranspR*, 2002, 27.

[49] Cf. Putzeys (1981), pp. 229 ff.

not exclude the right to consideration,[50] as the trip is completed, even if the obligation to bring it to an end within the stipulated time remains unfulfilled. However, although this nonfulfillment may lead to compensation for the prejudice, according to Article 23, fifth paragraph, the transfer is completed, as demonstrated by the redelivery, with the related acceptance by the consignee and with the resultant right of the carrier to the consideration.

In essence, full autonomy in determining the timeframes and methods of payment is different from the identification of the prerequisite for the rise of the right, which is linked to the completion of the trip and achievement of the corresponding economic benefits, regardless of the fact that the transfer is partial or late. In any case, the operation achieves its purpose contemplated by the Convention. There is no contradiction between this idea and the introduction in CMR of a compensatory obligation, deriving precisely from the transporter's breach, as the contract is implemented, albeit not perfectly. *A fortiori*, compensation is due if the journey does not reach its scheduled end, without the carrier's responsibility and for circumstances deemed outside his sphere of control, on the basis of the uniform law. Then, if the loss is total, in a physical[51] or economic[52] sense, but there is no responsibility on the transporter's part, the contract fails to fulfill its purpose and the consideration is not due, without prejudice to the nonexistence of a compensatory obligation.

Finally, in the event of partial fulfillment, the consideration must not be restructured in proportion to the part of the undamaged goods. Thus, if some packages arrive intact, the fee is not reduced, but it is necessary to refer to the contractual will and, if a total price is provided, it must be paid in full, always subject to compensation for prejudices, if due. The agreement rarely states a fee proportional to the quantity or weight of the goods and, indeed, based on commercial practices, this eventuality is marginal, in line moreover with the centrality of the result in the consensual program. This element offers little importance to quantitative criteria, rarely considered in the identification of the consideration, which is mostly unitary and all-inclusive. Therefore, in the event of partial fulfillment, the payment is usually due in full, unless an opposite contractual indication can be reconstructed.

6.2.2 *The Carrier's Charges and the Manner in Which They May Be Levied*

The prerequisite for the consideration is the completion of the trip, and the uniform law contemplates fee as an essential element, as, for Article 1, only contracts for fee

[50] Cf. Cass. com. France 6 October 1975, in *Bull. transp.*, 1975, 478, which, wrongly, rejected the carrier's request for payment of the consideration on the grounds that delivery was delayed.

[51] Cf. BGH 10 December 2009, in *TranspR*, 2010, 78; BGH 13 February 1980, in *VersR*, 1980, 533; BGH 15 October 1992, in *TranspR*, 1993, 137.

[52] Cf. Putzeys (1981), pp. 229 ff.

fall within its scope. Regulation of the implementing aspects is left to contractual autonomy; for example, the parties decide whether the consideration is unitary or proportional to the weight and number of packages or whether payment is anticipated or deferred, as well as identify the place of fulfillment.

The carrier can undertake repeated journeys for the same sender, and the fees can be distinguished for each service or take the form of a global sum or the same one for each route. Therefore, the pecuniary obligation must be defined in the agreement in all its aspects, without legal limits with regard to the deadline, repetition of the services, presence of terms or conditions and any other relevant profile, with various solutions, *a fortiori* in this epoch of feverish recourse to electronic means and innovative financial and organizational solutions. All that remains is to trace back the regulation of credit to the Convention, without the operation of the national law.

Once the goods in custody have been received, the carrier does not always arrange at once for their transfer and, pending the order from the shipper, may keep them in storage before departure. In this case, the consideration might relate to the entire operation, including the phase prior to the journey narrowly understood. In fact, the supposed logistics contract[53] has made the structure of operators more complex, with an expansion of traditional functions in terms of storage, packaging, preparation of goods and their arrangement in anticipation of distribution. These operations are components of an activity focused on transport and, for this more sophisticated organization, the consideration reflects the greater articulation of services, enriched by functions that are heterogeneous and yet connected in a consequential manner. Sometimes, the fee can be global, i. e., aimed at remunerating the entire service, coupled with initiatives preliminary or subsequent to the trip.

Pursuant to Article 41, however, the uniform law is mandatory and pertains only to transport. Therefore, if this is a segment of a more articulated intervention, the Convention cannot be applied to the overall activity, but the beginning of the transfer is identified with the movement of the load until its redelivery. The uniform law applies to these operations, regardless of consensual indications, precisely due to the mandatory nature of Article 41. The consideration can be global, as there is no obstacle to such a consensual choice, and it can refer to all services, even if they are part of related, but different contractual models. However, the Convention must be implemented with regard to consideration for the carriage and the related obligations, although it could be difficult to distinguish the part of the credit regulated by it. Article 41 imposes this solution, as, although it is a component of more articulated services, transport refers to an imperative regulation with sectorial features, for example in terms of prescription, all the more so in common law countries, considering the clear derivation of the provision from a continental tradition. This is not an obstacle to the integration of several services and does not prevent the related business strategy; however, it forces contractual solutions that are confronted with the specific regulation of road transport. The case of mere ancillary services to carriage that fall within the scope of the relative contract is different, with the

[53] Cf. Brignardello (2013), pp. 1521 ff.; Logan (2000), pp. 21 ff.; Knemeyer et al. (2003), pp. 77 ff.

consequent application of CMR. It can be difficult to distinguish the two scenarios, but it pertains to the interpretation of agreements.

6.2.3 *Payment of Charges by the Consignee*

According to Article 13, second paragraph, before receiving the goods, the consignee must pay the credits relating to the consideration, the amount of which has been indicated in the consignment note.[54] By express provision, the transporter may carry the burden of collecting the fee from the consignee,[55] provided that the sum is set. According to Article 13, first paragraph, in this case, if he decides to exercise his right to redelivery, the recipient must request the release of the second copy of the transport document and, thus, is aware of the fact that, if he wants the goods, he must first pay the consideration, if thus agreed. If he refuses, the carrier can retain the goods until payment has been made in his favor.

Since the fee may undergo changes during the trip, as in the cases described in Article 16, it is questionable whether these charges can also be requested pursuant to Article 13, second paragraph. The rule refers to the "charges shown to be due on the consignment note"[56] and, therefore, the consignee is bound to pay the amount clarified in the same consignment note. For subsequent expenses, the carrier should contact the sender, also because they are undetermined at departure and there is no documentary confirmation on the credit and its quantification, in any case, left to the initiative of a subject not chosen by the consignee.

It is different if nothing emerges from the consignment note. According to some,[57] albeit in the presence of a freight collection clause, the consignee would not be required to pay, since, pursuant to Article 13, second paragraph, he would be bound only to the indicated amount, failing which nothing could be expected, but the thesis is not convincing.[58] The obligation to pay is connected to exercise of the right to redelivery and the consignee must pay the consideration although the amount is not mentioned in the consignment note, provided that there is an original agreement and the recipient is aware of it, as, just because he claims the goods, he undertakes to satisfy the carrier's credit. After all, pursuant to Article 4, omission of the consignment note or one of its provisions does not affect the validity of the contract and its clauses. The problem of the lack of the transport document is only evidential and the transporter must prove in another way that he has concluded with the shipper an agreement on the supposed "freight collect" and, then, must prove that, before

[54] Cf. Temme (2013b), pp. 358 ff.; Supreme Court of Poland 19 December 2013, II CSK 70/2013.

[55] Cf. LG Koblenz 20 March 2015, in *TranspR*, 2015, 166.

[56] The French text reads, "*le montant des créances résultant de la lettre de voiture*".

[57] Cf. App. Paris 19 November 1981, in *Bull. transp.*, 1982, 81; BGH 25 April 1991, in *TranspR*, 1991, 312; OLG Munich 9 October 1992, *ibid.*, 1993, 75.

[58] Cf. Maccarone (1987), pp. 62 ff.

delivery, the recipient is forewarned and, within a reasonable time, can reflect on the advisability of accepting, in relation to the amount of the fee.

If redelivery occurs without prior collection, the carrier may still act in any event against the consignee only, as the latter undertakes to pay as a result of the same redelivery, if the corresponding provision appears in the note or, failing that, if he is aware of the shipper and carrier's agreement.[59] It does not matter at what time the transporter asks for compliance; the fact that, usually, the request precedes the unloading is part of a rational choice by the carrier, who, in this manner, can count on the residual remedy of retention, in the face of any resistance from the recipient, as the invitation to pay after redelivery has a low persuasive force. If the consignee refuses to pay the fee, despite being obliged, the transporter is entitled to institute legal action. In fact, Article 13, second paragraph, provides for a specific method of collection, without thereby intervening on the structure of the contract. In fact, by agreement between the sender and carrier, the fee is charged to the consignee and unconditional redelivery removes any obligation from the shipper. This voluntary behavior, in fact, has a releasing effect, without prejudice to the recipient's continuing liability, with an action disciplined by the Convention in all respects, for example with regard to prescription, arbitration and jurisdiction.

On the contrary, if, having learned of his obligations, the consignee refuses the redelivery, he has no obligation and only the sender's one remains. From a structural viewpoint, according to Article 13, second paragraph, the agreement between the shipper and carrier conditions the exercise of the right to payment of consideration to redelivery and the consignee's obligation is based on the contract, as conduct due for him to obtain the goods.[60] The economic explanation lies in the commercial relations between the sender and recipient, unrelated to carriage and the Convention. Regardless of the express mention in Article 13, second paragraph, the obligation is linked to the redelivery by virtue of the original agreement, which explains the choice of CMR.

In case of refusal, based on the general principle of correspondence, as the carrier performs his service, the creditor is whoever entrusts it to him, that is, the shipper, since the scheduled fulfillment by the consignee is lacking. Therefore, the sender is not a guarantor of the recipient, but the passive subject of the original obligation, against the consignee's refusal. Once again, the whole transaction falls under the uniform law, and the focal point is the transporter's failure to collect his fee, because he can withhold the goods if the recipient does not pay him. This is his right *vis-à-vis* the consignee, precisely in relation to legitimate retention, but it is also an *onus* toward the shipper, who has no obligation if the carrier makes an unconditional redelivery, albeit in good faith, for example for a misplaced trust in the recipient.

[59] The English text of Article 13, second paragraph, reads, "the consignee who avails himself of the rights (...) shall pay the charges shown to be due on the consignment note". The French text of Article 13, second paragraph, reads, "*le destinataire qui se prévaut des droits* (...) *est tenu de payer le montant des créances résultant de la lettre de voiture*".

[60] Cf. Letacq et al. (2006), pp. 653 ff.; Wesolowski (2013), pp. 341 ff.

Then, according to Article 13, second paragraph, if disputes arise on the amount of credits, the transporter conducts the redelivery only after having received a deposit.[61] The consignee has the additional obligation to provide an adequate guarantee and, intelligibly, for some,[62] this is an excessive measure because it could be invoked by the carrier regardless of an actual objection from the recipient.

References

Brignardello M (2013) Il contratto di servizi di logistica. In: Morandi F (ed) Aa. Vv., I contratti del trasporto. Bologna, 1519 ff.

Clarke MA (2014) International carriage of goods by road, VI edn. CMR, New York

De la Motte H, Temme J (2013) Geltungsbereit. In: Thume KH (ed) Aa. Vv., CMR: über den Beförderungsvertrag im internationalen Strassengüterverkehr, III edn. Frankfurt am Main, pp 86 ff.

Fillers A (2020) The CMR in the practice of Latvian courts. Unif Law Rev, 169 ff.

Jung C (1997) The Convention on the contract for the International carriage of goods by road (CMR): survey, analysis and trends of recent German case law. Unif Law Rev, 148 ff.

Knemeyer AM, Corsi TM, Murphi PR (2003) Logistics outsourcing relationships: customer perspectives. J Bus Logis, 77 ff.

Letacq F, Putzeys J, Bonnevie P (2006) Recouvrement de créances, action directe contro le destinataire en paiement du fret e la CMR. Unif Law Rev, 653 ff.

Loewe R (1976) Commentary on the Convention of 19 may 1956 on the contract for the international carriage of goods by road. Eur Transp Law 11:311 ff.

Logan MS (2000) Using agency theory to design successful outsourcing relationship. Int J Logist Manag, 21 ff.

Maccarone S (1987) The right of disposal und CMR. In: Theunis J (ed) Aa. Vv., International carriage of goods by road CMR. London, pp 62 ff.

Messent A, Glass DA (2018) CMR: contracts for the international carriage of goods by road, IV edn. New York

Putzeys J (1981) Le contrat de transport routier de marchandises. Bruxelles

Rodière R (1971) The Convention on road transport. Eur Transp Law 6:307 ff.

Silingardi G, Corrado A, Meotti A, Morandi F (1994) La disciplina uniforme del contratto di trasporto di cose su strada. Turin

Temme J (2013a) Article 12. In: Thume KH (ed) Aa Vv CMR: über den Beförderungsvertrag im internationalen Strassengüterverkehr, III edn. Frankfurt am Main, pp 304 ff.

Temme J (2013b) Article 16. In: Thume KH (ed) Aa Vv CMR: über den Beförderungsvertrag im internationalen Strassengüterverkehr, III edn. Frankfurt am Main, pp 349 ff.

Wesolowski K (2013) A review of judicial decisions of the Polish Supreme Court within the scope of CMR. Eur Transp Law 48:341 ff.

[61] Cf. Supreme Court of Poland 19 December 2013, II CSK 70/2013. Generally, see Wesolowski (2013), pp. 341 ff.

[62] Cf. Messent and Glass (2018), pp. 116 ff., according to whom "this provision is potentially unsatisfactory insofar as it appears to place an obligation on the consignee to furnish security, regardless of the absolute existence of a legitimate claim by the consignee against the carrier".

Chapter 7
Liability of the Carrier

Contents

C. Tincani, *Contract for the International Carriage of Goods by Road*, Law for Professionals, https://doi.org/10.1007/978-3-031-08487-4_7

7.1 The Carrier's Responsibility Regime

7.1.1 The Principles of Shared Responsibility

The first paragraph of Article 17 of the Convention regulates the liability of the carrier; in fact, for this provision, he is liable for "*la perte total ou partielle ou de avarie, qui se produit entre le moment de la prise en charge de la marchandise et celui de la livraison, ainsi que du retard à la livraison*".[1] To this end, the total or partial loss and damage occurring between the entrusting of the goods and their redelivery are relevant.[2] The delay follows the same fate, although, unlike the first three cases, it does not concern the integrity of the load, but the performance of the service and its chronological dimension.

The carrier takes on an obligation and undertakes to bring the cargo to its destination[3] in the conditions found at the time of delivery to himself and, if previously agreed, within the established deadline or, failing that, before the necessary one.[4] The transporter is responsible for the failure to achieve one of these objectives[5] and, in general, the liability of Article 17, first paragraph, is not modulated on fault; in fact, the arguments[6] according to which there is a presumption of responsibility have been overcome. Rather, it is objective, and all the risks involved

[1]This is how Article 17, first paragraph, reads in the French version. The English version reads, "for the total or partial loss of the goods and for damage thereto occurring between the time when he takes over the goods and the time of delivery, as well as for any delay in delivery". See Thume (2013), p. 362 ff.; Cass. Greece 1885/2005; Cass. Belgium 23 January 2014, in *Europ. transp. law,* 2014, no. 49, 337, according to which the CMR applies to the cases of loss, damage and delay in the delivery of the load; all other prejudices (for example, damage to goods other than the load) are governed by domestic law.

[2]Cf. Messent and Glass (2018), p. 134 ff.; Libouton (1973), p. 33 ff.; Wesolowski (2013), p. 33 ff.; Thume (2013), p. 380 ff. Cf. LG Düsseldorf 28 March 2017, in *TranspR*, 2017, 311, according to which, in order to assert the liability of the carrier, the person entitled must prove the delivery of the goods and all their characteristics.

[3]However, see OLG Cologne 17 March 1998, in *TranspR,* 2000, 80, according to which in transport with Iran, there is a usage according to which the liability of the carrier ceases with the delivery to customs.

[4]Cf. Putzeys (1981), p. 216 ff., according to whom "*l'obligation de faire implique un résultat.*" See also Messent and Glass (2018), p. 133 ff.; Clarke (2014), p. 181 ff.; Cabrera Cànovas (2012), p. 139 ff.; Van Ryn (1966), p. 654 ff.

[5]Cf. Cabrera Cànovas (2012), p. 139 ff., according to whom "*the responsabilidad del transportista originates when, existiendo su culpa, falla en cumplir su obligación fundamental de hacer llegar la mercancía to the consignee en buen estado, íntegra y inside de plazo*". Cf. Cass. Greece 1025 / 2018.

[6]Cf. Putzeys (1981), p. 217 ff.

are borne by the carrier.[7] As is replied,[8] Article 17, first paragraph, would only create "*a système de présomption de faute contre le transporteur et au profit de l'ayant droit*",[9] often due to the latter's difficulty in identifying "*le fait fautif du transporteur qui est à l'origine de l'avarie ou de la perte*".[10] The approach is not convincing although, in continental legal systems, such a solution would perhaps have been more consistent with the overall view of liability for nonfulfillment of such obligations. However, Article 17 does not contemplate any presumption at the textual level, as, in the first paragraph, the concept does not appear; in the second, specific exemptions are identified, with an exhaustive list and with the further provision of the so-called special risks of the fourth paragraph.

In addition to proving the stipulation of the contract, the shipper or the consignee must give evidence of the prejudice[11] and of the moment in which it occurred in relation to what is regulated by Article 30 and the reserves. In particular, the evidence may concern the difference between the shipped goods and those that actually arrived.[12] Again, it is sufficient to demonstrate that the delay is significant[13] and "*la faute du transporteur*" is not assumed.[14] On the contrary, Article 17, first paragraph, applies, without prejudice to the allegation and the demonstration of one of the cases regulated in the second paragraph.[15] The relative rules are mandatory and are identified in the conduct of the entitled person, in his order, in a defect of the goods or in circumstances that the carrier could not have avoided and the consequences whereof he could not have overcome. Usually, this last term refers to two

---

[7]Cf. Loewe (1976), p. 361 ff., according to whom "the liability *régime* established by Article 17 is not a system of liability for wrongful act or neglect, with reversal of the burden of proof, but a system of objective liability"; Thume (2013), p. 381 ff. Cf. also the Supreme Court of Poland 26 November 2019, IV CSK 415/2018.

[8]Cf. Putzeys (1981), p. 217 ff., according to whom "*the fait de ne pas avoir procuré le résultat promis crée une présomption de responsabilité*".

[9]Cf. Putzeys (1981), p. 222 ff.

[10]Cf. Putzeys (1981), p. 222 ff.

[11]Cf. OLG Cologne 4 June 2020, in *TranspR,* 2021, 15, according to which, as soon as the carrier becomes aware of the loss of the goods, it is his responsibility to adopt specific countermeasures and to document them, in order to be able to demonstrate them in a subsequent proceeding.

[12]Cf. Clarke (2014), p. 181 ff.; Rodière (1971), p. 13 ff., according to whom "the mere fact of goods arriving damaged, delayed, or short - delivered, is sufficient to make the carrier liable (. . .), to raise a presumption of his liability". See also Cass. Italy 2 October 2003, n. 14680, in *Dir. mar.,* 2005, 864.

[13]Cf. Clarke (2014), p. 181 ff. See also Cass. com. France 18 January 2000, in *Bull. transp. logist.,* 2000, 74.

[14]Cf. Putzeys (1981), p. 223 ff.; Cabrera Cànovas (2012), p. 140 ff., according to whom, "*si la mercancía no es entregada en destino íntegra y en buenas condiciones, se presume que hay incumplimiento por parte del transportista*".

[15]Cf. Clarke (2014), p. 181 ff.; Cabrera Cànovas (2012), p. 139 ff., according to whom the carrier, "*para exonerarse de esa responsabilidad, tendrá que demostrar la existencia de una causa o circumstancia concreta, de entre las que en lista taxativa enumera el Convenio CMR en el Article 17*"; Silingardi et al. (1994), p. 117 ff.; Sánchez Gamborino (2001a), p. 645 ff.; Abromavicius (2017), p. 54 ff.; Kolacz (2017), p. 48 ff. See also Cass. Belgium 9 December 1999, in *Unif. law rev.*, 2000, 851.

distinct situations, defined by civil law systems as fortuitous events or *force majeure,*[16] that is, events outside the sphere of control of the transporter, although not relevant in terms of the fault, but of the objective imputability of the nonfulfillment in relation to the transporter's possibilities of intervention. A rigorous burden of proof is incumbent on him, as he must demonstrate the existence of one of the specifically indicated causes and the etiological link with the prejudice.[17] In fact, he cannot avoid liability by simply declaring that he has acted with professional diligence, nor that the event has been determined by factors unrelated to those of Article 17, second paragraph, without prejudice to the provision of the fourth. For the second paragraph to operate, the prejudice must be attributable to one of the prescribed situations;[18] on the other hand, the unknown or different-from-those-established causes[19] do not release the carrier from any liability.

Therefore, although such theoretical classifications are of minor importance when discussing uniform law, Article 17 does not focus on compliance with precautionary rules and the suitability of the transporter's conduct according to axiological criteria, but on analytically disciplined cases. However, by virtue of the considerable experience in ordinary risks outside the control of the carrier in international transport, Article 17, second paragraph, groups known situations, wherein execution of the service cannot be demanded. This justifies the traditional mention of fault,[20] but this statement is sometimes considered to be based on the idea that, if the circumstances of Article 17, second paragraph, occur, the fulfillment goes beyond what can be expected from a diligent transporter.

Although these considerations grasp concepts inherent in Article 17, second paragraph, the conclusion is not convincing, because both the regulation of liability and that of the grounds for exemption are limited to the objective profile, without judicial assessments on the diligence and adequacy of the organization and the carrier's commitment. Therefore, the application of Article 17 must remain generally bound to the description of the facts, without trespassing on the intent and, in any case, on the psychological condition of the transporter.

---

[16] Cf. Messent and Glass (2018), p. 132 ff.

[17] Cf. Antapasis (2017), p. 44 ff. See Cass. Greece 1025 / 2018; App. Piraeus 45 / 1997, in *Pireus law rev.,* 1997, 58; RB Roermond 19 March 2014, in *Europ. transp. law,* 2016, no. 51, 223; App. Barcelona 18 September 2918, no. 580, in *Jur,* 2018, 253561.

[18] Cf. BGH 26 April 2018, in *TranspR*, 2018, 384, according to which the application of Article 17, second paragraph, implies the positive identification of an insuperable cause.

[19] Cf. App. Madrid 28 March 2001, in *Jur,* 2001, 158657; App. Barcelona 18 September 2018, no. 580, *ibid.,* 2018, 253561; OLG Cologne 3 March 1999, in *TranspR,* 2001, 122, according to which, if the original cause of the damage remains unknown, the carrier cannot attach its inevitable nature, pursuant to Article 17.

[20] Cf. Putzeys (1981), p. 223 ff.

7.1.2 *The First Three Cases of Exemption from Liability, the Conduct or an Order of the Person Entitled to Redelivery, and the Defect of the Goods*

Article 17, second paragraph, identifies four causes for the carrier's exemption from liability, the "*faute de l'ayant droit, un ordre de celui - ci ne résultant pas d'une faute du transporteur, un vice propre de la marchandise, ou des circonstances que le transporteur ne pouvait pas éviter et aux conséquences desquelles il ne pouvait pas obvier*".[21] The "*faute de l'ayant droit*"[22] excludes "*insuffisance d'emballage*",[23] "*la défectuosité de chargement*"[24] and "*imperfection de l'étiquetage*",[25] as they are special risks pursuant to Article 17, fourth paragraph.[26] The "*faute de l'ayant droit*" is recognized in the incomplete compilation of the consignment note, in the indication of an incorrect address, in the failure to deliver a document necessary for the completion of customs operations or in the transmission of an inaccurate one.[27]

Article 17, second paragraph, groups cases relating to events that occurred in the execution and so significant as to prevent the achievement of the goal.[28] However, because of their objective characteristics, they exclude liability as the situation that arose is beyond the carrier's control[29] and, even if it occurred during the journey and while the goods were under his care, the harmful event is not attributable to him, as it is unrelated to his obligations and his intervention, for the fulfillment of the obligation assumed.

In particular, the shipper cannot invoke the transporter's liability if he insists that the transporter places perishable goods on the vehicle despite the malfunctioning of

[21]This is how Article 17, second paragraph, reads in the French version. The English text, reads, "the wrongful act or neglect of the claimant, the instructions of the claimant given otherwise than as the result of a wrongful act or neglect on the part of the carrier, by inherent vice of the goods or through circumstances which the carrier could not avoid and the consequences of which he was unable to prevent".

[22]Cf. Eckardt (2017), p. 39 ff., according to whom "the position in Germany is that the claimant might be either the sender or the consignee"; Rodière (1971) 15 ff. Cf. also BGH 15 January 2007, in *TranspR*, 2007, 314; BGH 9 September 2010, *ibid.*, 2011, 178.

[23]Cf. *Le Lamy transp.*, 2020, vol. I, 493.

[24]Cf. *Le Lamy transp.*, 2020, vol. I, 493.

[25]Cf. *Le Lamy transp.*, 2020, vol. I, 493.

[26]Cf. Clarke (2014), p. 217 ff., according to whom "there (. . .) remains only a small cluster of cases in which the defense, act or neglect of the claimant has been invoked"; Rodière (1971), p. 15 ff.; Messent and Glass (2018), p. 143 ff.

[27]Cf. App. Paris 2 December 1981, in *Bull. transp.*, 1982, 73; App. Paris 18 October 1995, in *Le Lamy transp.*, 2020, vol. I, 494; App. Lyon 7 May 1981, in *Bull. transp.*, 1981, 410; App. Montpellier 20 February 1992, in *Le Lamy transp.*, 2020, vol. I, 494.

[28]Cf. Otte (2018), p. 1280 ff.

[29]For a singular scenario, cf. BGH 3 July 2000, in *Europ. transp. law,* 2000, no. 35, 678, according to which, if the carrier asks the shipper to collaborate, and while complying with the request, he does not actually cooperate, the sender is not liable pursuant to Article 17, second paragraph.

the refrigeration system,[30] does not correctly pre-cool the cargo subjected to a controlled temperature[31] or does not adequately guard the returned damaged load for repair.[32] Furthermore, the sender cannot ask for compensation if he does not report hidden defects whereof he is aware, such as, for example, the unusual height of the center of gravity of a machine,[33] the risk of spontaneous combustion[34] or the structural sensitivity to frost.[35] On the contrary, the shipper cannot be blamed if he does not check the accuracy of the known address of a regular customer[36] or, if in breach of recent instructions, the carrier is objected to refusal at the time of redelivery.[37] Furthermore, the stop attributable to the negligent conduct of the sender that causes the freezing of the load does not exclude the responsibility of the transporter because the latter must take all the necessary measures to protect the cargo according to the external temperature.[38]

Moreover, this cause for exemption must be in direct and exclusive connection with the damage, and it is not enough that the sender's conduct contributes to the creation of the conditions for the prejudice, but must provoke it directly, at least according to the ideas of some Scholars.[39] Thus, the carrier's liability for the theft of the vehicle despite the forced stop at night is due to the disorganization of the shipper, who should have delivered the goods to the same transporter the night before.[40] If anything, the delay can force the carrier to stop, but that is not the direct cause of the theft. In the same sense, there is no conduct attributable to the sender if the load gets wet during a prolonged stop at customs, due to his delay in transmitting the necessary documents.[41] In these situations, the carrier is not exempted from the obligation to safeguard the cargo from external events, such as theft or bad weather, and this is possible and must be done despite the extension of the journey.

[30] Cf. App. Grenoble 4 December 1996, in *Bull. transp. logist.*, 1997, 120. Cf. Koller (2019), p. 1 ff.

[31] Cf. App. Paris 14 February 1991, in *Bull. transp. logist.*, 1991, 289; App. Lyon 6 April 2017, *ibid.*, 2017, 262.

[32] Cf. Cass. com. France 16 March 1993, in *Bull. transp. logist.*, 262.

[33] Cf. Cass. com. France 5 July 1977, in *Bull. transp.*, 1977, 402. See also Libouton (1973), p. 34 ff.

[34] Cf. Cass. com. France 23 May 1989, in *Le Lamy transp.*, 2020, vol. I, 494.

[35] Cf. App. Paris 26 March 1969, in *Bull. transp.*, 1969, 174; App. Nîmes 18 May 1988, *ibid.*, 1988, 472.

[36] Cf. App. Paris 9 November 2011, in *Bull. transp. logist.*, 2011, 703.

[37] Cf. App. Montpellier 25 January 2011, in *Bull. transp. logist.*, 2011, 94.

[38] Cf. App. Paris 30 September 1987, in *Bull. transp.*, 1988, 59.

[39] Cf. Messent and Glass (2018), p. 140 ff.; Gerspacher and Thalmann (2017), p. 57 ff.

[40] Cf. App. Paris 4 July 1989, in *Le Lamy transp.*, 2020, vol. I, 494.

[41] Cf. App. Paris 3 November 1977, in *Le Lamy transp.*, 2020, vol. I, 494; Cass. Belgium 12 December 1980, in *Unif. law rev.*, 1981, 250. But see App. Paris 6 July 1995, in *Le Lamy transp.*, 2020, vol. I, 494, which granted the benefit of Article 17, second paragraph, in the case of theft of part of the goods during lunch break, as the unloading could have been completed earlier.

Some different elements are found in many German decisions,[42] where, on the one hand, they apply Article 17, fifth paragraph, on the concurrence between the behavior of the sender and that of the carrier.[43] On the other hand, they are perhaps influenced by the concept of good faith and reconstruct the organizational duties of the transporter in relation to the immediate warning by the shipper on the existence of factors that impose derogatory organizational measures, specifically regarding the protection of safety.[44] This is particularly true for safeguarding expensive cargoes from theft or robbery. Because German case law[45] is rigorous in this regard, the problems multiply and, sometimes, the application of Article 17, second paragraph, leads to the identification of a concurrent behavior of the sender and the transporter and the latter's liability is not excluded. In particular, this was decided in a case where the carrier was found guilty of willful misconduct, with the consequent unlimited responsibility of Article 29.[46] The solution is convincing because the seriousness of his nonfulfillment did not prevent the causal relevance of the shipper's conduct.

The second type of case for exemption refers to the "*ordre de l'ayant droit*", that is, to the instructions of whoever has the right to dispose of the goods. Despite opposing arguments,[47] the sender's information is no more significant after the power of counter-order passes to the consignee. It is the shipper's duty to use the fastest means of communication and transmit instructions on time as long as he can adopt them. There should be no effective problem of timeliness, at least given modern-day tools. Instead, the statements in the consignment note about regulating the refrigeration system are really significant.[48] Therefore, the carrier benefits from

[42] Cf. BGH 9 October 2003, in *TranspR*, 2004, 175, according to which the sender is responsible for failing to inform and declare the value of the goods if it is believed that, in case the value of the goods is known, the carrier would have better fulfilled the precautionary rules he should have received and followed.

[43] Cf. BGH 13 July 2000, in *TranspR*, 2000, 409, according to which, although the carrier is responsible for a correct delivery of the goods, he can attach a relevant conduct of the sender in relation to the fulfillment of his duties of collaboration, if necessary to achieve the negotiation program; thus, the shipper's failure to reply may lead to the application of Article 17, fifth paragraph, on concurrence between the sender's and the carrier's responsibility; LG Munich 6 February 2014, in *TranspR*, 2014, 295; OLG Munich 6 June 2019, in *VersR*, 2020, 591, according to which, if the sender has contributed to creating the conditions for which a third party could take possession of the goods, to the detriment of the carrier, there is a concurrence of his responsibility, for the conduct both of the shipper and the carrier.

[44] Cf. LG Karlsruhe 30 April 2015, in *TranspR*, 2016, 195, according to which it is the responsibility of the sender to explicitly warn the carrier of the specific risks inherent in transport.

[45] Cf. BGH 9 October 2003, in *TranspR*, 2004, 175.

[46] Cf. BGH 19 May 2005, in *TranspR*, 2006, 114; BGH 3 March 2005, *ibid.*, 2006, 114.

[47] Cf. Putzeys (1981), p. 250 ff.; Clarke (2014), p. 219 ff.; Loewe (1976), p. 362 ff.; Rodière (1971), p. 16 ff., according to whom "the carrier cannot (...) seek to cover himself by means of instructions from the consignee which should have dispatched to him earlier on, or conversely, by means of instructions from the sender which he would only receive after the power of acting in this matter had passed from the sender to the consignee".

[48] Cf. Cass. com. France 19 April 1982, in *Bull. transp.*, 1982, 309.

the provision of Article 17, second paragraph, if the shipper's inaccurate behaviors lead to an unusual stop at customs with a consequent delay due only to this circumstance.[49] The opposite principle applies if the sender's information is the result of inadequate intervention by the transporter.[50]

Furthermore, the latter would not be liable for the damage caused by a maneuver ordered by the consignee, so that the unloading can take place in the best conditions.[51] This solution is not convincing as, in performing the service, the carrier has decision-making independence.[52] Therefore, he is not required to execute a maneuver if he deems it incorrect and furthermore likely to cause damage to the cargo. However, depending on the actual unfolding of the events, Article 17, second paragraph, can be applied if the consignee's suggestion originates from a better and consolidated knowledge on some aspects that could be unknown to the carrier and on which he has limited and less experience.

Then, the transporter can avoid liability by invoking the defect of the goods. This is defect inherent in the load that[53] predisposes it to deterioration, as in the case of an animal suffering from a disease or a load of fruit compromised by a bacterium or a parasite.[54] However, despite the presence of worms and molds in perishable goods, the transporter cannot invoke this cause for exemption if temperature problems emerge during the journey.[55] The solution is convincing, as the alteration can be provoked by external agents developed by the nonfunctioning of the refrigeration system, while, with one that does work properly, the integrity of the goods would not be compromised. The doubt about the actual causal link excludes the application of this case of exemption as no evidence of a connection between the deterioration and the intrinsic defect exists.

Instead, the chemical reaction produced by acid in contact with the ferrous metal of the tank is rightly considered an intrinsic defect, provided that the carrier is neither

---

[49] Cf. App. Paris 15 December 1988, in *Le Lamy transp.*, 2020, vol. I, 494; App. Paris 25 January 1989, *ibid.*, 2020, vol. I, 494; Trib. com. Aix - en – Provence 23 June 2003, in *Bull. transp. logist.*, 2003, 494.

[50] Cf. Cass. com. France 5 July 1976, in *Le Lamy transp.*, 2020, vol. I, 495. See also Clarke (2014), p. 219 ff.; Putzeys (1981), p. 251 ff.

[51] Cf. App. Paris 25 November 1977, in *Bull. transp.*, 1978, 66. The appeal was rejected by Cass. com. France 8 October 1979, *ibid.*, 1979, 545.

[52] For a partially similar solution, cf. Messent and Glass (2018), p. 145 ff., according to whom "liability was shared, however, where the carrier's driver must have known that the stability of the load was such that it could not tolerate the instruction given by the consignee". As far as the latter is concerned, cf. OLG Hamburg 26 October 1994, in *TranspR,* 1945, 293.

[53] Cf. Clarke (2014), p. 221 ff., according to whom "most things carry within them the seeds of their own destruction or decay"; Loewe (1976), p. 362 ff.; Libouton (1973), p. 34 ff.; Gruber (2017), p. 38 ff.; Messent and Glass (2018), p. 145 ff.

[54] Cf. App. Aix - en - Provence 21 June 1985, in *Le Lamy transp.*, 2020, vol. I, 495. See also Clarke (2014), p. 181 ff., according to whom "the vice must be inherent when the goods are taken over by the carrier".

[55] Cf. App. Rouen 1 March 2012, in *Bull. transp. logist.,* 2012, 201.

informed of this particularity nor invited to take the necessary countermeasures.[56] Finally, the proof must result from a precise finding and cannot be based on a generic allegation, as in the case where it is stated that "*il est incompréhensible que des fruits ne puissent supporter un délai de transport de six jours*".[57]

7.1.3 The Circumstances that Have Arisen and Are Unavoidable. Theft

For the identification of the fourth cause of exemption, Article 17, second paragraph, states that the transporter is not liable "through circumstances which the carrier could not avoid and the consequences of which he was unable to prevent".[58] Because of how it is formulated, this expression seems to recall the notion of *force majeure* despite the lack of the element of unpredictability alongside that of inevitability.[59] From a practical perspective, many continental decisions emphasize equivalence with *force majeure,*[60] although they often recognize the cause of exemption in the absence of unpredictability.[61] In fact, according to some, "*il suffit que l'événement ait été inévitable dans sa cause et que ses effets aient été insurmountable*".[62]

The omission of an explicit reference to "*force majeure*" would express the will of uniform law not to use "concepts established in national law",[63] in favor of a formula described as "a step halfway between accidental loss and *force majeure*".[64] In fact, the institution of Article 17, second paragraph, is heterogeneous to *force majeure*[65] understood in common sense. In particular, the events of the latter group

[56] Cf. App. Paris 28 October 1969, in *Bull. transp.,* 1970, 7.

[57] Cf. App. Rennes 5 November 1974, in *Bull. transp.,* 1974, 514.

[58] Thus, Article 17, second paragraph, in the English version. The French version reads, "*des circonstances que le transporteur ne pouvait pas éviter et aux conséquences desquelles il ne pouvait pas obvier*".

[59] Cf. Messent and Glass (2018), p. 147 ff.

[60] Cf. Defossez (2016), p. 87 ff.

[61] Cf. Cass. com. France 27 January 1981, in *Bull. transp.,* 1981, 219; Cass. com. France 31 May 2011, in *Le Lamy transp.*, 2020, vol. I, 495; App. Paris 6 May 1998, *ibid.,* 2020, vol. I, 495; App. Lyon 7 September 2017, *ibid.,* 2020, vol. I, 495, according to which "*la définition de ce cas d'exonération ne retient pas, par rapport aux critères de la force majeure tels qu'entendus en droit français, celui de l'imprévisibilité*"; App. Orléans 1 February 2018, in *Bull. transp logist.,* 2018, 92; OGH 2 October 2013, in *Europ. transp. law,* 2014, no. 49, 334. See also Krings (1999), p. 770 ff.

[62] Cf. App. Pau 24 June 2013, in *Le Lamy transp.*, 2020, vol. I, 495.

[63] Cf. Clarke (2014), p. 227 ff.

[64] Cf. Clarke (2014), p. 227 ff.; Messent and Glass (2018), p. 147 ff.; Loewe (1976), p. 362 ff.; Rodière (1971), p. 17 ff.

[65] Cf. Eckardt (2017), p. 41 ff., according to whom "the Federal Supreme Court has repeatedly held that the legislator misunderstood the Convention and that the German understanding of *force majeure* should not be relevant here"; Kolacz (2017), p. 50 ff. Cf. Loewe (1976), p. 362 ff.; Wesolowski (2013), p. 343 ff.

are outside the sphere of control of the carrier, and the criterion selected by uniform law can include situations relating to his organization.[66] For example, while not integrating *force majeure* in the proper sense, the strike could be relevant for Article 17, second paragraph. With *a contrario* reasoning, this is confirmed in the third paragraph, wherefor the transporter cannot avoid his liability by demonstrating the imperfection of the vehicle.

According to some,[67] the inevitability of Article 17, second paragraph, cannot be evaluated in the same way as the "reasonable care" criterion defined according to current practice, as the concept was known in 1956 and, therefore, if it had been endorsed, there would have been explicit reference in the CMR. Moreover, Article 17, second paragraph, presupposes greater diligence than ordinary, and the carrier must demonstrate that he has adopted all the necessary measures imposed by the best scientific knowledge of the moment, in relation to the circumstances[68] and possible initiatives of his auxiliaries.[69] Therefore, the reference to the "utmost care"[70] criterion, as a parameter for evaluating conduct, is convincing and this is consistent with cases for exemption anchored to an objective profile, without any reference to diligence. Ultimately, we are discussing professional initiatives to be conducted with the employment of the maximum resources available for complex operations.[71]

For example, theft is a recurring event regarding the debate on Article 17, second paragraph. In the case of a vehicle parked in broad daylight with the doors closed in front of the customs offices in Milan,[72] there is no possible exemption. The theft of a truck, whose doors are forced open with a simple break-in and whose alarm is easily deactivated,[73] is not an inevitable circumstance. It is the same if the theft is committed when the carrier is engaged in the presentation of documents.[74] Not

---

[66] Cf. Clarke (2014), p. 228 ff.; Kolacz (2017), p. 51 ff.; Messent and Glass (2018), p. 147 ff.; Loewe (1976), p. 362 ff.

[67] Cf. Clarke (2014), p. 228 ff.

[68] Cf. Clarke (2014), p. 230 ff.

[69] Cf. OLG Thuringia 30 March 2007, in *TranspR,* 2007, 201.

[70] Cf. Eckardt (2017), p. 41 ff., according to whom "the carrier has to prove that the loss could not have been prevented even if the utmost care possible under circumstances had been taken"; Antapasis (2017), p. 45 ff., according to whom "Greek courts use a 'competent prudent professional carrier' standard in order to examine the carrier's conduct"; Jung (1997), p. 156 ff.; Mayer (1997), p. 173 ff.; Libouton (1973), p. 35 ff. See also Cass. 1518 / 2001, in *Elldik,* 44, 1619; Cass. 826 / 2004, *ibid.,* 45, 1656; App. Tessaloniki 730 / 2005, in *EmpD,* 2005, 528.

[71] Cf. Czerwenka (2016), p. 536 ff., according to whom "German courts consider an event 'unavoidable' (...) only if the carrier could not prevent it from occurring despite exercising the utmost possible and reasonable care, attention, skill and prudence".

[72] Cf. Cass. com. France 31 March 1987, in *Bull. transp.,* 1987, 280; App. Paris 15 March 1990, in *Le Lamy transp.*, 2020, vol. I, 495; OGH 15 December 1981, in *TranspR,* 1984, 262.

[73] Cf. App. Paris 29 February 1996, in *Le Lamy transp.*, 2020, vol. I, 495; OLG Munich 27 March 1981, in *VersR,* 1982, 264; OLG Munich 17 July 1991, in *TranspR,* 1991, 427; Hof Gent 5 April 2004, in *Europ. transp. law,* 2005, no. 40, 846, according to which "a 'king pin' does not qualify as a suitable anti - theft device protecting both the vehicle and the load". Cf. Thume (2013), p. 430 ff.

[74] Cf. App. Paris 4 July 1984, in *Bull. transp.,* 1985, 158.

even the choice of leaving a dog to guard the cabin is sufficient;[75] moreover, the transporter is responsible for the theft of a vehicle parked in a protected area during the night, albeit with adequate lighting.[76]

In general, to apply Article 17, second paragraph, the need to abandon the truck and the impossibility of arranging it in any other way must be demonstrated,[77] so that there is no exemption if the drivers leave the vehicle without being forced by the situation, i.e., if it is a more convenient conduct but not essential. Furthermore, Article 17, second paragraph, does not apply to the theft of goods delivered to a different consignee following a false communication transmitted during the journey that was not verified[78] or if the carrier has all the information necessary for the exact identification of the recipient.[79] Likewise, the transporter is liable for theft that occurred at night on the weekend on a vehicle parked at his home.[80]

Moreover, it is not enough to prove that, due to its size, the truck could not be housed in a guarded parking lot.[81] On the contrary, the theft of the vehicle parked at customs is inevitable while the carrier is waiting for the necessary documents to be sent, if he can prove that the load was adequately protected.[82] In fact, the wait was not predicted but imposed by the negligent conduct of the shipper and, at any rate, in relation to this situation, further measures could not have been expected.[83] Instead,

---

[75]Cf. App. Paris 14 June 1977, in *Bull. transp.,* 1977, 354.

[76]Cf. App. Douai 17 December 2015, in *Bull. transp. logist.,* 2016, 79; Trib. Prato 14 May 2005, in *Dir. mar.,* 2006, 267, according to which the carrier is liable for the theft of the vehicle which occurred at night in a fenced parking lot; OLG Hamburg 7 December 1965, in *TranspR,* 1996, 238. See also Thume (2013), p. 428 ff.

[77]Cf. Cass. com. France 2 May 2001, in *Bull. transp. logist.,* 2001, 362.

[78]Cf. Cass. com. France 2 May 2001, in *Bull. transp. logist.,* 2001, 362. More incisively, cf. OLG Hamburg 28 July 1999, in *TranspR,* 2000, 176, according to which, since the frequency of criminal acts in the regions around Moscow is known, the carrier must ensure precisely the identity and right of the consignee, failing which, he cannot invoke the cause of exemption from liability of Article 17, second paragraph; cf. LG Berlin 26 January 2000, in *TranspR,* 2000, 255, according to which the carrier whose driver violates the specific indication to however ascertain the identity of the employee of the consignee, unknown to him, incurs liability in a risk area such as Moscow.

[79]Cf. OLG Stuttgart 13 October 1999, in *TranspR,* 2001, 127.

[80]Cf. OGH 29 June 1983, in *Unif. law rev.,* 1984, 526; Hof Antwerp 30 May 1979, *ibid.,* 1981, 236; Hof Antwerp 20 December 1999, in *Europ. transp. law,* 2000, no. 35, 687; Cass. com. France 6 January 1998, in *Bull. transp.,* 1998, 39. Cf. Humphreys and De Peuteur (1992), p. 738 ff.

[81]Cf. App. Aix - en – Provence 11 March 1969, in *Bull. transp.,* 1969, 389; App. Paris 15 February 1977, *ibid.,* 1978, 53; App. Poitiers 5 February *2016, ibid.,* 2016, 112, according to which the theft committed in spite of two drivers is not inevitable; App. Brussels 12 December 1977, *ibid.,* 1978, 39, according to which the carrier cannot invoke the provision of Article 17, second paragraph, in the case of destruction of the vehicle due to an arson by unknown persons, as it could have been taken to a guarded parking lot. See also BGH 5 June 1981, in *Europ. transp. law,* 1982, no. 17, 301; App. Limoges 1 March 1983, in *Bull. transp.,* 1983, 331, according to which the carrier is liable for the theft of the vehicle parked at his home because, despite having closed it, he could have adopted further measures, such as the installation of the alarm.

[82]Cf. App. Lyon 22 March 2018, in *Bull. transp. logist.,* 2018, 189.

[83]In an opposite sense, see App. Paris 4 July 1989, in *Le Lamy transp.*, 2020, vol. I, 494.

the carrier is liable in the event of a prolonged stop of the truck in an area facing the highway toll collection stations.[84]

In general, theft does not exempt,[85] except in sporadic cases,[86] the transporter, who is almost never considered without responsibility, although he is diligent, as in the situation already mentioned of a theft committed with the vehicle parked in a protected and illuminated area.[87] In this case, it is difficult to imagine the further steps that should have been taken except for the simultaneous presence of two drivers. From this perspective, the objective nature of the case for exemption is demonstrated in the common interpretation.

In other situations, the conduct prior to the theft is considered and placed in relation to the degree of probability of the event.[88] Thus, the carrier is held responsible if he leaves the vehicle in an unsupervised and crowded place to go to the hospital and have a wound treated and if the theft occurs during the absence of a couple of hours.[89] The solution is correct as such circumstances are not inevitable; in fact, the truck could have been better guarded and, once again, there should have been a second driver, who could have controlled both the vehicle and the goods. However, the decision would be excessive if the injuries to the driver's safety were so serious as to cause an actual concern, enough to justify the second driver's sudden reaction and his contemporary presence in hospital.

Furthermore, if the pilot falls ill during the journey, the disease requires hospitalization and causes the subsequent removal of the cargo, it is not an inevitable fact capable of excluding the liability of the carrier if, before admission, the driver is able to inform his employer.[90] Then, the transporter is responsible if, aware of the danger in traveling to some Italian regions, he negligently fails to prepare an itinerary with stops in protected and supervised areas[91] or if, after activating the security system, he leaves the keys in an inappropriate place.[92] Therefore, the contractual clauses that

---

[84] Cf. OLG Hamburg 7 June 2001, in *TranspR,* 2002, 108.

[85] Cf. Silingardi et al. (1994), p. 159 ff.; Fillers (2020), p. 189 ff.; RB Antwerp 16 May 1997, in *Europ. transp. law,* 1999, n, 34, 119; RB Antwerp 29 April 1999, *ibid.,* 1999, no. 34, 851; App. Barcelona 4 September 2013, no. 322, in *Jur,* 2013, 340805; App. Barcelona 2 September 2008, no. 300, *ibid.,* 2009, 42600.

[86] Cf. Silingardi et al. (1994), p. 159 ff., nt. 141.

[87] Cf. App. Douai 17 December 2015, in *Bull. transp. logist.,* 2016, 79.

[88] Cf. BGH 21 February 2008, in *TranspR*, 2008, 249, according to which the carrier is liable for the failure to adopt the necessary security measures, despite the sender's warning on the specific value and therefore on the strong risks related to the journey.

[89] Cf. Antapasis (2017), p. 47 ff. Cf. OLG Düsseldorf 13 May 2020, in *Europ. transp. law,* 2021, no. 61, 53, according to which "illness and hospitalization of the driver during the carriage does not justify unavoidability in the sense of Article 17, second paragraph, for the subsequent theft of the goods to the extent that the driver is still able to advise his employer before is brought to hospital".

[90] Cf. OLG Düsseldorf 13 June 2020, in *TranspR,* 2021, 151.

[91] Cf. Cass. Netherlands 24 June 1997, in *Europ. transp. law,* 1998, no. 33, 52; HR Netherlands 17 April 1998, *ibid.,* 1999, no. 34, 82.

[92] Cf. OLG Saar 5 April 2006, in *TranspR,* 2007, 63.

require drivers to stop in areas monitored and controlled by cameras, with unlimited liability of the carrier if they do not comply, are valid and effective.[93]

There is a considerable severity of judgment on the inevitability of the theft and, usually, the diligent transporter is liable, despite guarding the truck by parking in a monitored area or by activating the most modern alarms. These measures are considered sufficient only if completed by the presence of two drivers on board[94]; thus, constant control of the vehicle[95] would be guaranteed and the departure of one of them would not undermine surveillance. In practice, it is difficult to respect the alternation between the two drivers when the stop is imposed for the satisfaction of normal needs, such as having a meal. The desire to spend the break in the company of a colleague is strong and understandable at a human level; therefore, although the simultaneous journey of two drivers is aimed at preventing the truck from being abandoned, albeit for a short period of time, caution never reaches its programmed goals and the transporter cannot be released from liability, pursuant to Article 17, second paragraph.[96] On the contrary, this measure is decisive in exceptional situations, such as, for example, in the event of a breakdown, where one driver seeks help while the other remains in the vehicle.

7.1.4 Robbery

With respect to theft, in addition to the stealing of goods, robbery involves aggression against the driver. The threat to safety leads to a less severe assessment of the carrier's liability, with an expansion of the number of decisions in his favor if Article 17, second paragraph, is invoked.[97] In fact, as it is believed, the transporter is not

[93]Cf. LG Bremen 5 June 2018, in *TranspR,* 2018, 390.

[94]Cf. Czerwenka (2016), p. 539 ff., who indicates the measures necessary for the theft to be considered an inevitable event; among them there is the presence of the second driver. See also Humphreys and De Peuteur (1992), p. 740 ff. Cf. OLG Cologne 25 August 2016, in *TranspR,* 2017, 62, according to which the carrier must adopt specific countermeasures to be able to demonstrate the inevitable nature of the fact, for example, the presence of a second driver.

[95]Cf. OLG Nuremberg 24 February 1999, in *TranspR,* 2000, 81, according to which, due to the risk of theft and robbery, in Italy, breaks and interruptions must be carried out in guarded parking areas, and if this is impossible with the presence of one driver only, two must be present, failing which, the carrier must compensate the entire prejudice, so that the forfeiture of the compensatory limit applies. But see OLG Stuttgart 26 July 2006, in *TranspR,* 2007, 320, according to which, on the occasion of a transport from Germany to Northern Italy, even if, for the mandatory breaks in the guide, no guarded parking areas can be found, it is not mandatory the use of the second driver.

[96]Cf. *Micheal Galley Footwear Ltd.* see *Dominic Iaboni,* in *All England report,* 1982, 200, according to which theft committed while both drivers were at lunch is not inevitable. See also Hof Antwerp 30 May 1979, in *Unif. law rev.,* 1981, 236.

[97]Cf. Jung (1997), p. 157 ff.; Antapasis (2017), p. 47 ff.

responsible if he is attacked while replacing a tire in a service area[98]; if he is surprised by three men as he sleeps in his cabin in a rest area, which, although not controlled, is still illuminated, with a restaurant open at night, with a constant presence of staff and customers.[99] The principle is applied in case of a stay imposed by the need to respect the prescribed rest periods when the closest protected area is not in proximity.[100] On the contrary, pursuant to Article 17, second paragraph, the fact that the attack occurred in a roundabout on an Italian road not known to be dangerous is relevant.[101] The fact that Italy is considered a destination at risk does not necessarily imply that the stop reveals a lack of caution, but it[102] must be demonstrated. Moreover, regardless of any assessment of crime in Italy, some interval in the mileage is required.

Finally, violence committed on a French highway while the driver is going back to the vehicle[103] or that executed by false controllers on a truck equipped with a siren are considered cases for exemption.[104] *A fortiori*, the carrier is not liable if he tries to resist the attackers but then succumbs in the face of a threat perpetrated with a large-caliber weapon[105] or after criminals break the windows of the

---

[98] Cf. Cass. com. France 10 December 1991, in *Le Lamy transp.*, 2020, vol. I, 496; Cass. com. France 21 June 1988, *ibid.*, vol. I, 496; App. Paris 1 July 1999, *ibid.*, 2020, vol. I, 496; App. Amiens 20 March 2014, *ibid.*, 2020, vol. I, 496.

[99] Cf. App. Paris 13 September 2002, in *Bull. transp. logist.*, 2002, 622; but see Cass. com. France 2 June 2004, in *Le Lamy transp.*, 2020, vol. I, 49, which overturned the decision. See also OLG Cologne 10 July 2012, in *TranspR*, 2015, 111, according to which the custody obligations of a vehicle are fulfilled when the driver does not leave it unattended for a long period and sleeps in the cabin; *Cicatiello* c. *Anglo European Shipping Services Ltd.*, in *Lloyd's rep.*, 1994, 678.

[100] Cf. Cass. com. France 9 April 2013, in *Bull. transp. logist.*, 2013, 271.

[101] Cf. Cass. com. France 14 June 2016, in *Le Lamy transp.*, 2020, vol. I, 496; OLG Karlsruhe 29 June 1995, in *VersR*, 1995, 1306; BGH 13 November 1997, in *TranspR*, 1998, 250; OLG Zweibrücken 17 December 1997, *ibid.*, 1997, 369.

[102] Cf. App. Lyon 30 May 2002, in *Bull. transp. logist.*, 2002, 437; App. Reims 9 December 2002, *ibid.*, 2003, 18, according to which the carrier attacked by an armed gang operating in Sicily, following an ambush near the consignee's plant, is not liable for robbery.

[103] Cf. App. Paris 29 March 2007, in *Bull. transp. logist.*, 2007, 274.

[104] Cf. App. Reims 27 June 2001, in *Le Lamy transp.*, 2020, vol. I, 496; App. Paris 17 June 1986, in *Bull. transp.*, 1987, 174. For a similar case, see OLG Stuttgart 1 August 2007, in *TranspR*, 2007, 322, according to which the fact that the fake policemen did not show the badges is not a relevant factor; OLG Karlsruhe 21 December 2000, *ibid.*, 2003, 347, according to which there is no liability of the carrier if the driver is stopped by a person wearing a police uniform and, on the occasion of an alleged check, he is immobilized by another criminal; LG Nuremberg—Freuth 21 January 1999, *ibid.*, 2000, 369, according to which the liability of the carrier is excluded when the driver is misled by alleged police officers in the Czech Republic, who invite him to follow them and then rob him. In such circumstances, the presence of a second driver would have been irrelevant; LG Hamburg 23 September 2001, *ibid.*, 2003, 351. In the same sense, see *Gamble (Health and Beauty Care) Ltd.* c. *Concordia Shipping Agency Ltd.*, in *C. L. C. C. (B. L.)*, 2000.

[105] Cf. App. Amiens 14 October 2010, *Le Lamy transp.*, 2020, vol. I, 496. See also Cass. com. France 21 June 1988, in *Bull. transp*, 1988, 437; OGH 19 January 1994, in *TranspR*. 1995, 65; BGH 13 November 1997, *ibid.*, 1998, 250; OLG Koln 3 December 1998, *ibid.*, 1998, 250; App. Riom 15 September 1999, in *Bull. transp.*, 1999, 746. But see OLG Bremen 11 May 2000, in

vehicle.[106] Then, the attack is relevant to Article 17, second paragraph, if the driver arrives at his destination one day in advance, is subsequently asked to redeliver the goods on the agreed one and decides to stop not *in loco* but in an area considered safe, as the nearest guarded parking lot is far too distant.[107]

In these cases, the transporter must be diligent in choosing the parking area[108]; in fact, the truck must be parked in an illuminated place,[109] although not always controlled,[110] despite the fact that German case law is not always unanimous on this latter detail.[111] The carrier must put in place measures that, if not sufficient to free him from responsibility for theft, are adequate if it is associated with violence or threat, for the fair balancing of the opposing interests, so that those of the creditor upon custody and redelivery must, in part, give in to the strongest need to safeguard life and safety.[112] However, robbery does not always involve the application of Article 17, second paragraph, as, at any rate, the driver must demonstrate that he acted prudently.[113] Therefore, the transporter is responsible if, after being a victim of

---

TranspR., 2001, 75, according to which the driver should not have stopped, despite the fact that a tire exploded in the rear axle of his trailer, because the so-called "tire trick" is known in Poland and therefore the driver should not have fallen in for deception.

[106] Cf. App. Paris 14 December 2011, in *Le Lamy transp.*, 2020, vol. I, 496.

[107] Cf. App. Versailles 3 September 2013, in *Bull. transp. logist.*, 2013, 526; but see Cass. com. France 10 March 2015, in *Le Lamy transp.*, 2020, vol. I, 496, who rejected the appeal.

[108] Cf. App. Barcelona 20 January 2005, no. 7, in *Jur*, 2005, 120240, according to which the carrier is responsible in case of robbery occurred while the vehicle, without anti-theft devices, was parked in an unsupervised area in the outskirts of Rome; App. Barcelona 31 December 2002, *ibid.*, 2004, 14170; App. Valencia 8 November 1997, no. 984, in *Ac*, 197, 2273. For a case of exemption from liability for robbery, see App. Valencia 4 July 2000, no. 555, *ibid.*, 2000, 285304.

[109] Cf. App. Valencia 3 February 2016, no. 50, in *Jur*, 2016, 143913; App. Balearic Islands 4 June 2018, no. 229, *ibid.*, 2018, 255961, according to which the carrier is liable for robbery as the vehicle was parked at the entrance to a parking lot and not inside it; Supreme Court of Spain 8 October 2003, no. 918, in *RJ*, 2003, 7383; App. Barcelona 6 May 2020, no. 726, in *Ac*, 2020, 1200.

[110] Cf. OLG Munich 27 October 2000, in *TranspR*, 2001, 125, according to which the robbery of a vehicle loaded with cigarettes parked in an illuminated but not guarded parking lot in Corsica, in front of the consignee's establishment, leads to the exclusion of the carrier's responsibility, if there is no protected parking nearby.

[111] Cf. OLG Bremen 11 January 2001, in *TranspR*, 2001, 66, according to which, if the property is deposited for the night at the factory of an Italian company, the German carrier fulfills his obligations not only if the structure is fenced, but when there both plant surveillance.

[112] Cf. BGH 8 October 1998, in *TranspR*, 1999, 59; BGH 18 January 2001, *ibid.*, 2001, 369; OLG Koln 3 December 1998, *ibid*, 2000, 462; OLG Stoccarda 1 August 2007, *ibid.*, 2007, 322; Hof Antwerp 6 June 2005, in *Europ. transp. law*, 2006, no. 41, 272. Cf. Sánchez Gamborino (2001b), p. 857 ff.

[113] Cf. *Logmill Corporation PLC* v. *Andrea Merzario Ltd.*, in *C. L. C. C. (B. L.)*, 1995; App. Salonicco 171 / 2005, in *DEE*, 2005, 984; Hof Antwerp 10 October 1995, in *Europ. transp law*, 1998, no. 33, 108; Hof Antwerp 7 November, 1995, *ibid*, 1998, no. 33, 114, according to which the carrier is not asked to perform heroic behavior, but it is necessary that his conduct does not contribute to the occurrence of the robbery, as in the case in which he continues the journey at night and stops in a dangerous area, increasing the risk; Hof Antwerp 6 February 1996, *ibid.*, 1998, no. 33, 118; HR Netherlands 24 April 2009, in *Europ. transp. law*, 2009, no. 44, 707; App. Almeria

aggression in a place, he does not take the necessary precautions when returning there[114]; if he leaves the highway and stops on the side of a secondary road to check the address of the consignee on the packages, unspecified in the consignment note[115] or if he stops in a service area on an Italian highway,[116] instead of entering a city, where he could find a guarded parking lot.[117]

The latter principle has been confirmed, but it is quite severe. In fact, on the one hand, Italian rest areas are busy even at night and, on the other hand, the difficulty of circulation in cities, especially in large ones, is underestimated and would probably lead to delays. Again, if an act of aggression perpetrated at a service station is usually inevitable, this is not the case if the driver can stop in one of the parking lots indicated by the insurance company[118] On the contrary, the transporter is not liable if he opts to rest in an unattended area even if at that moment it was busy with other people, as, according to his experience, the same place would not be dangerous; however, he is attacked during his sleep,[119] the decision considers irrelevant the fact that the parking lot was not monitored, the vehicle was not equipped with an alarm and there was no second driver, who could have avoided the interruption of the journey. Perhaps, greater acumen can be expected on the part of the carrier.

---

23 October 2000, no. 376, in *Jur*, 2001, 44610, according to which the carrier is liable if he does not demonstrate that he has adopted sufficient diligence in order to avoid the robbery; Cass. France 5 July 2005, in *Unif. law rev.*, 2005, 920. See also Messent and Glass (2018), p. 163 ff.; Wesolowski (2913), p. 342 ff.; Krings (1999), p. 770 ff.; Mayer (1997), p. 173 ff.; Gruber (2017), p. 38 ff.

[114]Cf. Cass. com. France 2 February 1999, in *Bull. transp.*, 1999, 175.

[115]Cf. Cass. com. France 16 May 2006, in *Bull. transp. logist.*, 2006, 400. For similar cases, Cf. BGH 13 April 2000, in *TranspR,* 2000, 407, in which the driver was forced to stop, despite the darkness, to ask for directions, as he did not have a map of the city. Cf. Eckardt (2017), p. 42 ff.

[116]Cf. Humphreys and De Peuteur (1992), p. 742 ff., according to whom many Italian places are "hot spots identified on the basis of an analysis of statistical data relating to committed thefts".

[117]Cf. Cass. com. France 18 March 1986, in *Bull. transp.*, 1986, 251; Cass. com. France 5 January 1988, *ibid.*, 1988, 103; Cass. com. France 20 March 1990, *ibid.*, 1990, 778; Cass. com. France 14 May 1991, *ibid.*, 1992, 11; Cass. com. France 2 February 1999, *ibid.*, 1999, 175; Cass. com. France 29 February 2000, in *Europ. transp. law,* 2000, no. 35, 769. See also RB Turnhout 30 June 1997, in *Europ. transp. law,* 1998, no. 33, 139, according to which the carrier is liable if the stops occur in an area with poor surveillance. In the same sense, cf. RB Gent 11 February 1997, *ibid.*, 1998, no. 33, 121. See Messent and Glass (2018), p. 161 ff.

[118]Cf. App. Paris 28 February 1996, in *Le Lamy transp.*, 2020, vol. I, 496; App. Poitiers 4 November 1987, in *Bull. transp.*, 1988, 426; App. Toulouse 26 May 1988, in *Le Lamy transp.*, 2020, vol. I, 496; App. Besançon 17 September 1993, *ibid.*, 2020, vol. I, 496, according to which "*un professionel de la route ne peut, sans imprudence, stationner de nuit sur une aire isolée et non gardée du Nord de l'Italie*". See also App. Paris 30 May 2001, in *Bull. transp. logist.*, 2001, 641; App. Paris 22 January 2003, in *Le Lamy transp.*, 2020, vol. I, 496.

[119]Cf. Cass. Greece 1518 / 2001, in *EMP*, 2004, 452; *G. L. Cicatiello Srl and others* v. *Anglo European Shipping Services Ltd. and others* in *Europ. transp. law,* 1996, no. 31, 218.

In general, the driver must not facilitate the attack in any way,[120] for example, by setting off too late in the evening[121] or by arranging a dangerous route so as to be forced to make an extra stop.[122] However, the driver's statements on the modalities of the robbery alone are not sufficient to establish whether the fact was inevitable, pursuant to Article 17, second paragraph.[123] After all, the impression of having suffered inhalation of gas through the seals of the cabin door during sleep[124] is not conclusive, and incomplete statements are irrelevant or counterproductive.[125] Finally, the presence of two drivers, on the one hand, guarantees uninterrupted surveillance and, on the other hand, it is not always suitable for preventing a robbery, as both must respect the scheduled rest periods.[126] However, the threat cannot be thwarted simply by assigning more than one driver, with obvious defense difficulties in case of aggression.[127] Therefore, the affirmation on the general lack of responsibility in case of robbery, sometimes proposed in forensic practice, is not reflected in a more articulated case law system, which focuses on the features of the single event.[128]

7.1.5 Road Traffic, Vehicle Integrity and Atmospheric Elements

With a mere ordering intent, this paragraph includes events relating to traffic, such as road accidents, fires and damage to the integrity of the load because of atmospheric phenomena, that is hail or other bad weather. Usually, the carrier is liable if, due to

[120] Cf. Letacq (2016), p. 546 ff., who lists the most frequent cases in which robbery does not exempt the carrier.

[121] Cf. App. Poitiers 23 April 1986, in *Bull. transp.*, 1987, 362. See also Clarke (2014), p. 236 ff.

[122] Cf. App. Antwerp 7 November 1995, in *Unif. law rev.*, 1998, 114. See also Cass. com. France 18 March 1986, in *Bull. transp.*, 1986, 251, according to which the carrier is liable if he decides to stop before the authorized driving period is completed.

[123] Cf. App. Versailles 14 September 2004, in *Bull. transp. logist.*, 2005, 102.

[124] Cf. App. Angers 2 December 2008, in *Bull. transp. logist.*, 2008, 782.

[125] Cf. App. Versailles 23 September 2014, in *Le Lamy transp.*, 2020, vol. I, 497.

[126] Cf. OGH 29 June 1983, in *Europ. transp. law*, 1984, no. 19, 526; OLG Cologne 3 December 1998, in *TranspR*, 2000, 462, according to which the attack was such that the presence of two drivers would not have prevented the fact. See also Silber c. *Islander Trucking*, in Lloyd's rep., 1985, 243. Cf. Messent and Glass (2018), p. 162 ff.

[127] Cf. OLG Hamm 6 January 1997, in *TranspR*, 2000, 176, according to which the carrier is not liable if he proves that the event would have occurred even with the presence of two drivers or that there was no availability of guarded rest areas in accessible places.

[128] Cf. HR Netherlands 24 April 2009, in Europ. *transp. law,* 2009, no. 44, 707; App. Almeria 23 October 2000, no. 376, in *Jur*, 2001, 44610; Cass. France 5 July 2005, in *Unif. law rev.*, 2005, 920.

sleepiness, he causes the collision[129]; in this situation, his conduct might be relevant pursuant to Article 29 as a default equated to willful misconduct.[130] If he miscalculates the height of the vehicle and damages it while crossing a bridge, he is responsible if he cannot prove that the relevant road sign is inaccurate[131] or that the route is scheduled by the shipper in a binding manner.[132] The latter solution is not convincing as, although the choice of itinerary can be left to the sender, this does not imply that he knows the route perfectly and does not exempt the carrier from verifying its adequacy on the basis of a visual observation.[133]

In general, the driver must be foresighted to avoid collisions because of inappropriate maneuvers of others. For example, if needed, the transporter can demonstrate that the necessity of sudden braking was imposed by atypical and unpredictable needs, given the particular traffic congestion.[134] On the contrary, the carrier is liable if he loses control of the vehicle due to excessive speed[135] or if he collides with the truck in front, which was forced to slow down following another accident.[136] In fact, the latter is a frequent traffic risk that can be overcome by respecting safety distances.

For it to be relevant pursuant to Article 17, second paragraph, the road accident must be exceptional and the circumstances must not be indeterminate.[137] Thus, the carrier is not liable if, while proceeding at an adequate speed, a vehicle swerves and invades his lane in the opposite direction or if the truck in front brakes suddenly and without warning moves to the overtaking area.[138] The same principle applies if someone else's improper maneuvers cause an accident while the carrier's vehicle is

---

[129] Cf. Clarke (2014), p. 236 ff.; Libouton (1973), p. 36 ff. Cf. RB Dordrecht 18 May 1966, in *Europ. transp. law,* 1968, no. 3, 416; OLG Munich 19 July 2000, in *TranspR,* 2000, 412; BGH 29 January 2004, *ibid.,* 2994, 213.

[130] Cf. Supreme Court of Spain 9 February 1999, no. 78, in *RJ,* 1999, 1054.

[131] Cf. Trib. com. Marseille 23 October 1987, in *Bull. transp.,* 1988, 43.

[132] Cf. OLG Celle 7 September 2000, in *TranspR,* 2001, 119.

[133] In this sense, see BGH 10 April 2003, in *Europ. transp. law,* 2003, no. 38, 782, according to which the carrier cannot rely, in all circumstances, on what is declared in an authorization regarding the indication of the maximum height.

[134] Cf. OLG Düsseldorf 14 March 2007, in *TranspR,* 2007, 199. See also Thume (2013), p. 434 ff.

[135] Cf. App. Versailles 5 April 2001, in *Bull. transp. logist.,* 2001, 339.

[136] Cf. App. Rouen 11 April 1991, in *Le Lamy transp.*, 2020, vol. I, 498.

[137] Cf. App. Paris 31 March 1994, in *Bull. transp. logist.,* 2020, vol. I, 498, according to which the carrier is liable, as the accident occurred in undetermined circumstances; App. Paris 30 June 2016, *ibid.*, 2016, 447, according to which the carrier is liable if the accident occurs as a result of his fainting and because he did not stop, feeling faint; Court Paris 7 February 1994, in *Le Lamy transp.*, 2020, vol. I, 498; App. Aix – en – Provence 9 January 1987, in *Bull. transp.,* 1987, 156, according to which the carrier is liable if the accident is caused during the braking test imposed by the technical inspection of the vehicle.

[138] Cf. OLG Munich 16 January 1974, in *Europ. transp. law,* 1974, no. 9, 620; OLG Düsseldorf 14 March 2007, in *TranspR,* 2007, 199; RB Antwerp 31 October 1997, in *Europ. transp. law,* 1998, no. 33, 835; RB Antwerp 30 January 1998, *ibid.,* 1998, no. 33, 842.

parked properly[139] or if, due to the imprudence of third parties, the accident occurs because of thick fog.[140] Again, the collision provoked by a sudden swerve, made by the truck in front of that of the carrier, who proceeds at normal speed, is attributable to the third party.[141]

Finally, the transporter is not always exempt from liability if, in an attempt to prevent a collision, he makes a sudden maneuver. He has the obligation of custody and he must arrange the load even in anticipation of violent action during the journey.[142] The sender is obliged to respect the same prudence if he is liable for the loading and stowing.[143] However, in the latter case, the carrier can invoke Article 17, fourth paragraph, letter c). In summary, his liability ceases if there is an unforeseeable circumstance[144] or behavior of a harmful third party. These criteria are correct and obvious, because, if the carrier is a specialist in transport and must guarantee its regular performance, the relative pitfalls are not to be underestimated and indeed are very frequent.

The destruction of the vehicle can depend on a fire.[145] Even in case the fire is malicious and provoked by third parties, the conduct of the carrier must be verified.[146] Therefore, he is liable if the truck is parked for several days in an unsupervised area although it can be in a controlled place.[147] Furthermore, the lack of clarity on how the fire developed does not exclude the transporter's liability, pursuant to Article 17, second paragraph,[148] for the irrelevance of unknown causes.

---

[139] Cf. Trib. Paris 13 December 1976, in *Bull. transp.*, 1977, 37. For similar cases, see App. Paris 13 December 1976, *ibid.*, 1977, 83; Cass. com. France 8 March 2017, *ibid.*, 2017, 173; App. Metz 30 October 1990, *ibid.*, 1991, 490.

[140] Cf. Trib. Brussels 31 May 1996, in *Europ. transp. law*, 1996, no. 31, 586.

[141] Cf. Trib. Mulhouse 30 January 2004, in *Bull. transp. logist.*, 2004, 136; App. Paris 16 January 2002, *ibid.*, 2002, 168, according to which the carrier is not liable if he collides with a vehicle moving on without the headlights on; Cass. com. France 22 July 1986, *ibid.*, 1986, 591, which recognized the carrier's liability to the extent of fifty percent for having braked late and not very sharply when a four hundred kilogram cast iron block fell from a previous vehicle.

[142] Cf. Clarke (2014), p. 237 ff.; OLG Karlsruhe 9 December 1998, in *TranspR*, 2000, 465, according to which, in the event of significant damage to an asset, the carrier must explain what measures he has taken to obviate the risk of road accidents and how he has checked and arranged the loading and stowage before the start of the journey.

[143] Cf. Trib. Rouen 11 April 1991, in *Bull. transp. logist.*, 1992, 11.

[144] Cf. App. Barcelona 15 October 2012, no. 329, in *Ac*, 2012, 2342; App. Barcelona 4 February 2016, no. 24, in *Ac*, 2016, 706, according to which the carrier is liable for the damage to the goods following a curve performed at an excessive speed.

[145] Cf. Abromavicius (2017), p. 54 ff. See App. Valencia 29 March 2006, no. 134, in *Jur*, 2006, 226817.

[146] Cf. Clarke (2014), p. 238 ff. See also BGH 5 June 1981, in *Europ. transp. law*, 1982, no. 17, 309; RB Zeeland – West - Brabant, 13 December 2017, *ibid.*, 2018, no. 53, 469.

[147] Cf. Cass. com. France 6 January 1998, in *Le Lamy transp.*, 2020, vol. I, 497; App. Brussels 12 December 1978, in *Bull. transp.*, 1978, 39; App. Versailles 7 September 1995, *ibid.*, 1995, 659; App. Antwerp 24 November 1982, in *Le Lamy transp.*, 2020, vol. I, 497.

[148] Cf. Cass. com. France 13 September 2011, in *Le Lamy transp.*, 2020, vol. I, 497; App. Rennes 6 May 2015 in *Bull. transp. logist.*, 2015, 316.

Moreover, the carrier is responsible if the fact is due to a maintenance defect[149] or because the vehicle is not equipped with the prescribed fire extinguisher.[150] The liability is excluded only if exceptional circumstances occur. Therefore, it must be considered whether, because of spontaneous combustion of the load, the fire spreads to the point of destroying other goods present in a second truck of the same transporter, parked next to the first.[151]

Bad weather can lead to the application of Article 17, second paragraph, only if exceptional. Therefore, frost in January is not unpredictable, but the risk of losing the goods falls on the shipper if he does not strengthen the packaging.[152] On the contrary, the responsibility lies with the carrier if he does not prevent freezing despite adequate packaging.[153] The transporter's opportunities to successfully invoke Article 17, second paragraph, increase if the sender does not perceive the particular sensitivity of some goods to being exposed to freezing, if the fragility of this load cannot be inferred in any other way.[154] However, these circumstances cannot be taken into account if freezing occurs after the deadline for redelivery and the shipper can demonstrate that the reinforced packaging would have been sufficient for a journey of the agreed duration.[155] Finally, the presence of violent winds accompanied by heavy rain, which tears the tarpaulin and wets the goods, is not a reason for exemption. However, the carrier can demonstrate the inability to find shelter.[156] If particularly strong winds give rise to the recognition of the state of natural disaster, Article 17, second paragraph, applies.[157]

---

[149] Cf. App. Versailles 14 November 2019, in *Le Lamy transp.*, 2020, vol. I, 497; OLG Düsseldorf 18 July 1971, in *VersR,* 1973, 177; OLG Zweibrücken 23 September 1966, *ibid.,* 1967, 1145.

[150] Cf. App. Pau 21 June 2013, in *Le Lamy transp.*, 2020, vol. I, 497.

[151] Cf. Cass. com. France 23 May 1989, in *Le Lamy transp.*, 2020, vol. I, 497; App. Versailles 8 April 2010, in *Bull. transp. logist.,* 2010, 255, according to which the carrier is not liable if the fire of one of the axles of the transport vehicle is caused by the rubbing of a foreign body that accidentally entered between the twin tires of the rear axle.

[152] Cf. App. Montpellier 28 February 1985, in *Bull. transp.,* 1985, 600; more generally, OGH 9 November 2016, in *TranspR,* 2017, 120, according to which the sender must assess the need for packaging considering the fact that the transport involves, in any case, an unavoidable exposure of the goods to negative effects caused by the elements.

[153] Cf. App. Amiens 28 October 1992, in *Bull. transp. logist.,* 1992, 766; App. Nîmes 18 May 1988, *ibid.,* 1988, 472.

[154] Cf. App. Paris 25 March 1969, in *Bull. transp.,* 1969, 174; see also App. Nîmes 18 May 1988, *ibid.,* 1988, 472.

[155] Cf. Cass. com. France 5 December 1989, in *Bull. transp.* 1990, 310.

[156] Cf. App. Versailles 11 June 2013, *Le Lamy transp.*, 2020, vol. I, 497.

[157] Cf. App. Paris 2 October 2014, in *Le Lamy transp.*, 2020, vol. I, 497.

7.1.6 The Facts of the Public Administration and Third Parties

In defining the unavoidable circumstances pursuant to Article 17, second paragraph, the legitimate conduct of third parties or the provisions of public administrations are included if their effects are reflected on the journey.[158] This is the case with strikes, although it is not always a reason for exemption, as the carrier must demonstrate that he could not have avoided the consequences. Thus, if he can cross the border elsewhere, a local customs officers' strike is not a case of *force majeure*.[159] Again, if perishable goods are redelivered late because of a strike and the transporter agrees to move them to a different location without first checking their condition, the strike cannot be invoked as an unavoidable circumstance.[160] Since going on strike without warning is sometimes considered commonplace in many countries, the carrier should predict its possible impact when organizing the journey.[161] This solution is not always adequate because considerable effort would be required from him. To tell the truth, the latter decisions are a little out of date, since, in various countries, compliance with the notice period is not only the subject of specific provisions, but also commonplace. The tasks of a due professional activity include that the transporter be expected to verify any strike, information whereof is sometimes disseminated in real time through some institutional sites.

On the contrary, a strike called by the port staff of Marseille is considered an inevitable circumstance if it delays the loading of a vehicle with perishable goods by several days and significantly extends the trip.[162] The transporter is not liable if, informed of a strike by the customs officers, he gets organized to arrive at the border when such event is over, but, along the journey, he learns that the same abstention from work has been extended. Moreover, in this case, the question arises as to whether the decision is in line with the reconciliation between the workers' interest in the strike with that in the regular development of the productive activity.[163] However, if the mentioned decisions are updated with respect to the current regulatory contexts, they are reasonable. At any rate, only the strike of public administration employees is relevant, not that of the carrier's workers, since, in this case, the requirement of inevitability is missing, and that is reserved for national initiatives, completely outside the control of an individual operator.

Article 17, second paragraph, regards the conduct of personnel during customs operations. For example, violent handling followed by loading performed without

---

[158] Cf. Jung (1997), p. 157 ff.

[159] Cf. App. Paris 1 July 1986, in *Le Lamy transp.*, 2020, vol. I, 498.

[160] Cf. Cass. com. France 9 October 1974, in *Le Lamy transp.*, 2020, vol. I, 498.

[161] Cf. App. Paris 21 January 1988, in *Le Lamy transp.*, 2020, vol. I, 498, which excluded *force majeure* in the event of a strike by the maritime personnel called after the goods had been loaded.

[162] Cf. App. Paris 1 July 1986, in *Le Lamy transp.*, 2020, vol. I, 498.

[163] Cf. Trib. com. Tours 2 September 1994, in *Le Lamy transp.*, 2020, vol. I, 498. The decision was confirmed by App. Orléans 12 November 1996, *ibid.*, 2020, vol. I, 498.

caution is a cause for exemption if the transporter demonstrates the impossibility of solving the problem or mitigating the consequences.[164] Then, a wait of 7 days imposed by customs with regard to the transfer of fresh plants excludes the responsibility of the carrier.[165]

More generally, events caused by third parties are inevitable if they do not leave any alternative to the transporter. For example, a double postponement of boarding due to a decision by the shipping company is not an insurmountable fact if recourse can be taken to a different one.[166] Although it is known, the political situation of a country does not exclude liability, so that the carrier can refuse to perform the service,[167] even more so in an era like ours, dominated by modern means of communication, which guarantee immediate information.

7.1.7 The Defective Condition of the Vehicle Used to Perform the Carriage

According to Article 17, third paragraph, "a defective condition of the vehicle" or "the wrongful act or neglect of the person from whom" the carrier "may have hired the vehicle or of the agents or servants of the latter" is not a cause of exemption.[168] This provision follows the one on exemption cases and precedes the regulation on special risks; for some,[169] the choice to include this rule here is not accidental but rather underlines how the truck defect would not be counted among the inevitable circumstances provided for by Article 17, second paragraph, and, at the same time, it would not be a special risk, since, otherwise, there would be a contradiction with the reference of Article 17, fourth paragraph, to Article 18, fourth paragraph, relating to transport performed with a vehicle equipped to protect the goods from heat, cold or changes in temperature.[170] According to Article 17, third paragraph, the carrier must guarantee the maintenance of the truck under any circumstances; thus, he is liable if

---

[164] Cf. App. Paris 7 April 1986, in *Le Lamy transp.*, 2020, vol. I, 499. Cf. Messent and Glass (2018), p. 165 ff.

[165] Cf. App. Agen 21 September 1983, in *Le Lamy transp.*, 2020, vol. I, 499. See Clarke (2014), p. 239 ff.; Messent and Glass (2018), p. 165 ff.

[166] Cf. App. Nîmes 20 December 1990, in *Le Lamy transp.*, 2020, vol. I, 499.

[167] Cf. App. Paris 6 February 1979, in *Bull. transp.*, 1979, 281; App. Paris 28 February 1981, *ibid.*, 1981, 270; App. Paris 9 July 1981, in *Le Lamy transp.*, 2020, vol. I, 499; Trib. com. Carpentras 19 February 1993, *ibid.*, 2020, vol. I, 499, on the delivery of goods to Jordan shortly before the ultimatum addressed to Iraq on withdrawal from Kuweit expired.

[168] This is how Article 17, third paragraph, in the English version, reads. In the French version, it reads, "*défectuosités du véhicule*" or "*de fautes de la personne dont" le transporteur "aurait loué le véhicule ou des préposés de celle – ci*".

[169] Cf. Clarke (2014), p. 241 ff.

[170] Cf. Clarke (2014), p. 241 ff.

the gearbox breaks[171] or if, due to a manufacturing defect, he does not realize that the vehicle is too high when compared to the height of a bridge[172] or if, because of the malfunction of the brakes, a fire breaks out and, in an attempt to contain it, the firefighters damage the load.[173]

Article 17, third paragraph, limits the application of both Article 17, second paragraph, and Article 17, fourth paragraph. Therefore, it circumscribes the scope of these two provisions, so that, in general, the control over the functionality of the vehicle falls within the direct and inevitable object of responsibility. This clarification is not useless because of the frequency of similar cases and because ensuring the functionality of the truck is the first step in reconstructing the obligations of the carrier. Nor is there a contradiction with Article 17, fourth paragraph, letter a), with regard to a derogatory event and deemed worthy of separate treatment. Even if Article 17, third paragraph, had not been inserted, the same conclusions could have been reached on the basis of the second paragraph, since the two rules are consistent with each other and not in contradiction. However, this does not exclude the relevance of Article 17, third paragraph, in clarifying the implicit concepts in the second one.

The sender or consignee has the burden to prove the causal link between the damage and the defect of the vehicle; at the same time, it is difficult for the carrier to demonstrate to the contrary because of the propensity of case law to charge the malfunction of the truck to its improper use. Thus, the transporter is responsible for the prejudice to a part of the load if provoked by fire following the explosion of a tire if this latter fact can be traced back to a maintenance defect.[174]

According to Article 17, third paragraph, the lack of integrity of the vehicle[175] is relevant; therefore, the carrier is liable if the damage is caused by the explosion of a nearly new[176] tire or by engine wear.[177] However, this provision is extended to cases

[171] Cf. Messent and Glass (2018), p. 166 ff.; Thume (2013), p. 435 ff.

[172] Cf. App. Colmar 26 January 2000, in *Bull. transp.*, 2000, 154. For a particular hypothesis, cf. Hof Antwerp 23 June 1992, in *Europ. transp. law,* 1993, no. 28, 293, according to which the carrier is not liable if the tugboat entrusted to him does not cross the bridge because it is a few meters higher than the height requirements; the carrier was unable to perceive the exact height of the vehicle on the basis of a simple visual feedback.

[173] Cf. App. Paris 10 March 2000, in *Bull. transp.*, 2000, 211.

[174] Cf. App. Brussels 17 June 1971, in *Europ. transp. law,* 1971, no. 6, 825.

[175] Cf. App. Paris 26 May 1982, in *Bull. transp.*, 1982, 502, according to which a torn sheet is a defect of the vehicle. In the same sense, see *Walek & Co.* v. *Ball, in Lloyd's rep.,* 1980, 279, according to which a cover with a faulty inclination falls under Article 17, third paragraph; OGH 13 February 2003, in *Europ. transp. law,* 2004, no. 39, 244.

[176] Cf. OGH 10 July 1991, in *Unif. law rev.*, 1992, 833, according to which there is insufficient proof that the tires were almost new (to the extent of eighty percent); App. Rennes 6 May 2015, in *Le Lamy transp.*, 2020, vol. I, 498; Hof Antwerp 19 October 2009, in *Europ. transp. law,* 2010, no. 45, 427, according to which "a tire puncture is a defect of the road vehicle in the sense of Article 17, third paragraph, of CMR as a result of which the carrier is relieved of his full liability".

[177] Cf. App. Versailles 14 November 2019, in *Le Lamy transp.*, 2020, vol. I, 498.

wherein the truck is unsuitable for receiving the cargo.[178] *A fortiori*, the legal notion of defect of the vehicle includes not only an original and structural one that makes the same vehicle dangerous, but also its inadequacy for a single load, which is a more frequent scenario that has to be placed at the same level, albeit with an objective reading of responsibility.[179]

This particular unsuitability presupposes prior knowledge of the characteristics of the goods, with the fulfillment by the sender of the obligation to collaborate in the smooth running of the journey and with detailed information inferable from the consignment note or from other ancillary sources.[180] This conception does not extend the responsibility, because, for accurate understanding of Article 17, third paragraph, the defect exists if the truck is not ready for the agreed journey and from the object of the same Article 17, third paragraph, the necessary connotations of the vehicle are derived, regardless of an express consensus or the fact that only the transferred asset is known, because, to that point, it aids the professional competence of the carrier. Then, if the goods are not identified in a consistent manner, there is no responsibility. For example, the transporter must ensure internal cleanliness, if necessary. Therefore, if the load is damaged due to the presence of residual chemical traces of a previous trip, the carrier is liable pursuant to Article 17, third paragraph.[181] The same principle applies in case of delivery of works of art on a truck with an interior that is too large, more suitable for the transfer of window frames.[182]

In general, for the vehicle to be considered unsuitable, the carrier must know the nature of the load;[183] thus, he must be aware of its sensitivity to exposure to cold[184]

---

[178] Cf. Clarke (2014), p. 242 ff.; Putzeys (1981), p. 256 ff., according to whom *"est assimilable à la défectuosité du véhicule son inaptitude à réaliser le transport comandé. Cette 'défectuosité' est alors relative, puisqu'elle dépend de la nature de la marchandise; pour qu'il soit responsable, le transporteur aura dû être (mis) au courant des nécessités inhérentes au contrat, par l'éxpediteur, par la convention";* see also Sánchez Gamborino (2001a), p. 645 ff. For an approach limited to vehicle defects only, see Libouton (1973), p. 39 ff.; Haak (1986), p. 151 ff.

[179] Clarke (2014), p. 242 ff.; Putzeys (1981), p. 256 ff.

[180] Cf. OLG Frankfurt am Main 3 December 2003, in *TranspR*, 2004, 125, according to which, since the risk of freezing the beer derives from an intrinsic characteristic of the product, it is the responsibility of the sender to disclose this fact and order a suitable vehicle.

[181] Cf. App. Amiens 28 November 1974, in *Bull. transp.*, 1975, 23; Federal Court of the Swiss Confederation 3 November 2008, in *the Information system of the Federal Court*; OGH 28 February 2001, in *Europ. transp. law*, 2003, no. 38, 131; Hof Antwerp 20 June 2011, *ibid.*, 2011, no. 45, 543, according to which there is responsibility of the carrier even if the damage from contamination extends from the goods loaded to those not transported.

[182] Cf. Cass. com. France 22 February 1994, in *Bull. transp.*, 1994, 263; OGH 21 February 1996, in *TransR*, 1996, 422. For an analogous case, see App. Barcelona 29 March 2007, no. 185, in *Jur*, 2007, 243690.

[183] Cf. Loewe (1976), p. 364 ff., according to whom, "if the vehicle is merely unsuitable for the carriage of certain types of goods, this constitutes a defective condition only in cases where the carrier is aware of the unsuitability". Cf. App. Madrid 19 January 2018, no. 59, in *Ac*, 2018, 316.

[184] Cf. Clarke (2014), p. 242 ff.; Messent and Glass (2018), p. 167 ff.

or be instructed by the shipper[185] that, as the cargo must be stored at a certain temperature, an adequate refrigeration system is required.[186] Therefore, the transporter is not liable for a hidden defect of a container supplied by the sender[187] or if the carrier accepts from him a vehicle with evident damage.[188] The latter solution is not convincing, as Article 17, third paragraph, implies a restrictive interpretation[189] and that the transporter must guarantee the proper functioning of the truck regardless of any acquiescent conduct of the sender. On the contrary, if the transporter usually carries certain goods, wherefrom some precautions are required, it is presumed that he knows the procedures for proper accommodation;[190] therefore, he cannot prove that he has not been informed, as experience helps.

Finally, according to Article 17, third paragraph, the carrier is liable if the imperfection depends on the negligent conduct of the person from whom the vehicle is rented. The same principle applies in the case of a subcarrier accepting a truck with a damaged tarpaulin from the main transporter.[191] This approach is convincing, because subtransport is an autonomous contract, albeit linked by a functional constraint to the main one, and the subcarrier must comply with the provisions of Article 17, third paragraph.

7.2 The Special Risks

7.2.1 The So-Called Special Risks

Like some civil law systems, the Convention opts for the most severe regime of objective liability, with a deviation from the model based on fault, as can be deduced from a reconstruction of Article 17, according to which the carrier is always liable if he does not demonstrate the causal connection between the prejudice and one of the exemption cases indicated exhaustively in Article 17, second paragraph. The

[185] Cf. App. Granada 7 March 2005, no. 150, in *Ac*, 2005, 1008, according to which the carrier is liable because he disregards the instructions of the shipper on the regulation of the thermostat.

[186] Cf. OLG Nuremberg 14 June 1965, in *Europ. transp. law,* 1971, no. 6, 247; App. Venice 31 October 1974, *ibid.,* 1974, no. 9, 242, according to which the carrier is not liable if he uses a nonrefrigerated vehicle suitable for the transport of bananas, if the shipper does not request a vehicle with these characteristics. Cf. App. Valencia 9 November 2009, no. 276, in *Ac,* 2010, 266; App. Barcelona 17 December 2013, no. 479, in *Jur*, 2014, 21232, according to which the carrier is responsible because he did not transport the medicines at a controlled temperature of minus twenty degrees, despite the warning to that effect on the packages themselves.

[187] Cf. Clarke (2014), p. 242 ff.

[188] Cf. Messent and Glass (2018), p. 168 ff.

[189] Cf. Rodière (1971), p. 18 ff.

[190] Cf. Messent and Glass (2018), p. 168 ff.

[191] Cf. *Walek & Co.* c. *Chapman & Ball*, in *Lloyd's rep.,* 1980, 279; Loewe (1976), p. 364 ff.; Messent and Glass (2018), p. 168 ff.

strategy is justified by the idea of composing "the needs of safeguarding users and (...) regulating the exercise of transport activities in relation to the incidence of business risk in a limited legislative framework".[192] Such theses are frequent in continental law and underline a certain preference for objective parameters, although there are other arguments that tend to emphasize fault.[193] However, apart from a general assessment of the best regulatory framework, Article 17 does not consider diligence.

Showing an innovative approach in road transport, the Convention mitigates liability by borrowing the category of so-called "excepted perils" from the experience gained in the maritime sector. In this last regard, Article 4, no. 2, of the 1924 Brussels Convention identifies mandatory cases that, if they occurred, would waive the carrier from the liability for loss or damage, as they are typical risks of navigation and extraneous to the carrier's control. Inspired by this model, Article 17, fourth paragraph, identifies in a binding manner six categories of perils for which the transporter is not responsible[194]; such scenarios do not fall within the scope of his business risk and, therefore, they are not controllable by himself or, in any case, these factors are not attributed to him.[195] There is no symmetry between the cases of exemption from liability of Article 17, second paragraph, and the special risks of the fourth one, because, unlike the former, the latter apply only for prejudices from loss or damage and not for those from delay.[196] In fact, according to Article 17, fourth paragraph, "the carrier shall be relieved of liability when the loss or damage arises from the special risks".[197]

Each case refers to the obligation to preserve the load and its custody, not to the duration of the journey and its overall execution. This conclusion is intuitively evident if one reflects on the structure of the provisions. Therefore, unlike the causes of exemption, the failure to achieve the agreed goal is not taken into account, but structural problems, such as to condition the transfer in an original way, are; these are problems mostly due to the characteristics of the goods, which are outside the possible intervention of the carrier. The difference from Article 17, second paragraph, can be clearly seen.

Pursuant to Article 18, second paragraph, to be able to invoke one of the so-called "special risks", the transporter must demonstrate that, from an etiological perspective, the damage is attributable to one of the cases referred to in Article 17, fourth paragraph.[198] For some decisions,[199] the alleged special risk should not necessarily

---

[192] Cf. Silingardi et al. (1994), p. 162 ff.

[193] Cf. Putzeys (1981), p. 217 ff.

[194] Cf. Putzeys (1981), p. 256 ff.; Libouton (1973), p. 39 ff.; Haak (1986), p. 153 ff.

[195] Cf. Jung (1997), p. 158 ff.

[196] Cf. Putzeys (1981), p. 256 ff.; Haak (1986), p. 154 ff.

[197] This is how Article 17 reads in the English version. The French version reads, *"le transporteur est déchargés de sa responsabilité lorsque la perte ou the avarie résulte des risques particuliers"*.

[198] Cf. BGH 15 June 2000, in *Europ. transp. law,* 2000, no. 35, 785.

[199] Cf. Cass. com. France 24 October 1990, in *Bull. transp.,* 1990, 99; App. Amiens 6 May 1981, *ibid.,* 1982, 271; App. Brussels 1 December 1997, in *Europ. transp. law,* 2000, no. 35, 125.

be the actual cause of the prejudice but a likely explanation.[200] Since the provision of Article 17, fourth paragraph, is in favor of the transporter, it would apply even if the damage could result from other scenarios contemplated by the same fourth paragraph and, therefore, the burden of proof would be less rigorous than that one which is inferred from Article 17, second paragraph, wherefor the unknown cause is irrelevant. This approach to Article 17, fourth paragraph, is not convincing, not only due to the lack of a coherent textual reference, but also because, by their nature, special risks can only be relevant if they are connected by a causal link to the fact. There can be no lessening of the burden of proof; either the etiological link exists and Article 17, fourth paragraph, applies, or the opposite principle has to be invoked. If anything, the provision does not require risk to be the sole cause, but only one of the determining causes, although the problem is not statistically relevant. This is not an exclusive feature of Article 17, fourth paragraph, because it also concerns the reasons for exemption, as can be seen in Article 17, fifth paragraph, about the shipper's obligations.

The CMR introduces an institution hitherto practically unknown in international road transport and the solution is clever, so much so that it has resisted for over 60 years, and radically solves known problems in the operational experience on the basis of objective criteria, with regard not so much to transport as an activity as to its scope. In turn, the entitled person can give proof to the contrary and demonstrate that one of the special risks, pursuant to Article 18, second paragraph, did not cause the damage.[201] The shipper or the consignee do not have to identify the fact that actually determined the loss or damage, but can limit themselves to refuting the carrier's argument; if this attempt is successful, the transporter can only refer to the reasons for exemption regulated by Article 17, second paragraph.

Pursuant to Article 29, the carrier cannot invoke special risks if he acts with willful misconduct or with equivalent fault, but, on this point, the burden of proof is on the person entitled, who must demonstrate the specific subjective condition of the transporter. If the sender or the consignee demontrates the carrier's willful misconduct or the equivalent fault, the same carrier cannot invoke the compensation limit and, furthermore, Article 17, fourth paragraph, does not apply. In fact, the special risks are relevant in a journey executed according to the rules of social normality and not with a significant deviation from the precautionary standards. This does not exclude the reference to Article 17, fourth paragraph, on objective parameters, because these are relevant in ordinary conditions. Willful misconduct or equivalent default shifts the transporter's liability to another level and, not surprisingly, the

[200] Cf. Cass. com. France 10 February 1969, in *Bull. transp.*, 1969, 107; Cass. com. France 4 February 1986, *ibid.*, 1986, 197; App. Paris 27 January 1970, *ibid.*, 1970, 100; App. Paris 23 December 1975, *ibid.*, 1976, 48. Cf. also Putzeys (1981), p. 256 ff., according to whom "*on ne rappellera jamais assez que le transporteur n'a pas à prouverla relation causale entre la perte, l'avarie (...) et le fait particulier, mais qu'il peut limiter sa démonstration à celle de la possibilité de causalité*".

[201] Cf. Pesce (1995), p. 225 ff.

corresponding circumstances require specific allegations and proofs from the person entitled to the compensation.

7.2.2 Open Vehicles and the Lack of or Defect in Packaging

Article 17, fourth paragraph, letter a), states as a first scenario of special risk the "*emploi de véhicules ouverts et non bâchés, lorsque cet emploi a été convenu d'une manière expresse et mentionné dans la lettre de voiture*".[202] Because of how the transfer is carried out, the goods may suffer prejudice owing to their exposure to bad weather, such as cold, frost, hail or rain, and the carrier can invoke this provision if the use of the open vehicle is agreed with the shipper. Therefore, Article 17, fourth paragraph, letter a), does not apply when, once a truck with a sheet has been made available to facilitate loading, the driver does not deem it necessary to restore it for the journey.[203] According to Article 17, fourth paragraph, letter a), the agreement must be explicitly outlined in the consignment note, but this provision must be interpreted consistently with the rule of the Convention concerning the optional nature of this document, that is, Article 4, wherefore and failing which it is possible to infer the will of the parties in another way, although the absence of the consignment note makes the proofing more difficult.

The carrier cannot invoke Article 18, third paragraph, if there is an atypical decrease in the number of goods or an atypical loss of packages. The reference to a "*manquant d'une importance anormale*" presupposes bulk cargo wherefor there is a dispersion of light material because of the effect of the wind. The shortfall must not be overly significant, but compatible with this mode of transport. Conversely, the carrier is liable for the loss of packages; Article 18 does not issue an investigation and, therefore, it is not relevant the fact as to whether they fall or are stolen. This is because, if the carrier agrees to transport the goods with an open vehicle, he must take the necessary measures to guarantee a safe journey.

Article 17, fourth paragraph, letter b), contemplates the lack or defect of packaging if the shipper has to prepare it.[204] Furthermore, the provision does not concern apparent defects in the packaging, as these must be addressed with justified reservations at the time of loading.[205] To apply Article 17, fourth paragraph, letter b), the absence or inadequacy of packaging must increase the risk, for example, due to frost

[202] Thus, Article 17, fourth paragraph, letter a), is in the French version. In the English version, it reads, "use of open unsheeted vehicles, when their use has been expressly agreed and specified in the consignment note".

[203] Cf. App. Rennes 18 January 1989, in *Le Lamy transp.*, 2020, vol. I, 500.

[204] Cf. Hof Gent 19 January 1999, in *Europ. transp. law,* 1999, no. 34, 264. See also Otte (2018), p. 1398 ff.

[205] Cf. Antapasis (2017), p. 48 ff., according to whom it is possible for the carrier to prove the packaging defect, despite not having made reservations at the time of receipt of the goods. See also App. Larissa 347 / 2006, in *EpiskED,* 2006, 548; App. Pireo 268 / 2001, in *EMD*, 2001, 327.

or oxidation; this must be a direct consequence of the lack of protection or the inadequate one and it must be practically assessed.[206] It is not possible to apply Article 17, fourth paragraph, letter b), for a material of large dimensions and heavy weight if it suffers a breakdown following a violent impact against the vault of a bridge,[207] because the case is completely heterogeneous with respect to the legal rule.

The same principle applies if coils of copper wire break due to the vehicle overturning[208] or if metal drums are damaged during unloading.[209] In fact, in these cases, there is no causal link between the damage and the lack of, or defect in, packaging. More generally, the carrier cannot invoke this risk if, by their nature, the goods are not subject to degeneration, despite the fact that, in the absence of protection or due to defective packaging, they are exposed to adverse weather conditions,[210] or if the prejudice is caused by the packaging usually used for cargo with those characteristics.[211] In the latter case, the carrier is not responsible, as an appropriate container is used.

On the contrary, Article 17, fourth paragraph, letter b), describes the case wherein the packaging is functional to the protection of the goods, but is not successful in safeguarding them.[212] Thus, if the conduct is attributable to the shipper, the transporter is not liable if aluminum elements sensitive to violent shocks or rubbing are held in place only by a plastic band[213]; if, in an inadequate way, separate parts of a textile machinery are protected, likely to being damaged by impact,[214] or, again, if polyester dividers are compromised during their transport in a sealed container.[215] *A fortiori*, the carrier can invoke Article 17, fourth paragraph, letter b), if, due to a

---

206 Cf. JMerc San Sebastian 26 June 2018, no. 214, in *Jur*, 2018, 273147, according to which the carrier is not liable if it is proven that the oxidation precedes the loading.

207 Cf. App. Poitiers 31 March 1971, in *Bull. transp.*, 1971, 168. Similarly, see App. Dijon 13 March 1985, in *Le Lamy transp.*, 2020, vol. I, 500; App. Orléans 18 January 1995, in *Bull. transp. logist.*, 1995 129.

208 Cf. App. Paris 13 February 1985, in *Le Lamy transp.*, 2020, vol. I, 500.

209 Cf. App. Grenoble 3 October 2001, in *Le Lamy transp.*, 2020, vol. I, 500.

210 Cf. App. Lyon 6 April 2017, in *Le Lamy transp.*, 2020, vol. I, 500.

211 Cf. App. Douai 16 December 2014, in *Le Lamy transp.*, 2020, vol. I, 500, for a case of beet seeds packaged in octabins, a typical container for these products.

212 Cf. App. Lleida 25 June 2015, no. 274, in *Jur*, 2015, 187564, according to which the carrier is not liable because the shipper did not display the *"no apilar"* notice on the packaging.

213 Cf. App. Paris 23 June 1975, in *Bull. transp.*, 1975, 360.

214 Cf. App. Grenoble 23 April 1980, in *Bull. transp.*, 1980, 301. In the same sense, see App. Versailles 19 May 2011, in *Le Lamy transp.*, 2020, vol. I, 500; App. Aix – en – Provence 10 November 2010, *ibid.*, vol. I, 500, for a case of inadequately stacked tubs of yogurt; App. Douai 21 October 2010, *ibid.*, vol. I, 500.

215 Cf. App. Paris 6 December 2007, in *Le Lamy transp.*, 2020, vol. I, 500. See also App. Besançon 7 February 1996, in *Bull. transp. logist.*, 1996, 682, for a case of cheeses arranged too tightly on a pallet.

defect in the packaging, goods sensitive to freezing, such as legumes or fruit, are damaged.[216]

7.2.3 *Maintenance, Loading, Unloading, and Stowage by the Sender or the Consignee*

According to Article 17, fourth paragraph, letter c), the carrier is not liable for prejudice caused during the "*manutention, chargement, arrimage ou déchargement*",[217] when they are entrusted to the shipper or the consignee[218]; however, if the transporter helps in the loading operations, he cannot invoke this special risk.[219] Thus, he is not required to compensate for the prejudice caused by the stacking of heavy crates on lighter ones if this is attributable to the sender.[220] For the carrier to benefit from the indication of Article 17, fourth paragraph, letter c), he cannot generally attach the inadequacy of such operations as the cause of the damage.[221] On the contrary, the fact that the goods move during the journey does not in itself imply a stowage defect,[222] but the transporter must prove precise

---

[216] Cf. App. Montpellier 28 February 1985, in *Bull. transp.*, 1985, 600.

[217] This is how Article 17, fourth paragraph, letter c), reads in the French version. In the English version, it reads, "handling, loading, stowage, or unloading". Cf. Putzeys (1981), p. 262 ff.; Libouton (1973), p. 42 ff.; Loewe (1976), p. 366 ff., according to whom "the mere existence of the special provision in paragraph fourth, letter c), shows clearly that under CMR *régime*, the operations mentioned therein may be performed by either of the contracting parties and that the authors of the Convention carefully avoided attributing any obligation in that respect to either party". Cf. Rodière (1970), p. 630 ff.; Thume (2013), p. 454 ff.

[218] Cf. App. Amiens 23 November 1990, in *Bull. transp. logist.*, 1991; App. Toulouse 17 February 2016, *ibid.*, 2016, 143; Hof 1 Antwerp March 1999, in *Europ. transp. law*, 2000, no. 35, 544; Hof Hertogenbosch 30 April 2019, *ibid.*, 2019, no. 54, 541; BGH 19 March 2015, *ibid.*, 2016, no. 51, 99; RB Leuven 23 October 1990, *ibid.*, 1992, no. 27, 272, according to which, if, during the journey, the carrier moves the goods, such as, for example, because of transshipment of the goods, he cannot invoke Article 17, fourth paragraph, letter c); OGH 20 October 2004, in *Unif. law rev.*, 2005, 625, according to which, in the absence of an agreement, the sender is responsible for stowage operations; App. Asturias 13 January 1998, no. 19, in *Ac*, 1998, 2980. See also Thume (2013), p. 455 ff.

[219] Cf. OLG Munich 28 January 2004, in *TranspR*, 2004, 324.

[220] Cf. App. Paris 13 January 1984, in *Le Lamy transp.*, 2020, vol. I, 503.

[221] Cf. Bamberg 29 July 2015, in *TranspR*, 2016, 155.

[222] Cf. App. Bourges 5 July 2012, in *Le Lamy transp.*, 2020, vol. I, 500; App. Lyon 18 September 2014, *ibid.*, 2020, vol. I, 500; App. Douai 16 December 2014, *ibid.*, 2020, vol. I, 500, for a scenario in which the carrier collaborates with the sender to perform the loading; App. Riom 29 January 2011, *ibid.*, 2020, vol. I, 500, with regard to a case in which the transporter carries out the transshipment of goods during the journey; App. Orléans 22 December 2005, *ibid.*, 2020, vol. I, 500.

situations that link the prejudice to the conduct of the shipper or the consignee[223] or are a plausible explanation for it.[224] In this last respect, the solution of the aforementioned decision is not convincing, because the etiological link must be ascertained and Article 17, fourth paragraph, letter c), does not lessen the burden of proof, as it is either given or lacking. Thus, if the cause of the prejudice is not identified, the demonstration of the fact that the stowage by the sender was such as to expose the goods at risk is irrelevant.[225] Moreover, the etiological link between overload and an accident is not demonstrated if the latter occurs in undetermined conditions.[226] In fact, Article 17, fourth paragraph, letter c), does not operate in the absence of evidence of a connection between the special risk and the event that occurred.

On the contrary, the carrier can invoke Article 17, fourth paragraph, letter c), if he identifies the circumstances that connect the damage to one of the operations indicated by the law.[227] For some decisions,[228] the "*chargement par l'expéditeur*" risk would only apply to the event of damage, as it would be difficult to demonstrate that the arrival of part of the goods is due to a defect in loading. The solution is not convincing, because it starts from an interpretation contrary to the literal sense of the provision, according to which the carrier is not liable for loss or damage if they arise from special risks. The difficulty of fulfilling the burden of proof does not mean that the less common scenarios are not considered in Article 17, fourth paragraph, letter c), if there is evidence of causation. Furthermore, by virtue of the effects of the consignment note, the transporter is required to verify the number of packages and must formally confirm their loading to a lesser extent than what was declared. Therefore, the sender cannot be attributed this shortfall if only the integrity of the container seals is reported, because experience shows that there are no inviolable

[223] Cf. App. Besançon 15 December 1982, in *Bull. transp.* 1983, 96; App. Aix – en – Provence 12 February 1992, in *Le Lamy transp.*, 2020, vol. I, 500; App. Brussels 11 October 1989, *ibid.*, 2020, vol. I, 500, according to which the fact that the goods are loaded by the sender is not sufficient for the carrier not to be liable. See Sánchez Gamborino (2001a), p. 645 ff.

[224] Cf. Putzeys (1981), p. 265 ff., who recalls *"une probabilité raisonnable"*. Cf. OGH 27 April 2016, in *Europ. transp. law,* 2016, no. 51, 565, according to which "it suffices that the possibility of the cause is proved".

[225] Cf. Cass. com. France 5 June 1972, in *Bull. transp.,* 1972, 484; App. Paris 29 April 1972, *ibid.*, 1972, 194; App. Paris 28 January 1987, in *Le Lamy transp.*, 2020, vol. I, 501.

[226] Cf. App. Amiens 27 May 1981, in *Bull. transp.,* 1982, 271; App. Aix - en - Provence 9 April 1992, *ibid.,* 1993, 527.

[227] Cf. Cass. com. France 5 May 2004, in *Bull. transp. logist.,* 2004, 371; App. Lyon 28 April 2016, *ibid.,* 2016, 303; App. Paris 21 March 2013, in *Le Lamy transp.*, 2020, vol. I, 501; App. Lyon 24 January 2013, *ibid.,* 2020, vol. I, 501; App. Paris 26 January 2006, *ibid.,* 2020, vol. I, 501; App. Paris 25 February 1986, *ibid.,* 2020, vol. I, 501; App. Paris 22 September 1986, *ibid.,* 2020, vol. I, 501. See also BGH 24 September 1987, in *TranspR,* 1988, 108; BGH 27 October 1978, in *VersR,* 1979, 417; OLG Düsseldorf 13 January 1972, *ibid.,* 1973, 178; OLG Hamburg 18 December 1986, *TranspR,* 1987, 413; OLG Hamm 4 November 1971, in *VersR,* 1973, 911; OLG Saarbrücken 23 August 1985, in *TranspR,* 1985, 382.

[228] Cf. App. Paris 5 March 1980, in *Bull. transp.,* 1980, 187.

seals,[229] and this case law principle is rational and conforms to what emerges from practice.[230]

For a constant French orientation,[231] the transporter would be required to additionally check the loading performed by the sender, although the text of the Convention does not expressly mention it. Therefore, the carrier would be liable for damages resulting from inadequate stowage by the shipper if the same carrier starts the journey despite visible defects.[232] This approach is persuasive, because it underlines the role of the transporter, a professional, who is required to comply with the relative precautionary rules,[233] and this point of view is followed by German case law.[234] The liability regime is based on objective criteria, but the special risk can be invoked if the sender's initiatives undergo immediate critical examination aimed at eliminating any obvious defect. Article 8 of the Convention deserves a broad interpretation and the verification of the transporter concerns loading and stowage, as well as packaging.[235] Furthermore, the person entitled to compensation has to prove the apparent nature of the defect in loading.[236]

[229] Cf. App. Rouen 11 February 1993, in *Bull. transp. logist.,* 1993, 583.

[230] Cf. BGH 13 September 2012, in *TranspR,* 2012, 56.

[231] Cf. Cass. com. France 3 May 1976, in *Bull. transp.,* 1976, 317; Cass. com. France 14 June 1976, *ibid.,* 1976, 342; Cass. com. France 23 February 1982, *ibid.,* 1982, 285; Cass. com. France 22 July 1986, *ibid.,* 1986, 516; Cass. com. France 1 December 1992, in *Le Lamy transp.*, 2020, vol. I, 502; Cass. com. France 28 March 2000, in *Bull. transp. logist.,* 2000, 276; Cass. com. France 11 June 2002, in *Le Lamy transp.*, 2020, vol. I, 502; App. Paris 23 June 1989, *ibid.,* 2020, vol. I, 502; App. Orléans 22 December 2005, *ibid.,* 2020, vol. I, 502; App. Pau 16 December 1987, in *Bull. transp.,* 1988, 653; App. Agen 29 June 1981, *ibid.*, 1981, 433; App. Paris 26 May 1981, *ibid.,* 1982, 503; App. Nancy 10 June 2015, *ibid.,* 2015, 413. The principle was posed by Cass. com. France 3 May 1975, in *Le Lamy transp.*, 2020, vol. I, 502. See also RB Brugge 12 October 1999, in *Europ. transp. law,* 2000, no. 35, 552, but see RB Antwerp 6 May 1993, *ibid.*, 1993, no. 28, 768, according to which there is no obligation of the carrier to check the loading, even if, later, he reaches the same conclusions, since the carrier should verify that the stowage is adequate and not dangerous for traffic. For an intermediate position, see OLG Munich 6 February 2014, in *Unif. law rev.,* 2014, 295, according to which, although not having an obligation to check the loading, the carrier should intervene if the loading defect is evident. Cf. Haak (1986), p. 165 ff.

[232] Cf. Krings (1999), p. 774 ff.

[233] Cf. Schelin (2016), p. 440 ff., according to whom, "in practice, the carrier is often the expert on how goods should be handled".

[234] Cfr. OLG Bremen February 8, *in TranspR,* 2008, 252, according to which, even if the loading and stowage are carried out by the sender's employees, the carrier must check the exact arrangement of the goods at the beginning of the journey.

[235] RB Antwerp 6 May 1993, in *Europ. transp law,* 1993, no. 28, 768, according to which "in accordance with Article 8 CMR the carrier has the duty to check the apparent condition of the goods and their packaging".

[236] Cf. Cass. com. France 22 July 1986, in *Bull. transp.,* 1986, 516; Cass. com. France 31 January 1995, in *Le Lamy transp.*, 2020, vol. I, 503; App. Metz 28 October 1987, *ibid.,* 2020, vol. I, 503; App. Aix – en – Provence 21 October 1988, in *Bull. transp.,* 1989, 436.

However, it is said,[237] if the carrier contributes to the determination of the damage, his liability would be concurrent with that of the sender or of the consignee, on the basis of their respective responsibilities, but this argument cannot be endorsed. In fact, if the damage does not depend on the conduct of the shipper, Article 17, fourth paragraph, letter c), cannot be invoked and, despite Article 17, fifth paragraph, the transporter is liable, because the prejudice is a direct result of his inertia. If there is no causal link with a risk of Article 17, fourth paragraph, letter c), his liability is full, and the omission of immediate control excludes the applicability of the institution without a mere reduction in its scope.

Furthermore, the carrier must show the apparent defect in loading or stowage with justified reservations[238] and, therefore, he cannot put on the consignment note only the words "*réserves faites sur l'arrimage et le calage*", because detailed observations are required,[239] but unlike the provisions of Article 8, the reservations must not be accepted, as there is no express provision on the matter.[240] According to some,[241] this solution would start from an unfounded interpretation of Article 8[242]; for these theses,[243] its violation would presume the perfect condition of the goods at the time of receipt, but this would not prevent the carrier from proving the contrary.[244] Likewise, the transporter could demonstrate the incorrect execution of one of the operations of Article 17, fourth paragraph, letter c), albeit at a later time. These observations cannot be endorsed, because Article 8, first paragraph, letter b), must be read in conjunction with Article 9, second paragraph, which, due to the way it is formulated, contemplates an absolute presumption, precluding proof to the contrary.

[237] Cf. Cass. com. France 10 October 1989, in *Bull. transp.,* 1989, 673; Cass. com. France 11 June 2002, in *Le Lamy transp.*, 2020, vol. I, 502; App. Paris 8 November 2000, in *Bull. transp. logist.,* 2004, 388; App. Lyon 18 January 2007, *ibid.,* 2007, 591; App. Lyon 16 March 2012, *ibid.,* 2012, 250; App. Versailles 25 March 2004, *ibid.,* 2004, 388. Cf. Putzeys (1981), p. 266 ff.

[238] Cf. App. Colmar 10 July 1970, in *Bull. transp.,* 1970, 358. For the opposite idea, see Putzeys (1981), p. 269 ff., according to whom *"l'expéditeur a, pour des motifs qui he sont propres, décidé librement de procéder lui - même à la manutention; il en supporte seul responsibility"*; RB Antwerp 15 March 2002, in *Europ. transp. law,* 2002, no. 37, 511.

[239] Cf. App. Aix – en – Provence 3 March 1987, in *Le Lamy transp.*, 2020, vol. I, 503; RB Mechelen 18 November 1999, in *Europ. transp. law,* 2000, no. 35, 432. But see Cass. Belgium 9 December 1999, *ibid.,* 2000, no. 35, 386, according to which the carrier does not need to formulate reasoned reservations. This argument cannot be endorsed.

[240] Cf. App. Rennes 18 January 1989, in *Le Lamy transp.*, 2020, vol. I, 503.

[241] Cf. Clarke (2014), p. 270 ff.

[242] Cf. Clarke (2014), p. 271, according to whom "this is an error which stems from a misunderstanding of Article 8. Breach of Article 8 has only one consequence; failure to check and consequent failure to enter reservations in the consignment note gives rise to an evidential presumption against the carrier that he received the goods in good condition (...). However, the effect is a rebuttable presumption and not estoppel".

[243] Cf. Clarke (2014), p. 270 ff.

[244] Cf. Thume (2013), p. 459 ff.

Some[245] do not recognize any obligation on the part of the carrier to verify the exact loading, failing which Article 17, fourth paragraph, letter c), would lose importance and would almost never be applied. Rather, according to these approaches,[246] defects in loading, stowage or unloading that affect only the fate of the goods and those that compromise traffic safety should be distinguished.[247] With regard to the former, the carrier should warn the shipper or the consignee if he is aware of it, but there would be no obligation to examine, as it would only be optional. Thus, if a cargo of eggs is damaged due to inadequate stowage performed by the sender, the transporter would not be liable although he expresses doubts about the arrangement, but then performs the service.[248] Again, the same conclusions should be reached if, after having suggested to the sender's employees how to place a load of frozen fish, compliance with the instructions given is not verified.[249] On the contrary, the transporter should in any case ensure that the load does not jeopardize traffic safety[250]; for example, he must avoid vehicle overturning.[251]

The argument can only be partially endorsed, because, as French case law[252] shows, the obligation to check is general. However, precisely by virtue of Article 17, fourth paragraph, letter c), despite detecting a defect in the preparatory operations performed by the sender and notifying it, the transporter can still execute the service without incurring liability. If the shipper does not adapt, Article 17, fourth paragraph, letter c), applies. However, in the case of groupage transport, this is valid only in the relationship with the liable party, without any consequence toward other senders. In such a case, the initiative of the imprudent shipper has no impact because the latter may have liability toward the injured party under domestic law, but the Convention does not apply. In any case, the carrier must oppose the incorrect indications of the sender if, despite immediate objections, he does not conform, with not only the goods, but also the entire journey in danger, to the premises for

---

245 Cf. Clarke (2014), p. 268 ff., according to whom "the carrier's defense in Article 17. 4 (c) would be largely nullified"; Putzeys (1981), p. 269 ff., according to whom, *"dès lors que l'expéditeur n'a pas demandé au transporteur de vérifier l'arrimage et s'est estimé suffisamment compétent, the initiative du transporteur ne pourrai pas se retrouver contre lui, malgré sa vérification, l'arrimage venait à lâcher*"; Rodière (1970), p. 311 ff.

246 Cf. Clarke (2014), p. 268 ff.

247 Cf. Clarke (2014), p. 268 ff.; Jung (1997), p. 158 ff.

248 Cf. OLG Hamm 19 February 1973, in *Europ. transp. law,* 1974, no. 9, 753;

249 Cf. OGH 8 October 1984, in *Strassengüterverkehr*, 1985, 28.

250 Cf. Clarke (2014), p. 271 ff. See also OGH 25 September 1968, in *Europ. transp. law,* 1973, no. 8, 309, with regard to a fall of a machine not properly fixed; RB Antwerp 7 March 1980, *ibid.*, 1981, no. 16, 466; OLG Hamm 19 February 1972, *ibid.*,1974, no. 9, 753; OLG Düsseldorf 25 March 1993, in *TranspR*, 1994, 439; OLG Munich 28 July 1995, *ibid.*, 1996, 240; BGH 27 October 1978, in *VersR*, 1979, 417.

251 See Cass. com. France 3 May 1976, in *Europ. transp. law,* 1978, no. 13, 106; Cass. com. France 26 October 1983, in *Bull. transp.*, 1984, 360; App. Paris 22 June 1982, *ibid.*, 1982, 432.

252 Cf. Cass. com. France 3 May 1976, in *Bull. transp.*, 1976, 317; Cass. com. France 14 June 1976, *ibid.*, 1976, 342; Cass. com. France 23 February 1982, *ibid.*, 1982, 285; Cass. com. France 22 July 1986, *ibid.*, 1986, 516.

prejudice of others. Among these are indeterminate third parties, such as car drivers, who could see their own life jeopardized by the overturning of the truck, although the related compensation actions have nothing to do with the Convention.[253]

In case of transport with packages destined to several consignees, if, at first, the same packages are arranged to form a stable whole, after each delivery the carrier must place the remaining load in such a way as to restore the lost balance, and the decision is correct, because, during the journey, the transporter must intervene in the event of any modification of the cargo.[254] This also applies if the risk of imbalance is the result of untimely instructions from the shipper[255] or if the goods move after a sudden stop.[256] Thus, if the originally hidden defect occurs immediately after departure, the carrier must return to the sender and cannot permanently rely on his temporary intervention if he can go back to the place of origin without a particular burden in the execution of the service.[257] This solution is consistent with Article 17, fourth paragraph, letter c).

More generally, the carrier is not liable for the hidden loading defect[258] or if it concerns a cargo in sealed containers placed on a semitrailer and then entrusted for transfer.[259] Thus, he must not know on his own the consistency of perishable goods and, therefore, he must be made aware of the methods of conservation of a load of chestnuts without having to acquire independent information.[260] Furthermore, he can invoke the special risk *"chargement par l'éxpediteur"* if he proves that the damage is provoked by a wrong maneuver performed by the employee of the shipper

[253] Cf. Putzeys (1981), p. 267 ff. For a particular case, see OLG Frankfurt am Main 20 April 2007, in *TranspR,* 2008, 472, according to which the compensation claims of a third party for an event that occurred during transport, in particular, for the explosion of a tire, are not regulated by the CMR.

[254] Cf. App. Dijon 13 March 1985, in *Le Lamy transp.*, 2020, vol. I, 502; Cass. com. France 10 June 1986, in *Bull. transp.,* 1986, 608; RB Gent 1 December 1998, in *Europ. transp. law,* 1999, no. 34, 392; App. Almeria 25 March 2013, no. 85, in *Jur,* 2013, 198313.

[255] Cf. App. Paris 10 October 1988, in *Bull. transp.,* 1989, 408.

[256] Cf. App. Dijon 13 September 1984, in *Le Lamy transp.*, 2020, vol. I, 502; RB Antwerp 1 February 1996, in *Europ. transp. law,* 1996, no 31, 579.

[257] Cf. App. Metz 28 October 1987, in *Le Lamy transp.*, 2020, vol. I, 502, which acknowledged the responsibility of one third of the carrier for the damage caused by the fall of a part of the load after only 2 h from when he had rearranged it.

[258] Cf. Cass. com. France 30 November 1982, in *Bull. transp.*, 1983, 129; Cass. com. France 31 January 1995, in *Le Lamy transp.*, 2020, vol. I, 503.

[259] Cf. App. Paris 25 February 1987, in *Le Lamy transp.*, 2020, vol. I, 503; App. Paris 3 February 2011, *ibid.,* 2020, vol. I, 503, with regard to a scenario of inadequate supports for travertine slabs; App. Barcelona 27 June 2005, no. 315, in *Jur,* 2006, 46130.

[260] Cf. App. Poitiers 1 March 1995, in *Le Lamy transp.*, 2020, vol. I, 503; App. Aix - en- Provence 20 December 1979, in *Bull. transp.*, 1980, 104; App. Aix - en- Provence 16 June 1983, in *Le Lamy transp.*, 2020, vol. I, 503, with regard to the nonlocking of the hooks from which the quarters of meat are suspended; App. Paris 21 March 2013, *ibid.*, 2020, vol. I, 503, with regard to the standing charge of two thermal batteries, when their packaging would have required a horizontal arrangement. See also App. Douai 6 October 1982, *ibid.*, 2020, vol. I, 503, regarding an inadequate loading of carpets, capable of exerting lateral pressure on the sheet; Trib. com. Paris 26 June 1981, in *Bull. transp.,* 1982, 142, with regard to the use of inadequate points for fixing the goods.

in charge during stowage. In fact, according to Article 17, fourth paragraph, letter c), the transporter is not liable even if the operations described are executed out by the "*personnes agissant pour le compte de l'expéditeur ou du destinataire*".[261] However, this provision cannot be invoked for damage resulting from violent handling during customs control as it is entrusted to public officials.[262]

7.2.4 Risks Inherent in the Nature of the Goods

The fourth case of special risk concerns the transport of goods that by their very nature are subject to loss or damage. This case is distinguished from the own defect of the cargo, provided for by Article 17, second paragraph, as a cause for exemption from liability.[263] The latter is an inherent defect in one of the goods that predisposes it to deterioration. On the contrary, for Article 17, fourth paragraph, letter d), to apply, the entire load must consist of substances of the same type that, due to their characteristics, are exposed to high dangers.[264] As an example, the rule contemplates breaking for fragile objects, such as those made of crystal or terracotta.[265] Other risks are rust for metals, natural and spontaneous decomposition for perishable goods, drying for fresh fruits, dripping for certain liquids, or natural decline due to evaporation. To apply Article 17, fourth paragraph, letter d), the carrier must demonstrate that the damage or loss is a consequence of the nature of the cargo,[266] but not the existence of this exclusive cause,[267] also because this proof is often, in fact, impossible.

The prejudices to tiles intended for covering are not included in the special risks because they are not fragile[268] to the point of not supporting the journey, nor are mirrors, if the breakage is due to their fall,[269] nor are fir trees if they wither following too long a journey accomplished with inadequate means. In fact, in these cases, the

[261] Cf. App. Paris 7 April 1986, in *Le Lamy transp.*, 2020, vol. I, 503. Cf. Messent and Glass (2018), p. 176 ff.; Putzeys (1981), p. 263 ff.

[262] Cf. App. Paris 7 April 1986, in *Le Lamy transp.*, 2020, vol. I, 503. Cf. Clarke (2014), p. 266 ff.

[263] Cf. Clarke (2014), p. 272 ff.; Messent and Glass (2018), p. 193 ff.; Otte (2018), p. 1383 ff.

[264] Cf. Clarke (2014), p. 277 ff.; Putzeys (1981), p. 270; Messent and Glass (2018), p. 198 ff.; Libouton (1973), p. 35 ff.; Rodière (1971), p. 16 ff.; Loewe (1976), p. 362 ff.; Haak (1986), p. 168 ff.; Thume (2013) 462 ff. Cf. OGH 3 July 2013, in *TranspR,* 2014, 427, according to which, on the basis of ordinary principles of experience, the provision must refer to the goods for which the risk is significant.

[265] But Cf. App. Paris 8 May 1976, in *Bull. transp.,* 1976, 270, according to which the fragility of a painting does not fall into this case.

[266] Cf. App. Castellón 8 April 2002, no. 111, in *Ac,* 2002, 997, according to which the carrier is liable if he does not prove that the damage was caused by the defect of the goods.

[267] Cf. Cass. com. France 4 February 1986, in *Bull. transp.,* 1986, 197.

[268] Cf. App. Colmar 7 November 1973, in *Le Lamy transp.*, 2021, vol. I, 524.

[269] Cf. Trib. com. Avignon 8 October 2004, in *Bull. transp. logist.,* 2004, 720.

cause of the injury is heterogeneous with respect to the original conformation of the load.[270] The use of an unsuitable vehicle was assessed differently for Article 17, fourth paragraph, letter d). Thus, the carrier is not liable for damage to a cargo of pineapple placed on an ordinary truck in the month of July for a journey of five hundred kilometers.[271] In fact, the distance was deemed too short for the absence of refrigeration or an isothermal system to prejudice the goods, although the principle is questionable, given the French summer heat. On the contrary, the transporter's responsibility has been recognized for the oxidation of steel products loaded in winter on an uncovered vehicle or with a torn tarpaulin[272] or for the degradation suffered by some works of art placed on a normal semitrailer,[273] without other precautions. However, the transporter is not required to pay compensation for damage provoked by frost with regard to goods the sensitivity of which to cold is not known, placed on a truck equipped with only one tarpaulin.[274] However, the decision leaves us perplexed because, owing to similarity, it would not have been impossible to identify the problem even in the absence of specific information.

Article 18, fourth paragraph, considers the particular case of transport performed with a means "*amenagé en vue de soustraire les marchandises à l'influence de la chaleur, du froid, des variations de température ou de l'humidité de l'air*".[275] This provision adopts a broader concept than that of a vehicle subjected to a controlled temperature and, in this situation, the carrier can benefit from Article 17, fourth paragraph, letter d), if he can prove that he has followed the shipper's instructions and that "*toutes les misures en lui incombant, compte tenu des circonstances, ont été prises en ce qui concerne le choix, l'entretien et l'emploi de (. . .) aménagements*" of the truck.

This provision would not be in line with Article 17, third paragraph, according to which the defect of the vehicle is not a cause for exemption from liability. Instead, the rule of Article 18, fourth paragraph, on the choice and use of a refrigeration system does not present problems of consistency with Article 17, third paragraph, because, although inappropriate, these devices do not affect the overall functionality of the vehicle. Instead, Article 17, fourth paragraph, letter d), could not be invoked in the event of inadequate maintenance of the refrigeration system, if, as happens mostly, it causes a breakdown or malfunction. For some,[276] this antinomy is resolved

---

[270] Cf. App. Grenoble 16 May 2019, in *Le Lamy transp.*, 2021, vol. I, 524.

[271] Cf. App. Versailles 29 February 1984, in *Bull. transp.,* 1984, 249.

[272] Cf. App. Paris 10 December 1971, in *Bull. transp.,* 1972, 35; App. Paris 3 February 1984, in *Le Lamy transp.*, 2021, vol. I, 524.

[273] Cf. Cass. com. France 22 February 1994, in *Bull. transp. logist.,* 1994, 236.

[274] Cf. App. Paris 25 March 1969 in *Bull. transp.,* 1967, 174.

[275] This is how Article 18, fourth paragraph, is in the French version. Cf. Cass. com. France 15 February 1982, in *Bull. transp.,* 1982, 182. See also Clarke (2014), p. 278 ff.; Messent and Glass (2018), p. 194 ff.; Haak (1986), p. 168 ff.

[276] Cf. Loewe (1976), p. 365 ff., according to whom "defects in such items of the vehicle's equipment as are designed to protect the goods from the weather are not dealt with in Article 17, third paragraph, but are subject of special rules contained in Article 18, fourth paragraph". See

with a restrictive interpretation of the notion of defective vehicle, to refer to the imperfection of the truck as such, so that the refrigeration system can fall within the exclusive object of Article 18, fourth paragraph. This solution is convincing, as Article 18, fourth paragraph, does not concern the vehicle itself, but the air conditioning or heating system, which are separate devices and the installation of which requires the intervention of experts. If this interpretation is endorsed, Article 18, fourth paragraph, does not overlap with the regulation of Article 17, third paragraph, but integrates it.

On the contrary, the malfunction of the electrical system is usually equated with a vehicle defect, pursuant to Article 18, fourth paragraph. At any rate, the carrier must demonstrate that the device is used correctly, including by regulating the temperature during the journey if it is possible,[277] and the conclusion is convincing. However, the transporter must prove that all necessary measures with regard to the "*choix, l'entretien et l'emploi de ces aménagements*" have been taken and that the instructions given by the shipper have been respected.[278] It is a heavy burden and, if it is not fulfilled, the carrier cannot invoke Article 17, fourth paragraph, letter d). Thus, he has to be held liable for the defrosting of frozen products,[279] for a system failure,[280] for its breakage,[281] or for the one of the thermometer installed on the device.[282] The same principle applies if the transporter takes ten hours to unload with a night temperature of six degrees Celsius if this results in a significant alteration inside and outside a container in a refrigerated vehicle,[283] if this time is completely disproportionate.

---

also Haak (1986), p. 173 ff., according to which "a meaningful interpretation of Article 18, fourth paragraph, of CMR means that Article 18, fourth paragraph, of CMR should refer to a defective condition of the specially equipped vehicle which is essential to the agreed carriage".

[277] Cf. OLG Hamm 2 November 1998, in *TranspR,* 2000, 361, according to which, if the parties agree to carry out a refrigerated transport, even in the absence of an indication in the consignment note, the burden of proving that he has not left the goods exposed to a temperature higher than that required.

[278] Cf. Sánchez Gamborino (2001b), p. 856 ff. Cf. Trib. Superiore Spain 4 July 2016, no. 455, in *RJ*, 2016, 167; OLG Brandenburg 29 March 2000, in *TranspR,* 2000, 220, according to which the injured party, who wants to seek compensation for damages, must attach and demonstrate in court the preventive indications given on the refrigeration of the goods.

[279] Cf. App. Paris 30 May 1973, in *Bull. transp.,* 1973, 304; App. Paris 20 November 1979, *ibid.,* 1980, 190; Cass. com. France 8 December 1998, *ibid.*, 1999, 352, for a similar case relating to the transport of meat.

[280] Cf. App. Paris 6 November 1979, in *Bull. transp.,* 1974, 574; App. Riom 16 October 1981, *ibid.,* 1982, 11.

[281] Cf. App. Aix – en – Provence 5 July 1983, in *Le Lamy transp.*, 2021, vol. I, 525.

[282] Cf. App. Lyon 20 June 1979, in *Bull. transp.* 1979, 561.

[283] Cf. App. Aix – en – Provence 10 June 1983, in *Le Lamy transp.*, 2021, vol. I, 525; App. Paris 4 March 1985, *ibid.,* 2021, vol. I, 525.

The carrier is responsible for a too-intense operation of the device if it causes the goods to freeze[284] although he cannot check the temperature inside the vehicle, because it is sealed,[285] or for the excessive heating of fruit or vegetables for a longer duration of the journey due to mechanical failure, unless he can prove that the system continued to operate at the required temperature for the entire time.[286] The same conclusions can be reached in the case of transport of live plants performed in the winter in a truck equipped with a heating appliance if the damage from freezing is due to inadequate control of the internal temperature.[287] Again, the carrier is liable for a load of chestnuts covered with mold and worms if excessive heating is not excluded from the causes of the event.[288] Furthermore, if the shipper covers strawberries placed in a refrigerated vehicle with a tarpaulin, with the intent of protecting the upper row from the risk of frost and, then, the same tarpaulin slips and obstructs a ventilation opening, liability is excluded if the tarpaulin was not needed.[289]

On the contrary, the carrier is not liable if, despite the system defect, the damage is due to the sender's conduct, as in the case of defrosting prior to placing on the vehicle[290] or if, having to execute the transport with a refrigerated truck, it is completed with a common one on account of the failure to transmit the necessary instructions.[291] The problem lies in the fact that the latter were essential and the need for precaution could not be understood differently.

---

[284] Cf. App. Murcia 30 October 2009, no. 580, in *Jur*, 2009, 475526, according to which the carrier is liable for the prejudice to the goods resulting from both excessive refrigeration and overheating.

[285] Cf. App. Aix – en – Provence 26 April 1977, in *Le Lamy transp.*, 2021, vol. I, 525; App. Rennes 26 November 1986, *ibid.*, 2021, vol. I, 525; App. Montpellier 27 October 1983, *ibid.*, 2021, vol. I, 525; App. Paris 28 March 1978, in *Bull. transp.*, 1978, 320, with regard to the lack of a grill for transporting meat with the intention of exploiting the space of the cold room.

[286] Cf. Aix – en – Provence 14 January 1992, in *Le Lamy transp.*, 2021, vol. I, 525.

[287] Cf. App. Toulouse 17 February 1971, in *Bull. transp.*, 1971, 353. Similarly, see OLG Zweibrücken 12 March 2019, in *Europ. transp. law,* 2019, n. 54, 449; App. Alicante 11 July 1994, in *Ac*, 1994, 1154; App. Alicante 22 March 2000, no. 313, in *Jur*, 2000, 153347.

[288] Cf. App. Rouen 1 March 2012, in *Bull. transp. logist.*, 2012, 201.

[289] Cf. App. Bordeaux 11 July 1986, in *Le Lamy transp.*, 2021, vol. I, 525. See also *Stef Transport Rennes – Stef International Ouest* v. *D & M Fraser* in *Europ. transp. law,* 2019, no. 54, 187, according to which the carrier is responsible for only a part of the damage caused by a faulty circulation of cold air inside the vehicle, if the malfunction is caused by inadequate stowage by the shipper.

[290] Cf. App. Aix – en – Provence 16 November 1989, in *Le Lamy transp.*, 2021, vol. I, 525; Aix – en – Provence 12 May 1987, in *Bull. transp.*, 1987, 400.

[291] Cf. App. Versailles 29 February 1984, in *Bull. transp.*, 1984, 249; App. Aix – en – Provence 10 November 1976, *ibid.*, 1977, 248.

7.2.5 *The Insufficiency or Imperfection of the Markings or Numbers of the Packages and the Transport of Live Animals*

Article 17, fourth paragraph, letter e), considers the insufficiency or imperfection of the markings and numbers of packages[292] as a special risk and, for the regulation to operate, the carrier must demonstrate the causal link between one of the situations described and the damage. Upon reception of the goods, he must challenge the apparent defects with an approach consistent with Article 8, first paragraph, and Article 9, second paragraph.[293] Usually the markings and numbers of the packages are indicated in the consignment note and, therefore, deficiency or imperfection has to be recognized on the basis of its results, failing which the carrier can prove the existence of defects in another way, although it is more difficult to give the evidence. However, although there is imperfect marking, he cannot invoke Article 17, fourth paragraph, letter e), just in case the problem can be solved.[294]

Article 17, fourth paragraph, letter f), concerns the transport of live animals, and the special risks are justified by their nature, as happens for injuries following a fall, kicks, bites, asphyxiation, escape, illness or contamination from a disease.[295] The transporter may invoke this provision for the death of animals due to stress,[296] provided this is not caused by inadequate accommodation or prolonged travel. In fact, he must demonstrate that all necessary measures have been taken and that the instructions of the sender have been implemented,[297] with a specific provision of Article 18, fifth paragraph,[298] to be integrated with Article 17, fourth paragraph, letter f).

---

[292] Cf. Putzeys (1981), p. 278 ff.; Thume (2013), p. 464 ff.

[293] But see Clarke (2014), p. 284 ff., for whom the failure to formulate reservations on apparent defects at the time of loading would not have a preclusive effect; Loewe (1976), p. 368 ff.

[294] Cf. App. Douai 16 December 2014, in *Le Lamy transp.*, 2021, vol. I, 526.

[295] Cf. Thume (2013), p. 482 ff.

[296] Cf. Cass. com. France 17 June 1997, in *Bull. transp. logist.*, 1997, 507.

[297] Cf. Clarke (2014), p. 285 ff.; Putzeys (1981), p. 281 ff.; Loewe (1976), according to whom, "when" the carrier "is able to furnish proof to this effect, the presumption under Article 18, second paragraph, is that the damage has been caused by special circumstances inherent in this type of carriage, since livestock are exposed to certain risks when transported".

[298] For a reconstruction of the proof of the fact in question according to the likelihood criteria, cf. Putzeys (1981), p. 226 ff., according to whom *"mais la vraisemblance, la possibilité suffit et il n'est pas question d'exiger la preuve de la causalité"*; Libouton (1973), p. 49 ff.; Wesolowski (2013), p. 342 ff.; Jung (1997), p. 159 ff. This would exclude the need to prove the causal link, see Putzeys (1981), p. 280 ff., according to whom *"l'Article 18, paragraph 5, ne déroge pas au système de preuve de Article 18, deuxième paragraphe, qui crée une présomption de causalité de dommage, dès que sont établis le fait libératoire et the possibilité de causalité"*. This approach is contested here, because, if the etiological link is not ascertained, the damage cannot be the consequence of one of the special risks and, therefore, the carrier is liable.

With regard to this risk, the CMR is said to require a lower diligence than that imposed by Article 18, fourth paragraph, according to which the "utmost care" criterion operates.[299] This argument is unfounded, because it is based on a literal interpretation. On the contrary, Article 18, in both fourth and fifth paragraphs, integrates the concept of special risks with full reference to the observance of precautionary rules, and there are no different degrees in this regard, but rather a homogeneous duty to perform all the functions necessary for the success of the transport, as can be deduced from case law,[300] which rightly gives a coherent and unitary vision of the problem.

7.2.6 The Burden of Proof

The Convention has opted for a liability regime for loss, damage and delay based on objective criteria, as can be seen from Article 17, second paragraph, wherefor the investigation into the causes of exemption is independent of the evaluation of the psychological factor. This regulation is integrated by that on the so-called special risks, disciplined by Article 17, fourth paragraph. According to Article 18, first paragraph, the carrier must demonstrate that the loss, damage or delay is caused by one of the facts strictly provided for by Article 17, second paragraph.[301] In particular, it is necessary to prove the connection between prejudice and one of the causes of exemption. Then, if the carrier can demonstrate that several factors caused the damage, he is liable to the extent that he contributed to it, pursuant to Article 17, fifth paragraph.[302]

The rule is questionable because, in case of several causes, it provides for proportional liability in relation to factors specific to the transporter's sphere of risk, with a criterion that does not question the objective nature of the regulation because it refers to the simple etiological link with the prejudice, with no consideration for fault. Indeed, the application of a proportional parameter is particularly difficult, because the extent of liability can only be established on an equitable basis

[299] Cf. Clarke (2014), p. 285 ff., according to whom, "whereas the duty of utmost care in respect of equipment is to take 'all steps incumbent', the duty in respect of livestock is to tale 'all steps normally incumbent', suggesting a benchmark of current practice which is below the level of duty imposed on a carrier by the duty of utmost care"; Loewe (1976), p. 370 ff.; Krings (1999), p. 775 ff.

[300] Cf. Cass. Denmark 10 September 1996, in *Europ. transp. law,* 1997, no. 32, 230.

[301] Cf. Libouton (1973), p. 48 ff.; Thume (2013), p. 466 ff.

[302] Cf. Krings (1999), p. 776 ff.; Jung (1997), p. 158 ff.; Thume (2013), p. 491 ff.; BGH 30 March 2006, in *Europ. transp. law,* 2006, no. 41, 668; BGH 25 January 2007, *ibid.,* 2007, no. 42, 766; RB 15 March 2002, *ibid.,* no. 37, 511; OGH 13 February 2003, *ibid.,* 2004, no. 39, 244; OGH 31 October 2018, *ibid.,* 2019, no. 54, 218; Hof Antwerp 19 February 2001, *ibid.,* 2001, no. 36, 242; OLG Vienna 19 June 2019, *ibid.,* 2011, no. 55, 547. In particular, cf. OLG Koln 30 May 2006, in *TransR,* 2007, 114, according to which the contribution of the sender is compatible with the unlimited liability of the carrier pursuant to Article 29.

and with discretionary appreciation. From a logical point of view, if there are several causes, it makes no sense to speak of proportion, as their simultaneous presence affects the occurrence of the damage, but there is no mathematical formula regarding their different relevance. Therefore, the concept of proportion refers to the appreciation of the judge or to the consent of the parties if they come to a settlement. Despite the different wording of the CMR, the proportion cannot be identified from either the logical perspective or the mathematical one.

Even for special risks, the burden of proof falls on the carrier and, if he demonstrates the teleological link with the loss or damage, the entitled person can give evidence of the contrary.[303] According to Article 18, second paragraph, a negative fact has to be proved because it must be excluded that the prejudice derives from the event indicated by the carrier, but the cause does not need to be identified. Despite some peculiar expressions of Article 18, second paragraph, the evidence concerns the reason for the prejudice from an objective point of view, without any concession to the notion of possibility.

In summary, the reconstruction of the CMR regulation in objective terms does not prevent consideration of the precautionary rules whereto the carrier is bound, as can be seen from Article 18, fourth and fifth paragraphs. Without trespassing on the psychological aspect, attention has to be paid to mere facts, like the causal link, with the correction of the forfeiture of the benefit of the compensation limit in the event of willful misconduct or equivalent default. This principle operates at a different level from that of Article 17 and, without altering it, the former completes the system. However, the analysis of the frequent operational problems and the correlated wide debate allow us to conclude that on the numerous issues related to experience, the objective conception supported here does not lead to conclusions different from those reached with the opposite view centered on fault.

However, the central point is the obligations of the carrier and, on the basis of a well-known consolidated professional experience, their reconstruction leads to reasonable conclusions. This aspect emerges in part from German case law,[304] which gives great emphasis to the fact that the transporter is aware of the value of the goods and, therefore, he is put in the condition to plan adequate security measures under a penalty, not only of liability in general, but also, often, of the unlimited one of Article 29. This specific position can be linked not only to the idea of good faith, but precisely to some implicit consideration of fault, at least indirectly, for dividing the risk.

[303] Cf. Libouton (1973), p. 49 ff.

[304] See BGH 3 May 2007, in *TranspR*, 2007, 419; BGH 1 December 2005, *ibid.*, 2006, 115; OGH 26 March 2004, *ibid.*, 2004, 364; LG Hamburg 9 September 2002, *ibid.*, 2005, 315.

7.2.7 *The Persons in Charge and Other Auxiliaries of the Carrier*

According to Article 3, "*le transporteur répond, comme des propres actes et omissions, de ses préposés et des autres personnes aux services desquelles il recourt pour l'exécution du transport, lorsque ces préposés ou ces personnes agissent dans l'exercice de leurs fonctions*".[305] In the French text, the reference to the persons in charge is intended in a broad sense and is independent from the role assumed by each one in the company hierarchy and the specific management or control position.[306] Uniform law does not investigate the limits of the representation power, as the purpose is to attribute responsibility to the carrier for the acts and omissions of the auxiliaries[307] and, in general, of all those whose activities he uses to perform the service.[308]

For the goals of Article 3, people who act in the name and on behalf of the transporter on an ongoing basis (the so-called "agents" in the English text) are also considered. The expression "*des autres personnes*" refers to the parties that cooperate in different ways to the success of the journey[309]; it includes subcarriers,[310] who can follow the entire route or part of it, the freight forwarder, the driver of the so-called tow truck, who rescues the vehicle with a breakdown, or the stevedore with whom the carrier gets in touch before departure or during the journey.[311] On the other hand, if the sender executes the loading, he is not in any case an auxiliary of the carrier, because, otherwise, Article 17, fourth paragraph, would lose its significance. In this context, there is not an "*autre personne*", but a different party of the relationship.[312]

According to the English version,[313] due to the way in which Article 3 is written, the carrier should be liable for the acts and omissions of the persons whose activities

---

[305] This is how Article 3 in the French version; the English text reads: "the carrier shall be responsible for the acts and omissions of the agents and servants and of any other persons of whose services he makes use for the performance of the carriage, when such agents, servants or other persons are acting within the scope of their employment". Cf. Haak (1986), p. 175 ff.; Libouton (1973), p. 22 ff.; Schmid (2013), p. 171 ff.

[306] Cf. Putzeys (1981), p. 49 ff.

[307] Cf. Schmid (2013), p. 175 ff.

[308] Cf. Schmid (2013), p. 173 ff.

[309] Cf. Schmid (2013), p. 177 ff.; Ferrari (2018), p. 1267 ff.

[310] Cf. OGH 29 March 2017, in *TranspR,* 2017, 315, according to which, pursuant to Article 3, the carrier is not liable only for his employees, but for any auxiliary he makes use of for the purpose of performing the trip and therefore of the sub-carrier, so that he has full responsibility for any event occurring during his activity, without prejudice to the action for recourse, since the subcontractor has no direct relationship with the sender, but has responsibility towards the transporter who has appointed him. Cf. Loewe (1976), p. 333 ff.; Ferrari (2018), p. 1270 ff.

[311] Cf. Putzeys (1981), p. 50 ff.

[312] Cf. Putzeys (1981), p. 50 ff.

[313] Cf. Loewe (1976), p. 333 ff.

are used in performing the transport and for all the conduct of those in charge and of the agents, even if not connected to the execution of the journey; in fact, from a grammatical point of view, the reference "for the performance of the carriage" is addressed only to "other persons".[314] To make the law consistent with the purpose for which it is designed, a forcing of the literal sense has been rightly proposed,[315] so that all the activities that have contributed to the execution of the service can be considered relevant for all the persons involved.

Article 3 considers the intervention of third parties with reference to the "*exécution du transport*" and includes the fulfillment of all the obligations incumbent on the carrier by virtue of a contract already stipulated. Therefore, if not authorized, the driver cannot accept a declaration of value or one of special interest in redelivery, because they impose a more severe obligation for compensation than that provided for by Article 23 of the Convention and are a new agreement, albeit linked to the original one.[316] Then, the carrier is liable if the prejudice is caused by collaborators in the performance of their duties. Therefore, he is responsible if the driver is caught expatriating people who could not leave the country, with the consequent seizure of the vehicle and the goods,[317] although it is a serious conduct, only occasioned by the performance of the service.[318]

Then, the driver who stows the load in a way that differs from the instructions received acts to fulfill the obligations from his employment contract; therefore, Article 3 applies.[319] According to some,[320] the conduct of the auxiliary must not be evaluated in isolation, but in its context,[321] and must be a way of performing the service entrusted to him; this is the case of imprudent driving, of someone who smokes while unloading flammable material,[322] or of someone who damages or steals goods intentionally.[323] On the other hand, an unauthorized deviation from the

[314]Cf. Haak (1986), p. 177 ff.

[315]Cf. Messent and Glass (2018), p. 82 ff.

[316]Cf. Putzeys (1981), p. 52 ff.

[317]Cf. OGH 22 November 1977, in *Unif. law rev.*, 1979, 284. See also OLG Munich 1 June 2011, in *TranspR*, 2011, 337.

[318]Cf. Haak (1986), p. 178 ff.

[319]Cf. App. Rouen 13 January 2005, in Messent and Glass (2018), p. 84 ff., nt. 18. See also BGH 27 June 1985, in *Europ. transp. law,* 1986, no. 21, 102; Hof Antwerp 31 January 2000, in *J. P. A.*, 2000, 247, according to which the *de facto* carrier acts in the exercise of his functions if he decides to retain the goods to protect his credit against his contractor.

[320]Cf. Clarke (2014), p. 388 ff.

[321]Cf. *Smith* v. *Stages,* in *AC,* 1989, 928.

[322]Cf. Clarke (2014), p. 390 ff.

[323]Cf. OLG Schleswig Holstein 18 December 2014, in *TranspR*, 2015, 157, according to which the carrier is fully liable, pursuant to Articles 3 and 29, of the voluntary appropriation of the goods by an unfaithful subcontractor. See also OGH 29 March 2017, in *Europ. transp. law,* 2017, no. 52, 643; RB Limburg 21 June 2017, *ibid.*, 2017, no. 52, 654.

predetermined route may be justified by the need to find a safe place to stop, refuel or execute any repairs. Conversely, Article 3 does not apply if the driver intentionally slows the truck for a strike strategy.

However, Article 3 does not extend the carrier's liability; thus, he can invoke the prescribed grounds for exemption if he proves that, for example, the damage caused by the subcontractor depends on an unavoidable event.[324] Likewise, Article 29 applies if the prejudice is provoked by the collaborator's conduct, based on willful misconduct or equivalent fault. Again, the transporter is liable if, using a "digital freight exchange platform", he assigns the journey to criminals who take advantage of the name of a subcarrier.[325] The question arises as to whether in Article 3 the scenario wherein the carrier hires the vehicle from a third party or his employees is included[326]; Article 3 does not operate[327] and the case is regulated by Article 17, third paragraph.

Overall, Article 3 is a wise and general rule, because it leads the transport back to the operator's organization and, therefore, to the preparation of various autonomous or subordinate collaborations for the achievement of final goals. In modern society, this conception is supported by the greater organizational complexity and, consequently, by the need to consider the activity as a whole as an expression of a rational predisposition of diverse professional contributions. The transporter makes use of them, but this defines his liability. Deviant conducts of collaborators not even caused by the journey are an exception. In the event of illegal immigrants aboard the vehicle, Article 3 is rightly invoked because the unlawful conduct is attributable to the driver at an administrative and criminal level, but the consequent seizure is detrimental to the entitled person and, therefore, in this perspective, the CMR applies with the responsibility of the carrier.

7.3 The Carriage of Dangerous Goods

7.3.1 Dangerous Goods

Article 22 considers the transport of dangerous goods, but does not give a definition. According to the one in use, "all goods are to be considered as dangerous, if, in normal road transport, they present an immediate risk".[328] This definition includes load with an intrinsic danger either because of its proximity to the remaining part of the cargo or because of the way in which it is transported. The European Agreement relating to the carriage of dangerous goods by road, signed in Geneva on

[324] Cf. Messent and Glass (2018), p. 84 ff.

[325] Cf. GH Hertogenbosch 15 April 2014, in *Europ. transp. law,* 2014, no. 49, 701.

[326] Cf. Messent and Glass (2018), p. 84 ff.

[327] Cf. *Le Lamy transp.*, 2021, vol. I, 510. See also Schmid (2013), p. 179 ff.

[328] Cf. Loewe (1976), p. 374 ff.

30 September 1957,[329] contains a non-exhaustive list of substances, a useful one also for the application of Article 22 of the CMR; however, the parties to the contract are free to identify the danger by consensus.[330]

According to Article 22, first paragraph, at the time of delivery, the sender must warn of this risk and, if necessary, he must indicate the precautions that have to be taken.[331] Any related instruction must be included in the consignment note,[332] failing which, it is up to the shipper to prove that the transporter was aware of the matter. If he cannot ignore the dangerousness of the cargo, easily recognizable,[333] in general, he is not obliged to intervene in the absence of instructions, because, according to Article 22, first paragraph, he does not have an active role, but must only be informed. If warned, he must not necessarily inspect the load to verify that it is made harmless unless this is required by practice or by the need to safeguard the integrity of the vehicle.[334]

If, lacking information, the transporter does not recognize the danger on his own, the carrier may decide to unload, destroy or make harmless the goods, without any obligation to pay compensation.[335] These measures respond to a general interest in the protection of public safety prevailing over that of the performance of the service. The intervention aimed at making the load harmless respects the reasons underlying the contract, but the carrier is asked to be cautious in adopting the measure, because, if excessive, he commits an illegitimate conduct, with the obligation to compensate for the prejudice.[336] In any case, the transporter must be aware if he is transferring dangerous goods; however, the nonfulfillment of the obligation to provide information by the shipper does not result in the inevitable abandonment of the load, which, in any case, is an extreme remedy for situations where it is essential.

Pursuant to Article 22, second paragraph, about dangerous goods, the sender is liable "for all expenses, loss, or damage arising out of their handing over for carriage or of their carriage";[337] however, he cannot benefit from the compensation limit

---

[329] The so-called ADR. Obviously, there is no coincidence between the States that have ratified the CMR and those such Agreement.

[330] Cf. Clarke (2014), p. 222 ff.; Putzeys (1981), p. 276 ff.

[331] Cf. Messent and Glass (2018), p. 227 ff.; Silingardi et al. (1994), p. 183 ff. Cf. BGH 16 October 1986, in *Europ. transp. law,* 1987, no. 22, 56; Trib. com. Paris 31 March 1992, in *Bull. transp.,* 1992, 331, according to which the shipper is not liable if he does not warn about the dangerousness of the goods, when for a similar load the same carrier had been informed; Cass. com. France 16 October 1990, *ibid.,* 1990, 797; App. Nancy 3 June 1998, *ibid.,* 1998, 550.

[332] There is an overlap of Article 22, first paragraph, with Article 6, first paragraph, letter f).

[333] Cf. Cass. com. France 20 June 1978, in *Bull. transp.,* 1978, 469, with regard to a load of gas cigarette lighters; App. Lyon 7 October 1976, *ibid.,* 1977, 84.

[334] Cf. Clarke (2014), p. 222 ff.

[335] Cf. Messent and Glass (2018), p. 227 ff.

[336] Cf. Loewe (1976), p. 374 ff.

[337] This is how Article 22, second paragraph, is in the English version. The French version reads, "*de tous frais et dommages résultant de leur remise au transport ou de leur transport*". Cf. Putzeys (1981), p. 276 ff.

provided for in favor of the transporter.[338] For some,[339] the compensation limit introduced by domestic law would apply, if any. This argument is not convincing, because the Convention regulates the case without referring to the individual legal systems, with a complete discipline, albeit of a negative nature. If the shipper does not inform the carrier or the latter fails to recognize the risk, the shipper's liability arises if the transporter proves the connection between the failure to warn and the damage.[340] Thus, in groupage transport, the sender is liable for the prejudice caused to goods destined for different parties.[341] Furthermore, he is responsible for any destruction of the vehicle, as can be seen from the broad formula of Article 22, second paragraph, aimed at including all prejudices and costs related with carriage as a whole.

Article 22, second paragraph, overlaps with Article 10, according to which the sender is liable to the carrier for prejudice to people, material or other goods and for costs caused by the imperfection of the packaging. Unlike this rule, Article 22, second paragraph, is said not to consider the transporter as the exclusive creditor. According to some,[342] although they are aware of the fact that the Convention regulates contracts of carriage only, if a third party suffers the damage, the transporter could assign this party his own rights toward the sender. On the contrary, despite irrelevant literal differences, Article 10 and Article 22 are homogeneous provisions, and the second takes up the principle of the first with regard to dangerous goods. As the Convention regulates only transport, the carrier is the sole holder of the action against the shipper, obviously on the basis of the CMR. This does not exclude questions from other parties centered on different regulations. In fact, the assignment of rights can take place on the basis of domestic law, but, in turn, it is not governed by uniform one, without prejudice to the fact that this assignment concerns the carrier's credit positions and, therefore, not the damage suffered by different parties.

---

[338] Cf. Putzeys (1981), p. 357 ff.

[339] Cf. Putzeys (1981), p. 356 ff., according to whom "*la réparation due par l'expéditeur au transporteur et, le cas échéant, aux tiers ayant droit à d'autres marchandises, n'est soumise qu'aux limitations de droit commun*"; Clarke (2014), p. 224 ff.

[340] But see Putzeys (1981), p. 276 ff., according to whom "*la possibilité d'une causalité*" would operate.

[341] Cf. App. Brussels 25 January 1978, in *Bull. transp.*, 1978, 429.

[342] Cf. Messent and Glass (2018), p. 228 ff.

7.4 The Party That May Assert the Carrier's Liability

7.4.1 The Action of the Sender and That of the Consignee

At the time of conclusion of the contract of carriage, the rights toward the transporter belong to the sender because of the bilateral structure of this relationship, and this is confirmed in Article 12, first paragraph, of the Convention, wherefor the shipper can exercise the counter-order and decide on the suspension of the trip, the modification of the place of destination, or the redelivery to a party other than the original consignee. It is necessary to identify the moment at which the rights are transferred to the recipient and Article 13, first paragraph, identifies it with the arrival of the goods, with the request for the release of the second copy of the consignment note, if this is drawn up, and, finally, with the request for redelivery. In this situation, related to the original relationship between the carrier and the shipper, the consignee replaces the second and, from that moment, he can exercise the rights due to him.

If the goods arrive damaged, the further question of determining who can take action to ask for compensation, namely, if it is up to the sender or the consignee,[343] arises. This issue cannot be solved by Article 13, although there have been conflicting voices, according to which "the one who (. . .) has the right to obtain the goods from the carrier is entitled to all actions resulting from the nonfulfillment of the obliged party, in this case, the carrier",[344] so that "the lack of a specific rule of attribution of the action against the carrier is irrelevant. The action follows the dynamics of the right to redelivery (. . .) which, during the transfer (. . .), is expressed by the right of disposal".[345]

Instead, Article 13 regulates the passage of rights, but does not imply any coincidence in the same person of the right of asking for redelivery and of the "*droit d'action*",[346] as there is no link between the latter and the power to dispose.[347] In fact, they are distinct subjective positions; the right to redelivery and the power to counter-order arise from the contract and belong to the sender or consignee. On the contrary, the right to act presupposes a pathological situation, that is, damage to the goods, and whoever suffers it is not always the one who disposes of the cargo or requests its redelivery.

The CMR does not provide any express criteria for identifying who can bring an action for compensation.[348] As the question depends on the qualification of the transport and the identification of its nature, uniform law is not the best context for its

[343] Cf. Schmidt (2019), p. 255 ff.

[344] Cf. Pesce (1995), p. 162 ff.

[345] Cf. Pesce (1995), p. 163 ff.; Haak (1986), p. 267 ff.; Libouton (1973), p. 30 ff.

[346] Cf. Putzeys (1981), p. 361 ff.

[347] Cf. Putzeys (1981), p. 361 ff.

[348] Cf. Putzeys (1981), p. 361 ff., according to whom "*le droit des transports en général et la CMR en particulier n'ont pas déterminé à qui appartenait le droit d'action contre le transporteur responsable de avarie, de la perte ou du retard*"; Clarke (2014), p. 115 ff., according to whom

examination, because a complete legal system would be necessary for this theoretical study. Many provisions of the Convention refer to the entitled person without further specification. For example, for Article 12, last paragraph, if the transporter does not perform the instructions derived from the exercise of the counter-order, he is liable toward the person entitled. Then, according to Article 16, following the occurrence of impediments during the journey or the redelivery, the transporter can execute the unloading or proceed with the sale of the cargo, again on behalf of the entitled person. Finally, the latter can demonstrate that the prejudice is not provoked by one of the special risks, pursuant to Article 18, second paragraph or, according to Article 20, he can consider the goods as lost if there is no redelivery within 30 days from the expiry of the delivery term, if agreed, failing which within 60 days of receipt of the load by the carrier.

At a theoretical level, it is complex to establish who can act between the sender and the consignee. A few years ago, I studied this topic and tried to give an answer from the Italian point of view,[349] but the approach followed in that research cannot be repeated here and implies a reflection based on different theoretical assumptions in the various legal systems. The CMR gives an indication of an operational nature, because the constant reference to the entitled person is combined with the alternative identification of the creditor as the sender or as the consignee,[350] depending on the party that has suffered the damage from the nonfulfillment of contract obligation.

This solution allows one or the other to seek compensation on the basis of the existence, against them, of compensable prejudice. This approach is convincing in general, because it makes the action depend on the actual harm to the sender's or consignee's assets rather than their conducts along the journey. It is useful to verify what interpretation, in the experience of these decades, has been given to the concept of entitled person, so that it can be established as to whether the aforementioned argument has been successful in the various States, it has allowed a linear definition of the injured party and, therefore, that of the holder of the action, with regard to traditional contractual liability, considered as a priority by the Convention.

"the CMR contains no general or definitive rule governing the identity of the person or persons entitled to sue the carrier".

[349] Cf. Tincani (2012), p. 5 ff.

[350] Cf. Cass. Belgium 21 January 2010, in *Europ. transp. law,* 2010, no. 45, 311, according to which, alternatively, both the sender and the consignee can act to request compensation for damages, and if the latter receives compensation from the insurance company, this can subrogate and act against the carrier.

7.4.2 *The Concept of Entitled Person in the Main Case Law Orientations and the Action of Compensation for Prejudice Due to Loss or Damage*

For French case law, as the CMR does not recognize exclusive ownership of the right of action, it would be the responsibility of the parties, identified in the formal shipper, in the freight forwarder, if he compensates the injured party, although he does not appear in the consignment note,[351] and in the consignee, who can request the redelivery even in the absence of the material arrival of the goods, as in the case of total or presumed loss,[352] provided that the deadline, if agreed upon, or that required for the relative presumption to arise, has expired. For the majority approach,[353] the proposition of competing actions by the sender and the consignee would be possible, but the carrier could never be exposed to compensate twice for the same damage.

Therefore, each claim should concern distinct components of the prejudice; for example, the sender could claim compensation for damage and the consignee for the delay. If the goods arrive and are received, the shipper suffers prejudice only if the decrease in value jeopardizes his assets on the basis of applicable regulations. It is necessary to refer to the agreements related to transport, not always the sales ones, and to consider the overall relationships between the shipper and the consignee, on the basis of which the transfer is organized. In fact, these relationships allow to identify the person who is affected by the prejudice. An alteration in the state of the goods or their disappearance may affect the sender's or the consignee's assets, depending on the contract connected to that of transport.

On the other hand, the seller who is neither the shipper nor the consignee cannot act against the carrier,[354] because only a contractual party can invoke compensation. Furthermore, the decision confirms that the right to act presupposes an assessment of the position of the sender and that of the consignee in the transport-related relationship. To this end, we must consider relevant the status of the seller, that of the buyer or, more generally, any other title that pertains to the relationship of the shipper and the consignee with the goods being transferred. This way, the patrimonial sphere susceptible to being injured is identified.

---

351 Cf. Cass. com. France 2 February 1993, in *Le Lamy transp.*, 2021, vol. I, 557.

352 Cf. App. Paris 2 December 1981, in *Bull. transp.,* 1982, 73; Cass. Belgium 13 June 1980, in *Le Lamy transp.*, 2021, vol. I, 557.

353 Cf. App. Aix – en – Provence 15 February 1983, in *Le Lamy transp.*, 2021, vol. I, 557; App. Antwerp 24 November 1982, *ibid.,* 2021, vol. I, 557; App. Brussels 7 February 1992, *ibid.,* 2021, vol. I, 557.

354 Cf. App. Versailles 2 July 2009, in *Bull. transp. logist.,* 2009, 547; App. Amiens 12 May 2009, *ibid.,* 2009, 368; App. Dijon 26 June 2008, in *Le Lamy transp.*, 2021, vol. I, 558; Hof Gent 28 June 1996, in *Europ. transp. law,* 1996, no. 31, 843.

Again, if the owner is a third party with respect to the transport, he can act against the carrier on an extra-contractual basis.[355] Similarly, if the name of the person authorized to accept service appears as the recipient in the consignment note, he cannot ask for compensation.[356] Secondly, a parent company that does not appear as a shipper cannot act instead of him if the former has a separate legal personality from that of its subsidiaries.[357] Only the parties can request compensation, according to CMR, subject to verification of the underlying relationship.

According to Polish case law,[358] the identification of the entitled person is left to domestic law, provided that CMR would not give any criteria and, as the decisions have rarely dealt with the problem, because for that system, the question is not very relevant in practice[359]; in fact, the judge does not investigate further if the action is brought by the sender or the consignee.[360] In this perspective, not only could one of the two ask for compensation, but so also could another person with a relevant interest.[361] For some decisions, the action would be linked to the power to dispose of the cargo, according to Article 12 of the Convention, after an investigation into the property.[362] Thus, with redelivery, the sender would lose the power to dispose of, but the consignee could not ask for compensation without an injury to his financial sphere.

This approach does not distinguish two levels: the power of disposition pertains to the execution of the journey and is justified on the basis of the bilateral structure of the relationship, while the action implies a prejudice and belongs to those who suffer from it. However, the latter is not always identified with the holder of the power of disposition. Albeit implicitly, the Supreme Court of Poland[363] reached the same conclusion when it ruled that, despite being able to exercise the counter-order, the consignee cannot invoke compensation if the assets are not his property.

---

[355] Cf. App. Toulouse 8 June 2004, in *Bull. transp. logist.*, 2004, 486; Trib. com. Paris 5 September 2005, *ibid.*, 2005, 623.

[356] Cf. App. Aix - en – Provence 28 May 1991, in *Le Lamy transp.*, 2021, vol. I, 558.

[357] Cf. App. Paris 28 March 2013, in *Le Lamy transp.*, 2021, vol. I, 558; App. Amiens 15 June 2017, *ibid.*, 2021, vol. I, 558.

[358] Cf. Wesolowski (2013), p. 344 ff.

[359] Cf. Wesolowski (2013), p. 344 ff.

[360] Cf. Wesolowski (2013), p. 344 ff., according to whom "the courts do not usually make inquiries into this matter on their own initiative as long as the claimants are either the sender or the consignee".

[361] The Belgian law seems to be oriented in this sense. Cf. Krings (1999), p. 784 ff., according to whom "*cet action peut être exercée par toute personne qui ya intérêt direct, c'est à dire non seulement l'expéditeur et le destinataire, mais aussi toute autre personne qui a soit un intérêt direct*".

[362] Cf. Wesolowski (2013), p. 344 ff., according to whom, "in the light of the Supreme Court's opinion, both the right to compensation for loss and damage of the goods and other damage are related to the right to dispose of the consignment. The latter cannot be considered without reference to the property of a particular person".

[363] Cf. Wesolowski (2013), p. 344 ff.

German case law also identifies the person entitled on the basis of the rules on the counter-order,[364] but does not exclude the concurrence of actions between the sender and the consignee.[365] In addition to the French, this approach is shared by the judges of Belgium,[366] Austria[367] and Holland.[368] Therefore, the acquisition of the rights by the recipient would not preclude the shipper from seeking compensation. However, there would be a risk for the carrier to be exposed to two actions for the compensation of the same damage. This question, for some,[369] should be resolved on the basis of domestic law, whereas, for others,[370] this question is answered with the demonstration of the existence of a relevant interest, for example, that an actual damage to property is caused. This second approach is well founded.

In Italy, according to the first argument,[371] the arrival of the goods and the request for redelivery by the recipient would determine the transfer of all rights inherent to transport, including that to act; therefore, a concurrence of actions could never be displayed. In fact, "the exclusive legitimacy of the consignee has been confirmed once he has requested the delivery of the goods, given that, with this request, that determines the replacement of the consignee for the sender, the former can exercise all the rights resulting from the contract (...), including those with a compensatory content (...), with the simultaneous loss of any concurrent legitimacy".[372] This

[364] Cf. BGH 6 July 1979, in *Europ. transp. law,* 1980, no. 15, 863; BGH 21 December 1973, *ibid.,* 1975, no. 10, 92; OLG Hamm 9 December 1999, in *TranspR,* 2000, 122. See Haak (1986), p. 257 ff.; Messent and Glass (2018), p. 117 ff.

[365] Cf. BGH 24 October 1991, in *Europ. transp law,* 1992, no. 27, 839; BGH 6 May 1981, *ibid.,* 1982, no. 17, 331; BGH 14 February 2008, in *TranspR,* 2008, 323; BGH 6 July 2006, in *Europ. transp. law,* 2006, no. 41, 796.

[366] Cf. Cass. Belgium 29 September 2006, in *Europ. transp. law,* 2007, no. 42, 390; Hof Antwerp 3 December 2008, *ibid.,* 2009, no. 44, 334; Hof Brussels 5 December 1968, *ibid.,* 1969, no. 4, 958; App. Brussels 30 October 1975, *ibid.,* 1976, no. 11, 238; RB Antwerp 7 December 1973, *ibid.,* 1976, no. 11, 295.

[367] Cf. OLG Linz 27 November 1989, in *Unif. law rev.,* 1990, 442.

[368] Cf. Messent and Glass (2018), p. 118 ff., nt. 52.

[369] Cf. OGH 22 March 2002, in *Europ. transp. law,* 2002, no. 39, 79; BHG 24 October 1991, *ibid.,* 1992, no. 27, 839.

[370] Cf. App. Versailles 7 March 1996, in *Bull. transp.,* 1996, 633, according to which, if the shipper receives the indemnity from its insurance company, he loses the right to act; App. Paris 3 February 2010, *ibid.,* 2010, 410; App. Montpellier 1 December 1987, *ibid.,* 1988, 13; App. Rouen 20 January 2005, *idid.,* 2005, 374; App. Paris 29 September 1999, *ibid.,* 1999, 747; App. Paris 12 January 2011, *ibid.,* 2011, 141; App. Paris 17 November 2004, *ibid.,* 2005, 86; App. Versailles 22 October 2008, *ibid.,* 2009, 16; Hof. Brussels 16 November 1977, in *Europ. transp. law,* 1980, no. 15, 319, according to which, in order for the buyer to act, the latter must not prove that he is the owner or that he runs the risk of damage to his assets. Cass confirmed the judgment. Belgium 13 June 1980, *ibid.,* 1980, no. 15, 851; Cass. Belgium 29 September 2006, *ibid.,* 2007, no. 42, 390.

[371] Cf. App. Milan 17 May 2018, in *Dir. mar.,* 2018, 683 ff.; Cass. Italia 26 October 1993, no. 10621, *ibid.,* 1994, 1070; Cass. Italy 14 July 2015, no. 14665, in *Giur. it. rep.,* 2018; Trib. Milan 9 April 2001, in *Dir. mar.,* 2003, 176; Cass. Italy 21 February 2006, in *Europ. transp. law,* 20007, no. 42, 383.

[372] Cf. App. Milan 17 May 2018, in *Dir. mar.,* 2018, 683 ff.

approach can hardly be subscribed to, because it implies that the contract identifies the person who can act, while the recipient does not always suffer prejudice. Rather, the identification of who actually is damaged is left to an assessment of the transport-related relationship. This orientation is more persuasive, because only a person facing a prejudice can ask for compensation; therefore, it would be the sender if he proves that the damage was made to his financial sphere.[373]

7.4.3 *The Action for Compensation for Prejudice Due to Delay*

The Convention provides for a liability of the carrier for the delay in redelivery, in particular, according to Article 19, when the goods are delivered after the deadline, if contemplated, failing which if they are delivered in a time longer than that deemed reasonable for a professional. The law does not identify the person who can invoke compensation, nor does it refer to the general notion of an entitled person. Although there is no organic regulation, it is possible to qualify this case on the basis of the general principles of uniform law.

As for loss and damage, the recipient is not granted an exclusive compensation action.[374] Those who suffer prejudice because of the delay can act and, therefore, it is necessary to consider the relationship connected to the transport. Thus, a possible deadline is perhaps in the interest of the shipper alone, and exceeding it does not always entail prejudice for the consignee. It is not necessarily trade that underlies the transfer; there may be other arrangements, and the recipient might have no interest in a timely arrival.

Think of the sending of the envelope intended for the correspondent of a lawyer for filing in court or of the project addressed to a public administration in charge of performing a selection procedure for the assignment of a task. In such situations, the interest in executing the transport is only that of the sender, and the consignee does not have a substantial expectation to assert. In fact, the violation of a deadline results in prejudice for the former, as the delay affects his interests, because the correspondent cannot file the deed or the municipality excludes from the competition whoever sends the request after the deadline. In particular, this last question received an incorrect solution from a well-known Italian decision[375] that concerned domestic law and a national journey, but the problem arises likewise with regard to the CMR.

[373]Cf. Cass. Italy 17 November 1999, no. 12744, in *Giur. it. rep.*, 1999; Cass. Italy 20 October 2010, no. 24400, *ibid.*, 2010; Cass. Italy 13 December 2010, no. 25110, *ibid.*, 2010; Cass. Italy 30 January 2014, no. 2075, *ibid.*, 2014.

[374]Cf. Trib. of the Swiss Confederation 2 June 1981, in the *Information system of the Federal Court,* according to which claims for damages against the carrier for late delivery can be asserted by the sender or by the consignee, while any claims between carriers fall within the scope of national regulations.

[375]Cf. App. Cagliari 20 May 1969, in *Giur. it rep.*, 1978.

In fact, the delivery term could be introduced in the interests of both the shipper and the consignee. As in the case of loss or damage, in the action for compensation for prejudice due to delay, it is necessary to check the relationships connected to the transfer.

Only the analysis of specific events and transport-related relationships allows us to identify who is harmed by undue extension of the journey. Then, as some French decisions point out,[376] one is led to think that the consignee is mostly affected by the prejudice caused by delay. This is the most frequent scenario, because, in a clear majority of cases, sold goods are transferred, and it is in the interest of the consignee–buyer to receive them in time, as has been said in an Anglo-Saxon[377] case when the load was essential for the proper functioning of an industrial plant. However, as demonstrated by the situation of the envelope sent by those who want to participate in a tender called by a public administration, there are events wherein the interest and the prejudice are those of the sender. Therefore, although the Convention does not use this expression, in case of a compensation of prejudice created by delay, the action pertains to the entitled person.

7.4.4 Identification of the Person Entitled to Compensation in the Person Who Suffers the Financial Damage

The transport is independent of the contracts relating to the transfer of the right of property over the goods and, in any case, to the relationship between the sender and the consignee. Anyway, if the shipper is interested in the load, there must be an economic reason that justifies such an organizational option, but the contract of carriage is independent from it. The reasons that lead the shipper to stipulate do not affect the corresponding obligations. Moreover, experience confirms this, because the transporter does not always know the purpose of the sender and for the most part is not interested in it. If anything, he deals with the rational preparation of the instrumental resources needed for the professional and effective fulfillment of the service.

Sometimes, the goods are the property of the sender, sometimes of the consignee and, in other cases, they are neither of one nor of the other, but of a third party unrelated to the contract and its execution. The different structure of the underlying relationships has led Italian case law[378] and in part that of other countries[379] to

[376] Cf. App. Aix – en – Provence 15 February 1983, in *Le Lamy transp.*, 2021, vol. I, 557.

[377] Cf. *Shell Chemicals UK Ltd.* v. *P & O Roadtanks Ltd.*, in *Lloyd's rep.*, 1993, 114.

[378] Cf. App. Milan 17 May 2018, in *Dir. mar.*, 2018, 683 ff.; Cass. Italy 26 October 1993, no. 10621, *ibid.*, 1994, 1070; Cass. Italy 14 July 2015, no. 14665, in *Giur. it. rep.*, 2018; Trib. Milan 9 April 2001, in *Dir. mar.*, 2003, 176.

[379] Cf. Cass. Belgium 29 September 2006, in *Europ. transp. law,* 2007, no. 42, 390; Hof Antwerp 3 December 2008, *ibid.*, 2009, no. 44, 334; OLG Linz 27 November 1989, in *Unif. law rev.*, 1990, 442.

recognize, at times, the compensation action either to the sender[380] alone or to the recipient[381] and even concurrence between the two.[382] These reconstructions start from the erroneous assumption that the transport would regulate the compensation claim, while, in itself, it has nothing to do with the property, nor with its transfer, nor with the arising or modification of other rights concerning the goods. Therefore, the contract of carriage cannot identify the person entitled in the event of a violation of these rights, because they are unrelated to the agreement, and the same applies to the delay.

The determination of who can ask for compensation is not a question that can be answered by the transport regulations, which have a more limited objective, namely, that of establishing the obligations that the carrier assumes. In the face of nonfulfillment, it is necessary to clarify who can act, whether the sender or the consignee, provided that, in the latter case, the counter-order is not exercised and he requests redelivery. It is not for the regulation of transport to establish who, between the shipper and the recipient, can invoke compensation, because, to this end, a compensable prejudice is required. Its identification implies the analysis of the right of either the sender or the consignee to the cargo. Therefore, it is necessary to identify the property or which subjective position has suffered an injury due to the carrier's behavior. Inevitably, the investigation shifts to the underlying relationships. In fact, it is necessary to grasp the prejudice to establish who can ask for compensation, and this is possible only on the basis of the contract that identifies the rights concerning the goods and the consequences of their injury.

Precisely because it is independent in relation to the ownership of the rights inherent in the goods and the inspiring reasons for their movement, the transport determines the compensable prejudice, but refrains from qualifying it and, therefore, it is necessary to go beyond the agreement and investigate the organizational and commercial relationships that are on different perspectives. It is no coincidence that, aware of these dynamics and consistent with their aims, the Convention rightly speaks of the entitled person and, if it does not, a consistent reading of the provisions is required, for example, about the delay. With this, the CMR does not renounce to pursue its goal, but defines the limits of its intervention, so that it is up to the analysis of the overall commercial relations to establish who the entitled person is.

[380]Cf. App. Aix - en – Provence 28 May 1991, in *Le Lamy transp.*, 2021, vol. I, 558.

[381]Cf. App. Paris 2 December 1981, in *Bull. transp.*, 1982, 73; Cass. France 3 October 2000, in *Europ. transp. law,* 2001, no. 36; Cass. Belgium 13 June 1980, in *Le Lamy transp.*, 2021, vol. I, 557.

[382]Cf. App. Aix – en – Provence February 151983, in *Le Lamy transp.*, 2021, vol. I, 557; App. Antwerp 24 November 1982, *ibid.*, 2001, vol. I, 557; App. Brussels 7 February 1992, *ibid.*, 2001, vol. I, 557.

7.4.5 *The Possible Concurrence of Claims Not Based on the Contract and of Noncontractual or Tort Liability*

Pursuant to Article 28, if, in accordance with domestic law, the person entitled requests extra-contractual compensation for prejudices resulting from loss, damage or delay, the carrier can apply the provisions of CMR that exclude his liability or those that determine or limit the due compensation.[383] The noncontractual action is an alternative to the contractual one and can be exercised only for the relief of prejudices occurring during a journey governed by uniform law. Reference is made to the categories of continental law, but, although these have inspired the Convention, there have been no particular difficulties in other systems. In fact, Article 28 considers "the cases in which (. . .) a noncontractual liability of the carrier for loss, damage or delay" can be identified, "with reference to those cases that fall within the provision (. . .) of Article 17".[384] Therefore, failure to perform the service does not fall within the scope of this regulation as it is a heterogeneous case with respect to loss, damage or delay.[385]

The purpose of the rule is to avoid circumvention of uniform law rules so that the carrier is not exposed to the risk of facing further actions.[386] This way, the CMR is the only source of discipline of the carrier's liability in international transport, although, for some,[387] this principle would not operate for the so-called special risks on the basis of a literal exegesis of Article 28. In fact, this rule would recall the ones that "exclude (. . .) liability or which fix or limit the compensation",[388] without there being any reference to Article 17, fourth paragraph, and the consequent reversal of the burden of proof, pursuant to Article 18, second paragraph. On the contrary, when the Convention wants to predict this scenario, it would do so expressly, as per Article 29, according to which the carrier cannot make use of the rules that reverse the burden of proof if he acts with willful misconduct or with equivalent fault. The proposed solution is not convincing. If the entitled person could act in an extra-contractual way for the prejudices connected to the special risks, the uniformity of the regulatory system of the carrier's liability would fail, and this disruption would not be rational.

---

[383] Cf. App. Chambéry 15 May 2001, in *Le Lamy transp.*, 2021, vol. I, 540; Hof Antwerp 19 February 2007, in *Europ. transp. law,* 2007, no. 42, 427,

[384] Cf. Silingardi et al. (1994), p. 191 ff.; Haak (1986), p. 238 ff.; Loewe (1976), p. 382 ff.; Libouton (1973), p. 58 ff.; Rodière (1971), p. 318 ff.

[385] Cf. Messent and Glass (2018), p. 262 ff.

[386] Cf. Haak (1986), p. 237 ff., according to whom "the absence of a protective construction such as that of Article 28 of CMR against an eventual reduction of the system would have constituted a permanent threat to legal certainty in this field"; Putzeys (1981), p. 339 ff.

[387] For a reconstruction of the criticized argument, Cf. Clarke (2014), p. 210 ff.; moreover, the same Author criticizes the same solution.

[388] This is how Article 28, first paragraph, reads in the English version.

To apply Article 28, whoever invokes noncontractual compensation protection must be one of the parties and, therefore, the regulation does not concern the third one,[389] as in the case of a delivery to a person other than the consignee who, during unloading, causes damage to the goods.[390] Article 28 applies if the action is brought against auxiliaries the activities of whom the carrier makes use of, pursuant to Article 3, provided that the prejudice occurs in the exercise of their functions, failing which the same Article 28 cannot be invoked.[391] However, usually, the person entitled acts against the carrier despite the performance being executed by his auxiliaries, precisely by virtue of Article 3. It offers protection in limited cases where the employee is a subsequent carrier and the entitled person decides to take action against him.[392]

References

Abromavicius G (2017) Article 17 CMR overview countries. In: Verheyen W (ed) Aa. Vv., CMR 60 years. Time for retirement or future proof? Paris, pp 54 ff

Antapasis MA (2017) Article 17 CMR overview countries. In: Verheyen W (ed) Aa. Vv., CMR 60 years. Time for retirement or future proof?, Paris, pp 43 ff

Cabrera Cànovas A (2012) Jurisprudencia del Tribunal Supremo español en materias reguladas por el Convenio C M R. In: Sánchez - Gamborino F, Cabrera Cànovas A (eds) El convenio CMR: el contrado de transporte internacional de mercancias por carretera, Barcelona, pp 129 ff

Clarke MA (2014) International carriage of goods by road: CMR, VI edn. New York

Czerwenka B (2016) The concept of 'unavoidable circumstances' in Article 17, para 2, of the CMR in light of German jurisprudence. Unif Law Rev 532 ff

Defossez D (2016) CMR: what if the courts got it wrong?, Unif Law Rev, 75 ff

Eckardt T (2017) Article 17 CMR overview countries. In: Verheyen W (ed) Aa. Vv., CMR 60 years. Time for retirement or future proof? Paris, pp 39 ff

Ferrari F (2018) Art. 3 der CMR. In: Aa. Vv., Internationales Vertragsrecht, Munich, 1266 ff

Fillers A (2020) The CMR in the practice of Latvian courts. Unif Law Rev 169 ff

Gerspacher L, Thalmann R (2017) Article 17 CMR overview countries, various authors, CMR 60 years. In: Verheyen W (ed) Time for retirement or future proof? Paris, pp 56 ff

Gruber A (2017) Article 17 CMR overview countries. In: Verheyen W (ed) Aa. Vv., CMR 60 years. Time for retirement or future proof? Paris, pp 37 ff

Haak KF (1986) The liability of the carrier under CMR. The Hague

[389] Cf. App. Paris 5 March 2009, in *Bull. transp. logist.*, 2009, 240; App. Paris 11 June 1974, *ibid.*, 1974, 319. Cf. Messent and Glass (2018), p. 260 ff. But see Loewe (1976), p. 381 ff., according to whom "Article 28 also applies to claims by persons who are not able to enforce the rights established by CMR against the carrier, for example, to claims by a principal who has used the services of a forwarding agent in cases where the latter's rights have not been assigned to him". This argument cannot be endorsed, as the Convention governs the contract of carriage and therefore only considers the parties to the agreement.

[390] Cf. App. Grenoble 22 October 2020, in *Le Lamy transp.*, 2021, vol. I, 540.

[391] Cf. Messent and Glass (2018), p. 262 ff.; Clarke (2014), p. 210 ff.; Rodière (1971), p. 318 ff.

[392] Cf. Haak (1096), p. 241 ff., according to whom "reference may be made to the fact that where an agent or servant acquires the capacity of successive carrier, he can be proceeded against directly in that capacity by the claimant".

Humphreys G, De Peuteur S (1992) Highway robbery in Europe. Theft under CMR. Eur Transp Law 27:753 ff

Jung C (1997) The Convention on the contract for the International carriage of goods by road (CMR): survey, analysis and trends of recent German case law. Unif Law Rev, 148 ff

Kolacz MK (2017) *Article 17 CMR overview countries*. In: Verheyen W (ed) Aa. Vv., CMR 60 years. Time for retirement or future proof? Paris, pp 48 ff

Koller I (2019) Die Beweislast für den ordnungsgemäßen Zustand des Gutes bei dessen Übernahme, insbesondere für die Vorkühlung, in TranspR, 1 ff

Krings E (1999) CMR: examen de la jurisprudence des Cours de Cassation de France et de Pays – Bas (première partie). Unif Law Rev 160 ff

Letacq F (2016) Notion de "circonstances inévitables" de l'Article 17 (2) de la CMR au sens de la jurisprudence française. Unif Law Rev, 542 ff

Libouton J (1973) International road transport. Convention on the contract for the international carriage of goods by road. Review of Court decisions 1965–1971. Eur Transp Law 8:6 ff

Loewe R (1976) Commentary on the Convention of 19 May 1956 on the contract for the international carriage of goods by road. Eur Transp Law 11:311 ff

Mayer CU (1997) CMR – aperçu et réflexions sur la jurisprudence autrichienne en dernier ressort (1994–1996). Unif Law Rev 159 ff

Messent A, Glass DA (2018) Cmr: contracts for the international carriage of goods by road, IV edn. New York

Otte K (2018) Art. 17 der CMR. In: Aa. Vv., Internationales Vertragsrecht. Munich, 1367 ff

Pesce A (1995) Il trasporto internazionale di merci. Turin

Putzeys J (1981) Le contrat de transport routier de marchandises, Brussels

Rodière R (1970) The Convention on road transport. Eur Transp Law 6:630 ff

Rodière R (1971) The Convention on road transport. Eur Transp Law 7:2 ff

Sánchez Gamborino FJ (2001a) La jurisprudence du Tribunal Supremo espagnol en matière de CMR. Unif Law Rev 644 ff

Sánchez Gamborino FJ (2001b) La Conventión Cmr según la Jurisprudencia del "Tribunal Supremo" de España. Eur Transp Law 36:842 ff

Schelin J (2016) CMR Convention in a law and economic perspective. Unif Law Rev 434 ff

Schmid R (2013) Art. 3. In: Thume KH (ed) Aa. Vv., Cmr: über den Beförderungsvertrag im internationalen Strassengüterverkehr, III edn. Frankfurt Am Main, pp 171 ff

Schmidt P (2019) Der Lohnfuhrvertrag im Lichte jüngerer Rechtsprechung. Fata Morgana order Realität? TranspR, 249 ff

Silingardi G, Corrado A, Meotti A, Morandi F (1994) La disciplina uniforme del contratto di trasporto di cose su strada, Turin

Thume KH (2013) Haftung des Frachtführers. In: Thume KH (ed) Aa. Vv., CMR: über den Beförderungsvertrag im internationalen Strassengüterverkehr, III edn. Frankfurt Am Main, pp 361 ff

Tincani C (2012) La natura del trasporto stradale di merci. Milan

Van Ryn J (1966) Une nouvelle étape dans l'élaboration du droit des transport: la Convention de 1956 relative au transport international de marchandises par route (CMR). Eur Transp Law 1: 639 ff

Wesolowski K (2013) A review of judicial decisions of the polish supreme court within the scope of CMR. Eur Transp Law 48:341 ff

Chapter 8
Damages and Compensation Limit

Contents

C. Tincani, *Contract for the International Carriage of Goods by Road*, Law for Professionals, https://doi.org/10.1007/978-3-031-08487-4_8

8.1 Specific Cases

8.1.1 Failure to Execute

Articles 17 and 18 of the Convention regulate the carrier's liability for prejudice to cargo, identified in loss, damage and delay. However, this three-fold division is not exclusive, as it does not cover all prejudices based on the uniform law. In fact, the text provides for further hypotheses, such as the consequences of breaching the obligation to demand cash on delivery. Nevertheless, concerning the harm inflicted on cargo, Articles 17 ff. are clear as they contemplate what can happen. The load can arrive in an altered manner, arrive after the deadline, never arrive, or arrive only partially.

The hypothesis of failure to execute the trip is discussed and understood as "nonfulfillment resulting from the total or partial failure to perform the transport by the carrier who (...) did not initiate the transfer (...) or interrupted the journey before the goods were (...) redelivered".[1] Since Articles 17 and 18 primarily regard liability for loss, damage and delay, nonfulfillment of the obligation to execute the carriage is said to have not been regulated by the Convention but by the national law.[2]

The approach is unconvincing, because different concepts overlap. In fact, the supposed non-execution identifies the conduct that causes nonfulfillment, that is, the violation of an obligation. As it is the origin of the prejudice, it cannot be confused with the latter, and the breach can manifest itself as a reflection of various behaviors, including nonexecution. The refusal to perform the carriage does not always lead to an unfulfillment of the obligation. For instance, the shipper can accept the transporter's decision, if it is communicated to him, so that, in this case, the contract is considered terminated. If the obligation to transfer the goods is not implemented, the prejudice is due to delay or loss and, in particular, the former operates if the situation is transitory and then ceases, and the latter if it is stable, in the sense that there is no redelivery within 30 days from the expiry of the deadline or within 60 days from receipt of the load, pursuant to Article 20, first paragraph.

The conduct which causes nonfulfillment can assume infinite variations, but all destined to create one of the prejudices mentioned by the Convention, that is loss, damage, delay or the prolonged one, likely to turn into a loss, with the simple passage of time, on the basis of Article 20, first paragraph. Failure to execute is an omission, but it does not overlap with the possible prejudices, exhaustively indicated in the Convention. Therefore, there can be no reference to the national law,[3] and the lack or refusal to perform the service must be assessed pursuant to the uniform one.

---

[1] Cf. Silingardi et al. (1994), p. 137 ff.; Messent and Glass (2018), p. 209 ff.; Clarke (2014), p. 191 ff.

[2] Cf. Silingardi et al. (1994), p. 137 ff. See also App. Milan 11 July 1975, in *Unif. law rev.*, 1977, 336.

[3] App. Reims 5 May 1980, in *Bull. transp.*, 1980, 299.

In particular, the supposed nonexecution can occur if, after receiving the cargo, the carrier does nothing, regardless of whether he is aware of the whereabouts of the goods or loses them. However, there is either a loss or a delay where Article 20, first paragraph, applies. The same conclusion must be reached if the carrier adopts an explicit position and declares his intention not to perform the transport. This manifestation will make the nonfulfillment clear and deliberately planned, without altering the structure of the prejudice, so that the previous considerations apply if a consensual agreement is not reached. Therefore, despite the doctrine[4] attempting to introduce further cases, the uniform law has a solid systematic structure that correlates liability to different forms of prejudice and lays down a specific set of regulations for each one of them, albeit focused on the compensatory limit. If the coherent elements of the regulation are evaluated, the operation of the national law, which is always the cause of serious implementing difficulties, is avoided.

The same reasoning applies to other obligations provided by the Convention; their nonfulfillment does not coincide with the prejudice, that is merely a consequence of it, so that there is no room for any reference to the national law, since only the CMR regulates the compensation. For instance, noncompliance with the obligation to execute the instructions of the countermand is a conduct that can involve prejudice and, if necessary, can result in loss, damage or delay. To identify the prejudice, an assessment is made whether such behavior affects the final outcome of the trip. In fact, with the counter - order, new indications instrumental to the achievement of a result partially diverging from the original one are provided and, therefore, noncompliance can cause one of the prejudices contemplated by Articles 17 ff. This applies to the other obligations disciplined by the uniform law, and the prejudice can always be referred to the typical models, which are regulated by the CMR. An exception is the failure to collect the payment, which has its own separate discipline, but, in that case, the CMR clearly governs the problem of cash on delivery.

8.1.2 Delay in Execution

According to Article 19, there is a delay when the redelivery is not performed within the stipulated deadline and the latter is not a necessary element of the contract; therefore, the parties can provide for it, but they are not obliged to do so, and this is inferred from the consignment note.[5] Regardless of its possible non-inclusion, the effects of which are governed by Article 4, Article 6 distinguishes the essential elements of the contract from the eventual ones with regard to its draft and inserts the deadline[6] among the latter, pursuant to Article 6, second paragraph, letter f).

[4] Cf. Silingardi et al. (1994), p. 137 ff.

[5] Cf. Messent and Glass (2018), p. 206 ff. V. also Thume (2013), p. 545 ff.

[6] See: Thume (2013), p. 549 ff.

Therefore, the consignment note can be completed without specifying the expected time for redelivery[7] and the same applies to agreements entered into in another manner, particularly oral ones. In fact, Article 19 is said to not apply if the carrier takes more time during loading, as the rule would refer to the "duration of the carriage" and, therefore, the delay in the phase prior to transfer narrowly understood is considered to be governed by the national law.[8] The thesis remains unconvincing, because, even if the impediment occurs before the start of the journey, it postpones redelivery and loses any autonomous connotation. The fundamental point is not when the difficulty occurs, but its ultimate consequences, which are only relevant to Article 19.

The deadline can be indicated in the consignment note with different formulas, for instance, with the expression "*pas après le*"[9] and, in some cases, these can give rise to uncertainties, such as the "*le matin*"[10] clause, although, usually, it is interpreted as equivalent to that of "*tôt le matin*" or "*le matin de bonne heure*", so that the redelivery should be made early in the morning and is considered late if completed at 11.30.[11] Then, for transport to London, if the carrier agrees to take the ferry on a predetermined day, there is delay in the event of noncompliance, even if it is related to an intermediate stage. The conclusion is correct, because, in their autonomy, the parties can establish similar interlocutory obligations, as the silence of the Convention is not equivalent to prohibition and Article 41 does not apply.[12]

If it is not provided in the consignment note, the deadline can be regulated by another instrument, entitled "*instructions aux transporteurs*", as it contributes to the definition of the contractual program.[13] Furthermore, the clause inserted in the "*commande d'affrètement*"[14] or communicated by *telex*, before the journey begins,

[7]Cf. App. Aix – en Provence 20 March 20 1985, in *Le Lamy transp.*, 2020, vol. I, 490. For the opposite view, cf. Messent and Glass (2018), p. 207 ff., according to whom the consignment note would be illegitimate if the deadline was not indicated. But, precisely because the deadline is included among the optional elements, its absence does not affect the legitimacy of the act. See also Thume (2013), p. 547 ff.

[8]Cf. also OLG Naumburg 16 June 1912, in *TranspR,* 2013, 235; OLG Hamm 20 March 1997, *ibid.,* 1998, 297; OLG Düsseldorf 23 December 1996, *ibid.,* 1998, 113.

[9]Cf. App. Paris 2 December 1981, in *Bull. transp.,* 1982, 73.

[10]Cf. App. Versailles 27 February 1997, in *Bull. transp. logis.,* 1997, 350.

[11]Cf. App. Versailles 27 February 1997, in *Bull. transp. logis.,* 1997, 350.

[12]Cf. App. Aix – en – Provence 20 December 1977, in *Bull. transp.,* 1978, 245. See OLG Hamburg 17 June 2004, in *TranspR,* 2005, 116, according to which an approximate assessment of the delivery date is not equivalent to indicating a deadline. For the same opinion, see OLG Stuttgart 27 September 1991, *ibid.,* 1992, 22, according to which the clause "as soon as possible" is not the same as a deadline.

[13]Cf. App. Paris 23 March 1978, in *Bull. transp.,* 1978, 265; App. Montpellier 19 February 1987, *ibid.,* 1987, 578. Cf. also App. Aix – en – Provence 20 December 1977, *ibid.,* 1987, 245. App. Amiens 19 June 1980, *ibid.*, 1980, 490.

[14]Cf. Trib. com. Bois 6 December 2002, in *Bull. transp. logis.,* 2003, 143.

is binding.[15] Then, the deadline would also apply if the *telex* were sent during the execution of the transport and the receipt would be equivalent to acceptance.[16] This last solution remains unconvincing, because it would allow the shipper to unilaterally modify the original agreement, and this cannot happen without the express consent of the carrier, as the receipt of a document is not equivalent to adhering to a proposal, even more so if this happens during execution.[17]

Failure to lay down the deadline requires a more detailed assessment of the delay. According to Article 19,[18] this occurs when more time than that granted to a diligent professional operator is consumed, according to the criteria of social normality that have to be checked based on specific situation in relation to the itinerary, distance and difficulties encountered during the journey.[19] The conduct should be considered on the basis of diligence and, therefore, of what could be expected from a carrier equipped with the necessary technical resources[20] and with the highest level of commitment and prudence. For assessment, the nationality of the transporter is also relevant, if complex administrative tasks have to be performed abroad to obtain special transit permits.[21] However, the transporter is deemed liable if he takes 3 months to deliver cargo from France to Syria when 15 days are considered sufficient.[22]

Proof of the delay must be given by the claimant for compensation.[23] Usually, the overrun of the deadline can be easily ascertained, if agreed, because the moment in which the redelivery occurs is undisputed; it is therefore easy to demonstrate the

---

[15]Cf. App. Montpellier 21 April 1988, in *Le Lamy transp.*, 2020, vol. I, 490. Cf. also App. Toulouse 29 July 1981, *ibid.,* 1981, 381; OLG Düsseldorf 27 February 1997, in *TranspR,* 1998, 194. Cf. Libouton (1973), p. 54 ff.

[16]Cf. App. Rennes 26 November 1986, in *Le Lamy transp.*, 2020, vol. I, 490. See also App. Toulouse 4 June 1987, in *Bull. transp.,* 1981, 381.

[17]Cf. App. Paris 2 October 1991, in *Bull. transp. logis.,* 1991, 717. See also OLG Stuttgart 27 September 1991, in *TranspR,* 1992, 22.

[18]The French text reads, "*le temps qu'il est rasonnable*". The English text reads, "the time it would be reasonable". See also Thume (2013), p. 550 ff.

[19]Cf. Trib. com. Bobigny 25 February 1994, in *Le Lamy transp.*, 2020, vol. I, 490, according to which the delay is determined with regard to that envisaged by the typical French contract. Cf. Putzeys (1981), p. 232 ff.

[20]Cf. App. Venice 31 October 1974, in *Europ. transp. law,* 1975, no. 10, 21, according to which the duration of a transport from Belgium to Italy at the time ranged from 35 to 40 h including stops and the time spent at customs to complete the related administrative formalities.

[21]Cf. Arrond. Utrecht 12 March 1980, in Messent and Glass (2018), p. 208 ff., nt. 20.

[22]Cf. App. Lyon 27 June 1980, in *Bull. transp.,* 1980, 509. See also App. Rennes 5 November 1974, *ibid.,* 1974, 514; App. Poitiers 3 February 1976, *ibid.,* 1976, 185, according to which 2 days are enough for a voyage from the Adriatic Sea to the French Vendée. See also OLG Munich 12 April 1990, in *TranspR,* 1990, 280, regarding a journey in Kuwait; OLG Hamburg 3 May 1984, *ibid.,* 1985, 37, regarding a journey in Iraq; OLG Berlin 4 May 1983, *ibid.,* 1985, 134; OLG Lubeck 17 March 1986, *ibid.,* 1986, 339, regarding a journey from Frankfurt am Main to Helsinki.

[23]Cf. App. Grenoble 13 March 1980, in *Bull. transp.,* 1981, 306. Cf. Clarke (2014), p. 194 ff., according to whom "it is the claimant who must prove that the goods have not delivered within a reasonable time". See also Thume (2013), p. 555 ff.

delay,[24] and reference must be made to the consignee's receipt. Presently, with technological innovation and the use of modern IT tools, it is possible to track down the carriage in all its phases, with the supposed traceability; therefore, it is possible to check the progress during intermediate stages and be informed in real-time of the problems that may cause a slowdown. In the face of these novelties, proof of the delay is simple, because the results of the carrier's information system can be used against him to demonstrate the time consumed.

If a deadline is not agreed upon, whoever requests compensation must give evidence of what is necessary, according to Article 19, that is, the required time for an organized and diligent carrier; only in some cases, the relative allegations are easy to make, and reference can be made to common knowledge, i.e., for the most frequent journeys and for the known routes according to general experience. This does not apply to the unusual ones, for which evidence must be given with reference to the most widely practiced behaviors, and the judge's assessment depends on the legal theory followed by the appointed court or tribunal, governing the whole probative aspect. Therefore, the uniform law is limited to apportioning the burden of proof, placing it on the party who relies on the delay. It is necessary to demonstrate when the goods arrive and provide the evaluation criteria referred to in Article 19, although this can sometimes be difficult, depending on the approach of the procedural law.

Compensation for prejudice can be requested while the cargo is in motion, even when it is running late. However, it can be expected that the latter turns into a loss, pursuant to Article 20, first paragraph, and that the time specified therein expires, so that the most favorable compensation limit, provided by Article 23, third paragraph, might apply.[25] More generally, such a rush in initiating legal action would be surprising, because, even if Article 20, first paragraph, is not applied, the situation is only known in its entirety and the extent of the delay can be assessed once the redelivery has been completed, not to mention the separate problem of demonstrating the compensable prejudice.

8.1.3 Determining the Prejudice Caused by Delay

For prejudice caused by delay, we have to refer to Article 23, first paragraph, which introduces the criterion for quantifying the compensation, based on the value of goods in the place and time in which the carrier receives them. Instead, Article

---

[24]Cf. Messent and Glass (2018), p. 207 ff. Cf. App. Bordeaux 9 February 1972, in *Bull. transp.*, 1972, 114. See also App. Trento 21 May 1998, in *Europ. transp. law,* 1999, no. 34, 280, according to which the difficulties connected with the crossing of Eastern European States before the normalization of commercial relations were significant.

[25]Cf. Loewe (1976), p. 371 ff. Cf. App. Colmar 7 November 2012, in *Bull. transp. logis.,* 2012, 711; App. Versailles 18 April 2017, *Le Lamy transp.*, 2020, vol. I, 516.

23, fifth paragraph,[26] is relevant, in terms of which the prejudice occurred must be proved.[27] This is inevitable, because, if Article 23, first paragraph, is irrelevant, the delay does not in itself involve any harm to the proprietary sphere of others and it is not enough to offer evidence of its existence, as its specific consequences must be demonstrated.[28] In this regard, the Convention is concise and only requires that the harm resulting from the illegitimate prolongation of the transport be established. Article 23, fifth paragraph, does not mention expressed criteria for the assessment of this prejudice, but the distribution of the burden of proof is regulated for demonstration of facts from which actual prejudice can have derived. However, this is not disciplined more comprehensively by the Convention and, although there is no reference thereto, the application of national law is inevitable, because Article 23, fifth paragraph, is insufficient.

Each legal system has its own notion of prejudice and compensation and, consequently, this is reflected in the implementation of Article 23, fifth paragraph, which is as concise as it could be. Moreover, the Convention could not have done much more, because the issue is far too complex for an extended regulation in the uniform law and needs to be supplemented further, especially in the most questionable cases. There could be a rare but not impossible scenario in which the delay causes consequences on the safety of a person, for instance, due to a medicine failing to arrive on time. However, if we remain within the patrimonial sphere which is narrowly understood, the expression of Article 23, fifth paragraph, remains insufficient to assess the most delicate facts and, if we are not mistaken, the judge draws inspiration from the domestic law.

For the delay, the Convention sets the compensation limit in an amount not exceeding the consideration stipulated for the transport, to a lesser extent than Article 23, third paragraph.[29] However, the general concept of prejudice is no less important, due to the possible forfeiture of the benefit of the limit or its inapplicability in the event of a declaration of special interest upon redelivery, pursuant to Article 26. In fact, it is necessary to demonstrate the harm to patrimonial integrity[30] and the loss of earnings[31] that could have been achieved with the use of the cargo. For instance,

[26] The French text reads, "*en cas de retard, si l'ayant droit prouve qu'un préjudice en est résulté, le transporteur est tenu de payer pour ce préjudice une indemnité qui ne peut pas dépasser le prix du transport*". The English text reads, "in the case of delay, if the claimant proves that the damage has resulted therefrom, the carrier shall pay compensation for such damage not exceeding that carriage charges".

[27] Cf. OLG Düsseldorf 9 October 1986, in *TranspR,* 1986, 429.

[28] Cf. OLG Cologne 14 March 1997, in *VersR,* 1997, 1033.

[29] Cf. Otte (2018b), p. 1460 ff.

[30] Cf. App. Versailles 9 April 2019, in *Le Lamy transp.*, 2020, vol. I, 515; App. Rouen 16 December 2004, in *Bull. transp. logist.,* 2005, 190. See Clarke (2014), p. 194 ff., according to whom "Article 23, fifth paragraph (...), contemplates a different kind of 'damage', namely damage to the claimant's pocket: 'purely' economic loss, and nothing else". Cf. also Putzeys (1981), p. 296 ff.; Haak (1986), p. 229 ff.

[31] Cf. Thume (2013), p. 558 ff.

the decrease in the value of goods compared with the market price and the loss of customers fall under this concept.

Deterioration of the integrity of the load is not delay, but damage,[32] with the result that Article 25 applies, so that the opposite theses[33] are unfounded, as one has to concentrate on the final moment of the journey. In fact, it is irrelevant to trace our steps back to the cause of the prejudice to distinguish the delay from the physical damage, as only the harm is focused upon. Therefore, if the prolongation of the transfer involves a decrease in the value of the cargo, considering that it loses its integrity, for example in the case of perishable goods, it is considered a damage with the inevitable application of the relative compensation limit.

The juxtaposition between delay and damage does not qualify the contractual breach, but rather the prejudice caused. If the journey takes too long and, for this reason, the goods deteriorate, the prejudice consists in this latter element, regardless of the behavior of the carrier. Therefore, the prejudice caused by delay must be different from that caused to the structure of the goods and, though not defined in detail by the Convention, it must be linked to the organizational consequences of the late arrival itself, rather than redelivery of the goods regardless of its impact on its physical integrity. For this reason, if its intrinsic value does not matter, the claimant must demonstrate from an organizational viewpoint what the use of the cargo would have been and must also do so by identifying the impact of the unfulfillment of the delivery deadline. Precisely, for this reason, on one hand, evidence must be articulated and, on the other hand, the judge will tend to refer to the national law. Moreover, if both the prejudice due to delay and the one due to damage occur, both will be compensated, although the hypothesis is rare.[34]

8.1.4 Damage

According to Article 17, first paragraph, the carrier is liable for damage,[35] which is an alteration of the internal or external quality of goods that leads to a decrease in

---

[32] Cf. Cass. com. France 5 December 1989, in *Bull. transp.,* 1990, 310; OGH 31 March 1982, in *TranspR,* 1984, 196; BGH 15 October1992, *ibid.,* 1992, 137; Putzeys (1981), p. 296 ff., according to whom "*la dépréciation de la marchandise à la suite d'un retard à la livraison est une avarie, la réparation étant accordée selon les règles de la avarie est non celles du retard*".

[33] Cf. Nickel – Lanz (1976), p. 167 ff., according to whom it would be necessary to distinguish the hypotheses in which the damage is the cause of the delay, which would fall within the scope of application of Article 23, first - fourth paragraphs, from those in which it is the delay that causes damage to the load, which would fall under Article 23, fifth paragraph.

[34] Cf. Hof Gent 19 December 2005, in *Europ. transp. law,* 2007, no. 42, 275, according to which there is also the concurrence of damage from delay and from loss, if due to the delay the goods are lost; BGH 19 September 2019, *ibid.,* 2020, no. 55, 277.

[35] Cf. Putzeys (1981), p. 230 ff., according to whom "*l'avarie est une détérioration de l'intégrité de la marchandise*". See also Rodière (1971), p. 12 ff.; Haak (1986), p. 201 ff., according to whom "by

value.[36] If it affects a component of the load, it is partial; if it extends to the cargo as a whole, it is total.[37] But in both cases, the goods must retain their usefulness. If their structural modification deprives them of any economic significance, there is no damage, but loss and, to this end, we must refer to the criteria of social normality and patrimonial reasons underlying the journey, so that only the significant and recognizable residual value, based on a plausible use, is relevant.

The Convention does not offer a definition of "*dépréciation*"[38] and does not identify the criteria for quantifying compensation. In general, it is the difference between the value of goods at the time of delivery to the carrier and the residual value after they are damaged.[39] However, with regard to a machine, the prejudice is represented by the expenses incurred for its repair[40] and there is no contradiction with the definition just given, because, if the damage is reversible, it must be eliminated and the harm consists in the relative expense. Then, if an asset destined for a commercial event is broken during the journey, the costs incurred for temporary repair, necessary to allow the exhibition, are charged to the carrier, and to these are added those for the final restoration.[41] Therefore, depending on the circumstances, there may be various successive interventions, and all the related expenses contribute to the quantification of the prejudice. Moreover, the transporter is liable for "*l'aggravation de la dépréciation*" of the goods until the moment in which, rejected by the consignee,[42] he takes them back to the sender. If, in fact, these are the instructions, the damage must be assessed upon extinction of the obligation and, in this case, this happens at the time of final redelivery. For instance, the delivery of dead animals is damage,[43] not loss, only if the cargo maintains some usefulness in respect of any reasonable use of the carcasses.

In essence, the damage is a material prejudice, which involves an alteration in the structure of the asset, but does not prevent it from reaching its destination and, above all, from satisfying a residual interest. For the quantification of the decrease in value, it must be established whether the qualitative modification concerns part of or all of the load, but it retains a material identity and an economic significance, albeit to a lesser extent. Sometimes, it can be used for the original purpose, in other cases the

---

damage one can understand the situation where substantial change in the condition of goods has been affected". See also Thume and Riemer (2013a), p. 691 ff.

[36] Cf. LG Bonn 27 March 2001, in *TranspR,* 2002, 77, according to which rust on goods is considered a damage.

[37] See Thume and Riemer (2013a), p. 692 ff.

[38] Cf. Article 25, first paragraph. In the English text, Article 25, first paragraph, reads: "the carrier shall be liable for the amount by which the goods have diminished in value".

[39] Cf. App. Aix – en Provence 27 February1985, in *Le Lamy transp*., 2020, vol. I, 509; App. Paris 12 February 2004, in *Bull. transp. logist.*, 2004, 178; App. Aix – en – Provence 15 January 1991, *Le Lamy transp*., 2020, vol. I, 509.

[40] Cf. App. Lyon 7 June 2007, in *Bull. transp. logist.*, 2007, 466.

[41] Cf. Aix – en - Provence 9 December 1980, in *Le Lamy transp*., 2020, vol. I, 509.

[42] Cf. App. Aix – en – Provence 27 June 1986, in *Le Lamy transp*., 2020, vol. I, 509.

[43] Cf. Cass. com. France 9 May 1995, in *Le Lamy transp*., 2020, vol. I, 509.

forms of use change, as it happens in the case of dead animals, but, anyway, there is possible exploitation of goods, which, in fact, are not lost.

If anything, in practice, more difficult questions arise in the case of repair, especially if expenses are high and the compensation limit does not apply, for example for fault equivalent to willful misconduct. The Convention does not resolve the problem in an express way and, as, for the most part, we are discussing machines and tools in general, it is reasonable to make the prejudice coincide with the costs necessary for the restoration, so that the interest of the sender or the consignee can be completely satisfied. However, although this solution, supported by the French case law,[44] is acceptable, it involves forcing things in relation to Article 25, first paragraph, with its reference to Article 23, first paragraph, as its provisions recall "*la valeur de la marchandise*",[45] and the cost of restoration is different. Anyway, although French decisions are influenced by the relevant national principles on damage, it is reasonable to make the relief coincide with what is necessary for repair, without prejudice to the compensation limit, if applicable. Instead, unlike what happens for the delay, the relief does not include the lost earnings hoped for and not realized,[46] as the difference between Article 23, first paragraph, and Article 25, first paragraph, is too wide.

8.2 The Concept of Loss

8.2.1 Partial and Total Loss

The Convention provides for loss as one of the consequential prejudices to the carrier's liability and, as for delay and damage, it does not offer a definition, limiting itself to contrast total loss with a partial one.[47] The former occurs when the carrier "*se trouve dans l'impossibilité de présenter tant soit peu de la marchandise à la livraison*".[48] In general, total loss is associated with the destruction of the cargo, with its removal following a theft or robbery or, in any case, with any event that definitively causes the physical structure of the load to be destroyed.[49] We have to include in total loss the hypothesis in which the fate of the cargo is unknown, as

[44]Cf. App. Lyon 7 June 2007, in *Bull. transp. logist.*, 2007, 466; Aix – en - Provence 9 December 1980, in *Le Lamy transp.*, 2020, vol. I, 509.

[45]The English text reads, "the value of the goods".

[46]Cf. Cass. com. France 14 March 1995, in *Bull. transp. logist.*, 1995, 248; App. Paris 13 February 1985, in *Le Lamy transp.*, 2020, vol. I, 509; App. Paris 15 June 1989, *ibid.*, 2020, vol. I, 509; App. Aix – en – Provence 12 September 2013, *ibid.*, 2020, vol. I, 509; App. Paris 24 March 2004, in *Bull. transp. logist.*, 2004, 340; App. Lyon 22 June 2012, *Le Lamy transp.*, 2020, vol. I, 509; App. Versailles 18 April 2017, *ibid.*, 2020, vol. I, 509.

[47]Cf. Thume and Riemer (2013b), p. 654 ff.

[48]Cf. Putzeys (1981), p. 228 ff.

[49]Cf. Silingardi et al. (1994), p. 128 ff.

inferred from Article 20, first paragraph, which identifies the presumed loss with the unjustified extension of the journey. In this situation, the cargo does not reach its destination and the carrier fails to demonstrate that "*la marchandise existe et qu'elle est entre les mains de l'une ou de l'autre partie au contrat de transport*".[50] Moreover, the idea that ignorance of the fate of the load is part of the loss is consistent with common language, and this concept is implicit in non-delivery.

The trait common to all losses in the physical sense is the lack of arrival; if the empty wrapping reaches its destination, there is a loss, as the redelivery of the packaging does not satisfy the consignee's interest. However, in this regard, there is no lack of discordant voices, which recognize, in this case, a total damage, since the loss would imply non-arrival.[51] The solution contrasts with the idea of damage, for which the structural modification of the commodity does not prevent it from having its own physical identity and from retaining economic importance. If only the wrapping is delivered, it is not a material alteration, but a non-arrival, as the packaging wraps the contents and has a different nature and, if it is delivered empty, there is no modification of the goods, but their disappearance; therefore, it is loss, not damage.

Furthermore, it is considered loss if the goods are redelivered to a person other than the consignee, as the final result is always different from the planned one. Although the load does not lose its identity, there is breach of the main obligation, and the same conclusion can be reached if the consignee traces the load[52] and identifies the holder, as it happens by the initiative of the recipient, who, at a later time, stops the noncompliance and eliminates the prejudice. If anything, the identification of who wrongly obtains the goods allows the recipient to plan a further journey and to have the cargo redelivered, but, in fact, it is another carriage, as the first one ended in a different manner from what was stipulated, and the claim for compensation against the initial transporter is always unaffected. Conversely, there is no loss if the goods are redelivered to the shipper as a result of the counter—order, as there is a unilateral modification of the agreement; in fact, failure to redeliver is not the result of nonfulfillment, but of compliance with the stated instructions.

Partial loss occurs when a component of the cargo reaches its destination, and the quantitative decrease must result from the comparison between the initial load and the one delivered, considering the parameters of social normality, for example, due to the possible decrease in the weight of live animals or for other natural phenomena, also in relation to atmospheric conditions. For the quantification of the prejudice, the unit of measurement selected by the carrier at the time of loading is applied, so that, if the packages have been counted, the same criterion must be used; for example, the

[50]Cf. Putzeys (1981), p. 229 ff.

[51]Cf. Putzeys (1981), p. 228 ff.

[52]Cf. BGH 27 October 1978, in *VersR,* 1979, 276. Cf. Haak (1986), p. 200 ff.

consignee cannot talk about a reduction of weight,[53] which is irrelevant. As for the damage, the Convention considers only the material prejudice, and the relief does not include the loss of earnings hoped for and not realized.[54] Therefore, if a piece of machinery intended for exhibition in a fair breaks down irreparably, the sender is entitled to compensation for the loss, not for the harm resulting from the fact that the prepared exhibition structure remains unused and the tool is not exhibited. Moreover, if the loss coexists with the damage, both prejudices[55] are compensated, based on the respective parameters.

8.2.2 *The Supposed Economic Loss*

There is a thin line between the notion of damage and that of loss. Not all cases of qualitative alteration of the goods fall into the first category, as they must have an economic utility, even if it does not coincide with the typical one. Thus, for example, there is a total loss if the prejudice to perishable goods renders them useless[56] despite reaching their destination, and the loss cannot be recognized only in the event of non-arrival, nor is there damage when it is *"a cet point grave qu'il faille considérer la marchandise comme perdue. Dans ces cas, il y a avarie totale (…), pas perte totale"*.[57] If the load is unusable and does not retain any usefulness, there is no damage[58] or qualitative alteration, but there is no possibility of identifying what has been transported on the basis of social normality criteria, as is the case for broken bottles, irreversibly perished fruits or vegetables, or garments that do not retain any plausible function, along with many similar examples, for which reference must be made to loss in an economic sense.

Damage presupposes that, although not in perfect condition, the asset can satisfy the interest of the consignee. For example, concerning frozen fish, there is a loss if the load arrives partially defrosted, but completely unsuitable for consumption; in a German case,[59] the sender's request for a return journey is discussed and it is

[53] Cf. Putzeys (1981), p. 230 ff., according to whom *"si, par example, il n'a été procédé qu'à un comptage, le transporteur ne répond pas d'un manquant en poids"*. See also Silingardi et al. (1994), p. 128 ff.

[54] Cf. App. Lyon 22 June 2012, in *Le Lamy transp.*, 2020, vol. I, 509; App. Paris 21 December 2006, in *Bull. transp. logist.*, 2007, 44; App. Montpellier 10 September 2019, in *Le Lamy transp.*, 2020, vol. I, 509.

[55] Cf. OLG Munich 27 February 1981, in *VersR*, 1982, 334. See also OLG Celle 13 January 1975, *ibid.*, 1975, 250. Cf. Haak (1986), p. 200 ff.

[56] Cf. BGH 10 December 2009, in *TranspR*, 2010, 78; BGH 13 February 1980, in *VersR*, 1980, 533; BGH 15 October 1992, in *TranspR*, 1993, 137.

[57] Cf. Putzeys (1981), p. 229 ff.

[58] Cf. BGH 30 October 2017, in *TranspR*, 2018, 146, according to which, from an economic point of view, the damage to a part of the goods can result in loss of the entire load.

[59] Cf. BGH 3 July 1974, in *Unif. law rev.*, 1974, 216.

instrumental that the load can be frozen again and sent to a different consignee. The compensation would include the expenses for the return carriage, those of storage, while waiting for the second treatment, and those incurred for an expert to examine the newly frozen goods, so that Article 23, fourth paragraph, was deemed applicable.[60] The approach remains unconvincing as, in this situation, the delivery to the consignee had taken place and this led to the termination of the relationship. Therefore, compensation for damages could have been requested for the first journey, and a possible return was the object of a different contract. As far as the nature of the harm is concerned, everything depends on the possibility of restoring the food, because, if it can occur, the prejudice is a damage and relief for it is equal to the expenses necessary for its elimination; otherwise, there is an economic loss, provided that due compliance is made with the administrative and criminal regulations on foods.

Ultimately, the non-arrival of goods, because they have been destroyed, stolen or lost, is not the only case of loss, nor Article 32 precludes this solution, as it concerns the expiry of the prescription period and has no impact on the classification of prejudices. If the load is stolen, there is a loss although it arrives, and in no way is this conclusion affected by Article 32, because the sole purposes of the expiry of the prescription period is for this provision where the economic loss is equated to the damage, while every hypothesis of loss is subject to the same compensatory regulation, on the basis of Article 23. Depending on the regulatory aims, the category assumes different meanings, because Article 32[61] considers the recognizability and Article 23 deals with the nature of the harm. It makes no sense to speak of damage if bottles are delivered broken, since they are useless and the prejudice is maximum. However, for the purposes of the beginning of the prescription period, the event is immediately identifiable in an effortless manner and, therefore, Article 32, first paragraph, letter b), must apply. The opposite approach[62] shifts from an idea that cannot be shared, i. e., the concept of loss should be unitary throughout the Convention, while a linear interpretation of Article 23 and Article 32 leads to different conclusions. Moreover, if the load is devoid of any utility, there is no question of damage and the loss of the social function of the asset entails its loss, because the object of the contract, which has disappeared irremediably, is no longer present.

A singular case of loss in an economic sense, in a different way from what has just been said, occurs in the hypothesis of seizure of the goods at customs,[63] due to a breach by the carrier of his obligations. In this case, the asset is intact and its location

[60]Cf. BGH 3 July 1974, in *Unif. law rev.*, 1974, 216.

[61]For another take on it, cf. Putzeys (1981), p. 229 ff., according to whom "*le texte de Article 32 CMR renvoie au cas où les marchandises sont disparues et non au cas où le fait dommageable a provoqué une perte économique totale*".

[62]Cf. Putzeys (1981), p. 229 ff.

[63]Cf. OLG Brandenburg 1 June 2011, in *TransR*, 2013, 29; OGH 29 January 2014, in *TranspR*, 2014, 375, according to which the seizure of goods occurred during customs operations is a loss for the purpose of fulfilling the obligations of the contract of carriage, since it prevents redelivery.

is known, but there is precisely a loss in an economic sense, because it is necessary to refer to the completion of the transport according to the criteria of social normality, unlike the situation in which the release from seizure is accomplished long after, for example, following the outcome of a trial or other defensive initiatives. Furthermore, there is total loss even if the costs of restoring the damaged goods exceed their value[64] or if the transporter causes a delay, through his own fault in the execution of the carriage, and violates the obligations toward the shipper to perform the journey, with the application of Article 17, first paragraph, and of Article 23, fifth paragraph, for the purposes of determining compensation.[65]

8.2.3 The Presumption of Total Loss

According to Article 20, first paragraph, the goods are presumed lost if they are not redelivered within 30 days from expiry of the deadline set in the contract, failing which, within 60 days from the receipt of the goods by the carrier,[66] with clear connection with Article 32, about prescription.[67] There is an absolute presumption of loss[68]; in fact, the law precludes the carrier from offering proof to the contrary, as he is held liable only for failure to deliver within the stipulated time frame provided by Article 20, first paragraph. It cannot be demonstrated that the load is not lost, but is, for example, in a warehouse, waiting to be delivered, as according to Article 20, there is no indication in this sense.[69] This is confirmed by Article 20, second paragraph, which refers to the hypothesis in which "*la marchandise est retrouvée*".[70]

In fact, Article 20, first paragraph, sets a binding maximum duration of the journey, with the effect of causing the compensation indicated for the loss and sanctioning its presumed existence, because, if the cargo does not arrive within the time provided by Article 20, first paragraph, its subsequent recovery is irrelevant,[71]

[64] Cf. BGH 30 October 2017, in *TranspR,* 2018, 146; OLG Munich 23 November 2017, *ibid.,* 2018, 113.

[65] Cf. OLG Munich 29 July 1998, in *TranspR*, 2000, 31.

[66] Cf. Libouton (1973), p. 54 ff.; Demuth (2013), p. 561 ff. Cf. also BGH 15 October 1998 in *VersR*, 1999, 646; OLG Düsseldorf 23 November 1989, in *TranspR*, 1990, 63.

[67] Cf. Demuth (2013), p. 563 ff.

[68] Cf. BGH 25 October 2001, in *TranspR,* 2002, 198; OLG Düsseldorf 23 November 1989, *ibid.,* 1990, 63.

[69] The French text reads, "*l'ayant droit peut, sans avoir à fournir d'autres preuves, considerer la marchandise comme perdu*". The English text reads, "the fact that goods have not been delivered (...) shall be conclusive evidence of the loss of the goods".

[70] So is stated in the French text. The English text reads, "the goods be recovered".

[71] Cf. OLG Munich 1 June 2011, in *TranspR,* 2011, 337, according to which, if a transport from Germany to England is interrupted due to an intervention by the public security authority, in relation to a hypothesis of smuggling, and ends with a year of delay, there is a total loss of the goods, pursuant to Article 20, first paragraph, and this event is not inevitable, pursuant to Article 17, second

without prejudice to what is established by the second paragraph. The consignee can demonstrate "proper delivery by all means allowed to him"[72] and, if it occurs, Article 20, first paragraph, is inapplicable. Therefore, redelivery after the deadline set in Article 20, first paragraph, has an impact only if the person entitled to dispose of the cargo exercises the power contemplated by Article 20, second paragraph, within the limits set by the third paragraph thereof.[73] Moreover, the loss in Article 20, first paragraph, is total.[74]

According to Article 20, second paragraph, at the time of receiving the compensation, the person entitled to dispose of the goods can request in writing to be warned in the event of the cargo being found within the year of payment. This request is acknowledged in writing.[75] The Convention recognizes the right of restitution,[76] confirming that, apart from this possibility, the presumption of Article 20 is absolute and the discovery of goods has no effect.[77] The opposite thesis[78] has no foundation, as it is against the clear wording of the provision. Article 20, second paragraph, concerns the case in which, regardless of compensation, there is a strong expectation to obtain restitution, due to the unsatisfactory nature of what is received and because of the relevance of the recovery of possession, if possible.

Therefore, if the transporter finds the load, he must notify the person entitled thereto, who has 30 days within which to decide whether to acquire the load back.[79] In the meantime, he might have lost interest, because, for example, the cargo no longer has any use or its value has decreased due to the fall in prices, or he might request its redelivery, as, on the contrary, the value has increased or a significant expectation, not only in an economic sense, endures. In the latter case, if he confirms the desire to obtain the goods, he must pay the "*créances resultant de la lettre de voiture*",[80] that is, the transport costs and all those that could have been claimed in case of execution of the contract, if contemplated. Simultaneously, he must return

---

paragraph. See also OGH 22 April 2014, in *TranspR,* 2014, 378, according to which, pursuant to Article 20, first paragraph, discovery of the asset does not eliminate the presumed loss.

[72] Cf. Silingardi et al. (1994), p. 133 ff., according to whom the presumption of total loss provided for by Article 20, first paragraph, would be relative, i. e. would admit evidence to the contrary.

[73] Cf. Loewe (1976), p. 372 ff.

[74] Cf. App. Colmar November 7 2012, in *Bull. transp. logist.*, 2012, 711.

[75] Cf. Demuth (2013), p. 565 ff.

[76] Cf. Putzeys (1981), p. 199 ff. See also Demuth (2013), p. 567 ff.

[77] Cf. BGH 25 October 2001, in *TranspR,* 2002, 198, according to which, if the person entitled to the goods does not ask to be notified of the discovery of the goods pursuant to Article 20, second paragraph, the relationship deriving from the contract of carriage terminates with payment of the amount due as a result of the presumed loss, pursuant to the first paragraph.

[78] Cf. Putzeys (1981), p. 199 ff., according to whom "*l'absence de demande écrite n'équivaut (...) même pas à un abandon du droit de récupérer la marchandise si celle – ci à être récupérée et qu'il l'apprend*".

[79] Cf. Putzeys (1981), p. 200 ff. See also Demuth (2013), p. 569 ff.

[80] So it reads in the French version of Article 20, third paragraph. The English version of Article 20, third paragraph reads: "charges shown to be due on the consignment note".

the compensation, after deducting expenses,[81] and he can ask for relief of the prejudice caused by delay, according to the general criteria of the Convention. The violation of the obligation to notify does not in itself involve the application of the national law, as some argue,[82] because the obligation is established in detail by the Convention and what specification would be needed is unclear. Therefore, the nonfulfillment causes the right to compensation to be quantified, on the basis of the principles applicable to delay.

According to Article 20, fourth paragraph, if the person entitled to the goods does not ask to be notified or does not provide instructions within the deadline of 30 days provided for by Article 20, third paragraph, or if 1 year passes from the payment of compensation for loss, the national law of the place where the goods are located shall apply.[83] The rule is questionable,[84] as only the carrier has control of the cargo; thus, he could denounce the discovery after the lapse of 1 year or fail to fulfill the obligation to notify on the strength of Article 20, second paragraph, hoping that the deadline provided for by Article 20, fourth paragraph, might expire. The effort made by those[85] who proposed to extend such scenarios of Article 30, first paragraph, is interesting, especially in the part which provides for an extension of the prescription period to 3 years in the event of willful misconduct or equivalent default, but the solution cannot be accepted; in fact, the two provisions are too different for an analogy to be justified.

Since the transporter finds the cargo, there is no control over where it is recovered and the relative geographical reference is irrational, as there is no real proof against the transporter's allegations. After all, the domestic law referred to by Article 20, fourth paragraph, could differ from that of the transporter and from that of the person entitled to the goods and, in any case, it is identified on the basis of a criterion that cannot be easily ascertained, if one does not believe what is alleged by the carrier. Moreover, there is no reference to the national legislation on transport, because, after 1 year, the relationship ends and there is no reason why a domestic law should be substituted for the uniform one. On the contrary, albeit indirectly, the Convention refers to the regulation of the right of property and related actions, since the prolonged unavailability of the goods causes the end of the transport, but can give rise to lingering disputes over the ownership. Even if the structure of Article 20, fourth paragraph, cannot be shared, it is very rare and concerns implausible cases.

---

[81] Cf. Putzeys (1981), p. 200 ff., according to whom "*ne sont pas restitués les frais (...) que l'ayant droit peut avoir exposeés à cause de l'avarie – perte, par exemple, les frais de la procédure, les droits de douane si la marchandise a été considerée comme mise en consommation parce qu'elle a été pedue après son passage de la frontière*".

[82] Cf. Clarke (2014), p. 330 ff., according to whom, "if the carrier fails to give notification, the consequences are not covered by the CMR but left to the national law". Cf. also Loewe (1976), p. 372 ff.

[83] Cf. Demuth (2013), p. 571 ff.

[84] Cf. Messent and Glass (2018), p. 217 ff.; Loewe (1976), p. 372 ff.

[85] Cf. Messent and Glass (2018), p. 217 ff.

8.2.4 Determination of Prejudice from Loss

Article 23, first, second, and fourth paragraphs, identify the criteria for determining the prejudice from loss, both total and partial.[86] In addition to cases of non-arrival following destruction or theft of the load,[87] losses in an economic sense are traceable back to this notion.[88] According to Article 23, first paragraph, the compensation is determined on the basis of the value of the goods in the place and time in which the carrier receives them.[89] The Convention considers the moment in which the load is delivered to the transporter,[90] referring to the country where he usually has his head office, so that he can perform an effective control and identify the maximum amount of compensation.[91]

The provision excludes the sender or the consignee from claiming a relief inclusive of the hoped-for profit.[92] Since these criteria also apply in the event of the carrier's unlimited liability, the compensation must be determined in accordance with Article 23, first, second, and fourth paragraphs, without any reference to the principles of the national law on further harm that can be liquidated; therefore, the expected profit cannot be taken into account. So, the opposite solution cannot be subscribed,[93] motivated by the argument that, in a competitive market, goods are produced and sold in anticipation of a future profit. The concept is heterogeneous when compared to the spirit and aim of Article 23.

---

[86]Cf. Messent and Glass (2018), p. 230 ff.

[87]Cf. Federal Court of the Helvetic Confederation 30 May 2001, *Sistema informatico del tribunale federale.*

[88]Cf. Clarke (2014), p. 294 ff. Cf. also BGH 25 October 2010, in *Europ. transp. law,* 2002, no. 37, 353; BGH 19 May 1995, *ibid.,* 1996, n. 31, 703.

[89]Cf. LG Thuringia 1 March 2001, in *TranspR,* 2002, 70, according to which the value of the goods is affected by the export costs.

[90]Cf. Loewe (1976) 375 ff.; Libouton (1973), p. 55 ff.; Van Ryan (1966), p. 660 ff.; Krings (1999), p. 778 ff.; Mayer (1997), p. 174 ff. See also OGH 13 July 1994, in *TranspR,* 1995, 285; Cass. com France 5 October 2010, in *Europ. transp. law,* 2011, no. 46, 110; LG Lubeck 25 January 2000, in *TranspR,* 2000, 222, according to which in the case of damage to property, on the basis of the prohibition of *venire contra factum proprium,* pursuant to Article 23, the person entitled to the goods can request only what is indicated at the time of the deposit.

[91]Cf. Mayer (1997), p. 174 ff., who highlighted how "*le OGH avait (...) choisi d'attribuer au calcul de la valeur du bien non pas la fonction de limiter le montant des dommages et intérêts à un maximal, mais celle de définir l'ampleur objective du dommage*". For another interpretation, cf. Clarke (2014), p. 295 ff., according to whom "the reason for the emphasis on dispatch value and the bias against making the carrier liable for economic loss is said to be (...) a desire to keep cost of transport low". The statement may also be true, but it does not invalidate the normative reconstruction whose principles are clear.

[92]Cf. BGH 10 December 2009, in *TranspR,* 2010, 78; OLG Düsseldorf 14 July 1983, *ibid.,* 1984, 16; OLG Hamm 2 December 1991, *ibid.,* 1992, 179; OGH 15 February 1979, in *Unif. law rev.,* 1979, 229; Cass.com France 3 February 1987, in *Bull. transp.,* 1987, 270. See also Clarke (2014), p. 295 ff.; Loewe (1976), p. 375 ff., according to whom "loss of earnings cannot be claimed under Article 23".

[93]Cf. OLG Nuremberg 4 February 2009, in *TranspR,* 2009, 256.

Furthermore, the reference to "*au lieu et à l'époque de la prise en charge*"[94] does not mean that the compensation can always be quantified on the basis of the price fixed in the invoice,[95] if the same is issued long before delivery to the carrier, so that, in the case of purchase and sale of a good that is still to be produced and which takes several months to manufacture, "*au moment de sa remise au transport*" its value increases. Therefore, the relief must be determined as the price at the time of delivery to the carrier. On the contrary, if the lost goods are replaced with more expensive ones, the relief must be quantified by reference to their original value on the day and in the place where the transport begins,[96] and does not recognize the cost incurred for the aforementioned replacement. Although these precedents are clear, in the judicial practice of many countries, starting with Italy, the indications of the invoice assume great importance, without prejudice to the motivated objection thereto.

In fact, Article 23, second paragraph, refers to the "*cours en bourse ou, à défaut, d'après le prix courant sur le marché ou, à défaut de l'un ou de l'autre, d'après la valeur usuelle des marchandises de même nature et qualité*".[97] The provision sets out three principles that are mutually exclusive and operate according to the order indicated, as can be deduced from the asides "*à défaut*"[98] and "*à défaut de l'un ou de l'autre*".[99] First, it is necessary to verify whether the goods are among those traded on the stock exchange[100] and the situation is quite rare, considering that road trips are discussed and, therefore, goods destined mostly for widespread trade and which are not listed; then, we must consider the current price on the market[101] and, finally, we turn to the "*valeur usuelle des marchandises de même nature et qualité*".[102] The

[94] Cf. Article 23, first paragraph. The English text reads "at the place and at the time at which they were accepted".

[95] Cf. App. Rennes 6 May 2015, in *Le Lamy transp.*, 2020, vol. I, 510; App. Montpellier 10 September 2019, *ibid.*, 2020, vol. I, 510; App. Aix – en –Provence 19 June 2014, in *Bull. transp. logist.*, 2014, 432; App. Paris 6 July 1988, in *Bull. transp.*, 1980, 270; OGH 8 July 2004, in *Europ. transp. law*, 2005, no. 40, 734. Cf. Messent and Glass (2018), p. 23 ff.

[96] Cf. App. Amiens 18 May 1981, in *Bull. transp.* 1982, 208. See also App. Paris 30 May 1984, *ibid.*, 1985, 75; Trib. com. Paris 5 September 2005, in *Bull. transp. logist.*, 2005, 23.

[97] So reads the French text of Article 23, second paragraph. The English version of Article 23, second paragraph, reads, "to the commodity exchange price or, if there is no such price, according to the current market price or, if there is no commodity exchange price or current market price, by reference to the normal value of goods of the same kind and quality". Cf. BGH 25 October 2001, in *TranspR*, 2002, 198; BGH 15 October 1992, *ibid.*, 1993, 137; OGH 13 July 1994, *ibid.*, 1995, 285; OLG Düsseldorf 24 July 2002, *ibid.*, 343; OLG Hamm 25 November 1993, *ibid.*, 1994, 61.

[98] The English text reads, "there is no such price".

[99] The English text reads, "or if there is no commodity exchange price or current market price". Cf. App. Amiens 11 October 2012, in *Le Lamy transp.*, 2020, vol. I, 510. Cf. also Loewe (1976), p. 375 ff.

[100] Cf. Sánchez - Gamborino (2001a), p. 641 ff.

[101] Cf. App. Montpellier 10 September 2019, in *Le Lamy transp.*, 2020, vol. I, 510; Cass. com Belgium 27 May 2011, in *Europ. transp. law*, 2012, no. 47, 83. See also Otte (2018a), p. 1424 ff.

[102] The English text reads, "the normal value of goods of the same kind and quality".

latter is a subsidiary criterion, with a somewhat uncertain content and of rare application; for example, it can be used when assessing the prejudice to a load that is no longer being manufactured, but for which there is still an interest.[103]

With reference to the current price, we focus on the selling one addressed to the usual local customers and the thesis is convincing, based on Article 23, second paragraph.[104] Therefore, for determining the compensation, the agreements under which the buyer benefits from discounts in consideration of the particular relationships with the seller are not relevant.[105] In fact, the current price can be established in any manner by means of a catalog, tariffs or market reports.[106] Therefore, the expression "*prix courant*"[107] does not mean the manufacturing cost,[108] as explicitly stated in Article 23. Thus, if goods destined for Ukraine suffer damage, then, for quantification, the resale invoice is addressed to the consignee, and the profit is included.[109] However, if it is issued after the start of the journey, it is not taken into account, but regard must be paid to that which relates to the purchase, which is issued when the journey starts.[110]

[103] Cf. App. Rennes 6 May 2015, in *Le Lamy transp.*, 2020, vol. I, 510; App. Paris 9 July 1980, in *Bull. transp.*, 1980, 449, according to which the system outlined by Article 23, second paragraph, is insufficient if we consider the loss of a prototype for which both the criterion of the market price and that of the usual value are irrelevant. In this case, the costs of designing, manufacturing and final detailing of the prototype itself should be considered for the purpose of determining the damage. On this matter, see also Cass.com France 18 March 1997, in *Le Lamy transp.*, 2020, vol. I, 511. The reasoning might be correct if all the criteria of Article 23, second paragraph, are considered inapplicable as they are irrelevant in the present case.

[104] Cf. App. Lyon 7 December 2017, in *Le Lamy transp.*, 2020, vol. I, 511; App. Lyon 16 January 2014, *ibid.*, 2020, vol. I, 511; App. Chambéry 19 February 2013, *ibid.*, 2020, vol. I, 511.

[105] Cf. Cass. com. France 10 January 1983, in *Bull. transp.*, 1983, 154; App. Lyon 7 December 2017, in *Le Lamy transp.*, 2020, vol. I, 511; App. Lyon 16 January 2014, *ibid.*, 2020, vol. I, 511; App. Chambéry 19 February 2013, *ibid.*, 2020, vol. I, 511. See also Krings (1999), p. 777 ff.

[106] Cf. App. Amiens 11 October 2012, in *Le Lamy transp.*, 2020, vol. I, 511.

[107] The English text reads, "the current market price".

[108] Cf. Cass. com. France 8 February 1982, in *Bull. transp.*, 1982, 152; App. Versailles 30 September 1987, in *Le Lamy transp.*, 2020, vol. I, 511; App. Anvers 9 October 1985, *ibid.*, 2020, vol. I, 511, according to which the profit margin cannot be deducted from the invoice. See also Krings (1999), p. 777 ff.

[109] In this sense, see also Trib. com. Paris 3 December 1996, in *Bull. transp logist.*, 1997, 182.

[110] Cf. App. Paris 12 March 1999, in *Bull. transp logist.*, 1999, 344, which overturned Trib. com. Paris December 3 1996, *ibid.*, 1997, 182. See however Clarke (2014), p. 297 ff., for a scenario of export goods (specifically whiskey) for whom the export price would apply, i. e. the price of the goods in the foreign market they are destined for. The thesis is unfounded, because it is in clear contrast with Article 23, second paragraph. On this matter, see also Messent and Glass (2018), p. 233 ff., who adhere to the thesis disputed here. In this regard, see *Buchanan & Co. Ltd. v. Babco Forwarding & Shipping (U. K.) Ltd.*, in *Loyd's Rep.*, 1978, 119; *Sandeman Coprimar S. A. v. Transitos y Transpotes Integrale S. L.*, in *Queen's bench reports*, 2003, 1270.

8.2.5 Prejudice from Loss, Supposed Expenses and Taxes

According to Article 23, fourth paragraph, the costs of transfer, customs duties and other expenses incurred must be reimbursed, proportionately if the loss is partial, or in full if it is total. With regard to the former notion, reimbursement relates to the return of the transport fee[111] and Article 23, fourth paragraph, does not present any practical difficulties of application.[112] Thus, for example, the costs related to the additional journey for delivery to a new consignee, after the justified refusal is opposed by the first, are borne by the carrier.[113] On the contrary, the expenses relating to the transfer performed to replace the lost goods[114] cannot be recovered, as a second, autonomous transport is being dealt with there.

Customs duties[115] are relevant both to the country of destination and to the one to be crossed, but where, for example, the theft occurs.[116] Then, it would not be obligatory to prove that the taxes have been paid and their stipulation would be sufficient to claim a refund.[117] However, the principle makes sense if the payment is certain and only its timing is postponed, as only actual disbursements are relevant.

Due to its heterogeneousness, the category that includes other expenses is more questionable.[118] The reference to the "*occasion du transport*"[119] underlines the necessary link between these costs and the journey.[120] Therefore, loading costs are "*autres frais*",[121] as opposed to packaging ones, which are included in the price.[122]

---

[111] Cf. App. Versailles 5 October 2006, in *Le Lamy transp.*, 2020, vol. I, 518, for a hypothesis of restitution of the price in the event of total loss. See also App. Versailles 29 January 2019, *ibid.*, 2020, vol. I, 519, for a hypothesis of partial reimbursement in the event of partial loss. See also App. Metz 21 February 2013, in *Bull. transp. logist.*, 2013, 179; App. Olréans 8 October 2009, *ibid.*, 2010, 59.

[112] The subject was dealt with in the chapter relating to the consideration.

[113] Cf. App. Rennes 19 March 1987, in *Bull. transp.*, 1988, 105.

[114] Cf. App. Paris 17 December 1984, in *Le Lamy transp.*, 2020, vol. I, 519; App. Nancy 2 July 2002, *ibid.*, 2020, vol. I, 519.

[115] Cf. Putzeys (1981), p. 293 ff.; Otte (2018b), p. 1453 ss..

[116] Cf. App. Paris 30 May 1984, in *Bull. transp.*, 1985, 75, for a case of theft that took place in Italy in which the goods were sent temporarily to be then transferred to their final destination, in France.

[117] Cf. App. Paris 29 January 2004, in *Bull. transp. logist.*, 2004, 104.

[118] Cf. Thume and Riemer (2013b), p. 666 ff. See also OLG Düsseldorf 14 July 1983, in *TranspR*, 1984, 16; OLG Munich 17 July 1991, *ibid.*, 1991, 427; OLG Hamburg 2 May 1985, in *VersR*, 1986, 865; OLG Hamburg 7 November 1985, in *TranspR*, 1986, 15; OLG Hamburg 16 January 1986, *ibid.*, 1986, 229; RB Gent 29 June 1999, in *Europ. transp. law*, 2000, no. 35, 566; Hof Antwerp 29 June 2009, *ibid.*, 2010, n. 45, 182; Hof Antwerp 15 June 2009, *ibid.*, 2009, n. 45, 199; BGH 10 December 2009, *ibid.*, 2010, n. 45, 294.

[119] The English text reads, "in respect of the carriage of goods".

[120] Cf. BGH 26 June 2003, in *Europ. transp. law*, 2004, no. 39, 93.

[121] The English text reads, "other charges". Cf. OLG Munich 21 November 2018, in *TranspR*, 2019, 212, according to which insurance costs, taxes paid and legal fees fall into the category of "*autres frais*".

[122] Cf. Rodière (1971), p. 315 ff.

On the contrary, the expenses of sorting, checking and redelivery the damaged packaging[123] or those attendant on storage of the goods while waiting for the vehicle to be repaired[124] are to be borne by the transporter. If the cargo is stolen, the costs sustained by an engineer rushed into the scene are refundable,[125] as well as those incurred when an expert is enabled to immediately repair a piece of machinery intended for a fair.[126] The same applies to expert appraisals,[127] for rents unnecessarily paid, or for those not received because of the damage,[128] as well as financial harm,[129] understood as the loss of interest on the capital represented by the damaged cargo, although this last statement is not persuasive, since, albeit indirectly, it involves the restoration of the desired advantage, which should instead be excluded.

According to a Dutch decision,[130] deposit costs would be reimbursable only if they prove useful in obtaining a better price in the market. The thesis is unacceptable considering that, if the expenses indirectly attributable to the carriage are also evaluated in the "*autres frais*",[131] their reimbursement must be admitted regardless of their impact on the entire operation. Then, insurance premiums, correspondence and telephone expenses are not refundable,[132] as they are not connected with transport, except in a broad manner, with an excessive extension of the concept of Article 23, fourth paragraph.

[123] Cf. App. Nancy 2 July 2002, in *Bull. transp. logist.*, 2003, 216.

[124] Cf. JMerc Córdoba 18 March 2005, n. 9, in *Jur,* 2005, 221895.

[125] Cf. App. Poitiers 23 August 1990, in *Bull. transp.*, 1990, 586; but see RB Amsterdam 12 April 1972 in *S & S*, 1972, 102.

[126] Cf. App. Aix – en Provence 9 December 1980, in *Bull. transp.*, 1981, 143.

[127] Cf. App. Riom 16 October 1981, in *Bull. transp.*,1982, 11; App. Paris 30 June 2016, in *Le Lamy transp.*, 2020, vol. I, 519; RB Mechelen 18 November 1999, in *Europ. transp. law,* 2000, no. 35, 432. But see App. Anvers 9 October 1985, *ibid.*, 2020, vol. I, 519, according to which "*les frais d'expertise privée unilatérale ne sont pas inhérents au transport*". See also App. Versailles 17 September 2013, *ibid.*, 2020, vol. I, 519; App. Montpellier 19 November 2002, in *Bull. transp. logist.*, 2003, 31; App. Rennes 6 May 2015, in *Le Lamy transp.*, 2020, vol. I, 519, for which "*les frais d'expertise judiciaire*" are not refundable. But see Hof Antwerp 23 March 1983, in *Europ. transp. law,* 1983, no. 18, 518; Hof. Antwerp 3 October 2005, in *Europ. transp. law,* 2006, no. 41, 284, according to which the costs incurred for an expert appraisal are not reimbursable if it did not contribute to keeping the load in a good condition, as they would not be connected with the transport.

[128] Cf. App. Paris 27 April 1993, in *Bull. transp. logist.*, 1992, 455; App. Aix – en – Provence 7 September 1995, in *Le Lamy transp.*, 2020, vol. I, 519.

[129] Cf. Cass. com. France 3 February 1987, in *Bull. transp.*, 1987, 270. See also App. Paris 28 January 1987, in *Le Lamy transp.*, 2020, vol. I, 519, for a hypothesis of reimbursement of the "*perte de change*".

[130] V. RB Rotterdam 20 February 1976, in *Europ. law digest,* 1978, no. 6, 291; Arrond. Rotterdam 12 April 1972, in *Uniform. law rev.*, 1976, 253.

[131] The English text reads, "other charges".

[132] Cf. OLG Düsseldorf 18 November 1971, in *Europ. transp. law,* 1973, no. 8, 510.

The tendency to interpret[133] "*les autres frais encourus à l'occasion du transport*"[134] in a broad sense can lead to exaggerated solutions, as in the case of a fire that destroys both the load and the vehicle and for which the carrier asks for reimbursement of the "*frais de levage, d'entreposage, de gardiennage, d'enlèvement des marchandises, la valeur residuelle de la semi-remorque endommagée, les frais d'intervention et de la remise en état de la chaussée par la société d'autoroute*".[135] In this manner, expenses that cannot be directly linked to the transport[136] would also be due, but the thesis is unpersuasive, because it would imply the relevance of the unrealized profit.

In fact, costs not attributable to the transfer, even in a mediated manner, cannot be claimed, as in the case of the carrier who, instead of chemicals, delivers a detergent that is then used in a refinery, causing damage, by mistake. Article 23, fourth paragraph, would not be applied because such costs relate to goods other than those to be transported, with the alleged reference to the national law,[137] but the solution is not persuasive, as regard should only be paid to Article 23, first paragraph, and to the value of the load on departure, even if the prejudice is of particular importance, as in the case of strong impact on the operation of the refinery. Moreover, if the opposite theses were followed, it would become more difficult for the transporter to quantify the maximum limit of compensation,[138] an objective pursued instead by Article 23, first paragraph. Nor does this rule concern only the cargo, because, on the contrary, it limits the compensation in entirety and absolutely excludes the hoped-for profit, regardless of whether it is related to the methods of use of the goods and of their employment in an existing plant.

Much discussed is the question of the possible refund of taxes. If the consignee refuses the redelivery, he cannot recover the indirect taxes paid for the imported goods, according to what is derived from a specific decision.[139] The solution is

[133] Cf. Haak (1986), p. 225 ff.; Messent and Glass (2018), p. 240 ff.; Clarke (2014), p. 305 ff.

[134] The English text reads, "other charges incurred in respect of the carriage of goods".

[135] Cf. App. Pau 19 September 2014, in *Bull. transp. logist.*, 2014, 606. Cf. also App. Paris 25 March 1988, in *Le Lamy transp.*, 2020, vol. I, 519, which reimbursed the costs incurred by a company to carry out the safety tests to which propane bottles were subjected following an accident during transport. Cf. also Loewe (1976), p. 377 ff., according to whom "the charges incurred in respect of carriage also include the costs occasioned by an accident".

[136] For a detailed analysis, cf. Putzeys (1981), p. 292 ff.

[137] Cf. Messent and Glass (2018), p. 231 ff.; Krings (1999), p. 778 ff. Cf. *Shell Chemicals UK Ltd. v. P & O Roadtanks Ltd.*, in *Lloyd's rep.*, 1993, 114.

[138] Cf. Clarke (2014), p. 305 ff.

[139] See App. Paris 30 March 1973, in *Bull. transp.*, 1973, 195, confirmed by Cass. com France 28 July 1975, *ibid.*, 1975, 442. See also Cass. com France 15 October 2002, *ibid.*, 2002, 697; App. Poitiers 23 August 1990, *ibid.*, 1990, 586; Trib. com. Paris 10 February 1993, *ibid.*, 1993, 332; OGH 25 January 1990, in *TranspR*, 1990, 235. See also App. Nancy 14 January 2004, in *Bull. transp.*, 2004, 616, according to which taxes on cigarettes are not refundable because they are already included in the value of the goods.

consistent with Article 23, fourth paragraph.[140] Furthermore, we cannot accept the approach according to which the excise duty could be refunded only if the load has not left the country of departure,[141] because this idea conflicts with the more extensive spirit of the Convention.

More generally, expenses incurred before the start of the journey, such as packaging costs,[142] those concerning the stipulation of an insurance contract or those necessary for the issue of certificates are not reimbursable, as they are inherent to the phase prior to the execution of the service, while the expenses incurred subsequently to the occurrence of the prejudice, such as those of custody or expert appraisals, fall under Article 23, fourth paragraph.[143] In a case of damage to a machine to be delivered in Italy and then returned to the sender in England,[144] the packaging and transport costs were reimbursed, but not those of custody, those relating to appraisals performed both in the place where the damage was caused and in that of actual redelivery and, finally, the costs incurred for the return of the load. With regard to the latter and the expenses of the second appraisal, the solution is acceptable, as they relate to a further contract, while the approach remains unconvincing when discussing the other costs that were not reimbursed. In fact, albeit indirectly, they were connected to the first carriage and, therefore, they should have been charged to the transporter.[145]

Likewise, with regard to frozen fish, in a German case,[146] the sender's request for redelivery was discussed, which was instrumental to the fact that the goods could be frozen again and sent to a different consignee. The compensation would include the costs for the return journey, those concerning storage while waiting for the new treatment and those incurred so that an expert could examine the frozen goods, making Article 23, fourth paragraph, relevant.[147] In the case in question, the delivery to the recipient had occurred and this had resulted in the termination of the relationship. The possible return was the subject of a different contract, so that no problem should have arisen for the "*autres frais*".[148]

---

[140] See Cass. com France 14 March 1995, in *Bull. transp.*, 1995, 248, according to which only transport costs are reimbursable.

[141] Cf. Arrond. Amsterdam 30 March 1977, in *Unif. law rev.*, 1978, 299. See however Cass. com Netherlands 4 May 1987, in *Europ. transp. law,* no. 29, 360; HR 14 July 2006, *ibid.*, 2006, no. 41, 804.

[142] Cf. Thume and Riemer (2013b), p. 666 ff.

[143] Cf. Loewe (1976), p. 376 ff.

[144] See *William Tatton & Co. Ltd. v. Ferrymasters Ltd.*, in *Lloyd's rep.*, 1974, 203.

[145] In this sense, cf. *ICI PLC v. MAT Transport Ltd.*, in *Lloyd's rep.*, 1987, 534, according to which the costs of carrying out an expert appraisal are refundable.

[146] Cf. BGH 3 July 1974, in *Unif. law rev.*, 1974, 216.

[147] Cf. BGH 3 July 1974, in *Unif. law rev.*, 1974, 216. See also OLG Celle 29 October 1998, in *TranspR,* 1999, 106.

[148] The English text reads, "other charges".

8.2.6 Sharing of Burden of Proof

Concerning damage, apportionment of the burden of proof is not governed by the principles about liability; in particular, the criteria of Article 18, first and second paragraphs, cannot be used, because they only concern demonstration of the nonfulfillment. The prejudice is its consequence and, therefore, the evidence of its existence is to be kept distinct; since they are on different levels, the two issues are governed by separate rules. With regard to the prejudice, the evidence must be provided by those who invoke relief, on the basis of Article 23, first and second paragraphs. The same principle concerns the delay and, in this regard, is indicated with greater precision by Article 19. Therefore, without prejudice to the distinction with regard to liability, where the burden of proof has a different set of regulations, the same criteria apply to the three types of compensable harm and evidence must be adduced by the person requesting compensation. The law of the trial does not operate, because the issue is of substantive law and entirely falls within the object of uniform one.

Moreover, the Convention provides for an articulated system of reservations. At the time of redelivery, their execution interferes with the issue of proof, but the relative discipline has a broader prescriptive content, dealt with exhaustively by Article 30. Alternatively, Articles 8 and 9 regulate the reservations in the start-up phase of the carriage. In particular, according to Article 8, the transporter must verify the apparent condition of the goods and their packaging. According to Article 9, the consignment note offers evidence of receipt of the load and its condition, unless proven otherwise. This system has two distinct profiles: the one relating to the state of the cargo affecting the proof of prejudice and the packaging defect concerning liability.

From a systematic viewpoint, the inadequacy of the packaging refers to Article 17, fourth paragraph, letter b). Verification of the condition of the load is instrumental to proof of prejudice, with the application of Article 23, because only if the conditions of the goods are established on departure it is possible to determine whether there is damage or loss. Therefore, Articles 8 and 9 interfere both with the issue of liability and with that of prejudice. However, to avoid speaking twice about the same provision in this research, Articles 8 and 9 are considered in a unitary manner with regard to liability, due to the greater importance of this aspect from the viewpoint of application.

8.3 The Compensatory Obligation

8.3.1 The Determination of Interest

Article 27, first paragraph, lays down the criterion for calculating the interest to be applied to the amount paid by way of compensation by the carrier[149] and identifies it as five percent *per annum.*[150] Simultaneously, it establishes that the interest may run from either "*du jour de la réclamation adresée par écrit au transporteur*"[151] or "*du jour de la demande en justice*".[152] The rule is clear[153] and sets the effective starting date from the day on which a written complaint is submitted.[154] Therefore, the 1 year deadline cannot begin running from the time when reservations are formulated, for example, by the shipper,[155] or from when they are orally communicated to the carrier.[156] Referring to the written complaint, Article 27, first paragraph, seems to recall Article 32, second paragraph, and it is necessary to refer to this provision with regard to the wording of the warning, in particular about its specificity.[157]

The literal interpretation excludes the application of the interest rate if the transporter obtains compensation following nonfulfillment by the shipper or the consignee,[158] as the hypothesis in which the former promotes action seeking relief

---

149 Cf. Thume and Riemer (2013c), p. 716 ff.; HR Netherlands 20 November 1998, in *Europ. transp. law,* 1999, no. 34, 254, according to which Article 27, first paragraph, applies, even if the carrier has lapsed from the compensation limit pursuant to Article 28.

150 Cf. Thume and Riemer (2013c), p. 724 ff.

151 Cf. Article 27, first paragraph. The English text reads, "from the date on which the claim was sent in writing to the carrier". Cf. Messent and Glass (2018), p. 258 ff.; Clarke (2014), p. 307 ff.

152 Cf. Article 27, first paragraph. The English text reads, "from the date on which legal proceedings were instituted". See Messent and Glass (2018), p. 258 ff.; Clarke (2014), p. 307 ff. See also App. Douai 13 April 2006, in *Le Lamy transp.*, 2020, vol. I, 517; App. Versailles 18 February 2010, *ibid.,* 2020, vol. I, 517; App. Paris 8 January 2015, *ibid.,* 2020, vol. I, 517.

153 Cf. BGH 27 November 2003, in *TranspR,* 2003, 79, according to which the principle of Article 27, first paragraph, on the interest rate of five per cent also regards loans regulated by Articles 34 and 37.

154 Cf. Thume and Riemer (2013c), p. 719 ff.

155 Cf. Trib. Salon de Provence 9 January 2009, in *Bull. transp. logist.,* 2009, 115. See also App. Rennes 29 June 2010, in *Le Lamy transp.*, 2020, vol. I, 517; App. Douai 20 January 2005, in *Bull. transp. logist.,* 2005, 106; App. Dijon 2 July 2004, in *Le Lamy transp.*, 2020, vol. I, 517.

156 Cf. Messent and Glass (2018), p. 258 ff. See also Clarke (2014), p. 307 ff., according to whom "the written claim (. . .) has been held to mean a general intimation that the claimant considers the carrier liable, without any specific quantification of the complaint". On the characteristics of the written complaint, the thesis is different from the one I endorse and it applies both for the purposes of Article 32 and to those of Article 27. The profile is examined with regard to prescription and the relevant analysis is not repeated here. See also *William Tatton & Co v. Ferrymasters,* in *Lloyd's rep.*, 1974, 207.

157 See: Clarke (2014), p. 307 ff.; Loewe (1976) 380 ff.; Haak (1986), p. 236 ff.

158 Cf. App. Lyon 18 January 2018, in *Le Lamy transp.*, 2020, vol. I, 517; App. Nîmes 16 May 2012, *ibid.*, 2020, vol. I, 517; App. Lyon 18 December 2008, in *Bull. transp. logist.,* 2009, 483;

for his prejudice falls outside the scope of application of Article 27.[159] Article 27, first paragraph, has a sectoral slant and concerns only actions against the carrier, considered the object of the most relevant provisions of the Convention, starting with Articles 17 and 18. Although the expression "*transporteur*"[160] is not repeated with regard to "*de la demande en justice*",[161] Article 27, first paragraph, is clear and has a selective structure that concerns only the interest paid by the transporter on the compensation due by him. Furthermore, if the latter brings a legal action to request the reimbursement of any prejudices or the consideration or, in any case, fulfillment of the obligations resting on others, the national law on rights ancillary to the main obligation is applied.

Overall, the Convention has the objective of determining a uniform annual rate and effective date, and dictates an exclusive regulation, if Article 27, first paragraph, which leaves no room for the national law, is applied, although there has been no lack of decisions in the opposite direction.[162] Thus, it is not possible to proceed with the capitalization of interest because this is in contrast with Article 27.[163] The expected annual rate is very high, especially when compared with current ones,[164] but its indication dates back to 1956. Precisely because its adequacy must be assessed with reference to that time, the rule is consistent with the inflation index of that period. Presently, Article 27, first paragraph, is a punitive provision for the carrier and its rationality can be doubted, as it involves a significant outlay, completely disproportionate to the contemporary economic situation. This is because, at least in the European Union and in other countries, inflation is minimal or nonexistent, at least before the last events occurred, when this book had already been written (February 2022).

Moreover, the Convention has never been changed on this point, and it would be difficult to do so, because, over time, various situations have arisen and others may emerge, which can make the amount established in Article 27 too high or too low, especially considering that nothing else is due apart from interest. If the prejudice

---

App. Toulouse 3 October 2012, in *Le Lamy transp.*, 2020, vol. I, 517; App. Mons 12 May 2006, in *Bull. transp. logist.*, 2006, 366.

[159] See Clarke (2014), p. 307 ff.; Haak (1986), p. 235 ff.

[160] The English text reads, "carrier".

[161] The English text reads, "legal proceedings".

[162] Cf. Cass. com. France 6 June 1995, in *Le Lamy transp.*, 2020, vol. I, 517; Cass. com. France 3 March 1998, in *Bull. transp. logist.*, 1998, 231; Cass. com. France 18 January 2000, in *Le Lamy transp.*, 2020, vol. I, 517; Cass. com. France 28 January 2003, *ibid.*, 2020, vol. I, 517; App. Rouen 1 March 2012, *ibid.*, 2020, vol. I, 517. See also Clarke (2014), p. 307 ff., nt. 135, according to whom "the idea is to make exposure predictable and to discourage *forum shopping*". See also Krings (1999), p. 779 ff.

[163] See Haak (1986), p. 236 ff. In a different sense, see Cass. com. France 17 March 1992, in *Bull. transp. logist.*, 1992, 253; App. Paris 25 June 2009, *ibid.*, 2009, 450; Cass. com. France 25 November 1997, in *Le Lamy transp.*, 2020, vol. I, 518; App. Douai 13 April 2006, *ibid.*, 2020, vol. I, 518; App. Paris 16 September 1992, *ibid.*, 2020, vol. I, 518.

[164] For example, in Italy the rate varies from year to year, but tends to zero, at least till year 2021.

from late payment is greater, there is no further compensation. Faced with the desire to include the matter in the uniform law, the somewhat drastic solution of Article 27 was inevitable. Presently, the rule appears quite unfair, not for the extent of the interest, but because there is no similar provision in favor of the carrier, who should be induced to carefully evaluate the opportunity to defend a legal action; should he fail, costs ancillary to the credit would be heavy indeed.

As the compensation is determined on the basis of the criteria identified by Article 23, first, second and third paragraphs, a question mark arises as to the application of the aforementioned rate to the "*frais annexes*" established by Article 23, fourth paragraph, divided into "*frais de transport*",[165] "*droits de douane*"[166] and "*autres frais encourus à l'occasion du transport*".[167] In fact, for this provision, these items are subject to a refund, and Article 27 cannot be applied, at least on the basis of its literal wording,[168] as compensation is expressly mentioned. However, the five percent interest rate applies from the day either the written complaint or the court application is filed, until actual payment is made.[169] On the contrary, interest does not run in the period preceding one of the two acts, nor can the national law be invoked, as Article 27 deals in an exhaustive manner with the problem of ancillary costs, and nothing else is due.[170] Interest payments are the only ancillary costs disciplined, and their effective date is sanctioned by the Convention, without any other remedy. The obligation starts to run from the two typical acts indicated by Article 27, first paragraph; before these, the creditor cannot claim anything else, as specified. Therefore, interest amounts are due only in the event of an adverse order against the transporter.

8.3.2 The Exchange

Article 27, second paragraph, indicates the exchange criteria to be applied if payment of the amount disbursed by way of compensation has to be made in a country other than that in which the significant elements for determining the relief must be assessed, according to Article 23, first and second paragraphs.[171] If payment takes place in a country other than that in which the load is delivered to the carrier, the

---

[165] The English text reads, "carriage charges".

[166] The English text reads, "custom duties".

[167] The English text reads, "other charges incurred in respect of the carriage".

[168] In a different sense, see Cass. com. France 15 October 2002, in *Bull. transp. logist.*, 2002, 697.

[169] See Messent and Glass (2018), p. 258 ff.; Clarke (2014), p. 307 ff.

[170] See Clarke (2014), p. 307 ff.

[171] See Messent and Glass (2018), p. 260 ff.; Thume and Riemer (2013c), p. 729 ff. See also Arrond. Amsterdam 19 January 1977, in *Europ. law digest,* 1979, 401; Hof Hertogenbosch 16 March 1988, *ibid.*,1990, 138; App. Paris 24 April 1997, in *Bull. transp.*, 1997, 468; BGH 4 July 2013, in *TranspR,* 2014, 27, according to which the clause of a contract of carriage which, to define the maximum value of a transported package, refers to the dollar and mentions exchange in the local

exchange rate is that of the date of payment. To establish the compensation, reference is made to the time and place of delivery to the transporter, but, if payment takes place in another State, the exchange rate is that of the date of payment.

Thus, as the judge adopts the adverse order, the exchange rate can vary and the total amount can be more or less burdensome for the debtor. We cannot agree with the solution that if, the sum is less, the carrier should pay additionally to bring the amount back to the level at the time of the decision.[172] Without any textual justification, the solution is opposite to that of the Convention; according to this thesis, a similar reasoning would not be proposed if the conversion were to be the detriment of the transporter himself, as "he has brought this upon himself and no adjustment is required".[173] Instead, Article 27, second paragraph, is clear, and does not provide any corrective measures and the consequences of determining the interest rate are automatic and, thus, it does not matter who benefits from or is damaged by this rule.

Article 27, second paragraph, has a critical consequence; if the decision is pronounced by a judge other than that of the place where the delivery to the carrier occurred, the compensation must be determined in the currency in which the parameters of Article 23, first and second paragraphs, apply, with the rule being mandatory in nature, so that it prevails over any different procedural principle, pursuant to Article 41. For example, if the goods leave the UK, the Italian judge must pronounce an adverse order in pounds. If he failed to do so, the exchange rate would be that of the date of the decision rather than that of the payment. If this occurs in the UK, the problem resolves itself. If that is not the case, the exchange must be taken into account on the day on which the payment is done.

The exchange of Article 27 should not be confused with that provided by Article 23, seventh paragraph, for the compensation limit. In the latter case, for the conversion of the unit of account into national currency, reference is made to the date of the decision or the stipulated one. The system may appear a bit cumbersome, but it has its logic, because the unit of account is an expression of the weighted average of many currencies and, therefore, its conversion reflects this average at any time. If the value of the goods is close to 8.33 units of account per kilogram, depending on the exchange rate, the actual compensation may be lower or higher than the compensation limit, and this must be determined not at the time of the decision, but at that of the payment. Therefore, the judge must indicate the actual value in compliance with Article 27, second paragraph, if need be in a foreign currency. When payment takes place, if the actual value is lower than the limit, the former applies. The case is rare, because it assumes that the price of the goods is approximately 8.33 units of account

---

currency, presupposes reference to the euro, and the European Central Bank exchange rate must be considered.

[172] See Clarke (2014), p. 308 ff.; Loewe (1976), p. 380 ff. But see Putzeys (1981), p. 296 ff., according to whom "*la CMR étant de droit impératif, il n'est pas possible de déroger à ses méthodes d'évaluation de prejudice subi*".

[173] See Clarke (2014), p. 308 ff.

per kilogram. If that were not the case, the fluctuation in the exchange rate of the national currency would be irrelevant. The conversion of Article 27 is automatic, similar to that of Article 23, seventh paragraph. Therefore, only if the load is worth approximately 8.33 units of account per kilogram, the judge must pronounce both an order to pay the limited compensation and one to pay full one, often in two different currencies, with an alternative order and with the possibility for the carrier to satisfy it in compliance with Article 27, second paragraph, by disbursing the sum that is most convenient to pay.

8.4 Types and Functions of the Compensation Limit

8.4.1 The Reasons for Including a Compensation Limit and the Evolution of the Geneva Convention

The compensation limit is not an unknown institution in the transport law.[174] It was already present at the international level in the Berne Convention of 14 October 1890 with regard to rail traffic, in the Brussels Convention of 25 August 1924, in relation to maritime transport and in the Warsaw Convention of 12 October 1929 about air transport. The CMR, too, regulates it; if it had not done so, the Convention would have created an unjustified difference in treatment on the basis of various means used. This would be to the detriment of the road carrier, who would have had to compensate the prejudice in full. This benefit contributed to the development of the then-nascent transport industry, which, being able to determine business risks, translated them into insurance costs more easily.[175]

On one hand, the provision of the limit safeguards the position of the carrier, and, on the other hand, the criterion for its determination must guarantee the person entitled to the goods a serious compensation, not a fictitious or symbolic one. With regard to the CMR, this benefit satisfies the need for a uniform regulation of international traffic, as aimed by the Convention.[176] Compensation calculated on the basis of a predefined criterion reduces litigation; rather, the parties undertake legal action to ascertain the transporter's liability for willful misconduct or equivalent fault as the Convention provides for forfeiture of the limit.[177]

---

[174] Cf. Putzeys (1981), p. 297 ff.

[175] Cf. Silingardi et al. (1994), p. 200 ff.; Putzeys (1981), p. 298 ff.

[176] Cf. App. Brescia 1 June 2001, in *Dir. transp.*, 2002, 676 ff., according to which the limits of liability provided for by CMR would not apply in the absence of the reference in the consignment note to the application of the Convention, as provided by Article 7, third paragraph. The thesis cannot be accepted, because it is founded on the idea that, in the transport document, an express reference to the Convention would be required, without which it would not operate; this approach is in clear contrast with the mandatory effect of CMR, pursuant to Article 41.

[177] Cf. Putzeys (1981), p. 298 ff.

The CMR introduces a double compensation, depending on whether it is compensation for loss or damage or, on the contrary, for delay. In the latter case, the repayment cannot exceed the consideration required for the carriage, pursuant to Article 23, fifth paragraph. Regarding the first hypothesis, in the original text, the unit of measurement was the germinal gold franc and, in its first version, according to Article 23, third paragraph, "compensation shall not, however, exceed twenty - five francs per kilogram of gross weight short. 'Franc' means the gold franc weighing 10/31 of a gram and being of millesimal fineness 900". This formula was conceived at a time when the price of gold was stable, so that it could act as a unit of account, not subject to variations from one country to another, despite the fluctuations in the exchange rate between individual currencies.[178]

In particular, the International Monetary Fund (IMF) developed a system of declared official parities for gold. However, starting from 1971, its price began to fluctuate freely. This generated a paradoxical situation in which there were two gold currencies, i. e., the official one created and the one determined by the free market, higher than the other and, in any case, doomed to constant fluctuation.[179] The Convention did not provide for any mechanism for converting franc germinal gold into the national currency and, therefore, as it was impossible to establish which of the two criteria should be applied to determine the maximum compensation limit, with the Protocol of 5 July 1978,[180] the CMR accepted the new unit of account proposed by the IMF.

Presently, according to Article 23, third paragraph, in the event of loss or damage, the indemnity cannot exceed 8.33 units of account for each kilogram of missing or damaged gross weight. According to Article 23, seventh paragraph, the unit of account consists in the special drawing right as defined by the IMF and is calculated on the basis of a basket of 16 currencies without being subject to fluctuation to the same extent as the currency, within the aforementioned basket. In essence, it is a unit of account free from currency fluctuations. However, the provision does not introduce a mechanism for periodic updating of the unit of account, aimed at preventing the risk of inflation; for States that have ratified the 1978 Protocol, it is possible to request a revision, pursuant to Article 10.[181] According to Article 23, seventh paragraph, the unit of account is converted into the national currency of the State of the court hearing the dispute, on the basis of the value that the currency has at the date of decision[182] or at the agreed one.[183] Therefore, the conversion date can be set at a later time than that on which the ruling is issued.[184]

[178] Cf. Messent and Glass (2018), p. 229 ff.; Thume and Riemer (2013d), p. 653 ff.

[179] Cf. Loewe (1976), p. 375 ff.; Rodière (1971), p. 313 ff.

[180] The Protocol of 5 July 1978 entered into force on 15 March 1982. Cf. Haak (1986), p. 211 ff.

[181] Cf. Loewe (1976), p. 435 ff.; Messent and Glass (2018), p. 235 ff.

[182] Cf. App. Grenoble 22 April 2004, in *Bull. transp. logist.*, 2004, 334.

[183] Cf. App. Paris 28 June 1991, in *Le Lamy transp.*, 2020, vol. I, 512.

[184] Cf. *Le Lamy transp.*, 2020, vol. I, 512.

Not all the signatory States have ratified the 1978 Protocol and, for the others, the gold franc continues to be applied as the unit of measurement, according to the original provision of Article 32, third paragraph.[185] There is controversy as to whether this gold franc should be considered in the official currency or determined by the free market.[186] A literal interpretation of Article 23, as amended by the 1978 Protocol, which shows the intention of its promoters to establish a fixed rate identified in 8.33 special drawing rights, is convincing. According to Article 23, seventh paragraph, States that are not members of the IMF can calculate the value of their currency in special drawing rights; if the national law does not allow it, they can set the liability limit of 8.33 special rights of drawing in twenty - five monetary units. However, according to Article 23, ninth paragraph, this conversion must translate the same value of 8.33 units of account into the national currency, provided for by Article 23, third paragraph, as much as possible. Therefore, for the States that have not signed the 1978 Protocol, the unit of measurement of the gold franc must be converted on the basis of a fixed rate and not a variable one, according to the change in the market, as this solution appears more consistent with the present prescriptive content of Article 23, seventh, eighth and ninth paragraphs.[187]

Finally, the parties may modify the limit of the carrier's compensatory obligation with an indication of the value of the goods transported or with a declaration of special interest on redelivery. According to Article 24, after paying an additional fee, the sender can declare a value higher than the limit indicated in Article 23, third paragraph. According to Article 26, he can ask for compensation for further damage on the basis of the amount of interest declared. At the time of the conclusion of the contract, the sender and the transporter cannot stipulate a clause modifying the limit for loss, damage or delay established by Article 23,[188] due to the mandatory nature of the Convention, pursuant to Article 41.[189]

It seems superfluous to discuss the reference of the limit to the weight of the load, because it is a known criterion in the transport law. This widespread experience makes it somewhat cloying to dispute the mechanism, although the weight is not indicative of the value, and goods of considerable bulk and of high specific weight can have a low price. However, because of the possible declaration of special interest upon redelivery and that of value, the limit does not apply in the event of willful misconduct or equivalent fault. Notwithstanding the fact that the relief in compliance with the limit is not symbolic, these corrective measures reinforce the overall impression of the rationality of the rule, which, not surprisingly, has been enforced for decades.

---

[185] It is what happens in Croatia. See Radionov (2016), p. 457 ff., who underlines how the reference to the current price of gold leads *de facto* to a repeal of the rules on the compensation limit.

[186] Cf. Messent and Glass (2018), p. 236 ff.

[187] Cf. Messent and Glass (2018), p. 236 ff.

[188] Cf. Silingardi et al. (1994), p. 208 ff.

[189] Cf. Cass. com. France 17 May 1983, in *Bull. transp.*, 1983, 445; Cass. com. France 22 November 1988, *ibid.*, 1989, 209.

8.4.2 Calculation of the Compensation Limit for Losses and Damages

According to Article 23, third paragraph, to calculate the compensation limit, the unit of account must refer to the missing or damaged gross weight.[190] In fact, in the event of partial prejudice, "*la limitation sur le poids manquant ou avarié et non pas (...) sur le tonnage total de l'expédition*"[191] applies and the burden of proving the partial nature of the same prejudice falls on the carrier.[192] If the transport includes several packages and only some are lost, but the consignment note indicates the mere total weight, the carrier must identify what is involved in the nonfulfillment; if he fails to do so, the judge applies an arithmetic criterion[193] of presumptive nature, although this case law is perplexing, because it conforms to substantial justice, but with a notable enhancement of the equitable power. Indeed, the Convention does not refer to a presumption and, if anything, would require precise evidence. However, the limit proportional to the weight must be referred to the actual one,[194] not to the lower one, if any, stated in the consignment note,[195] consistent with Article 9, according to which, unless proven otherwise, the document demonstrates the conditions of the contract and of the receipt of the load.

In fact, Article 23, third paragraph, does not specify whether the limit proportional to the gross weight must relate to the individual assets or the overall loss or damage, with different compensation consequences. Thus, for example, if a part of the cargo, consisting of goods of different weights and value, is destroyed during the journey, the determination of the limit concerning the overall loss can allow full compensation for wrapping packages with valuable pieces. On the contrary, if one looks at the individual elements, it is inevitable that the relief will only be partial. As Article 23, third paragraph, indicates the "*kilogramme du poids brut manquant*",[196] the expression could lead us to consider only the value of each kilogram of the compromised item. Perhaps the most persuasive solution is to evaluate the specific

190 Cf. Thume and Riemer (2013d), p. 660 ff.; Rogov (2002), p. 286 ff.; Otte (2018b), p. 1450 ff.

191 Cf. Cass. com. France 22 April 1986, in *Le Lamy transp.*, 2020, vol. I, 512; App. Versailles 4 November 1987, *ibid.*, 2020, vol. I, 512.

192 Cf. App. Paris 22 January 1986, in *Le Lamy transp.*, 2020, vol. I, 512.

193 Cf. App. Paris 16 May 1991, in *Le Lamy transp.*, 2020, vol. I, 512; App. Paris 24 October 1991, *ibid.*, 2020, vol. I, 512; App. Paris 14 November 2002, *ibid.*, 2020, vol. I, 512; App. Versailles 30 March 1995, *ibid.*, 2020, vol. I, 512.

194 Cf. OLG Dresden 10 January 2018, in *TranspR*, 2018, 144, according to which containers are to be considered envelopes, as it happens for other custodial instruments, so that their weight must not be taken into account for the purposes of applying the compensation limit.

195 Cf. Trib. Bobigny 13 June 1996, in *Le Lamy transp.*, 2020, vol. I, 512.

196 This is how Article 23, third paragraph, reads in the French version. The English text reads, "kilogram of gross weight short".

situation and, in any case, guarantee adequate relief, as proved by decisions taking the opposite stance,[197] which were inspired by a prudent fact analysis.

In groupage transport, the packages are from different shippers and, in addition to indicating the total weight in the consignment note, that of the individual package has to be specified. In this scenario, with a unanimous judicial orientation,[198] the limit is determined on the basis of the weight of the lost or damaged goods, as each sender is linked to the carrier separately and the fate of the load is mutually disconnected, although, from the organizational viewpoint, all the items are involved in the same operation.

Article 25 sets the compensation limit in case of damage and establishes the relative criterion. Through the reference to Article 23, first, second and fourth paragraphs, relating to compensation for prejudice from loss, the relief is calculated on the basis of the value of goods at the place and time of receipt, being a value established in relation to the price on the stock exchange, at the current market price and, if that is not applicable, to the ordinary one of goods of the same nature and quality, pursuant to Article 23, first and second paragraphs.[199] In the event of total damage, the compensation can never exceed the sum due for the destruction and, in case of partial damage, the one provided for the loss of the depreciated part, pursuant to Article 25, second paragraph, letters a) and b).[200] Furthermore, through the reference of Article 25 to Article 23, fourth paragraph, in addition to the fee, customs duties and any expenses incurred during the trip are reimbursed in proportion to the compensation.

Finally, the prejudice created to a machine can present difficulties in terms of application of the CMR regulation. If several units are damaged, the limit is determined with regard to the overall weight, as the parts are constituent elements of the same machine and, if compromised, make it unusable or significantly affect its value.[201] A similar conclusion must be reached if the asset is disassembled and

---

[197] Cf. BGH 30 January 1981, in *Europ. transp. law*, 1981, no. 16, 455; App. Paris 15 June 1984, in *Bull. transp.*, 1984, 545, for which the criterion of the limit in relation to the total missing gross weight operates; App. Paris 10 December 1971, in *Bull. transp.*, 1972, 19; App. Paris 25 June 2009, *ibid.*, 2009, 450, for which the compensation limit is calculated with reference to the weight of the damaged package. See also Messent and Glass (2018), p. 237 ff.

[198] Cf. App. Paris 10 December 1971, in *Bull. transp.*, 1972, 19; App. Paris 25 June 2009, *ibid.*, 2009, 450. See also Cass. Belgium 3 June 1976, in *Le Lamy transp.*, 2020, vol. I, 513, which applied the same criterion in a case of "*groupage ferroviaire international*". Cf. Haak (1986), p. 215 ff.

[199] Cf. Loewe (1976), p. 378 ff.; Thume and Riemer (2013d), p. 656 ff.

[200] Cf. Rodière (1971), p. 317 ff. For a special scenario, see BGH 11 October 2018, in *Europ. transp. law*, 2018, no. 53, 453, according to which reused packaging represents an element independent of the goods and, therefore, its value is separate from that of the load. Therefore, if not damaged, its evaluation is not considered for the determination of the gross weight for the purposes of applying the compensation limit, pursuant to Article 15, second paragraph, letter b), and Article 23, third paragraph.

[201] Cf. App. Paris 31 January 1984, in *Bull. transp.*, 1984, 543; App. Aix – en – Provence 25 September 1990, in *Le Lamy transp.*, 2020, vol. I, 513; App. Besançon 12 December 1995,

transferred through different trips; in fact, the damage to the element as such is irrelevant, unlike the one to the more complex structure, as the piece contributes to guaranteeing the functionality of the equipment.[202] Regardless of this particular hypothesis, the same considerations raised with regard to the limit for loss would be valid for some writers.[203] If, in the shipment, there are goods of different value, the limit of Article 25, second paragraph, would not apply to the individual components with regard to the respective damages, but to the total value corresponding to the estimate of the damaged parts of the goods, so that full compensation is guaranteed for the more expensive ones. We can repeat the same conclusion, insisting on an adequate assessment of the situation.

8.4.3 The Compensation Limit and Delays

According to Article 23, fifth paragraph, the prejudice due to delay cannot lead to compensation exceeding the price of the transport[204] and the provision introduces a principle different from that of Article 23, third paragraph, in case of loss, as the relief is commensurate with 8.33 units of account for each kilogram of missing or damaged gross weight. As the remuneration is usually determined on the basis of distance and weight, the provision of Article 23, fifth paragraph, can generate a considerable amount.[205] Above all, the different structure of the uniform law, which opts for a determination of compensation on the basis of criteria different from those of Article 23, third paragraph, is surprising. Moreover, this is reflected in the different quantification of the relief, as the identification of the prejudice caused by delay generally follows a separate prescriptive path. Although the limit established by Article 23, fifth paragraph, is not low in itself, the reference to the consideration anchors the limit to the economic value of the operation; moreover, in case of delay, the weight could in no way be taken into account.

---

ibid., 2020, vol. I, 513; App. Orléans 18 January 1995, in *Bull. transp.,* 1995, 123; OLG Stuttgart 15 September 1993, in *TranspR*, 1994, 156; BGH 6 February 1997, in *Europ. transp. law,* 1998, no. 33, 701, according to which there is no loss of the overall value, if the repair of the damaged piece is possible and complete. Cf. Loewe (1976), p. 377 ff.; Thume and Riemer (2013d), p. 654 ff.

[202] Cf. Cass. com. France 15 October 2002, in *Bull. transp. logist.,* 2002, 697; App. Aix – en – Provence 5 October 1989, in *Le Lamy transp.*, 2020, vol. I, 513. Cf. also Haak (1986), p. 217 ff.; Clarke (2014), p. 301 ff.; but see Trib. com. Lyon 10 November 1975, in *Bull. transp.,* 1976, 175, then reformed by App. Lyon 21 July 1977, *ibid.*, 1977, 97, according to which the limit would apply with regard to individual pieces.

[203] Cf. Loewe (1976), p. 378 ff.

[204] Cf. Thume and Riemer (2013d), p. 674 ff.

[205] Cf. Haak (1986), p. 228 ff., according to whom, "having regard to the fact that the freight price is normally calculated by reference to distance and weight, this can amount to a subtantial sum".

For determining the limit for delay, Article 23 stresses the agreed upon fee for the entire journey and the portion corresponding to the fraction of it[206] in which the deadline is violated, not due to a literal interpretation of Article 23, fifth paragraph, but because this provision refers to the overall economic significance of the service. Thus, in cumulative carriage, if some transporters have not fulfilled their obligations, the relief must be contained in the overall price and not in that due to the carrier directly involved.[207]

As a parameter pursuant to Article 23, fifth paragraph, the notion of payment does not include customs duties or expenses incurred, as these items fall within the different assessment of Article 23, fourth paragraph,[208] and the price of the carriage is the maximum limit. Whoever requests compensation has to prove that the prejudice is such as to guarantee a relief equal to the agreed consideration.[209] In any case, a penalty clause is null and void, because it violates Article 41 and its related mandatory principle.[210] It does not matter that this clause would allow the penalty to be invoked without evidence of prejudice and that it would entail compensation up to the maximum limit provided for by Article 23, fifth paragraph,[211] because the inclusion of the penalty would introduce a consensual regime on the determination of relief, in conflict with Article 23, fifth paragraph. The clause cannot be equated to the declaration of special interest upon redelivery or that of value, and the principle applies not only to delay, but also to loss or damage.

8.5 Cases wherein the Compensation Limits Do Not Apply

8.5.1 Willful Misconduct

Similar to all conventions relating to transport, in addition to providing for a compensation limit, the CMR orders its forfeiture. Thus, with a provision borrowed from Article 25 of the Warsaw Convention in its original version,[212] for Article

[206] Cf. Messent and Glass (2018), p. 249 ff.; Krings (1999), p. 777 ff.

[207] Cf. App. Paris 18 October 1973, in *Bull. transp.*, 1973, 488.

[208] Cf. Loewe (1976), p. 377 ff.; Messent and Glass (2018), p. 249 ff. Cf. Cass. France 26 June 1984, in *Bull. transp.*, 1984, 610.

[209] Cf. Cass. com. France 6 October 1975, in *Bull. transp.* 1975, 478; App. Amiens 19 June 1980, *ibid.*, 1980, 490; OLG Düsseldorf 15 December 1994, in *TranspR*, 1995, 244.

[210] Cf. Trib. com. Paris 15 June 1978, in *Bull. transp.*, 1978, 420.

[211] Cf. OLG Munich 26 July 1985, in *TranspR*, 1985, 395.

[212] For the original Article 29 of the Warsaw Convention "*le transporteur n'aura pas le droit de se prévaloir ces dispositions de la présente Convention qui excluent ou limitent sa responsabilité si le dommage provient de son dol ou d'une faute qui, d'après la loi du tribunal saisi, est considerée come équivalente au dol*". Cf. Haak (1986), p. 243 ff.; Loewe (1976), p. 383 ff.; Rodière (1971), p. 317 ff.; Tuma (2006), p. 589 ff.; Jung (1997), p. 159 ff.; Mayer (1997), p. 174 ff.; Pesce (1995), p. 207 ff.

29, the carrier cannot avail himself of this benefit "*si le dommage provient de son dol ou d'une faute qui lui est imputable et qui, d'après la loi de la juridiction saisie, est considerée comme équivalente au dol*".[213] Forfeiture presupposes that the carrier acts with willful misconduct or with equivalent default.[214] According to Article 29, second paragraph, the same principle applies with regard to the work of the employees of the transporter or of the persons whose activities are used.[215] The burden of proof rests on whoever invokes Article 29 and the latter must demonstrate the existence of the causal link between the event and the willful misconduct or conduct characterized by equivalent fault.[216]

The notion of willful misconduct indicates the intention to cause damage, i. e., "*une fraude. C'est l'infidélitée du transporteur*".[217] Precisely because it requires an act executed with the will to harm, i. e., with a specific illegal resolution, the conduct is not frequent[218] and, almost always, attributable to theft committed by the driver, as evidenced by a constant French case law orientation.[219] Especially in the common

[213] So states the CMR in the French version. The English version of Article 29 reads, "if the damage was caused by his willful misconduct or by such default on his part as, in accordance with the law of the court or tribunal seised of the case, is considered as equivalent to willful misconduct".

[214] Cf. RB Rotterdam 8 March 2017, in *Europ. transp. law,* 2017, no. 52, 574, which specifies how the burden of proof falls on the owner of the goods; *Datect Electronic Holdings Limited and Others* v. *United Parcels Service Limited and Another,* in *Unif. law rev.,* 2005, 624; App. Barcelona 19 December 2006, n. 598, in *Ac,* 2007, 1526, according to which the compensation limit is applied if it is not shown that the damage derives from the intentional or negligent conduct of the carrier. The thesis is not convincing because only the person entitled to redelivery is relevant.

[215] Cf. Loewe (1976), p. 384 ff.; Van Ryn (1966), p. 667 ff.; Harms (2013), p. 757 ff. See also Hof Gravenhage 28 November 2007, in *Europ. transp. law,* 2008, no. 43, 364.

[216] Cf. Wesolowski (2013), p. 343 ff.; Sánchez - Gamborino (2001a, b), p. 646 ff. Cf. OLG Bamberg 31 January 2008, in *TranspR,* 2008, 469, according to which the unlimited liability of the carrier presupposes that the entitled person demonstrates specific and qualified fault profiles of the same carrier. Therefore, he does not forfeit the benefit when the circumstances are uncertain; OLG Hamburg 5 March 2015, in *TranspR,* 2017, 113.

[217] Cf. Putzeys (1981), p. 314 ff.; Cabrera Cánovas (2012), p. 149 ff.; Gruber (2017), p. 61 ff., according to whom, "for the carrier's actions to amount to willful misconduct, they must have acted willfully with the intention to breach the contract".

[218] Cf. App. Barcelona 14 November 2006, in *Jur,* 2007, 144550, according to which the compensation limit is applied as the "*sustracción se realizó sin que el conductor fuera consciente, impidiendo advertir intencionalidad por su parte*".

[219] Cf. Cass. com. France 22 March 2016, in *Le Lamy transp.*, 2020, vol. I, 516, which assessed the driver's participation in the theft of goods organized by an armed gang as willful misconduct. See also App. Lyon 30 March 2017, *ibid.,* 2020, vol. I, 516; App. Orléans 27 March 2014, *ibid.,* 2020, vol. I, 517. See also Hof Gent 7 February 2007, in *Europ. transp. law,* 2007, no. 42, 774.

law systems, but not limited to it,[220] there have been attempts[221] to extend the concept of willful misconduct to include the scenarios in which the author consciously accepts the consequences of a negligent conduct. Thus, those who do not evaluate the overall bulk of the load, which, due to its size, is close to the maximum height and then collides with a bridge, would act willfully. In the same sense, the behavior of someone who falls asleep while driving would be "willful misconduct", even if the prejudice is caused by the explosion of a tire.[222] Neither solution is acceptable; in the former case, there is no unlawful intention, only the violation of precautionary rules, and the same holds true for the latter case, in which the causal link is lacking.

According to the aforementioned overall approach, which is being criticized here, one should distinguish fault with foreseeability from negligence understood as a simple violation of the precautionary rules and consider the former as willful misconduct. If the driver dozes off because he is driving much longer than allowed, he would act with intent, as he would be aware of the illegitimate conduct and, if he persisted, he would show indifference to the possible harmful consequences.[223] Thus, it would be "willful misconduct" if the transporter left the vehicle unattended, "appreciating that it was risky and wrong to do so or being recklessly indifferent",[224] or if periodic maintenance was neglected, making the truck unsafe.[225] Thus, for "willful misconduct" to arise, it would be enough to accept the risk while foreseeing

[220] Cf. Cass. Belgium 30 March 2000, in *Europ. transp. law,* 2000, no. 35, 392; Hof Bruxelles 19 February 2021, *ibid.,* 2021, n. 61, 34, according to which the carrier who, after having concluded an insurance contract on behalf of the owner of the goods, settles with the insurance company following the theft, forfeits the limit, as he would have been aware of its importance and, therefore, would have acted willfully; HR Netherlands 22 February 2002, *ibid.,* 2004, no. 39, 658.

[221] Cf. Messent and Glass (2018), p. 274 ff.; *Laceys Footwear (Wholesale) Ltd.* v. *Bowler International Freight Ltd. and Another*, in *Europ. transp law,* 1998, no. 33, 79.

[222] Cf. *Sidney G. Jones Ltd.* v. *Martin Bencher Ltd.*, in *Lloyd's rep.,* 1986, 54.

[223] Cf. *Sidney G. Jones Ltd.* v. *Martin Bencher Ltd.*, in *Lloyd's rep.,* 1986, 54, according to which "the driver was well aware of the regulations. He chose to ignore them and he did so deliberately. He knew that by ignoring them, he exposed the load that he was carrying to a greater risk than if he had complied with the regulations. He appreciated that he was acting wrongfully, persisted in so acting and was wholly indifferent to the consequences". See also *TNT Global S. p. A.* v. *Denfleet International Ltd., ibid.,* 2007, 504; for the first instance judge "a driver who fell asleep at the wheel would, before falling asleep, have appreciated that he was sleepy, and that knowledge coupled with the decision to continue driving enabled him to hold that the circumstances amounted to willful misconduct".

[224] Cf. *Texas Instruments Ltd.* v. *Nasan (Europe) Ltd.*, in *Lloyd's rep,* 1991, 146. Cf. also *Lacey's Footwear (Wholesale) Ltd.* v. *Bowler Int. Freight Ltd., ibid.,* 1997, 369, according to which the carrier who disregarded the instructions acted fraudulently, delivering to a different place, without having time to verify the identity of the consignee.

[225] Cf. *Alena* v. *Harlequin*, in *Europ. transp. law,* 2003, no. 38, 218, according to which "a persistent failure by the owners to maintain the lorry over a period of time would clearly be willful misconduct because every one engaged in the transport business must know that a persistent lack of maintenance may cause the vehicle to be in a dangerous condition".

the negative consequences,[226] regardless of the degree of probability of the occurrence of the prejudice.[227]

The thesis is unfounded, although it has been supported both in the UK[228] and in Italy,[229] because the violation of the precautionary rules, in any case, determines only a fault, in the absence of intentional conduct.[230] Though involving the forfeiture of the limit, the relevant fault pursuant to Article 29 can have different articulations, particularly according to actual foreseeability or the possibility of anticipating the damaging fact. However, this has nothing to do with willful misconduct, characterized by the determination to give prejudice to others, and no other realistic case can be imagined than that of embezzlement or fraud.

8.5.2 Equivalent Default

According to Article 29, first paragraph, forfeiture of the compensation limit presupposes the proof of "default (. . .) as, in accordance to the law of the Court or Tribunal seized, it is considered equivalent to willful misconduct".[231] The Convention does not define equivalent fault[232] and, as has rightly been observed,[233] "the level of conduct that determines the exclusion" of the limit "is (. . .) expressed in the uniform rules in ways and concepts that can give rise to different assessments not only in relation to the letter of the individual norms but also to the language in which they are expressed". Indeed, the CMR refers to the definition elaborated by the different legal systems,[234] with the consequent disarticulation of the concept, due to

[226]Cf. Clarke (2014), p. 318 ff., according to whom "there is the willful misconduct if the misconduct increases the risk and in addition the carrier was aware of this"; Clarke (2016), p. 574 ff.; *Denfleet International Ltd. & Another* v. *TNT Global Spa Another,* in *Lloyd's law rep.,* 2007, 504; V. also Tuma (2006), p. 599 ff.; see also Hof Antwerp 9 March 1998, in *Europ. transp. law,* 1998, no. 33, 707, according to which the carrier would be responsible for "willful misconduct", if, before delivering, he does not verify the identity of the consignee.

[227]Cf. Clarke (2014), p. 318 ff., according to whom "the objective probability of loss or damage is relevant but not decisive".

[228]Cf. Clarke (2014), p. 318 ff.; Messent and Glass (2018), p. 274 ff.

[229]Cf. Silingardi et al. (1994), p. 227 ff., according to whom "the notion of 'willful misconduct' (. . .) must be made to coincide, in practice, with the notion of 'fault with foreseeability'".

[230]Cf. Hof Gent 10 May 2000, in *Europ. transp. law*, 2000, no. 35, 428, according to which "failure to fulfill the duty of care and surveillance of the goods, even in the case of goods at risk, does not itself constitute proof of willful misconduct by the carrier".

[231]This is how Article 29, first paragraph, reads in the English version. The French text reads, "*d'une faute qui lui est imputable et qui, d'après la loi de la jurisdiction saisie, est considerée comme équivalente au dol*".

[232]Cf. Schelin (2004), p. 107 ff.; Otte (2018d), p. 1502 ff.

[233]Cf. Pesce (1995), p. 209 ff.; Harms (2013), p. 744 ff.

[234]Cf. Supreme Court of Poland 10 September 2020, II CASK 125 / 2019, according to which there is forfeiture in the event of willful misconduct or gross negligence; OGH 30 January 2019, in

its non-unequivocal meaning. The provision is in contrast with the need for a uniform regulation toward which the Convention aims.[235]

Some interpreters[236] have rejected the idea that the CMR would have liked to introduce an equation between willful misconduct and "*faute lourde*", because, failing to do so, "*une interprétation laxiste et une assimilation pure et simple de la faute lourde au dol parce que telle est la tradition (...), allant jusqu'à abandonner l'élément international ou volontaire*".[237] The thesis is not extremely convincing, because, in a right or wrong manner, Article 29 refers to different legal systems. This is its fundamental weakness, with the consequent, unjustified disarticulation of the category. However, this defect cannot be eliminated by postulating a univocal concept of equivalent fault, contrary to the uniform law. Fortunately, as the application-related issues are similar, in several countries the case law conclusions are not so different, as the problems that have emerged in practice are often the same and their evaluation can achieve consistent results in light of comparable experience criteria. This is the result of an empirical approach rather than a homogeneous theoretical model, but, anyway, the results can be appreciated in a more coherent manner than one might imagine from a simple reading of Article 29.

Sometimes, a reconstruction of the equivalent fault is proposed[238] with the analysis of other rules of the uniform law, in particular Article 25 of the Warsaw Convention, in its 1955 Protocol version, a provision that refers to an "act or omission (...) done with intent to create damage or recklessly and with the knowledge that damage would probably result". Alongside willful misconduct, there is a reckless behavior supported by the foreseeability of the prejudice,[239] and it is up to the judge to assess whether "*le dol ou une faute qui confine au dol*"[240] occurs, that is, the default of whoever acts with the awareness that damage may take place. The carrier would go against the assumption of the protection provided in his favor by the uniform rules, as there would be either the intention to cause unjust prejudice or the acceptance of the relative risk. This should refer to the CMR, which should be read in conformity with the Warsaw Convention.[241] The already criticized Anglo-Saxon position is inspired by similar criteria, for which a violation of the precautionary rules with anticipation of the possible occurrence of the damage would be included under willful misconduct. Both theses are unfounded; as much as the

---

TranspR, 2019, 390, according to which Article 29 and Article 32 have the same approach in referring to the national law of the judge seized with the matter for the purposes of identifying negligence as equivalent to willful misconduct and, therefore, equivalent default. See also Fillers (2020), p. 194 ff.; Lecaroz and Michon (2016), p. 558 ff.; Defossez (2016), p. 89 ff. More generally, see Wijffels (2001a), p. 653 ff.; Wijffels (2001b), p. 27 ff.

[235] Cf. Rodière (1971), p. 318 ff.; Smeele (2000), p. 330 ff.

[236] Cf. Putzeys (1981), p. 316 ff.; Pesce (1995), p. 209 ff.

[237] Cf. Putzeys (1981), p. 316 ff.

[238] Cf. Pesce (1995), p. 209 ff.

[239] Cf. Pesce (1995), p. 217 ff.; Tuma (2007a), p. 157 ff.; Tuma (1998), p. 15 ff.

[240] Cf. Putzeys (1981), p. 320 ff. Cf. also Van Ryn (1966), p. 666 ff.

[241] Cf. Pesce (1995), p. 217 ff.

approach of the Warsaw Convention can be appreciated, Article 29 is different and this aspect must be accepted, not ignored. We have already argued about the indications of common law jurists, and we have confirmed the structural distinction between willful misconduct and fault.

According to Article L. 133 - 8 included in the "*Code du commerce*", with *Loi* n. 2009 - 1503 of 8 December 2009, "*seule est équipollente au dol, la faute inexcusable du voiturier. Est inexcusable, la faute délibérée qui implique la consience de la probabilité du dommage et son acceptation téméraire sans raison veritable. Toute clause contraire est réputée non écrite*". The new French regulation has overcome the previous orientation, according to which "*culpa lata dolo aequiparatur*", i.e., a clear fault or a gross negligence would be sufficient to determine the forfeiture of the limit.[242] Presently, according to the French domestic law, it is necessary to prove that the carrier knowingly accepts the risk that his conduct could cause damage and, therefore, the fundamental element is foreseeability.[243] For applying Article 29 of the CMR, this overall indication has a strong relevance, although, unlike the aforementioned approaches of the Anglo-Saxon studies, the French rule remains anchored to fault and does not trace the violation of precautionary rules with foreseeability of damage to willful misconduct.

A comparable regulatory evolution can be found in the German law;[244] at first, this had identified equivalent negligence in the supposed "*grosse Fahrlässigkeit*"[245] and Article 29 applied especially in the event of a clear violation of precautionary rules. Therefore, a huge deviation of the behavior from the required parameters of diligence, expertise and prudence was needed;[246] thus, the carrier who, after an accident, had reloaded the fallen medicines, combining them with those still on the vehicle, was ruled to be in clear fault, since, as was evident, this could have determined the contamination of those medicines not involved in the accident.[247] Presently, according to § 435 HGB,[248] the carrier must accept the risk that damage

---

[242] Cf. Krings (1999), p. 781 ff. See App. Paris 26 January 2000, in *Europ. transp. law*, 2000, no. 35, 416.

[243] Cf. Gruber (2017), p. 62 ff.

[244] Cf. Fremuth (2004), p. 99 ff.; Tuma (2002), p. 139 ff.

[245] Cf. Eckardt (2017), p. 63 ff.; Harms (2013), p. 745 ff.

[246] Cf. Messent and Glass (2018), p. 270 ff.; Jung (1997), p. 160 ff.

[247] Cf. BGH 28 May 1998, in *TranspR*, 1998, 454. See also BGH 16 July 1998, in *Europ. transp. law*, 1999, no. 34, 360; BGH 17 April 1997, in *TranspR*, 1998, 65; OLG Cologne 4 July 1995, *ibid.*, 1996, 284; BGH 17 July 1997, *ibid.*, 1998, 25. For another interpretation, cf. LG Freiburg 3 September 2004, in *TranspR*, 2005, 315, according to which, if due to a road accident the individual goods, in particular medical devices, fall from their container and the driver puts them back randomly, there is unlimited liability for the carrier, regardless of the nature of the fault in the occurrence of the original event.

[248] According to §435 HGB, "*die in diesem Unterabschnitt und im Frachtvertrag vorgesehenen Haftungsbefreiungen und Haftungsbegrenzungen gelten nicht, wenn der Schaden auf eine Handlung oder Unterlassung zurückzuführen ist, die der Frachtführer oder vanntlicte in § 428 genannte Person vorsätzlich*". Cf. Harms (2013), p. 744 ff.

may arise from his conduct[249] and, once again, this criterion affects the application of Article 29. Actually, in the aforementioned case of medicines dumped on the road, the solution would be the same, because both the clear deflection from the precautionary rules[250] and the inevitable anticipation of the harm are present. However, German decisions are quite homogeneous,[251] despite the evolution of the law.[252]

In Spanish system, judicial precedents[253] sometimes distance themselves from the concept of "*culpa lata*" and consider that accompanied by foreseeability[254] equivalent to willful misconduct, on the basis of recent provisions[255]; Dutch law

---

[249] Cf. BGH 1 July 2010, in *TranspR*, 2011, 78; BGH 6 June 2007, *ibid.*, 2007, 423; OLG Düsseldorf 18 December 2013, *ibid.*, 2014, 291; OLG Düsseldorf 17 December 2014, *ibid.*, 2016, 391; OLG Stuttgart 25 February 2015, *ibid.*, 2015, 191; OLG Koblenz 3 July 2013, *ibid.*, 2014, 154; OLG Düsseldorf 21 November 2012, *ibid.*, 2013, 115; OLG Hamm 21 November 2013, *ibid.*, 2014, 290; BGH 20 September 2010, *ibid.*, 2010, 45; OLG Koblenz 20 May 2010, *ibid.*, 2010, 442; BGH 21 March 2007, *ibid.*, 2007, 361; BGH 13 June 2012, in *Europ. transp. law*, 2013, no. 48, 199. Cf. also Harms (2013), p. 752 ff.

[250] Cf. Harms (2013), p. 753 ff.

[251] Cf. OLG Stuttgart 28 May 2008, in *TranspR*, 2008, 259, according to which, in a carriage related to the production methods of the automobile company and called just in time, the carrier is liable without limitation if he does not take the necessary precautions to abide by the defendant's delivery deadline.

[252] Cf. OLG Düsseldorf 4 July 2001, in *TranspR*, 2002, 158, according to which, if the carrier does not disclose how he has protected the goods against the risk of theft, he falls into the fault equated to willful misconduct; OLG Munich 27 July 2001, *ibid.*, 2002, 161, according to which a negligent organization of parking in the carrier's plant is recognized when there are limited controls on the exit of goods and there is mixed parking of various companies operating in nearby areas; OLG Stuttgart 11 June 2003, in *TranspR*, 2003, 308, according to which full compensation can be recognized only if the organizational defect is the original cause of the damaging event and there is considerable negligence on the part of the carrier; OLG Munich 28 October 2015, in *TranspR*, 2016, 193, according to which a clear violation of the precautionary rules necessary for a specific transport involves the loss of the compensation limit.

[253] Cf. Hendrickse (2017), p. 158 ff.; Cass. Spain 12 March 1998, in *Europ. transp. law*, 1999, no. 34, 100.

[254] Ma v. Sánchez - Gamborino (2016), p. 568 ff., according to whom "there is also an 'indirect' way of committing willful misconduct, which occurs when, without the intention of failing to comply with the contract, the person responsible is aware that his act or omission will probably give rise to such noncompliance and, even so, decides to go ahead, often (...) for reasons of mere convenience"; App. Barcelona 5 July 1999, in *Ac*, 1999, 1850, according to which "*no es precisa una voluntad deliberadamente rebelde: basta que el infractor se represente como posibile, a consecuencia de su acción, el resultado prohibido y, pese a ello, consienta en llevar a cabo la misna*". These approaches adhere to the extensive notion of willful default, criticized here, and identify in the *culpa lata* that which is equated with willful default. In this respect, see also App. Barcelona 18 June 1999, *ibid.*, 1999, 1200.

[255] For Article 62 LCTTM (Ley 15 de 2009, de noviembre, del contrato de transporte terrestre de mercancías): "*no se applicarán las normas del presente capítulo que excluyan o limiten la responsabilidad del porteador o que inviertan la carga de la prueba, cuando el daño o perjuicio haya sido causando por èl or por sus auxiliares, dependientes o independientes, con actuacíon dolosa o con una infracción dolosa o con una infracción consciente y voluntaria del deber jurídico asumido que produzca daños que, sin ser directamente queridos, sean consecuencia necesaria de la acción*". For an analysis of the jurisprudence prior to 2009, cf. Sánchez - Gamborino (2001a, b),

works in the same way.[256] On the contrary, the Polish legal system is linked to the "*culpa lata dolo aequiparatur*" principle and, therefore, equivalent fault is encountered when the most elementary rules of diligence are violated.[257] A similar position is applied in Norway,[258] Austria,[259] Switzerland[260] and Italy,[261] except for those theses close to the Anglo-Saxon ones.[262]

On one hand, these different approaches should not be surprising, because they are consequences of the reference to national legislation, as Article 29 takes for granted an influence of the principles of the domestic law with regard to CMR implementation. This approach is one of the strategic limits of the Convention, but the outcome is inevitable, based on a plain literal interpretation. On the other hand, if it has developed in French and German law and if it is underlined by common law judicial precedents, the idea of default with foreseeability of harm is not considered as essential or exclusive by Article 29 and is not imposed in all countries and, thus, the differing position of some States cannot be criticized. In particular, it remains unclear why the analysis of Article 29 should be influenced by the theses on the Warsaw Convention[263] when considering a completely different system. It is one thing to express hope for a different structure of the Geneva Convention and another to think that the Warsaw one refers to road transport, albeit in a mediated or indirect manner.

However, the concept of macroscopic discrepancy from precautionary rules is not so different from their violation with foreseeability of possible damage, because there is no need for proof of its actual anticipation in the mind of the carrier or his assistants, considering that the only reference is to his plausible contemplation, according to the criteria of social normality, as a possible outcome of negligent or imprudent behavior. In fact, the significant violation of precautionary rules is an indication of specific neglect for the interest of the person entitled to the cargo.

---

p. 646 ff.; Sánchez - Gamborino (2001b), p. 866 ff.; Sánchez - Gamborino (2010), p. 227 ff. For the following one, see Cabrera Cánovas (2012), p. 149 ff.

[256] Cf. HR Netherlands 5 January 2001, in *Europ. transp. law,* 2001, no. 36, 116; Smeele (2001), p. 37 ff.

[257] Cf. Wesolowski (2013), p. 344 ff., according to whom "it should be noticed that the concept of Polish law does not require from the carrier (. . .) the necessity of being aware of the causing of damage".

[258] Cf. Supreme Court of Norway, 16 March 1995, in *Europ. transp. law,* 1996, no. 31, 563, according to which "the degree of culpability which excludes the limitation of liability laid down in article 29 CMR consists of gross negligence".

[259] Cf. OGH 30 January 2019, in *Europ. transp. law*, 2020, no. 55, 441; OGH 21 March 2018, *ibid.,* 2019, no. 54, 106; Tuma (2007b), p. 366 ff.; Tuma (1993), p. 649 ff. More generally, see Jesser – Huß (2004), p. 111 ff.; Otte (2018d), p. 1513 ff.

[260] Cf. HG Canton of Argau 7 June 2011, in *TranspR,* 2012, 339, according to which, under the law of the Swiss Confederation, gross default entails the unlimited liability of the carrier.

[261] Cf. Orrù (2017), p. 78 ff.; Tuma (2007b), p. 367 ff.

[262] Cf. Silingardi et al. (1994), p. 227 ff.

[263] Cf. Pesce (1995), p. 209 ff.; Tuma (2007a), p. 157 ff.

Regardless of whether reference is made to foreseeability of the harm or the intensity of the deviation from the standards for the correct execution of the professional activity, the overall results are homogeneous. The aforementioned German case on the hasty collection of medicines dumped on the roadway is an obvious example, because, whatever concept of default or negligence is to be adopted, the limit does not apply. On one hand, there is a clear violation of the precautionary rules. On the other hand, there is foreseeability of the prejudicial consequences, and German case law precisely has a lot of consistency in evaluating similar phenomena, regardless of the legislative evolution.

8.5.3 Cases Where Equivalent Default Is Possible: Theft

There is a recurring case of theft while the vehicle is parked at night in an unsupervised area, despite the fact that there is a guarded parking lot nearby.[264] In this situation, the carrier is often considered to be indulging in equivalent default, as he clearly violates the normal precautionary rules on the strength of which the more prudent solution should be opted for. On one hand, it would not give him an absolute guarantee to prevent theft and, on the other hand, it would protect him from being extremely superficial and negligent. The same conclusion is reached when, having committed himself to transport expensive photographic equipment, a carrier spends the night in an unattended area adjacent to an Italian motorway, despite the high risk known at that time.[265] Analysis of Article 29 would lead to similar conclusions if the degree of deviation from the precautionary rules is not considered, but rather the easy foreseeability of the damage is.

According to some rulings,[266] anyone who stops in an open and unsupervised area for the whole weekend, during which the load is stolen or subjected to

[264] Cf. Cass. com. France 30 June 2004, in *Unif. law rev.*, 2005, 634; Cass. com. France 22 January 2002, in *Bull. transp. logist.*, 2002, 110; Cass. com. France 13 September 2011, *ibid.*, 2011, 555; Cass. France 3 October 2000, in *Europ. transp. law*, 2001, no. 36, 92; *Texas Instruments Ltd.* v. *Nason (Europe) Ltd.*, in *Lloyd's rep.*, 1991, 146. For a singular hypothesis, cf. Cass. France 24 June 2008, in *Europ. transp. law*, 2008, no. 43, 740, according to which the carrier who transfers the goods to "*une remorque placée en position arrière contre le quai de déchargement de l'enceinte d'un entrepôt dans lequel jamais aucun vol n'avait eu lieu*" is not grossly negligent and does not therefore forfeit the compensation limit; OGH 2 July 2008, *ibid.*, 2009, no. 44, 299.

[265] Cf. OLG Cologne 10 December 2002, in *TranspR*, 2003, 459; OLG Cologne 27 September 2005, *ibid.*, 2007, 316; RB Bruxelles 8 June 1990, in *Europ. transp. law*, 1990, no. 26, 362, according to which the carrier who leaves the vehicle with a valuable load during the weekend in a deserted and unsupervised area and does not make sure that the next carrier moves the vehicle forfeits the compensation limit. Cf. Jung (1997), p. 162 ff.; Harms (2013), p. 760 ff.

[266] Cfr OLG Hamburg 17 January 2001, in *TranspR*, 2002, 238; OLG Cologne 27 September 2005, *ibid.*, 2007, 316; RB Bruxelles 25 May 1992, in *Europ. transp. law*, 1993, no. 28, 762; *Texas Instrument Ltd. and others* v. *Nason (Europe) Ltd. and others*, in *Europ. transp. law*, 1991, no. 26, 671, according to which "a carrier is guilty of willful misconduct in requiring a trailer to

vandalism, would act with willfulness.[267] Illicit premeditation is lacking in this conduct, as the transporter has no intention of causing prejudice, unless one wishes to adhere to the thesis,[268] criticized here, for which even fault with foreseeability would be traced back to willful misconduct. However, the harmful consequences of such behavior cannot escape the carrier; by ignoring them, he accepts the risk and, in any case, clearly and inexcusably violates the criteria of prudence. If the driver proves that, due to bad weather, he cannot reach a protected parking lot, the demonstrated difficulty can justify the conduct and exclude the application of Article 29, although contrary decisions were issued in some cases.[269]

Sometimes,[270] for Article 29 not to be applied, the presence of two drivers[271] is requested, so that it is possible to avoid the situation where only one is forced to stop in an unsupervised area, being too tired to reach a guarded parking lot. Furthermore, the presence of a single driver does not cause forfeiture of the compensation limit if the shipper is familiar with the carrier's usual practice and knows that he travels to Italy with a driver, without the sender raising any objections.[272] In general, assessment of the compliance by the behavior with the precautionary rules is more severe with regard to the transport of valuable goods and, for their better protection, the carrier must install a satellite tracking device.[273] Professional diligence necessitates that precautions should be undertaken in relation to specific circumstances,[274] according to the characteristics of the load. Therefore, the driver who parks the vehicle in front of his hotel without an anti-theft alarm, with a valuable cargo on board,[275] acts with equivalent fault, as, precisely because of its particular value, he

---

be left in a car park without inquiring whether that was a safe place for it having regard to the risk of theft".

[267] Cf. OLG Munich 12 May 1989, in *TranspR,* 1990, 427.

[268] Cf. Silingardi et al. (1994), p. 227 ff.; Clarke (2014), p. 318 ff.; Messent and Glass (2018), p. 274 ff.

[269] Cf. OLG Hamm 9 May 1996, in *TranspR,* 1997, 190; OLG Nuremberg 22 March 1995, *ibid.,* 1996, 381.

[270] Cf. OLG Munich 29 November 1995, in *TranspR,* 1997, 190; OLG Nuremberg 24 February 1999, *ibid.,* 2000, 81; Audiencia Provincial de Barcelona 6 April 1999, in *Unif. law rev.,* 1999, 1040; OLG Vienna 26 March 2004, in *TranspR,* 2004, 364.

[271] Cf. Cass. Italy 20 May 2020, n. 9266 in *Giur. it rep.,* 2020, according to which the carrier is liable for the careless entrusting of the goods to a single driver.

[272] Cf. OLG Hamm 19 November 1998, in *TranspR,* 2000, 363.

[273] Cf. App. Reims 16 October 2012, in *Bull. transp. logist.,* 2012, 712.

[274] Cf. App. Versailles 30 October 2003, in *Bull. transp. logist.,* 2003, 83; OLG Munich 29 November 1995, in *TranspR,* 1997, 190; OLG Nuremberg 24 February 1999, *ibid.,* 2000, 81; OLG Munich 23 September 2004, *ibid.,* 2005, 254; App. Segovia 10 November 1999, n. 288, in *Ac,* 1999, 8028; App. Barcelona 11 June 1999, *ibid.,* 1999, 6126; LG Berlin 13 October 2010, in *TranspR,* 2011, 188, according to which the carrier is not saddled with unlimited liability when staying a night in an unguarded parking lot whose fences are however controlled by satellite and when he sleeps on board; LG Erfurt 25 September 2015, *ibid.,* 2018, 120.

[275] Cf. Krings (1999), p. 781 ff.; Otte (2018d), p. 1507 ff.

should place it in a protected and supervised area, above all if the truck does not have an adequate anti-theft device.

The same does not apply if the driver, being unaware of the nature of the goods and not realizing their value, does not evaluate the danger to which they are exposed; thus, it would be willful misconduct if, carrying expensive perfumes, a transporter stopped in an unattended lay-by, but near a police station.[276] The solution cannot be endorsed, as there is no intentional conduct and the presence of high-priced goods only aggravates the wrongfulness of infringing those precautionary rules the breaching of which involves the application of Article 29 on the subject of fault, if this deviation is of particular importance and implies the reasonable foreseeability of the damage. In this sense, anyone who, during the night, leaves the vehicle in a fenced but unguarded parking lot at the inn where he sleeps acts with equivalent fault.[277]

For instance, the "*faute lourde*" is excluded if the transporter parks in a "*gare routière*" without activating the alarm, as access is forbidden to the public and is considered a safe place,[278] or when the vehicle stops for a few minutes in the courtyard of the sender's company, while the carrier acquires the necessary documents, although the truck is not locked and the keys are in the passenger compartment.[279] However, the specific case needs to be examined, as circumstances may vary, leading to a different opinion. The lack of indication by the transporter of the situation in which the loss of the package occurs[280] leads to forfeiture of the limit; as the event falls within the carrier's sphere of control and knowledge, it would be impossible to prove equivalent fault. Precisely for this reason, a detailed description of the fact is required. However, the theft committed by the person to whom the driver gives a ride during the journey does not always cause the forfeiture of the limit, but it is necessary to examine the whole situation[281] and, in particular, to determine whether, on the basis of professional diligence, any operator would have formulated the same opinion on the passenger's reliability.

Despite the strong presence of criminal acts on the motorways in several countries, case law is strict and demands that these illicit plots are contrasted with the use of what is offered by modern technologies, organizational resources, or protected night rest spaces. The substantial coherence of the decisions of the various States

[276] Cf. Cass. com. France 2 October 2012, in *Bull. transp. logist.*, 2012, 601.

[277] Cf. Trib. Prato 14 May 2005, in *Dir. mar.*, 2006, 567; App. Milan 20 April 2005, in *Dir. trasp.*, 2006, 1009.

[278] Cf. Cass. com. France 26 February 1985, in *Bull. transp.*, 1985, 270; Cass. com. France 5 January 1988, *ibid.*, 1988, 102; App. Paris 28 September 2006, *ibid.*, 2006, 665; App. Versailles 14 November 2002, *ibid.*, 2002, 792; Cass. France 4 May 2017, in *Europ. transp. law*, 2018, no. 53, 297.

[279] Cf. Cass. com. France 25 June 1985, in *Bull. transp.*, 1985, 436; App. Paris 24 January 2001, *ibid.*, 2001, 194; OLG Düsseldorf 22 November 1990, in *TranspR*, 1991, 59.

[280] Cf. Trib. Bassano del Grappa 25 November 1997, in *Dir. trasp.*, 1999, 249.

[281] Cf. OLG Hamm 22 November 2004, in *TranspR*, 2005, 123.

confirms the limited relevance of the different conceptions of fault or of gross negligence.

8.5.4 Cases Where Equivalent Default Is Possible: Defective Packaging, Improper Handling, Stowage and Others

The overload can lead to the instability of the vehicle and, if caused in violation of the relative technical provisions and with a conduct that strays from professional diligence, it can cause the application of Article 29.[282] Furthermore, if an asset of a certain value suffers damage as a result of an inappropriate arrangement by an inexperienced carrier, there is forfeiture of the limit, as this profile falls within the ordinary knowledge of the operation and of safety of the truck, so that noncompliance therewith is serious and, in particular, inexperience cannot justify the violation of the fundamental precautionary rules. Then, in groupage transport, insufficient controls on the ways in and out of the warehouse lead to the forfeiture of the limit.[283]

Moreover, the carrier is liable without the benefit of the limit if he places the heat-sensitive load in a part of the vehicle that is not refrigerated, with a high risk that it will be damaged;[284] similarly, the placement of heavy goods on top of more fragile ones is considered an instance of "*faute lourde*".[285] In both cases, the transporter is fully liable for a behavior that does not comply with the parameters of prudence, but, as is inevitable in such cases, the damage is easily foreseeable. Thus, anyone who uses a truck with an unsuitable refrigeration system, compromising the load of meat,[286] is grossly negligent and falls in equivalent fault, while the same reasoning does not apply in the case of a sudden breakdown if the device is in good condition and has undergone the necessary maintenance. On the contrary, the lack of adequate control over the loading procedures executed by the sender causes the application of Article 29 if the wrong accommodation creates prejudice to the load,[287] provided that the problem is clearly detectable.

Anyone who intentionally violates the rules of road traffic acts in gross negligence and falls in equivalent fault. For example, Article 29 applies in scenarios

[282] Cf. Cass. com. France 15 June 2007, in *Bull. transp. logist.*, 2007, 183.

[283] Cf. OLG Nuremberg 18 October 1999, in *TranspR*, 2000, 126.

[284] Cf. Cass. com. France 18 March 1986, in *Bull. trasnsp. logist.*, 1986, 336; Cass. com. France 13 October 1981, in *Europ. transp. law*, 1982, no. 17, 288.

[285] Cf. App. Paris 27 May 1986, in *Bull. transp.*, 1986, 676.

[286] Cf. OLG Hamburg 23 June 1999, in *TranspR*, 2000, 175; OLG Vienna 19 June 2019, in *Europ. transp. law*, 2011, no. 55, 547; OLG Munich 22 March 2006, in *TranspR*, 2006, 310, according to which the carrier is unlimitedly liable for a carriage of foodstuffs with the refrigeration system broken and at an outside temperature of thirty degrees centigrade. Cf. Harms (2013), p. 773 ff.

[287] Cf. OGH 21 March 1977, in *Unif. law rev.*, 1978, 292.

where, crossing the road with the red light on, the driver is in the belief that there are no vehicles with right-of-way approaching from a side road, with the carrier causing an accident, as "he took a risk which he knew he ought not to have taken and, in that circumstance, he could be rightly found to have committed an act of willful misconduct".[288] The thesis is convincing, although it is a case of equivalent fault and not one of willful misconduct for the reasons already set forth. The conscious transgression of road rules does not imply the intention to damage the goods; rather, there is negligence coupled with foreseeability of the harm, traceable back to fault or, better, fault equated to willful misconduct provided by Article 29. In this sense, we have to consider the conduct of those who drive under the influence of alcohol,[289] cause an accident due to fatigue,[290] or fall asleep while driving.[291] In the latter case, the carrier would only be liable if he realizes that he is about to fall asleep;[292] conversely, he must always behave prudently and avoid reaching a level of tiredness that could compromise his ability to drive.

Furthermore, "*une faute particulièrement lourde*" is committed by anyone who swerves too fast, regardless of whether he is sober or drunk, tired or rested, since, in any case, the normal rules of prudence are breached,[293] similar to someone who hits a bridge[294] or drives too fast on a difficult road.[295] Finally, the carrier who deviates from the predetermined route and becomes stranded on a railway track during its crossing is in equivalent fault,[296] although the case is surprising and unclear as to how this can happen. Furthermore, there is an equivalent fault if the driver ventures onto a narrow road in the woods and ends up in a ditch.[297] Similarly, the driver who performs the redelivery without ascertaining the identity of the consignee is grossly negligent, but he is not showing willful misconduct.[298]

[288] Cf. *Sidney G. Jones Ltd.* v. *Martin Bencher Ltd.* in *Lloyd's rep.*, 1986, 54 ff.

[289] Cf. OGH 31 July 2001, in *TranspR*, 2002, 113.

[290] Cf. OLG Karlsruhe 17 February 1995, in *TranspR*, 1995, 439; OLG Munich 19 July 2000, *ibid.*, 2000, 412.

[291] Cf. OLG Karlsruhe 17 February 1995, in *TranspR*, 1995, 439.

[292] Cf. *TNT Global S. p. a.* v. *Denfleet*, in *Lloyd's rep.*, 2007, 404.

[293] Cf. App. Nancy 21 January 1987, in *Bull. transp.*, 1987, 344; Cass. com. France 3 March 1998, *ibid.*, 1998, 231.

[294] Cf. Cass. com. France 16 April 1996, in *Bull. transp. logist.*, 1996, 334.

[295] Cf. Cass. com. France 22 September 1983, in *Bull. transp.*, 1983, 566.

[296] Cf. Sánchez - Gamborino (2001a), p. 646 ff.

[297] Cf. OLG Düsseldorf 26 July 2004, in *TranspR*, 2005, 118.

[298] Cf. App. Paris 26 January 2000, in *Europ. transp. law*, 2000, no. 34, 415; Cass. Italy 7 October 2008, in *Giur. it. mass.*, 2008; LG Berlin 26 January 2000, in *TranspR*, 2000, 255.

8.5.5 *The Criteria for Determining the Unlimited Compensation*

In general, forfeiture of the compensation limit presupposes conduct of the carrier aimed at causing damage or behavior in violation of the precautionary rules, with foreseeability of the possible occurrence of prejudice. The transporter's conduct in relation to the event is assessed and a check has to be conducted on whether all the necessary measures are undertaken. Thus, parking in an unguarded but illuminated car park is almost always considered imprudent, pursuant to Article 29. However, a German approach went further and identified an obligation of the transporter to inform the sender, with its own relevance in the assessment of the carrier's liability; in this manner, there may be a concurrence between the unlimited liability of the latter and the negligent behavior of the shipper.[299] For example, for fear of an increased consideration, the latter keeps silent about the true value of goods, thereby preventing the other party, who is unaware of it, from adopting more stringent protective measures.[300] There can be a relevant conduct of the sender only if, by not denouncing the enormous value of the load, such omission affects the damaging event from a causal viewpoint.[301] In other cases, the question arises as to whether the transporter would have better complied with the precautionary rules if he had been aware of the importance of the cargo.[302]

So, the unlimited liability pursuant to Article 29 presupposes, before the conclusion of the contract, the explanation of the special risks connected with its execution,[303] in particular with regard to the value of the assets.[304] Therefore, Article 29 applies if the carrier does not adopt the necessary security measures, despite the sender's warning on the specific value of the load and, therefore, on the strong risks related to the journey.[305] In this case, it has been stated that the person entitled to the goods could disregard the indications of CMR and ask for relief under the national law, even if the aggrieved party could always opt for application of the uniform law

---

[299] Cf. BGH 3 May 2007, in *TranspR,* 2007, 419, according to which account must be taken of the concurrence of responsibility even in the case of unlimited liability under Article 29 of the CMR.

[300] Cf. BGH 1 December 2005, in *TranspR,* 2006, 115; OGH 26 March 2004, *ibid.,* 2004, 364, according to which the inevitable character of the fact for the purposes of exempting the carrier from liability is not a connotation to be seen in an absolute sense. Night theft in an unsupervised parking area, despite the considerable presence of vehicles, does not involve the carrier's liability if the shipper refuses an increase in the fee for guaranteeing the presence of a second driver.

[301] Cf. LG Hamburg 9 September 2002, in *TranspR,* 2005, 315.

[302] Cf. BGH 9 December 2003, in *TranspR,* 2004, 175.

[303] Cf. BGH 20 January 2005, in *TranspR,* 2005, 311.

[304] Cf. BGH 19 May 2005, in *TranspR,* 2006, 114; BGH 3 March 2005, *ibid.,* 2006, 114, according to which, if Article 29 applies, reference can be made to national law for the purpose of determining the compensable damages, bypassing the specific regulations of Articles 18–28 of the CMR.

[305] Cf. BGH 21 February 2009, in *TranspR,* 2008, 249.

text and, in particular, the rules provided by Articles 17–28.[306] However, the solution is not persuasive, because, although there is full liability, the CMR still applies and so does its system laid down in Articles 17–28.

On the contrary, the carrier who does not know the value and the exact nature of the cargo (as in the case of transport of expensive perfumes) does not lose the benefit of the limit if he travels on a closed vehicle and, for the night rest, chooses an unattended parking spot in a high traffic area where part of the load is stolen.[307] This conclusion is possible only if we agree with the German reconstruction according to which, alongside the obligations of the job, the carrier envisages a specific obligation of the sender to inform about the characteristics of the cargo. If this shipper's obligation is fulfilled, the transporter is almost always liable in an unlimited manner; in fact, his behavior is assessed in relation to the damage caused and, on the basis of verification of the circumstances, there are always more stringent safety measures that he could have adopted.

For the German approach, the shipper must report the value of goods and, if found to be of value, he can demand that the carrier takes special precautions. Thus, for example, for a transfer of computer material of immense importance, if at the border there is no envisaged protection by law-enforcement officers, the theft is inevitable only if the transporter consults the sender and, having obtained his consent, secures a private escort.[308] Similar conclusions are reached if a shipment of cameras and other technological tools are left unattended for 3 h.[309] Conversely, the overnight stop by the driver in Southern Italy in an illuminated but unguarded area, in the presence of other vehicles, is not a fault equated to willful misconduct, in consideration of the modest value of the load.[310]

However, in all these situations, the carrier must be informed; if that does not happen, Article 29 does not apply.[311]Thus, in the case of the theft of goods intended for smokers, the fact that they were expensive and subject to the related taxes does not constitute a sufficient warning to justify the unlimited liability of the transporter with regard to the presence of a second driver and stopping only in areas equipped with security and surveillance measures.[312] In essence, the declaration of value becomes an element supplementing the shipper's obligations and loses part of its distinctive features enshrined in Article 24 of the Convention. Therefore, the

---

[306]Cf. BGH 30 September 2010, in *TranspR,* 2010, 437; BGH 3 March 2005, *ibid,* 2005, 253.

[307]Cf. OLG Saar December 12 2000, in *TranspR,* 2001, 169.

[308]Cf. OLG Hamburg 4 October 2001, in *TranspR,* 2002, 109.

[309]Cf. OLG Saar 17 July 2008, in *TranspR,* 2008, 471. See also OLG Stuttgart 11 May 2016, *ibid.,* 2017, 10, according to which unlimited liability attaches to the carrier who, when warned of the particular value of the goods, stumbles into a theft by parking in an unattended area; OLG Nuremberg 14 August 2017, *ibid.,* 2018, 118; LG Hamburg 15 April 2016, in *TranspR,* 2017, 32, according to which the carrier who leaves a vehicle with known valuables parked over the weekend is liable in an unlimited sense.

[310]Cf. OLG Nuremberg 17 April 2002, in *TranspR,* 2002, 243.

[311]Cf. OLG Munich 26 October 2017, in *TranspR,* 2018, 56.

[312]Cf. LG Stuttgart 15 December 2014, in *TranspR,* 2015, 163.

delivery of goods without specifying their value not only excludes the full liability of the carrier for the failure to provide the declaration of value, but also leads to a concurrent negligent behavior of the shipper and the carrier.[313]

8.6 Special Interests in Delivery

8.6.1 The Declaration of Value

The compensation limit for loss, damage and delay cannot be waived with specific contractual provisions. It can only be changed with a declaration of value or with that of special interest upon redelivery, which are hypotheses governed by Articles 24 and 26.[314] According to Article 24, after paying an additional fee, the sender can indicate in the consignment note a value of the cargo higher than the limit set in Article 23, third paragraph, and the amount stated is substituted for it.[315] For a consolidated approach,[316] "*la declaration de valeur spéciale doit être faite dans la lettre de voiture*", so that an indication of it in other documents could not produce the effects of Article 24.[317] The thesis remains unconvincing, as, according to the CMR, the consignment note is optional and failure to draft it does not preclude the will from being inferred in another manner, according to Article 4; in this sense, the *fax message* of the carriage order produces the same effects as present in Article 24.[318] In the absence of the consignment note, it is more difficult to offer evidence of the declaration made, particularly with regard to the position of the next carrier, who may not be aware of a different agreement between the shipper and the first one on the criteria for calculating the compensable prejudice.

On the contrary, the indication present in a document drawn up to fulfill the administrative obligations at the customs offices is not a declaration of value, as it does not relate to the carriage.[319] However, there are options on particular conditions, including those regarding the obligations of the transporter in the computer

[313]Cf. LG Fulda 18 November 2009, in *TranspR,* 2010, 192.

[314]Cf. Van Ryn (1966), p. 662 ff.

[315]Cf. Thume and Riemer (2013e), p. 689 ff.; Otte (2018c), p. 1466 ff.

[316]Cf. Putzeys (1981), p. 306 ff.; Messent and Glass (2018), p. 253 ff.; Clarke (2014), p. 309 ff.; Thume and Riemer (2013e), p. 685 ff.

[317]Cf. App. Reims 13 July 1977, in *Bull. transp.,* 1977, 406.

[318]Cf. App. Paris 28 September 2006, in *Bull. transp. logist.,* 2006, 664; App. Aix - en - Provence 16 November 2006, *ibid.,* 2006, 744; App. Versailles 4 November 1993, *ibid.,* 1994, 19; App. Paris 9 April 2009, *ibid.,* 2009, 307.

[319]Cf. App. Versailles 6 July 1994, in *Bull. transp.,* 1994, 759; App. Paris 5 March 1986, in *Le Lamy transp.*, 2020, vol. I, 514; Cass. com. France 10 July 1989, in *Bull. transp.,* 1989, 591. Cf. also Krings (1999), p. 770 ff. But see App. Nancy 29 October 1987, *Le Lamy transp.*, 2020, vol. I, 514, according to which the indication of the agreed and accepted price would not be necessary for the validity of the declaration of value.

systems for booking travels and entering into agreements, with increasing frequency. As the declaration of value outside the consignment note is considered a possibility, only the interpretation of the agreed solution can allow its qualification. In general, Article 24 can be implemented with the simple use of electronic communication.

The declaration of value is not a unilateral act of the shipper[320] and, although he issues it, it must be accepted by the carrier; this is confirmed in Article 23, for which the surcharge must be agreed upon and, therefore, the declaration presupposes a complex agreement, including the determination of the consideration.[321] Thus, the declaration cannot be made in an instrument prepared by the sender, not signed by the carrier, and with an illegible signature of the former.[322] Furthermore, the validity and effectiveness of the declaration itself are not subject to payment of the surcharge, as it is sufficient that the same be agreed upon;[323] in fact, the phrase "against payment of a surcharge to be agreed upon"[324] underlines the need to agree on a higher payment for the greater commitment undertaken, but does not require advance payment.

The declared value replaces the limit of Article 23, third paragraph, for which the compensation cannot exceed 8.33 units of account for each kilogram of missing gross weight, so that the same compentation has to be calculated on the real value of goods; the function of the declaration is "*d'élever le plafond de l'indemnité pour dommage matériel*".[325] Its close connection with this provision means that, in the event of willful misconduct or equivalent fault, the carrier cannot limit the relief to the declared amount, because, in any case, Article 29 applies. However, unlike the declaration of special interest on redelivery, that of value involves a variation of the limit only in the event of loss or damage, but does not extend to compensation for delay, provided for by Article 23, fifth paragraph.[326] Finally, the burden of proof rests upon the person entitled to dispose of the goods and, therefore, if he demonstrates that the value is higher than the limit, the difference is compensated to the extent of what was declared, pursuant to Article 24.[327]

---

[320] Cf. OGH 26 April 2001, in *Europ. transp. law,* 2002, no. 37, 497, according to which the implicit or express acceptance of the carrier is necessary; BGH 17 December 2020, in *TranspR,* 2021, 154.

[321] Cf. App. Lyon 16 March 2012, in *Le Lamy transp.*, 2020, vol. I, 514.

[322] Cf. App. Paris 15 December 1977, in *Bull. transp.,* 1978, 53; App. Lyon 16 March 2012, in *Le Lamy transp.*, 2020, vol. I, 514.

[323] Cf. App. Paris 28 February 2001, in *Bull. transp. logist.,* 2001, 210; App. Paris 28 September 2006, *ibid.,* 2006, 664. See also Loewe (1976), p. 377 ff., according to whom "the surcharge is not a prerequisite for the validity of a declaration made in accordance with Article 24".

[324] So reads the English text. In the French text, Article 24 reads, "*contre paiement d'un supplément de prix à convenir*".

[325] Cf. *Le Lamy transp.*, 2020, vol. I, 513.

[326] Cf. Loewe (1976), p. 377 ff.

[327] Cf. Putzeys (1981), p. 308 ff.

8.6.2 The Declaration of Special Interest upon Redelivery

According to Article 23, fourth paragraph, in addition to compensation for loss or damage, "*d'autres dommages ne sont pas dûs*" and "*les indemnités plus élevées ne peuvent être réclamées qu'en cas de déclaration de la valeur de la marchandise ou de déclaration d'inérêt spécial à la livraison*", pursuant to Article 23, sixth paragraph. The carrier cannot pay a refund exceeding the carriage price for the damage caused by delay, pursuant to Article 23, fifth paragraph, but the declaration of special interest on redelivery allows compensation "*du préjudice autre*".[328] In general, with regard to its structure, the considerations highlighted for the declaration of value are valid. Therefore, it can be inserted in documents other than the consignment note, as long as they are related to the carriage.[329] Furthermore, it is not a unilateral act of the shipper, as the transporter must provide his consent,[330] a price supplement[331] must be agreed upon and the different limit within which liability attaches to the carrier must be indicated.

In fact, Article 26, first paragraph, considers further prejudice to that resulting from loss, damage and delay;[332] the latter is understood as exceeding the agreed term, with the exclusion of the other hypothesis of Article 19, in which the transporter does not perform the redelivery within the time that should reasonably be accorded to a diligent carrier. In fact, in this case, no declaration can be made, as can be inferred from Article 26, as the chronological limit is established *a posteriori*. In the event of loss or damage, the person entitled to the goods can request compensation for "*préjudice commercial*"[333] or for the "*perte d'un marché, la destruction d'autres marchandises, la diminuition d'une production*"[334] or even for the "*préjudice immatériel ou moral*".[335] Again, reference to the national law is necessary for determining compensation. Delay, in the given meaning, can cause one prejudice after the other, for which a refund within the limits of the carriage price would not be adequate.[336] Finally, the eligible claimant bears the burden of proving the further prejudice for which he claims relief.

---

[328] Cf. Putzeys (1981), p. 309 ff., according to whom "*le dommage supplémentaire*" of Article 26, second paragraph, is identified in the "*préjudice autre*". See also Thume and Riemer (2013c), p. 707 ff.

[329] Cf. App. Paris 23 March 1978, in *Bull. transp.*, 1978, 265; App. Montpellier 19 February 1987, *ibid.*, 1987, 578. See on the other hand BGH 14 July 1993, in *Europ. transp. law*, 1993, no. 28, 917, according to which the declaration of special interest upon redelivery should be inserted in the consignment note.

[330] Cf. BGH 17 December 2020, in *TranspR*, 2021, 154.

[331] Cf. Cass. com. France 10 July 1989, in *Bull. transp.*, 1989, 591.

[332] Cf. Thume and Riemer (2013f), p. 711 ff.

[333] Cf. *Le Lamy transp.*, 2020, vol. I, 514.

[334] Cf. Putzeys (1981), p. 309 ff.

[335] Cf. Putzeys (1981), p. 309 ff.

[336] Cf. Putzeys (1981), p. 309 ff.

References

Cabrera Cánovas A (2012) Jurisprudencia del Tribunal Supremo español en materias reguladas por el Convenio CMR. In: Sánchez - Gamborino F, Cabrera Cànovas A (eds) El convenio CMR: el contrado de transporte internacional de mercancias por carretera, Barcelona, 129 ff

Clarke MA (2014) International carriage of goods by road: CMR, VI edn. New York

Clarke MA (2016) Willful misconduct under English law. Unif Law Rev, 575 ff

Defossez D (2016) CMR: what if the courts got it wrong?. Unif Law Rev, 75 ff

Demuth K (2013) Article 20. In: Thume KH (ed) Aa. Vv., CMR: über den Beförderungsvertrag im internationalen Strassengüterverkehr, III edn.Frankfurt am Main, pp 561 ff

Eckardt T (2017) Article 29 CMR overview countries. In: Verheyen W (ed) Aa. Vv., CMR 60 years. Time for retirement or future proof?, Paris, pp 61 ff

Fillers A (2020) The CMR in the practice of Latvian courts. Unif Law Rev, 169 ff

Fremuth F (2004) Haftungsbegrenzungen und deren Durchbrechung im allgemeinen deutschen Frachtrecht und nach der CMR. TranspR, 99 ff

Gruber A (2017) Article 29 CMR overview countries. In: Verheyen W (ed) Aa. Vv., CMR 60 years. Time for retirement or future proof? Paris, pp 61 ff

Haak KF (1986) The liability of the carrier under CMR. The Hague, 1986

Harms C (2013) Article 29. In: Thume KH (ed) Aa. Vv., CMR: über den Beförderungsvertrag im internationalen Strassengüterverkehr, III edn. Frankfurt am Main, pp 741 ff

Hendrickse M (2017), Evaluation of article 29. Should one adapt article 29 CMR?. In: Verheyen W (ed) Aa. Vv., CMR 60 years. Time for retirement or future proof? Paris, pp 153 ff

Jesser – Huß M (2004) Haftungsbegrenzungen und deren Durchbrechung im allgemeinen Frachtrecht und nach der CMR in Österreich. TranspR, 111 ff

Jung C (1997) The Convention on the contract for the International carriage of goods by road (CMR): survey, analysis and trends of recent German case law. Unif Law Rev, p 148 ff

Krings E (1999) CMR: examen de la jurisprudence des Cours de Cassation de France et de Pays – Bas (deuxième partie). Unif Law Rev, 767 ff

Lecaroz J, Michon N (2016) L'article 29 de la CMR en pratique. Unif Law Rev, 548 ff

Libouton J (1973) International road transport. Convention on the contract for the international carriage of goods by road. Review of Court decisions 1965–1971. Eur Transp Law 8:6 ff

Loewe R (1976) Commentary on the convention of 19 may 1956 on the contract for the international carriage of goods by road. Eur Transp Law 11:311 ff

Mayer CU (1997) CMR – aperçu et reflections sur la jurisprudence autrichienne en dernier ressort (1994–1996). Unif Law Rev, 159 ff

Messent A, Glass DA (2018) CMR: contracts for the international carriage of goods by road, IV edn. New York

Nickel – Lanz (1976), La Convention relative au contrat de transport international de marchandises par route (CMR), Hamburg

Orrù E (2017) Article 29 CMR overview countries. In: Verheyen W (ed) Aa. Vv., CMR 60 years. Time for retirement or future proof? Paris, pp 79 ff

Otte K (2018a) Art. 20 der CMR. In: Aa. Vv., Internationales Vertragsrecht, Munich, 1424 ff

Otte K (2018b) Art. 23 der CMR. In: Aa. Vv., Internationales Vertragsrecht, Munich, 1438 ff

Otte K (2018c) Art. 24 der CMR. In: Aa. Vv., Internationales Vertragsrecht, Munich, 1465 ff

Otte K (2018d) Art. 29 der CMR. In: Aa. Vv., Internationales Vertragsrecht, Munich, 1500 ff

Pesce A (1995) Il trasporto internazionale di merci, Turin

Putzeys J (1981) Le contrat de transport routier de marchandises, Bruxelles

Radionov N (2016) Limitation of liability right in road freight carriage in Croatia: an extinct institute. Unif Law Rev, 457 ff

Rodière R (1971) The convention on road transport. Eur Transp Law 6:307 ff

Rogov S (2002) Paradoxon der dualen Haftungsobergrenze des Article 23, Abs. 3 CMR. TranspR, 296 ff

Sánchez - Gamborino FJ (2001a) La jurisprudence du Tribunal Supremo espagnol en matière de CMR. Unif Law Rev, 644 ff
Sánchez - Gamborino FJ (2001b) La Convention Cmr según la Jurisprudencia del "Tribunal Supremo" de España, in Europ. transp. law, n. 36, 842 ss
Sánchez - Gamborino FJ (2010) New Spanish law on contracts for the land carriage of goods: act 15 / 2009 dated 11 November 2009, a faithful son of the CMR with some discrepancies. Eur Transp Law 45:227 ff
Sánchez - Gamborino FJ (2016) Article 29 of the CMR Convention concerns nothing but willful miscondacut of the carrier. Unif Law Rev, 560 ff
Schelin J (2004) Haftungsbegrenzung und ihre Durchbrechung nach der CMR in den skandinavischen Staaten und Finnland. TranspR, 107 ff
Silingardi G, Corrado A, Meotti A, Morandi F (1994) La disciplina uniforme del contratto di trasporto di cose su strada, Turin
Smeele FGM (2000) Dutch case law on article 29, CMR. Eur Transp Law 35:329 ff
Smeele FGM (2001) Dutch case law on Article 29, CMR revisited. Eur Transp Law 36:37 ff
Thume KH (2013) Article 19. In: Thume KH (ed) Aa. Vv., CMR: über den Beförderungsvertrag im internationalen Strassengüterverkehr, III edn. Frankfurt am Main, pp 545 ff
Thume KH, Riemer JB (2013a) Article 25. In: Thume KH (ed) Aa. Vv., CMR: über den Beförderungsvertrag im internationalen Strassengüterverkehr, III edn. Frankfurt am Main, pp 691 ff
Thume KH, Riemer JB (2013b) Article 23. In: Thume KH (ed) Aa. Vv., CMR: über den Beförderungsvertrag im internationalen Strassengüterverkehr, III edn. Frankfurt am Main, pp 667 ff
Thume KH, Riemer JB (2013c) Article 27. In: Thume KH (ed) Aa. Vv., CMR: über den Beförderungsvertrag im internationalen Strassengüterverkehr, III edn. Frankfurt am Main, pp 716 ff
Thume KH, Riemer JB (2013d) Article 23. In: Thume KH (ed) Aa. Vv., CMR: über den Beförderungsvertrag im internationalen Strassengüterverkehr, III edn. Frankfurt am Main, pp 653 ff
Thume KH, Riemer JB (2013e) Article 24. In: Thume KH (ed) Aa. Vv., CMR: über den Beförderungsvertrag im internationalen Strassengüterverkehr, III edn. Frankfurt am Main, pp 685 ff
Thume KH, Riemer JB (2013f) Article 26. In: Thume KH (ed) Aa. Vv., CMR: über den Beförderungsvertrag im internationalen Strassengüterverkehr, III edn. Frankfurt am Main, pp 707 ff
Tuma OJ (1993) Article 29 CMR Bestandsaufnahme und Ausblick. Eur Transp Law 28:649 ff
Tuma OJ (1998) Article 29 CMR – Die unendliche Geschichte? Eur Transp Law 33:13 ff
Tuma OJ (2002) Ist grobe Fahrlässigkeit ein Tatbestand des Article 29 CMR? Eur Transp Law 37: 139 ff
Tuma OJ (2006) The degree of fault under article 29. Unif Law Rev 584 ff
Tuma OJ (2007a) Degré de la faute suivant l'Article 29 de la CMR. Eur Transp Law 42:153 ff
Tuma OJ (2007b) Degré de la faute suivant l'Article 29 de la CMR II – aperçu par pays. Eur Transp Law 42:355 ff
Van Ryn J (1966) Une nouvelle étape dans l'élaboration du droit des transport: la Convention de 1956 relative au transport international de marchandises par route (CMR). Eur Transp Law 1: 639 ss
Wesolowski K (2013) A review of judicial decisions of the polish supreme court within the scope of CMR. Eur Transp Law 48:341 ff
Wijffels R (2001a) Introduction to the CMR with regard to linguistic inaccuracies. Eur Transp Law 36:653 ff
Wijffels R (2001b) Article 29, Abs. 1, CMR – Belgische Störung der Uniformität. Eur Transp Law 33:27 ff

Chapter 9
Rights Protection

Contents

9.1 Joint Assessment of the Condition of Goods

9.1.1 Apparent Losses and Damage

For Article 30, first paragraph, in the event of patent loss or damage at the time of redelivery, the consignee must verify the condition of the goods along with the carrier. In this case, verification results in a shared description of prejudices found or in the affixing of unilateral reservations.[1] In fact, the prejudice detected must be identified in detail, but this control is not of a contractual nature, as neither is any act of disposal conducted nor is a contract of assessment of the situation, in the legal

[1] Cf. Cabrera Cánovas (2012), p. 151 ff., according to whom, "*se si opta por la comprobación, esta ha de ser bilateral, esto es: con la partecipatión no solo del destinatario, sino también del transportista (...), como es lógco y acorde con el carácter bilateral del proprio contrato de transporte*"; Sánchez - Gamborino (2001b), p. 869 ff. See also Otte (2018a), p. 1519 ff.

C. Tincani, *Contract for the International Carriage of Goods by Road*, Law for Professionals, https://doi.org/10.1007/978-3-031-08487-4_9

systems in which it is envisaged, entered into. Rather, a declaration of unilateral or unanimous knowledge, whereby the state of cargo is certified, is made.

This act is mostly adopted by employees or collaborators dedicated to material operations, such as the driver or the warehouse worker, for instance. Entrepreneurs rarely intervene, the more so in large companies. This does not pose any problem, precisely due to the lack of contractual components of the declaration, although the Convention uses expressions such as "ascertained", which could lead to misunderstandings. Not surprisingly, for Article 30, first paragraph, there may be a different conclusion by persons who intervened, and the consignee can and must append his reservations even if there are divergent opinions. His silence has preclusive effects.

Only upon redelivery[2] can the verification be conducted, and the first must be effective, as evidenced by the use of the French term "*livraison*",[3] different from the concept of making something available. Therefore, late reservations cannot be formulated if facts are apparent and further discovery of any prejudices is of no importance.[4] This is because, according to Article 30, first paragraph, in the event of omitted objection, the consignee is presumed to receive goods in the state described in the consignment note.[5] However, the judge must consider the recipient's declaration that he has checked the load in the presence of the transporter sufficient, even though the latter does not confirm it. Indeed, a unilateral act is enough, if only for the reference in the Convention to the unequivocal concept of reservation and, in such case, it is up to the carrier to elicit his dissent.[6]

In summary, if the recipient[7] does not raise any objection, the cargo has to be considered to have arrived according to the description given in the consignment

[2] Cf. OGH 28 March 2000, in *Europ. transp. law,* 2003, no. 38, 231, according to which "there was a delivery within Article 30 where the consignee consented to the discharge of goods in the working space under his control even though the carrier was engaged in the subsequent transfer of the goods to their depot".

[3] In the English text: "if the consignee takes delivery".

[4] See Messent and Glass (2018), p. 285 ff., according to whom, "if no such reservation is sent within the prescribed time, then effectively any damage subsequently discovered will be unrecoverable, since evidence contradicting the result of the checking will be inadmissible".

[5] See Messent and Glass (2018), p. 284 ff., according to whom, "if the consignee fails to give a reservation as required by Article 30, then taking delivery amounts to *prima facie* evidence that he has received the goods in the condition described in the consignment note". Cf. Cass. Greece 61/2011, according to which with Article 30, first paragraph, there is a presumption in favor of the carrier; App. Alava 7 July 2005, no. 102, in *Jur,* 2005, 233598.

[6] Cf. OGH 6 October 2000, in *Europ. transp. law,* 2003, no. 38, 236, according to which "an admission 'that the condition of the goods was checked in the presence of the carrier' is not a (simple) question of fact but also (at least also) a decision in law for the appeal judge, who formally held that 'the checking of the condition of the goods in the presence of the carrier' was also a matter for decision by the court of".

[7] Cf. Silingardi et al. (1994), p. 247 ff.

note[8] or, in any case, in the state in which it was at departure.[9] A different assessment by the judge presupposes proof, with the *onus* of evidence resting on the consignee himself. Instead, for Article 30, first paragraph, if there is a disagreement by the transporter, the reservations exclude the so-called presumption of conformity,[10] but the burden of proof continues to rest on the person requesting compensation.[11] In fact, if unilateral, the declaration prevents the forfeiture from taking place, but has no consequence on demonstration of the prejudice, which is postponed to the next, eventual proceedings. Alternatively, if the consignee formulates no remark, the goods are presumed delivered in the state in which they were shipped, unless otherwise proved. Report of the loss or damage prevents this effect, that is, it is a relative presumption, using this concept according to the discipline of the most civil law countries. The means of proof are governed by the national procedural system. Depending on different regulations, in many States, the contrary evidence permitted in general by Article 30, first paragraph, could be given in a difficult way. If, then, following the recipient's dispute, the transporter's consent is recorded, we have the shared evaluation provided for by Article 30, second paragraph.

For Article 30, first paragraph, the consignee must indicate "in a general way" the nature of the loss or damage.[12] For some, the description should not be detailed or too broad.[13] This approach is hardly convincing;[14] if, in fact, the prejudice were not identified with a certain precision, it would also be possible to trace it back to those detected at a later stage, in contrast with the precise chronological limit established for reservations on apparent prejudices. In this sense, the expression "*sous réserve de contrôle au déballage, marchandises mouillées*"[15] was deemed inadequate, as it does not clarify the damage occurred, requiring further analysis. Thus, with good

[8]See Libouton (1973), p. 61 ff., according to whom "reservations sent within the proper time to the seller of the goods do not come under the time – limit laid down in article 30, first paragraph, since they are not binding on the carrier, not having sent to him".

[9]Cf. App. Paris 28 October 1969, in *Bull. transp.*, 1970, 7; App. Angers 13 June 2017, *ibid.*, 2017, 424; Aix – en – Provence 4 September 1996, in *Le Lamy transp.*, 2020, vol. I, 524; App. Douai 7 June 1994, in *Bull. transp.*, 1994, 623. Contrary proof is not precluded, cf. Cass. com. France 27 September 2011, *ibid.*, 2011, 583; Cass. com. France 22 March 2016, *ibid.*, 2016, 219; LG Baden – Baden 22 October 1999, in *TranspR*, 2000, 254, according to which Article 30, first paragraph, is applicable even in absence of a consignment note.

[10]See Messent and Glass (2018), p. 286 ff.

[11]See Silingardi et al. (1994), p. 247 ff.

[12]The French text reads: as follows: "*adressé des réserves au transporteur indiquant la nature générale de la perte ou de l'avarie*". The English text reads as follows: "giving a general indication of the loss or damage".

[13]See Loewe (1976), p. 384 ff., according to whom "the description of the damage need not be extremely detailed; however, it cannot, for example, be validly confined to a mere statement of 'loss' or 'damage'".

[14]Cf. Rodière (1971), p. 323, according to whom "Article 30, first paragraph, should be read as requiring the interested party to indicate to carrier the exact nature of the loss or damage of which he is complaining".

[15]Cf. App. Aix en Provence 22 February 1979, in *Bull. transp.*, 1979, 387.

reason, the reference to prejudice suffered by 25% of the load was considered incorrect, as the nature of the event and the identity of the load involved were not specified.[16] Furthermore, with regard to a delivery of 20 tons, the reservation "*vingt tonnes nets*" was deemed inadequate, as the lost packages[17] should have been identified, at the very least with a minimum of clarity.

Again, the expression "*sous réserve contrôle, colis ouvert*" was considered too general, unlike "*accepté sous réserve colis ouvert, il manqué trois pieces*".[18] Instead, indicating that two hundred and sixty packages out of two thousand one hundred had been destroyed was deemed sufficient,[19] although this thesis is not convincing. For the decision, the function of reservations would only be to preserve the right to take legal action and, therefore, a concise expression, such as the one reported, was accepted. On the contrary, the reservation presupposes a binding identification of what happened[20] and the term "general" of Article 30, first paragraph, should not mislead, as it wants to exclude the need for ritual expressions, but one has to specify what is essential to achieve the objective of the rule. Therefore, in order to avoid forfeiture, the incident must be identified and French case law is appropriately vigilant in this regard.[21] It is not enough to mention a problem, as it must be clarified in its conformation and in its object.[22]

If there is no consignment note, the condition of goods at the time they were entrusted to the carrier is anyway relevant.[23] The decision is surprising, because, at the time of receipt, the consignee is unaware of the original state of the load and must only highlight the loss or the damage, that is, the negative situations, without wondering at what moment they arose. The related problem is entrusted to the proceedings, once the presumption of Article 30, first paragraph, in any case with the possibility of proof to the contrary, has been rebutted.

---

[16] Cf. App. Paris 23 March 1979, in *Bull. transp.*, 1979, 387. See also App. Paris 11 December 1996, in *Le Lamy transp.*, 2020, vol. I, 524, which considered the following reservations inadequate: "*en visant que l'état des emballages, savoir 'pallettes défectueuses, cartons énventrés*". See also App. Lyon 7 January 2016, in *Bull. transp.*, 2016, 45; App. Douai 16 January 1997, *ibid.*, 1997, 103, according to which "*la mention 'endommagement très sérieux de la marchandise*'" is not sufficient.

[17] Cf. App. Paris 10 November 1999, in *Bull. transp.*, 1999, 823. See also App. Caen 1 December 2011, *ibid.*, 2012, 19. But see Cass. com. France 16 May 2006, in *Le Lamy transp.*, 2020, vol. I, 524.

[18] Cf. App. Pau 18 June 2007, in *Bull. transp.*, 2007, 432.

[19] Cf. App. Brussels 27 February 1996, in *Europ. transp. law*, 1996, no. 31, 833. Cf. also App. Paris 1 June 2005, in *Bull. transp.*, 2005, 454, according to which "*doivent être regardées comme suffisantes les réserves du destinataire mentionnant 'reçue soixante colis tous ouverts*'".

[20] Cf. Hof Antwerp 15 November 1978, in *Europ. transp. law*, 1979, no. 14, 661.

[21] Cf. App. Aix en Provence 22 February 1979, in *Bull. transp.*, 1979, 387; App. Paris 23 March 1979, *ibid.*, 1979, 387; App. Caen 1 December 2011, *ibid.*, 2012, 19; App. Douai 16 January 1997, *ibid.*, 1997, 103.

[22] See Demuth (2013), p. 820 ff.

[23] Cf. App. Limoges 2 June 1967, in *Bull. transp.*, 1967, 273.

The rule is affected by its time, marked by limited means of communication. For this reason, immense attention has been paid to the immediate intervention of the consignee, so that, at the end of the journey, the existence of a problem can be established, without delay, if it is evident. This follows the logic of a Convention concluded when information circulated with difficulty and allowing written objections subsequently raised would have entailed problems. At present, this issue is felt less and there is no such urgent need to guarantee the driver to return to the base with a consignment note including the reservation, as an e-mail or fax message could precede him.

However, with the declared option of immediate complaint, Article 30, albeit slightly dated, is in force and must be interpreted as it was intended. If anything, the importance of the specificity of description is downsized from the point of view of application. In fact, in many cases, a photograph is sufficient and, indeed, is the best way to explain the nature of damages claimed.[24] Nor is there any prohibition to insert it as an attachment to the consignment note or to the reservation, precisely because this would pursue the purpose of Article 30. Indeed, with good reason,[25] lack of provisions on the format leaves ample room to the consignee, provided that the spirit of Article 30 is complied with, and the possible insertion of the reservation in the consignment note is functional above all to guarantee the timeliness of the control, which is the true purpose of Article 30.

Therefore, reservations for patent damages may be oral,[26] but this could raise problems of proof.[27] For example, the carrier's failure to contest a letter in which reference was made to a previous telephone call in which reservations had been expressed was deemed sufficient.[28] The question is of a procedural nature and falls outside the scope of the Convention, being part of the matter devolved to the relevant national law. However, despite the freedom of format, written reservations make it easier for the recipient to prove their existence and timeliness.[29]

---

[24] Cf. OLG Hamburg 27 January 2004, in *TranspR,* 2004, 215, according to which an efficient reservation pursuant to Article 30, first paragraph, is not only provided with a remark affixed to the consignment note but also by a photographic reproduction of the goods.

[25] See Demuth (2013), p. 824 ff.; Otte (2018a), p. 1521 ff.

[26] Cf. Libouton (1973), p. 60 ff., according to whom, "in a case of loss or visible damage reservations made verbally not later than the time of delivery are valid even if they are made by telephone". See also R.B. Antwerp 1 April 1980, in *Europ. transp. law,* 1980, no. 15, 461, according to which "oral reservation proved by the fact that the carrier took steps in his own warehouses to find out what happened to the missing goods".

[27] Cf. Libouton (1973), p. 60 ff., according to whom "it is duty of the party interested in the goods to bring proof of verbal reservations; sufficient proof of this will be offered if the facts connected with them are not disputed".

[28] Cfr. Hof Antwerp 21 June 1978, in *Europ. transp. law.*, 1978, no. 13, 601. Cf. also Cass. com. France 29 April 1975, in *Bull. transp.,* 1975, 298.

[29] Cf. Messent and Glass (2018), p. 288 ff., according to whom "it will always be in the consignee's interests to ensure that the reservation is in writing, since it will be for him to show that the reservation has been properly made, although this may not be necessary where the carrier

The communication sent by post the next day, after the unloading operations had concluded at 8 pm, was considered adequate.[30] Although the solution responds to an evident equitable logic, it leaves some doubts, because it violates the principle of immediacy and, although the hour was late, it does not take much time to draft a precise text. The decision should be based on Article 30, fourth paragraph, for which the delivery date is not considered in the calculation of the timeframes of the entire Article. However, these timeframes are seven and 21 days, but, when Article 30, first paragraph, uses the expression "at the latest at the time of delivery",[31] Article 30, fourth paragraph, does not operate and the check must be done immediately, also to allow the driver to leave promptly.[32]

9.1.2 The Adversarial Principle

Adversarial and joint examination postulates a concurrent assessment by carrier and consignee on the condition of goods, and there must be a shared declaration on any loss or damage.[33] Both parties can agree on the fact that the cargo has arrived in a certain state, but they do not conduct acts of disposal and limit themselves to describing the load and, therefore, there is a joint declaration of knowledge.[34] Article 30, second paragraph, attaches to it a foreclosure effect and, in any future proceedings, it will be no longer possible to discuss the state of the cargo at the time of delivery, because contrary evidence cannot be adduced.[35] In accordance with the categories of various civil law countries, it is an absolute presumption,[36] and the joint and adversarial examination implies sharing an opinion on the condition of the load. There is only a declaration of knowledge, but what has been inspected can no longer be disputed, without prejudice to Article 30, second paragraph, with the exception of non-apparent damage.[37]

---

subsequently fails to dispute with reasonable promptness that an oral reservation was made at the proper time".

[30] Cf. App. Paris 22 June 1966, in *Bull. transp.,* 1966, 298.

[31] The French text reads: *"au plus tard au moment de la livraison"*. The English text reads as follows: "not later than the time of delivery".

[32] Cf. Cass. com. France 29 April 1975, in *Bull. transp.,* 1975, 298, according to which *"les réserves doivent être formulées séance tenante"*.

[33] Cf. Otte (2018a), p. 1525 ff.

[34] Cf. Loewe (1976), p. 386 ff., according to whom "the purpose of the checking by the consignee and the carrier for the second paragraph, is to establish the nature and the scope of the damage that has occurred but not the cause of the damage".

[35] Cf. App. Aix – en Provence 26 January 2017, in *Bull. transp.,* 2017, 88.

[36] Cf. Silingardi et al. (1994), p. 254 ff., according to whom "it seems better to refer to total presumption of conformity between the results of the cross-verification and the actual state of the goods".

[37] Cf. Trib. com. Elbeuf 7 May 2004, in *Bull. transp.,* 2004, 410.

For others,[38] it is a preclusion linked to the prohibition to give contrary evidence.[39] It was stated that "it is similar to a time-limit, but is not strictly one",[40] and it was then added that "the text states that evidence to the contrary may not be introduced. But this does not exclude on the one hand either the admission of the defendant, a fundamental principle, really, or the chance for the plaintiff to establish, above all, that his good faith has been abused by a scheming carrier".[41] Basically, willful misconduct, violence or, perhaps, even error are said to be relevant, so that the effects of a flawed verification can be removed. However, this argument is unconvincing, as the act has no contractual character, but is a description, which classifies the situation in a definitive way.

The problem of fraud does not arise, unlike what has been stated, arguing that "the willful misconduct of the carrier may consist of hiding damage by the expedient of re-packing, or of having taken the advantage of the recipient's trust by making him sign a checking statement which does not correspond to what has been mutually agreed".[42] If the malicious behavior of the transporter conceals the damage, Article 30, second paragraph, on non-apparent prejudice, applies, and the Convention solves the problem by itself, in the most linear manner. In fact, if the Article 30 joint declaration could be questioned by willful misconduct or by error, the uniform law system would be altered, because the first case is governed by Article 30, second paragraph, and the second is the object of the specific provision of Article 30, first paragraph, which does not offer any significance to the error.

If the consignee commits it due to his shortcomings, however, he cannot prove that the patent damage had not been detected at once. A borderline situation with no known comparisons in case law is that of violence; however, in this extreme scenario, there is no effective agreement and Article 30 does not work, precisely due to the nonexistence of the shared description. On the contrary, if the consignee fails to check the goods, despite having the opportunity, due to negligence or excessive trust in the other party, his declaration or lack of a reservation bind him in a manner that can no longer be overcome.

For Article 30, second paragraph, the joint examination of the cargo can only be surmounted in the case of non-apparent damage, provided that the consignee communicates the written reservations within 7 days. Article 30, first paragraph, does not say anything about the format of the joint declaration and the parties can "proceed amicably" and are "required to comply with criteria of loyalty, honesty and correctness".[43] According to some,[44] the Convention would allow recourse to procedures governed by national law. However, this argument is unconvincing, because

[38] Cf. Rodière (1971), p. 321 ff.

[39] See Putzeys (1981), p. 192 ff.

[40] Cf. Rodière (1971), p. 321 ff.

[41] Cf. Rodière (1971), p. 321 ff.

[42] Cf. Rodière (1971), p. 322 ff.

[43] Cf. Silingardi et al. (1994), p. 253 ff.

[44] Cf. Silingardi et al. (1994), p. 253 ff.

domestic law could not have a specific relevance, and there is no need to supplement the CMR, which has a sufficient articulation and allows for linear application. A specification based on the regulations of each country would jeopardize the expeditious implementation of Article 30 in every legal system, with reference to procedural regulations of which economic operators would not have any precise and homogeneous knowledge.

A mooted point is the silence of the carrier, that is, reservations made only by the consignee, but in the presence of the driver. In this case, there is no shared evaluation, but the unilateral reservations are inserted in a moment of dialogue and the transporter does not express himself on the remarks made by the recipient. As it has been stated,[45] in a way we can endorse, silence implies acceptance, as, although able to do so, the carrier refrains from any observation and does not formulate any objections.[46] There is no joint and adversarial verification properly so-called, as the explicit declaration is lacking; however, his behavior toward the reservations of the other party provokes acceptance.[47] This principle is correct, because it provides an extensive interpretation of Article 30, first paragraph, but in line with its objective, that is, to gather the perspectives of the consignee and carrier. Moreover, without this reading, the latter would only need to remain inert because the former cannot force him to take a position. The case of conflicting statements is different, with the judge called to settle the dispute.

If the recipient formulates a reservation without any objection from the driver, who takes part in the inspection, what has been declared is indisputable, precisely because an opposite version is not provided, except for Article 30, second paragraph, for hidden damages. In summary, Article 30, first paragraph, refers to the joint verification intended as a concomitant check and as simultaneous presence of the parties, called to assume an active role in the control. This does not imply an excessive liability of the employees of the carrier and of the consignee, without prejudice to the fact that they should be accustomed to conducting a professional activity and with the related training. The Convention does not have in mind the occasional recipient, but normal commercial traffic aimed at consolidated organizations with adequate capacity to check the status of goods. Therefore, the rigorous description required by Article 30, first paragraph, is proportionate to the average

[45] Cf. Loewe (1976), p. 385 ff.; Libouton (1973), p. 61 ff.

[46] Cf. App. Paris 24 March 1972, in *Bull. transp.*, 1972, 205, according to which there is a statement during the cross-examination for the report submitted by a health service in which it is stated that the ascertainment of damaged food took place in the presence of the carrier. Cf. also App. Paris 28 March 1978, *ibid.*, 1978, 320, for the acknowledgment of damage carried out by the insurance company's expert and in presence of the carrier once the goods had arrived to destination. Furthermore, v. App. Aix – en Provence 4 June 1976, in *Le Lamy transp.*, 2020, vol. I, 524.

[47] Cf. Hof Antwerp 21 June 1978, in *Europ. transp. law.*, 1978, no. 13, 601. See also Cass. com. France 29 April 1975, in *Bull. transp.*, 1975, 298. Cf. also Cabrera Cánovas (2012), p. 152 ff., according to which *"el tribunal declara que basta con la presencia pasiva del conductor para considerer la verificación hecha contradictoriamente, conforme prevé el Convenio CMR"*. Cf. also Sánchez - Gamborino (2001a), p. 644 ff.

competence of operators and a careful analysis is enough, without prejudice to the specific regulation of hidden damages.

9.1.3 Non-apparent Losses and Damage

The Convention defines neither patent nor hidden loss or damage.[48] The former consists in prejudice to the goods or in a packaging defect detectable at the time of redelivery,[49] and a realistic possibility of immediate and visual understanding of the problem is required.[50] Therefore, late reservations are not justified, because complete documentation is awaited, although the recipient can verify the integrity of the load at an earlier time.[51] The decision is convincing and the patent loss or damage pertains to the prejudices found on arrival, on the basis of ordinary powers of control. As mentioned,[52] the detection of prejudice to the packaging does not imply that the goods are in the same condition and the consignee must check whether the contents arrive unharmed or whether, as a result of the packaging problem, they suffer damage.[53]

For example, the prejudice to plants affected by the cold is hidden; in fact, such pathological phenomena appear at a later stage.[54] In a similar vein and with good reason, it was held[55] in respect of prejudice due to the presence of fine dust, which had penetrated into packaging.[56] Thus, the damage to a machine is hidden if it

[48]Cf. Clarke (2014), p. 201 ff.

[49]Cf. Messent and Glass (2018), p. 285 ff.; Krings (1999), p. 783 ff.

[50]Cf. App. Paris 9 July 1959, in *Droit mar. fran.*, 1959, 690, according to which "*un dommage est apparent lorsque au moment de la délivrance le réceptionnaire peut s'en rendre compte par un examen rapide, à l'aide des sens dont chacun dispose, éventuellement complété par des moyens normaux*". Cf. also Cass. com. France 15 July 1986, in *Bull. transp.*, 1986, 542, according to which "*le destinataire établit suffisamment la réalité des avaries ou des manquants*". See also App. Aix – en Provence 6 March 1991 in *Le Lamy transp.*, 2020, vol. I, 524.

[51]Cf. OLG Linz 27 November 1989, in *Unif. law rev.*, 1990, 442.

[52]Cf. App. Bordeaux 28 April 1997, in *Bull. transp.*, 1998, 417.

[53]Cf. Cass. com. France 2 June 1987, in *Le Lamy transp.*, 2020, vol. I, 522; App. Reims 3 March 1980, in *Bull. transp.*, 1980, 237; App. Lyon 22 April 1988, *ibid.*, 1989, 176, for which non-apparent damage includes any problem that can be ascertained only once the packages have been opened. Similarly, as regards the replacement of goods, see App. Grenoble 29 September 2014, *ibid.*, 2014, 605. Cf. also App. Douai 7 June 1994, *ibid.*, 1994, 623, in relation to a scenario in which the packaging is damaged without apparent consequences for the content.

[54]Cf. App. Toulouse 26 March 1969, in *Europ. transp. law,* 1971, no. 6, 131. Cf. also App. Besançon 27 October 1999, in *Bull. transp.*, 2000, 94.

[55]Cf. App. Paris 2 December 1981, in *Bull. transp.*, 1982, 73.

[56]Cf. App. Rouen 21 February 1991, in *Bull. transp.*, 1991, 507, which considers the case of some dust that entered a tank.

emerges only with operation.[57] Indeed, in this case, one may wonder whether the time limit granted by Article 30, first and second paragraphs, is sufficient, because prolonged tests and in-depth analyses may be necessary, although such scenarios are rare.

The question arises as to whether the consignee should open the packaging immediately, without any possibility of making reservations by the next deadline. In particular, the problem is relevant with regard to the transport of a significant number of packages. According to some,[58] the carrier could not be expected to wait for a cylinder weighing about 27 tons to be checked before setting off. Therefore, any defects found later would not be patent and the solution is correct, because it balances the transporter's interest in moving away with the consignee's one in completing his investigations calmly. In fact, to contain costs and guarantee adequate income, the carrier has a strong expectation to reduce stops, the extension of which translates into an increase in expenses; thus, an expansion of the concept of hidden loss or damage allows the driver to leave immediately and the recipient to avoid forfeiture. However, the length of the ascertainment is not the only significant aspect; visual verification must still be difficult, because the Convention refers to the hidden nature of the problem rather than to the duration of the check.

According to a French approach,[59] the consignee would not have the burden of ascertaining the contents of the package. In this manner, the carrier would not have to wait for complete control; however, the argument is unconvincing. In fact, without any connection in the text, in the presence of packages the loss or damage would always be hidden, while the time required to open them can be limited and the recipient must do so in an adversarial inspection, to protect the commitment of the transporter, who, within reasonable limits, has the right to attend the verification. Therefore, patent damages concern both the packaging and its contents, as long as they can be detected immediately. In this case, the recipient is saddled with the burden of verifying the integrity of goods and must perform an analysis, the intensity of which depends on the number of packages, in any case without being exempted from opening them.[60]

[57] Cf. App. Paris 16 September 1992, in *Bull. transp.*, 1992, 651. See also App. Douai 7 September 1994, *ibid.*, 1994, 623; App. Douai 16 January 1997, *ibid.*, 1997, 103. See also Krings (1999), p. 783 ff.

[58] Cf. App. Bordeaux 28 April 1997, in *Bull. transp.*, 1998, 417. For a similar case, see App. Barcelona 30 November 2016, no. 267, in *Jur*, 2017, 1684.

[59] Cf. App. Grenoble 25 September 2014, in *Bull. transp.*, 2014, 605; App. Reims 3 March 1980, *ibid.*, 1980, 237; App. Lyon 22 April 1988, *ibid.*, 1989, 176, Cass. France 24 November 1987, *ibid.*, 1988, 42; App. Lyon 16 October 1998, *ibid.*, 1999, 782.

[60] In a conflicting sense, Cf. RB Antwerp 30 September 1994, in *Europ. transp. law*, 1995, no. 30, 233, according to which "it is insufficient if, at the moment of receipt of the goods, the consignee issues the reservations concerning damaged packaging. It is also necessary that, within 7 days of delivery, he formulates a protest with regard to the contents". On the contrary, if the verification is possible, any reservation on the packaging is insufficient and the wrapping must be opened immediately.

Reservations for hidden prejudices ought to be made in writing[61] and can be included in the consignment note[62] or communicated by post,[63] telegram,[64] or fax,[65] with a broad interpretation of the concept of written act, in the spirit of the Convention, so that an e-mail message is sufficient, regardless of the different national regulations governing this form of correspondence. Article 30, first paragraph, does not clarify whether the communication must be sent or received within the prescribed timeframe, although the expression "*adressé*" suggests sending, in line with the English version in which the word "sent" appears.

Complaints can be sent not only to the carrier, but also to his "agents or servants",[66] while a reservation addressed to the shipper[67] is ineffective, because it falls outside the contract of carriage and, if anything, it can refer to the purchase and sale agreement. In general, reserves for hidden defects can only be made by the consignee, pursuant to Article 30, first paragraph, but his act can benefit the sender, if the latter can ask for the compensation and, in any case, he does. The recipient has an obligation of diligent conduct; to avoid forfeiture, with prejudice to the shipper's right to relief, he must report any hidden defects within 7 days, failing which the presumption of conformity of the state of goods with what is described in the consignment note operates.

In addition, with regard to non-apparent losses or damages, the reservation must indicate the "*nature generale*"[68] of the problem. However, the ideas proposed on the disputes formulated on arrival apply and, if anything, strictness in the interpretation must be accentuated. In fact, the carrier is no longer present and, with sufficient articulation, the declaration must put him in a position to unambiguously understand the alleged prejudice. Not surprisingly, Article 30, first paragraph, requires the written format and this must be combined with adequate specificity.

If the reservations object to a finding during joint ascertainment, the breach of the seven-day deadline prevents proof to the contrary from being adduced.[69] Article

---

[61] Cf. Clarke (2014), p. 201 ff., according to which "no particular form or formula is required for reservations, as long as the import is clear. For example, reservations may be scribbled on the copy of the consignment note retained by the carrier; however, any other written form will suffice". Cf. App. Grenoble 29 September 2014, in *Bull. transp.,* 2014, 605.

[62] Cf. Cass. France 29 April 1975, in *Bull. transp.,* 1975, 298.

[63] Cf. App. Paris 22 June 1966, in *Bull. transp.,* 1966, 330.

[64] Cf. Messent and Glass (2018), p. 288 ff.

[65] Cf. Cass. France 24 November 1987, in *Bull. transp.,* 1988, 42; App. Lyon 16 October 1998, *ibid.*, 1999, 782.

[66] Cf. Loewe (1976), p. 384 ff.

[67] Cf. Loewe (1976), p. 384 ff., according to whom "a reservation addressed (. . .) to the sender will have no legal effects". See also Libouton (1973), p. 61 ff. Cf. Cass. com. France 26 October 1999, in *Le Lamy transp.*, 2020, vol. I, 524, according to which any reservations for hidden defects sent to the forwarding agent are not effective. See, furthermore, App. Paris 13 January 1988, *ibid.*, 2020, 524.

[68] The English text mentions "a general indication of the loss or the damage".

[69] Cf. Trib. com. Elbeuf 7 May 2004, in *Bull. transp.,* 2004, 410.

30, second paragraph, allows the effects of the unanimous statement to cease; however, complaints for hidden prejudices must be sent within the short term indicated therein. Moreover, Article 30, second paragraph, and its prohibition of adducing evidence to the contrary operate only if there is a joint declaration, and this does not always happen. In other cases, Article 30, second paragraph, is not applicable, but the consignee must still send the reservation within 7 days. If he fails to do so, the presumption of conformity of the condition of goods with that described in the consignment note arises, but the contrary can be proved, pursuant to Article 30, first paragraph.

According to the expression used in some civil law systems, the presumption of Article 30, second paragraph, is absolute, whereas that of the first paragraph is relative.[70] In particular, Article 30, second paragraph, is inapplicable if, despite the "*livraison*"[71] mentioned in the first paragraph, there is no joint declaration, because the consignee and the carrier are in disagreement. In this case, if there are hidden damages, the complaint must be made within 7 days; however, exceeding this deadline would trigger off the relative presumption of Article 30, first paragraph, and the consignee or shipper can prove the contrary.

In general, for Article 30, fifth paragraph, there is a duty to collaborate[72] in performing checks, and both the consignee and the carrier must behave correctly. Thus, the former must perform the control in a reasonable time and in a manner that does not result in an excessively long pause, and the transporter must allow him adequate time, considering the nature of goods. Moreover, if the investigation is too complex, the recipient can submit reservations in the following 7 days. With good reason, violation of Article 30, fifth paragraph, was found if the destruction of the cargo rendered the verification of an expert[73] useless, since summoning him would have created unnecessary expenses. Moreover, the carrier cannot complain if he does not communicate his intention to use an expert and the consignee sells the goods and keeps the proceeds.[74] In fact, if the damage is patent, a delay in necessary initiatives would be unjustified, in the absence of an explicit request from the transporter to appoint a trusted technician.

[70]Cf. Libouton (1973), p. 62 ff., according to whom, "if the damage is apparent, absence of reservations made at time of delivery implies an assumption *juris tantum* that the goods were in proper condition". Cf. also Putzeys (1981), p. 196 ff.

[71]The English text reads as follows: "delivery".

[72]Cf. Libouton (1973), p. 63 ff., according to whom "it is sufficient for the parties to give each other every reasonable facility for making the requisite investigation".

[73]Cf. RB Amsterdam 24 November 1976.

[74]Cf. Hof Antwerp 21 June 1978, in *Europ. transp. law,* 1978, no. 13, 601.

9.1.4 Disputing Delays

For Article 30, third paragraph, the action for compensation of prejudice caused by delay presupposes a written reservation, to be formulated within 21 days from the moment the load is made available to the consignee,[75] regardless of whether there is actual delivery, with a clear difference from the content of the first paragraph, which refers to the "*livraison*" in the French text.[76] Although the third paragraph uses the expression "reservation", which is also employed in the first, the two provisions are different, as the act of the third paragraph does not want to highlight the delay, which is for the most part indisputable. Whoever intends to request compensation for such a prejudice must not formulate a declaration of knowledge, but manifest the compliant will, that is, affirm the existence of the damage and the intent to enforce the credit in court. For this reason, the time limit of the third paragraph is longer and, since it is an act of disposal, the reservation presupposes ownership of the relative power, unlike what happens for the mere declaration of knowledge of Article 30, first and second paragraphs. Therefore, in companies, complaints regarding delays must come from the legal representative or a person who has the relative power.

The third paragraph operates only if the goods are made available,[77] but there also may be delays in other cases, for example, if, forewarned of the expiry of the delivery deadline before departure, the sender exercises the power of countermand and waives transport. If the so-called "making available" is lacking, there are no forfeiture and no requirement for a reservation. On the contrary, if the third paragraph is applicable, an advance communication before arrival[78] is sufficient, as the deadline is in favor of the consignee and not the carrier. Furthermore, for goods delivered late, losses or damage, the first and second paragraphs of Article 30[79] must be complied with, because the compensation differs in function from that of Article 30, third paragraph, referring only to the prejudice connected to exceeding the delivery deadline.

Although the third paragraph speaks of an offer to the consignee, it does not state who should be the author of the reservation, unlike Article 30, second paragraph, and the argument according to which the act could only stem from the recipient is

---

[75] Cf. App. Trento 21 May 1998, in *Europ. transp. law,* 1999, no. 34, 381. Cf. also App. Paris 6 June 2002, in *Bull. transp.,* 2002, 580.

[76] The English text, Article 30, third paragraph, reads as follows: "no compensation shall be payable for delay in delivery, unless a reservation has been sent in writing to the carrier, within twenty-one days from the time that the goods were placed at the disposal of the consignee".

[77] Cf. App. Aix en – Provence 26 November 1980 in *Bull. transp.,* 1981, 185; OGH 19 September 2002, in *Europ. transp. law,* 2004, no. 39, 400; HR The Netherlands 4 October 2002, *ibid.,* 2004, no. 39, 669, according to which if, in the case of a theft, the goods are delivered by the deadline of Article 20, first paragraph, Article 30, third paragraph, applies.

[78] Cf. OLG Dusseldorf 18 January 1979.

[79] Cf. Clarke (2014), p. 203 ff., according to whom, "if delay causes damage to the goods, the more general view is that the case is not one of delay regulated by Article 30, third paragraph, but one of damage regulated by article 30, first paragraph".

supported by some Authors.[80] However, it is unconvincing, because it does not coincide with the spirit of the provision. The possible author can be the shipper; in fact, he can seek compensation, but only if there is no forfeiture.[81] If anything, as Article 30 is expressed in general terms, the recipient's initiative benefits the shipper and the reciprocal principle applies.[82] However, there must be a timely challenge, regardless of who initiates or invokes it. Then, the sender may be in difficulty in respecting the deadline of Article 30, third paragraph, if he has no news of the delay and possible damage. As the goods must be made available to the consignee, the latter has an obligation of diligent conduct, or to formulate the objection, or to allow the shipper to attend to this.

The act must be written,[83] failing which it will not prevent forfeiture. The Convention does not clarify whether, within the scheduled deadline, the communication should be sent or received, while greater precision would have been desirable. However, the expression "*adressé*" suggests that sending the reservation is considered sufficient,[84] in line with what has been stated about the first paragraph, and the word "sent" appears in the English text.

According to some,[85] unlike the deadline provided for in Article 30, first and second paragraphs, the 21 day deadline would include Sunday and public holidays, and this is derived from Article 30, second paragraph, which states the opposite principle, as the concept is not addressed in the third paragraph. The difference between the two provisions is evident and it is difficult not to consider the treatment of holidays as distinct. One can wonder about the reason behind this choice and a possible explanation could be the desire of not extending the already long period of 21 days. For Article 30, fourth paragraph, the initial day is never considered in the calculation of deadlines provided for by the entire provision, for each of its scenarios.[86]

Although the expression "reservation" is used in all three paragraphs and a peremptory term is provided, imposing the forfeiture, the effects are different. In

---

[80] Cf. Messent and Glass (2018), p. 290 ff., according to whom, "in such circumstances, the sender is dependent on the consignee for prompt action".

[81] Cf. Rodière (1971), p. 324 ff., according to which, "as far as the legal character of the rule laid down in paragraph 3 is concerned, this must be regarded as a true procedure of limitation (. . .). The interested party is time – barred".

[82] Cf. App. Limoges 7 November 1977, in *Bull. transp.,* 1977, 537, according to which any delay in reservations can be formulated by the sender.

[83] Cf. App. Limoges 7 November 1977, in *Bull. transp.,* 1977, 537, according to which the requirement of the written form is respected with the addition of reservations set out on the consignment note or sent by telex. See also App. Aix - en - Provence 26 November 1980 in *Bull. transp.,* 1981, 185.

[84] Cf. App. Aix - en - Provence 26 November 1980 in *Bull. transp.,* 1981, 185.

[85] Cf. Loewe (1976), p. 386 ff., according to whom, "unlike the seven-day time-limit mentioned in first and in second paragraph, Sundays and public holidays have to be included in calculating the time-limit of twenty - one days". See also Rodière (1971), p. 323 ff.

[86] See Clarke (2014), p. 203 ff.

fact, for Article 30, third paragraph, in the event of a violation, the action can no longer be instituted and any appointed judge must dismiss the application.[87] This does not happen for late reservations for non-apparent prejudices, pursuant to the first paragraph, as, if it is assumed that the state of goods is what is described in the consignment note, evidence to the contrary is always admitted, without prejudice to the stricter presumption of Article 30, second paragraph.

9.2 The Period of Limitation

9.2.1 The Time Limit

Article 32, first paragraph, provides a one-year term known as "*prescription*",[88] except for an extension to 3 years in some circumstances,[89] for the exercise of actions arising from carriages regulated by the Convention. The choice would be justified by the nature of the service and the organization of professional transporters.[90] Performing many services, the operator would find it difficult to maintain track of the documents of all trips for a protracted time, and this was more evident in 1956, when there were no computers to perform these tasks. Although similar ideas are widespread,[91] they are very benevolent toward the Convention, despite the fact that the short prescription is a well-known solution in road transport, especially in continental legal systems.[92] To be honest, despite there being many journeys, it is certainly not impossible to store documents and the short term benefits the carriers on the basis of at least questionable needs.

The French expression "*prescription*" helps interpretation in civil law countries, making it clear that prescription is what is being discussed, as has been specified in Spain,[93] Germany,[94] France,[95] and Italy.[96] In common law areas, the institution has been brought back to the concept of period of limitation[97] and a questionable

[87] Cf. Clarke (2014), p. 203 ff., according to whom "failure to send reservation results in more than a presumption in favour of the carrier: it bars the recovery of compensation". See also Libouton (1973), p. 63 ff. See also BGH 14 November 1991, in *Europ. transp. law,* 1993, no. 28, 265.

[88] In the English text as follows: "the period of limitation".

[89] See Haak (1986), p. 296 ff.; Cabrera Cánovas (2012), p. 153 ff.

[90] See Silingardi et al. (1989), p. 145 ff. See also Jung (1997), p. 164 ff.

[91] See Pesce (1995), p. 181 ff.

[92] Cf. Cabrera Cánovas (2012), p. 153 ff.

[93] Cf. Cabrera Cánovas (2012), p. 153 ff.

[94] See Demuth (2013), p. 885 ff.; Otte (2018b), p. 1550 ff.

[95] See Putzeys (1981), p. 386 ff.; Haak (1986), p. 293 ff.

[96] See Silingardi et al. (1989), p. 145 ff.

[97] In the English text article 32, first paragraph, reads as follows: "the period of limitation for an action arising out of carriage under the Convention shall be one year".

procedural nature has been postulated.[98] It is discussed whether, in continental States, prescription extinguishes the subjective right or the action, a theoretically complicated profile that does not have to be resolved in the same manner in every legal system. However, prescription is anchored to substantive law. Reference to a category proper to the continental tradition justifies some unease that has emerged in the typical interpretations of Anglo-Saxon countries.[99]

Article 32 applies both for actions against the carrier and for those in his favor.[100] In a Dutch decision,[101] the restrictive, unacceptable argument was upheld, according to which Article 32 would only concern actions against the transporter, as the provision would be consistent with those on liability,[102] while Article 32, second paragraph, would relate to disputes brought against the carrier. On the contrary, as a whole, the rule concerns all actions, without any distinction between those who promote them, and the opposite argument would create unfounded differences.

Thus, any actions instituted by the carrier or those initiated between transporters are subject to Article 32,[103] provided that the relationship falls within the scope of the Convention, and "consequently the rule governing the period of limitation also applies to a claim under a guarantee brought by a carrier against a sub-transporter",[104] and, in the same way, "the period of limitation of the direct action of the carrier by road against the consignee is subject to the provisions of Article 32".[105] It is irrelevant whether the dispute is one of guarantee.[106] In Germany, Article 32 was applied to the action relating to the recovery of overpaid

[98] See Clarke (2014), p. 123 ff.

[99] See Clarke (2014), p. 123 ff.

[100] Cf. Haak (1986), p. 295 ff.; Cabrera Cánovas (2012), p. 153 ff. Cf. App. Lyon 6 January 1984, in *Le Lamy transp.*, vol. I, 2020, 529.

[101] See Trib. Amsterdam 4 June 1974, in *Bull. transp.*, 1975, 531. In the sense criticized herein, see also Cass. Belgium 7 January 2000, in *Unif. law. rev.*, 2000, 852 ff. For the opposite view, see BGH 11 December 1981, in *Europ. transp. law,* 1983, no. 18, 63 ff.; HR The Netherlands 11 February 2000, no. C 98/207, *ibid.*, 2000, no. 35, 381.

[102] In the sense criticized herein, see Cass. Greece 1714/2014.

[103] See OGH 20 June 2000, in *Europ. transp. law,* 2004, no. 39, 86; HR The Netherlands 11 February 2000, in *Europ. transp. law,* 2000, no. 35, 381, according to which Article 32 is applied to all actions initiated by the carrier, not just those filed for the purpose of obtaining the consideration.

[104] See Cass. Belgium 19 February 2004, no. 202, in *Europ. transp. law,* 2004, no. 39, 521.

[105] See Cass. France 24 March 2004, *ibid.*, 2004, no. 39, 53. See also RB Antwerp 1 October 2004, no. AR 2/14272, *ibid.*, 2006, no. 41, 102, according to which "a claim for payment of a customs debt by reason of the loss or incorrect use by the carrier of documents remitted to him is subject to the period limitation laid down in article 32".

[106] Cf. App. Dijon 26 January 1983, in *Bull. transp.*, 1982, 43; App. Paris 30 May 1984, *ibid.*, 1984, 89. Cf. also App. Paris 6 May 2004, in *Le Lamy transp.*, 2020, vol. I, 531; App. Douai 8 December 2016, in *Bull. transp. logis.*, 2017, 15; App. Paris 6 September 2012, in *Le Lamy transp.*, 2020, vol. I, 531. The longer term of 3 years is applied in case of damage or equivalent fault, cf. App. Paris 17 December 2008, *ibid.*, 2020, 531.

expenses[107] and to the one with which the transporter requested compensation for damage following the prolonged stop at customs, as the sender had provided incomplete documents.[108] The principles are correct; both claims belong to the execution of the agreement and fall within the scope of the Convention. In a similar manner, it was decided for an action brought by the freight forwarder against the transporter for the relief of damage caused to the former's trailer.[109] However, in this case, it is necessary that the prejudice inflicted on the vehicle is connected to the contract of carriage, as, failing that, the problem would not be covered by the Convention.[110]

Article 39, fourth paragraph, resolves any doubt on the identification of the deadline for recourse actions in transport with multiple carriers, referring to Article 32.[111] The opposite principle applies to disputes in which the *commissionnaire,*[112] or whoever manages warehouses,[113] or the owner of the vehicle[114] is a party, or if the dispute arises between the transporter and the consignee who promises to arrange a load for the return trip, without the subsequent stipulation of the contract.[115] This is because these facts may concern in a broad sense the transfer of goods from the material point of view, but the agreement is not discussed and, therefore, the Convention does not operate. Alternatively, in combined carriage,[116] Article 32 applies if the injury occurs during the road trip.[117]

Article 32 can be invoked for extra-contractual liability,[118] regardless of its configuration in individual legal systems, if it is enforced against the transporter for loss or damage, as, in any case, it is disciplined by the Convention, pursuant to

---

[107] See BGH 18 February 1972, in *Europ. transp. law,* 1972, no. 7, 860.

[108] See BGH 11 December 1981, in *Europ. transp. law,* 1983, no. 18, 63. See also BGH 28 February 1975, in *Unif. law rev.,* 1975, 372.

[109] See App. Paris 7 March 1990, in *Bull. transp.,* 1991, 118. Actions between forwarding agents do not fall within the scope of the CMR, cf. App. Paris 20 March 1972, *ibid.,* 1972, 182; App. Paris 11 October 1989, *ibid.,* 1990, 294, and, in the same sense, it applies for the actions in guarantee conducted by the forwarding agents toward the recipient or charger, cf. App. Paris 21 September 1987, in *Le Lamy transp.*, 2020, vol. I, 531.

[110] See Demuth (2013), p. 885 ff.

[111] Cf. App. Versailles 3 September 2013, in *Bull. transp. logist.,* 2013, 539; Cass. com. France 25 January 1972, in *Bull. transp.,* 1972, 148; App. Nancy 29 November 1994, in *Le Lamy transp.*, 2020, vol. I, 531.

[112] See Trib. comm. Paris 29 June 1970, in *Bull. transp.,* 1970, 325. See also Cass. France 21 June 1982, *ibid.,* 1982, 416, according to which an action performed by the forwarding agent in the role of the sender is subjected to Article 32. The conclusion is correct because, in that case, the forwarding agent acts like the sender.

[113] See App. Paris 12 June 1970, in *Bull. transp.,* 1970, 228; BGH 13 January 1978, in *Europ. transp. law,* 1978, no. 13, 402.

[114] See Silingardi et al. (1989), p. 146 ff..

[115] See App. Amiens 19 June 1980, in *Bull. transp.,* 1980, 490.

[116] See RB Antwerp 23 September 1975, in *Europ. transp. law,* 1976, no. 11, 279.

[117] See Demuth (2013), p. 885 ff.

[118] See Haak (1986), p. 294 ff.

Article 28, first paragraph. The same principle does not apply if such action is performed by a third-party; for example, Article 32 cannot be invoked in reply to the request for compensation by a pedestrian injured by the movement of a vehicle[119] or an action brought by someone who is in any case unrelated to transport, albeit with an indirect interest, despite the fact that there are different precedents in various countries.[120]

In fact, there is no regard for the material transfer if the proceedings involve parties other than the contractual ones. The action is one of extra-contractual liability, but is instituted by a third-party and is heterogeneous compared to both the Convention and its Article 32. The latter does not relate to carriage as a physical fact, but to the contract,[121] in accordance with Article 1, first paragraph. It makes no difference that Article 28, first paragraph, resolves the problem of concurrence between contractual and extra-contractual liability. However, the second action refers to Article 32 provided that the parties to the proceedings are the sender, the carrier or the consignee, and the Convention does not concern the non-contractual responsibility of other parties or to third-parties.

Furthermore, "a declaratory action from the carrier to declare that he is not or limitedly liable for damage or loss of the goods falls under the scope of Article 32".[122] This argument is correct, because the action brought by the transporter is regulated by the CMR. Indeed, "the applicability of Article 32 to actions brought by the carrier is not limited to those for payment of his charges".[123]

We discuss the operation of Article 32 in relation to disputes concerning the incorrect execution of custom operations. For some French decisions,[124] the Convention is irrelevant, as the transporter is an agent and the activity is not subject to uniform law.[125] Instead, even for these cases, Article 32 must be invoked, as they are functions ancillary to the transfer of assets, regulated in any event by Article 11, third

[119] See Clarke (2014), p. 126 ff.

[120] See *Shell chemicals U. K. Ltd. v. P. & O. Roadtanks Ltd.*, in *Lloyd's rep.*, 1993, I, 114; OGH 15 March 2005, no. 21/5b, in *Europ. transp. law,* 2005, no. 40, 878, according to which "all claims for compensation which do not fall under Article 17 and Article 28 of the CMR and to which chapter IV of the CMR is therefore inapplicable, are also time-barred in accordance with Article 31, first paragraph, of the CMR".

[121] See Demuth (2013), p. 883 ff.

[122] See HR The Netherlands 18 December 2009, no. 7/11057, in *Europ. transp. law,* 2010, no. 45, 101.

[123] See HR The Netherlands 11 February 2000, no. C98/207, in *Europ. transp. law,* 2000, no. 35, 381.

[124] See App. Amiens 19 June 1980, in *Bull. transp.,* 1980, 490; App. Paris 24 February 1993, *ibid.,* 1994, 52.

[125] See Cass. France 28 May 2002, in *Europ. transp. law*, 2002, no. 37, 508, according to which "the period of limitation laid down in Article 32 is not applicable to actions arising from the performance of a mandate given to the carrier for the performance of customs formalities". Cf. also App. Reims 24 September 1990, in *Bull. transp.,* 1991, 471; App. Paris 4 January 1978, *ibid.,* 1978, 177.

paragraph.[126] According to a minority approach,[127] Article 32 would be relevant only if custom operations were performed by the carrier pursuant to a specific obligation; on the contrary, this would not happen if the latter made use of an assistant. In reality, Article 32 does not operate for actions against a third-party, even if chosen by the transporter, because the scenarios are not disciplined by the Convention, but the opposite is true for disputes brought by the sender or consignee against the transporter, pursuant to Article 11, third paragraph, regardless of whether he employs others for the fulfillment of the undertaken obligations. Reference can be made to regulations on the mandate; nevertheless, the action remains within the perimeter of the CMR. Furthermore, the action instituted by the carrier to recover the tax paid falls within the scope of Article 32.[128] Similar ideas apply for the collection of cash on delivery,[129] in turn governed by the Convention, pursuant to Article 21.

One wonders if Article 32 can be recalled if the sender does not make the goods available or presents them in conditions that do not allow the transfer, so that this does not begin.[130] The Convention concerns the contract and this reasoning, *a fortiori*, is consistent with Article 32. If the aforementioned facts occur before the stipulation and preclude it, the related actions are not governed by uniform law, as they do not concern the nonfulfillment of obligations assumed; however, it is the opposite if the agreement is concluded and its execution is discussed. In fact, the idea that Article 32 refers to the material operation and not to the contract is unfounded. On the basis of a literal exegesis of the expression "*transport*",[131] it is considered indicative of the activity and not of the concluded agreement. This reconstruction is not convincing, because Article 32, first paragraph, refers to the contract, albeit in a synthetic manner, in line with the Convention. A restrictive argument first of all contrasts with Article 1, first paragraph, and with its explicit reference to the agreement. Therefore, the concept did not have to be repeated with the same words, much less in Article 32, first paragraph.

In summary, for all matters regulated by the Convention, Article 32 must be invoked. However, according to part of the case law,[132] this article has a broader

---

[126] See Demuth (2013), p. 883 ff. See also App. Lyon 6 July 1983, in *Bull. transp.*, 1984, 339; App. Versailles 25 November 1999, *ibid.*, 2000, 274; App. Colmar 9 November 1979, in *Le Lamy transp.*, 2020, vol. I, 529, according to which "*les formalités douanières ne sont que l'accessoire nécessaires du contrat de transport lorqu'elles sont accomplies par le transporteur lui – même. Il convient de souligner, à ce propos, que l'artcle 11 de la CMR se situe dans un chapitre intitulé 'conclusion et exécution du contrat de transport'*".

[127] See Trib. Orleans 24 March 1987, in *Bull. transp.*, 1987, 662.

[128] See Cass. France 28 May 2002, in *Bull. transp.*, 2002, 403.

[129] See Cass. com. France 6 February 1985, in *Le Lamy transp.*, 2020, vol. I, 480.

[130] See Pesce (1995), p. 183 ff., nt. 129.

[131] For the approach criticized here, see Pesce (1995), p. 183 ff. The English text reads as follows: "carriage".

[132] See OGH 15 March 2005, in *Europ. transp. law*, 2005, no. 40, 878.

scope. The case of the action against the carrier for incomplete non-execution[133] is controversial, according to some not regulated by the Convention (in this research, it is argued that this case does not exist or, better put, has no autonomy with regard to loss, damage or delay). For those who believe that the issue is recognizable and is within the scope of uniform law,[134] there is no problem about the operation of Article 32, which certainly applies. This is all the more true if we share the approach herein preferred. Anyway, the opposite is not true, as, according to a decision,[135] wrongly oriented to exclude liability for failure to perform from the scope of the Convention and to refer it to national law, Article 32 would still be applicable. This reductive interpretation, which cannot be endorsed in its basis, is literal, that is, deduced from the text of Article 32, first paragraph, which would concern all actions related to transport, regardless of whether domestic law must be implemented, as some believe,[136] in an unfounded way, with regard to complete failure to perform.

9.2.2 Willful Misconduct and Equivalent Default

Article 32 provides for an extension to 3 years of the term "*dans le cas de dol ou de faute considérée, d'après la loi de la juridiction saisie, comme équivalent au dol*".[137] On the notion of willful misconduct and equivalent default, there are no reasons why the interpretation should differ from that of Article 29, first paragraph.[138] The short term guarantees the rapid stability of relations and requires the timely initiation of disputes. These requirements do not collide much with an extension, as they do with one based on assumptions that are difficult to evaluate in advance, most of which is left to the discretion of the judge, with wide fluctuations in the decisions. If Article 32 wants to promote certainty, without prejudice to the full discretion of the Convention, it is contradictory to anchor the extension to an analysis of the conduct with such broad nuances and with reference to questionable judicial choices, which

[133] See BGH 18 February 1972, in *Europ. transp. law,* 1972, no. 7, 860; Polish Supreme Court 7 March 2017, II CSK 242/2016.

[134] See Greiter (1986), p. 280 ff.

[135] See *Shell chemicals U. K. Ltd. v. P. & O. Roadtanks Ltd.*, in *Lloyd's rep.*, 1993, I, 114.

[136] See Messent and Glass (2018), p. 310 ff.

[137] The English text reads as follows: "in the case of willful misconduct or such default as in accordance with the law of the court or tribunal seized of the case, is considered as equivalent to willful misconduct". Cf. Cass. France 12 December 1989, in *Europ. transp. law,* 1991, no. 26, 359, for a scenario of extension of the prescription terms for serious misconduct; App. Alicante 13 December 2013, no. 466, in *Jur,* 2014, 172739; OLG Düsseldorf 20 March 2013, in *TranspR,* 2013, 196; Hof Hertogenbosch 13 February 2018, in *Europ. transp. law,* 2018, no. 53, 460, that applied the extension of the prescription term in case of willful misconduct; OLG Hamburg 7 March 2018, *ibid.,* 2018, no. 53.

[138] Cf. OGH 30 January 2019, in *TranspR,* 2019, 390, according to which Article 29 and Article 32 have the same approach in referring to the national law of the place where legal proceedings were instituted to identify the default equated to willful misconduct and, therefore, equivalent default.

become indisputable only after the decision. This can lead to instrumental actions,[139] in which those who do not respect the annual deadline invoke the more extensive legal framework. Thus, the procedural opposition is harsh,[140] but it is less reasonable than the one that occurred when the compensation limit was set, based on identical concepts of willful misconduct and equivalent fault. If, in this case, it is rational to guarantee full compensation for prejudice, owing to the greater seriousness of the behavior,[141] the same reasoning remains unconvincing when discussing the prescription, whose regulation should be linear, precisely for the benefit of certainty.[142]

Furthermore, Article 32, first paragraph, does not consider that willful misconduct or equivalent default may depend on the conduct of employees or assistants. In fact, there is no indication similar to that of Article 29, second paragraph, and this leads some[143] to adhere to the restrictive argument on the alleged inapplicability of the extended term for the behavior of collaborators. By virtue of Article 3,[144] prescription period is 3 years even if the willful misconduct or one characterized by equivalent default takes place with the intervention of a person, employed in or connected to the organization.

In fact, Article 3 codifies a general principle, relating to all cases concerning illegitimate behavior. Essentially, the rule has shown foresight, as, in 1956, the structural system of the average operator was certainly not so advanced as it is today. Therefore, Article 3 invites us to evaluate the activity as a whole, rather than the discrete actions of an entrepreneur or a corporate director, and any restrictive interpretation would lead to paradoxical consequences. For example, in established companies, there would never be a willful misconduct or an equivalent fault, because it is unthinkable that the directors deal with single transport, and the intervention of employees or, in any case, of assistants is inevitable and entirely reasonable.

Finally, there is no reason to exclude the extension of the deadline if the willful misconduct or equivalent fault is specific to the consignee or the sender. The case is

---

[139] See Haak (1986), p. 296 ff., according to whom "the escape offered here has been tested many times, although generally in vain". See App. Paris 25 June 2009, in *Bull. transp.,* 2009, 498, which, having ascertained that the carrier had acted in respect of precautionary rules, did not apply the extension of the prescription term. See also Cass. France 7 January 2003, in *Europ. transp. law,* 2003, no. 38, 788, according to which "serious misconduct is not committed, in the course of a carriage by road in Italy, where the carrier had stationed his vehicle and was guarding it in the evening in front of the place of delivery and his was attacked at that moment by four armed men who threatened him, took him hostage, and made off with his lorry". Furthermore, see Trib. Milano 14 June 2001, in *Dir. transp.,* 2003, 674, for which "the behavior of a driver who left the vehicle close to the restaurant where he stopped for lunch in a non-surveyed but not isolated area" it is not "a serious misconduct"; OLG Hamburg 7 March 2018, in *Europ. transp. law,* 2018, no. 53, 305.

[140] See App. Grenoble 22 April 2004, in *Bull. transp.,* 2004, 335; Cass. France 7 March 2007, *ibid.,* 2007, 259; Cass. Paris 16 January 2007, *ibid.,* 2007, 79; Cass. France 10 March 2004, *ibid.,* 2004, 207; App. Paris 3 March 2004, *ibid.,* 2004, 207.

[141] Cf. App. Paris 28 May 2003, in *Unif. law rev.,* 2004, 208. See also Krings (1999), p. 787 ff.

[142] See Clarke (2014), p. 128 ff.

[143] See Dorrestein (1977), p. 435 ff.

[144] See Haak (1986), p. 296 ff.

rare, but the extensive expression of Article 32, first paragraph, is clear, and there is no need to compare the contrasting positions of different parties. If they fall within the prescribed aggravated liability, the extension operates in any case.

9.2.3 The Effective Date

Article 32, first paragraph, identifies three different moments from which the prescription period can run. The choice is strange, because considerable complexities derive from it, and it is the source of great case law debate,[145] with numerous question marks,[146] while nothing has stood in the way of an unequivocal clarification. Furthermore, there are significant differences in the time allowed for action, up to a quarter of the ordinary time limit. The carrier, whose initiatives mostly fall within the provision of Article 32, first paragraph, letter c), benefits from this,[147] with some necessary criticism of rationality of the text and its balance.[148]

Besides, the Convention shows its age, due to references that are inconsistent with the current season of the so-called "traceability" of many itineraries. In fact, from Article 32, first paragraph, letter b), we can infer the implicit belief that the journey could last for several weeks and could begin 30 days after the goods have been delivered to the transporter. This implies a significant discrepancy from the current technical context and indirectly heightens the intensity of the debate on provisions that are often suspected of being irrational and causing injustice. As there are three systems on identifying the effective date, in the same proceedings the term can be fulfilled for one party to the trial, but not for the other. In any case, often two rules operate in the same proceeding.[149]

According to Article 32, first paragraph, letter a), in the event of partial loss, damage or delay, the limitation period begins on the day the goods are redelivered.[150] Despite the opposite traditional argument,[151] the concept of redelivery must not be accorded as a unitary value throughout the Convention. In fact, for the limited purposes of Article 32, first paragraph, only the consignee's full knowledge of the damage is relevant. For Article 32, first paragraph, letter a), if the

---

145 See Messent and Glass (2018), p. 311 ff.; Sánchez - Gamborino (2001b), p. 871 ff.

146 Cf. Wesolowsky (2013), p. 344 ff.

147 Cf. Haak (1986), p. 299 ff., according to whom "it may perhaps create the impression that the carrier is in a better position as regards the period of limitation than claimant having regard to the fact that he has an extra three months available to him".

148 Cf. Clarke (2014), p. 132 ff.; Loewe (1976), p. 392 ff.

149 Cf. Cabrera Cánovas (2012), p. 153 ff.

150 Cf. App. Paris 20 February 2003, in *Le Lamy transp.*, 2020, vol. I, 531; App. Nîmes 13 December 2007, *ibid.,* 2020, 531; App. Versailles 18 February 2010, *ibid.,* 2020, 531, for a case in which the goods were returned after having been found following a theft. See also OGH 1 July 2009, in *TranspR,* 2010, 348; Otte (2018b), p. 1555 ff.

151 See Messent and Glass (2018), p. 311 ff.

recipient has material disposal of goods, there is no reason to postpone the beginning of the term, with a reading consistent with that of Article 30, first paragraph. In fact, the same expression is used in Article 30, first paragraph, "*livraison*",[152] unlike the concept of "making available" of Article 30, third paragraph.[153]

For a Dutch decision,[154] there would be no redelivery with the sole bailment of goods in the warehouse prior to the withdrawal by the consignee. However, according to a Swedish ruling,[155] the situation in which, after having refused the load because it is damaged, the recipient agrees to keep it on behalf of the sender would fall under letter a). For the first decision, a manifestation of will is required; for the second, material availability is sufficient. The last solution is convincing, because, for these purposes, the redelivery is identified with knowledge of the prejudice, that is, with the arrival in a place where the recipient comes into contact with the load. At that point, he can verify it and take any action.

In a British case when the cargo arrived damaged, it was refused and returned to the sender as per his instructions.[156] It was considered that the situation did not fall under Article 32, first paragraph, letter a), and national regulations were applied. In general, for the action by the recipient, awareness of the prejudice is relevant and, consequently, the refusal to accept subsequent to his knowledge of the state of the load is irrelevant. In this regard, although this cannot be said for other principles of the Convention, the redelivery must be understood in a material sense and the refusal indicates a possible control over the condition of goods, so that there is no reason to postpone the start of the prescription period.[157]

In case the sender requests the return of the cargo, the power of countermand is exercised and a new journey begins, albeit within the scope of the same convention. In this new journey, the shipper is at the same time the consignee, with the obvious need to pay a second consideration; as regards the first transfer, Article 32, first paragraph, letter a), applies and domestic law may not be invoked. The same ideas apply to a dispute that arose in Belgium, in which the consignee refused to accept the load, which was partly destroyed during the journey, and the goods were returned to the sender after arrival, following the refusal of the recipient.[158]

In case of damage to a load still in transit, the shipper could exercise the counter - order, provided for by Article 12, and request the return of goods in his favor; for the

---

[152]The English text reads as follows: "takes delivery".

[153]The English text reads as follows: "placed at disposal", whereas in the French one we read as follows: "*à la disposition*".

[154]Cf. Hof Hertogenbosch 21 December 1965, in *Europ. transp. law,* 1966, no. 1, 698; GH Gravenhage 10 May 1978, *ibid.*, 1978, no. 13, 606.

[155]Cf. App. Western Sweden 9 April 1974.

[156]See *Moto Vespa S. A. v. Mat (Britannia express) Ltd.*, in *Lloyd's rep.*, 1979, 175.

[157]For the opposite sense, see App. Lyon 18 September 2014, in *Le Lamy transp.*, 2020, vol. I, 531; App. Besançon 8 January 2014, in *Bull. transp. logist.*, 2014, 51; App. Paris 4 June 2008, *ibid.*, 2008, 433, according to which prescription begins to run "*du jour du déchargement en entrepôt, après retour en France, de la marchandise refuséè à l'étranger*".

[158]See App. Brussels 28 June 1969, in *Europ. transp. law,* 1969, no. 4, 925.

purposes of Article 32, first paragraph, letter a),[159] the modification of the place of destination or the indication of a different consignee are an expression of the aforementioned power and the journey takes place, albeit with a different itinerary from the initial one. When the cargo arrives at the sender, who requests it, there is a redelivery and the prescription starts, always in the execution of the same contract.[160]

Furthermore, during a carriage of several goods to the same consignee, an item was lost, found after more than a year. According to a German decision,[161] it would not be a definitive loss and, as the object was recovered, the case was qualified as a delay, with the consequent application of Article 32, first paragraph, letter a), starting from the redelivery, which took place 12 months later. This argument is unconvincing, as it is a scenario of presumed loss, pursuant to Article 20. The prescription begins after the loss. Following the discovery, Article 20, third paragraph, applies.

Likewise, Article 32, first paragraph, letter a), operates if, in a carriage of two packages to the same person, one is lost, and the limitation period starts from the delivery of stored goods, if the loss is certain, because it is unnecessary to wait for the term of Article 20. Finally, if a single journey leads to several arrivals close to each other, the prescription begins from the last one.[162] There is no contradiction with what has been stated about the German case,[163] as the chronological consistency of the two redeliveries causes a delay and not a partial loss; it all depends on the operation of Article 20.

It matters little that the consignee informs the sender of the cases mentioned in Article 32, first paragraph, letter a), as knowledge of the former starts the term for anyone wishing to act. If the inertia affects a possible initiative of the shipper, he can ask the recipient for compensation, on the basis of national law, with a situation that is extraneous to uniform one, but that does not have any impact on the possible fulfillment of the term. In fact, Article 32, first paragraph, letter a), does not impose any communication of the recipient to the sender and this is irrelevant for the prescription.

According to a French decision,[164] there is a delay if, after having fallen during the journey, an item is returned to the shipper and by the latter to the consignee himself, after repair. The term would run from the final arrival and not from the moment of the accident, despite the fact that more than a year has passed. However, we are forgetting Article 20. This solution remains unconvincing, as the recipient should act within the limits of Article 32, first paragraph, letter a), after having ascertained a partial loss, without prejudice to the consequences of the expiry of the

[159] Cf. *Worldwide carriers Ltd. v. Ardtran international Ltd.*, in *Lloyd's rep.*, 1983, 61.

[160] Cf. App. Lyon 12 May 2016, in *Le Lamy transp.*, 2020, vol. I, 532; App. Pau 11 February 1991, overturned by Cass. com. France 16 March 1993, in *Bull. transp. logist.*, 1993, 262.

[161] Cf. OLG Düsseldorf 23 November 1989.

[162] See Trib. com. Paris 5 May 2004, in *Bull. transp. logist.*, 2005, 391.

[163] Cf. OLG Düsseldorf 23 November 1989.

[164] Cf. App. Orleans 22 December 2005, in *Bull. transp.*, 2006, 15.

thirty-day term of Article 20. The one that took place a year later is a new carriage and, if necessary, the term of letter a) runs only for the prejudices that occurred in the second journey.

Article 32, first paragraph, letter b), concerns total loss, in the presence of which the prescription operates from the thirtieth day following the expiry of the term agreed for the completion of the operation[165] or, failing that, from the sixtieth day after receipt of the goods by the carrier.[166] The loss in an economic sense[167] would also be included in this scenario, for some; however, the solution is unconvincing.[168] In fact, delivery must be understood as the moment in which the consignee is informed of the condition of the load to be able to evaluate it. Therefore, it does not matter whether the cargo arrives damaged or permanently destroyed. In both cases, the recipient can immediately take action, and letter b) is designed only for cases in which the goods do not arrive,[169] also in relation to the expiry of the thirty-day term of Article 20. In fact, the difficulty of acquiring information justifies the recognition of an additional period, before the beginning of the prescription. This is always viewed against the background of the organizational methods of 1956, for which the so-called traceability was unthinkable. For other purposes, the loss in an economic sense can be equated to a physical one, but not with regard to Article 32, when, if ever, the comparison must be made between the first and the damage.

In case of transport to multiple consignees, the fate of each individual package[170] is relevant; if only one is lost, letter b) applies, although the others arrive, while there is partial loss and letter a) operates if there is only one recipient. With regard to transport with multiple carriers, the question arises as to how we should determine the so-called take-over to make the 60 days run. As it can be observed, "the appropriate date is that on which the goods were taken over by that carrier" and the solution is convincing, although it may not be easy to identify the relative moment.[171]

---

[165] Cf. Spain Supreme Court 13 May 2008, no. 327, in *RJ,* 2008, 3066; App. Versailles 14 November 2019, in *Le Lamy transp.*, 2020, vol. I, 532; App. Paris 28 March 2019, *ibid.,* 2019, 532; App. Riom 12 June 2002, in *Bull. transp. logist.,* 2003, 83. Cf. App. Paris 13 April 2018, *ibid.,* 2020, 252, according to which the term must be stated in the consignment note or written on an invoice, but the same is not relevant if it is included in the sale agreement. See also Otte (2018b), p. 1556 ff.

[166] Cf. App. Paris 18 June 1997, in *Bull. transp. logist.,* 1997, 523; App. Riom 10 October 2001, *ibid.,* 2001, 745; App. Pau 10 September 2007, in *Le Lamy transp.*, 2020, vol. I, 532; App. Tolosa 26 November 2014, *ibid.,* 2020, 532; App. Douai 8 December 2016, in *Bull. transp. logist.,* 2017, 15.

[167] See *Thermo engineers Ltd. v. Ferrymasters Ltd.*, in *Lloyd's rep.,* 1981, 200.

[168] Along similar lines, see *William Tatton & Co. Ltd. v. Ferrymasters Ltd.*, in *Lloyd's rep.,* 1974, 203; *Worldwilde carriers Ltd. v. Ardtran international Ltd., ibid.,* 1983, 61.

[169] Cf. Cass. France 18 November 1953, in *Bull. transp.,* 1954, 136; Cass. France 7 February 1955, *ibid.,* 1955, 207; Trib. com. Bobigny 29 January 1993, in *Le Lamy transp.*, 2020, vol. I, 532.

[170] Cf. Hof Brussels 16 November 1977, in *Europ. transp. law,* 1980, no. 15, 319; RB Brussels 28 February 1975, *ibid.,* 1975, no. 10, 419.

[171] See Messent and Glass (2018), p. 315 ff.

Article 32, first paragraph, letter c), has a residual value and includes all the cases not attributable to letter a) or letter b), so that the term runs 3 months after the conclusion of the contract.[172] According to some,[173] letter c) would not be applicable to loss, damage or delay, not attributable to the previous cases and, in particular, to that of letter a), with the consequence that one should refer to national law. However, the problem does not arise, because either the goods arrive and so letter a) operates, or reference has to be made to letter b), and letter c) include certain actions undertaken by the sender or the consignee. It could be for example a claim for compensation on the subject of cash on delivery[174] or one for restitution of the excess amount paid by way of consideration.[175] The provision refers to the action for recovery of the undue payment[176] if, by mistake, the recipient pays the costs twice.

Usually, letter c) concerns the rights of the carrier, both for his consideration[177] and for the redress of prejudices, for example, defects in packaging or loading, negligent behavior of the sender,[178] or damage suffered by the vehicle and provoked by the movement of the load during the transfer, in case they are attributable to the shipper.[179] The same is true when the transporter requests relief for the suffered damage, because he holds the vehicle at the customs office pending the completion of related operations,[180] for violation of tax regulations, attributable to the sender. For this reason, the provision is often considered an indirect protection of the carrier.[181]

In fact, he can often count on a three-month extension of the term, as it remains the same, but the starting date is postponed. Nowadays, in particular, the beginning of the journey is almost always immediate or very close to the stipulation of the contract, and it is unjustified to leave such a long reaction period. These objections on the transporter's advantage are not always convincing; although in rare cases, he

---

[172] Cf. Hof Antwerp 22 February 2021, in *Europ. transp. law,* 2020, no. 61 56. See also Otte (2018 b), p. 1557 ff.

[173] See *Moto Vespa S. A. v. Mat (Britannia express) Ltd.,* in *Lloyd's rep.,* 1979, 175

[174] Cf. GH Hertogenbosch 13 January 1970, in *Europ. transp. law,* 1971, no. 6, 817.

[175] See BGH 18 February 1972, in *Europ. transp. law,* 1972, no. 7, 860.

[176] See LG Graz 5 April 2000, 5 R 40/00, in *Europ. transp. law,* 2002, no. 37, 360.

[177] Cf. App. Paris 22 May 2002, in *Bull. transp. logist.,* 2002, 567; App. Paris 21 November 2007, in *Le Lamy transp.*, 2020, vol. I, 532; App. Tolosa 22 December 2016, in *Bull. transp. logist.,* 2017, 79; App. Grenoble 18 September 2014, in *Le Lamy transp.*, 2020, vol. I, 532; App. Besançon 6 January 2013, *ibid.,* 2020, 532; App. Nîmes 16 May 2012, *ibid.,* 2020, 532; Federal Tribunal of the Swiss Confederation 19 December 1985, in Federal Informatic System; LG Lübeck 8 February 2001, in *TranspR,* 2001, 171, according to which prescription of Article 31, first paragraph, is applied for the repayment of undue compensation paid with regard to a journey in which damage has occurred.

[178] See App. Paris 4 March 2010, in *Bull. transp.,* 2010, 655; App. Lyon 18 December 2008, *ibid.* 2009, 483.

[179] See App. Lyon 18 December 2008, in *Bull. transp.,* 2009, 483.

[180] See BGH 11 December 1981, in *Europ. transp. law,* 1983, no. 18, 63. Cf. also App. Colmar 23 November 2016, in *Bull. transp. logist.,* 2016, 722.

[181] See Demuth (2013), p. 909 ff.

is placed in a difficult situation, because the transport lasts more than 3 months.[182] However, the circumstance is irrelevant on a systematic level. Due to its residual nature, Article 32, first paragraph, letter c), includes all actions not attributable to the previous provisions, since, as a whole, Article 32 proposes an organic regulation,[183] albeit referring only to the situations disciplined by the Convention and, for example, not to the action of unjust enrichment.[184]

Finally, before the conclusion of the deal, the carrier can hold the goods for another reason, for example in custody, under a storage or logistics contract, according to organizational models much more widespread today than in 1956 and, perhaps for this reason, not taken into adequate consideration by the Convention. Both to establish the date of conclusion of the transport agreement, pursuant to letter b), and, above all, to define the so-called "assumption of responsibility", mentioned by letter c), the storage or logistics contract must be distinguished from the one on carriage. Failing that, if previous possession were considered relevant, the prescription could always be enforced, if this preparatory phase continued for a long time, with an irrational solution.

Therefore, for the purposes of letter b), only the stipulation of the contract must be taken into account and the previous custody has no effect. With regard to letter c), the order in which the sender arranges the transfer must be evaluated, regardless of whether the goods are already in the material availability of the carrier. In fact, the concept of "assumption of responsibility" must not be given a physical interpretation. If the transporter holds in the interest of others, he takes charge of the load for the purposes of the Convention when he receives the order to transfer, despite picking the cargo from his warehouse, regardless of IT methods used to make such contact with the shipper and to receive his instructions.

Finally, and rightly so, it is believed that the reference to "*le jour indiqué ci - dessus comme point de départ de la prescription n'est pas compris dans le délai*"[185] concerns not only Article 32, first paragraph, letter c), but all cases covered by the entire provision.[186]

9.2.4 The Relevance of the Period of Limitation

Article 32, first paragraph, letter b) and letter c), creates a space of time in which the prescription does not run.[187] During this period, you can exercise the action without

[182] See BGH 11 December 1981, in *Europ. transp. law,* 1983, no. 18, 63.

[183] See App. Brussels 28 June 1969, in *Europ. transp. law,* 1969, no. 4, 925.

[184] In the opposite sense, see LG Graz 5 April 2000, in *Europ. transp. law,* 2002, no. 37, 360.

[185] The English text reads as follows: "the day on which the period of limitation begins to run shall not be included in the period".

[186] See Messent and Glass (2018), p. 318 ff.; Putzeys (1981), p. 388 ff.

[187] See Haak (1986), p. 301 ff.

waiting for the term to begin. However, in this case, neither the suspension nor the possible interruption operates, although there are opposing opinions.[188] In fact, it was observed that, "if a claimant submits a claim before the actual period of limitation begins to run, it would however be unfair to deny him the effects provided for in paragraph 2; however, these effects must then be regarded as occurred from the moment when the actual period of limitation has begun to run".[189] On the contrary, a prescription period that has not yet started cannot be interrupted or suspended.[190] To this end, the previous period indicated by Article 32, first paragraph, letter b) and letter c), must be concluded, and the prescription must have begun; the solution may also be unjust,[191] but it is inevitable, because the interpretation is literal, at least for the continental law.

The national law of the trial regulates the exercise of the action or the raising of an "*exception*", without any interference from the Convention. This is reasonable, as such matters do not belong to substantive regulation, but only to procedural one. Therefore, in many continental countries, the "*exception*" of prescription can only be formulated by the party and cannot operate *ex officio*, as it has rightly been stated in France[192] and as it must be held in Italy.

If anything, surprisingly, Article 32, fourth paragraph, does not apply the rule deriving from the well-known maxim "*quae temporalia ad agendum, perpetua ad excipiendum*", stating that the term refers not only to the exercise of the action, but also to the formulation of the "*exception*", with a questionable solution, such as to influence many parties accustomed to some continental laws to make frequent errors. Furthermore, as is inevitable, "*exceptions*" are raised after the commencement of the trial, sometimes after a certain time period, according to the relative legal framework and the duration of the trials.

Therefore, the limitation period of "*exceptions*", coinciding with that of the actions, acquires importance, without prejudice to various regimes on the effective date. For instance, this would be the case of a carrier who asks for payment of the consideration, taking advantage of Article 32, first paragraph, letter c), and placing the sender or the consignee in a predicament, despite the failure to punctually fulfill the redelivery obligations. The latter parties may have their "*exceptions*" extinguished, so that they are unable to invoke the termination of the contract or, in any case, to assert their credit, even for the purposes of set-off.[193] Nor is it worth

---

[188] Cf. Loewe (1976), p. 392 ff. Cf. App. Amiens 11 October 2012, in *Le Lamy transp.*, 2020, vol. I, 533. For an opposite view, App. Angers 1 March 2016, *Bull. transp. logist.*, 2016, 175.

[189] See Loewe (1976), p. 392 ff.

[190] See Libouton (1973), p. 66 ff.; RB Antwerp 16 May 2003, in *Europ. transp. law,* 2003, no. 38, 360.

[191] Cf. Libouton (1973), p. 66 ff.

[192] See Cass. France 25 September 1970, in *Bull. transp.*, 1970, 32.

[193] For the applicability of Article 32 to the counterclaim, cf. Hof Antwerp 24 October 2005, in *Europ. transp. law,* 2006, no. 41, 297.

arguing that they could interrupt or suspend the running of the limitation period, because they could be satisfied by a damage insurer.

The traditional maxim on the prescription of the action and not of the "*exception*" is intended to prevent such situations. It is unclear why this should not be adapted to international transport, in which, in cases such as the one described, if one does not want to rely on the suspension or on the interruption of the limitation period, it is necessary to act preventively, within the limits of prescription, in the same way as the national law of the court seized with the matter. Especially if we consider the often small amount of the carrier's credits, with the advantage of the delayed effect of the prescription period, the application of the "*quae temporalia ad agendum, perpetua ad excipiendum*" maxim would have allowed the consignee or the sender that serene defense, unbothered by the running of the prescription period, which the same principle seeks to guarantee. In fact, this is in the interest of justice.

9.2.5 The Written Claim and Its Effects

According to Article 32, second paragraph, the first "*réclamation écrite*"[194] addressed to the carrier suspends the running of the prescription period, until he replies, again in writing, thereby returning any documents attached to the notice.[195] The time prior to sending of the letter is added to the subsequent one with regard to the effects of the suspensive event.[196] The rule does not concern the prescription of rights of the transporter, due to the clear wording, so that the provision is unfavorable to him and has been designed for the most serious cases of nonfulfillment, i. e., loss, damage or delay.

However, the transporter can lodge a complaint pursuant to Article 32, second paragraph, against another one, in the event of participation by more than one of them.[197] Article 32, second paragraph, focuses on the party against whom the claim is addressed and identifies him with the "*transporteur*",[198] but the fact that the sender, consignee or another carrier is making the complaint is irrelevant.[199] Article

[194] The English text reads as follows: "a written claim".

[195] Cf. App. Barcellona 26 May 2006, in *Jur*, 2007, 72368.

[196] See Putzeys (1981), p. 394 ff.; Cabrera Cánovas (2012), p. 155 ff.

[197] Cf. Gragnoli (1990), p. 67. In senso contrario, v. Demuth (2013), p. 917 ff.

[198] The English text reads as follows: "carrier". Cf. Cass. com. France 14 April 1992, in *Bull. transp.*, 1981, 538; App. Paris 28 April 1987, *ibid.*, 1987, 424; App. Aix - en - Provence 15 February 1979, *ibid.*, 1979, 352, according to which any action instituted by the carrier against the shipper or the consignee recipient, for instance for the payment of transport fees or for compensation for damage caused to the vehicle, does not equate to a complaint and, therefore, are not capable of suspending the prescription.

[199] Cf. BGH 8 July 2004, in *TranspR*, 2004, 357, according to which an attorney can send the warning pursuant to Article 32, second paragraph, as long as he clarifies the grounds for his intervention; LG Aachen 28 November 2006, *ibid.*, 2007, 40. See also Otte (2018b), p. 1558 ff.

32, second paragraph, does not specify whether the formal claim submitted by the shipper or the consignee can suspend the prescription period in favor of the other party. The restrictive solution is the most convincing, because it is consistent with the principle according to which interruptive or suspensive acts have effect only in favor of those who put them in place,[200] although this solution is the least favorable for the carrier, who could witness the two claims simultaneously communicated to him, for example, one from the sender for damage and the other from the consignee for delay.

Later, the claim can be presented by the insurer who has subrogated the rights of others,[201] and it is discussed whether it is necessary that this subrogation precedes the sending of the letter. For some French decisions, this is indispensable[202] and the argument is rational, because this subrogation is the prerequisite for the notification. Furthermore, it can come from the shipper's-commission agent, as the sender's "*mandataire qualifié*",[203] although it must only be received by the carrier[204] and not by the "*commissionaire du transport*";[205] likewise, the letter received by the transporter's insurer does not suspend the term.[206] With regard to travel with multiple carriers,[207] the claim addressed to one of them would not suspend the term against the others, even if it concerned compensation for the entire damage. The

[200] Cf. App. Paris 21 December 2006, in *Bull. transp. logist.*, 2007, 44; App. Toulouse 7 December 1989, in *Le Lamy transp.*, 2020, vol. I, 535; Cass. com. France, 9 January 1990, in *Bull. transp.*, 1990, 362.

[201] Cf. Cass. France 4 October 1982, in *Bull. transp.*, 1982, 549; App. Lyon 2 March 1978, *ibid.*, 1978, 382. Cf. also App. Paris 31 March 2004, in *Bull. transp. logist.*, 2004, 297; App. Paris 17 November 2004, *ibid.*, 2005, 86; App. Poitiers 3 April 2012, in *Le Lamy transp.*, 2020, vol. I, 534. See also App. Agen 19 March 1980, in *Bull. transp.*, 1980, 502, according to which the complaint can be submitted by an "*agent général d'assurence*"; App. Dijon 26 January 1983, in *Le Lamy transp.*, 2020, vol. I, 534, for which the complaint can be submitted by a "*le Comité des assureurs maritimes*".

[202] Cf. App. Agen 19 March 1980, in *Bull. transp.*, 1980, 502; Cass. France 4 October 1982, *ibid.*, 1982, 549; confirms the need for the insurer's preventive subrogation in the charger or recipient's rights. App. Aix en Provence 8 October 1968, *ibid.*, 1969, 18.

[203] Cf. App. Paris 22 January 1986, in *Bull. transp.*, 1986, 482. See also App. Paris 14 December 2011, in *Le Lamy transp.*, 2020, vol. I, 534; App. Paris 3 December 2008, in *Bull. transp. logist.*, 2008, 781; App. Toulouse 26 November 2014, in *Le Lamy transp.*, 2020, vol. I, 534. See also App. Paris 24 October 1989, *ibid.*, 2020, 534, according to which there is a suspension when the complaint, sent to the forwarding agent, is also transmitted to the carrier. Cf. furthermore App. Versailles 2 December 2010, *ibid.*, 2020, 534, according to which a complaint addressed to the carrier as well as to the forwarding agent has suspensive effects towards the former only.

[204] Cf. Cass. com. France 4 March 2003, in *Bull. transp. logist.*, 2003, 199.

[205] Cf. App. Paris 7 November 1975, in *Bull. transp.*, 1975, 515; App. Paris 23 June 1976, *ibid.*, 1976, 332.

[206] Cf. App. Lyon 2 March 1978, in *Bull. transp.*, 1978, 382. For a contrary position, cf. Libouton (1973), p. 66 ff.; Cabrera Cánovas (2012), p. 157 ff., according to whom the Supreme Court "*establece que la reclamación escrita dirigida solo al transpotista suspende la prescripción también para el asegurador de este*".

[207] Cf. *Worldwide carriers Ltd. v. Ardtran international Ltd.*, in *Lloyd's rep.*, 1983, 61.

solution remains unconvincing, because there is a passive joint responsibility between the carriers and, if the action can be proposed for the whole relief against a co-debtor, the claim must be effective for all with the same consequence.

The "*réclamation*" must be made in writing[208] and it is not necessary to attach supporting documents,[209] but the carrier should return them, if transmitted.[210] The Convention is exhibiting its age, as photocopying machines were not widely available in 1956; in fact, it was stated, "at the time when the CMR was drawn up, photocopies were unknown or fairly rare. There were difficulties in the production of copies of long documents and the law of procedure of many countries required the time-consuming and expensive business of certification. It was therefore quite normal practice to send the carrier original documents".[211] At present, the idea of replication with the physical movement of documents (completely superfluous) is quite odd, as whoever sends any document keeps a copy, and this attention to irrelevant aspects makes no sense. The rule is too severe in sanctioning restitution of the photocopies, often attributable to simple forgetfulness.

It would be necessary to return the original documents,[212] but the transmission of photocopies has been considered sufficient.[213] There is an ongoing debate as to whether photocopied documents should be returned as well, and this is excessive, because the creditor is in the possession of the originals.[214] *A fortiori*, if there is a partial acceptance of the complaint based on the silence of the Convention, the shipment of the material becomes irrelevant.[215] These doubts are sometimes difficult to resolve, because the wording is clear; however, the consequences are unreasonable. An abrogative interpretation of the provision is not possible, but, at least, the failure to return photocopies can be considered ineffective and the operation of the rule is limited to cases, at present to be considered very rare, in which the originals

---

[208] Cf. Demuth (2013), p. 113 ff. See also Mayer (1997), p. 175 ff. See also Cass. Italy 6 July 2020, n. 13811, in *Giur. it. rep.*, 2020.

[209] Cf. App. Paris 25 March 1982, in *Bull. transp.*, 1982, 434; App. Paris 31 March 2004, in *Le Lamy transp.*, 2020, vol. I, 533; App. Grenoble 3 October 2001, in *Bull. transp. logist.*, 2001, 711; App. Versailles 2 December 2010, *ibid.*, 2010, 735; App. Grenoble 3 October 2001, in *Le Lamy transp.*, 2020, vol. I, 534, according to which, "*le seul formalisme imposé par le CMR est l'écrit*"; App. Brussels 27 February 1996, in *Europ. transp. law,* 1996, no. 31, 833.

[210] Cf. Trib. com. Chartres 1 April 2003, in *Bull. transp. logist.,* 2003, 422; Cass. Belgium 27 September 1984, in *Le Lamy transp.*, 2020, vol. I, 536; App. Reims 22 March 1976, in *Bull. transp.,* 11979, 84; App. Krakow 22 July 2020, according to which the carrier must return the documents attached to the complaint; Hof Antwerp 2 June 2003, in *Europ. transp. law,* 2004, no. 39, 407; Spain Supreme Court 24 February 1995, no. 143, in *Rj,* 1995, 1111, according to which Article 32, second paragraph, "*no declara ineficaz la interrupción cuando no se acompañan documentos*".

[211] Cf. Loewe (1996), p. 435 ff. See also De Beule (1988), p. 654 ff.; Radionov (2020), p. 16 ff.

[212] Cf. RB Roermond 15 October 1970, in *Europ. transp. law,* 1971, no. 6, 839.

[213] Cf. *Microfine Minerals & Chemicals Ltd. v. Transferry Shipping Co. Ltd.*, in *Lloyd'd rep.*, 1991, 630; Hof Antwerp 2 June 2003, in *Europ. transp. law,* 2004, no. 39, 407.

[214] Cf. BGH 21 November 1996, in *Europ. transp. law,* 1997, no. 32, 442.

[215] Cf. OLG Celle 13 January 1975, 1975, in *Europ. transp. law,* 1975, no. 10, 410.

have been transmitted. Moreover, with a careful reading of the current economic evolution, the sending of the "*reclamation*" by fax[216] or e-mail[217] has been deemed adequate.

There is no certainty about the moment in which the suspensive effect occurs, whether from the sending of the notice or from its arrival,[218] although this latter option is to be preferred,[219] as it emphasizes knowledge on the part of the carrier.

With regards to the content of the complaint, the confirmation of reservations formulated at the time of redelivery[220] is insufficient, but an indication of costs incurred to remedy the damage is said to be adequate.[221] Thus, it is necessary to quantify the prejudice, although a precise reconstruction of facts is not required.[222] The claim must contain sufficient information to guide the carrier's decision,[223] as, failing that, there would be no adversarial discussion. A notice in which it is

---

[216] Cf. Cass. Belgium 12 December 1980, in *Europ. transp. law,* 1981, no.16, 250. More in general, Cf. App. Aix – en – Provence 11 March 1969, in *Bull. transp.*, 1969, 389.

[217] Cf. RB Antwerp 8 November 2013, in *Europ. transp. law,* 2014, no. 49, 222.

[218] Cf. Trib. com. Paris 25 June 1979, in *Bull. transp.* 1979, 403; App. Paris 17 November 2004, in *Bull. transp. logist.,* 2005, 86; App. Besançon 13 January 2015, in *Le Lamy transp.*, 2020, vol. I, 533; App. Brussels 20 September 1995, *ibid.,* 2020, vol. I, 535; App. Paris 26 February 1997, *ibid.,* 2020, vol. I, 536, according to which the proof of receipt of a written complaint can be provided with any means. See also Cass. com. France 3 March 1998, in *Bull. transp. logist.,* 1998, 112.

[219] See Messent and Glass (2018), p. 328 ss.; Loewe (1976), p. 394 ff.; Demuth (2013), p. 921 ff. See also Cass. France 20 July 1983, in *Bull. transp.,* 1984, 236; App. Paris 25 March 1982, *ibid.,* 1982, 434; Cass. France 3 March 1998, *ibid.,* 1998, 212. Cf. also *Zerowatt S.p.a.* v. *International Express Company Limited*, in *Europ. transp. law,* 1991, no. 26, 530, according to which letters sent by mail in England with a first class shipping are intended to be received the day following the shipping and the prescription is suspended from that date.

[220] Cf. App. Reims 3 March 1980, in *Bull. transp.,* 1980, 237. Cf. also App. Brussels 20 September 1995, in *Le Lamy transp.*, 2020, vol. I, 535.

[221] Cf. App. Reims 3 March 1980, in *Bull. transp.,* 1980, 237; Trib. Albertville 4 March 1975, *ibid.,* 1976, 217. See also App. Paris 19 June 1997, in *Le Lamy transp.*, 2020, vol. I, 535; Trib. com. Chartres 1 April 2003, *ibid.*, 2020, 535. See also App. Anvers 2 December 1981, *ibid.*, 2020, 535, according to which there are suspending effects if a telex or a letter describes the damages charged to the carrier and the value of goods are indicated therein. See also App. Paris 22 January 1986, in Bull. transp., 1986, 482; App. Paris 26 October 2005, in *Bull. transp. logist.,* 2005, 718; App. Paris 2 April 1991, *ibid.,* 1991, 428.

[222] Cf. App. Paris 22 January 1986, in *Bull. transp.,* 1986, 482; Cass. Belgium 19 June 2010, in *Europ. transp. law,* 2010, no. 45, 623; OLG Karlsruhe 28 September 2001, in *TranspR,* 2004, 33, according to which, in the claim, it is not required to specify in detail the nature and cause of the damage or ground for the claim. Therefore, it is not necessary to quantity the requested compensation; OLG Frankfurt am Main 5 October 2004, *ibid.,* 2005, 256, according to which the claim does not have to be specific with regard to the claims put forward during the proceedings.

[223] Cf. Hof Brussels 7 December 2012, in *Europ. transp. law,* 2013, no. 48, 201; OGH 29 August 1994, *ibid.,* 1996, no. 31, 211. See also Cass. com. France 15 May 2001, in *Le Lamy transp.*, 2020, vol. I, 535; App. Paris 24 September 1997, *ibid.,* 2020, 535; App. Paris 28 March 2019, *ibid.,* 2020, 535. See, moreover, App. Aix - en - Provence 7 February 1990, in *Bull. transp.,* 1990, 698; App. Paris 6 July 1994, in *Le Lamy transp.*, 2020, vol. I, 535; App. Nancy 29 November 1994, *ibid.,* 2020, 535; App. Versailles 2 December 2010, in *Bull. transp. logist.,* 2010, 735, according to which a complaint anticipated by complete documentation, never sent, is entitled to suspend the

highlighted that the goods have arrived damaged for 80 or 90%[224] is not enough, if, on the basis of relative indications, the transporter is unable to identify the prejudice.[225] Moreover, if this is not reconstructed exactly, the act suspends the prescription term provided that the information is in the carrier's possession or acquired immediately after the claim,[226] with a very benevolent approach toward the creditor. A modification of this thesis does not undermine the suspensive effect.[227] In general, the communication must specify the carriage it refers to and the request for compensation.[228] For Article 32, second paragraph, only the first complaint suspends the prescription period and when, this effect ends, it is not possible to propose a second act with the same purpose.[229]

The suspension ceases with the negative response of the transporter,[230] who has neither an obligation to reply nor a burden in a technical sense. However, it is in his interest to intervene if he wants to prevent the suspensive effects[231] from being prolonged. Implicitly, the provision invites the establishment of an adversarial discussion by soliciting an out-of-court settlement of the disputes or, better, by creating conditions for a documented dialogue on the basis of a detailed claim, which can be a prelude to an agreement.[232]

According to a particular reconstruction of Article 32, second paragraph,[233] the suspension would be stopped even if the carrier did not intervene within a reasonable period from three to 6 months. The solution cannot be endorsed, because it leaves the

---

prescription, if the content is precise enough; Cass. Belgium 7 December 2012, in *Europ. transp. law,* 2013, no. 48, 210.

[224]Cf. App. Toulouse 22 November 1989, in *Bull. transp.,* 1990, 427. See also App. Riom 15 September 1999, *ibid.,* 1999, 746.

[225]Cf. Cass. com. France 12 July 1994, in *Le Lamy transp.*, 2020, vol. I, 535, according to which a letter without a compensation request does not have a suspending effect. See also App. Reims 3 March 1980, *ibid.*, 2020, 535.

[226]Cf. Trib. com. Liege 25 November 1982, in *Europ. transp. law,* 1982, no. 17, 843.

[227]Cf. OLG Munich 24 April 1992, in *TranspR*, 1992, 360; Putzeys (1981), p. 396 ff.

[228]Cf. BGH 7 November 1985, in *Europ. transp. law,* 1986, no. 21, 266; App. Paris 22 January 1986, in *Bull. transp.,* 1986, 482. See however, for the opposite view, Cass. Italy, sez. un., 24 November 2009, no. 24680, in *Giur. it. rep.,* 2009.

[229]Cf. Cass. Italy 29 January 2003, no. 1272, in *Dir. mar.,* 2005, 498; Cass. Italy 7 April 2005, no. 7258, in *Dir. trasp.,* 2007, 497; App. Cordóba 19 November 2012, no. 269, in *Ac,* 2013, 2236.

[230]Cf. Spain Supreme Court 9 June 1998, no. 653, in *RJ,* 1998, 5282, according to which the objection by the carrier's lawyer does not equate to the answer, pursuant to Article 32, second paragraph; App. Cordóba 19 November 2012, no. 269, in *Ac,* 2013, 2236.

[231]Cf. Polish Supreme Court 20 February 2018, V CSK 205/2017, according to which, until the events of Article 32, second paragraph, take place, the suspension effects continue; Polish Supreme Court 22 November 2007, III CSK 150/2007.

[232]Cf. Gragnoli (1990), p. 70 ff.

[233]Cf. Radionov (2020), p. 19 ff., who proposes a teleological reading of Article 32, second paragraph, so that "the rejection does not have to be made in writing for the suspension to end. If there has been no rejection and both parties have ceased all activities on settling the claim, a reasonable period should be applied, between three and six months, for the suspension to end".

identification of this term to a discretionary assessment without any provision in the CMR, in contrast with the logic of the institution of prescription, aimed at offering certainty to relationships.

Like the claim, the answer does not invoke particular formal requirements, but it must be clear.[234] Thus, the carrier's request for further documents or more information[235] is irrelevant, being an act that does not make the suspension to cease. Furthermore, if, on the same day, the creditor receives two letters with which the carrier first denies his liability and subsequently communicates the intention of his insurance company to pay the indemnity, the suspension does not stop,[236] as per a reasonably resolved singular case. In fact, the second note changes what has been said by the first and their arrival is simultaneous.

Finally, in the event of partial adhesion to the claim, the limitation period begins to run again for rights not subject to out-of-court settlement.[237] According to a literal interpretation,[238] the running of the term would remain suspended, at most definitively, for recognized credits, as the right would be subject to a suspended term for an indefinite time. If Article 32, second paragraph, wants the out-of-court settlement, the prescription must also run for uncontested credits and, to this end, partial acceptance must be evaluated according to the national law "*de la juridiction saisie*",[239] pursuant to Article 32, third paragraph. Moreover, the problem is of limited practical importance, because, if a general agreement is reached, it should be performed without further difficulties.

The carrier's reply[240] that does not result in a precise denial of the opposing theses is equivalent to an admission. Thus, we cannot consider a denial, but an

---

[234] Cf. App. Bordeaux 24 October 2018, in *Le Lamy transp.*, 2020, vol. I, 536; App. Lyon 2 November 1983, *ibid.*, 2020, 536; App. Paris 27 January 1986, *ibid.*, 2020, 536, according to which a carrier who states he will refund the damage within the compensation limits provided for by the Convention does not reject the complaint; Trib. com. Brussels 2 April 1990, in *Europ. transp. law*, 1990, no. 26, 541, according to which the carrier's reply must be clear and formal. See also *Microfine Minerals and Chemicals Ltd. and Walker Chemie GmbH* v. *Transferry Shipping Co. Ltd.*, *ibid.*, 1992, 118, according to which, to stop the suspension, it is not sufficient for a carrier to write a letter informing that he has contacted his insurance company and, while waiting for an answer, the carrier does not consider himself liable based on the information he has received. See also App. Versailles 2 December 2010, *ibid.*, 2020, 536; App. Krakow 22 July 2020, according to which the carrier must reply in writing.

[235] Cf. Supreme Court Spain 29 June 1998, no. 635, in *Europ. transp. law*, 1999, no. 34, 692. Cf. also Cabrera Cánovas (2012), p. 156 ff.

[236] Cf. RB Rotterdam 12 May 1978, in *Europ. law digest*, 1989, no. 407; Hof Antwerp 2 June 2003, in *Europ. transp. law*, 2004, no. 39, 407.

[237] Cf. App. Riom 12 June 2002, in *Bull. transp. logist.*, 2003, 83; App. Colmar 23 November 2016, *ibid.*, 2016, 722. See also App. Reims 3 March 1980, in *Bull. transp.*, 1980, 237, according to which a carrier's note with which his insurance company declares to pay half of the amount requested through the complaint does not have any suspension effects.

[238] Cf. Gragnoli (1990), p. 91 ff.

[239] The English text reads as follows: "by the law of the court or tribunal seized of the case".

[240] See Messent and Glass (2018), p. 331 ff.

admission the declarations of two carriers "*dont le conseil répond qu'il convient déduire de la somme reclamée la valeur du sauvatage de la marchandise*"[241] and "*qui indique qu'il procedera au remboursement*" and "*qui indique qu'il procedera au remboursement du dommage conformément aux limitations de responsabilité de la CMR et sur la base du rapport*".[242]

Finally, pursuant to Article 32, second paragraph, the burden of proving receipt rests on those who have an interest in doing so,[243] and the rule does not change the conclusions that could have been reached based on general principles, but creates complete homogeneity before any jurisdiction and in respect of any national law.

9.2.6 The Laws of Individual Countries

Article 32, third paragraph, remits to the national law "*de la juridiction saisie*"[244] the regulation of other cases of suspension and interruption[245]; these categories, too, must be understood on the basis of the continental law.[246] The discipline is entrusted to the one of the "*juridiction saisie*", despite the fact that the provisions are of substantive law. In fact, the Convention governs the first claim and could have been focused on all cases of suspension and interruption, thereby avoiding application difficulties. Such a uniform regulation would have prevented sensitive issues, thereby facilitating the task of the parties and their defenders.

Thus, according to French law, for a claim for compensation to interrupt the limitation period, one must look at the moment in which the document is sent "*par l'huissier de justice à autorité étrangère*" and not "*à la date de remise de l'assignation*".[247] In Italian law, the opposite solution applies. Both approaches are consistent with Article 32, third paragraph, which leaves the regulation to domestic law, and this testifies to the difficulties in proposing a correct defense for those who do not possess the mastery of the "*loi de la juridiction saisie*", especially because, at

---

[241] Cfr. Cf. App. Lyon 2 November 1983, in *Bull. transp.,* 1983, 23.

[242] Cf. App. Paris 27 January 1986, in *Bull. transp.,* 1986, 45.

[243] Cf. Cass. com. France 15 May 2001, in *Bull. transp. logist.,* 2001, 418; App. Aix - en - Provence, 23 June 2010, *ibid.,* 2010, 657; App. Pau 24 June 2013, in *Le Lamy transp.*, 2020, vol. I, 536; App. Bordeaux 24 October 2018, *ibid.,* 2020, 536, according to which it is the carrier's responsibility to try to reject the complaint and return the documents.

[244] The English text reads as follows: "the law of the court or tribunal seized of the case".

[245] Cf. Cass. Greece 487/2008; Cass. Greece no. 1411/2018, according to which, in case of an insurer's subrogation, the beneficiary's claims *vis-à-vis* third-parties in the insurance contract are prescribed within 6 months from the subrogation, as per Greek law.

[246] Cf. Cass. France 13 May 2014, in *Bull. transp.*, 2014, 344; App. Reims 11 June 2013, *ibid.,* 2013, 608; App. Lyon 6 March 2008, *ibid.,* 590; App. Paris 21 December 2006, *ibid.,* 2007, 44; Cass. France 28 September 2004, *ibid.,* 2004, 668; App. Aix en Provence 12 February 2004, *ibid.*, 2004, 451; Cass. Belgium 13 October 2011, in *Europ. transp. law,* 2012, no. 47, 221.

[247] Cf. Trib. Chambéry 13 April 2007, in *Bull. transp.,* 2007, 320.

the time of the claim, it could be difficult to identify exactly in front of which judge the case will appear.

Then, the rules on transport with multiple carriers[248] are not applied in a dispute in which the contractual one acts against his subtransporter; as Article 32, third paragraph, does not operate, the regulation of suspensive and interrupting events is not identified based on the national law of the "*juridiction saisie*".

For legal systems, such as the Italian one, in which the out-of-court complaint has an interrupting effect, there are coordination problems with Article 32, second paragraph, which fully regulates the first claim for compensation, a claim to which only suspensive effects can be connected. In fact, if, for any reason, the act is not suitable to provoke them (for example, because it is generic), there is no effect on the prescription. Article 32, second paragraph, does not refer to the national law and there can be no interrupting consequences other than suspensive ones. This does not apply to subsequent letters, regulated instead by the domestic law, which is responsible for determining whether they can interrupt the course of the limitation period.

If the shipper or consignee provides an initial claim and causes the suspension, for the legal systems for which a formal complaint interrupts the limitation period one must ask whether this also applies to the suspended one.[249] The case is much more frequent than one might imagine and, for example, occurs when, in the event of a delay in response, a reminder is sent with possible interrupting effects according to some national laws. Considering the silence of Article 32, second paragraph, the question is devolved to the "*loi de la juridiction saisie*", because it does not depend on the interpretation of the uniform law, but on the domestic one.[250] For example, according to an Italian contribution,[251] the claims subsequent to the first would interrupt the prescription, even if suspended, although this conclusion is motivated on the basis of domestic law and cannot assume general significance.[252] This shows what obstacles stand in the way of the application of Article 32, third paragraph, and to the choices of economic operators, who cannot have in-depth knowledge of various regulatory systems.

In common law countries, Article 32, third paragraph, leads to conclusions that are not always consistent. Thus, it was stated that, after the first complaint, the parties could extend the limitation period; however, the argument is unfounded, due to the mandatory nature of the Convention.[253] Article 32, third paragraph, entrusts to national law the regulation of only the interruptive and suspensive cases other than

[248] Cf. App. De Mons 14 May 2002, in *Europ. transp. law,* 2004, no. 39, 99.

[249] Cf. Cass. Italy 7 April 2005, no. 7258, in *Dir. mar.*, 2007, 1145, according to which "a complaint following the first or, in any case, a compensation claim addressed to the carrier after the first complaint can disclose the requisites of a letter of formal demand on the basis of the law of the court seized with the case and, therefore, produce the effect of interrupting prescription". For the opposite direction, see Cass. Italy 29 January 2003, no. 1272, *ibid.*, 2005, 498.

[250] Cf. Krings (1999), p. 787 ff.

[251] Cf. Gragnoli (1990), p. 91 ff.

[252] Cf. Cass. Italy 7 April 2005, no. 7258, in *Dir. mar.,* 2007, 1145.

[253] Cf. Messent and Glass (2018), p. 334.

the first claim. Failing that, domestic law cannot intervene and a valid agreement cannot be stipulated, due to the mandatory nature of the Convention, pursuant to Article 41. Therefore, the clause that extends or shortens the term envisaged by Article 32, first paragraph, is null and void. Precisely due to their heterogeneous nature, it is not possible to recall the institutes of estoppel or waiver, typical of Anglo-Saxon countries.[254] These principles cannot be traced back to either suspensive or interruptive events and the "*loi de la juridiction saisie*" does not operate.

References

Cabrera Cánovas A (2012) Jurisprudencia del Tribunal Supremo español en materias reguldas por el Convenio CMR. In: Sánchez Gamborino FJ, Cabrera Cánovas A (eds) El convenio CMR: el contrado de transporte internacional de mercancias por carretera, Barcelona, pp 131 ff

Clarke MA (2014) International carriage of goods by road: CMR, VI edn. New York

De Beule D (1988) L'article 32, second paragraph, CMR. Eur Transp Law 28:654 ff

Demuth K (2013) Reklamationen und Klagen. In: Thume KH (ed) Aa. Vv., CMR: Über den Beförderungsvertrag im internationalen Strassengüterverkehr, III edn. Frankfurt am Main, pp 815 ff

Dorrestein HJ (1977) Recht van het internationale wegvervoer, Zwolle

Gragnoli E (1990) La sospensione del decorso del termine di prescrizione per i debiti del vettore nella CMR. Dir Trasp, 63 ff

Greiter I (1986) CMR – Gerichtsurteile, Eisenstadt

Haak KF (1986) The liability of the carrier under CMR. The Hague

Jung C (1997) The Convention on the contract for the International carriage of goods by road (CMR): Survey, analysis and trends of recent German case law. Unif Law Rev, 148 ff

Krings E (1999) CMR: Examen de la jurisprudence des Cours de Cassation de France et de Pays – Bas (deuxième partie). Unif Law Rev, 767 ff

Libouton J (1973) International road transport. Convention on the contract for the international carriage of goods by road. Review of Court decisions 1965 – 1971. Eur Transp Law 8:6 ff

Loewe R (1976) Commentary on the Convention of 19 may 1956 on the contract for the international carriage of goods by road. Eur Transp Law 11:311 ff

Loewe R (1996) La CMR à 40 ans. Unif Law Rev 429 ff

Mayer CU (1997) CMR – Aperçu et reflections sur la jurisprudence autrichienne en dernier ressort (1994 – 1996). Unif Law Rev 159 ff

Messent A, Glass DA (2018) CMR: contracts for the international carriage of goods by road, IV edn. New York

Otte K (2018a) Art. 30 der CMR, in Aa. Vv., Internationales Vertragsrecht, Munich, pp 1519 ff

Otte K (2018b) Art. 32 der CMR, in Aa. Vv., Internationales Vertragsrecht, Munich, pp 1550 ff

Pesce A (1995) Il trasporto internazionale di merci, Turin

Putzeys J (1981) Le contrat de transport routier de marchandises, Brussels

Radionov N (2020) Suspension of the period of limitation under the CMR and silence of the carrier: new approach. Eur Transp Law 55:3 ff

Rodière R (1971) The Convention on road transport. Eur Transp Law 6: 307 ff

Sánchez - Gamborino FJ (2001a) La jurisprudence du Tribunal Supremo espagnol en matière de CMR. Unif Law Rev, 644 ff

[254] Cf. Clarke (2014), p. 150, according to whom "the time limitation will not be enforced against the claimant if the other party has waived the period or is estopped from pleading it".

Sánchez - Gamborino FJ (2001b) La Conventión CMR según la Jurisprudencia del "Tribunal Supremo" de España. Eur Transp Law 36:842 ff

Silingardi G, Riguzzi M, Gragnoli E (1989) Trasporto internazionale merci su strada e CMR, Rome

Silingardi G, Corrado A, Meotti A, Morandi F (1994) La disciplina uniforme del contratto di trasporto di cose su strada, Turin

Wesolowsky K (2013) A review of judicial decisions of the polish supreme court within the scope of CMR. Eur Transp Law 48:337 ff

Chapter 10
The Jurisdiction

Contents

10.1 The Relationship Between the Geneva Convention and Legal Systems of Individual Countries

10.1.1 The Scope of Application of Article 31

For disputes concerning international transport, Article 31, first paragraph, indicates the criteria for identifying judges who have jurisdiction.[1] This rule replaces the

[1]Cf. Legros (2016), pp. 585 ff., according to whom "*la liberté des parties est assez grande, celles – ci pouvant même être mise à profit pour pratiquer le* forum shopping, *notamment en insérant des clauses attributives de juridiction donnant compétence à des fors qui connaissent les actions*

C. Tincani, *Contract for the International Carriage of Goods by Road*, Law for Professionals, https://doi.org/10.1007/978-3-031-08487-4_10

principles of international procedural law, in line with the overall choice of the Convention.[2] Article 31 applies to all disputes relating to transfers that fall within the scope of the CMR and concerns both contractual and noncontractual liability actions,[3] in particular those of Article 28.[4] Article 31 considers both claims of the person entitled to redelivery and those of the carrier and subtransporter.[5] Furthermore, these actions may focus on ascertaining the nonexistence of the transfer obligation and, in this case, Article 31, second paragraph, can be applied.[6] On the contrary, claims falling outside the scope of the Convention are excluded. According to an approach challenged herein,[7] the action for breach of contract consisting in the failure to complete performance of the service would be regulated by domestic law.[8] This argument is based on the unfounded assertion that the CMR concerns the cases of loss, damage and delay and not those of failure to perform; however, this reconstruction has already been criticized.[9]

Then, Article 31 would not apply if the carrier did not take charge of the goods, provided that Article 31, first paragraph, letter b), would make a binding reference to the place of receipt of the load or to that envisaged for redelivery.[10] The approach remains unconvincing,[11] as Article 31 pertains to any contract regulated by the CMR,[12] whether or not the cargo is transmitted to the carrier, an irrelevant circumstance;[13] it does not influence the stipulation of the agreement and, thus, the

préventives en déclaration de non responsabilité ou encore qui adoptent une conception restrictive de la faute équipollente au dol de l'article 29 de la CMR"; Ferrari (2002), pp. 693 ff.; Defossez (2016), pp. 93 ff.

[2]Cf. Haak (1986), pp. 275 ff., according to whom, "in order to further and to guarantee substantive legal unity, the Convention presents in Article 31 (. . .) of the CMR a mandatory law regulation of a procedural law nature"; Messent and Glass (2018), pp. 291 ff. Cf. OGH 12 June 2001, in *Europ. transp. law,* 2003, no. 38, 357.

[3]Cf. BGH 31 May 2001, in *Europ. transp. law,* 2002, no. 37, 80; OGH 25 February 2015, in *TranspR,* 2015, 399, according to which Article 31 applies in disputes related to applications concerning annexed noncontractual liability in relation to the carriage. Cf. Koller (2002), pp. 133 ff.

[4]Cf. Loewe (1976), pp. 387 ff.; Putzeys (1981), pp. 373 ff.

[5]Cf. Cass. Belgium 19 February 2004, in *Europ. transp. law,* 2004, no. 39, 521; Clarke (2014), pp. 151 ff.

[6]Cf. Federal Tribunal of the Swiss Confederation 25 September 2012, in *Sistema informatico federale.*

[7]Cf. App. Milan 11 July 1975, in *Unif. law rev.,* 1977, 336; App. Lyon 16 September 2011, in *Bull. transp.,* 2011, 571; Messent and Glass (2018), pp. 293 ff.; Loewe (1976), pp. 387 ff.

[8]In the opposite sense, cf. Silingardi et al. (1994), pp. 263 ff.

[9]In the sense supported in the text, cf. OGH 25 February 2015, in *TranspR,* 2015, 399, according to which Article 31 also applies to disputes related to claims deriving from failure to perform services agreed upon.

[10]Cf. OLG Vienna 3 April 1984, in *TranspR,* 1984, 152; Loewe (1976), pp. 389 ff.

[11]Cf. Clarke (2014), pp. 155 ff.

[12]Cf. Putzeys (1981), pp. 373 ff.

[13]Cf. Putzeys (1981), pp. 373 ff., according to whom "*le transport proprement dit n'ayant encore reçu un début d'exécution, on ne peut dire quel le litige (. . .) soit issu du transport*".

operation of Article 31, since this initial conduct in any case implements a contract concluded earlier. Therefore, the provision pertains to any action based on the agreement,[14] such as that of the transporter who wants to be refunded for the costs incurred for customs duties.[15] This also applies if, as a result of the judgment, liability is ascertained on the basis of domestic law,[16] rather than Article 17 of the Convention. This is regardless of the fact that the decision is convincing, because this aspect concerns the merits and not the allocation of jurisdiction.

For Article 31, the party, therefore the carrier, shipper or consignee, must act, the last one if he asks for redelivery. Conversely, Article 31 cannot be invoked by a party extraneous to the relationship, albeit the owner of the goods.[17] On the contrary, according to French case law,[18] the provision would also concern the actions of third-parties. However, this thesis is unfounded, because it is in contrast with the overall object of the CMR, which is inherent solely to the contract. Then, in groupage transport, the carrier can bind himself to make multiple deliveries and some may be subject to the Convention, others to domestic law, but, for the latter, Article 31 may not be relied upon.[19] The same conclusions must be reached with regard to transport combined with breaking of the load, as this scenario is not regulated by Article 2 and, therefore, the CMR does not apply.[20]

10.1.2 The Consensual Identification of Jurisdiction

For Article 31, first paragraph, the parties may indicate the jurisdiction of a signatory State.[21] Thus, the designation of a country that has not adhered to the Convention is void, because Article 31 is mandatory, pursuant to Article 41.[22] Article 31 does not specify whether it mentions the parties with regard to those to the contract or those to the dispute. The problem is relevant, because we must establish whether the

[14] Cf. Putzeys (1981), pp. 373 ff., according to whom "*aussi croyons – nous qu'il est plus raisonnable d'appliquer les règles de compétence (...) à toutes litiges auxquels donnent lieu les contrats de transports soumis*".

[15] Cf. Putzeys (1981), pp. 374 ff. In the opposite sense, see Loewe (1976), according to whom, "when the carrier has incurred expenses on behalf of the person entitled to dispose of the goods and those expenses are not directly related to the carriage, for example, if he has paid custom duties on the goods, Article 31 in not applicable to the legal proceedings which might arise".

[16] Cf. Clarke (2014), pp. 155 ff.

[17] Cf. Loewe (1976), pp. 387 ff.; Messent and Glass (2018), pp. 293 ff.

[18] Cf. Cass. com. France 11 October 2011, in *Bull. transp. logist.,* 2011, 603.

[19] Cf. Messent and Glass (2018), pp. 293 ff.

[20] Cf. Messent and Glass (2018), pp. 293 ff.

[21] Cf. Messent and Glass (2018), pp. 292 ff.; Crignon-Dumoulin (2006), pp. 610 ff.; Demuth (2013a), pp. 851 ff.; App. Aix-en-Provence 4 September 1996, in *Bull. transp.,* 1997, 277; Cass. Italy 14 March 2017, no. 6484, in *Giur. it. rep.,* 2017.

[22] Cf. Putzeys (1981), pp. 375 ff.

consignee can conclude the jurisdiction agreement with the carrier, even if there was no indication in the original contract. As there is no provision in favor of the restrictive solution, which would allow the pact on jurisdiction only at the time of the stipulation of the original contract, the agreement about jurisdiction may be concluded at a later stage, provided that the selected country has adhered to the Convention.[23]

The jurisdiction indicated by consensus is an alternative to that of Article 31, first paragraph, letter a) and letter b), as the relative provisions are "in addition"[24] to the consensual option.[25] Therefore, a clause on jurisdiction that conceives it as exclusive is void pursuant to Article 41,[26] which makes the opposite solution of Article 31 mandatory.[27] As some authors believe,[28] an exclusive agreement could be stipulated only if it followed the rise of the dispute and with a separate act from the initial contract of carriage, because, at that point, Article 31[29] would not operate. However, this thesis underestimates the peremptory nature of Article 31,[30] and the opposite and more restrictive solution has instead to be preferred.

Article 31, first paragraph, does not impose any explicit requirements for an agreement concerning jurisdiction.[31] It is not possible to refer to domestic law[32] in the absence of an indication by the CMR, even if the opposite argument has been supported[33] and, from that angle, it has been investigated whether reference should

[23] Cf. Messent and Glass (2018), pp. 293 ff.; *British American Tobacco Denmark A/S* v. *Kazemier Transport B. See* in *Lloyd's rep.,* 2016, 463.

[24] This is how Article 31 reads in the English text. The French text of Article 31 reads as follows: "*en dehors des juridictions des pays contractants désignées d'un commun accord par les parties*".

[25] Cf. Messent and Glass (2018), pp. 292 ff., according to whom "the fact that the parties have agreed a jurisdiction does not exclude the alternative jurisdiction based on the provisions of Article 31, first paragraph, letters a) and b), since it is provided that the latter shall be 'in addition' to the former"; Loewe (1976), pp. 388 ff.; Putzeys (1981), pp. 374 ff.; Sànchez Gamborino (2001a), pp. 647 ff.; Sànchez Gamborino (2001b), pp. 868 ff.; Ferrari (2002), pp. 693 ff. See also Cass. Belgium 8 December 2006, in *Europ. transp. law*, 2007, no. 42, 401, according to which "the contractual election of *forum* does not prevail"; RB Antwerp 8 November 2013, *ibid.,* 2014, no. 49, 223.

[26] Cf. OLG Cologne 25 February 2014, in *TranspR,* 2015, 115; BGH 18 December 2003, *ibid.,* 2004, 169; OLG Hamburg 11 October 2001, *ibid.,* 2002, 111; OGH 27 November 2008, *ibid.,* 2009, 413. Cf. also Loewe (1976), pp. 388 ff.; Clarke (2014), pp. 161 ff.; Haak (1986), pp. 282 ff.; Putzeys (1981), pp. 374 ff.

[27] Cf. Puetz (2018), pp. 122 ff., according to whom "the nullity is only partial, in the sense that the exclusive choice is turned into an additional one".

[28] Cf. Putzeys (1981), pp. 374 ff.

[29] Cf. Putzeys (1981), pp. 376 ff., according to whom "*il s'agit là, non plus d'une clause d'un contrat de transport, mais d'une véritable transaction, donc le contenu est librement décidé par les parties. Cette transaction implique renonciation aux atres possibilités*".

[30] Cf. Clarke (2014), pp. 161 ff.

[31] Cf. Puetz (2018), pp. 122 ff.; Demuth (2013a), pp. 857 ff.

[32] Cf. Polish Supreme Court 14 March 2019, IV CSK 6/2018, according to which Article 31, first paragraph, of the CMR also prevails on Article 25 of regulation EU 1215/2012.

[33] Cf. Loewe (1976), pp. 388 ff.; Messent and Glass (2018), pp. 295 ff.

be made to the law of the State to whose jurisdiction the agreement refers to or to the one in which the contract was stipulated. The approach is unconvincing, because, in the absence of an opposite solution, according to Article 31, the format freedom must be accepted and it is unclear why national regulations[34] should be invoked. Failure to include the clause in the consignment note is irrelevant pursuant to Article 4 of the CMR, although a greater probative effort is needed in that case.[35] For example, in cumulative carriage, the knowledge of the consignee who adheres to the relationship[36] or of the next carrier must be demonstrated.[37] Thus, the provision on jurisdiction cannot be raised against the recipient if it is reported in the documents he has viewed, but is illegible, and this is a balanced solution to a peculiar case.[38]

For some,[39] it would be necessary to include the consensual indication on jurisdiction in the consignment note, as the consignee would enter the relationship only by accepting the same consignment note and, therefore, the contract. This approach remains unconvincing, due to the optional and probative nature of the draft of the note,[40] as well as because of the fact that Article 31 agreement is not mentioned by Article 6.[41] In general, the recipient who is unaware of the agreement upon jurisdiction is not bound by it, unless the shipper acts on his behalf or, *a fortiori*, if, at the time of redelivery, the same recipient accepts the note with the relative indication.[42]

In general, the jurisdiction agreement is concluded by the carrier. Therefore, if the clause is included in a sales contract with respect to which the transporter is a third-party, it has no binding effect on him if he is unaware and, thus, does not adhere to it.[43] Then, in combined carriage, if the claim for compensation for loss, damage or delay concerns the road section, any jurisdiction clause placed in the bill of lading is inapplicable, if in contrast with Article 31.[44] Finally, the agreement may be included in a separate or subsequent manifestation of will compared to the original contract

[34]Cf. Puetz (2018), pp. 122 ff. See also Cass. Belgium 29 April 2004, in *Europ. transp. law,* 2004, no. 39, 688.

[35]Cf. Loewe (1976), pp. 368 ff.; Putzeys (1981), pp. 375 ff.; Puetz (2018), pp. 122 ff.

[36]Cf. Putzeys (1981), pp. 375 ff.; Silingardi et al. (1994), pp. 265 ff.

[37]Cf. Clarke (2014), pp. 160 ff.

[38]Cf. App. Colmar 26 November 2001, in *Bull. transp. logist.,* 2002, 15; App. Parigi 14 November 1969, in *Unif. law rev.,* 1970, 133.

[39]Cf. App. Parigi 14 November 1969, in *Bull. transp.,* 1969, 363.

[40]Cf. Putzeys (1981), pp. 375 ff., according to whom "*la lettre de voiture n'est qu'un instrument de preuve; elle n'est pas une formalité solennelle, indispensable à la conclusion du contrat et par conséquent, d'aucun accord s'inscrivant dans le contrat*".

[41]Cf. Messent and Glass (2018), pp. 294 ff.; Hof Gent 7 March 2005, in *Europ. transp. law,* 2006, no. 41, 570; Cass. Belgium 29 April 2004, in *Bull. transp. logist.,* 2005, 213, according to which a clause on jurisdiction included in an invoice and not challenged by the consignee binds him.

[42]Cf. Clarke (2014), pp. 160 ff.

[43]Cf. Putzeys (1981), pp. 372 ff.; Messent and Glass (2018), pp. 294 ff.

[44]Cf. RB Antwerp 23 September 1975, in *Europ. transp. law,* 1976, no. 11, 279.

and, although some are of different opinions,[45] these latter scenarios are in any case not governed by domestic law, as the approach of the Convention is all-encompassing and does not require other provisions.

10.1.3 The Alternative Criteria on the Identification of the Judge Having Jurisdiction and Their Scope

As an alternative to the jurisdiction agreement, Article 31, first paragraph, letters a) and b), indicates two criteria. While the agreement must concern the jurisdiction of a signatory State, this does not apply to the parameters of Article 31, first paragraph, letter a) and letter b).[46] Moreover, the judge of a nonsignatory country could find it difficult to apply provisions of a treaty unknown to himself or, in any case, extraneous to his legal system. For this reason, it is hoped[47] that the action is exercised in a signatory State, "since the enforcement provisions of Article 31, paragraph 3, only apply in respect of a judgment by a court of a contracting party",[48] and the approach can be fully endorsed. Then, according to a majority argument,[49] Article 31, first paragraph, is mandatory, so that "any basis of jurisdiction provided by national law are excluded, unless consistent with CMR".[50]

Article 31, first paragraph, does not refer to the national law on the same jurisdiction,[51] but determines the criteria for identifying the State and its judges;[52] instead, the domestic provisions on territorial competence apply.[53] Thus, the jurisdiction of the Italian court applies in case of a liability action brought against the German carrier if the place of delivery is in Italy.[54] Again, for a transport from Paris to Antwerp,[55] Article 31, first paragraph, letter b), recognizes French and Belgian

---

[45] Cf. Clarke (2014), pp. 159 ff.

[46] Cf. Demuth (2013a), pp. 853 ff.

[47] Cf. Messent and Glass (2018), pp. 292 ff.

[48] Cf. Messent and Glass (2018), pp. 292 ff.; Clarke (2014), pp. 156 ff.

[49] Cf. Messent and Glass (2018), pp. 292 ff. Cf. *Arctic Electronics Co. (U.K.) Ltd.* v. *McGregor Sea & Air Services Ltd.*, in *Lloyd's rep.*, 1985, 510.

[50] Cf. Messent and Glass (2018), pp. 292 ff.

[51] However, see Haak (1986), pp. 275 ff., who highlights that in the Netherlands, Article 31, first paragraph, is interpreted as a rule referring to domestic law; Demuth (2013a), pp. 850 ff.

[52] Cf. OGH 27 November 2008, in *TranspR*, 2009, 414, according to which Article 31, first paragraph, governs jurisdiction and not authority or allocation within a federal State and, within its scope of application, it is a *lex specialis*.

[53] Cf. Clarke (2014), pp. 152 ff., according to whom "determination of appropriate court in England is a matter for English law"; Demuth (2013a), pp. 860 ff.

[54] Cf. App. Milano 18 March 1994, in *Riv. dir. priv. proc.*, 1995, 141.

[55] Cf. App. Bordeaux 12 October 2016, in *Le Lamy transp.*, 2021, vol. I, 558.

jurisdiction in general terms, deferring the identification of the judge with authority to domestic law in each countries.[56]

In fact, Article 31, first paragraph, refers to the "*jurisdictions du pays*".[57] The intention to leave the selection of the competent judge to the State and its legal system is obvious, even if it has not adhered to the Convention.[58] Thus, in the case of Germany, as a federal State, Article 31 identifies the federal State with jurisdiction,[59] whereas the domestic law establishes the judge.[60] If the individual legal system does not determine him, for some,[61] Article 31 would apply as a subsidiary criterion aimed at filling the gap.[62] This argument is unacceptable, as the rule concerns jurisdiction only.[63] Therefore, in the absence of an internal provision on the identification of the judge, the rule about jurisdiction itself does not operate.[64]

Once the jurisdiction has been identified, the judge would be required to decide, although domestic law does not resolve the issue of territorial competence.[65] In fact, as it has been incorrectly stated,[66] "*les jurisdictions françaises n'hesitent pas, en*

[56]Cf. Cass. com. France 17 January 1995, in *Le Lamy transp.*, 2021, vol. I, 558; App. Bourges 12 February 2002, in *Bull. transp. logist.*, 2003, 103; App. Amiens 7 March 1997, *ibid.*, 1997, 261; App. Versailles 10 November 2005, *ibid.*, 2005, 813.

[57]Article 31, first paragraph, of the French text reads as such. Article 31, first paragraph, of the English text reads as follows: "courts or tribunals".

[58]Cf. Cass. com. France 17 January 1995, in *Le Lamy transp.*, 2021, vol. I, 558; App. Bourges 12 February 2002, in *Bull. transp. logist.*, 2003, 103; App. Amiens 7 March 1997, *ibid.*, 1997, 261. Cf. also Krings (1999), pp. 785 ff.; Crignon-Dumoulin (2006), pp. 610 ff., according to whom "*la CMR règle uniquement la compétence internationale en déterminant le pays dans lequel une action peut être introduite. Le Tribunal de l'Etat ainsi désigné est déterminé en application des dispositions nationales*".

[59]Cf. OGH 27 November 2008, in *TranspR*, 2009, 414, according to which Article 31, first paragraph, governs jurisdiction and not authority or allocation within a federal State.

[60]Cf. Clarke (2014), pp. 152 ff.

[61]Cf. OLG Hamburg 22 January 1979, in *Unif. law rev.*, 1980, 266; App. Aix-en-Provence 3 March 1994, in *Bull. transp. logist.*, 1994, 451; App. Angers 4 December 1995, *ibid.*, 1996, 337.

[62]Cf. Loewe (1976), pp. 389 ff., according to whom "it was not the intention of the authors of the Convention to permit actions to be brought before the courts or tribunals mentioned in paragraph 1 (a) and (b) only in cases where the national law (. . .) itself provided that they were competent. The situation, on the contrary is that CMR compels contracting States to place their courts or tribunals at the disposal of the parties in cases covered by sub-paragraphs (a) and (b), on the understanding that it is for the national law to determine which court or tribunal will be competent *ratione materiae* and *ratione loci*".

[63]Cf. BGH 6 February 1981, in *Europ. transp. law*, 1982, no. 17, 50.

[64]Cf. Haak (1986), pp. 276 ff., according to whom, "when in such a case the law of the court petitioned possesses no rules of competence in tune with article 31, paragraph 1, letters a) and b), CMR (. . .), should the sender be obliged to petition another, generally foreign court".

[65]Cf. Cass. France 20 December 2000, in *Bull. transp. logist.*, 2001, 54; Cass. com. France 11 December 2001, *ibid.*, 2002, 15; Cass. France 20 September 2000, in *Europ. transp. law*, 2001, no. 36, 236.

[66]Cf. App. Orléans 9 December 1999, in *Bull. transp. logist.*, 2000, 12; Cass. com. France 15 May 2001, *ibid.*, 2001, 418; App. Aix-en-Provence 6 June 2013, *ibid.*, 2013, 461; App. Parigi 24 June

carence de (leur) droit processuel, à s'arroger compétence, lors même qu'elles devraient opérer renvoi vers les juridictions étrangères".[67] This argument is unfounded, because Article 31 clearly refers to jurisdiction alone and a different solution would impose an arbitrary interpretation in contrast with a plain textual indication, as well as confusion between different categories, with no justification in the objectives of uniform law. If the territorial competence is indeterminable, the national judge cannot decide and, in any case, it is a problem internal to each State, so the CMR does not apply.

10.1.4 The Two Criteria for Identifying the Country with Jurisdiction

Article 31, first paragraph, letter a), identifies the jurisdiction of the State in which "the defendant is ordinarily resident, or has his principal place of business, or the branch or agency through which the contract of carriage was made".[68] The provision refers to the habitual residence and not to the domicile[69] of the defendant, understood as a natural person,[70] whereas, for the legal one, it concerns the head office, without clarifying whether it is the actual or registered one. In this last respect, the interpretation is not left to the competent judge[71] and, in any case, it is not discretionary, because nothing hinders a convincing extensive reading, aimed at encompassing both solutions.[72] If it had wanted only a binding one, the Convention would have made it clear. Therefore, "the principal place of business" is the center from which orders are issued or effective control is exercised. A factual analysis aimed at

2010, *ibid.,* 2010, 482; App. Lyon 17 July 2002, *ibid.,* 2002, 548; App. Colmar 26 November 2001, *ibid.,* 2002, 15.

[67] Cf. Cass. com. France 8 January 2008, in *Le Lamy transp.*, 2021, vol. I, 558, according to which "*la disposition de l'Article 31 de la CMR doit s'interpreter comme permettant la saisine de l'ordre juridictionnel national du lieu de cette livraison, sans que l'application subséquente des règles de compétence territoriale interne à cet ordre puisse avoir pour effet d'écarter la compétence générale expréssement voulue par le Traité international*".

[68] Article 31, first paragraph, letter a), of the English text reads as such. The French text of Article 31, first paragraph, letter a), reads as follows: "*le défendeur a sa résidence habituelle, son siège principal ou la succursale ou l'agence par l'intermédiare de laquelle le contrat de transport a été conclu*".

[69] Cf. Silingardi et al. (1994), pp. 268 ff.; Rodière (1971), pp. 575 ff.

[70] Cf. Clarke (2014), pp. 157 ff., according to whom, "by inference, ordinary residence refers to natural persons".

[71] But cf. Loewe (1976), pp. 388 ff., according to whom "the provision does not settle the question whether 'principal place of business' means the statutory or actual place of business; and the absence of an answer to this question may lead to differing interpretations in contracting States".

[72] Cf. Messent and Glass (2018), pp. 295 ff.

establishing where managerial power is exercised is required.[73] In fact, the equation between the registered and administrative office corresponds to the objective of founding the jurisdiction in a place consistent with the organizational establishment of the defendant.

Then, Article 31, first paragraph, letter a), refers to the notion of defendant without further qualification; this provision does not apply if the party to the contract assigns his rights to a third-party.[74] The purpose of the provision is to confer jurisdiction on the judges of the State in which there is a direct relationship with the dispute. This would be evaded if the assignee could identify the jurisdiction, as this could move the dispute to a State that is heterogeneous compared to the interests of contractual parties.[75] Ultimately, the defendant's location should involve selecting a country in which the other party also has significant interests.

Some interpretative doubts arise with regard to the expression "branch or agency"[76] as, due to the manner in which it is formulated, it remains unclear whether it refers only to the branch or peripheral structure of the defendant, or even to those of the plaintiff, if they operate for the conclusion of the contract.[77] The more restrictive interpretation has to be preferred, as it is consistent with the entire provision.[78] Indeed, it would not make sense to base the jurisdiction on the place where a party outside the direct control of the defendant has his seat or residence, as this could transfer the case away from his interests, in a way contrary to the objectives of uniform law. It is not only the place where the branch or the peripheral structure of the carrier is located that must be considered, as the defendant is not always the transporter.[79] Although such a situation occurs frequently, it is not true in itself, because he can bring an action, for example, to obtain payment of the

[73] Cf. Clarke (2014), pp. 157 ff., for whom "the principal place of business is 'the centre from which instructions are given, and from which control is exercised, and the centre from which the company is managed without any further control'".

[74] Cf. Messent and Glass (2018), pp. 295 ff.; *Hatzl* c. *XL Insurance Co. Ltd.*, in *Lloyd's rep.*, 2009, 555.

[75] Cf. Messent and Glass (2018), pp. 296 ff.

[76] Article 31, first paragraph, letter a), of the English text reads as such. Article 31, first paragraph, letter a) of the French text reads as follows: "*la succursale ou l'agence*."

[77] Cf. Clarke (2014), pp. 158 ff., according to which "in some sense the branch or agency must be the defendant's own branch or agency rather than an independent one merely mandated to make the contract of carriage."

[78] Cf. Messent and Glass (2018), pp. 296 ff., according to whom "the question (...) arises as to whether the 'branch and agency' referred to in Article 31, paragraph 1 (a) refers to a branch or agency of the defendant or whether it would also cover an agency of the plaintiff (...). In other words, it might be argued that the possessive pronoun, appearing as it does only in relation to 'principal place of business' qualifies only that phrase and not the words 'branch or agency.' However, the words 'the defendant (...) has' must necessarily qualify both phrases, as otherwise the second half paragraph (a) makes no grammatical sense at all"; Silingardi et al. (1994), pp. 268 ff.; Loewe (1976), pp. 389 ff.

[79] However, cf. Loewe (1976), pp. 388 ff., according to whom "the branches and agencies must therefore be branches or agencies of the carrier".

consideration, and it is disciplined by Article 31. Jurisdiction, however, is defined with regard to the defendant's condition, despite being the shipper.

Article 31, first paragraph, letter b), identifies the jurisdiction of the State with reference to the place of receipt of the goods by the carrier or to that intended for redelivery.[80] Usually, the latter is indicated in the consignment note, unless it is modified following the exercise of the power of counter-order.[81] Furthermore, the fact that the goods do not arrive at their destination, because, for example, they are stolen,[82] does not preclude the possible application of this criterion.[83] In general, it is a parameter in favor of the consignee and it prevails although the actual unloading place is different from the scheduled one.[84] Alternatively, the generic indication of the French State as the place of arrival and location of the recipient remains insufficient to give rise to the jurisdiction of the judges of that country.[85] In fact, an imprecise draft affects the evidential function of the consignment note, pursuant to Article 6, first paragraph, letter d). Conversely, specifying the consignee's address identifies the jurisdiction.[86] Then, although Article 31, first paragraph, letter b), refers to the "place where the goods were taken over by the carrier",[87] the criterion also applies in the event of failure to perform, especially if a delivery deadline is envisaged. In fact, non-arrival is a delay and, as such, falls within the scope of the Convention.[88] Finally, for a German ruling, the sender or consignee can take action against the transporter's liability insurer, if national law allows such direct action with the application of Article 31.[89] A similar possibility is granted to the damage insurer, who, subrogated on the basis of a provision of the individual State, acts against the carrier.[90]

---

[80] Cf. Otte (2018), pp. 1533 ff.

[81] Cf. OLG Hamburg 7 April 1994, in *TranspR,* 1995, 115; OLG Monaco 19 July 1994, *ibid.,* 1995, 116; Clarke (2014), pp. 159 ff.

[82] Cf. App. Bordeaux 12 October 2016, in *Le Lamy transp.*, 2021, vol. I, 558; Trib. com. Boulogne-sur-Mer, 24 November 2017, *ibid.,* 2021, vol. I, 558.

[83] Cf. App. Parigi 24 October 1991, in *Bull. transp.,* 1991, 779; BGH 18 December 2003, in *Europ. transp. law,* 2004, no. 39, 684, according to which the place of redelivery is decisive pursuant to Article 31, first paragraph, letter b), also if the goods are not delivered, but returned because they are damaged.

[84] Cf. Putzeys (1981), pp. 378 ff., according to whom the criterion of the scheduled place of redelivery excludes "*celui du lieu réel de déchargement lorsque le lieu prévu n'est pas atteint. Cette règle dispose évidemment en faveur du destinataire*".

[85] Cf. App. Versailles 23 February 2006, in *Bull. transp.,* 2006, 384.

[86] Cf. Cass. com. France 8 January 2008, in *Le Lamy transp.*, 2021, vol. I, 558.

[87] Article 31, first paragraph, letter b), of the English text reads as such. Article 31, first paragraph, letter b), of the French text reads as follows: "*le lieu de la prise en charge de la marchandise ou celui prévu pour la livraison*".

[88] Cf. Messent and Glass (2018), pp. 297 ff., nt. 88.

[89] Cf. BGH 29 May 2019, in *TranspR,* 2019, 499.

[90] Cf. BGH 29 May 2019, in *VerkersR,* 2020, 148.

10.1.5 Jurisdiction, Multicarrier and Multimodal Transport

Article 31, first paragraph, presents application issues in relation to transport with multiple carriers. In particular, in cumulative carriage, the jurisdiction agreement binds the shipper and the first transporter, but not the subsequent ones, if this agreement is not contemplated by the consignment note or is not communicated in any other manner at the time of receipt of goods.[91] For Article 36, the liability action for loss, damage or delay may be brought against the first, the last or the carrier along whose route the event causing the prejudice occurs. The same action can be conducted simultaneously against some transporters.

From a joint reading of Article 36 and Article 31, first paragraph, letter b), it appears that, to identify the jurisdiction, it is necessary to refer to the place of receipt of goods and to the one envisaged for redelivery. The first criterion may refer, abstractly speaking, either to the place of transmission to the first carrier at the time of entering into the contract or to the passage of the load to the next one. The preferable argument identifies the jurisdiction with regard only to the position of the original transporter.[92] In fact, whoever initiates an action does not always easily know where the goods will be delivered to the next carrier. If anything, the probative difficulties already highlighted in the event of failure to or irregular draft of the consignment note arise again. It is unacceptable to refer Article 31, first paragraph, letter b), to the place of transmission of the load to the next transporter, as there is no indication to this effect in the CMR. If it had wanted to contemplate this possibility, it would have done so explicitly. Silence militates in favor of the binding identification of the jurisdiction with regard to the delivery of the cargo in direct implementation of the original contract only.

Again, pursuant to Article 36, Article 31, first paragraph, letter a), diversifies the choice of jurisdiction on the basis of the defendant's residence or head office. However, the criterion concerning "the branch or agency through which the contract of carriage was made" presupposes reference to the original parties. Therefore, the position of the first transporter is the only relevant, as the successive ones take part in the relationship through a simple manifestation of their will; in fact, they do not

[91]Cf. *British American Tobacco Denmark A/S* v. *Kaziemer Transport BV,* in *Lloyd's rep.,* 2016, 463, according to which "a successive carrier will not be bound by jurisdiction clause agreed between the consignor and the first carrier unless it is identified in the consignment note" (or unless, of course, the successive carrier binds himself to it by agreement in some other way); Messent and Glass (2018), pp. 368 ff.; Puetz (2018), pp. 122 ff.; Lamont-Black (2016), pp. 488 ff. However, see Loewe (1976), pp. 388 ff., according to whom "the designation of a jurisdiction, in accordance with the first sentence of Article 31, paragraph 1, by the parties who originally concluded the contract of carriage produces its effects with respect to the successive carriers even where such designation does not appear on the consignment note". This argument cannot be subscribed to.

[92]Cf. *British American Tobacco Denmark A/S* v. *Kaziemer Transport BV,* in *Lloyd's rep.,* 2016, 463, according to which "it is common ground (...) that paragraph, letter b), refers to the places of taking over by the carrier and designated for delivery under CMR made between the consignor and the first carrier"; OGH 25 May 2004, in *TranspR,* 2004, 359; Messent and Glass (2018), pp. 368 ff.

interfere with the initial agreement.[93] Finally, once the jurisdiction has been identified on the basis of Article 31, first paragraph, letter a) and letter b), Article 36, last paragraph, consolidates the jurisdiction over possible further actions, which, on the contrary, could involve proceedings in another State. In this manner, Article 36, last paragraph, avoids the exercise of several actions in succession.[94]

In internal relations, pursuant to Article 39, second paragraph, the carrier bringing an action for recovery may opt for the jurisdiction of the State in which one of the other transporters has his habitual residence, head office or branch or a peripheral structure through which the contract is concluded.[95] Compared to Article 31, first paragraph, Article 39, second paragraph, provides for a less wide choice of countries with jurisdiction. As for Article 36, last paragraph, once the State to which one of the aforementioned criteria applies has been identified, Article 39, second paragraph, centralizes the judgment of the case brought against all carriers, regardless of whether the parameters set out by the Article 39, second paragraph, apply to all of them.[96] In this way, duplication of proceedings and decisions is avoided.[97]

Alternatively, subtransport is a recurring organizational model. The main carrier is the sole party bound to the sender and may decide to use one or more operators for performance of the service. The first transporter remains solely liable for the journey to the shipper and consignee. Given the particular structure of the contract, Article 31, first paragraph, letter b), identifies the jurisdiction considering the position of the main transporter, without giving any relevance to the different receipt of goods by the subtransporter.[98] On the contrary, in the internal relations between the two carriers, delivery to the latter is considered, if the CMR is applied. In fact, the subcarriage is an autonomous contract, instrumentally linked to a previous one; however, from a structural viewpoint, it is identical to the first. Therefore, for the purposes of Article 31, first paragraph, letter b), with regard to subtransport only and to the legal actions related to it, the position of the subcarrier is relevant.[99]

---

[93] Cf. *British American Tobacco Denmark A/S* v. *Kaziemer Transport BV,* in *Lloyd's rep.,* 2016, 463, according to which "CMR makes them a party by statute in consequence of their accepting the goods and the consignment note".

[94] Cf. *British American Tobacco Denmark A/S* v. *Kaziemer Transport BV,* in *Lloyd's rep.,* 2016, 463, according to which, Article 36, last paragraph, confirms that "there is no need to pursue them sequentially"; Clarke (2014), pp. 159 ff. Lamont-Black (2016), pp. 493 ff.

[95] Cf. Crignon-Dumoulin (2006), pp. 613 ff. Cf. Cass. Denmark 24 March 2000, in *Europ. transp. law,* 2000, no. 35, 772; RB Limburg 28 March 2017, *ibid.,* 2018, no. 53, 87.

[96] Cf. Messent and Glass (2018), pp. 387 ff., according to whom "all other successive carriers can be joined in the same action, regardless of whether an action against them in that country would otherwise have been permitted by Article 39, paragraph 2".

[97] Cf. Messent and Glass (2018), pp. 387 ff.

[98] Cf. BGH 31 May 2001, in *TranspR*, 2001, 452; BGH 9 October 2003, *ibid.,* 2004, 166; BGH 20 November 2008, *ibid.,* 2009, 26; OGH 1 April 1999, *ibid.,* 2000, 34; *Moto Vespa S. A.* v. *MAT (Brittania Express) Ltd.,* in *Lloyd's,* 1979, 175.

[99] Cf. BGH 13 March 2014, in *TranspR,* 2014, 370.

Multimodal transport is implemented in at least two different ways under a contract with which a single carrier, the so-called multimodal transport operator, assumes responsibility for the entire transfer. As a whole, the agreement regulates the journey from the moment of receipt of goods until delivery. In case of a transnational transfer, it is necessary to consider individual sections into which the entire itinerary is divided. So, where appropriate, the CMR operates for the part entrusted to the road transporter and, within these restricted limits, Article 31 can be applied. Therefore, it can only be invoked for internal relations between the multimodal operator[100] and the road hauler, and it is not possible to extend the relevance of the rule to other cases.[101]

10.2 Exercise of the Legal Action

10.2.1 Remedies for the Possible Duplication of Proceedings

Article 31, first paragraph, identifies various States with jurisdiction. To avoid a duplication of proceedings and judgments,[102] according to Article 31, second paragraph, if an action is brought before the judge of the country with jurisdiction pursuant to the first paragraph or if the dispute has already been decided,[103] parties cannot initiate a new one, unless the decision issued by the judge seized in the first proceeding cannot be enforced in the country where the second lawsuit is started.[104] This latter scenario is relevant if the State in which the original proceeding began has not ratified the Convention.[105] However, if there are more trials, the prescription period provided for by Article 32 must be complied with for each action.[106] Article 31, second paragraph, concerns a coincidence of the actions in respect to both the object and parties, regardless of the procedural position. In this manner, the carrier, at first a defendant, can be the plaintiff in the subsequent case, always with the application of Article 31, second paragraph.[107]

The Convention does not clarify when the "action is pending", but assumes that it had some beginning; in fact, it is stated, "*une action est en instance devant une*

[100] Cf. Laimer and Perathoner (2019), pp. 40 ff.; Puetz (2018), pp. 122 ff.

[101] Cf. Demuth (2013a), pp. 849 ff.

[102] Cf. Clarke (2014), pp. 161 ff.; Haak (1986), pp. 291 ff.; Putzeys (1981), pp. 379 ff.

[103] Cf. Putzeys (1981), pp. 379 ff., who highlights that the rule of "*lis alibi pendens*" is applied only if there is a decision that has not become *res judicata* as yet; Demuth (2013a), pp. 869 ff.

[104] Cf. Haak (1986), pp. 291 ff.; Putzeys (1981), pp. 379 ff.

[105] Cf. Loewe (1976), pp. 390 ff.

[106] Cf. Messent and Glass (2018), pp. 299 ff.

[107] Cf. Messent and Glass (2018), pp. 299 ff., according to whom "this prohibition applies to any new action 'between the same parties', so it will apply equally to attempts by the defendant to counterclaim in another jurisdiction"; Loewe (1976), pp. 389 ff.; Otte (2018), pp. 1539 ff.

jurisdiction".[108] In this regard, the CMR does not propose any regulation; therefore, the solution of complex and inevitable application problems cannot be found there. It must be inferred from other sources and, within the European Union, Regulation (EU) 1215/2012[109] assumes specific importance. However, this reference is partial, as the scope of application of the CMR is much more extensive from a territorial viewpoint. Consequently, from time to time, depending on the States involved, it is necessary to establish relevant sources and, on this basis, the concept of the supervened exercise of the action. It is not possible here to examine all the possibilities and it seems sufficient to underline that the CMR does not solve the problem and refers to other regulatory indications,[110] especially of a procedural nature.

For Article 31, second paragraph, a new action "between the same parties on the same grounds"[111] is precluded. This formula was considered ambiguous, but the criticisms are unfounded.[112] The provision relates to the subsequent exercise of the same action and, therefore, its object is relevant, at least in relation to the continental law. The identity of the action presupposes that not only of the parties but also of the object, although the exact interpretation of this reference, proposed in a synthetic manner by the CMR, is a delicate issue. Therefore, despite the perspicuity of Article 31, second paragraph, and its consistency with the overall logic of continental legal systems, the judges of various countries are certainly influenced by their procedural law. Without prejudice to the synthetic reference to the uniqueness of the dispute, it would be an exaggeration to expect uniform solutions on such a complex topic, characterized by individual legal systems to such an extent.

In cumulative carriage, if the parties to the subsequent proceedings are the same, the negative ascertainment of the liability of one of the transporters precludes the possibility that he can be sued by the party entitled to the goods, as the case falls under Article 31, second paragraph.[113] In fact, if such proceedings arise from relationships governed by the Convention, negative declaration actions also fall under Article 31, first paragraph. Therefore, they involve the application of

[108] Article 31, second paragraph of the French text reads. Article 31, second paragraph, of the English text reads as follows: "before a court or tribunal". Cf. Messent and Glass (2018), pp. 300 ff., according to whom "the specific reference to 'before a court or a tribunal' must mean that at least some step in the action has been taken".

[109] Cf. *Royal & Sun Alliance Insurance Plc.* v. *MK Digital FZE (Cyprus) Ltd.*, in *Lloyd's rep.*, 2005, 679, which applied Article 31, first paragraph, letter a), of Regulation (EU) 1215/2012, which identifies the beginning of the *lis alibi pendens* with the filing of the judicial application.

[110] Cf. Messent and Glass (2018), pp. 300 ff., who highlight that in the United Kingdom, the beginning of the *lis alibi pendens* was made to correspond with the notification of the judicial application, by reference to national law. Cf. *Andrea Merzario Ltd.* v. *Internationale Spedition Leitner Gesellschaft GmbH*, in *Lloyd's rep.*, 2001, 490, which recognized the jurisdiction of the United Kingdom, although the proceedings were subsequent to a matter started before an Austrian judge. This is because, in such case, the pleading had been filed, but not yet notified.

[111] Thus, Article 31, second paragraph of the English text read.

[112] Cf. Clarke (2014), pp. 162 ff.

[113] Cf. *Andrea Merzario Ltd.* v. *Internationale Spedition Leitner Gesellschaft GmbH*, in *Lloyd's rep.*, 2001, 490.

Article 31, second paragraph.[114] For example, they are identical to those targeted at securing payment of the consideration.[115]

On the contrary, Article 31, second paragraph, does not operate if the action is exercised in a State whose jurisdiction is not identified on the basis of one of the criteria of Article 31, first paragraph,[116] for example, as determined by a specific agreement. A further exception could arise because "a court may feel compelled to accept proceeding on the basis of doubts as to the meaning of where a claim can be said to be 'pending' in another jurisdiction for the purposes of Article 31, paragraph 2".[117] This argument remains unconvincing, as the second judge must decide on the existence of conditions for the operation of Article 31, second paragraph, and cannot simply state that he has doubts.

10.2.2 Enforcement of Decisions

For Article 31, third paragraph, a decision pronounced by a judge of a signatory country that has become enforceable is also such for other contracting States, as long as, if need be, the formalities prescribed by the legal system in which the foreign decision is to be executed are fulfilled.[118] In this way, the Convention guarantees to anyone who obtains a favorable ruling that it will be executed in other States that are party to the CMR.[119] The provision does not eliminate the control of judges of the second country, as the formalities required must be fulfilled.[120]

In any case, it is up to the judge of the State in which the decision is to be executed to verify that it is enforceable in the country where the proceeding was initiated.[121] However, this cannot entail any revision of the decision on the merits; once resolved, the same dispute cannot be reexamined. Thus, possible varied outcomes are

[114] Cf. Court of Justice, third section, 19 December 2013, C-no. 452 del 2012, *NipponKoa Insurance Co. (Europe) Ltd.* c. *Inter – Zuid Transport BV e DTC Surhuisterveen BV*; BGH 25 July 2019, in *TranspR*, 2019, 508, according to which Article 31, second paragraph, applies also if, in one of the two Stated, an application for negative declaration is brought. Cf. also Lamont-Black (2016), pp. 498 ff.

[115] Cf. Puetz (2018), pp. 118 ff.

[116] Cf. Messent and Glass (2018), pp. 302 ff.; BGH 25 July 2019, in *TranspR*, 2019, 508.

[117] Cf. Messent and Glass (2018), pp. 302 ff.

[118] Cf. Rodière (1971), pp. 577 ff.; Haak (1986), pp. 291 ff.; Demuth (2013a), pp. 873 ff.

[119] See Silingardi et al. (1994), pp. 275 ff.; Messent and Glass (2018), pp. 303 ff., according to which "the plaintiff wishes to enforce a decision otherwise than in the country in which it was obtained".

[120] It is the analysis conducted by each domestic legislation that must verify which formalities are necessary for the nature of writ of execution to be conferred on the foreign pronouncement. Cf. Messent and Glass (2018), pp. 303 ff.: Loewe (1976), pp. 391 ff.

[121] Cf. Messent and Glass (2018), pp. 303 ff.; Loewe (1976), pp. 391 ff.

avoided.[122] Furthermore, as Article 31, third paragraph, concerns the States that have joined the CMR,[123] the jurisdictions chosen according to Article 31, first paragraph, can be of noncontracting countries. In this case, Article 31, third paragraph, does not apply.[124] The purpose of this last provision is to ensure that, once it has become enforceable in one State, a decision has the same force in all other signatory countries.[125]

For Article 31, fourth paragraph, judgments after trial, those made *in absentia* and judicial settlements fall within the scope of Article 31, third paragraph, provided that the latter are enforceable in the State in which they are adopted.[126] However, the rulings which, after dismissing the plaintiff's claim, order him to pay compensation for prejudices, in addition to the reimbursement of expenses, are excluded from the structure of Article 31, fourth paragraph,[127] in accordance with the principles of each legal system. For the latter scenarios, the immediate and direct recognition of the decision as an enforceable one, pursuant to Article 31, third paragraph, does not apply. However, Article 31, fourth paragraph, does not preclude the fact that, in a legal system other than that in which the decision is made, an executive order can be obtained for damages and expenses, but only "makes it clear [that] the awards of costs must, as such, be recognized and enforced".[128]

Finally, Article 31, fifth paragraph, excludes that the "*caution*"[129] is due by citizens of signatory countries who reside or have a place of business in another contracting State.[130] The purpose of the rule is to facilitate access to justice, preventing any obstacle from domestic provisions.[131] Referring to the "nationals of contracting countries",[132] Article 31, fifth paragraph, seems to exclude citizens of the same State from its scope of application.[133] However, no element of a systematic

[122] See Silingardi et al. (1994), pp. 276 ff.; Rodière (1971), pp. 577 ff.

[123] Cf. Clarke (2014), p. 162, according to whom, "evidently, the 'country concerned' is the other contracting State in which the judgment is to become enforceable".

[124] See Silingardi et al. (1994), pp. 276 ff.

[125] See Silingardi et al. (1994), pp. 276 ff.; Clarke (2014), pp. 162 ff.

[126] Cf. Loewe (1976), pp. 391 ff., according to whom "settlements confirmed by order of a court will have to be recognized and enforced only if, in the State on whose territory they have been concluded, they constitute enforceable acts"; Demuth (2013a), pp. 875 ff.

[127] Cf. Putzeys (1981), pp. 380 ff., according to whom "*les dommages – intérêts (...) sont les dommages – intérêts parfois allués pour procés téméraires et vexatoires*".

[128] Cf. Loewe (1976), pp. 391 ff. See also Silingardi et al. (1994), pp. 276 ff.

[129] Article 31, fifth paragraph, of the French text reads as such. Article 31, fifth paragraph, of the English text reads as follows: "security for costs."

[130] Cf. Rodière (1971), pp. 577 ff.

[131] See Silingardi et al. (1994), pp. 277 ff.

[132] Article 31, fifth paragraph, of the English text reads as such. Article 31, fifth paragraph, of the French text reads as follows: "*pays contractants*".

[133] Cf. Messent and Glass (2018), pp. 306 ff. For a restrictive reading of Article 31, fifth paragraph, cf. Loewe (1976), pp. 392 ff., for whom "it cannot be inferred from the provision that it exempts

nature emerges for such a restrictive interpretation, as Article 31, fourth paragraph, generally favors the reasons of the defense.

10.2.3 The Arbitration Clause

For Article 33, the parties can include a specific clause aimed at referring the dispute to an arbitration tribunal in the contract of carriage; however, it must provide for the application of the CMR.[134] Although the provision does not mention formal requirements expressly, the agreement may not be oral.[135] After all, the consignee is bound only if the written clause is included in the contract.[136] Moreover, the arbitration tribunal must implement the Convention,[137] as the purpose of the provision is to ensure the operation of the CMR,[138] so that any intermediate carriers are also aware of the agreement and, even more so, the consignee. In the absence of the written form, the clause is void.[139]

With good reason, an agreement[140] that referred the dispute to arbitrators exclusively and did not provide for reference to the Convention[141] was considered null and void; this consequence was derived from the violation of Article 33 owing to the inaccuracy of the content. However, there was also noncompliance with Article 31, as, in the agreement, the power of the arbitration tribunal was considered

---

nationals of the State of the court or tribunal who are resident in that State from the obligation to furnish security".

[134] Cf. OGH 20 March 2007, in *TranspR,* 2007, 326, according to which the arbitration clause is valid and effective if it envisages the applicability of the CMR by the arbitrators; Demuth (2013b), 941 ff.; Herrero de Egaña Muñoz-Cobo (2016), pp. 590 ff.

[135] Cf. Messent and Glass (2018), pp. 336 ff., according to whom "it would seem that the agreement as to arbitration should be in writing"; Demuth (2013b), pp. 940 ff.

[136] Cf. Clarke (2014), pp. 164 ff.; Haak (1986), pp. 283 ff.

[137] Cf. App. Paris 12 January 2011, in *Bull. transp.,* 2011, 141, according to which "*la clause doit stipuler, en de termes dénués d'impécision, que ce tribunal arbitral appliquera la Convention CMR*"; App. Aix-en-Provence 2 September 2004, *ibid.,* 2004, 614; App. Aix-en-Provence 19 November 2015, *ibid.,* 2015, 700; App. Toulouse 22 December 2016, *ibid.,* 2017, 79; HR The Netherlands 25 January 2008, in *Europ. transp. law,* 2008, no. 43, 498, according to which, if the dispute does not fall within the scope of the CMR, the arbitration clause must not conform to the provisions of Article 33. Cf. Fillers (2020), pp. 172 ff., who draws the same conclusions on the basis of a recognition of Lithuania jurisdiction.

[138] Cf. Haak (1986), pp. 281 ff.

[139] Cf. Messent and Glass (2018), pp. 336 ff.; Loewe (1976), pp. 395 ff.

[140] For a null and void case, see *A. B. Bofors – UVA* v. *A. B. Skandia Transport*, in *Lloyd's rep.,* 1982, 410; Arrond. Rotterdam 31 January 1967, in *S & S.,* 1967, no. 56.

[141] Cf. Haak (1986), pp. 284 ff.

exclusive.[142] In fact, similar to the jurisdiction agreement, the arbitration clause cannot be exclusive, based on an extensive interpretation of Article 31. Instead, we have to consider valid the clause according to which the arbitrators "should observe the applicable imperative legal stipulations, including the provisions of international transport treaties".[143]

Although Article 33 does not mention an agreement following the beginning of a dispute, its stipulation is considered legitimate[144] and it should not comply with Article 33;[145] therefore, it must not specifically refer to the CMR. The regulation of the arbitration clause does not imply the prohibition of concluding an agreement after the prejudice occurred; the Convention only aims at ensuring the full awareness of the sender, carrier and consignee. Such problems are irrelevant in the case of an agreement stipulated after the beginning of the dispute, and this justifies the silence of the CMR, which does not deal with the topic. The Convention signed in New York on 10 June 1958 operates for the execution of arbitration awards for the States that have ratified it.[146]

10.3 The Relationship Between the Geneva Convention and European Union Regulations

10.3.1 Article 31, First Paragraph, and the Regulation (EU) 1215/2012

For EU Member States that have joined the CMR, Article 31, first paragraph, must be read in the light of Regulation (EU) 1215/2012 on the jurisdiction, recognition and enforcement of decisions in civil and commercial matters. It replaced the previous Regulation (EC) 44/2001,[147] which, in turn, had intervened on the Brussels

142 In this sense, see OGH 5 May 2010, in *TranspR,* 2010, 383; RB Antwerp 8 November 2013, in *Europ. transp. law,* 2014, no. 49, 222. In the sense criticized herein, see OLG Koblenz 22 February 2007, in *TranspR,* 2007, 249.

143 Cf. *Inco Europe Ltd.* c. *First Choice Distribution,* in *All England Reports*, 1999, 820; but see OLG Hamm 29 June 1998, in *TranspR,* 1999, 201, which considered a clause with the same content illegitimate.

144 Cf. Messent and Glass (2018), pp. 337 ff., according to whom, "once the claim has arisen, on the basis of the normal contractual principle that any compromise of an action is binding on the parties, the parties may dispose of it in any way they agree".

145 Cf. Loewe (1976), pp. 395 ff., according to whom, "after the damage has occurred, arbitration agreements may be concluded without any restriction whatever"; Putzeys (1981), pp. 382 ff., according to whom "*il ne faut pas la confondre avec le compromis après naissance du litige et qui est soumis au droit des partes litigants* '*sans restriction aucune*'".

146 Cf. Messent and Glass (2018), pp. 338 ff.

147 Cf. OGH 13 December 2002, in *Europ. transp. law,* 2003, no. 38, 656.

Convention of 27 September 1968.[148] For Article 71 of Regulation (EU) 1215/2012, this "shall not affect any conventions to which the Member States are parties and which, in relation to [a] particular matter, govern jurisdiction or the recognition or the enforcement of judgments". The provision refers only to conventions on a "particular matter". Therefore, those which, in general terms, regulate jurisdiction, recognition and enforcement of decisions are excluded. Moreover, this principle had already been ruled by Article 69 of Regulation (EC) 44/2001.

In fact, Article 71 not only operates for conventions ratified by all Member States, but also for those to which only some have adhered. So, the aim is to prevent EU countries from breaking their commitments at the international level, and the rule is without prejudice to agreements previously stipulated.[149] However, while Article 57 of the 1968 Brussels Convention considered "any conventions to which contracting States are or will be parties", the current regulation allows the derogation with regard to existing treaties, but not to future ones. In particular, the conventions ratified and executed before the enforcement of Regulation (EC) 44/2001 fall within the scope of Article 71. In fact, according to the thirty-six recital of Regulation (EU) 1215/2012, "this Regulation should not affect the application of bilateral conventions and agreements between a third State and a Member State concluded before the date of entry into force of Regulation (EC) 1215/2012, which concern matters governed by this Regulation".

The CMR became enforceable on 2 July 1961 and almost all European Union countries had joined before the enforcement of Regulation (EC) 44/2001. The only exceptions were Cyprus and Malta, which ratified the CMR in 2003 and 2007.[150] With reference to the previous Regulation (EC) 44/2001, the Court of Justice[151] interpreted Article 31, first paragraph, of the CMR in the sense that, if a dispute falls within the scope of application of both the Regulation and the Convention, in compliance with the provisions of Article 71, first paragraph, of the Regulation, a State applies the rules on jurisdiction provided for by Article 31, first paragraph, of

[148] Cf. BGH 27 January 2003, in *Europ. transp. law,* 2003, no. 38, 653; BGH 10 September 2003, *ibid.,* 2004, no. 39, 74.

[149] Cf. OGH 7 January 2003, in *Europ. transp. law,* 2003, no. 38, 658; OGH 10 January 2003, *ibid.,* 2003, no. 38, 661. See also Otte (2018), pp. 1536 ff.

[150] Cf. Puetz (2018), pp. 117 ff.

[151] Cf. Court of Justice, first chamber, 4 September 2014, Cause C-no. 157 of 2013, *Nickel & Goeldner Spedition GmbH* v. *"Kintra" UAB*; Trib. Milan 17 April 2014, in *Riv. dir. int. priv. proc.,* 2017, 128. Although in a different field of international maritime transport of goods, cf. Cass. Italy 9 March 2015, no. 4686, in *Riv. dir. int. priv. proc.,* 2016, 509, according to which, with regard to the request for refund of damage resulting from the collision of two vessels, occurred in Croatian waters, the jurisdiction is determined pursuant to the Brussels Convention of 10 May 1956 for the unification of some rules concerning the civil jurisprudence competent for cases of collision between vessels. The prevalence of the conventional framework is stated by Article 71, first paragraph, of Regulation (EC) 44/2001, now replaced by Regulation (EU) 1215/2012. With regard to the 1968 Brussels Convention, for a similar pronouncement by the Court of Justice, see Court of Justice, third chamber, 28 October 2004, Cause C-no. 148 of 2003, *Nürberger Allgemeine Versicherungs AG,* v. *Portbridge Transport International BV.*

the CMR.[152] The argument of the Court of Justice is well founded and is based on a literal reading of Regulation (EU) 1215/2012, consistent with its objectives, which are also stated precisely.

In general, Article 31, first paragraph, concerns the relationship between the carrier and shipper or consignee, depending on who holds the right of redelivery.[153] On the contrary, the rules on jurisdiction of Regulation (EU) 1215/2012 for disputes with the shipper apply as long as he is a citizen of another EU country.

10.3.2 Article 31, Second and Third Paragraphs, and Regulation (EU) 1215/2012

Article 31, second and third paragraphs, of the CMR poses delicate problems of coordination with the analogous provisions of Regulation (EU) 1215/2012.[154] Although with regard to the previous Regulation (EC) 44/2001, the Court of Justice ruled on a preliminary question concerning the interpretation of Article 71 in relation to the indications of Article 31, second and third paragraphs, of the CMR.[155] In particular, the question arose whether, following an application for execution filed pursuant to Article 31, third paragraph, of the CMR, the judge of the State called to implement a decision could have ascertained the fact that the judge of the country of origin had violated the principle of Article 31, second paragraph, of the CMR. Basically, the question arose if the rules of the CMR should prevail over that of the Regulation.

The Court reached a complex solution and interpreted Article 71 of Regulation (EC) 44/2001 in the sense that the judges of EU member States have to apply the rules on jurisdiction, recognition and enforcement of decisions provided for by a convention relating to a particular matter, such as the CMR, provided they present a high degree of predictability, facilitate a good administration of justice, attempt to reduce the risk of multiple pending proceedings and ensure the execution of decisions in civil and commercial matters and mutual trust within the Union, in

[152] Cf. BGH 27 February 2003, in *TranspR,* 2003, 302, according to which the jurisdictional principles of Article 31, first paragraph, prevail on European regulations; OLG Düsseldorf 17 June 1999, *ibid.,* 2002, 237; OLG Schleswig 20 December 2001, *ibid.,* 2002, 76; OLG Hamburg 30 September 2002, *ibid.,* 2003, 23; OGH 8 April 2002, *ibid.,* 2003, 67. Cf. also Demuth (2013a), pp. 852 ff.

[153] Cf. App. Lyon 21 October 1976, in *Bull. transp.,* 1977, 110; Trib. com. Paris 9 February 1999, *ibid.*, 1999, 445.

[154] Cf. *Sony Computer Entertainment Ltd.* v. *RH Freight Services Ltd. and Others*, in *Lloyd's law rep.,* 2007, 463; the case considers the Regulation (EC) 44/2001.

[155] Cf. Court of Justice, Grand Chamber, 4 May 2012, C-no. 533 of 2008, *TNT Express Nederland BV* v. *AXA Versicherung AG.* In the sense indicated by the Court of Justice, see RB Limburg 25 March 2020, in *Europ. transp. law,* 2021, no. 61, 45.

conditions equally favorable to those provided for by the aforementioned Regulation.[156] In essence, its provision would not necessarily be conditioned by the rules laid down by treaties on particular matters; however, there would be a margin for discretionary adaptation.[157]

The principle was reiterated;[158] in particular, the Court was again asked to establish whether Article 31, second paragraph, of the CMR could operate if an action for negative declaration is conducted in front of a judge.[159] For the Court, "the Article 71 of Regulation EC 44/2001 must be interpreted as meaning that it precludes an interpretation of Article 31, second paragraph, 'of the CMR', according to which an action for negative declaration or a negative declaratory judgment in one Member State does not have the same cause of action as an action for indemnity between the same parties in another Member State".

The approach is unacceptable, as negative declaration actions also fall within the scope of the CMR.[160] In fact, they pertain to international transport, as stipulated by Article 31, first paragraph. Therefore, the principle of Article 31, second paragraph, operates even in this case.[161] This approach is confirmed by a German orientation, according to which, pursuant to Article 31, second paragraph, an action for damages is precluded by the fact that in another State where the CMR applies there is a pending trial dealing with an action for negative declaration between the same parties and for the same fact,[162] although there is no shortage of opposite solutions.[163]

[156] Cf. Belintxon Martín (2016/2017), pp. 586 ff.; Carbone (2016), pp. 15 ff., who, while sharing the approach of the Court of Justice, highlights that the coordination clause, incorporated in Article 71, must be interpreted as "addressed to favor the application of special conventions only if and to the extent in which they do not cause prejudice to the fundamental rules of the legal space".

[157] Cf. Belintxon Martín (2016/2017), pp. 586 ff., according to whom "this suggests that there is a margin of discretion, a room for judicial interpretation of the rule of speciality, that will depend on the circumstances of the particular case"; Defossez (2016), pp. 78 ff.

[158] Cf. Court of Justice, third chamber, 19 December 2013, C-no. 452 del 2012, *NipponKoa Insurance Co. (Europe) Ltd.* v. *Inter – Zuid Transport BV and DTC Surhuisterveen BV.*

[159] Cf. Belintxon Martín (2016/2017), pp. 587 ff.

[160] Cf. *Andrea Merzario Ltd.* v. *Internationale Spedition Leitner Gesellschaft GmbH,* in *Lloyd's rep.,* 2001, 490. Cf. Carbone (2016), pp. 16 ff.; Herber (2003), pp. 19 ff.; Heuer (2002), pp. 222 ff.; Shariatmadari (2006), pp. 105 ff. See also BGH 20 November 2003, in *Europ. transp. law,* 2004, no. 39, 255.

[161] Cf. OGH 17 February 2006, in *TranspR,* 2006, 257, according to which a preventive action for negative declaration entails the applicability of Article 31, second paragraph, in relation to the subsequent action instituted by the party entitled to compensation.

[162] Cf. OLG Nurimberg 6 March 2002, in *TranspR,* 2002, 402; OLG Düsseldorf 9 October 2018, in *TranspR,* 2019, 140, according to which Article 31, second paragraph, operates if, in the Netherlands, an action for negative declaration is proposed and, in Germany, a claim for an order is initiated.

[163] Cf. OLG Cologne 8 March 2002, in *TranspR,* 2002, 239, according to which the exercise of an action for negative declaration in a different State that has adhered to the CMR does not preclude the action from being brought in Germany; OLG Hamburg 7 November 2002, *ibid.,* 2003, 25.

In general, the overall viewpoint offered by the Court is unconvincing, as it contradicts the clear spirit of Article 71, which has remained unchanged in the current Regulation (EU) 1215/2012, for which the conventions on particular matters governing the jurisdiction, recognition and enforcement of decisions must be applied, with no room for restrictive interpretations.[164] Based on the aforementioned Article 71, Article 31, second and third paragraphs, of the CMR should always prevail. To be honest, it is unclear why the Court did not grasp the divergence of its interpretation from Article 71 of Regulation (EU) 1215/2012 and took such a creative stance that is inconsistent with unequivocal textual indications.[165]

Then, for Article 31, second paragraph, of Regulation (EU) 1215/2012, if an agreement reserves jurisdiction exclusively to the judge of a Member State, the one of the country seized at a later time must suspend the proceeding until the first judge declares his eventual lack of jurisdiction. This provision cannot be applied to international transport governed by the CMR, as the latter opts for a nonexclusive jurisdictional agreement, pursuant to Article 31, first paragraph.

Finally, for Article 31, third paragraph, of the CMR, a decision that has become enforceable in one contracting State is such in all the others, provided that, where regulated, the formalities required in the country in which the decision is to be enforced are fulfilled. For the ratifying States that are members of the European Union, formal requirements are determined by Article 71, second paragraph, letter b), of Regulation (EU) 1215/2012.[166] Therefore, the recognition or enforcement of decisions can be denied only on the basis of Article 45 of the same Regulation,[167] for example, if there are statements contrary to public order or the ruling is incompatible with that issued between the same parties in the Member State where enforcement is sought.

[164] In the opposite sense, see Carbone (2016), pp. 17 ff., according to whom, "in order to prevail over Brussels regulation I – *bis,* any provision prescribed by international conventions cannot 'limit itself' to regulating civil procedural issues emerged in a specific case in an exclusive manner. Firstly and mostly, they need to envisage a solution that, *prima facie*, seems consistent with the logic behind the Union's legislation and instrumental to the pursuit of its objectives".

[165] Cf. Wesolowski (2011), pp. 141 ff., who, with similar arguments, does not share the solution of the Court of Justice. According to the Author, "it is possible that domestic courts applying the CMR will refer the Court's judgment (. . .) also to the matters regulated by the provisions of this Convention. Such understanding of the Court's judgment would (. . .) mean that it contains impermissible (. . .) interpretation of CMR. Such interpretation is not legally binding".

[166] For Article 71, second paragraph, letter b), "any decision taken in a Member State by a jurisdictional authority that has based its jurisdiction on a dispute related to a specific matter is recognized and enforced in other Member States in compliance with this regulation".

[167] Cf. Puetz (2018), pp. 123 ff.

10.3.3 The Convention Relating to Jurisdiction, Recognition and Enforcement of Judgments in Civil and Commercial Matters, Signed in Lugano on 30 October 2007

The Lugano Convention relating to the jurisdiction, recognition and enforcement of judgments in civil and commercial matters was signed on 30 October 2007, by the then European Community, Denmark, and the States members of the European Free Trade Association (the so-called EFTA), namely, Switzerland, Norway and Iceland.[168] In turn, it replaces the 1988 Lugano Convention, which recalled in content the 1968 Brussels Convention. Before becoming a member of the European Union, Poland had joined the 1988 Lugano Convention, by virtue of its Article 62, first paragraph, letter b), which also regulated the application for non-EU countries that did not belong to the European Free Trade Association.[169]

In terms of its content, the Lugano Convention of 2007 follows Regulation (EC) 44/2001. On the basis of directives issued by the Council in 2002, the Commission participated in the definition of the aforementioned treaty with the aim of facilitating, as far as possible, the alignment of its provisions with those of the Regulation. In contrast to the 1988 Convention, the 2007 Convention included the then European Community as a contractual party rather than individual Member States.[170] This was possible following the intervention of the Court of Justice,[171] which, after being summoned by the Council to rule over the parties authorized to conclude this agreement, recognized the then Community's exclusive authority to stipulate the Convention.

The particular position of Denmark[172] has to be considered. By virtue of the provisions of Protocol no. 22 annexed to the Treaty on the Union and to the Treaty on Functioning, Denmark cannot manifest any accession to acts of the European Union. Therefore, neither Regulation (EC) 44/2001, pursuant to the 21st recital, nor Regulation (EU) 1215/2012, pursuant to the 41st recital, bind it. Moreover, the 1968 Brussels Convention would govern civil or commercial disputes with that State on the basis of the 21st recital of Regulation (EC) 44/2001. Denmark signed an agreement on 1 July 2007, with the then European Community to avoid discrepancies in regulations between Member States. Under this agreement, the provisions of Regulation (EC) 44/2001 were also applied to such country. With the entry into force of Regulation (EU) 1215/2012, Denmark notified the Commission of its decision to implement it.[173]

---

[168] Cf. Carbone (2016), pp. 5 ff.; Pocar (2008), pp. 2 ff.; Tebbens (2001), pp. 2 ff.

[169] Cf. Carbone (2016), pp. 5 ff.

[170] Cf. Carbone (2016), pp. 6 ff.

[171] Cf. Court of Justice 7 February 2006, opinion 1/03.

[172] Cf. Carbone (2016), pp. 9 ff.

[173] Cf. Carbone (2016), pp. 10 ff.

Furthermore, to establish the respective fields of application of Regulation (EU) 1215/2012, the Denmark–European Community agreement and the latest Lugano Convention, the defendant's domicile is relevant, pursuant to Article 64, second paragraph, of the Lugano Convention; if the domicile is located in a Member State, the Union regulation or the aforementioned agreement with Denmark shall apply, on the basis of the identified criteria. If the defendant is in Switzerland, Iceland or Norway, the Lugano Convention operates.[174]

Like Regulation (EU) 1215/2012, the Lugano Convention does not affect the treaties that in particular matters govern the jurisdiction, recognition and enforcement of decisions, as provided for by Article 67, first paragraph, of the same Convention.[175] Therefore, Article 31 of the CMR must prevail in all disputes in which either a Member State, pursuant to Article 71 of Regulation (EU) 1215/2012, or Denmark, on the basis of the aforementioned agreement, or Switzerland, Iceland or Norway, pursuant to the aforementioned Article 67 of the Lugano Convention, are involved.[176]

References

Belintxon Martín U (2016/2017) The CMR 1956 Convention: some specific issues from a private international law perspective. Yearb Priv Int Law, 570 ff.

Carbone SM (2016) Il nuovo spazio giudiziario europeo in materia civile e commerciale: il regolamento Ue no. 1215/2012. Turin

Clarke MA (2014) International carriage of goods by road: CMR, VI edn. New York

Crignon-Dumoulin S (2006) Article 31 de la CMR. Unif Law Rev, 609 ff.

Defossez D (2016) CMR: what if the courts got it wrong? Unif Law Rev, 75 ff.

Demuth K (2013a) Art. 31. In: Thume KH (ed) Aa. Vv., CMR: Über den Beförderungsvertrag im internationalen Strassengüterverkehr, III edn. Frankfurt Am Main, pp 847 ff.

Demuth K (2013b) Art. 33. In: Thume KH (ed) Aa. Vv., CMR: Über den Beförderungsvertrag im internationalen Strassengüterverkehr, III edn. Frankfurt Am Main, pp 940 ff.

Ferrari F (2002) Forum shopping despite international uniform contract law conventions. Int Comp Law Q, 689 ff.

Fillers A (2020) The CMR in the practice of Latvian courts. Unif Law Rev, 169 ff.

Haak KF (1986) The liability of the carrier under CMR. The Hague

Herber R (2003) Probleme um Art. 31 CMR endlich ein Ende des Mißbrauchs durch negative Feststellungsklage des Frachtführers? TranspR, 19 ff.

Herrero de Egaña Muñoz-Cobo MI (2016) Spain's juntas arbitrales de transporte: a special dispute adjudication regime for small claims in land transport. Unif Law Rev, 591 ff.

[174] Cf. Trib. Varese 27 October 2012, in *Riv. dir. int. priv. proc.*, 2013, 455, according to which the 2007 Lugano Convention endorses the principle *actor sequitur forum rei* and, therefore, remains anchored to the defendant's domicile in a signatory State of the Convention, with the exception of derogations introduced by its Article 5.

[175] Cf. Ferrari (2002), pp. 693 ff.

[176] Cf. OGH 18 December 2000, in *Europ. transp. law,* 2003, no. 38, 354; RB Rotterdam 3 July 2019, *ibid.,* 2020, no. 55, 41.

Heuer K (2002) CMR und EuGVÜ: nochmals zur Frage der internationalen Zuständigkeit (Art. 31, Abs. 1, CMR/Art. 20 EuGVÜ) und zur Einrede der Rechtschängigkeit bei negative Feststellungsklage (Art. 31, Abs. 2, CMR./Art. 21 EuGVÜ). TranspR, 221 ff.

Koller I (2002) Gehilfen des CMR – Frachtführers und Art. 31 CMR. TranspR, 133 ff.

Krings E (1999) CMR: examen de la jurisprudence des Cours de Cassation de France et de Pays – Bas (première partie). Unif Law Rev, 160 ff.

Laimer S, Perathoner C (2019) Jurisdiction based on place of performance in the case of a multimodal transport. Priv Int Law Int Civ Proc, 39 ff.

Lamont-Black S (2016) The UK Supreme Court on jurisdiction over successive CMR Convention carriers and European Union rules. Unif Law Rev 2016:487 ff.

Legros C (2016) Les difficultés posées par les règles de compétence jurisdictionnelle et d'arbitrage de la CMR. Unif Law Rev, 576 ff.

Loewe R (1976) Commentary on the Convention of 19 may 1956 on the contract for the international carriage of goods by road. Eur Transp Law 11:311 ff.

Messent A, Glass DA (2018) CMR: contracts for the international carriage of goods by road, IV edn. New York

Otte K (2018) Art. 31 der CMR. In Aa. Vv., Internationales Vertragsrecht. Munich, pp 1528 ff.

Pocar F (2008) The new Lugano Convention on jurisdiction and the recognition and enforcement of judgments in civil and commercial matters. Yearb Priv Int Law, 2 ff.

Puetz A (2018) Rules on jurisdiction and recognition or enforcement of judgments in specialized Conventions on transport in the aftermath of TNT: dynamite or light in the dark? Eur Legal Forum, 117 ff.

Putzeys J (1981) Le contrat de transport routier de marchandises. Brussels

Rodière R (1971) The Convention on road transport. Eur Transp Law 7:2 ff.

Sànchez Gamborino FJ (2001a) La jurisprudence du Tribunal Supremo espagnol en matière de CMR. Unif Law Rev 644 ff.

Sànchez Gamborino FJ (2001b) La Conventión CMR según la Jurisprudencia del "Tribunal Supremo" de España. Eur Transp Law 36:842 ff.

Shariatmadari SH (2006) Die internationale Zuständigkeit bei Nichteinlassung des Beklagten zur Sache und die Einrede der Rechtshängikeit bei negativer Feststellungsklage im Rahmen des Art. 31 CMR im Lichte der neueren Rechtsprechung des EuGH und des BGH. TranspR, 105 ff.

Silingardi G, Corrado A, Meotti A, Morandi F (1994) La disciplina uniforme del contratto di trasporto di cose su strada. Turin

Tebbens HD (2001) Judicial interpretation of the 1988 Lugano Convention. Yearb Priv Int Law, 2 ff.

Wesolowski K (2011) The unclear relations between CMR and European Union law in respect of jurisdiction and enforcement of foreign judgments. Eur Transp Law 46:133 ff.

Table of Cases

Austria
OGH 25 September 1968, in *Europ. transp. law,* 1973, n. 8, 309;
OGH 21 March 1977, in *Unif. law rev.,* 1978, 292;
OGH 5 July 1977, in M. A. Clarke (2014), *International carriage of goods by road: Cmr,* New York, ed. VI, 286 ss., nt. 344;
OGH 22 November 1977, in *Unif. law rev.,* 1979, 284;
OGH 15 December 1977, in *VersR,* 1978, 980;
OGH 15 February 1979, in *Unif. law rev.,* 1979, 229;
OGH 15 December 1981, in *TranspR,* 1984, 262;
OGH 31 March 1982, in *TranspR,* 1984, 196;
OGH 2 April 1982, in *TranspR,* 1984, 151;
OGH 18 May 1982, in *TranspR,* 1983, 48;
OGH 29 June 1983, in *Unif. law rev.,* 1984, 526;
OGH 8 September 1983, in *Europ. transp. law,* 1985, n. 20, 282;
OGH 8 October 1984, in *Strassengüterverkehr*, 1985, 28;
OGH 4 June 1987, in *Europ. transp. law,* 1988, n. 23, 714 ss.;
OGH 25 January 1990, in *TranspR,* 1990, 235;
OGH 10 July 1991, in *Unif. law rev.,* 1992, 833;
OGH 14 July 1993, in *TranspR,* 1994, 189;
OGH 19 January 1994, in *TranspR* 1995, 65;
OGH 13 July 1994, in *TranspR,* 1995, 285;
OGH 29 August 1994, in *Europ. transp. law,* 1996, n. 31, 211;
OGH 21 February 1996, in *TranspR,* 1996, 422;
OGH 1 April 1999, in *TranspR,* 2000, 34:
OGH 24 June 1999, in *TranspR,* 2000, 370;
OGH 28 March 2000, in *Europ. transp. law,* 2003, n. 38, 231;
OGH 20 June 2000, in *Europ. transp. law,* 2004, n. 39, 86;
OGH 6 October 2000, in *Europ. transp. law,* 2003, n. 38, 236;
OGH 18 December 2000, in *Europ. transp. law,* 2003, n. 38, 354;
OGH 28 February 2001, in *Europ. transp. law,* 2003, n. 38, 131;

C. Tincani, *Contract for the International Carriage of Goods by Road*, Law for Professionals, https://doi.org/10.1007/978-3-031-08487-4

OGH 26 April 2001, in *Europ. transp. law,* 2002, n. 37, 497;
OGH 12 June 2001, in *Europ. transp. law,* 2003, n. 38, 357;
OGH 31 July 2001, in *TranspR,* 2002, 113;
OGH 29 January 2002, in *Europ. transp. law,* 2002, n. 37, 809;
OGH 22 March 2002, in *Europ. transp. law,* 2002, n. 39, 79;
OGH 8 April 2002, in *TranspR,* 2003, 67;
OGH 15 May 2002, in *Europ. transp. law,* 2003, n. 38, 512;
OGH 16 May 2002, in *TranspR,* 2002, 403;
OGH 19 September 2002, in *Europ. transp. law,* 2004, n. 39, 400;
OGH 13 December 2002, in *Europ. transp. law,* 2003, n. 38, 656;
OGH 7 January 2003, in *Europ. transp. law,* 2003, n. 38, 658;
OGH 10 January 2003, in *Europ. transp. law,* 2003, n. 38, 661;
OGH 13 February 2003, in *Europ. transp. law,* 2004, n. 39, 244;
OGH 26 March 2004, in *TranspR,* 2004, 364;
OGH 25 May 2004, in *TranspR,* 2004, 359;
OGH 8 July 2004, in *Europ. transp. law,* 2005, n. 40, 734;
OGH 20 October 2004, in *Unif. law rev.,* 2005, 625;
OGH 15 March 2005, in *Europ. transp. law,* 2005, n. 40, 878;
OGH 17 February 2006, in *TranspR,* 2006, 257;
OGH 20 March 2007, in *TranspR,* 2007, 326;
OGH 2 July 2008, in *Europ. transp. law,* 2009, n. 44, 299;
OGH 27 November 2008, in *TranspR,* 2009, 413;
OGH 1 July 2009, in *TranspR,* 2010, 348;
OGH 5 May 2010, in *TranspR,* 2010, 383;
OGH 19 January 2011, in *TranspR,* 2011, 255;
OGH 18 February 2013, in *TranspR,* 2013, 344;
OGH 3 July 2013, in *TranspR,* 2014, 427;
OGH 2 October 2013, in *Europ. transp. law,* 2014, n. 49, 334;
OGH 29 January 2014, in *TranspR,* 2014, 375;
OGH 22 April 2014, in *TranspR,* 2014, 378;
OGH 25 February 2015, in *TranspR,* 2015, 399;
OGH 27 April 2016, in *Europ. transp. law,* 2016, n. 51, 565;
OGH 9 November 2016, in *TranspR,* 2017, 120;
OGH 29 March 2017, in *TranspR,* 2017, 315;
OGH 21 March 2018, in *Europ. transp. law,* 2019, n. 54, 106;
OGH 31 October 2018, in *Europ. transp. law,* 2019, n. 54, 218;
OGH 19 December 2018, in *TranspR,* 2019, 324;
OGH 30 January 2019, in *Europ. transp. law* 2020, n. 55, 441;
OGH 20 January 2020, in *Europ. transp. law,* 2021, n. 61, 67;

OLG Vienna 3 April 1984, in *TranspR,* 1984, 152;
OLG Linz 27 November 1989, in *Unif. law rev.,* 1990, 442;
OLG Vienna 26 March 2004, in *TranspR,* 2004, 364;
OLG Vienna 19 June 2019, in *Europ. transp. law,* 2011, n. 55, 547;

LG Graz 5 April 2000, in *Europ. transp. law,* 2002, n. 37, 360.

Belgium

Cass. 3 June 1976, in *Le Lamy transp.*, 2020, vol. I, 513;
Cass. 30 May 1980, in *Europ. transp. law,* 1980, n. 15, 79;
Cass. 13 June 1980, in *Le Lamy transp.*, 2021, vol. I, 557;
Cass. 12 December 1980, in *Europ. transp. law,* 1981, n.16, 250;
Cass. 9 April 1981, in *E. L. D.*, 1983, n. 11, 31;
Cass. 27 September 1984, in *Le Lamy transp.*, vol. I, 2020, 536;
Cass. 17 September 1987, in *Europ. transp. law,* 1998, n. 23, 201;
Cass. 18 February 1994, in *Europ. transp. law,* 1994, n. 29, 464;
Cass. 30 June 1995, in *Europ. transp. law,* 1996, n. 31, 544;
Cass. 3 January 1997, in *Europ. transp. law,* 1998, n. 33, 825;
Cass. 9 December 1999, in *Unif. law rev.,* 2000, 851;
Cass. 7 January 2000, in *Unif. law. Rev.,* 2000, 852 ss.;
Cass. 30 March 2000, in *Europ. transp. law,* 2000, n. 35, 392;
Cass. 19 February 2004, in *Europ. transp. law,* 2004, n. 39, 521;
Cass. 29 April 2004, in *Europ. transp. law,* 2004, n. 39, 688;
Cass. 8 November 2004, in *Europ. transp. law,* 2006, n. 41, 228;
Cass. 29 September 2006, in *Europ. transp. law,* 2007, n. 42, 390;
Cass. 8 December 2006, in *Europ. transp. law*, 2007, n. 42, 401;
Cass. 21 January 2010, in *Europ. transp. law,* 2010, n. 45, 311;
Cass. 19 June 2010, in *Europ. transp. law,* 2010, n. 45, 623;
Cass. 27 May 2011, in *Europ. transp. law,* 2012, n. 47, 83;
Cass. 13 October 2011, in *Europ. transp. law,* 2012, n. 47, 221;
Cass. 7 December 2012, in *Europ. transp. law,* 2013, n. 48, 210;
Cass. 12 April 2013, in *Europ. transp. law,* 2014, n. 49, 109;
Cass. 23 January 2014, in *Europ. transp. law,* 2014, n. 49, 337;

App. Liège 18 December 1967, in *Europ. transp. law,* 1969, n. 4, 965;
App. Bruxelles 28 June 1969, in *Europ. transp. law,* 1969, n. 4, 925;
App. Bruxelles 17 June 1971, in *Europ. transp. law,* 1971, n. 6, 825;
App. Bruxelles 30 October 1975, in *Europ. transp. law,* 1976, n. 11, 238;
App. Bruxelles 12 December 1977, in *Bull. transp.,* 1978, 39;
App. Bruxelles 25 January 1978, in *Bull. transp.,* 1978, 429;
App. Gent 20 June 1986, in *Europ. transp. law,* 1986, n. 22, 371;
App. Bruxelles 20 September 1995, in *Le lamy transp.,* 2020, vol. I, 535;
App. Antwerp 7 November 1995, in *Unif. law rev.,* 1998, 114;
App. Bruxelles 27 February 1996, in *Europ. transp. law,* 1996, n. 31, 833;
App. Bruxelles 1 December 1997, in *Europ. transp. law,* 2000, n. 35, 125;
App. De Mons 14 May 2002, in *Europ. transp. law,* 2004, n. 39, 99;

Hof Hertogenbosch 21 December 1965, in *Europ. transp. law,* 1966, n. 1, 698;
Hof Bruxelles 5 December 1968, in *Europ. transp. law,* 1969, n. 4, 958;
Hof Bruxelles 21 January 1969, in *Europ. transp. law,* 1969, n. 4, 943;
Hof Bruxelles 23 December 1971, in *Europ. transp. law,* 1972, n. 7, 865;
Hof Bruxelles 13 January 1972, in *Europ. transp. law,* n. 7, 151;
Hof Bruxelles 19 October 1972, in *Europ. transp. law,* 1973, n. 8, 503;

Hof Bruxelles 26 June 1974, in *Europ. transp. law,* 1975, n. 10, 235;
Hof Bruxelles 16 November 1977, in *Europ. transp. law,* 1980, n. 15, 319;
Hof Bruxelles 17 November 1977, in *Europ. transp. law,* 1980, n. 15, 319;
Hof Antwerp 21 June 1978, in *Europ. transp. law.*, 1978, n. 13, 601;
Hof Antwerp 15 November 1978, in *Europ. transp. law*, 1979, n. 14, 661;
Hof Antwerp 30 May 1979, in *Unif. law rev.,* 1981, 236;
Hof Antwerp 23 March 1983, in *Europ. transp. law,* 1983, n. 18, 518;
Hof Antwerp 16 October 1985, in *Europ. transp. law,* 1986, n. 21, 377;
Hof Antwerp 8 November 1989, in *Europ. transp. law,* 1990, n. 25, 83;
Hof Antwerp 23 June 1992, in *Europ. transp. law,* 1993, n. 28, 293;
Hof Liège 27 October 1992, in *J. T.*, 1993, 538;
Hof Gent 13 September 1995, in *Europ. transp. law,* 1997, n. 32, 602;
Hof Antwerp 10 October 1995, in *Europ. transp. law,* 1998, n. 33, 108;
Hof Antwerp 7 November, 1995, in *Europ. transp. law,* 1998, n. 33, 114;
Hof Antwerp 6 February 1996, in *Europ. transp. law,* 1998, n. 33, 118;
Hof Gent 28 June 1996, in *Europ. transp. law,* 1996, n. 31, 843;
Hof Gent 30 April 1997, in *Europ. transp. law,* 1997, n. 32, 606;
Hof Antwerp 9 March 1998, in *Europ. transp. law,* 1998, n. 33, 707;
Hof Gent 19 January 1999, in *Europ. transp. law,* 1999, n. 34, 264;
Hof Antwerp 1 March 1999, in *Europ. transp. law,* 2000, n. 35, 544;
Hof Antwerp 20 December 1999, in *Europ. transp. law,* 2000, n. 35, 687;
Hof Antwerp 31 January 2000, in *J. P. A.*, 2000, 247;
Hof Gent 10 May 2000, in *Europ. transp. law*, 2000, n. 35, 428;
Hof Antwerp 19 February 2001, in *Europ. transp. law*, 2001, n. 36, 242;
Hof Antwerp 2 June 2003, in *Europ. transp. law,* 2004, n. 39, 407;
Hof Gent 5 April 2004, in *Europ. transp. law,* 2005, n. 40, 846;
Hof Gent 7 March 2005, in *Europ. transp. law,* 2006, n. 41, 570;
Hof Antwerp 3 October 2005, in *Europ. transp. law,* 2006, n. 41, 284;
Hof Antwerp 24 October 2005, in *Europ. transp. law,* 2006, n. 41, 297;
Hof Antwerp 6 June 2005, in *Europ. transp. law,* 2006, n. 41, 272;
Hof Gent 19 December 2005, in *Europ. transp. law,* 2007, n. 42, 275;
Hof Antwerp 15 May 2006, in *Europ. transp. law,* 2006, n. 41, 658;
Hof Gent 7 February 2007, in *Europ. transp. law,* 2007, n. 42, 774;
Hof Antwerp 19 February 2007, in *Europ. transp. law,* 2007, n. 42, 427;
Hof Antwerp 14 May 2007, in *Europ. transp. law,* 2008, n. 43, 99;
Hof Antwerp 3 December 2008, in *Europ. transp. law,* 2009, n. 44, 334;
Hof Antwerp 15 June 2009, in *Europ. transp. law,* 2010, n. 45, 199;
Hof Antwerp 29 June 2009, in *Europ. transp. law,* 2010, n. 45, 182.
Hof Antwerp 19 October 2009, in *Europ. transp. law,* 2010, n. 45, 427;
Hof Gent 20 June 2011, in *Europ. transp. law,* 2011, n. 45, 543;
Hof Antwerp 31 October 2011, in *Europ. transp law,* 2013, 48, 82;
Hof Bruxelles 7 December 2012, in *Europ. transp. law,* 2013, n. 48, 201;
Hof Antwerp 6 January 2014, in *Europ. transp. law,* 2014, n. 49, 341;
Hof Antwerp 1 October 2018, in *Europ. transp. law,* 2018, n. 53, 386;

Hof Bruxelles 19 February 2021, in *Europ. transp. law,* 2021, n. 61, 34;
Hof Antwerp 22 February 2021, in *Europ. transp. law,* 2020, n. 61 56;

RB Antwerp 28 March 1966, in *Europ. transp. law,*1966, n. 1, 708;
RB Dordrecht 18 May 1966, in *Europ. transp. law,* 1968, n. 3, 416;
RB Antwerp 27 February 1967, in *Europ. transp. law,* 1968, n. 3, 1244;
RB Antwerp 27 October 1972, in *Europ. transp. law,* 1972, n. 7, 1054;
RB Mechelen 14 February 1973, in *Europ. transp. law,* 1973, n. 8, 630;
RB Antwerp 7 December 1973, in *Europ. transp. law,* 1976, n. 11, 295;
RB Bruxelles 28 February 1975, *Europ. transp. law,* 1975, n. 10, 419;
RB Antwerp 16 April 1975, in *Europ. transp. law,* 1975, n. 10, 548;
RB Antwerp 23 September 1975, in *Europ. transp. law,* 1976, n. 11, 279;
RB Antwerp 7 January 1977, in *Europ. transp. law,* 1977, n. 12, 420;
RB Bruxelles 12 February 1977, in *Europ. transp. law,* 1978, n. 13, 285;
RB Antwerp 3 April 1977, in *Europ. transp. law,* 1977, n. 12, 411;
RB Antwerp 4 May 1977, in *Europ. transp. law,* 1978, n. 13, 478;
RB Antwerp 7 March 1980, in *Europ. transp. law,* 1981, n. 16, 466;
RB Antwerp 1 April 1980, in *Europ. transp. law,* 1980, n. 15, 461;
RB Antwerp 28 January 1985, in *Europ. transp. law,* 1990, n. 25, 211;
RB Bruxelles 8 June 1990, in *Europ. transp. law,* 1990, n. 26, 362;
RB Gent 19 June 1990, in *Europ. transp. law,* 1991, n. 26, 377;
RB Leuven 23 October 1990, *Europ. transp. law,* 1992, n. 27, 272;
RB Bruxelles 25 May 1992, in *Europ. transp. law,* 1993, n. 28, 762;
RB Antwerp 6 May 1993, in *Europ. transp law*, 1993, n. 28, 768;
RB Antwerp 30 September 1994, in *Europ. transp. law,* 1995, n. 30, 233;
RB Antwerp 1 February 1996, in *Europ. transp. law,* 1996, n. 31, 579;
RB Antwerp 17 January 1997, in *Europ. transp. law,* 1998, n. 33, 53;
RB Gent 11 February 1997, in *Europ. transp. law,* n. 33, 1998, 121;
RB Antwerp 16 May 1997, in *Europ. transp. law,* 1999, n, 34, 119;
RB Turnhout 30 June 1997, in *Europ. transp. law,* 1998, n. 33, 139;
RB Antwerp 31 October 1997, in *Europ. transp. law,* 1998, n. 33, 835;
RB Antwerp 30 January 1998, in *Europ. transp. law,* 1998, n. 33, 842;
RB Gent 1 December 1998, in *Europ. transp. law,* 1999, n. 34, 392;
RB Gent 29 June 1999, in *Europ. transp. law,* 2000, n. 35, 566;
RB Brugge 12 October 1999, in *Europ. transp. law,* 2000, n. 35, 552;
RB Mechelen 18 November 1999, in *Europ. transp. law,* 2000, n. 35, 432;
RB Antwerp 25 February 2000, in *Europ. transp. law,* 2000, n. 35, 527;
RB Antwerp 15 March 2002, in *Europ. transp. law,* 2002, n. 37, 511;
RB Antwerp 16 May 2003, in *Europ. transp. law,* 2003, n. 38, 360;
RB Antwerp 1 October 2004, in *Europ. transp. law,* 2006, n. 41, 102;
RB Antwerp 8 November 2013, in *Europ. transp. law,* 2014, n. 49, 222;

Trib. com. Bruxelles 10 November 1971, in *J. P. A.*, 1971, 227;
Trib. com. Antwerp 20 April 1972, in *J. B. C.,* 1972, 466;
Trib com. Bruxelles 26 October 1972, in *Europ. transp. law,* 1973, n. 8, 516;
Trib. com. Liège 25 November 1982, in *Europ. transp. law,* 1982, n. 17, 843;

Trib. com. Bruxelles 2 April 1990, in *Europ. transp. law,* 1990, n. 26, 541;
Trib. Bruxelles 31 May 1996, in *Europ. transp. law,* 1996, n. 31, 586;

Arrond. Antwerp 18 November 1987, in *Europ. transp. law,* 1990, n. 25, 251.

Danmark

Cass. 10 September 1996, in *Europ. transp. law,* 1997, n. 32, 230;
Cass. 24 March 2000, in *Europ. transp. law,* 2000, n. 35, 772.

Corte marittima e commerciale di Copenhagen 16 September 1996, in *Europ. transp. law,* 1998, n. 33, 71.

France

Cass. 18 November 1953, in *Bull. transp.,* 1954, 136;
Cass. 7 February 1955, in *Bull. transp.,* 1955, 207;
Cass. 27 November 1962, in J. Putzeys (1981), *Le contrat de transport routier de marchandises,* Bruxelles, 349 ss., nt. 853;
Cass. 18 July 1966, in *Bull. transp.,* 1966, 286;
Cass. 6 November 1967, in J. Putzeys (1981), *Le contrat de transport routier de marchandises,* Bruxelles, 349 ss., nt. 852;
Cass. com. 10 February 1969, in *Bull. transp.,* 1969, 107;
Cass. com. 16 February 1970, in *Bull. transp.,* 1970, 144
Cass. com. 17 February 1970, in *Bull. transp.,* 1970, 158;
Cass. 21 October 1970, in *Bull. transp.,* 1970, 367;
Cass. com. 25 January 1972, in *Bull. transp.,* 1972, 148;
Cass. com. 5 June 1972, in *Bull. transp.,* 1972, 484;
Cass. com. 9 October 1974, in *Le Lamy transp.*, 2020, vol. I, 498;
Cass. com. 29 April 1975, in *Bull. transp.,* 1975, 298;
Cass. com. 3 May 1975, in *Le Lamy transp.*, 2020, vol. I, 502;
Cass. 28 July 1975, in *Bull. transp.,* 1975, 442;
Cass. com. 6 October 1975, in *Bull. transp.,* 1975, 478;
Cass. com. 27 October 1975, in *Bull. transp.,* 1975, 526;
Cass. com. 19 January 1976, in *Bull. transp.,* 1976, 149;
Cass. com. 3 May 1976, in *Bull. transp.,* 1976, 317;
Cass. com. 10 June 1976, in *Bull. transp.,* 1986, 402;
Cass. com. 14 June 1976, in *Bull. transp.,* 1976, 342;
Cass. com. 5 July 1976, in *Le Lamy transp.*, 2020, vol. I, 495;
Cass. 19 July 1976, in *Bull. transp.,* 1976, 3641;
Cass. com. 22 July 1976, in *Bull. transp.,* 1976, 416;
Cass. com. 23 May 1977, in *Bull. transp.,* 1977, 388;
Cass. com. 5 July 1977, in *Bull. transp.,* 1977, 402;
Cass. com. 20 June 1978, in *Bull. transp.,* 1978, 469;
Cass. com. 8 October 1979, in *Bull. transp.,* 1979, 545;
Cass. com. 23 October 1980, in *Bull. transp.,* 1980, 598;
Cass. com. 27 January 1981, in *Bull. transp.,* 1981, 219;
Cass. com. 12 May 1981, in *Bull. transp.,* 1981, 355;

Cass. com. 16 June 1981, in *Bull. transp.*, 1981, 419;
Cass. com. 13 October 1981, in *Europ. transp. law,* 1982, n. 17, 288;
Cass. com. 2 February 1982, in *Bull. transp.*, 1982, 152;
Cass. com. 8 February 1982, in *Bull. transp.*, 1982, 152;
Cass. com. 15 February 1982, in *Bull. transp.*, 1982, 182;
Cass. com. 23 February 1982, in *Bull. transp.*, 1982, 285;
Cass. com. 19 April 1982, in *Bull. transp.*, 1982, 309;
Cass. 21 June 1982, in *Bull. transp.*, 1982, 416;
Cass. 4 October 1982, in *Bull. transp.*, 1982, 549;
Cass. com. 30 November 1982, in *Bull. transp.* 1983, 129;
Cass. com. 13 December 1982, in *Bull. transp.*, 1983, 64;
Cass. com. 10 January 1983, in *Bull. transp.*, 1983, 154;
Cass. com. 17 May 1983, in *Bull. transp.*, 1983, 445;
Cass. 20 July 1983, in *Bull. transp.*, 1984, 236;
Cass. com. 22 September 1983, in *Bull. transp.*, 1983, 566;
Cass. com. 5 October 1983, in *Le Lamy transp.*, 2020, vol. I, 472;
Cass. com. 26 October 1983, in *Bull. transp.*, 1984, 360;
Cass. com. 15 May 1984, in *Bull. transp.*, 1984, 526;
Cass. com. 29 May 1984, in *Le Lamy transp.*, 2020, vol. I, 476;
Cass. 26 June 1984, in *Bull. transp.*, 1984, 610;
Cass. com. 6 February 1985, in *Le Lamy transp.*, 2020, vol. I, 480;
Cass. com. 26 February 1985, in *Bull. transp.*, 1985, 270;
Cass. com. 5 May 1985, in *Bull. transp.*, 1986, 350;
Cass. com. 25 June 1985, in *Bull. transp.*, 1985, 436;
Cass. com. 4 February 1986, in *Bull. transp.*, 1986, 197;
Cass. com. 18 March 1986, in *Bull. transp.*, 1986, 607;
Cass. com. 22 April 1986, in *Le Lamy transp.*, 2020, vol. I, 512;
Cass. com. 10 June 1986, in *Bull. transp.*, 1986, 608;
Cass. com. 15 July 1986, in *Bull. transp.*, 1986, 542;
Cass. com. 22 July 1986, in *Bull. transp.*, 1986, 591;
Cass. 3 February 1987, in *Bull. transp.*, 1987, 270;
Cass. com. 31 March 1987, in *Bull. transp.*, 1987, 280;
Cass. com. Francia 12 May 1987, in *Bull. transp.* 399;
Cass. com. 2 June 1987, in *Le Lamy transp.*, vol. I, 2020, 522;
Cass. com. 24 November 1987, in *Bull. transp.*, 1988, 42;
Cass. com. 20 December 1987, in *Le Lamy transp.*, 2020, vol. I, 483;
Cass. com. 5 January 1988, in *Bull. transp.*, 1988, 102;
Cass. com. 3 March 1988, in *Bull. transp. logist.*, 1998, 231;
Cass. com. 21 June 1988, in *Le Lamy transp.*, vol. I, 496;
Cass. com. 5 July 1988, in *Bull. transp.*, 1988, 530;
Cass. com. 22 November 1988, in *Bull. transp.*, 1989, 209;
Cass. com. 23 May 1989, in *Le Lamy transp.*, 2020, vol. I, 494;
Cass. com. 10 July 1989, in *Bull. transp.*, 1989, 591;
Cass. com. 10 October 1989, in *Bull. transp.*, 1989, 673;
Cass. com. 5 December 1989, in *Bull. transp.*,1990, 310;

Cass. 12 December 1989, in *Europ. transp. law,* 1991, n. 26, 359;
Cass. com. 9 January 1990, in *Bull. transp.,* 1990, 362;
Cass. com. 20 March 1990, in *Le Lamy transp.*, 2020, vol. I, 484;
Cass. com. 24 April 1990, in *Le Lamy transp.*, 2020, vol. I, 476;
Cass. com. 10 July 1990, in *Bull. transp. logist.,* 1990, 697;
Cass. com. 16 October 1990, in *Bull. transp.,* 1990, 797;
Cass. com. 24 October 1990, in *Bull. transp.,* 1990, 99;
Cass. com. 14 May 1991, in *Bull. transp. logist.,* 1992, 11;
Cass, com. 12 November 1991, in *Le Lamy transp.*, 2020, vol. I, 454;
Cass. com. 10 December 1991, in *Le Lamy transp.*, 2020, vol. I, 496;
Cass. com. 17 March 1992, in *Bull. transp. logist.,* 1992, 253;
Cass. com. 14 April 1992, in *Bull. transp.,* 1981, 538;
Cass. com. 1 December 1992, in *Le Lamy transp.*, 2020, vol. I, 467;
Cass. com. 2 February 1993, in *Le Lamy transp.*, 2021, vol. I, 557;
Cass. com. 16 March 1993, in *Bull. transp. logist.,* 1993, 262;
Cass. com. 6 July 1993, in *Le Lamy transp.*, 2021, vol. I, 475;
Cass. com. 22 February 1994, in *Bull. transp.,* 1994, 263;
Cass. com. 5 July 1994, in *Bull. transp. logist.,* 1994, 690;
Cass. com. 12 July 1994, in *Le Lamy transp.*, 2020, vol. I, 535;
Cass. com. 17 January 1995, in *Le Lamy transp.*, 2021, vol. I, 558;
Cass. com. 31 January 1995, in *Le Lamy transp.*, 2020, vol. I, 503;
Cass. com. 14 March 1995, in *Bull. transp. logist.,* 1995, 248;
Cass. com. 9 May 1995, in *Le Lamy transp.*, 2020, vol. I, 509;
Cass. com. 6 June 1995, in *Le Lamy transp.*, 2020, vol. I, 517;
Cass. 21 November 1995, in *Unif. law rev.,* 1996, 594;
Cass. com. 16 April 1996, in *Bull. transp. logist.,* 1996, 334
Cass. com. 19 November 1996, in *Bull. transp. logist.,* 1996, 878;
Cass. com. 7 January 1997, in *Le Lamy transp.*, 2021, vol. I, 482;
Cass. 18 March 1997, in *Le Lamy transp.*, 2020, vol. I, 511;
Cass. com. 25 March 1997, in *Le Lamy transp.*, 2021, vol. I, 475;
Cass. com. 20 May 1997, in *Le Lamy transp.*, 2020, vol. I, 483;
Cass. com. 17 June 1997, in *Bull. transp. logist.,* 1997, 507;
Cass. com. 25 November 1997, in *Le Lamy transp.*, 2020, vol. I, 518;
Cass. com. 6 January 1998, in *Bull. transp.,* 1998, 39;
Cass. 3 March 1998, in *Bull. transp.,* 1998, 212;
Cass. com. 8 December 1998, in *Bull. transp.,* 1999, 352;
Cass. com. 2 February 1999, in *Bull. transp.,* 1999, 175;
Cass. com. 26 October 1999, in *Le Lamy transp.*, 2020, vol. I, 524;
Cass. com. 18 January 2000, in *Le Lamy transp.*, 2020, vol. I, 517;
Cass. com. 28 March 2000, in *Bull. transp. logist.,* 2000, 276;
Cass. 3 October 2000, in *Europ. transp. law,* 2001, n. 36, 92;
Cass. 20 September 2000, in *Europ. transp. law,* 2001, n. 36, 236;
Cass. 20 December 2000, in *Bull. transp. logist.,* 2001, 54;
Cass. com. 2 May 2001, in *Bull. transp. logist.,* 2001, 362;
Cass. com. 15 May 2001, in *Le Lamy transp.*, 2020, vol. I, 535;

Cass. com. 13 November 2001, in *Bull. transp. logist.,* 2001, 804;
Cass. com. 11 December 2001, in *Bull. transp. logist.,* 2002, 15;
Cass. 22 January 2002, in *Bull. transp.,* 2002, 110;
Cass. com. 5 February 2002, in *Bull. transp.,* 2002, 52;
Cass. 28 May 2002, in *Europ. transp. law*, 2002, n. 37, 508;
Cass. com. 11 June 2002, in *Le Lamy transp.*, 2020, vol. I, 502;
Cass. 15 October 2002, in *Bull. transp.,* 2002, 697;
Cass. 7 January 2003, in *Europ. transp. law,* 2003, n. 38, 788;
Cass. com. 28 January 2003, in *Le Lamy transp.*, 2020, vol. I, 517;
Cass. com. 4 March 2003, in *Bull. transp. logist.,* 2003, 199;
Cass. 10 March 2004, in *Bull. transp.,* 2004, 207;
Cass. 24 March 2004, in *Europ. transp. law,* 2004, n. 39, 53;
Cass. com. 5 May 2004, in *Bull. transp. logist.,* 2004, 371;
Cass. com. 2 June 2004, in *Le Lamy transp.*, 2020, vol. I, 49;
Cass. com. 30 June 2004, in *Uniform. law rev.,* 2005, 634;
Cass. 28 September 2004, in *Bull. transp.,* 2004, 668;
Cass. 5 July 2005, in *Unif. law rev.,* 2005, 920;
Cass. com. 16 May 2006, in *Le Lamy transp.*, vol. I, 2020, 524;
Cass. com. 13 June 2006, in *Bull. transp.* 2006, 452;
Cass. 16 January 2007, in *Bull. transp.,* 2007, 79;
Cass. 7 March 2007, in *Bull. transp.,* 2007, 259;
Cass. com. 15 June 2007, in *Bull. transp. logist.,* 2007, 183;
Cass. com. 18 September 2007, in *Bull. transp. logist.,* 2007, 587;
Cass. com. 11 December 2007, in *Bull. transp. logist.,* 2007, 771;
Cass. com. 8 January 2008, in *Le Lamy transp.*, 2021, vol. I, 558;
Cass. 14 May 2008, in *Europ. transp. law,* 2008, n. 43, 611;
Cass. 24 June 2008, in *Europ. transp. law,* 2008, n. 43, 740;
Cass. com. Francia 30 June 2009, in *Bull. transp. logist.,* 2009, 447;
Cass. 5 October 2010, in *Europ. transp. law,* 2011, n. 46, 110;
Cass. com. 1 February 2011, in *Bull. transp. logist.,* 2011, 107;
Cass. com. 31 May 2011, in *Le Lamy transp.*, 2020, vol. I, 495;
Cass. com. 13 September 2011, in *Bull. transp. logist.,* 2011, 555;
Cass. com. 27 September 2011, in *Bull. transp. logist.,* 2011, 583;
Cass. com. 11 October 2011, in *Bull. transp. logist.,* 2011, 603;
Cass. 21 November 2011, in *Bull. transp. logist.,* 2006, 728;
Cass. com. 2 October 2012, in *Bull. transp. logist.,* 2012, 601;
Cass. 16 October 2012, in *Bull. transp. logist.,* 2012, 632;
Cass. com. 9 April 2013, in *Bull. transp. logist.,* 2013, 271;
Cass. 13 May 2014, in *Bull. transp. logist.*, 2014, 344;
Cass. com. 23 September 2014, in *Bull. transp. logist.,* 2014, 517;
Cass. com. 10 March 2015, in *Le Lamy transp.*, 2020, vol. I, 479;
Cass. com. Francia 1 March 2016, in *Le Lamy transp.*, 2021, vol. I, 475;
Cass. com. 22 March 2016, in *Bull. transp. logist.*, 2016, 219;
Cass. com. 14 June 2016, in *Le Lamy transp.*, 2020, vol. I, 496;

Cass. com. 8 March 2017, in *Bull. transp. logist.*, 2017, 173;
Cass. 4 May 2017, in *Europ. transp. law,* 2018, n. 53, 297;

App. Paris 9 July 1959, in *Droit mar. fran.,* 1959, 690;
App. Paris 22 June 1966, in *Bull. transp.,* 1966, 298;
App. Limoges 2 June 1967, in *Bull. transp.,* 1967, 273;
App. Aix en Provence 8 October 1968, in *Bull. transp.,* 1969, 18;
App. Aix – en – Provence 11 March 1969, in *Bull. transp.,* 1969, 389;
App. Paris 25 March 1969, in *Bull. transp.,* 1969, 174;
App. Toulouse 26 March 1969, in *Europ. transp. law,* 1971, n. 6, 131;
App. Paris 26 March 1969, in *Bull. transp.,* 1969, 174;
App. Paris 28 October 1969, in *Bull. transp.,* 1970, 7;
App. Paris 14 November 1969, in *Unif. law rev.,* 1970, 133;
App. Paris 27 January 1970, in *Bull. transp.,* 1970, 100;
App. Paris 12 June 1970, in *Bull. transp.,* 1970, 228;
App. Colmar 10 July 1970, in *Bull. transp.,* 1970, 358;
App. Paris 21 October 1970, in *Bull. transp.,* 1970, 307;
App. Paris 4 December 1970, in *Bull. transp.,* 1970, 407;
App. Paris 17 December 1970, in *Bull. transp.,* 1971, 49;
App. Paris 6 January 1971, in *Bull transp.,* 1971, 40;
App. Paris 27 January 1971, in *Bull. transp.,* 1971, 115;
App. Toulouse 17 February 1971, in *Bull. transp.,* 1971, 353;
App. Poitiers 31 March 1971, in *Bull. transp.,* 1971, 168;
App. Paris 10 December 1971, in *Unif. law rev.*, 1972, 274;
App. Paris 19 December 1971, in *Bull. transp.,* 1972, 35;
App. Bordeaux 9 February 1972, in *Bull. transp.,* 1972, 114;
App. Paris 20 March 1972, in *Bull. transp.,* 1972, 182;
App. Paris 24 March 1972, in *Bull. transp.,* 1972, 205;
App. Paris 29 April 1972, in *Bull. transp.,* 1972, 194;
App. Rouen 16 June 1972, in *Europ. transp. law,* 1972, n. 7, 1040
App. Colmar 16 June 1972, in *Bull. transp.,* 1972, 320;
App. Paris 27 June 1972, in *Europ. transp. law,* 1972, n. 7, 1040;
App. Paris 26 January 1973, in *Bull. transp.,* 1973, 73;
App. Paris 30 March 1973, in *Bull. transp.,* 1973, 195;
App. Paris 30 May 1973, in *Bull. transp.,* 1973, 304;
App. Paris 18 October 1973, in *Bull. transp.,* 1973, 488;
App. Colmar 7 November 1973, in *Le Lamy transp.*, 2021, vol. I, 524;
App. Paris 8 February 1974, in *Bull. transp.,* 1974, 104;
App. Paris 11 June 1974, in *Bull. transp.,* 1974, 49;
App. Rennes 5 November 1974, in *Bull. transp.,* 1974, 514;
App. Amiens 28 November 1974, in *Bull. transp.*, 1975, 23;
App. Paris 23 June 1975, in *Bull. transp.*, 1975, 360;
App. Paris 7 November 1975, in *Bull. transp.,* 1975, 515;
App. Paris 23 December 1975, in *Bull. transp.,* 1976, 48;
App. Poitiers 3 February 1976, in *Bull. transp.,* 1976, 185;

App. Reims 22 March 1976, in *Bull. transp.,* 11979, 84;
App. Paris 8 May 1976, in *Bull. transp.,* 1976, 270;
App. Aix – en Provence 4 June 1976, in *Le Lamy transp.*, vol. I, 2020, 524;
App. Paris 23 June 1976, in *Bull. transp.,* 1976, 332;
App. Lyon 7 October 1976, in *Bull. transp.,* 1977, 84;
App. Lyon 21 October 1976, in *Bull. transp.,* 1977, 110;
App. Aix – en – Provence 10 November 1976, in *Bull. transp.,* 1977, 248;
App. Paris 13 December 1976, in *Bull. transp.,* 1977, 83;
App. Paris 15 February 1977, in *Bull. transp.,* 1978, 53;
App. Paris 17 March 1977, in *Bull. transp.,* 1977, 196;
App. Aix – en – Provence 26 April, 1977, in *Le Lamy transp.*, 2021, vol. I, 525;
App. Paris 14 June 1977, in *Bull. transp.,* 1977, 354;
App. Reims 13 July 1977, in *Bull. transp.,* 1977, 406;
App. Lyon 21 July 1977, in *Bull. transp.,* 1977, 97;
App. Paris 3 November 1977, in *Le Lamy transp.*, 2020, vol. I, 494;
App. Limoges 7 November 1977, in *Bull. transp.,* 1977, 537;
App., Paris 25 November 1977, in *Bull. transp.,* 1978, 66;
App. Paris 14 December 1977, in *Bull. transp.,* 1978, 289;
App. Paris 15 December 1977, in *Bull. transp.,* 1978, 53;
App. Aix – en – Provence 20 December 1977, in *Bull. transp.,* 1978, 245;
App. Paris 4 January 1978, in *Bull. transp.,* 1978, 177;
App. Paris 19 January 1978, in *Bull. transp.,* 1978, 161;
App. Lyon 2 March 1978, in *Bull. transp.,* 1978, 382;
App. Paris 23 March 1978, in *Bull. transp.,* 1978, 265;
App. Paris 28 March 1978, in *Bull. transp.,* 1978, 320;
App. Paris 27 April 1978, in *Bull. transp.,* 1978, 408;
App. Anvers 21 June 1978, in *Europ. Transp. law.,* 1978, 601;
App. Bruxelles 12 December 1978, in *Bull. transp.,* 1978, 39;
App. Paris 6 February 1979, in *Bull. transp.,* 1979, 281;
App. Aix en Provence 22 February 1979, in *Bull. transp.,* 1979, 387;
App. Paris 23 March 1979, in *Bull. transp.,* 1979, 387;
App. Lyon 20 June 1979, in *Bull. transp.* 1979, 561;
App. Paris 6 November 1979, in *Bull. transp.,* 1974, 574;
App. Colmar 9 November 1979 in *Le Lamy transp.*, vol. I, 2020, 529;
App. Paris 20 November 1979, in *Bull. transp.,* 1980, 190;
App. Aix - en- Provence 20 December 1979, in *Bull. transp.,* 1980, 104;
App. Pau 16 January 1980, in *Bull. transp.,* 1980, 91;
App. Paris 22 February 1980, in *Bull. transp.*, 1980, 239;
App. Reims 3 March 1980, in *Bull. transp.,* 1980, 237;
App. Paris 5 March 1980, in *Bull. transp.,* 1980, 187;
App. Grenoble 13 March 1980, in *Bull. transp.,* 1981, 306
App. Agen 19 March 1980, in *Bull. transp.,* 1980, 502;
App. Grenoble 23 April 1980, in *Bull. transp.,* 1980, 301;
App. Paris 27 May 1980, in *Bull. transp.,* 1980, 435;
App. Amiens 19 June 1980, in *Bull. transp.,* 1980, 490;

App. Lyon 27 June 1980, in *Bull. transp.,* 1980, 509;
App. Paris 9 July 1980, in *Bull. transp.,* 1980, 449;
App. Aix en – Provence 26 November 1980 in *Bull. transp.,* 1981, 185;
Aix – en - Provence 9 December 1980, in *Le Lamy transp.*, 2020, vol. I, 509;
App. Paris 28 February 1981, in *Bull. transp.,* 1981, 270;
App. Amiens 6 May 1981, in *Bull. transp.,* 1982, 271;
App. Lyon 7 May 1981, in *Bull. transp.,* 1981, 410;
App. Amiens 18 May 1981, in *Bull. transp.,* 1982, 208;
App. Paris 26 May 1981, in *Bull. transp.,* 1982, 503;
App. Amiens 27 May 1981, in *Bull. transp.,* 1982, 271;
App. Paris 26 June 1981, in *Bull. transp.,* 1981, 395;
App. Agen 29 June 1981, in *Bull. transp.*, 1981, 433;
App. Paris 9 July 1981, in *Le Lamy transp.*, 2020, vol. I, 499;
App. Toulouse 29 July 1981, in *Le Lamy transp.*, vol. I, 2020, 381;
App. Paris 23 September 1981, in *Bull. transp.,* 1981, 538;
App. Paris 28 September 1981, in *Le Lamy transp.*, 2020, vol. I, 472;
App. Riom 16 October 1981, in *Bull. transp.,* 1982, 11;
App. Aix - en - Provence 6 November 1981, in *Bull. transp.,* 1982, 258;
App. Paris 19 November 1981, in *Bull. transp.,* 1982, 81;
App. Paris 2 December 1981, in *Bull. transp.,* 1982, 73;
App. Paris 7 December 1981, in *Bull. transp.,* 1982, 73;
App. Aix – en – Provence 12 January 1982, in *Le Lamy transp.*, 2021, vol. I, 481;
App. Orléans 20 January 1982, in *Bull. transp.,* 1982, 233;
App. Paris 15 February 1982, in *Bull. transp.,* 1982, 141;
App. Douai 11 March 1982, in *Bull. transp.,* 1982, 199;
App. Paris 25 March 1982, *Bull. transp.,* 1982, 434;
App. Paris 26 May 1982, in *Bull. transp.,* 1982, 502;
App. Nîmes 26 May 1982, in *Bull. transp.,* 1982, 407;
App. Chambéry 22 June 1982, in *Le Lamy transp.*, 2020, vol. I, 484;
App. Paris 22 June 1982, in *Bull. transp.,* 1982, 432;
App. Douai 6 October 1982, in *Le Lamy transp.*, 2020, vol. I, 503;
App. Anvers 24 November 1982, in *Le Lamy transp.*, 2020, vol. I, 497;
App. Benançon 15 December 1982, in *Bull. transp.* 1983, 96;
App. Dijon 26 January 1983, in *Le Lamy transp.*, vol. I, 2020, 534;
App. Paris 31 January 1983, in *Bull. transp.,* 1983, 83;
App. Bordeaux 7 February 1983, in *Le Lamy transp.*, 2020, vol. I, 466;
App. Aix – en – Provence 15 February 1983, in *Le Lamy transp.*, 2021, vol. I, 557;
App. Limoges 1 March 1983, in *Bull. transp.,* 1983, 331;
App. Lyon 3 March 1983, in *Bull. transp.,* 1983, 359;
App. Lyon 24 March 1983, in *Bull. transp.*, 1984, 166;
App. Paris 21 April 1983, in *Le Lamy transp.*, 2020, vol. I, 484;
App. Aix – en – Provence 10 June 1983, in *Le Lamy transp.*, 2021, vol. I, 525;
App. Aix - en- Provence 16 June 1983, in *Le Lamy transp.*, 2020, vol. I, 503;
App. Aix – en – Provence 5 July 1983, in *Le Lamy transp.*, 2021, vol. I, 525;
App. Lyon 6 July 1983, in *Bull. transp.,* 1984, 339;

App. Aix – en – Provence 12 July 1983, in *Le Lamy transp.*, 2021, vol. I, 481;
App. Agen 21 September 1983, in *Le Lamy transp.*, 2020, vol. I, 499;
App. Montpellier 27 October 1983, in *Le Lamy transp.*, 2021, vol. I, 525;
App. Lyon 2 November 1983, in *Bull. transp.,* 1983, 23;
App. Paris 17 November 1983, in *Bull. transp. logist.,* 1984, 390;
App. Toulouse 8 December 1983, in *Bull. transp.,* 1984, 457;
App. Lyon 6 January 1984, in *Le Lamy transp.*, vol. I, 2020, 529;
App. Paris 13 January 1984, in *Le Lamy transp.*, 2020, vol. I, 503;
App. Paris 31 January 1984, in *Bull. transp.,* 1984, 543;
App. Paris 3 February 1984, in *Le Lamy transp.*, 2021, vol. I, 524;
App. Versailles 29 February 1984, in *Bull. transp.,* 1984, 249;
App. Paris 24 April 1984, in *Le Lamy transp.*, 2020, vol. I, 543 ss.;
App. Paris 30 May 1984, in *Bull. transp.,* 1985, 75;
App. Aix – en – Provence 13 June 1984, in *Le Lamy transp.*, 2021, vol. I, 481;
App. Paris 15 June 1984, in *Bull. transp.,* 1984, 545;
App. Paris 4 July 1984, in *Bull. transp.,* 1985, 158;
App. Dijon 13 September 1984, in *Le Lamy transp.*, 2020, vol. I, 502;
App. Paris 17 December 1984, in *Le Lamy transp.*, 2020, vol. I, 519;
App. Paris 13 February 1985, in *Le Lamy transp.*, 2020, vol. I, 509;
App. Paris 15 February 1985, in *Le Lamy transp.*, 2020, vol. I, 484;
App. Montpellier 28 February 1985, in *Bull. transp.,* 1985, 600;
App. Aix – en Provence 27 February 1985, in *Le Lamy transp.*, 2020, vol. I, 509;
App. Paris 4 March 1985, in *Le Lamy transp.*, 2021, vol. I, 525;
App. Dijon 13 March 1985, in *Le Lamy transp.*, 2020, vol. I, 500;
App. Aix – en – Provence 19 March 1985, in *Le Lamy transp.*, 2021, vol. I, 482;
App. Aix – en Provence 20 March 1985, in *Le Lamy transp.*, 2020, vol. I, 490;
App. Lyon 22 March 1985, in *Le Lamy transp.*, 2020, vol. I, 468;
App. Paris 30 April 1985 in *Le Lamy transp.*, 2020, vol. I, 480;
App. Aix - en - Provence 21 June 1985, in *Le Lamy transp.*, 2020, vol. I, 495;
App. Anvers 9 October 1985, in *Le Lamy transp.*, 2020, vol. I, 511;
App. Lyon 18 October 1985, in *Bull. transp.,* 1986, 744;
App. Versailles 20 November 1985, in *Bull. transp.,* 1986, 264;
App. Versailles 15 January 1986, in *Bull. transp.,* 1986, 741;
App. Paris 21 January 1986, in *Bull. transp.,* 1986, 742;
App. Paris 22 January 1986, in *Bull. transp.,* 1986, 482;
App. Paris 27 January 1986, in *Bull. transp.,* 1986, 45;
App. Paris 25 February 1986, in *Le Lamy transp.*, 2020, vol. I, 501;
App. Paris 5 March 1986, *Le Lamy transp.*, 2020, vol. I, 514;
App. Paris 13 March 1986, in *Le Lamy transp.*, 2020, vol. I, 484;
App. Paris 7 April 1986, in *Le Lamy transp.*, 2020, vol. I, 499;
App. Poitiers 23 April 1986, in *Bull. transp.,* 1987, 362;
App. Paris 27 May 1986, in *Bull. transp.,* 1986, 676;
App. Paris 10 June 1986, in *Le Lamy transp.*, 2021, vol. I, 482;
App. Paris 17 June 1986, in *Bull. transp.*, 1987, 174;
App. Aix – en – Provence 27 June 1986, in *Le Lamy transp.*, 2020, vol. I, 509;

App. Paris 1 July 1986, in *Le Lamy transp.*, 2020, vol. I, 498;
App. Bordeaux 11 July 1986, in *Le Lamy transp.*, 2021, vol. I, 525;
App. Montpellier 18 September 1986, in *Le Lamy transp.*, 2020, vol. I, 466;
App. Paris 22 September 1986, in *Le Lamy transp.*, 2020, vol. I, 501;
App. Paris 13 October 1986, in *Bull. transp.,* 1986, 689;
App. Paris 15 October 1986, in *Bull. transp.,* 1987, 72;
App. Rennes 26 November 1986, in *Le Lamy transp.*, 2020, vol. I, 490;
App. Toulouse 6 January 1987, in *Bull. transp.,* 1988, 78;
App. Aix – en – Provence 9 January 1987, in *Bull. transp.,* 1987, 156;
App. Nancy 21 January 1987, in *Bull. transp.,* 1987, 344;
App. Paris 28 January 1987, in *Le Lamy transp.*, 2020, vol. I, 519
App. Montpellier 19 February 1987, in *Bull. transp.,* 1987, 578;
App. Paris 25 February 1987, in *Le Lamy transp.*, 2020, vol. I, 503;
App. Aix – en – Provence 3 March 1987, in *Le Lamy transp.*, 2020, vol. I, 503;
App. Rennes 19 March 1987, in *Bull. transp.,* 1988, 105;
App. Paris 28 April 1987, in *Bull. transp.,* 1987, 424;
Aix – en – Provence 12 May 1987, in *Bull. transp.,* 1987, 400;
App. Toulouse 4 June 1987, in *Bull. transp.,* 1981, 381
App. Paris 21 September 1987, in *Le Lamy transp.*, 2020, vol. I, 531;
App. Versailles 30 September 1987, in *Le Lamy transp.*, 2020, vol. I, 511;
App. Paris 30 September 1987, in *Bull. transp.,* 1988, 59;
App. Metz 28 October 1987, in *Le Lamy transp.*, 2020, vol. I, 502;
App. Nancy 29 October 1987, *Le Lamy transp.*, 2020, vol. I, 514;
App. Versailles 4 November 1987, in *Le Lamy transp.*, 2020, vol. I, 512;
App. Poitiers 4 November 1987, in *Bull. transp.,* 1988, 426;
App. Aix – en – Provence 17 November 1987, in *Bull. transp.*, 1987, 624;
App. Montpellier 1 December 1987, in *Bull. transp.,* 1988, 13;
App. Pau 16 December 1987, in *Bull. transp.,* 1988, 653;
App. Paris 13 January 1988, in *Le Lamy transp.*, 2020, vol. I, 524;
App. Paris 21 January 1988, in *Le Lamy transp.*, 2020, vol. I, 498;
App. Paris 25 March 1988, in *Le Lamy transp.*, 2020, vol. I, 519;
App. Montpellier 21 April 1988, in *Le Lamy transp.*, 2020, vol. I, 490;
App. Lyon 22 April 1988 in *Bull. transp.,* 1989, 176;
App. Paris 23 March 1988, in *Bull. transp.,* 1988, 265;
App. Nîmes 18 May 1988, in *Bull. transp.,* 1988, 472;
App. Rennes 25 May 1988, in *Le Lamy transp.*, 2020, vol. I, 467;
App. Toulouse 26 May 1988, in *Le Lamy transp.*, 2020, vol. I, 496;
App. Paris 6 July 1988, in *Bull. transp.,* 1980, 270;
App. Paris 10 October 1988, in *Bull. transp.,* 1989, 408;
App. Aix – en – Provence 21 October 1988, in *Bull. transp.,* 1989, 436;
App. Digione 22 November 1988, in *Bull. transp.,* 1989, 566;
App. Paris 15 December 1988, in *Le Lamy transp.*, 2020, vol. I, 494;
App. Rennes 18 January 1989, in *Le Lamy transp.*, 2020, vol. I, 500;
App. Poitiers 18 January 1989, in *Bull. transp.,* 1990, 101;
App. Paris 25 January 1989, in *Le Lamy transp.*, 2020, vol. I, 494;

App. Lyon 27 January 1989, in *Le Lamy transp.*, 483;
App. Paris 21 April 1989, in *Le Lamy transp.*, 2020, vol. I, 483;
App. Paris 15 June 1989, in *Le Lamy transp.*, 2020, 509;
App. Paris 23 June 1989, in *Le Lamy transp.*, 2020, vol. I, 502;
App. Paris 27 June 1989, in *Le Lamy transp.*, 2020, vol. I, 543 ss.;
App. Paris 4 July 1989, in *Le Lamy transp.*, 2020, vol. I, 494;
App. Aix – en – Provence 12 September 1989, in *Le Lamy transp.*, 2021, vol. I, 480;
App. Aix – en – Provence 13 September 1989, in *Le Lamy transp.*, 2021, vol. I, 482;
App. Aix – en – Provence 5 October 1989, in *Le Lamy transp.*, 2020, vol. I, 513;
App. Paris 11 October 1989, in *Bull. transp.*, 1990, 294;
App. Bruxelles 11 October 1989, in *Le Lamy transp.*, 2020, vol. I, 500;
App. Paris 24 October 1989, in *Le Lamy transp.*, vol. I, 2020, 534;
App. Aix – en – Provence 16 November 1989 in *Le Lamy transp.*, 2021, vol. I, 525;
App. Touluose 22 November 1989, in *Bull. transp.*, 1990, 427;
App. Toulouse 7 December 1989, in *Le Lamy transp.*, vol. I, 2020, 535;
App. Aix – en – Provence 16 January 1990, in *Le Lamy transp.*, 2021, vol. I, 480,
App. Aix - en - Provence 7 February 1990, in *Bull. Transp.*, 1990, 698;
App. Paris 7 March 1990, in *Bull. transp.*, 1991, 118;
App. Paris 15 March 1990, in *Le Lamy transp.*, 2020, vol. I, 495;
App. Aix - en – Provence 22 March 1990, in *Bull. transp.*, 1990, 796;
App. Paris 5 April 1990, in *Bull. transp. logist.*, 1991, 223;
App. Poitiers 23 August 1990, in *Bull. transp.*, 1990, 586
App. Reims 24 September 1990, in *Bull. transp.*, 1991, 471;
App. Aix – en – Provence 25 September 1990, in *Le Lamy transp.*, 2020, vol. I, 513;
App. Metz 30 October 1990, in *Bull. transp.*, 1991, 490;
App. Amiens 23 November 1990, in *Bull. transp.*, 1990, 292;
App. Nîmes 20 December 1990, in *Le Lamy transp.*, 2020, vol. I, 499;
App. Aix – en – Provence 15 January 1991, *Le Lamy transp.*, 2020, vol. I, 509;
App. Paris 16 January 1991, in *Bull. transp.*, 1991, 173;
App. Pau 11 February 1991, in *Bull. transp. logist.*, 1993, 262;
App. Paris 14 February 1991, in *Bull. transp. logist.*, 1991, 289;
App. Rouen 21 February 1991, in *Bull. transp.*, 1991, 507;
App. Lyon 21 February 1991, in *Bull. transp.*, 1992, 166;
App. Aix – en Provence 6 March 1991 in *Le Lamy transp.*, vol. I, 2020, 524;
App. Paris 2 April 1991, in *Bull. transp. logist.*, 1991, 428;
App. Rouen 11 April 1991, in *Le Lamy transp.*, 2020, vol. I, 498;
App. Paris 16 May 1991, in *Le Lamy transp.*, 2020, vol. I, 512;
App. Aix - en – Provence 28 May 1991, in *Le Lamy transp.*, 2021, vol. I, 558;
App. Aix – en – Provence 19 June 1991, in *Le Lamy transp.*, 2021, vol. I, 482;
App. Paris 28 June 1991, in *Le Lamy transp.*, 2020, vol. I, 512;
App. Paris 2 October 1991, in *Bull. transp. logis.*, 1991, 717;
App. Paris 24 October 1991, in *Le Lamy transp.*, 2020, vol. I, 512;
Aix – en – Provence 14 January 1992, in *Le Lamy transp.*, 2021, vol. I, 525;
App. Bruxelles 7 February 1992, in *Le Lamy transp.*, 2021, vol. I, 557;
App. Aix – en – Provence 12 February 1992, in *Le Lamy transp.*, 2020, vol. I, 500;

App. Montpellier 20 February 1992, in *Le Lamy transp.*, 2020, vol. I, 494;
App. Paris 10 March 1992, in *Bull. transp.,* 1992, 647;
App. Aix - en - Provence 9 April 1992, in *Bull. transp. logist.,* 1993, 527;
App. Aix – en- Provence 12 May 1992, in *Le Lamy transp.*, 2021, vol. I, 476;
App. Aix – en – Provence 10 September 1992, in *Bull. transp.,* 1993, 349;
App. Rouen 4 June 1992, *Le Lamy transp.*, 2020, vol. I, 467;
App. Paris 16 September 1992, in *Bull. transp.,* 1992, 651;
App. Versailles 15 October 1992, in *Bull. transp. logist.*, 1993, 239;
App. Amiens 28 October 1992, in *Bull. transp. logist.,* 1992, 766;
App. Rouen 11 February 1993, in *Bull. transp. logist.,* 1993, 583;
App. Paris 24 February 1993, in *Bull. transp.,* 1994, 52;
App. Paris 17 March 1993, in *Bull. transp.,* 1993, 488;
App. Toulouse 27 April 1993, in *Bull. transp.,* 1993, 32;
App. Paris 27 April 1993, in *Bull. transp. logist.,* 1992, 455;
App. Besançon 17 September 1993, in *Le Lamy transp.*, 2020, vol. I, 496;
App. Paris 7 October 1993, in *Bull. transp. logist.,* 1993, 741;
App. Versailles 4 November 1993, in *Bull. transp. logist.*, 1994, 19;
App. Aix – en – Provence 6 January 1994, in *Le Lamy transp.*, 2021, vol. I, 481;
App. Aix – en - Provence 3 March 1994, in *Bull. transp. logist.,* 1994, 451;
App. Paris 31 March 1994, in *Bull. transp. logist.,,* 2020, vol. I, 498;
App. Douai 7 June 1994, in *Bull. transp.,* 1994, 623;
App. Paris 6 July 1994, in *Le Lamy transp.*, 2020, vol. I, 535;
App. Versailles 6 July 1994, in *Bull. transp.,* 1994, 759;
App. Paris 7 July 1994, in *Le Lamy transp.*, 2020, vol. I, 468;
App. Lyon 7 October 1994, in *Bull. transp. logist.,* 1994, 757;
App. Nancy 29 November 1994, in *Le Lamy transp.*, 2020, vol. I, 535;
App. Orléans 18 January 1995, in *Bull. transp.,* 1995, 123;
App. Poitiers 1 March 1995, in *Le Lamy transp.*, 2020, vol. I, 503;
App. Versailles 30 March 1995, in *Le Lamy transp.*, 2020, vol. I, 454;
App. Paris 6 July 1995, in *Le Lamy transp.*, 2020, vol. I, 494;
App. Aix – en – Provence 7 September 1995, in *Le Lamy transp.*, 2020, vol. I, 519;
App. Versailles 7 September 1995, in *Bull. transp.,* 1995, 659;
App. Paris 18 October 1995, in *Le Lamy transp.*, 2020, vol. I, 494;
App. Paris 25 October 1995, in *Bull. transp.,* 1995, 362;
App. Paris 8 November 1995, in *Bull. transp.,* 1996, 132;
App. Angers 4 December 1995, in *Bull. transp.,* 1996, 337;
App. Besançon 12 December 1995, in *Le Lamy transp.*, 2020, vol. I, 513;
App. Besançon 7 February 1996, in *Bull. transp. logist.,* 1996, 682;
App. Paris 28 February 1996, in *Le Lamy transp.*, 2020, vol. I, 496;
App. Paris 29 February 1996, in *Le Lamy transp.*, 2020, vol. I, 495;
App. Versailles 7 March 1996, in *Bull. transp.,* 1996, 633;
App. Aix – en – Provence 4 September 1996, in *Le Lamy transp.*, 2020, vol. I, 524;
App. Paris 23 October 1996, in *Bull. transp.,* 1997, 106;
App. Versailles 24 October 1996, in *Bull. transp.,* 1997, 491;
App. Orléans 12 November 1996, in *Bull. transp.,* 1997, 159;

App. Grenoble 4 December 1996, in *Bull. transp. logist.,* 1997, 120;
App. Aix – en – Provence 5 December 1996, in *Le Lamy transp*., 2021, vol. I, 482;
App. Paris 11 December 1996, in *Le Lamy transp*., vol. I, 2020, 524;
App. Paris 18 December 1996, in *Bull. transp.,* 1997, 570;
App. Douai 16 January 1997, in *Bull. transp.,* 1997, 103;
App. Paris 26 February 1997, in *Le Lamy transp*., vol. I, 2020, 536;
App. Versailles 27 February 1997, in *Bull. transp. logis.,* 1997, 350;
App. Amiens 7 March 1997, in *Bull. transp.,* 1997, 261
App. Paris 24 April 1997, in *Bull. transp.,* 1997, 468;
App. Bordeaux 28 April 1997, in *Bull. transp.,* 1998, 417;
App. Paris 18 June 1997, in *Bull. transp. logist.,* 1997, 523;
App. Paris 19 June 1997, in *Le Lamy transp*., vol. I, 2020, 535;
App. Paris 24 September 1997, in *Le Lamy transp*., vol. I, 2020, 535;
App. Paris 22 October 1997, in *Bull. transp.,* 1997, 779;
App. Paris 6 May 1998, in *Le Lamy transp.,* 2020, vol. I, 495;
App. Nancy 3 June 1998, in *Bull. transp.,* 1998, 550;
App. Lyon 16 October 1998, in *Bull. transp*., 1999, 782;
App. Paris 12 March 1999, in *Bull. transp logist.,* 1999, 344;
App. Paris 1 July 1999, in *Le Lamy transp.,* 2020, vol. I, 496;
App. Riom 15 September 1999, in *Bull. transp.,* 1999, 746;
App. Paris 29 September 1999, in *Bull. transp.,* 1999, 747;
App. Besançon 27 October 1999, in *Bull. transp.,* 2000, 94;
App. Paris 10 November 1999, in *Bull. transp.,* 1999, 823;
App. Versailles 25 November 1999, in *Bull. transp.,* 2000, 274;
App. Orléans 9 December 1999, in *Bull. transp. logist.,* 2000, 12;
App. Paris 26 January 2000, in *Europ. transp. law,* 2000, n. 34, 415;
App. Colmar 26 January 2000, in *Bull. transp.,* 2000, 154;
App. Aix en Provence 2 March 2000, in *Le Lamy transp*., 2020, vol. I, 480;
App. Versailles 2 March 2000, in *Le Lamy transp*., 2020, vol. I, 483;
App. Paris 10 March 2000, in *Bull. transp*., 2000, 211;
App. Montpellier 21 March 2000, in *Bull. transp logist*., 2000, 350;
App. Paris 31 May 2000, in *Le Lamy transp*., 2020, vol. I, 543;
App. Paris 8 November 2000, in *Bull. transp. logist.,* 2004, 388;
App. Paris 24 January 2001, in *Bull. transp. logist.,* 2001, 194;
App. Paris 28 February 2001, in *Bull. transp. logist.,* 2001, 210;
App. Versailles 5 April 2001, in *Bull. transp. logist.,* 2001, 339;
App. Montpellier 24 April 2001, in *Bull. transp. logist.,* 2001, 525;
App. Chambéry 15 May 2001, in *Le Lamy transp*., 2021, vol. I, 540;
App. Paris 30 May 2001, in *Bull. transp. logist.,* 2001, 641;
App. Reims 27 June 2001, in *Le Lamy transp*., 2020, vol. I, 496;
App. Grenoble 3 October 2001, in *Bull. transp. logist.,* 2001, 711;
App. Riom 10 October 2001, in *Bull. transp. logist.,* 2001, 745;
App. Colmar 26 November 2001, in *Bull. transp. logist.,* 2002, 15;
App. Versailles 29 November 2001, in *Bull. transp. logist.,* 2002, 127;
App. Paris 16 January 2002, in *Bull. transp. logist.,* 2002, 168;

App. Versailles 17 January 2002, in *Bull. transp. logist.,* 2002, 1999;
App. Bourges 12 February 2002, in *Bull. transp. logist.,* 2003, 103;
App. Paris 28 March 2002, in *Le Lamy transp.*, 2021, vol. I, 475;
App. Paris 22 May 2002, in *Bull. transp. logist.,* 2002, 567;
App. Lyon 30 May 2002, in *Bull. transp. logist.,* 2002, 437;
App. Paris 6 June 2002, in *Bull. transp.,* 2002, 580;
App. Riom 12 June 2002, in *Bull. transp. logist.,* 2003, 83;
App. Nancy 2 July 2002, in *Le Lamy transp.*, 2020, vol. I, 519;
App. Lyon 17 July 2002, in *Bull. transp. logist.,* 2002, 548;
App. Paris 13 September 2002, in *Bull. transp. logist.,* 2002, 622;
App. Paris 14 November 2002, in *Le Lamy transp.*, 2020, vol. I, 512;
App. Versailles 14 November 2002, in *Bull. transp.,* 2002, 792;
App. Montpellier 19 November 2002, in *Bull. transp. logist.,* 2003, 31;
App. Reims 9 December 2002, in *Bull. transp. logist.,* 2003, 18;
App. Paris 22 January 2003, in *Le Lamy transp.*, 2020, vol. I, 496;
App. Paris 20 February 2003, in *Le Lamy transp.*, vol. I, 2020, 531;
App. Paris 26 February 2003, in *Bull. transp.*, 2003, 289;
App. Paris 21 May 2003, in *Bull. transp.,* 2003, 438;
App. Montpellier 27 May 2003, in *Bull. transp. logist.,* 2003, 437;
App. Paris 28 May 2003, in *Unif. law rev.,* 2004, 208;
App. Paris 25 September 2003, in *Bull. transp. logist.,* 2003, 793;
App. Versailles 30 October 2003, in *Bull. transp. logist.,* 2003, 83;
App. Nancy 14 January 2004, in *Bull. transp.,* 2004, 616;
App. Paris 29 January 2004, in *Bull. transp. logist.,* 2004, 104;
App. Paris 12 February 2004, in *Bull. transp. logist.,* 2004, 178;
App. Aix - en - Provence 12 February 2004, in *Bull. transp.,* 2004, 451;
App. Grenoble 22 April 2004, in *Bull. transp. logist.,* 2004, 334;
App. Paris 3 March 2004, in *Bull. transp.,* 2004, 207;
App. Paris 24 March 2004, in *Bull. transp. logist.,* 2004, 340;
App. Versailles 25 March 2004, in *Bull. transp. logist.,* 2004, 388;
App. Paris 31 March 2004, in *Le Lamy transp.*, vol. I, 2020, 533;
App. Grenoble 22 April 2004, in *Bull. transp.,* 335;
App. Paris 6 May 2004, in *Le Lamy transp.*, vol. I, 2020, 531;
App. Toulouse 8 June 2004, in *Bull. transp. logist.,* 2004, 486;
App. Douai 17 June 2004, in *Bull. transp. logist.,* 2004, 508;
App. Versailles 24 June 2004, in *Bull. transp. logist.,* 2004, 595;
App. Dijon 2 July 2004, in *Le Lamy transp.*, 2020, vol. I, 517;
App. Aix – en – Provence 2 September 2004, in *Bull. transp. logist.,* 2004, 614;
App. Versailles 14 September 2004, in *Bull. transp. logist.,* 2005, 102;
App. Lyon 28 October 2004, in *Bull transp. logist.,* 2005, 525;
App. Paris 17 November 2004, in *Bull. transp. logist.,* 2005, 86;
App. Rouen 16 December 2004, in *Bull. transp. logist.,* 2005, 190;
App. Rouen 13 January 2005, in Messent – Glass (2018), 84 ss., nt. 18;
App. Douai 20 January 2005, in *Bull. transp. logist.,* 2005, 106;
App. Rouen 20 January 2005, in *Bull. transp. logist.,* 2005, 374;

App. Paris 1 June 2005, in *Bull. transp.*, 2005, 454;
App. Paris 26 October 2005, in *Bull. transp. logist.,* 2005, 718;
App. Versailles 27 October 2005, in *Le Lamy transp.*, 2020, vol. I, 479;
App. Versailles 10 November 2005, in *Bull. transp. logist.,* 2005, 813;
App. Orléans 22 December 2005, in *Bull. transp.,* 2006, 15;
App. Paris 26 January 2006, in *Le Lamy transp.*, 2020, vol. I, 501;
App. Versailles 23 February 2006, in *Bull. trasnp.,* 2006, 384;
App. Douai 13 April 2006, in *Le Lamy transp.*, 2020, vol. I, 517;
App. Lyon 11 May 2006, in *Bull. transp.,* 2007, 78;
App. Mons 12 May 2006, in *Bull. transp. logist.,* 2006, 366;
App. Paris 28 September 2006, in *Le Lamy transp.*, 2020, vol. I, 454;
App. Versailles 5 October 2006, in *Le Lamy transp.*, 2020, vol. I, 518;
App. Aix - en - Provence 16 November 2006, in *Bull. transp. logist.,* 2006, 744;
App. Paris 21 December 2006, in *Bull. transp.,* 2007, 44;
App. Lyon 18 January 2007, in *Bull. transp. logist.,* 2007, 591;
App. Reims 22 January 2007, in *Bull. transp. logist.,* 2007, 95;
App. Paris 29 March 2007, in *Bull. transp. logist.,* 2007, 274;
App. Paris 4 April 2007, in *Bull. transp. logist.,* 2007, 388;
App. Lyon 7 June 2007, in *Bull. transp. logist.,* 2007, 466;
App. Pau 18 June 2007, in *Bull. transp.,* 2007, 432;
App. Pau 10 September 2007, in *Le Lamy transp.*, vol. I, 2020, 532;
App. Paris 21 November 2007, in *Le Lamy transp.*, vol. I, 2020, 532;
App. Paris 6 December 2007, in *Le Lamy transp.*, 2020, vol. I, 500;
App. Nîmes 13 December 2007, in *Le Lamy transp.*, 2020, vol. I, 531;
App. Lyon 6 March 2008 in *Bull. transp.,* 590;
App. Paris 9 April 2008, in *Le Lamy transp.*, 2020, vol. I, 454;
App. Pau 5 May 2008, in *Bull. transp. logist.,* 2008, 559;
App. Paris 4 June 2008, in *Bull. transp. logist.,* 2008, 433;
App. Dijon 26 June 2008, in *Le Lamy transp.*, 2021, vol. I, 558;
App. Versailles 22 October 2008, in *Bull. transp. logist.,* 2009, 16;
App. Douai 18 November 2008, in *Bull. transp.,* 2008, 735;
App. Angers 2 December 2008, in *Bull. transp. logist.,* 2008, 782;
App. Paris 3 December 2008, in *Bull. transp. logist.,* 2008, 781;
App. Paris 17 December 2008, in *Le Lamy transp.*, vol. I, 2020, 531;
App. Lyon 18 December 2008, in *Bull. transp.,* 2009, 483;
App. Paris 5 March 2009, in *Bull. transp. logist.,* 2009, 240;
App. Paris 11 March 2009, in *Bull. transp.,* 2009, 290;
App. Paris 9 April 2009, in *Bull. transp.,* 2009, 307;
App. Amiens 12 May 2009, in *Bull. transp. logist.,* 2009, 368;
App. Paris 25 June 2009, in *Bull. transp. logist.,* 2009, 450;
App. Versailles 2 July 2009, in *Bull. transp. logist.,* 2009, 547;
App. Olréans 8 October 2009, in *Bull. transp. logist.,* 2010, 59;
App. Versailles 5 November 2009, in *Bull. transp.,* 2010, 61;
App. Paris 3 February 2010, in *Bull. transp.,* 2010, 410;
App. Lyon 16 February 2010, in *Le Lamy transp.*, 2020, vol. I, 484;

App. Versailles 18 February 2010, in *Le Lamy transp.*, 2020, vol. I, 531;
App. Paris 4 March 2010, in *Bull. transp.*, 2010, 655;
App. Versailles 8 April 2010, in *Bull. transp. logist.*, 2010, 255;
App. Aix - en - Provence 23 June 2010, in *Bull. transp. logist.*, 2010, 657;
App. Paris 24 June 2010, in *Bull. transp. logist.*, 2010, 482;
App. Rennes 29 June 2010, in *Le Lamy transp.*, 2020, vol. I, 517;
App. Montpellier 14 September 2010, in *Le Lamy transp.*, 2020, vol. I, 466;
App. Amiens 14 October 2010, *Le Lamy transp.*, 2020, vol. I, 496;
App. Douai 21 October 2010, in *Le Lamy transp.*, vol. I, 500;
App. Aix – en – Provence 10 November 2010, in *Le Lamy transp.*, vol. I, 500;
App. Chambéry 16 November 2010, in *Bull. transp. logist.*, 2012, 632
App. Versailles 2 December 2010, in *Bull. transp. logist.*, 2010, 735;
App. Paris 12 January 2011, in *Bull. transp. logist.*, 2011, 141;
App. Montpellier 25 January 2011, in *Bull. transp. logist.*, 2011, 94;
App. Riom 29 January 2011, in *Le Lamy transp.*, 2020, vol. I, 500;
App. Paris 3 February 2011, in *Le Lamy transp.*, 2020, vol. I, 503;
App. Nancy 16 February 2011, in *Bull. transp. logist.*, 2011, 205;
App. Versailles 19 May 2011, in *Le Lamy transp.*, 2020, vol. I, 500;
App. Nîmes 26 May 2011, in *Le Lamy transp.*, 2021, vol. I, 478;
App. Paris 14 September 2011, in *Bull. transp. logist.*, 2011, 539;
App. Lyon 16 September 2011, in *Bull. transp.*, 2011, 571;
App. Paris 9 November 2011, in *Bull. transp. logist.*, 2011, 703;
App. Caen 1 December 2011, *Bull. transp.*, 2012, 19;
App. Paris 14 December 2011, in *Le Lamy transp.*, vol. I, 2020, 534;
App. Grenoble 17 January 2012, in *Bull. transp.*, 2012, 97;
App. Rouen 1 March 2012, in *Le Lamy transp.*, 2020, vol. I, 517;
App. Lyon 16 March 2012, in *Bull. transp. logist.*, 2012, 250;
App. Poitiers 3 April 2012, in *Le Lamy transp.*, 2020, vol. I, 534;
App. Versailles 10 May 2012, in *Bull. transp. logist.*, 2012, 378.;
App. Angers 15 May 2012, in *Le Lamy transp.*, 2021, vol. I, 478;
App. Nîmes 16 May 2012, in *Le Lamy transp.*, 2020, vol. I, 532;
App. Lyon 22 June 2012, *Le Lamy transp.*, 2020, vol. I, 509;
App. Bourges 5 July 2012, in *Le Lamy transp.*, 2020, vol. I, 500;
App. Paris 6 September 2012, in *Le Lamy transp.*, 2020, vol. I, 531;
App. Montpellier 18 September 2012, in *Le Lamy transp.*, 2020, vol. I, 454;
App. Toulouse 3 October 2012, in *Le Lamy transp.*, 2020, vol. I, 517;
App. Paris 10 October 2012, in *Bull. transp.*, 2012, 647;
App. Amiens 11 October 2012, in in *Le Lamy transp.*, 2020, vol. I, 533;
App. Reims 16 October 2012, in *Bull. transp. logist.*, 2012, 712;
App. Colmar 7 November 2012, in *Bull. transp. logis.*, 2012, 711;
App. Besançon 6 January 2013, in *Le Lamy transp.*, 2020, vol. I, 532;
App. Lyon 24 January 2013, in *Le Lamy transp.*, 2020, vol. I, 501
App. Chambéry 19 February 2013, in *Le Lamy transp.*, 2020, vol. I, 511;
App. Metz 21 February 2013, in *Bull. transp. logist.*, 2013, 179;
App. Paris 21 March 2013, in *Le Lamy transp.*, 2020, vol. I, 501;

App. Paris 28 March 2013, in *Le Lamy transp.*, 2021, vol. I, 558;
App. Aix – en – Provence 6 June 2013, in *Bull. transp. logist.,* 2013, 461;
App. Reims 11 June 2013, in *Bull. transp.,* 2013, 608;
App. Versailles 11 June 2013, *Le Lamy transp.*, 2020, vol. I, 497;
App. Pau 21 June 2013, in *Le Lamy transp.*, 2020, vol. I, 497;
App. Pau 24 June 2013, in *Le Lamy transp.*, 2020, vol. I, 536;
App. Versailles 3 September 2013, in *Bull. transp.,* 2013, 518;
App. Aix – en – Provence 12 September 2013, in *Le Lamy transp.*, 2020, vol. I, 509;
App. Versailles 17 September 2013, in *Le Lamy transp.*, 2020, vol. I, 519;
App. Metz 5 December 2013, in *Bull. transp. logist.,* 2014, 15;
App. Besançon 8 January 2014, in *Bull. transp. logist.,* 2014, 51;
App. Lyon 16 January 2014, in *Le Lamy transp.*, vol. I, 2020, 511;
App. Amiens 20 March 2014, in *Le Lamy transp.*, 2020, vol. I, 496;
App. Orléans 27 March 2014, in *Le Lamy transp.*, 2020, vol. I, 517;
App. Paris 10 April 2014, in *Bull. transp. logist.,* 2014, 698;
App. Paris 22 May 2014, in *Le Lamy transp.*, 2020, vol. I, 543;
App. Aix – en –Provence 19 June 2014, in *Bull. transp. logist.,* 2014, 432;
App. Lyon 18 September 2014, in *Le Lamy transp.*, vol. I, 2020, 531;
App. Grenoble 18 September 2014, in *Le Lamy transp.*, vol. I, 2020, 532;
App. Pau 19 September 2014, in *Bull. transp. logist.,* 2014, 606;
App. Versailles 23 September 2014, in *Le Lamy transp.*, 2020, vol. I, 497;
App. Grenoble 25 September 2014, in *Bull. transp.,* 2014, 605;
App. Grenoble 29 September 2014, in *Bull. transp.,* 2014, 605;
App. Paris 2 October 2014, in *Le Lamy transp.*, 2020, vol. I, 497;
App. Aix – en – Provence 30 October 2014, in *Bull. transp. logist.,* 2014, 694;
App. Toulouse 26 November 2014, in *Le Lamy transp.*, 2020, vol. I, 532;
App. Douai 16 December 2014, in *Le Lamy transp.*, 2020, vol. I, 500;
App. Paris 8 January 2015, in *Le Lamy transp.*, 2020, vol. I, 517;
App. Besançon 13 January 2015, in *Le Lamy transp.*, vol. I, 2020, 533;
App. Rennes 6 May 2015, in *Le Lamy transp.*, 2020, vol. I, 510;
App. Nancy 10 June 2015, in *Bull. transp. logist.,* 2015, 413;
App. Aix – en – Provence 19 November 2015, in *Bull. transp. logist.,* 2015, 700;
App. Douai 17 December 2015, in *Bull. transp. logist.,* 2016, 79;
App. Lyon 7 January 2016, in *Bull. transp.,* 2016, 45;
App. Poitiers 5 February 2016, in *Bull. transp. logist.,* 2016, 112;
App. Toulouse 17 February 2016, in *Bull. transp. logist.,* 2016, 143;
App. Angers 1 March 2016, in *Bull. transp. logist.,* 2016, 175;
App. Lyon 28 April 2016, in *Bull. transp. logist.,* 2016, 303;
App. Lyon 12 May 2016, in *Le Lamy transp.*, vol. I, 2020, 532;
App. Paris 30 June 2016, in *Le Lamy transp.*, 2020, vol. I, 519;
App. Bordeaux 12 October 2016, in *Le Lamy transp.*, 2021, vol. I, 558;
App. Colmar 23 November 2016, in *Bull. transp. logist.,* 2016, 722;
App. Douai 8 December 2016, in *Bull. transp. logis.,* 2017, 15;
App. Bordeaux 12 December 2016, in *Bull. transp. logis.,* 2017, 14;
App. Toulouse 22 December 2016, in *Bull. transp. logist.,* 2017, 79;

App. Aix – en - Provence 26 January 2017, in *Bull. transp.,* 2017, 88;
App. Lyon 30 March 2017, *Le Lamy transp.*, 2020, vol. I, 516;
App. Lyon 6 April 2017, in *Bull. transp. logis.,* 2017, 262;
App. Douai 6 April 2017, in *Bull. transp. logist.,* 2017, 259;
App. Versailles 18 April 2017, *Le Lamy transp.*, 2020, vol. I, 516;
App. Angers 13 June 2017, in *Bull. transp.,* 2017, 424;
App. Amiens 15 June 2017, in *Le Lamy transp.*, 2021, vol. I, 558;
App. Rouen 29 June 2017, in *Bull. transp. logist.,* 2017, 451;
App. Lyon 7 September 2017, *Le Lamy transp.*, 2020, vol. I, 495
App. Lyon 30 November 2017, in *Bull. transp. logist.,* 2017, 739;
App. Lyon 7 December 2017, in *Le Lamy transp.*, 2020, vol. I, 511;
App. Lyon 18 January 2018, in *Le Lamy transp.*, 2020, vol. I, 517;
App. Orléans 1 February 2018, in *Bull. transp logist.,* 2018, 92;
App. Lyon 22 March 2018, in *Bull. transp. logist.,* 2018, 189;
App. Paris 13 April 2018, in *Bull. transp. logist.,* 2018, 252;
App. Douai 28 June 2018, in *Bull. transp. logist.,* 2018, 413;
App. Bordeaux 24 October 2018, in *Le Lamy transp.*, 2020, vol. I, 536;
App. Versailles 29 January 2019, in *Le Lamy transp.*, 2020, vol. I, 519;
App. Paris 28 March 2019, in *Le Lamy transp.*, 2020, vol. I, 532;
App. Versailles 9 April 2019, in *Le Lamy transp.*, 2020, vol. I, 515;
App. Grenoble 16 May 2019, in *Le Lamy transp.*, 2021, vol. I, 524;
App. Paris 23 May 2019, in *Le Lamy transp.*, 2020, vol. I, 483;
App. Montpellier 10 September 2019, in *Le Lamy transp.*, 2020, vol. I, 509;
App. Versailles 14 November 2019, in *Le Lamy transp.*, 2020, vol. I, 532;
App. Montpellier 10 September 2019, in *Le Lamy transp.*, 2020, 466;
App. Grenoble 10 September 2020, in *Le Lamy transp.*, 2021, vol. I, 473;
App. Grenoble 22 October 2020, in *Le Lamy transp.*, 2021, vol. I, 540;

Trib. Charleroi 1 October 1968, in *Unf. Law rev.,* 1969, 327;
Trib. comm. Paris 29 June 1970, in *Bull. transp.,* 1970, 325;
Trib. com. Paris 12 October 1971, in *Unif. law rev.,* 1973, 268;
Trib. Albertville 4 March 1975 in *Bull. transp.,* 1976, 217;
Trib. com. Lyon 10 November 1975, in *Bull. transp.,* 1976, 175;
Trib. Paris 13 December 1976, in *Bull. transp.,* 1977, 37;
Trib. comm. Charleroi 26 June 1977, in *Europ. transp. law,* 1977, n. 12, 776;
Trib. com. Paris 15 June 1978, in *Bull. transp.,* 1978, 420;
Trib. comm. Tarbes 5 February 1979, in *Bull. transp logist.,* 1979, 196
Trib. com. Paris 25 June 1979, in *Bull. transp.,* 1979, 403;
Trib. com. Paris 26 June 1981, in *Bull. transp.,* 1982, 142;
Trib. com. Pontoise 22 February 1983, in *Le Lamy transp.*, 2021, vol. I, 559;
Trib. com. Paris 11 March 1983, in *Europ. transp. law,* 1990, n. 25, 2017;
Trib. com. Paris 14 September 1983, in *Europ. transp. law,* 1990, n. 25, 212;
Trib. Poitiers 7 December 1983, in *Bull. transp.* 1985, 425;
Trib. com. Marseille 4 February 1986, in *Europ. transp. law,* 1990, n. 25, 223;
Trib. Orléans 24 March 1987, in *Bull. transp.,* 1987, 662;

Trib. com. Marseille 23 October 1987, in *Bull. transp.,* 1988, 43;
Trib. com. Paris 31 March 1992, in *Bull. transp.,* 1992, 331;
Trib. com. Bobigny 29 January 1993, in *Le Lamy transp.*, vol. I, 2020, 532;
Trib. com. Paris 10 February 1993, in *Bull. transp.,* 1993, 332;
Trib. com. Carpentras 19 February 1993, in *Le Lamy transp.*, 2020, vol. I, 499,
Trib. Paris 7 February 1994, in *Le Lamy transp.*, 2020, vol. I, 498;
Trib. com. Bobigny 25 February 1994, in *Le Lamy transp.*, 2020, vol. I, 490;
Trib. com. Tours 2 September 1994, in *Le Lamy transp.*, 2020, vol. I, 498;
Trib. Bobigny 13 June 1996, in *Le Lamy transp.*, 2020, vol. I, 512;
Trib. com. Marseille 30 April 1996, in *Le Lamy transp.*, 2020, vol. I, 466;
Trib. com. Paris 3 December 1996, in *Bull. transp logist.,* 1997, 182;
Trib. com. Paris 9 February 1999, in *Bull. transp logist.,* 1999, 445;
Trib. com. Beauvais 4 July 2002, in *Bull. transp logist.,* 2002, 603
Trib. com. Bois 6 December 2002, in *Bull. transp. logis.,* 2003, 143;
Trib. com. Chartes 1 April 2003, in *Le Lamy transp.*, vol. I, 2020, 535;
Trib. com. Aix - en – Provence 23 June 2003, in *Bull. transp. logist.,* 2003, 494;
Trib. Mulhouse 30 January 2004, in *Bull. transp. logist.,* 2004, 136;
Trib. com. Paris 5 May 2004, in *Bull. transp. logis,* 2005, 391;
Trib. com. Avignon 8 October 2004, in *Bull. transp. logist.,* 2004, 720;
Trib. com. Paris 5 September 2005, in *Bull. transp. logist.,* 2005, 23;
Trib. Lyon 18 April 2006, in *Bull. transp.,* 2006, 667;
Trib. Chambéry 13 April 2007, in *Bull. transp.,* 2007, 320;
Trib. Salon de Provence 9 January 2009, in *Bull. transp. logist.,* 2009, 115;
Trib. com. Boulogne - sur - Mer, 24 November 2017, in *Le Lamy transp.*, 2021, vol. I, 558.

Germany

BGH 18 February 1972, in *Europ. transp. law,* 1972, n. 7, 860;
BGH 21 December 1973, in *Europ. transp. law,* 1975, n. 10, 92;
BGH 3 July 1974, in *Unif. law rev.,* 1974, 216;
BGH 28 February 1975, in *Unif. law rev.,* 1975, 372;
BGH 13 January 1978, in *Europ. transp. law,* 1978, n. 13, 402;
BGH 27 October 1978, in *VersR,* 1979, 276;
BGH 9 February 1979, in *Europ. transp. law,* 1980, n. 15, 215;
BGH 6 July 1979, in *Europ. transp. law,* 1980, n. 15, 863;
BGH 13 February 1980, in *VersR,* 1980, 533;
BGH 30 January 1981, in *Europ. transp. law,* 1981, n. 16, 455;
BGH 6 February 1981, in *Europ. transp. law,* 1982, n. 17, 50;
BGH 6 May 1981, in *Europ. transp. law,* 1982, n. 17, 331;
BGH 5 June 1981, in *Europ. transp. law,* 1982, n. 17, 301;
BGH 11 December 1981, in *Europ. transp. law,* 1983, n. 18, 63;
BGH 10 January 1982, in *Europ. transp. law,* 1983, n. 18, 32;
BGH 27 January 1982, in *Europ. transp. law,* 1985, 20, 249;
BGH 27 June 1985, in *Europ. transp. law,* 1986, n. 21, 102;
BGH 7 November 1985, in *Europ. transp. law,* 1986, n. 21, 266;

BGH 16 October 1986, in *Europ. transp. law,* 1987, n. 22, 56;
BGH 24 September 1987, in *TranspR,* 1988, 108;
BGH 10 October 1991, in *Europ. transp. law,* 1992, n. 27, 262;
BGH 25 April 1991, in *TranspR,* 1991, 312;
BGH 10 October 1991, in *Europ. transp. law,* 1992, n. 27, 262;
BGH 24 October 1991, in *Europ. transp law,* 1992, n. 27, 839;
BGH 14 November 1991, in *Europ. transp. law,* 1993, n. 28, 265;
BGH 15 October 1992, in *TranspR,* 1992, 137;
BGH 14 July 1993, in *Europ. transp. law*, 1993, n. 28, 917;
BGH 19 May 1995, in *Europ. transp. law*, 1996, n. 31, 703;
BGH 25 October 1995, n *Europ. transp. law,* , 1996, n. 31, 404;
BGH 21 November 1996, in *Europ. transp. law,* 1997, n. 32, 442;
BGH 6 February 1997, in *Europ. transp. law,* 1998, n. 33, 701;
BGH 17 April 1997, in *Unif. law rev.,* 1999, 206;
BGH 17 July 1997, in *TranspR,* 1998, 25;
BGH 13 November 1997, in *TranspR,* 1998, 250
BGH 28 May 1998, in *TranspR,* 1998, 454;
BGH 16 July 1998, in *Europ. transp. law,* 1999, n. 34, 360;
BGH 8 October 1998, in *TranspR,* 1999, 59;
BGH 15 October 1998 in *VersR,* 1999, 646;
BGH 13 April 2000, in *TranspR,* 2000, 407;
BGH 15 June 2000, in *Europ. transp. law,* 2000, n. 35, 785;
BGH 3 July 2000, in *Europ. transp. law,* 2000, n. 35, 678;
BGH 13 July 2000, in *TranspR,* 2000, 409;
BGH 18 January 2001, in *TranspR,* 2001, 369;
BGH 31 May 2001, in *Europ. transp. law,* 2002, n. 37, 80
BGH 25 October 2001, in *TranspR,* 2002, 198;
BGH 4 July 2002, in *Europ. transp. law,* 2002, 37, 817;
BGH 27 January 2003, in *Europ. transp. law,* 2003, n. 38, 653;
BGH 27 February 2003, in *TranspR,* 2003, 302;
BGH 10 April 2003, in *Europ. transp. law,* 2003, n. 38, 782;
BGH 26 June 2003, in *Europ. transp. law,* 2004, n. 39, 93;
BGH 10 September 2003, in *Europ. transp. law,* 2004, n. 39, 74;
BGH 9 October 2003, in *TranspR,* 2004, 175;
BGH 20 November 2003, in *Europ. transp. law,* 2004, n. 39, 255;
BGH 27 November 2003, in *TranspR,* 2003, 79;
BGH 9 December 2003, in *TranspR,* 2004, 175;
BGH 18 December 2003, in *Europ. transp. law,* 2004, n. 39, 684;
BGH 29 January 2004, in *TranspR,* 2004, 213;
BGH 4 March 2004, in *TranspR,* 2004, 460;
BGH 8 July 2004, in *TranspR,* 2004, 357;
BGH 20 January 2005, in *TranspR,* 2005, 311;
BGH 3 March 2005, in *TranspR,* 2006, 114;
BGH 19 May 2005, in *TranspR,* 2006, 114;
BGH 1 December 2005, in *TranspR,* 2006, 115;

BGH 30 March 2006, in *Europ. transp. law,* 2006, n. 41, 668;
BGH 19 January 2006, in *TranspR,* 2006, 121
BGH 6 July 2006, in *Europ. transp. law,* 2006, n. 41, 796;
BGH 15 January 2007, in *TranspR,* 2007, 314;
BGH, 25 January 2007, in *Europ. transp. law,* 2007, n. 42, 766.
BGH 21 March 2007, in *TranspR,* 2007, 361;
BGH 19 April 2007, in *Europ. transp. law,* 2008, n. 43, 94;
BGH 3 May 2007, in *TranspR,* 2007, 419;
BGH 6 June 2007, in *TranspR,* 2007, 423;
BGH 14 February 2008, in *Europ. transp. law,* 2008, n. 43, 1227;
BGH 21 February 2008, in *TranspR,* 2008, 249;
BGH 17 July 2008, in *Europ. transp. law.,* 2009, n. 44, 196;
BGH 20 November 2008, in *TranspR,* 2009, 26;
BGH 21 February 2009, in *TranspR,* 2008, 249;
BGH 26 March 2009, in *TranspR,* 2010, 76;
BGH 10 December 2009, in *TranspR,* 2010, 78;
BGH 1 July 2010, in *TranspR,* 2011, 78;
BGH 9 September 2010, in *TranspR,* 2011, 178;
BGH 20 September 2010, in *TranspR,* 2010, 45;
BGH 30 September 2010, in *TranspR,* 2010, 437;
BGH 25 October 2010, in *Europ. transp. law,* 2002, n. 37, 353;
BGH 15 December 2011, in *TranspR,* 2012, 330;
BGH 13 June 2012, in *Europ. transp. law,* 2013, n. 48, 199;
BGH 13 September 2012, in *TranspR,* 2012, 56;
BGH 25 October 2012, in *TranspR,* 2013, 239;
BGH 4 July 2013, in *TranspR,* 2014, 27;
BGH 13 March 2014, in *TranspR,* 2014, 370;
BGH 22 May 2014, in *TranspR,* 2015, 33;
BGH 19 March 2015, in *Europ. transp. law*, 2016, n. 51, 99;
BGH 21 September 2017, in *TranspR,* 2018, 11;
BGH 30 October 2017, in *TranspR,* 2018, 146;
BGH 28 February 2018, in *TranspR,* 2013, 290;
BGH 26 April 2018, in *TranspR,* 2018, 384;
BGH 11 October 2018, in *Europ. transp. law,* 2018, n. 53, 453;
BGH 29 May 2019, in *TranspR,* 2019, 499;
BGH 25 July 2019, in *TranspR,* 2019, 508;
BGH 19 September 2019, in *Europ. transp. law,* 2020, n. 55, 277;
BGH 17 December 2020, in *TranspR,* 2021, 154;

OLG Nuremberg 14 June 1965, in *Europ. transp. law,* 1971, n. 6, 247;
OLG Hamburg 7 December 1965, in *TranspR,* 1996, 238;
OLG Zweibrücken 23 September 1966, in *VersR,* 1967, 1145;
OLG Düsseldorf 8 May 1969, in *Europ. transp. law,* 1970, n. 5, 446;
OLG Düsseldorf 18 July 1971, in *VersR,* 1973, 177;
OLG Hamm 4 November 1971, in *VersR,* 1973, 911;

OLG Düsseldorf 18 November 1971, in *Europ. transp. law,* 1973, n. 8, 510;
OLG Düsseldorf 13 January 1972, *VersR,* 1973, 178;
OLG Hamm 19 February 1972, in *Europ. transp. law,* 1974, n. 9, 753;
OLG Hamm 19 February 1973, in *Europ. transp. law,* 1974, n. 9, 753;
OLG Düsseldorf 18 October 1973;
OLG Hamm 12 November 1973;
OLG Munich 16 January 1974, in *Europ. transp. law,* 1974, n. 9, 620;
OLG Celle 13 January 1975, in *Europ. transp. law,* 1975, n. 10, 410;
OLG Düsseldorf 18 January 1979;
OLG Hamburg 22 January 1979, in *Unif. law rev.,* 1980, 266;
OLG Hamburg 3 July 1980, in *VersR,* 1980, 1075;
OLG Hamburg 6 November 1980, in *VersR,* 1982, 556;
OLG Munich 27 February 1981, in *VersR,* 1982, 334;
OLG Munich 27 March 1981, in *VersR,* 1982, 264;
OLG Berlin 4 May 1983, in *TranspR,* 1985, 134;
OLG Düsseldorf 14 July 1983, in *TranspR,* 1984, 16;
OLG Hamburg 3 May 1984, in *TranspR,* 1985, 37;
OLG Düsseldorf 3 May 1984, in *TranspR,* 1984, 198;
OLG Hamburg 28 February 1985, in *TranspR*, 1985, 436;
OLG Hamburg 2 May 1985, in *VersR,* 1986, 865;
OLG Munich 26 July 1985, in *TranspR,* 1985, 395;
OLG Saarbrüchen 23 August 1985, in *TranspR,* 1985, 382;
OLG Hamburg 7 November 1985, in *TranspR,* 1986, 15;
OLG Hamburg 16 January 1986, in *TranspR,* 1986, 229;
OLG Lübeck 17 March 1986, in *TranspR,* 1986, 339;
OLG Düsseldorf 9 October 1986, in *TranspR,* 1986, 429;
OLG Hamburg 18 December 1986, *TranspR,* 1987, 413;
OLG Düsseldorf 30 May 1988, in *TranspR*, 1988, 423;
OLG Munich 12 May 1989, in *TranspR,* 1990, 427;
OLG Hamburg 18 May 1989, in *TranspR,* 1990, 188;
OLG Munich 5 July 1989, in *TranspR,* 1990, 16;
OLG Düsseldorf 23 November 1989, in *TranspR*, 1990, 63;
OLG Munich 12 April 1990, in *TranspR,* 1990, 280;
OLG Düsseldorf 22 November 1990, in *TranspR,* 1991, 59;
OLG Düsseldorf 3 December 1990, in *TranspR,* 1991, 91;
OLG Munich 12 April 1991, in *TranspR,* 1991, 298;
OLG Munich 17 July 1991, in *TranspR,* 1991, 427;
OLG Stuttgart 27 September 1991, in *TranspR,* 1992, 22;
OLG Hamm 2 December 1991, in *TranspR,* 1992, 179;
OLG Munich 24 April 1992, in *TranspR,*1992, 360;
OLG Düsseldorf 24 September 1992, in *TranspR,* 1993, 54 ss.;
OLG Munich 9 October 1992, in *TranspR,* 1993, 75;
OLG Düsseldorf 25 March 1993, in *TranspR*, 1994, 439;
OLG Stuttgart 15 September 1993, in *TranspR,* 1994, 156;
OLG Hamm 25 November 1993, in *TranspR,* 1994, 61;

OLG Hamburg 7 April 1994, in *TranspR,* 1995, 115;
OLG Düsseldorf 21 April 1994, in *TranspR,* 1995, 67;
OLG Munich 19 July 1994, in *TranspR,* 1995, 116;
OLG Hamburg 26 October 1994, in *TranspR,* 1945, 293;
OLG Düsseldorf 15 December 1994, in *TranspR,* 1995, 244;
OLG Karlsruhe 17 February 1995, in *TranspR,* 1995, 439;
OLG Nuremberg 22 March 1995, in *TranspR,* 1996, 381;
OLG Karlsruhe 29 June 1995, in *VersR*, 1995, 1306;
OLG Cologne 4 July 1995, in *TranspR,* 1996, 284;
OLG Munich 28 July 1995, in *TranspR,* 1996, 240;
OLG Munich 29 November 1995, in *TranspR,* 1997, 190;
OLG Hamm 9 May 1996, in *TranspR,* 1997, 190;
OLG Munich 4 December 1996, in *TranspR,* 1997, 195;
OLG Düsseldorf 23 December 1996, in *TranspR,* 1998, 113;
OLG Hamm 6 January 1997, in *TranspR*, 2000, 176;
OLG Düsseldorf 27 February 1997, in *TranspR,* 1998, 194;
OLG Cologne 14 March 1997, in *VersR,* 1997, 1033;
OLG Hamm 20 March 1997, *TranspR,* 1998, 297;
OLG Düsseldorf 23 December 1997, in *TranspR,* 1997, 422;
OLG Zweibrücken 17 December, 1997, in *TranspR,* 1997, 369;
OLG Cologne 17 March 1998, in *TranspR,* 2000, 80;
OLG Munich 31 March 1998, in *TranspR,* 1998, 353;
OLG Hamm 29 June 1998, in *TranspR,* 1999, 201;
OLG Munich 29 July 1998, in *TranspR*, 2000, 31;
OLG Celle 29 October 1998, in *TranspR,* 1999, 106;
OLG Hamm 2 November 1998, in *TranspR,* 2000, 361;
OLG Hamm 19 November 1998, in *TranspR,* 2000, 363;
OLG Cologne 3 December 1998, in *TranspR,* 1998, 462;
OLG Karlsruhe 9 December 1998, in *TranspR,* 2000, 465;
OLG Nuremberg 24 February 1999, in *TranspR,* 2000, 81;
OLG Cologne 3 March 1999, in *TranspR,* 2001, 122;
OLG Hamm 14 June 1999, in *TranspR,* 2000, 29;
OLG Düsseldorf 17 June 1999, in *TranspR,* 2002, 237;
OLG Hamburg 23 June 1999, in *TranspR,* 2000, 175;
OLG Hamburg 28 July 1999, in *TranspR,* 2000, 176;
OLG Hamburg 18 August 1999, in *TranspR,* 2000, 220;
OLG Stuttgart 13 October 1999, in *TranspR,* 2001, 127;
OLG Nuremberg 18 October 1999, in *TranspR,* 2000, 126;
OLG Hamm 9 December 1999, in *TranspR,* 2000, 122;
OLG Hamburg 9 March 2000, in *TransR,* 2000, 253;
OLG Brandenburg 29 March 2000, in *TranspR,* 2000, 220;
OLG Bremen 11 May 2000, in *TranspR,* 2001, 75;
OLG Munich 19 July 2000, in *TranspR,* 2000, 412;
OLG Celle 7 September 2000, in *TranspR,* 2001, 119;
OLG Munich 27 October 2000, in *TranspR,* 2001, 125;

OLG Saar 12 December 2000, in *TranspR,* 2001, 169;
OLG Karlsruhe 21 December 2000, in *TranspR,* 2003, 347;
OLG Bremen 11 January 2001, in *TranspR*, 2001, 66;
OLG Hamburg 17 January 2001, in *TranspR,* 2002, 238;
OLG Hamburg 7 June 2001, in *TranspR,* 2002, 108;
OLG Düsseldorf 4 July 2001, in *TranspR,* 2002, 158;
OLG Munich 27 July 2001, in *TranspR,* 2002, 161;
OLG Karlsruhe 28 September 2001, in *TranspR,* 2004, 33;
OLG Hamburg 4 October 2001, in *TranspR,* 2002, 109;
OLG Hamburg 11 October 2001, in *TranspR,* 2002, 111;
OLG Munich 18 October 2001, in *TranspR,* 2002, 27;
OLG Düsseldorf 14 November 2001, in *TranspR,* 2002, 73;
OLG Schleswig Holstein 20 December 2001, in *TranspR,* 2002, 76;
OLG Nuremberg 6 March 2002, in *TranspR,* 2002, 402;
OLG Cologne 8 March 2002, in *TranspR,* 2002, 239;
OLG Nuremberg 17 April 2002, in *TranspR,* 2002, 243;
OLG Düsseldorf 24 July 2002, in *TranspR,* 2002,343;
OLG Hamburg 7 November 2002, in *TranspR,* 2003, 25.
OLG Cologne 10 December 2002, in *TranspR,* 2003, 459;
OLG Stuttgart 11 June 2003, in *TranspR,* 2003, 308;
OLG Frankfurt 3 December 2003, in *TranspR,* 2004, 125;
OLG Hamburg 27 January 2004, in *TranspR,* 2004, 215;
OLG Munich 28 January 2004, in *TranspR,* 2004, 324;
OLG Cologne 25 March 2004, in *TranspR,* 2004, 358;
OLG Hamburg 17 June 2004, in *TranspR,* 2005, 116;
OLG Düsseldorf 26 July 2004, in *TranspR,* 2005, 118;
OLG Munich 23 September 2004, in *TranspR,* 2005, 254;
OLG Frankfurt 5 October 2004, in *TranspR,* 2005, 256;
OLG Hamm 22 November 2004, in *TranspR,* 2005, 123;
OLG Munich 25 November 2004, in *TranspR,* 2005, 473;
OLG Cologne 28 May 2005, in *TranspR,* 2005, 472;
OLG Cologne 27 September 2005, in *TranspR,* 2007, 316;
OLG Munich 22 March 2006, in *TranspR,* 2006, 310;
OLG Saar 5 April 2006, in *TranspR,* 2007, 63;
OLG Cologne 30 May 2006, in *TranspR,* 2007, 114;
OLG Stuttgart 26 July 2006, in *TranspR,* 2007, 320;
OLG Düsseldorf 13 December 2006, in *TranspR,* 2007, 25;
OLG Bremen 8 February 2007, in *TranspR*, 2008, 252;
OLG Koblenz 22 February 2007, in *TranspR,* 2007, 249;
OLG Stuttgart 22 February 2007, in *TranspR,* 2007, 249;
OLG Düsseldorf 14 March 2007, in *TranspR,* 2007, 199;
OLG Thuringia 30 March 2007, in *TranspR,* 2007, 201;
OLG Frankfurt sul Meno 20 April 2007, in *TranspR,* 2008, 472;
OLG Stuttgart 1 August 2007, in *TranspR,* 2007, 322;
OLG Düsseldorf 21 November 2007, in *TranspR,* 2008, 36;

OLG Bamberg 31 January 2008, in *TranspR,* 2008, 469;
OLG Stuttgart 28 May 2008, in *TranspR,* 2008, 259;
OLG Saar 17 July 2008, in *TranspR,* 2008, 471;
OLG Karlsruhe 17 October 2008, in *TranspR,* 2008, 471;
OLG Nuremberg 4 February 2009, in *TranspR*, 2009, 256;
OLG Stuttgart 11 November 2009, in *TranspR,* 2010, 149;
OLG Munich 5 May 2010, in *VersR,* 2010, 1521;
OLG Koblenz 20 May 2010, in *TranspR,* 2010, 442;
OLG Munich 23 December 2010, in *TranspR,* 2011, 158;
OLG Düsseldorf 12 January 2011, in *Europ. transp. law,* 2012, n. 47, 87;
OLG Hamm 27 January 2011, in *TranspR,* 2011, 181;
OLG Munich 8 March 2011, in *TranspR,* 2013, 31;
OLG Karlsruhe 24 March 2011, in *VersR*, 2011, 1546;
OLG Hamburg 14 April 2011, in *TranspR,* 2011, 181;
OLG Brandenburg 1 June 2011, in *TranspR,* 2013, 29;
OLG Munich 1 June 2011, in *TranspR,* 2011, 337;
OLG Naumburg 15 June 2012, in *TranspR,* 2013, 235;
OLG Cologne 10 July 2012, in *TranspR,* 2015, 111;
OLG Düsseldorf 21 November 2012, in *TranspR,* 2013, 115;
OLG Düsseldorf 20 March 2013, in *TranspR,* 2013, 196;
OLG Munich 23 April 2013, in *TranspR,* 2015, 449;
OLG Koblenz 3 July 2013, in *TranspR,* 2014, 154;
OLG Hamm 21 November 2013, in *TranspR,* 2014, 290;
OLG Düsseldorf 18 December 2013, in *TranspR,* 2014, 291;
OLG Munich 6 February 2014, in *Unif. law rev.,* 2014, 295;
OLG Cologne 25 February 2014, in *TranspR,* 2015, 115;
OLG Düsseldorf 3 December 2014, in *TranspR,* 2016, 456;
OLG Düsseldorf 17 December 2014, in *TranspR,* 2016, 391;
OLG Schleswig Holstein 18 December 2014, in *TranspR,* 2015, 157;
OLG Stuttgart 25 February 2015, in *TranspR,* 2015, 191;
OLG Hamburg 5 March 2015, in *TranspR,* 2017, 113;
OLG Cologne 16 April 2015, in *TranspR,* 2015, 449;
OLG Munich 28 October 2015, in *TranspR,* 2016, 193;
OLG Munich 2 December 2015, in *TranspR,* 2016, 69;
OLG Koblenz 9 March 2016, in *TranspR,* 2017, 109;
OLG Stuttgart 11 May 2016, in *TranspR,* 2017, 10;
OLG Munich 21 July 2016, in *TranspR,* 2017, 25;
OLG Munich 21 July 2016, in *VersR*, 2017, 583,
OLG Cologne 25 August 2016, in *TranspR,* 2017, 62;
OLG Karlsruhe 15 December 2016, in *TranspR,* 2017, 217;
OLG Munich 16 March 2017, in *TranspR,* 2017, 367;
OLG Nuremberg 14 August 2017, in *TranspR,* 2018, 118;
OLG Munich 26 October 2017, in *TranspR,* 2018, 56;
OLG Düsseldorf 18 November 2017, in *TranspR,* 2018, 197;
OLG Dresden 10 January 2018, in *TranspR,* 2018, 144;

OLG Hamburg 7 March 2018, in *Europ. transp. law,* 2018, n. 53, 305;
OLG Düsseldorf 5 September 2018, in *TranspR,* 2019, 73;
OLG Düsseldorf 9 October 2018, in *TranspR,* 2019, 140;
OLG Munich 21 November 2018, in *TranspR,* 2019, 212;
OLG Zweibrücken 12 March 2019, in *Europ. transp. law,* 2019, n. 54, 449;
OLG Munich 6 June 2019, in *VersR,* 2020, 591;
OLG Düsseldorf 13 May 2020, in *Europ. transp. law,* 2021, n. 61, 53;
OLG Cologne 4 June 2020, in *TranspR,* 2021, 15;
OLG Düsseldorf 13 June 2020, in *TranspR,* 2021, 151;

LG Duisburg 10 May 1968, in *Europ. transp. law,* 1969, n. 4, 979;
LG Nuremberg – Freuth 21 January 1999, in *TranspR,* 2000, 369;
LG Baden – Baden 22 October 1999, in *TranspR,* 2000, 254;
LG Lübeck 25 January 2000, in *TranspR,* 2000, 222;
LG Berlin 26 January 2000, in *TranspR,* 2000, 255;
LG Lübeck 8 February 2001, in *TranspR,* 2001, 171;
LG Thuringia 1 March 2001, in *TranspR,* 2002, 70;
LG Bonn 27 March 2001, in *TranspR,* 2002, 77;
LG Hamburg 23 September 2001, in *TranspR,* 2003, 351;
LG Düsseldorf 23 November 2001, in *TranspR,* 2002, 28;
LG Bonn 20 December 2001, in *TranspR,* 2002, 443,
LG Hamburg 9 September 2002, in *TranspR,* 2005, 315;
LG Hamburg 5 December 2007, in *TranspR,* 2008, 264;
LG Cottbus 8 July 2008, in *TranspR,* 2008, 368;
LG Giessen 31 July 2008, in *TranspR,* 2008, 370;
LG Fulda 18 November 2009, in *TranspR,* 2010, 192;
LG Berlin 13 October 2010, in *TranspR,* 2011, 188;
LG Munich 6 February 2014, in *TranspR,* 2014, 295;
LG Stuttgart 15 December 2014, in *TraspR,* 2015, 163;
LG Koblenz 20 March 2015, in *TranspR,* 2015, 166;
LG Karlsruhe 30 April 2015, in *TranspR,* 2016, 195;
LG Erfurt 25 September 2015, in *TranspR,* 2018, 120;
LG Hamburg 15 April 2016, in *TranspR,* 2017, 32;
LG Aachen 21 March 2017, in *TranspR,* 2018, 22;
LG Düsseldorf 28 March 2017, in *TranspR,* 2017, 311;
LG Bremen 5 June 2018, in *TranspR,* 2018, 390.

Greece
Cass. 1518 / 2001, in *Elldik*, 44, 1619;
Cass. 826 / 2004, in *Elldik*, 45, 1656;
Cass. 1885 / 2005;
Cass. 471 / 2006;
Cass. 487 / 2008;
Cass. 61 / 2011;
Cass. 1714 / 2014;

Cass. 1025 / 2018
Cass. 1411 / 2018

App. Piraeus 45 / 1997, in *Pireus law rev.,* 1997, 58;
App. Piraeus 173 / 2011;
App. Piraeus 268 / 2001, in *EMD*, 2001, 327;
App. Thessaloniki 171 / 2005, in *DEE*, 2005, 984;
App. Tessaloniki 730 / 2005, in *EmpD,* 2005, 528;
App. Larisa 347 / 2006, in *EpiskED,* 2006, 548;

Italy
Cass. 28 November 1975, n. 3983, in *Giur. it. rep.,* 1975;
Cass. 1 March 1978, n. 1034, in *Giur. it. rep.,* 1978;
Cass. 14 May 1979 n. 2773, in *Giust. civ.*, 1979, I, 1899;
Cass. 26 November 1980, n. 6272, in *Giur. it. rep.,* 1980;
Cass. 10 May 1989, n. 2137, in *Dir. trasp.,* 1990, 345;
Cass. 17 April 1992, n. 4728, in *Arch. giur. circ.*, 1992, 825
Cass. 13 July 1993, n. 7697, in *Arch. civ.,* 1994, 631;
Cass. 26 October 1993, n. 10621, in *Dir. mar.,* 1994, 1070;
Cass. 21 January 1994, n. 561, in *Dir. trasp.,* 1995, 273;
Cass. 26 April 1995 n. 4620, in *Nuova giur. civ. comm.,* 1996, I, 263;
Cass. 17 November 1999, n. 12744, in *Giur. it. rep.,* 1999;
Cass. 29 January 2003, n. 1272, in *Dir. mar.,* 2005, 498;
Cass. 10 February 2003, n. 1935, in *Europ. transp. law,* 2003, n. 38, 776;
Cass. 2 October 2003, n. 14680, in *Giur. it. rep.,* 2003;
Cass. 7 April 2005, n. 7258, in *Dir. trasp.,* 2007, 497;
Cass. 7 February 2006, n. 2529, in *Giur. it. rep.,* 2006;
Cass. 21 February 2006, n. 3665, in *Europ. transp. law,* 20007, n. 42, 383;
Cass. 2 March 2006, n. 4656, in *Giur. it rep.,* 2006;
Cass. 7 October 2008, in *Giur. it. mass.,* 2008;
Cass. 28 September 2009, n. 20756, in *Giur. it rep.,* 2009;
Cass., sez. un., 24 November 2009, n. 24680 in *Giur. it. rep.,* 2009.
Cass. 20 October 2010, n. 24400, in *Giur. it. rep.,* 2010;
Cass. 13 December 2010, n. 25110, in *Giur. it. rep.,* 2010;
Cass. 30 January 2014, n. 2075, in *Giur. it. rep.,* 2014;
Cass. 9 March 2015, n, 4686, in *Riv. dir. int. priv. proc.,* 2016, 509;
Cass. 14 July 2015, n. 14665, in *Giur. it. rep.,* 2018;
Cass. 14 March 2017, n. 6484, in *Giur. it. rep.,* 2017;
Cass. 5 March 2019, n. 6316, in *Giur. it. rep.,* 2019;
Cass. 20 May 2020, n. 9266 in *Giur. it rep.,* 2020;
Cass. 6 July 2020, n. 13811, in *Giur. it. rep.,* 2020.

App. Cagliari 20 May 1969, in *Giur. it rep.,* 1978;
App. Venice 31 October 1974, in *Europ. transp. law,* 1975, n. 10, 21;
App. Milan 11 July 1975, in *Unif. law rev.,* 1977, 336;
App. Florence 2 February 1981, in *Giur. it. rep.,* 1981;

App. Milan 18 March 1994, in *Riv. dir. priv. proc.,* 1995, 141;
App. Trento 21 May 1998, in *Europ. transp. law,* 1999, n. 34, 381;
App. Brescia 1 June 2001, in *Giur. it. rep.,* 2001;
App. Milan 20 April 2005, in *Dir. trasp.,* 2006, 1009;
App. Milan 17 May 2018, in *Dir. mar.,* 2018, 683 ss.;

Trib. Bassano del Grappa 25 November 1997, in *Dir. trasp.,* 1999, 249;
Trib. Milan 9 April 2001, in *Dir. mar.,* 2003, 176;
Trib. Milan 14 June 2001, in *Dir. trasp.,* 2003, 674;
Trib. Tortona 8 May 2005, in *Giur. it. rep.,* 2005;
Trib. Prato 14 May 2005, in *Dir. mar.,* 2006, 567;
Trib. Bari 20 November 2008, in *Giur. it. rep.*, 2008;
Trib. Varese 27 October 2012, in *Riv. dir. int. priv. proc.*, 2013, 455;
Trib. Lucca 24 April 2013, in *Giur. it. rep.,* 2013;
Trib. Milan 17 April 2014, in *Riv. dir. int. priv. proc.,* 2017, 128.

Norway
Cass. 16 March 1995, in *Europ. transp. law,* 1996, n. 31, 563.

The Netherlands
Cass. 4 May 1987, in *Europ. transp. law,* n. 29, 360;
Cass. 27 April 1989, in *Europ. transp. law,* 1989, n. 24, 345;
Cass. 29 June 1990, in *Le Lamy transp*., 2021, vol. I, 480;
Cass. 14 June 1996, in *Europ. transp. law,* 1996, n. 31, 558:
Cass. 24 June 1997, in *Europ. transp. law,* 1998, n. 33, 52;
Cass. 17 April 1998, in *Europ. transp. law,* 1999, n. 34, 82;
Cass. 20 November 1998, in *Europ. transp. law,* 1999, n. 34, 254;
Cass. 11 February 2000, in *Europ. transp. law,* 2000, n. 35, 381;
Cass. 5 January 2001, in *Europ. transp. law,* 2001, n. 36, 116;
Cass. 22 February 2002, in *Europ. transp. law,* 2004, n. 39, 658;
Cass. 4 October 2002, in *Europ. transp. law,* 2004, n. 39, 669;
Cass. 14 July 2006, in *Europ. transp. law,* 2006, n. 41, 804;
Cass. 25 January 2008, in *Europ. transp. law,* 2008, n. 43, 498;
Cass. 24 April 2009, in *Europ. transp. law,* 2009, n. 44, 707;
Cass. 18 December 2009, in *Europ. transp. law,* 2010, n. 45, 101;
Cass. 8 November 2011, in *Unif. law rev.,* 2005, 628;
Cass. 1 June 2012, in *TranspR,* 278;
Cass. 11 September 2015, in *Europ. transp. law,* 2016, n. 51, 109;

Hof Hertogenbosch 21 December 1965, in *Europ. transp. law,* 1966, n. 1, 698;
Hof Hertogenbosch 13 January 1970, in *Europ. transp. law,* 1971, n. 6, 817;
Hof Gravenhage 10 May 1978, *Europ. transp. law,* 1978, n. 13, 606;
Hof Hertogenbosch 16 March 1988, in *Europ. law digest,* 1990, 138;
Hof Gravenhage 28 November 2007, in *Europ. transp. law,* 2008, n. 43, 364;
Hof Amsterdam 28 August 2008, in *S&S,* 2011, 79;

Hof Hertogenbosch 13 February 2018, in *Europ. transp. law,* 2018, n. 53, 460,
Hof Hertogenbosch 30 April 2019, in *Europ. transp. law,* 2019, n. 54, 541;

RB Dordrecht 18 May 1966, in *Europ. transp. law,* 1968, n. 3, 416;
RB Roermond 15 October 1970, in *Europ. transp. law,* 1971, n. 6, 839;
RB Amsterdam 12 April 1972 in S & S, 1972, 102;
RB. Amsterdam 4 June 1974, in *Bull. transp.,* 1975, 531;
RB Rotterdam 20 February 1976, in *Europ. law digest,* 1978, n. 6, 291;
RB Amsterdam 24 November 1976;
RB Rotterdam 12 May 1978, in *Europ. law digest,* 1989, n. 407;
RB Rotterdam 6 July 2011, in *Europ. transp. law,* 2011, n. 46, 655;
RB Roermond 19 March 2014, in *Europ. transp. law,* 2016, n. 51, 223;
GH Hertogenbosch 15 April 2014, in *Europ. transp. law,* 2014, n. 49, 701;
RB Rotterdam 8 March 2017, in *Europ. transp. law,* 2017, n. 52, 574;
RB Limburg 28 March 2017, in *Europ. transp. law,* 2018, n. 53, 87;
RB Limburg 21 June 2017, in *Europ. transp. law,* 2017, n. 52, 654;
RB Zeeland – West - Brabant 13 December 2017, in *Europ. transp. law,* 2018, n. 53, 469;
RB Limburg 28 February 2018, in *Europ. transp. law,* 2018, n. 53, 481.
RB Rotterdam 19 June 2019, in *Europ. transp. law,* 2020, n. 55, 309;
RB Rotterdam 3 July 2019, in *Europ. transp. law,* 2020, n. 55, 41;
RB Limburg 25 March 2020, in *Europ. transp. law,* 2021, n. 61, 45;

Arrond. Rotterdam 31 January 1967, in *S & S.,* 1967, n. 56;
Arrond. Breda 16 February 1969, in *Europ. transp. law,* 1970, n. 5, 67;
Arrond. Rotterdam 12 April 1972, in *Uniform. law rev.,* 1976, 253;
Arrond. Amsterdam 19 January 1977, in *Europ. law digest,* 1979, 401;
Arrond. Amsterdam 30 March 1977, in *Unif. law rev.,* 1978, 299.

Poland

Supreme Court 22 November 2007, III CSK 150 / 2007;
Supreme Court 19 December 2013, II CSK 70 / 2013;
Supreme Court 4 December 2015, I CSK, 1063 / 2014;
Supreme Court 18 February 2016, II CSK 111 / 2015.
Supreme Court 13 October 2916, V CSK 712 / 2015;
Supreme Court 7 March 2017, II CSK 242 / 2016;
Supreme Court 20 February 2018, V CSK 205 / 2017;
Supreme Court 14 March 2019, IV CSK 6 /2018;
Supreme Court 27 August 2019, V CSK 191 / 2018;
Supreme Court 26 November 2019, IV CSK 415 / 2018
Supreme Court 10 September 2020, II CASK 125 / 2019;

App. Warsaw 17 December 2014, I ACa 971 / 2014;
App. Bialystok 25 March 2015, I ACa 952 / 2014;
App. Poznań 8 September 2017, I Aca 281 / 2017;

App. Krakow 12 October 2017, I ACa 510 / 2017;
App. Krakow 22 July 2020.

Portugal

Supremo Tribunal Da Justiça, Portugal, 17 November 1994, in *Unif. law rev.*, 1997, 200.

United Kingdom

Marston Excelsior v. *Arbuckle, Smith & Co,* in *Lloyd's rep.*, 1971, 306;
William Tatton & Co. Ltd. v. *Ferrymasters Ltd.*, in *Lloyd's rep.*, 1974, 203;
Muller Batavier Ltd. v. *Laurent Transport Co. Ltd.*, in *Lloyd's rep.*, 1977, 411;
Buchanan & Co. Ltd. v. *Babco Forwarding & Shipping (U. K.) Ltd.*, in *Loyd's Rep.*, 1978, 119;
Moto Vespa S. A. v. *Mat (Britannia express) Ltd.*, in *Lloyd's rep.*, 1979, 175;
Walek & Co. v. *Chapman & Ball (International) Ltd.*, in *Lloyd's rep.*, 1980, 279
Tetroc Ltd v. *Cross – con (Intrenational) Ltd,* in *Lloyd's rep.*, 1981, 192;
Thermo engineers Ltd. v. *Ferrymasters Ltd.*, in *Lloyd's rep.*, 1981, 200.
Micheal Galley Footwear Ltd. v. *Dominic Iaboni,* in *All England report*, 1982, 200;
B. Bofors – UVA v. *A. B. Skandia Transport,* in *Lloyd's rep.*, 1982, 410;
Eastern Kayam Carpets Ltd. v. *Eastern United Freght Ltd.*, Lexis citation, 1983, 1311;
Silber v. *Islander Trucking*, in *Lloyd's rep.*, 1985, 243;
Arctic Electronics Co. (UK) Ltd. v. *McGregor Sea & Air Services Ltd.*, in *Lloyd's rep.*, 1985, 510;
Sidney G. Jones Ltd. v. *Martin Bencher Ltd.*, in *Lloyd's rep.*, 1986, 54;
Worldwide carriers Ltd. v. *Ardtran international Ltd,* in *Lloyd's rep.*, 1983, 61;
ICI PLC v. *MAT Transport Ltd.*, in *Lloyd's rep.*, 1987, 534;
City Vintages Ltd v. *SCAC Transport International,* in *Lloyd's rep.*, 1987, 1053;
Smith v. *Stages,* in *AC,* 1989, 928;
Dresser UK Ltd. v. *Falcongate Freight Management Ltd.*, in *Europ. transp. law,* 1991, n. 26, 798;
Microfine Minerals & Chemicals Ltd. v. *Transferry Shipping Co. Ltd.*, in *Lloyd's rep.*, 1991, 630 e in *Europ. transp. law,* 1992, 118;
Zerowatt Spa v. *International Express Company Ltd.*, in *Europ. transp. law,* 1991, n. 26, 530;
Texas Instrument Ltd. and others v. *Nason (Europe) Ltd. and others,* in *Europ. transp. law,* 1991, n. 26, 671 and, in *Lloyd's rep.*, 1991, 146;
Shell Chemicals UK Ltd. v. *P & O Roadtanks Ltd.*, in *Lloyd's rep.*, 1993, 114;
Harrison & Sons Ltd. v. *R. T. Steward Transport Ltd.*, in *Europ. transp. law,* 1993, n. 28, 747;
Logmill Corporation Plc. v. *Andrea Merzario Ltd.*, in *C. L. C. C. (B. L.)*, 1995;
G. L. Cicatiello Srl. and others v. *Anglo European Shipping Services Ltd. and others,* in *Lloyd's rep.*, 1994, 678, and in *Europ. transp. law,* 1996, n. 31, 218;
Laceys Footwear (Wholesale) Ltd. v. *Bowler International Freight Ltd. and Another*, in *Europ. transp. law,* 1998, n. 33, 79, and in *Lloyd's rep.*, 1997, 369;

Inco Europe Ltd. v. *First Choice Distribution,* in *All England Reports*, 1999, 820;
Gamble (Health and Beauty Care) Ltd. v. *Concordia Shipping Agency Ltd.*, in *C. L. C. C. (B. L.)*, 2000;
Andrea Merzario Ltd. v. *Internationale Spedition Leitner Gesellschaft GmbH.,* in *Lloyd's rep.,* 2001, 490;
Quantum Ltd. v. *Plane Trucking Ltd.,* in *Lloyd's rep.,* 2001, 131;
Parr v. *Clark & Rose Ltd.,* in *S. C. R. L.*, 2002, 222;
Sandeman Coprimar S. A. v. *Transitos y Transpotes Integrale S. L.,* in *Queen's bench reports*, 2003, 1270;
Alena v. *Harlequin*, in *Europ. transp. law,* 2003, n. 38, 218;
Royal & Sun Alliance Insurance Plc. v. *MK Digital FZE (Cyprus) Ltd.,* in *Lloyd's rep.,* 2005, 679;
Rosewood Trucking Ltd. v. *Brian Balaam,* in *Unif. law rev.*, 2005, 624;
Datect Electronic Holdings Limited and others v. *United Parcels Service Limited and Another,* in *Unif. law rev.*, 2005, 624;
T Comedy (UK) Ltd. v. *Easy managed Transport Ltd.,* in *Lloyd's rep.*, 2007, 397;
Sony Computer Entertainment Ltd. v. *RH Freight Services Ltd. and Others*, in *Lloyd's law rep.,* 2007, 463;
TNT Global S. p. A. v. *Denfleet International Ltd.,* in *Lloyd's rep.,* 2007, 504;
Hatzl v. *XL Insurance Co. Ltd.,* in *Lloyd's rep.,* 2009, 555;
British American Tabacco Denmark A / S v. *Kazemier* in *Lloyd's rep.,* 2016, 463;
Stef Transport Rennes – Stef International Ouest v. *D & M Fraser,* in *Europ. transp. law,* 2019, n. 54, 187.

Spain

Cass. 12 March 1998, in *Europ. transp. law,* 1999, n. 34, 100;
Cass. 29 June 1998, n. 635, in *Europ. transp. law,* 1999, n. 34, 692;
Cass. 9 February 1999, n. 78, in *RJ,* 1999, 1054;
Cass. 8 October 2003, n. 918, in *RJ,* 2003, 7383;
Cass. 13 May 2008, n. 327, in *RJ,* 2008, 3066;
Cass. 4 July 2016, n. 455, in *RJ,* 2016, 167;

App. Alicante 11 July 1994, in *Ac*, 1994, 1154;
App., Valencia 8 November 1997, in *Ac,* 197, 2273;
App. Asturias 13 January 1998, in *Ac,* 1998, 2980;
App. Barcelona 11 June 1999, in *Ac,* 1999, 6126;
App. Barcelona 18 June 1999, in *Ac,* 1999, 1200;
App. Barcelona 5 July 1999, in *Ac,* 1999, 1850;
App. Segovia 10 November 1999, in *Ac,* 1999, 8028;
App. Alicante 22 March 2000, in *Jur,* 2000, 153347;
App. Valencia 4 July 2000, in *Jur,* 2000, 285304;
App. Almeria 23 October 2000, in *Jur*, 2001, 44610;
App. Madrid 28 March 2001, in *Jur,* 2001, 158657;
App. Castellón 8 April 2002, *Ac,* 2002, 997;
App. Barcelona 31 December 2002, in *Jur,* 2004, 14170;

App. Barcelona 13 February 2003, in *Jur,* 2004, 14188;
App. Barcelona 20 January 2005, in *Jur,* 2005, 120240;
App. Granada 7 March 2005, in *Ac,* 2005, 1008;
App. Barcelona 27 June 2005, in *Jur,* 2006, 46130;
App. Alava 7 July 2005, in *Jur,* 2005, 233598;
App. Valencia 29 March 2006, in *Jur,* 2006, 226817;
App. Barcelona 26 May 2006, in *Jur,* 2007, 72368;
App. Barcelona 14 November 2006, in *Jur,* 2007, 144550;
App. Barcelona 19 December 2006, in *Ac,* 2007, 1526;
App. Barcelona 29 March 2007, in *Jur,* 2007, 243690;
App. Barcelona 2 September 2008, in *Jur,* 2009, 42600;
App. Murcia 30 October 2009, in *Jur,* 2009, 475526;
App. Valencia 9 November 2009, in *Ac,* 2010, 266;
App. Barcelona 4 September 2013, in *Jur,* 2013, 340805;
App. Barcelona 15 October 2012, in *Ac,* 2012, 2342;
App. Cordóba 19 November 2012, in *Ac,* 2013, 2236;
App. Almeria 25 March 2013, in *Jur,* 2013, 198313;
App. Alicante 13 December 2013, in *Jur,* 2014, 172739;
App. Barcelona 17 December 2013, in *Jur,* 2014, 21232,
App. Lleida 25 June 2015, in *Jur,* 2015, 187564;
App. Valencia 3 February 2016, in *Jur,* 2016, 143913;
App. Barcelona 4 February 2016, in *Ac,* 2016, 706;
App. Barcelona 18 September 2918, in *Jur,* 2018, 253561;
App. Madrid 19 January 2018, in *Ac,* 2018, 316;
App. Alicante 25 October 2019, in *Jur,* 2020, 88714;
App. Barcelona 6 May 2020, in *Ac,* 2020, 1200;

JMerc Córdoba 18 March 2005, n. 9, in *Jur,* 2005, 221895;
JMerc Donostia 26 June 2018, n. 214, in *Jur,* 2018, 273147;

Audiencia Provincial de Barcelona 6 April 1999, in *Unif. law rev.,* 1999, 1040;
Audienca Provinciale de Alicante 15 June 2005, citata da Messent – Glass (2018), 221, nt. 106.

Swiss

Trib. federale 2 June 1981, in *Sistema informatico federale;*
Trib. federale 22 November 1983, in *Sistema informatico federale;*
Trib. federale 19 December 1985, in *Sistema informatico federale;*
Trib. Federale 30 May 2001, *Sistema informatico federale;*
Trib. Federale 3 November 2008, in *Sitema informatico federale;*
Trib. federale 25 September 2012, in *Sistema informatico federale;*

AG Cantone della Città di Basilea 12 May 2000, in *TranspR,* 2000, 372;
HG Cantone Argau7 June 2011, in *TranspR,* 2012, 339.

European Union

Court of Justice, third section, 28 October 2004, Causa C – n. 148 del 2003, *Nürberger Allgemeine Versicherungs AG* v. *Portbridge Transport International BV;*

Court of Justice, Grande Chambre, 4 May 2012, C – n. 533 del 2008, *TNT Express Nederland BV* v. *AXA Versicherung AG;*

Court of Justice, second section, 6 September 2012, Causa C- n. 273 del 2011, *Mecsek – Gabona Kft* v. *Nemzeti Adó – és Vámhivatal Dél – dunántùli Regionális Adó Foigazgatósága;*

Court of Justice, third section, 19 December 2013, C – n. 452 del 2012, *NipponKoa Insurance Co. (Europe) Ltd.* c. *Inter – Zuid Transport BV e DTC Surhuisterveen BV;*

Court of Justice, first section, 4 September 2014, Causa C – n. 157 del 2013, *Nickel & Goeldner Spedition GmbH* c. *"Kintra" UAB;*

Court of Justice, fourth section, 20 October 2016, Causa C – n. 24 del 2015, *Josef Plöckl* v. *Finanzamt Schrobenhausen*;

Court of Justice, fourth section, 10 June 2021, Causa C - n. 279 del 2019, *The Commissioners for Her Majesty's Revenue and Customs.*

MIX
Papier aus verantwortungsvollen Quellen
Paper from responsible sources
FSC® C105338

If you have any concerns about our products,
you can contact us on
ProductSafety@springernature.com

In case Publisher is established outside the EU,
the EU authorized representative is:
Springer Nature Customer Service Center GmbH
Europaplatz 3, 69115 Heidelberg, Germany

Printed by Libri Plureos GmbH
in Hamburg, Germany